Lecture Notes in Computer Science   14013

Founding Editors

Gerhard Goos
Juris Hartmanis

Editorial Board Members

The series Lecture Notes in Computer Science (LNCS), including its subseries Lecture Notes in Artificial Intelligence (LNAI) and Lecture Notes in Bioinformatics (LNBI), has established itself as a medium for the publication of new developments in computer science and information technology research, teaching, and education.

LNCS enjoys close cooperation with the computer science R & D community, the series counts many renowned academics among its volume editors and paper authors, and collaborates with prestigious societies. Its mission is to serve this international community by providing an invaluable service, mainly focused on the publication of conference and workshop proceedings and postproceedings. LNCS commenced publication in 1973.

Masaaki Kurosu · Ayako Hashizume
Editors

Human-Computer Interaction

Thematic Area, HCI 2023
Held as Part of the 25th HCI International Conference, HCII 2023
Copenhagen, Denmark, July 23–28, 2023
Proceedings, Part III

Springer

Editors
Masaaki Kurosu
The Open University of Japan
Chiba, Japan

Ayako Hashizume
Hosei University
Tokyo, Japan

ISSN 0302-9743   ISSN 1611-3349 (electronic)
Lecture Notes in Computer Science
ISBN 978-3-031-35601-8   ISBN 978-3-031-35602-5 (eBook)
https://doi.org/10.1007/978-3-031-35602-5

This Springer imprint is published by the registered company Springer Nature Switzerland AG
The registered company address is: Gewerbestrasse 11, 6330 Cham, Switzerland

Foreword

Human-computer interaction (HCI) is acquiring an ever-increasing scientific and industrial importance, as well as having more impact on people's everyday lives, as an ever-growing number of human activities are progressively moving from the physical to the digital world. This process, which has been ongoing for some time now, was further accelerated during the acute period of the COVID-19 pandemic. The HCI International (HCII) conference series, held annually, aims to respond to the compelling need to advance the exchange of knowledge and research and development efforts on the human aspects of design and use of computing systems.

The 25th International Conference on Human-Computer Interaction, HCI International 2023 (HCII 2023), was held in the emerging post-pandemic era as a 'hybrid' event at the AC Bella Sky Hotel and Bella Center, Copenhagen, Denmark, during July 23–28, 2023. It incorporated the 21 thematic areas and affiliated conferences listed below.

A total of 7472 individuals from academia, research institutes, industry, and government agencies from 85 countries submitted contributions, and 1578 papers and 396 posters were included in the volumes of the proceedings that were published just before the start of the conference, these are listed below. The contributions thoroughly cover the entire field of human-computer interaction, addressing major advances in knowledge and effective use of computers in a variety of application areas. These papers provide academics, researchers, engineers, scientists, practitioners and students with state-of-the-art information on the most recent advances in HCI.

The HCI International (HCII) conference also offers the option of presenting 'Late Breaking Work', and this applies both for papers and posters, with corresponding volumes of proceedings that will be published after the conference. Full papers will be included in the 'HCII 2023 - Late Breaking Work - Papers' volumes of the proceedings to be published in the Springer LNCS series, while 'Poster Extended Abstracts' will be included as short research papers in the 'HCII 2023 - Late Breaking Work - Posters' volumes to be published in the Springer CCIS series.

I would like to thank the Program Board Chairs and the members of the Program Boards of all thematic areas and affiliated conferences for their contribution towards the high scientific quality and overall success of the HCI International 2023 conference. Their manifold support in terms of paper reviewing (single-blind review process, with a minimum of two reviews per submission), session organization and their willingness to act as goodwill ambassadors for the conference is most highly appreciated.

This conference would not have been possible without the continuous and unwavering support and advice of Gavriel Salvendy, founder, General Chair Emeritus, and Scientific Advisor. For his outstanding efforts, I would like to express my sincere appreciation to Abbas Moallem, Communications Chair and Editor of HCI International News.

July 2023   Constantine Stephanidis

HCI International 2023 Thematic Areas and Affiliated Conferences

Thematic Areas

- HCI: Human-Computer Interaction
- HIMI: Human Interface and the Management of Information

Affiliated Conferences

- EPCE: 20th International Conference on Engineering Psychology and Cognitive Ergonomics
- AC: 17th International Conference on Augmented Cognition
- UAHCI: 17th International Conference on Universal Access in Human-Computer Interaction
- CCD: 15th International Conference on Cross-Cultural Design
- SCSM: 15th International Conference on Social Computing and Social Media
- VAMR: 15th International Conference on Virtual, Augmented and Mixed Reality
- DHM: 14th International Conference on Digital Human Modeling and Applications in Health, Safety, Ergonomics and Risk Management
- DUXU: 12th International Conference on Design, User Experience and Usability
- C&C: 11th International Conference on Culture and Computing
- DAPI: 11th International Conference on Distributed, Ambient and Pervasive Interactions
- HCIBGO: 10th International Conference on HCI in Business, Government and Organizations
- LCT: 10th International Conference on Learning and Collaboration Technologies
- ITAP: 9th International Conference on Human Aspects of IT for the Aged Population
- AIS: 5th International Conference on Adaptive Instructional Systems
- HCI-CPT: 5th International Conference on HCI for Cybersecurity, Privacy and Trust
- HCI-Games: 5th International Conference on HCI in Games
- MobiTAS: 5th International Conference on HCI in Mobility, Transport and Automotive Systems
- AI-HCI: 4th International Conference on Artificial Intelligence in HCI
- MOBILE: 4th International Conference on Design, Operation and Evaluation of Mobile Communications

List of Conference Proceedings Volumes Appearing Before the Conference

1. LNCS 14011, Human-Computer Interaction: Part I, edited by Masaaki Kurosu and Ayako Hashizume
2. LNCS 14012, Human-Computer Interaction: Part II, edited by Masaaki Kurosu and Ayako Hashizume
3. LNCS 14013, Human-Computer Interaction: Part III, edited by Masaaki Kurosu and Ayako Hashizume
4. LNCS 14014, Human-Computer Interaction: Part IV, edited by Masaaki Kurosu and Ayako Hashizume
5. LNCS 14015, Human Interface and the Management of Information: Part I, edited by Hirohiko Mori and Yumi Asahi
6. LNCS 14016, Human Interface and the Management of Information: Part II, edited by Hirohiko Mori and Yumi Asahi
7. LNAI 14017, Engineering Psychology and Cognitive Ergonomics: Part I, edited by Don Harris and Wen-Chin Li
8. LNAI 14018, Engineering Psychology and Cognitive Ergonomics: Part II, edited by Don Harris and Wen-Chin Li
9. LNAI 14019, Augmented Cognition, edited by Dylan D. Schmorrow and Cali M. Fidopiastis
10. LNCS 14020, Universal Access in Human-Computer Interaction: Part I, edited by Margherita Antona and Constantine Stephanidis
11. LNCS 14021, Universal Access in Human-Computer Interaction: Part II, edited by Margherita Antona and Constantine Stephanidis
12. LNCS 14022, Cross-Cultural Design: Part I, edited by Pei-Luen Patrick Rau
13. LNCS 14023, Cross-Cultural Design: Part II, edited by Pei-Luen Patrick Rau
14. LNCS 14024, Cross-Cultural Design: Part III, edited by Pei-Luen Patrick Rau
15. LNCS 14025, Social Computing and Social Media: Part I, edited by Adela Coman and Simona Vasilache
16. LNCS 14026, Social Computing and Social Media: Part II, edited by Adela Coman and Simona Vasilache
17. LNCS 14027, Virtual, Augmented and Mixed Reality, edited by Jessie Y. C. Chen and Gino Fragomeni
18. LNCS 14028, Digital Human Modeling and Applications in Health, Safety, Ergonomics and Risk Management: Part I, edited by Vincent G. Duffy
19. LNCS 14029, Digital Human Modeling and Applications in Health, Safety, Ergonomics and Risk Management: Part II, edited by Vincent G. Duffy
20. LNCS 14030, Design, User Experience, and Usability: Part I, edited by Aaron Marcus, Elizabeth Rosenzweig and Marcelo Soares
21. LNCS 14031, Design, User Experience, and Usability: Part II, edited by Aaron Marcus, Elizabeth Rosenzweig and Marcelo Soares

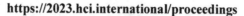

https://2023.hci.international/proceedings

Preface

Human-Computer Interaction is a Thematic Area of the International Conference on Human-Computer Interaction (HCII). The HCI field is today undergoing a wave of significant innovation and breakthroughs towards radically new future forms of interaction. The HCI Thematic Area constitutes a forum for scientific research and innovation in human-computer interaction, addressing challenging and innovative topics in human-computer interaction theory, methodology, and practice, including, for example, novel theoretical approaches to interaction, novel user interface concepts and technologies, novel interaction devices, UI development methods, environments and tools, multimodal user interfaces, human-robot interaction, emotions in HCI, aesthetic issues, HCI and children, evaluation methods and tools, and many others.

The HCI Thematic Area covers four major dimensions, namely theory and methodology, technology, human beings, and societal impact. The following four volumes of the HCII 2023 proceedings reflect these dimensions:

- Human-Computer Interaction (Part I), addressing topics related to design and evaluation methods, techniques and tools, and interaction methods and techniques
- Human-Computer Interaction (Part II), addressing topics related to children-computer interaction, emotions in HCI, and understanding the user experience
- Human-Computer Interaction (Part III), addressing topics related to human-robot interaction, chatbots and voice-based interaction, and interacting in the metaverse
- Human-Computer Interaction (Part IV), addressing topics related to supporting health, quality of life and everyday activities, as well as topics related to HCI for learning, culture, creativity, and societal impact.

Papers of these volumes are included for publication after a minimum of two single-blind reviews from the members of the HCI Program Board or, in some cases, from members of the Program Boards of other affiliated conferences. We would like to thank all of them for their invaluable contribution, support, and efforts.

July 2023

Masaaki Kurosu
Ayako Hashizume

Human-Computer Interaction Thematic Area (HCI 2023)

Program Board Chairs: **Masaaki Kurosu**, *The Open University of Japan, Japan* and **Ayako Hashizume**, *Hosei University, Japan*

Program Board:

- Salah Ahmed, *University of South-Eastern Norway, Norway*
- Valdecir Becker, *Federal University of Paraiba, Brazil*
- Nimish Biloria, *University of Technology Sydney, Australia*
- Zhigang Chen, *Shanghai University, P.R. China*
- C. M. Nadeem Faisal, *National Textile University, Pakistan*
- Yu-Hsiu Hung, *National Cheng Kung University, Taiwan*
- Jun Iio, *Chuo University, Japan*
- Yi Ji, *Guangdong University of Technology, P.R. China*
- Hiroshi Noborio, *Osaka Electro-Communication University, Japan*
- Katsuhiko Onishi, *Osaka Electro-Communication University, Japan*
- Mohammad Shidujaman, *Independent University, Bangladesh, Bangladesh*

The full list with the Program Board Chairs and the members of the Program Boards of all thematic areas and affiliated conferences of HCII2023 is available online at:

http://www.hci.international/board-members-2023.php

Human-Computer Interaction Thematic Area (HCI 2023)

HCI International 2024 Conference

The 26th International Conference on Human-Computer Interaction, HCI International 2024, will be held jointly with the affiliated conferences at the Washington Hilton Hotel, Washington, DC, USA, June 29 – July 4, 2024. It will cover a broad spectrum of themes related to Human-Computer Interaction, including theoretical issues, methods, tools, processes, and case studies in HCI design, as well as novel interaction techniques, interfaces, and applications. The proceedings will be published by Springer. More information will be made available on the conference website: http://2024.hci.international/.

General Chair
Prof. Constantine Stephanidis
University of Crete and ICS-FORTH
Heraklion, Crete, Greece
Email: general_chair@hcii2024.org

https://2024.hci.international/

Contents – Part III

Chatbots and Voice-Based Interaction

Interacting in the Metaverse

Human Robot Interaction

Towards Diversity, Equity, and Inclusion in Human-Robot Interaction

Jessica K. Barfield[✉]

School of Information Sciences, University of Tennessee, Knoxville, USA
Jbarfiel@vols.utk.edu

Abstract. As robots become smarter and interact with people in different social contexts it has become necessary to design robots that accommodate the information needs and values of a diverse group of users. This is an important topic of research for human-robot interaction given people who interact with robots vary by race, ethnicity, and gender. However, recent discussions within the robotics community suggest that current robots may not be designed to reflect the values and diversity of the users who interact with robots and thus may not be inclusive for different user populations. Drawing on Social Identity Theory, this paper focuses on whether users assign an ethnic identity to a robot and if so, which characteristics of robots lead to such decisions. From information on how users place robots into social categories, guidelines can be developed for interfaces between humans and robots that accommodate the ethnic diversity of users expected to interact with robots in social contexts.

Keywords: Human-Robot Interaction · Equity · Inclusion · Social Identity Theory

1 Introduction

In human-robot interaction the goal of research is to design robots that interact with humans in user-friendly and predicable ways often resembling how humans interact with each other in social contexts. However, as more people interact with robots the diversity of the users has increased encompassing different cultures, religions, and ethnicities. For that reason, an important research question for robotics is whether the design of current robots, and particularly the human-robot interface, accommodates the diversity of the different user populations interacting with robots. At its essence, this question focuses on whether individual's categorize robots into different social classes and whether the social class of the robot contributes to the goal of achieving diversity, equity, and inclusion in human-robot interaction.

To orient the reader, ethnicity is thought to be the quality of belonging to a population group or subgroup made up of people who share a common cultural background or descent. Thus, ethnicity may refer to the cultural expression and identification of people of different geographic regions, including their customs, history, language, and religion (Bentley, 1987). Within robotics, there is an evolving stream of research to suggest

© The Author(s), under exclusive license to Springer Nature Switzerland AG 2023
M. Kurosu and A. Hashizume (Eds.): HCII 2023, LNCS 14013, pp. 3–17, 2023.
https://doi.org/10.1007/978-3-031-35602-5_1

that people categorize robots into classes based on race and gender, and to a lesser extent categorized by ethnicity. Further, given the interest of this paper is to discuss diversity, equity, and inclusion in human-robot interaction, diversity can be described as the variety of differences that can exist amongst people including their race, nationality, gender and sexual identity, disability, and others (see Grubbs, 2020). Further, equity can be thought of as the practice of providing fair opportunities to people based on individual needs, thus aiming to "level the playing field" (Walster et al., 1976). Finally, inclusion is aimed at ensuring that individuals can find opportunities to participate, regardless of their differences (Goodin, 1996).

Guided by predictions from Social Identity Theory (Tajfel et al., 1979) which describes how humans place other humans into social categories, this paper discusses how social robots are categorized as a function of robot design features signaling ethnicity, and how robots can be designed to accommodate users with different ethnicities. Thus, in this paper, the discussion focuses on whether people who interact with robots categorize the robot based on the social characteristic of ethnicity, and if so the implications for diversity, equity, and inclusion in robotics and particularly for human-robot interaction.

2   Background Literature

2.1   Social Classification of Robots

Whether users place robots into social categories has implications for achieving diversity, equity, and inclusion in human interaction with robots and thus for human-robot interface design. In this section of the paper I review past research on the social categorization of robots. The basic position I take is that by placing a robot into a social category, the user is interacting with a robot which either matches or not the social characteristics of the user. More specifically, I propose that matches in ethnicity will lead to the impression that the user is interacting with a similar (or in-group) social entity, which could lead to the experience of diversity, equity, and inclusion in human-robot interaction.

Evidence that we place robots in social categories is provided by recent studies showing that people tend to react to robots as if they had a race or gender (Eyssel and Kuchenbrandt, 2012). For example, Sparrow (2020) commented that robots are often viewed as white and designed to reflect western cultural values. Additionally, Bartneck et al. (2018) found that people reacted to robots using racial stereotypes and would shoot faster at a darker colored robot than a lighter colored one (see Louise et al., 2018). Contributing to this line of research Barfield (2021) performed studies to determine how the surface color of a robot influenced the evaluation of the robot theorizing that darker colored robots would evoke racial stereotypes. Further, Bartneck et al. (2018) and Piske (1998) commented that when forming opinions about other people we often rely on social cues such as age, gender, and race (see also Brahnman and De Angeli, 2012).

Based on the results of past studies, the human tendency to classify robots into social classes may lead them to stereotype robots along racial lines which is a growing concern for the goal of achieving diversity, equity, and inclusion in human interaction with social robots (see generally Eyssel and Loughnan, 2013; Louine et al. 2018). For example, Eyssel and Hegel (2012) have shown that people use a variety of cues to categorize non-human entities and that there is also a tendency to place robots into racial and ethnic categories. Eyssel and Kuchenbrandt (2012) studying bias against robots, used German citizens to evaluate robots that were given a Turkish or German identity. The results of their study indicated that the robot introduced to the German citizens as a Turkish product compared to the same robot introduced to subjects as an in-group, or German product, received significantly less preference among German citizens. Further, De Angeli et al. (2006) found that people are more likely to engage in antisocial behaviors when interacting with technology designed with humanlike and engendered forms, and that robots designed with female gender cues could be the subject of unintended sexual attention and harassment (see Brahnman and De Angeli, 2012). Additionally, Bartneck et al. (2018) noted that manipulations of robot shape and hairstyle often elicited gender stereotypical responses. Given that robots may be perceived as representing a particular gender, these findings raise interesting design questions; as an example, whether it is ethical to create female appearing robots that are designed to serve gender roles in society (Bernotat et al. 2017). If such robots were the subject of gender discrimination, surely this would not be perceived as achieving an equitable and inclusive human-robot experience.

The placing of robots into different social categories could lead to several outcomes either positive or negative in human-robot interaction. For example, with robots becoming more humanoid in appearance, intelligent, and social in behavior, there is a growing effort to investigate whether people discriminate against robots and respond to them based on whether they view them as having a gender, race, or ethnicity. For example, Eyssel and Hegel (2012) investigating the effect of facial cues on the perception of robot gender asked whether a robot designed as gendered female would be stereotyped as female, and whether a robot designed as gendered male would be stereotyped as male. Their findings indicated that the same gender stereotypes which bias social perceptions of humans, are also applied to robots. For example, "male appearing" robots were ascribed more agency related traits, and "female appearing" robots were ascribed more communal traits (Eyssel and Hegel, 2012). More recently, Otterbacher and Talias (2017) found that people responded with stereotypical responses to robots thought to represent a particular gender. Using videos of male or female appearing robots, participant's evaluations of the female gendered robots were categorized as being emotionally warm and the male gendered robots as being more agentic (Otterbacher and Talias, 2017).

In addition to gender, there are other factors which influence how an individual evaluates another person and whether they exhibit a bias against that person. For example, it has been shown that people are evaluated more positively if they are perceived as part of the evaluator's "in-group" and negatively if not (Turner, 1978). This in-group bias effect was tested in the domain of social robots by Eyssel and Longham (2013). In their study, participants who identified as Caucasian, were asked to rate robots whose appearance resembled the participants in-group or resembled a social out-group designed with "afrocentric features". Contrary to expectations, more agency was attributed to the out-group robots, and as an explanation, Eyssel and Longham (2013) attributed the unexpected finding to the participants desire to appear egalitarian and unprejudiced. The extent to which this represents a consistent response to social robots remains to be determined in future studies. Eyssel and Kuchenbrandt (2012) also investigated the effect of social category membership on the evaluation of humanoid robots. Their results showed that subjects who rated a robot which was designed to represent either their in-group or a national out-group not only rated the in-group robot more favorably but used social categorization processes and differential social evaluations to evaluate the robots (Eyssel and Kuchenbrandt, 2012). Thus, from these results it is evident that people categorize robots and do so by social cues. Taken together, the above studies suggest that achieving diversity, equity, and inclusion in human-robot interaction may be dependent of the social categorization of robots.

On the topic of robot categorizations resulting in discrimination and the stereotyping of robots, Louine et al. (2018) investigated the perception of robots of certain colors. Respondents were presented with pictures of black, yellow, and neutral-colored robots and were asked to indicate their evaluation of the robot along a number of dimensions. The results suggested that black colored robots were viewed as significantly stronger than yellow robots, that respondents were more likely to move away from black colored robots, and that yellow robots were viewed as more affable than black robots. Further, using the shooter-bias paradigm, Bartneck et al. (2018) provided strong evidence that people discriminate against robots thought to represent a different race than the observer. In their study, subjects viewed white or black colored robots that either had a gun or other object in their hand. Bartneck and colleagues found that people shot quicker if the robot was darker than if it was lighter. And in a related study, Barfield (2021) showed that robot color can evoke an emotional response from people in various situations. Varying the surface color of robots, she found that participants thought society would discriminate against a black or rainbow colored robot more so than a robot colored as white. Further, a black colored robot was thought to be stronger than a white or yellow colored robot and participants indicated that a red or black colored robot would be selected more often to commit an assault than the other robots.

In another study, Esposita et al. (2020) investigated the extent to which robots' degree of human likeness, gender and ethnicity affected elders' attitude towards using robots as healthcare assistants. Two groups of seniors were asked to watch video clips showing three speaking female and male robots, respectively. The robots consisted of two androids, one with Caucasian and one with Asian features, and one humanoid robot. It was found that androids were clearly more preferred than humanoid robots no matter their gender. Further, seniors' preferences were for female android robots with Asian traits and male android robot with Caucasian traits suggesting that both gender and ethnic features interacted in defining robot's appearance that generate seniors' acceptance.

One overarching conclusion from the above studies is that human observers are able to place robots into different social categories based on their appearance an observation which has implications for achieving diversity, equity, and inclusion in human-robot interaction. Remarkedly, categorizing robots by appearance is a human skill developed at an early age. For example, Matsuda, Ishiguro, and Hiraki (2015) used robots to examine infant discrimination ability between humans, an android robot, and a more "mechanical-looking" robot. Subjects consisted of three groups, 6 to 8-month, 9 to 11-month, and 12 to 14-month-old infants. In the study, a human and robot image, or the two robot images, were presented side-by-side in the visual field facing the infants and using eye tracking equipment the infant's time spent focusing on each of three areas of the images were recorded. The results provided by Matsuda and colleagues showed that infants that were within the 6 to 14-month age range were able to distinguish between a mechanical appearing robot from a human but were not able to distinguish between an android robot and human (Matsuda, Ishiguro, and Hiraki, 2015). This result is particularly interesting for human-robot interaction given that psychologists have concluded from extensive research that people learn to discriminate against other people early in their lives (Bolgatz, 2005; Skinner, 2019).

2.2 Social Identity Theory

The above literature review indicated that people categorize robots based on a number of social cues. The process of making a social categorization decision is described by Social Identity Theory. According to the theory, people tend to categorize other people either as a member of their in-group or as an out-group member based on social characteristics (Tajfel et al. 1979). An important question for human-robot interaction is whether the same holds true for robots as how we evaluate robots influences how we interact with them. Additionally, the Social Identity Theory has particular significance to several contexts in which people interact with robots (Reynolds, 2018; Robertson, 2014; Tamburrini, 2009). For this paper, an idea expressed is that the social classification of robots as described by the Social Identity Theory influences whether diversity, equity, and inclusion is achieved in human-robot interaction. Basically, Social Identity theory is an explanatory framework on how members are determined to be part of a group. The key premise to Social Identity Theory is that it emphasizes the importance of group belongingness (Tajfel et al., 1979) with the focus being in-group behavior and self-categorization within the group.

From the Social Identity Theory perspective, social identity is displayed in group membership, and supported and sustained by group membership (Coeckelbergh, 2021) and social identity makes group behavior possible (Suraj, 2005). The concept of social identities can be broken down into the concepts of social identity salience, nested identities, and cross-cutting identities. The idea of identity salience focuses on the salience of social identities rather than individual identities (Callero, 1985). The salience of a particular social identity is dependent on the group context. Individuals perform the social identity most relevant to their perception of the social setting. In keeping with the idea of identity salience, there is an identity hierarchy, which means a given identity is invoked in a given context (Callero, 1985). Therefore, an individual's salient social identity in one group might not be the same in a different group. As shown in Fig. 1, in the first step of Social Identity Theory, the social world is divided into social categories, in the next step people are motivated to obtain a positive identity through positive intergroup social comparisons, and in the last step of the model, a positive social identity serves basic needs such as self-esteem (Fig. 1). The processes of Social Identity Theory are further summarized in Table 1 with examples to human-robot interaction.

As indicated, according to Social Identity Theory, people tend to categorize other people either as a member of their in-group or as an out-group member (Tajfel et al., 1979); which I propose has significance for achieving diversity, equity, and inclusion in interactions with social robots. In my research on perceived robot ethnicity and its role in achieving diversity, equity, and inclusion, Social Identity Theory provides the theoretical

Social Identity Theory

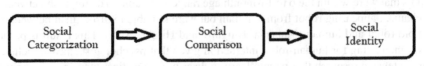

Fig. 1. The three stages of Social Identity Theory.

framework guiding my studies as it applies directly to the process of social categorization; a task I ask participants to do based on the robots' perceived ethnicity. Essentially, under Social Identity Theory, people view and evaluate another person's identity when they interact with them. We are social beings; thus, we have social identities and we have a tendency to categorize other people based on their identity (Gruber and Hancock, 2021; Tajfel et al. 1979). In Table 1, I give examples of the different stages comprising Social Identity Theory in the context of human-robot interaction.

Table 1. Stages of Social Identity Theory with human-robot interaction example.

Stages of Social Identity Theory	Description	Human-Robot Interaction Example	Reference
Social Categorization	In the first stage we categorize objects to understand and identify them. Similarly, we discover things about ourselves by knowing what categories we belong to. The process through which individuals may be grouped is based upon social information, such as gender, race, and age, but numerous other dimensions are categorized as well, such as social status, and occupation	The social category membership on the evaluation of humanoid robots that either belonged to an individual's in-group or to a national out-group in terms of robot anthropomorphism (e.g., mind attribution, warmth), psychological closeness, contact intentions, and design showed that participants not only rated the in-group robot more favorably importantly, people also anthropomorphized it more strongly than the out-group robot. Thus, people may apply social categorization processes and subsequent differential social evaluations to robots	Eyssel, F., and Kuchenbrandt, D., Social Categorization of Social Robot: Anthropomorphism as a Function of Robot Group Membership, British Journal of Social Psychology, Vol. 51(4), 724–731, 2012

(*continued*)

Table 1. (*continued*)

Stages of Social Identity Theory	Description	Human-Robot Interaction Example	Reference
Social Identification	In the second stage, through the process of social identification, we adopt the identity of the group we have categorized ourselves as belonging to. Thus, we conform to the norms of the group. There is an emotional significance to social identification with a group, and self-esteem is affected by group membership	Does the introduction of robots as teammates have an impact on in-group. Two samples from the United States were asked to imagine a hypothetical situation in which they were assigned to a work team at a new job. The studies examined perceived in-group identification. Having a robot on the work team had a negative impact on in-group identification. The results suggest that when humans are members of minority subgroup within a work team, their subgroup identity is threatened. Identification with a work team including robot members is associated with individual factors such as attitude towards robots, technological expertise, and personality Robot navigation in environments shared with humans should take into account social structures and interactions. A hierarchical clustering method for grouping individuals into free standing conversational groups (FSCS), utilizing their position and orientation was proposed	Savela, N., Kaakinen, M., (…)., and Oksanen, A., Sharing a Work Team with Robots: The Negative Effect of Robot Co-workers on In-group Identification with the Work Team, Computers in Human Behavior, 115, 2021
		Robot navigation in environments shared with humans should take into account social structures and interactions. A hierarchical clustering method for grouping individuals into free standing conversational groups (FSCS), utilizing their position and orientation was proposed	Kollakidou, A; Naik, L; (…); Bodenhagen, L, Enabling Robots to Adhere to Social Norms by Detecting F-Formations, 30th IEEE International Conference on Robot and Human Interactive Communication (RO-MAN), 110–116, 2021

(*continued*)

Table 1. (*continued*)

Stages of Social Identity Theory	Description	Human-Robot Interaction Example	Reference
Social Comparison	The third stage of SIT consists of social comparison. Once an individual has categorized themselves as part of a group and have identified with that group they then tend to compare that group with other groups. If our self-esteem is to be maintained our group needs to compare favorably with other groups	Understanding human-robot social comparison is critical for creating robots that do not cause psychological discomfort; however, there has been scant research examining social comparison processes in HRI. For HRI, using a humanoid robot, a model was developed to describe the mechanisms involved in social comparisons	Gruber, M.E., and Hancock, P.A., The Self-Evaluation Maintenance Model in Human-Robot Interaction: A Conceptual Replication, 13th International Conference on Social Robotics (ICSR) – Robotics in Our Everyday Lives, 280, 2021

An important question for human-robot interaction is whether the same social categorization process that occurs for humans holds true for robots as how we categorize robots influences how we experience them and interact with them (Eyssel and Kuchenbrandt, 2012). As indicated previously, evidence that we evaluate and place robots in social categories is provided by studies showing that people react to robots as if they had a race or gender (Eyssel and Hegel, 2012). For example, Sparrow (2020) commented that robots are often viewed as white and designed to reflect western cultural values which suggests that such robots do not support the goal of achieving diversity, equity, and inclusion in human-robot interaction. Additionally, as discussed above, Bartneck et al. (2018) found that people reacted to robots using racial stereotypes (indicating that a social categorization process occurs) and would shoot faster at a darker colored robot than a lighter colored one in the same social context.

Given the paper discusses the role that perceived robot ethnicity plays in contributing to diversity, equity, and inclusion, the following figure shows basic factors which contribute to the perception of robot ethnicity. From these there are socioeconomic factors, cultural factors (which are the focus of this paper), behavioral factors, and communicative factors. From the figure it is evident that many factors could contribute to the process of a robot being categorized by ethnicity (Fig. 2).

Next, an experiment on robot ethnicity and its role in achieving diversity, equity, and inclusion is presented. The data are still undergoing analysis, and thus the results presented here are descriptive.

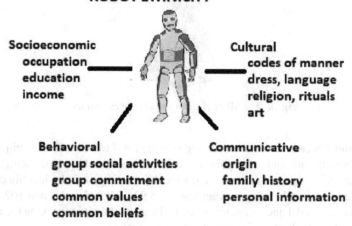

Fig. 2. Factors which may contribute to the perception of robot ethnicity.

3 Experiment: Robot Ethnicity

3.1 Methodology

Research Questions

RQ1: Will users who view a robot as the same ethnicity as themselves evaluate the robot as being more inclusive compared to a robot presented with a different ethnic identity? RQ2: Will robot ethnic voice accent influence the perception of robot ethnicity?

Experiment Design. The study was run as a 2 × 3 between subject design with robot voice (male, female) and robot ethnicity (American, Chinese, Hispanic) serving as independent variables. The robot voices were downloaded from an internet site which contained voice templates. The voices spoken by the Misty II robot, were obtained from text to speech software which included several voice accents reflecting different ethnicities.

Creating Robot Ethnicity. The robot used in the study was the Misty II robot which is a programmable robot platform designed for developers. Misty can speak, has mobility, facial recognition ability, responds to touch, and has expressive eyes (Fig. 3). Robot ethnicity was created using a voice with an ethnic accent and consisted of a spoken narrative by the robot with the narrative containing cues to ethnicity as follows. *"Hi. I am a robot (male or female voice) named (Karen, Guadalupe, Cheng) and I was built in the (United States, Mexico, China). I can speak (English and another language; Spanish and English; Mandarin and English). I will be assisting you in an information search and retrieval task. We have been given an assignment to do which will start as soon as I ask you a few questions about working with me. I look forward to working with you."*

Fig. 3. The Misty II robot used in the experiment.

Subjects and Procedure. After receiving IRB approval to run subjects, subjects were recruited from mTurk and were paid a small renumeration for participating. In total for the data analysis presented here there were 327 participants who identified with an American ethnicity and having a mean age of 35.93 with 225 males and 102 females. Participants accessed a questionnaire online and viewed the robot speaking the narrative online. The study took approximately 10 min to complete.

Response Measure. The response measure consisted of answers to a questionnaire with questions written to investigate diversity, equity, and inclusion in human-robot interaction. In the description of the data below, the specific question will be provided.

4 Results

When participants were asked "Would you prefer to work with a robot that matches your specific ethnicity?" when the robot's narrative was presented as American and the spoken robot voice was male, the mean response (using a 1–7 Likert scale) indicated that this combination was most preferred among participants (Mean = 5.67, sd = 0.94), followed by the Hispanic robot male narrative (Mean = 5.50, sd = 1.05), then the Chinese male robot narrative (Mean = 5.31, sd = 1.20). Thus, American participants viewing a robot whose combination of ethnicity cues when spoken with a male gendered voice was more preferred compared to the other robot ethnicities. Interestingly, when presented with a female voice and Chinese or Hispanic narrative, the American participants showed a tendency to prefer these ethnic combinations over a robot presented with American ethnic cues: China female narrative (Mean = 5.57, sd = 1.32); Hispanic female narrative (Mean = 5.53, sd = 1.10); and American female narrative (Mean 5.13, sd = 1.39).

Further, when asked "Do you prefer to work with a robot that matches your gender identity?" the American narrative with a male voice led to the strongest preference (Mean = 5.60, sd = 1.12) compared to the Hispanic (Mean = 5.48, sd = 1.04) and Chinese narrative presented with a male voice (Mean = 5.24, sd = 1.11). Interestingly, the lowest evaluation among the six ethnic possibilities was the American narrative presented in a female voice (Mean = 5.07, sd = 1.27). When asked "How similar do you feel to the robot?" it was interesting that for the Chinese female robot narrative (Mean = 5.52, sd = 1.10) the participants responded with the lowest mean rating. Further, when asked "How connected do you feel to the robot?" the response pattern was similar to the above questions and is displayed in Fig. 4. What is interesting to note about the figure is the increase or decrease response pattern across ethnicities for male and female ethnic voices to present the robot narrative.

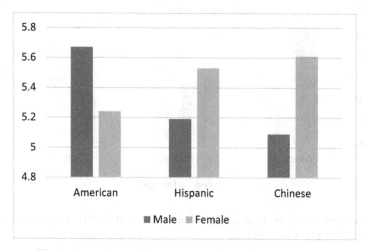

Fig. 4. Responses to "How connected do you feel to the robot?"

Participants were also asked whether they thought the robot had a personality, "To what extent do you think the robot has a personality?", the participants who viewed the American narrative spoken with a male voice responded more strongly (Mean = 5.65, sd = 1.27) than for the Hispanic (Mean = 5.27, sd = 1.34) or Chinese robot narrative spoken with a male voice (Mean = 5.15, sd = 1.07). Further, it is interesting to note the responses to the question, "To what extent would working with a robot of a different ethnicity increase diversity in society?". The responses were as follows; American narrative with male voice (Mean = 5.35, sd = 0.93); Hispanic narrative with male voice (Mean = 5.10, sd = 1.16; Chinese narrative with male voice (Mean = 5.09, sd = 1.09). And considering the robot with the female voice the responses were American narrative presented with female voice (Mean = 5.13, sd = 1.02); Hispanic narrative presented with a female voice (Mean = 5.33, sd = 1.11; and Chinese narrative presented with a female voice (Mean = 5.59, sd = 0.59). Here we see again the monotonic increase or decrease in the mean response as a function of the gender of the robot voice.

It was also of interest to evaluate whether working with a robot presented with a particular ethnic voice spoken as male or female influenced other aspects of diversity, equity, and inclusion. When asked "To what extent do you believe it is more inclusive for you to work with a robot that matches your ethnicity?" the general response pattern across the different robots was similar to the order of responses to the above questions. For example, the American ethnic narrative spoken with a male voice was (Mean = 5.65, sd = 0.88); followed by the Hispanic ethnic male narrative (Mean 5.15, sd = 1.35), and the Chinese ethnic male narrative (Mean = 5.09, sd = 1.26). For the female voice the results were: Chinese narrative (Mean = 5.71, sd = 1.00; Hispanic narrative (Mean =

5.40, sd = 1.21, and American narrative (Mean = 5.29, sd = 1.10). These results are presented graphically in Fig. 5.

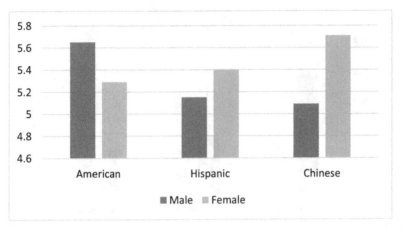

Fig. 5. Responses for "To what extent do you believe it is more inclusive for you to work with a robot that matches your ethnicity?"

In terms of a robot with a perceived ethnicity being more equitable, the following question was asked, "To what extent would human-robot interaction be more equitable if the robot's ethnicity was the same as yours?". The responses were: American narrative spoken with male voice (Mean = 5.50, sd = 1.04); Hispanic narrative with male voice (Mean = 5.40, sd = 1.24); Chinese narrative with male voice (Mean = 5.22, sd = 1.04); American narrative with female voice (Mean = 5.36, sd = 1.22); Hispanic narrative with female voice (Mean = 5.24, sd = 1.37); and Chinese narrative spoken with female voice (Mean = 5.46, sd = 1.03).

5   Discussion and Conclusions

The primary purpose of this paper was to introduce the idea that individuals who interact with robots in various social contexts may assign an ethnic identity to the robot based on cues theorized *a priori* to signal robot ethnicity. In the current study this was done in two main ways – by the use of an ethnic voice accent spoken by the robot and by cues presented in the robot's narrative thought to signal ethnicity which consisted of robot place of origin, ethnic name, and knowledge of the major religion practiced within American, Hispanic, or Chinese cultures. From the questionnaire interesting response patterns emerged. For example, the robot presented with the American ethnic cues using a male voice consistently led to a higher mean response across the questions. Thus, indicating that for the set of ethnic cues which were presented in the current study, there seemed to be a stronger perceived match in ethnicity when an American ethnicity narrative was spoken with a male voice, compared to the Hispanic or Chinese narrative spoken with a male gendered voice.

The mean response to the questions also showed that the gender of the voice speaking the robot narrative mattered across the questions especially when robot ethnicity and inclusion as expressed in the robot narrative was considered. Of interest to my current research agenda to design robots that accommodate the values of diverse populations, and as indicated previously, when the robot presented the American ethnicity narrative, the male voice narrative was always rated higher than the female voice regardless of the question. However, for the Hispanic and Chinese narratives, for almost all questions, the female voice narrative led to higher mean ratings for the questions than the male voice narrative. This provides preliminary evidence that voice accent combined with robot ethnic narrative cues is a strong combination signaling robot ethnicity. Further, as a conjecture, a robot voice with an ethnic accent may be more salient in signaling robot ethnicity than "just" the cues presented in the narrative (ethnic name, location of origin outside the U.S., and knowledge of religious principles associated with a particular ethnicity). This is an area of research that I am more fully exploring in other studies.

Additionally, it seems apparent that participants viewed the robots as expressing an ethnicity, thus I postulate that the Social Identity Theory is applicable to robot ethnicity decisions and subject to the three stages of the model, although this remains to be empirically evaluated in more depth in future studies. However, it does appear that robot voice gender (spoken with an accent) and robot ethnicity cues presented in the narrative are factors participants consider when evaluating the ethnicity of a robot. From this, an emerging picture on guidelines for robots is beginning to emerge and briefly discussed below. An interesting question to pose is how the above results apply to the goal of achieving diversity, equity, and inclusion within society? On this, a number of observations can be made. From the data, tradeoffs emerged for diversity and inclusion within human-robot interaction. For example, an American narrative with a male voice which matched the participants American ethnicity was preferred. However, given the participants in the data analysis identified with an American ethnicity, to create the impression of inclusion, a Chinese ethnicity with a female voice was thought to increase inclusivity. Perhaps the participants thought the latter robot to be most unlike them, and thus more likely to represent an inclusive robot interface. However, to achieve the goal of an equitable human-robot interaction, no clear pattern from the participant's responses emerged.

To some extent in this exploratory study, given the questions asked, American partic- ipants showed that they would accommodate robots designed with different ethnic cues under different circumstances. For example, as a conjecture they might think a robot designed with an American ethnicity to be preferred over the Chinese ethnicity robot when the issue is working with a robot that matches their ethnicity; but otherwise think that a Chinese ethnic robot supports inclusivity. Future studies will need to look for tradeoffs between the use of different robot ethnicities and task performance, and how such robots contribute to diversity, equity, and inclusion in human interaction with social robots. As preliminary thoughts on guidelines for human-robot interaction to achieve diversity, equity, and inclusion, American participants seemed to prefer interacting with a robot whose ethnicity cues and spoken accent matched their own. However, given the participants rated the Chinese female robot as producing an inclusive human-robot interaction, the results are promising that people may be willing to accept other robot ethnicities in their social interactions with robots. However, these are preliminary results and conclusions and thus in need of future research.

Going forward, I plan to use participants of different ethnicities and have them interact with the robot to determine how different user populations view ethnicities as accommodating their values. From such studies I expect to propose design guidelines which would allow users to select ethnic cues which would lead to a human-robot experience that accommodate their ethnic values and thus contributes to diversity, equity, and inclusion within society.

Acknowledgement. The author thanks the University of Tennessee-Knoxville for support during the writing of this paper and for the funds to purchase the robot used in the study.

References

Barfield, J.K.: Discrimination and stereotypical responses to robots as a function of robot colorization. In: Adjunct Proceedings of the 29th ACM Conference on User Modeling, Adaptation and Personalization (UMAP 2021 Adjunct), Utrecht, The Netherlands, pp. 109–114 (2021)

Bartneck, C., et al.: Robots and racism. IN: ACM/IEEE International Conference, pp. 1–9 (2018)

Bentley, G.: Ethnicity and practice. Comp. Stud. Soc. Hist. **29**(1), 24–55 (1987)

Bernotat, J., Eyssel, F., Sachse, J.: Shape it – the influence of robot body shape on gender perception in robots. In: International Conference on Social Robotics (ICSR), pp. 75–84 (2017)

Bolgatz, J.: Revolutionary talk: elementary teacher and students discuss race in a social studies class. Soc. Stud. **96**(6), 259–264 (2005)

Brahnman, S., De Angeli, A.: Gender affordances in conversational agents. Interact. Comput. **24**(3), 139–153 (2012)

Callero, P.L.: Role-identity salience. Soc. Psychol. Q. **48**(3), 203–215 (1985)

Coeckelbergh, M.: How to use virtue ethics for thinking about the moral standing of social robots: a relational interpretation in terms of practices, habits, and performance. Int. J. Soc. Robots **13**, 31–40 (2021)

De Angeli, A., Brahnman, S., Wallis, P., Dix, A.: Misuse and use of interactive technologies In: CHI 2006 Extended Abstracts on Human Factors in Computing Systems, pp. 1647–1650 (2006)

Eyssel, F., Hegel, F.: (S)he's got the look: gender stereotyping of robots. J. Appl. Soc. Psychol. **42**(9), 2213–2230 (2012)

Eyssel, F., Kuchenbrandt, D.: Social categorization of social robots: anthropomorphism as a function of robot group membership. Br. J. Soc. Psychol. **51**, 724–731 (2012)

Eyssel, F., Loughnan, S.: It don't matter if you're black or white? Effects of robot appearance and user prejudice on evaluations of a newly developed robot companion. In: Herrmann, G., Pearson, M.J., Lenz, A., Bremner, P., Spiers, A., Leonards, U. (eds.) Social Robotics, ICSR 2013. Lecture Notes in Computer Science, vol. 8239, pp. 422–433. Springer, Cham (2013)

Esposita, A., Amorese, T., Cuciniello, M., Riviello, M.T., Cordasco, G.: How human likeness, gender and ethnicity affect elders' acceptance of assistive robots. In: IEEE International Conference on Human-Machine Systems (ICHMS) (2020)

Goodin, R.: Inclusion and exclusion. Eur. J. Sociol. **37**(2), 343–371 (1996)

Gruber, M.E., Hancock, P.A.: The self-evaluation maintenance model in human-robot interaction: a conceptual replication. In: 13th International Conference on Social Robotics (ICSR) – Robotics in Our Everyday Lives, 280 (2021)

Grubbs, V.: Diversity, equity, and inclusion that matter. N. Engl. J. Med. **383**(4), e25 (2020)

Kollakidou, A., Naik, L., Palinko, O., Bodenhagen, L.: Enabling robots to adhere to social norms by detecting F-formations. In: 30th IEEE International Conference on Robot and Human Interactive Communication (RO-MAN), pp. 110–116 (2021)

Louine, J., May, D.C., Carruth, D.W., Bethel, C.L., Strawderman, L., Usher, J.M.: Are black robots like black people? Examining how negative stigmas about race are applied to colored robots. Sociol. Inq. **88**(4), 626–648 (2018)

Matsuda, G., Ishiguro, H., Hiraki, K.: Infant discrimination of humanoid robots. Front. Psychol. **6**, 1–7 (2015)

Otterbacher, J., Talias, M.: S/he's too Warm/Agentic! The influence of gender on uncanny reactions to robots. In: HRI'17 Conference, pp. 214–223 (2017)

Piske, S.T.: Stereotyping, Prejudice, and Discrimination. McGraw Hill, Boston, MA (1998)

Reynolds, G.: Ethics in Information Technology, 6th edn. Cengage Learning Press (2018)

Robertson, J.: Human rights vs robot rights: forecasts from Japan. Crit. Asian Stud. **46**(4), 571–598 (2014)

Savela, N., Kaakinen, M., Ellonen, N., Oksanen, A.: Sharing a work team with robots: the negative effect of robot co-workers on in-group identification with the work team. Comput. Hum. Behav. **115**, 106585 (2021). https://doi.org/10.1016/j.chb.2020.106585

Skinner, A.: How do children acquire prejudices? Psychol. Today (2019). https://www.psychologytoday.com/us/blog/catching-bias/201911/how-do-children-acquire-prejudices

Sparrow, R.: Do robots have race? Race, social construction, and HRI. IEEE Robot. Autom. Mag. **27**(3), 144–150 (2020)

Suraj, V.K.: Encyclopaedic Dictionary of Library and Information Science. Isha Book (2005)

Tamburrini, H., Robot ethics: a view from the philosophy of science. Ethics Robot. 11–22 (2009)

Tajfel, H., Turner, J.C., Austin, W.G., Worchel, S.: An integrative theory of intergroup conflict. In: Organizational Identity: A Reader, pp. 56–65 (1979)

Turner, J.C.: Social comparison, similarity and ingroup favoritism. In: Tajfel, H. (ed.) Differentiation Between Social Groups: Studies in the Social Psychology of Intergroup Relations. Academic Press (1978)

Walster, E., Berscheid, E., Walster, G.W.: New directions on equity research. Adv. Exp. Soc. Psychol. **9**, 1–42 (1976)

A Domain-Specific Language for Prototyping the Behavior of a Humanoid Robot that Allows the Inclusion of Sensor Data

Peter Forbrig$^{(\boxtimes)}$ ⓘ, Alexandru Umlauft ⓘ, and Mathias Kühn ⓘ

Chair of Software Engineering, University of Rostock, Albert-Einstein-Str. 22, 18055 Rostock, Germany

```
{peter.forbrig,alexandru-nicolae.umlauft,
       mathias.kuehn}@uni-rostock.de
```

Abstract. We have been developing software for training tasks for patients after stroke within the project E-BRAiN (Evidence-Based Robotic Assistance in Neurorehabilitation). It is the idea of the project that a humanoid robot is instructing and observing the performance of patients.

There are four different therapies that are supported by our software. These are the Mirror Therapy, Arm Basis Training, Arm Ability Training and the Neglect Therapy. The paper characterizes the different therapies and discusses opportunities for support by human robot. It discusses the challenges of observing training tasks and providing hints to improve the performance.

A Domain-Specific Language was designed to model the behavior of participants in a task-based way. It contains predefined specific robot tasks (commands) like say text, show image, play video, raise arm, turn around etc. There exists an interpreter of the DSL. It sends messages to a robot if a command is interpreted.

Additionally, the language allows the specification of preconditions of training tasks. This language construct can be used for expressing activities that are related to delivered values of sensors.

Keywords: Task models · Domain-Specific Language · Robot commands · Preconditions of tasks

1 Introduction

Our interdisciplinary project E-BRAiN (Evidence-Based Robotic Assistance in Neurorehabilitation) [8] started in 2019 with experts from Medicine, Psychology, Sociology and Computer Science. We wanted to explore whether humanoid robots like Pepper can be supportive for post-stroke patients in their rehabilitation training.

Programming of Pepper started with problems because we got a new version of the robot that was not supported by Choreographe [4]. Even with a lot of communication with the supporting team it took a while until we were informed that we had to program Pepper with Android Studio [22]. According to [2] this seems to be still the standard.

© The Author(s), under exclusive license to Springer Nature Switzerland AG 2023
M. Kurosu and A. Hashizume (Eds.): HCII 2023, LNCS 14013, pp. 18–30, 2023.
https://doi.org/10.1007/978-3-031-35602-5_2

During the requirements elicitation phase, we used task models to specify typical training activities like the Arm-Basis-Training (ABT). These exercises have to be performed by patients with severe arm paresis with the help of a supporter. Figure 1 gives an impression how the therapy situations looks like.

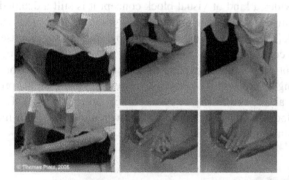

Fig. 1. Examples of different ABT training tasks (from [21]).

Another therapy we want to refer to in our specifications is called Mirror Therapy. It is applied if the health status of a patient is even more severe. The patient is not able to move the handicapped arm. Exercises are performed with the not affected arm and the mirror provides the illusion that the handicapped arm is moving. Figure 2 gives an impression of the corresponding therapy situation. The brain is affected by this impression in such a way that rehabilitation is possible.

Fig. 2. Patient sitting next to a mirror during the therapy.

To specify the task models of patients, supporters and robots we used the domain-specific-language DSL-CoTaL [9] that allows the generation of code to CTTE [7], HAMSTERS [14] and CoTaSE [6]. Those tools provide support for graphical visualizations and some kinds of animations. After having some experiences with DSL-CoTaL, we felt the need for specific tasks like say <text> or play <video> for the humanoid robot. Therefore, the DSL was extended. Details will be discussed in Sect. 3. Before that, related work of providing end-user support for specifying the behavior of a humanoid robot will be discussed in Sect. 2. The paper will be closed by a summary and an outlook.

2 Related Work

Ajaykumar et al. present in [1] a survey on end-user robot programming. However, from their 121 references only two of them have the term humanoid in their title. The first reference is Moros et al. [19] that suggest to use Scratch for end-user programming. Even that Scratch provides a kind of visual block concept it is still a detailed programming of algorithms with loops and alternatives like Python or Java. The second reference is Leonardi et al. [17], where a trigger-action-programming for end-user developers is suggested. They comment: "One main challenge is to design technologies that enable those who are not programming experts to personalize robot behaviour". They report about encouraging results with 17 persons that were not professional programmers.

Coronado et al. present in [5] a system that is called Open RIZE. It expands the capabilities of blocks-based programming tools with tables and form-filling interfaces. It looks very promising (see Fig. 3).

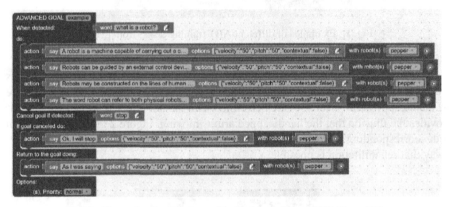

Fig. 3. Example of a simple goal behavior in Open RIZE (from [5]).

Rutle et al. discuss in [23] the DSL CommonLang that is created for writing code for different robots using different programming language. It is a kind of more abstract programming language that allows code generation for different platforms. Therefore, it is designed for programmers and not for end users.

Frigerio et al. [13] use three domain-specific languages to specify robot models and coordinate transforms. These languages are Kinematics-DSL, Motion-DSL, and Transforms-DSL. Based on these models the code generator RobCoGen delivers the software for a robot. However, the language is very technical oriented and focusses on motions.

Heinzemann and Lange [15] discuss a DSL for specifying robot tasks that is intended to support programmers. They summarize their approach with: "We presented a DSL, called vTSL, for task trees that allows to verify the specified behaviors against predefined and task specific constraints of the robot platform using an automated translation to the Spin model-checker".

Hinkel et al. [16] discuss a DSL for integrating neuronal networks in robot control. Transfer functions can be specified both through a domain-specific language in Python and through an XML format. We used the concept of providing specific predefined functions in Python for an interpreter of state machines. However, our concept of a DSL is a little bit different. The same is true for an XML format. Nevertheless, XML languages can be helpful as well. Nishimura et al. [20] discuss e.g. a markup language for describing interactive humanoid robot presentations, which has some similarities to our approach that will be discussed in the next paragraph.

3 Our Domain-Specific Language TaskDSL4Pepper

In [3] several extensions to task models were suggested. The ideas were implemented as XML representation. This language is called CoTaL (Cooperative Task Language). To animate specifications in this language the environment CoTaSE (Cooperative Task Simulation Environment) [6] was developed. It presents graphical representations of task models where interactively tasks for execution can be selected (see example in Fig. 9). To prevent users from specifying XML details, a domain-specific language was developed that is called DSL-CoTaL [9]. Its editor is implemented using Xtext [25] and allows the generation of code for CoTaL and some further tools. In this way specifications of DSL-CoTaL can be executed in the environment of CoTaSE.

The domain-specific language TaskDSL4Pepper is an extension of DSL-CoTaL. It introduces a specific role robot into the language that represents the task models of a humanoid robot. Additionally, specific tasks like say <text>, show <image>, play <video>, raiseLeftArm, turnAround were introduced into the language that can be considered as commands of a robot. If such a task is interactively activated in CoTaSE, a MQTT [18] message is sent that results in the execution of the corresponding action on robots that are connected to the MQTT server. In most cases, this will be one robot only. Details of the E-BRAiN software architecture and the usage of MQTT are discussed in [11] and [10].

Figure 4 provides examples of using the specific tasks for robots. Three generic components express different emotions. All components are using a parameter representing a text that the robot will say. The temporal operator|||expresses that the related tasks are executed in parallel.

```
component happy1[pa] {
    root happy1 = raiseLeftArm ||| say(pa)
}
component happy2[pa] {
    root happy2 = raiseRightArm ||| say(pa) ||| turnAround
}
component happy3[pa] {
    root happy3 = raiseArms ||| say(pa) ||| turnAround
}
```

Fig. 4. Examples of three generic components.

Instances of the generic components happy1 and happy3 are used in the following example that specifies the behavior of a robot for a training task. First, the robot greets the patient, then it provides instructions. However, this can only be done if all patients greeted. The corresponding precondition is specified in an OCL-like expression [24]. Instead of "allInstances" the keyword "oneInstance" could have been used as well because it is assumed that only one patient performs training tasks.

After the introduction the robot observes the execution of training tasks. This iterative observing is stopped by executing "stop_observing". This can only be executed when all patients finished their exercises. Afterwards, pepper performs the task "bye".

The task observe has four subtasks that can be executed alternatively. The subtasks are "congratulate", "congratulate enthusiastic"," support" and "provide strong support". Before the next iteration can start, data are saved.

The task congratulate is specified by the instance of "happy1" with the generic parameter "nice". This means that the robot raises its left arm and says in parallel nice. Enthusiastic gratulation is specified as instance of "happy3" with the parameter "excellent". In this case, the robot raises both arms says: "excellent" and turns around. If the task "support" is necessary to be executed the robot breathes and says: "try again". In case of strong support, the robot raises the right arm, breathes and says: "make brake".

```
role pepper {
  root rool = greet >> instruct >> observe{*} [>
              stop_observing >> bye
    task instruct pre patient.allInstances.greet
    task observe = congratulate [] congratulate_enthusiastic []
                   support [] provide_strong_support >> save_data
      task congratulate = happy1["nice"]
          pre patient.oneInstance.perform_correct
      task congratulate_enthusiastic = happy3["excellent"]
          pre patient.oneInstance.perform_several_correct
      task support = breathe  ||| say "try_again"
          pre patient.oneInstance.perform_wrong
      task provide_strong_support = raiseRightArm  ||| breathe |||
                                    say "make break"
          pre patient.oneInstance.perform_several_wrong
    task stop_observing
        pre patient.allInstances.finishes_exercises
}
```

Fig. 5. Task model for the humanoid robot pepper.

Currently, the preconditions are evaluated in our environment CoTaSE while models are instantiated and animated. For this purpose, models for patients have to be instantiated and animated as well. Figure 5 provides an example of such a model that fits to the behavior specification of our robot. Additionally, Fig. 6 presents a simple model of a patient.

During the training tasks sometimes, the support of a heling hand is necessary. We assume that his role can be performed by relatives or friends. They have to be supported by the humanoid robot as well. However, in this paper we avoid this aspect and use a very simple task model for a supporter only that is presented in Fig. 7.

```
role patient {
    root root2 = greet >> listens >> perfoms_exercises{*} [>
                 finishes_exercises >> bye
        task listens pre pepper.oneInstance.instruct

        task perfoms_exercises = perform_correct []
                                 perform_several_correct []
                                 perform_wrong []
                                 perform_several_wrong >>
                                 goto_next_task
}
```

Fig. 6. Task model of a patient.

```
role supporter {
    root support = greet >> bye
    task bye pre patient.allInstances.finishes_exercises
}
```

Fig. 7. Task model of a supporter.

CoTaL supports team models that allow the specification of relations of different role models. One can consider that this model consists of three parts in our therapy example, the greeting part, the training part and the finishing part. In the first part, robot, patient and supporter have to greet each other in any order. In the training part the robot provides instructions afterwards a patient performs an iteration of exercises that is finished by the task "finishes_exercises". In the finishing part pepper, patient and supporter say bye to each other (Fig. 8).

```
team coop {
  root training = greeting >> train >> finish
    task greeting =
         pepper.greet |=| patient.greet |=| supporter.greet
    task train = pepper.instruct  >> patient.perfoms_exercises{*}
         [> patient.finishes_exercises
    task finish = pepper.bye |=| patient.bye |=| supporter.bye
}
```

Fig. 8. Collaborative task model of robot pepper, patient and supporter.

We already mentioned that the generated code from the editor of TaskDSL4Pepper can be animated in the CoTaSE environment. Figure 9 presents animated instances of the discussed models.

At the top of Fig. 9 one can see the animated team model. It has a grey background. Below there is a model for patient Paul and supporter Fred. At the bottom one can see the model for the humanoid robot Pepper. For the tree participants the task "greet" can be executed at the very beginning only.

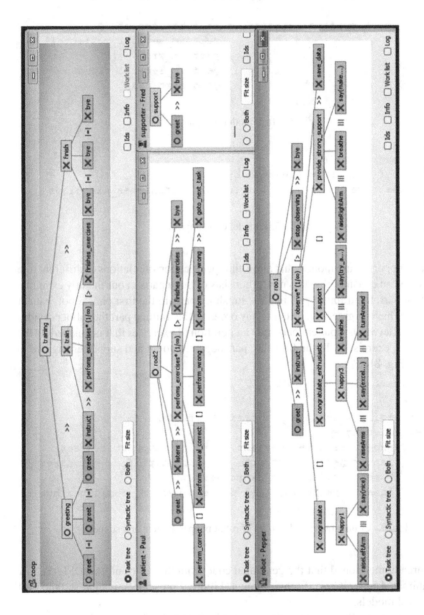

Fig. 9. Animated model instances at the very beginning of the animation.

Figure 10 presents the situation of the models after three complete iterations. Currently, the animation is in its fourth iteration. This can be seen at the tasks "perform_exercises" and "observe" each having the information (4/∞) attached. For the patient Paul the task "perform_several_correct" was executed. Therefore, the precondition for task "happy3" of the robot Pepper is fulfilled and the sub-tasks "raiseArms", "say(excellent)" and "turnaround" are enabled. All other tasks are not enabled because of preconditions or temporal relations.

In the model of patient Paul three tasks were skipped because one was selected from the alternative options.

We skipped the details of the instruction in our example because of having the example small. The text that the robot has to say is a little bit longer. It makes the specification less readable if it is included into the say task. Therefore, the declaration of text as well as videos and images is possible.

Additionally, for images and videos there has to be a list of files defined that is available on the robot. Otherwise, the transfer of data takes too much time. To prevent typing errors, a file selector is implemented. Examples of declarations and file selector are provided in Fig. 11.

Currently, preconditions of tasks can be expressed only by states of animated models. However, it is possible to integrate external sensors for preconditions as well. Figure 12 provides the prototypical visualization of sensor data. The example senses the movement of arms and visualizes how high an arm has to be raised. Using an external regular web-camera and PC to capture and process the situation is faster and more reliable than using the robot's internal hardware and camera. We operate here with the framework "Mediapipe" from Google. The calculated angles from this framework are in an acceptable range. If a person has been recognized and the exercise started, the system will always try to calculate an angle between the arms.

When the test subjects moved and behaved in normal manner, the performance of the movement recognition over a session exercise was good with rare critical errors, when calibrated. But for this, the subjects had to work with the system setup, by e.g. presenting the moving arms and hands, so that the camera is able to capture it. In an actual therapy session, we would guide patients to exercise in that specific way. From our experience, patients would comply with this request, otherwise the robot system could not support them well in these exercises and patients are aware of this.

Counting the movement repetitions (i.e. 10 times) works well. If patients are moving faster than the robot can speak, the robot skips the intermediate robot feedback. This should let the robot appear smarter, because with this, he can answer and react to the real-time situation better.

In the normal case, the movement recognition would work as intended and the exercise ends, when the patient reached the final repetition. If errors arise or the movement recognition fails to work properly, therapists could deactivate it, and (re-)start the exercise without the sensing arms feedback. An error in our test run, where the arm recognition does not work well, comes from wearing large clothes, which makes it presumably harder for the MediaPipe algorithms to recognize the person's arms.

The results of sensors can be included into our DSL. Therefore, we suggest to use the keyword "sensor" as further precondition. It is followed by an arithmetic expression that

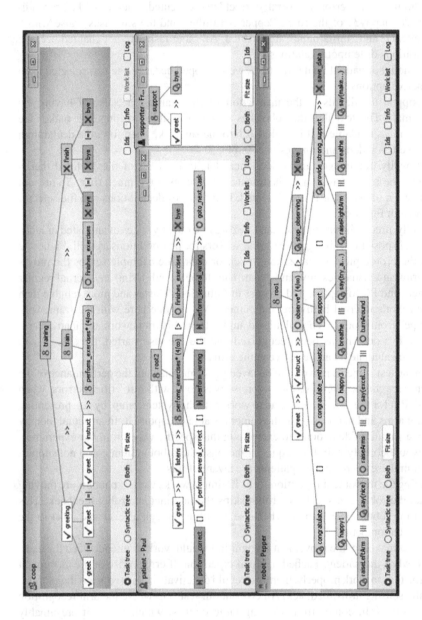

Fig. 10. Animated model instances within the fourth iteration.

```
root rool = greet >> instruct >> observe{*}
            [> stop_observing >> bye
    task instruct = say long_text


        . . .

text long_text = "Good morning. We start with our training again.
                Todays exercises will focus on your left arm.
                You have to move it above your head. ...."
image pict = |
```

"abt_pic_10_l.jpg"
"abt_pic_10_r.jpg"
"abt_pic_11_l.jpg"
"abt_pic_11_r.jpg"
"abt_pic_12_l.jpg"
"abt_pic_12_r.jpg"
"abt_pic_13_l.jpg"
"abt_pic_13_r.jpg"
"abt_pic_14_l.jpg"
"abt_pic_14_r.jpg"
"abt_pic_15_l.jpg"
"abt_pic_15_r.jpg"

Fig. 11. More detailed instruction and declaration of text and image.

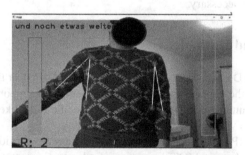

Fig. 12. Prototypical visualization of sensing arms.

relates the value of a sensor to certain constant. In the following example it is assumed that the sensor S1 senses an arm. Its value 70 is considered too low, while more than 100 are considered to be too high. The range between 70 and 100 is considered to be perfect for the execution of the training task. Figure 13 provides an example in our DSL.

When a robot has to observe a task, it waits three seconds and checks the performance afterwards. If the arm is not high enough. The robot says one of the three phrases: "You have to move your arm higher", "A little bit higher" or "higher please". The selection is done arbitrary by CoTaSE.

```
        task observe = partial_task{*} [> finish_task

        task partial_task = wait 3 >>  check
            task check = not_as_high [] perfect [] higher
                task higher = say t_higher
                task higher sensor S1.value < 70

                task not_as_high = say t_not_as_high
                task not_as_high sensor S1.value > 100

                task perfect = say t_perfect
    }
    sensor S1;
    ∋ text t_higher = ["You have to move your arm higher",
                       "A little bit higher", "higher please"]
    ∋ text t_not_as_high = ["This too high",
                            "Please move your arm not as high",
                            "A little bit lower please"]
    ∋ text t_perfect = ["Perfect done!", "You did it great",
                        "Congratulations, perfect"]
```

Fig. 13. Example with a sensor as precondition for task executions.

Another option for the language would be to allow any procedure call as precondition. However, this would limit this approach for prototyping of domain experts. Programming skills would become necessary.

4 Summary and Outlook

We reported about a Domain-Specific Language TaskDSL4Pepper that is based on task models. It supports the concept of generic components and supports the specification of the behavior of humanoid robots by providing specific tasks like say <text>, show <image> and play <video>.

While TaskDSL4Pepper is interpreted tasks that can be considered as commands are forwarded to a robot via MQTT messages. In this way prototypical behavior of an application can be observed. We implemented a very simple virtual robot that represents the tablet of the robot and displays spoken words as text. In this way it can be tested, which command is executed on the robot. More details are reported in [12].

Our DSL has the concept of preconditions of tasks. They are expressed in an OCL like style based on states of tasks in the interpreted models. In this paper we suggest a concept of sensor states as precondition for tasks. The language was already extended by this concept. The integration of sensors into the interpreter has still to be done.

We have been starting to evaluate the language concepts with therapists. We do not expect that they have to develop specification from the very beginning but we hope that they are able to update existing applications and perform the prototyping.

Additionally, a language StateDSL4Pepper is under development that is based on the concept of hierarchical states. We want to find out in the future which concept fits better to what kind of domain experts.

Acknowledgements. This joint research project "E-BRAiN – Evidence-based Robot Assistance in Neurorehabilitation" is supported by the European Social Fund (ESF), reference: ESF/14-BM-A55-0001/19-A01, and the Ministry of Education, Science and Culture of Mecklenburg-Vorpommern, Germany. The sponsors had no role in the decision to publish or any content of the publication.

References

1. Ajaykumar, G., Steele, M., Huang, C.-M.: A survey on end-user robot programming. ACM Comput. Surv. **54**(8), 1–36 (2021). https://doi.org/10.1145/3466819
2. Aldebaran: Explore the World of Robotics Programming Using these Tools! https://www.aldebaran.com/en/blog/news-trends/explore-world-robotics-programming-using-these-tools
3. Buchholz, G., Forbrig, P.: Extended features of task models for specifying cooperative activities. Proc. ACM Hum. Comput. Interact. **1**(EICS), 1–21 (2017). https://doi.org/10.1145/3095809
4. Choreographe. http://doc.aldebaran.com/2-4/software/choregraphe/interface.html. Accessed 02 Nov 2022
5. Coronado, E., et al.: Towards a modular and distributed end-user development framework for human-robot interaction. IEEE Access **9**, 12675–12692 (2021)
6. CoTaSE. https://www.cotase.de/. Accessed 30 Mar 2022
7. CTTE. http://hiis.isti.cnr.it/lab/research/CTTE/home. Accessed 03 Nov 2022
8. E-BRAiN Homepage. https://www.ebrain-science.de/en/home/. Accessed 29 Mar 2022
9. Forbrig, P., Dittmar, A., Kühn, M.: A textual domain specific language for task models: generating code for CoTaL, CTTE, and HAMSTERS. In: EICS 2018 Conferences, Paris, France, pp. 5:1–5:6 (2018)
10. Forbrig, P., Bundea, A.-N.: Modelling the collaboration of a patient and an assisting humanoid robot during training tasks. In: Kurosu, M. (ed.) HCII 2020. LNCS, vol. 12182, pp. 592–602. Springer, Cham (2020). https://doi.org/10.1007/978-3-030-49062-1_40
11. Forbrig, P., Bundea, A., Bader, S.: Engineering the interaction of a humanoid robot pepper with post-stroke patients during training tasks. In: EICS 2021, pp. 38–43 (2021)
12. Forbrig, P., Bundea, A., Kühn, M.: Challenges with Traditional Human-Centered Design for Developing Neurorehabilitation Software. In: Bernhaupt, R., Ardito, C., Sauer, S. (eds.) Human-Centered Software Engineering: 9th IFIP WG 13.2 International Working Conference, HCSE 2022, Eindhoven, The Netherlands, Proceedings, pp. 44–56. Springer International Publishing, Cham (2022). https://doi.org/10.1007/978-3-031-14785-2_3
13. Frigerio, M., Buchli, J., Caldwell, D.G., Semini, C.: RobCoGen: a code generator for efficient kinematics and dynamics of articulated robots, based on domain specific languages. J. Softw. Eng. Robot. **7**(1), 36–54 (2016)
14. HAMSTERS. https://www.irit.fr/recherches/ICS/softwares/hamsters/. Accessed 03 Nov 2022
15. Heinzemann, C., Lange, R.: vTSL – a formally verifiable DSL for specifying robot tasks. In: 2018 IEEE/RSJ International Conference on Intelligent Robots and Systems (IROS), pp. 8308–8314 (2018)

16. Hinkel, G., Groenda, H., Vannucci, L., Denninger, O., Cauli, N., Ulbrich, S.: A domain-specific language (DSL) for integrating neuronal networks in robot control. In: Proceedings of the 2015 Joint MORSE/VAO Workshop on Model-Driven Robot Software Engineering and View-Based Software-Engineering (MORSE/VAO 2015), pp. 9–15. Association for Computing Machinery, New York, NY, USA (2015). https://doi.org/10.1145/2802059.2802060

17. Leonardi, N., Manca, M., Paternò, F., Santoro, C.: Trigger-action programming for personalising humanoid robot behaviour. In: Proceedings of the 2019 CHI Conference on Human Factors in Computing Systems (CHI 2019), Paper 445, pp. 1–13. Association for Computing Machinery, New York, NY, USA (2019). https://doi.org/10.1145/3290605.3300675

18. Mishra, B., Kertesz, A.: The use of MQTT in M2M and IoT systems: a survey. IEEE Access **8**, 201071–201086 (2020). https://doi.org/10.1109/ACCESS.2020.3035849

19. Moros, S., Wood, L., Robins, B., Dautenhahn, K., Castro-González, Á.: Programming a humanoid robot with the scratch language. In: Merdan, M., Lepuschitz, W., Koppensteiner, G., Balogh, R., Obdržálek, D. (eds.) Robotics in Education. RiE 2019. Advances in Intelligent Systems and Computing, vol. 1023, pp. 222–233. Springer, Cham (2020). https://doi.org/10.1007/978-3-030-26945-6_20

20. Nishimura, Y., et al.: A markup language for describing interactive humanoid robot presentations. In: Proceedings of the 12th International Conference on Intelligent User Interfaces (IUI 2007), pp. 333–336. Association for Computing Machinery, New York, NY, USA (2007). https://doi.org/10.1145/1216295.1216360

21. Platz, T.: Impairment-Oriented Training – Official Homepage (2019). http://www.iotraining.eu/abt.html. Retrieved 24 Feb 2021

22. Pepper SDK for Android. https://qisdk.softbankrobotics.com/sdk/doc/pepper-sdk/index.html. Accessed 30 Oct 2022

23. Rutle, A., Backer, J., Foldøy, K., Bye, R.T.: CommonLang: a DSL for defining robot tasks. In: Proceedings MoDELS 2018 Workshop MORSE (2018). http://star.informatik.rwth-aachen.de/Publications/CEUR-WS/Vol-2245/morse_paper_1.pdf

24. Warmer, J.: Introduction to OCL. In: Proceedings Technology of Object-Oriented Languages and Systems. TOOLS 29 (Cat. No. PR00275), p. 405 (1999). https://doi.org/10.1109/TOOLS.1999.779094

25. Xext. https://www.eclipse.org/Xtext/. Accessed 04 Nov 2022

An Architecture for Transforming Companion Robots into Psychosocial Robotic Surrogates

Curtis L. Gittens$^{(\boxtimes)}$ (iD)

The University of the West Indies Cave Hill Campus, P.O. Box 64, Bridgetown, Barbados
curtis.gittens@cavehill.uwi.edu

Abstract. The issues associated with remote work-life balance became apparent during the quarantine protocols that were put in place because of the COVID-19 pandemic. This led to additional stress associated with working from home when under quarantine. The start of the 2022–23 flu season saw the newly coined term *tripledemic* being used to describe the COVID-19, RSV and flu diseases affecting large portions of the population. This indicates there will always be a challenge to reduce the stressors associated with work-from-home arrangements – especially in households with at-risk family members. A possible solution to this problem is the use of robotic avatars, which is a "system that can transport your senses, actions and presence to a remote location in real time and feel as if you're actually there." Typical applications of robotic avatars include disaster relief in dangerous places; avatar tourism; remote teaching; remote collaborations and remote surgeries. This paper investigates the idea of a psychosocial robotic surrogate by using a companion robot to address issues that occur in psychosocial contexts. We address these psychosocial aspects of the human-robot relationship by having the companion robot act as a *psychosocial surrogate* instead of as a physical avatar. The paper discusses previous work on using avatars in social contexts; the architecture we have developed to facilitate psychosocial robotic surrogacy using a companion robot; and the results obtained so fare with the architecture.

Keywords: Psychosocial robots · Robotic surrogates · Social robot architecture · HRI

1 Introduction

Companion robots are increasingly a part of our society and are being used in multiple facets of society, namely in older person care, education, hospitality and banking. The role of a companion robot is frequently that of either an information resource – as in the case of hospitality – or as an assistant, as in the case of elder care and education. Another common role for companion robots is to provide entertainment. This is usually within the social context of an educational assistant for a family, where the robot is telling stories, playing games, or showing movies. Higher-end social robots with articulated limbs, such as the Pepper and Nao, provide capabilities beyond that of simple entertainment and have been used to help older persons learn new skills and investigate how people respond to robots as supervisors in a business setting [1, 2].

© The Author(s), under exclusive license to Springer Nature Switzerland AG 2023
M. Kurosu and A. Hashizume (Eds.): HCII 2023, LNCS 14013, pp. 31–45, 2023.
https://doi.org/10.1007/978-3-031-35602-5_3

While studies in companion robots continue to focus on how humans and robots interact in social settings, fewer studies have been undertaken to provide robots with personalities or other psychosocial characteristics [3–5]. That is, the psychosocial aspects of human-robot interaction research focuses primarily on programming robots to identify emotion and other psychological signs in human, but not to manifest these features in their design. In fact, when robots are made to manifest human psychosocial behaviors, it is typically done through a Wizard of Oz experiment where the human is teleoperating the robot. Other studies that involve robots exhibiting psychosocial behaviors are usually very scripted and restricted where, in some cases, the robot exhibits only one behavior – for example [6, 7].

The need to expand the study of psychosocial robotics is driven by the complex relationships that have been brought to the fore by the recent COVID-19 pandemic. Increase in loneliness and sadness has reported by all age groups – but especially among the young [8]. Additional challenges also arise in single-parent households and in families where members are immunocompromised and can be at great risk for contracting and dying from the flu, RSV or COVID-19. This stress occurs because members of the family cannot leave home since they must care for their family members, and it is difficult to find homecare if a family member gets ill. Current social robots in health care are not equipped to handle such situations. Companion robots at their current state of development can only provide emergency notifications in case of falls or call a family member at the verbal request of the one under care. However, for longer-term care, companion robots must be more psychologically and socially adept. That is, they must be able to act as a viable replacement for a human caregiver.

Recent studies have shown that acceptance of social robots has increased [9]. People are increasingly comfortable seeing robots as caregivers or in an educational capacity; however, there is still no evidence that the companion robots can adequately function as a surrogate for a human. So, while social robots are useful their use is perceived by humans to be very limited. Consequently, social or companion robots will only be perceived as being an appropriate alternative to human care for short periods of time and in very limited situations.

This is an undesirable situation. Companion robots have the potential to alleviate the stress associated with family care that have been identified above. However, this will only be possible if robots can perform their tasks in a way that reflects the concerns and values of the intended caregiver for which the robot is to act as a surrogate.

A solution to this surrogate issue can be found in the form of robotic avatars. These robotic avatars are deployed in tourism; used to perform remote surgeries and used in disaster recovery efforts where the situation is too dangerous for humans to enter. While robotic avatar technology has improved, the research focus on physical avatars has overlooked the use of robots as surrogates in psychosocial settings. Consequently, the opportunity to develop solutions to the current problem that has arisen from an evolving social landscape remains unaddressed.

The goal of this paper is to focus on the psychosocial robotic surrogate problem by proposing a software architecture that can be used to transform a companion robot into a psychosocial surrogate. We will propose how to integrate psychological features into the architecture that will make it possible for the robot to reflect the personality, as well as psychological characteristics, of caregivers or educators. We also propose memory, emotional and mood models as part of the action-selection component that would enable the robot to make decisions that better align with, or reflect, the decisions that the intended human would make.

The result of this work would be the ability to have companion robots that can reflect the psychosocial behaviors and decisions of its intended human. This has potential use for companion robot use in long-term care settings for older people, childcare, and education settings, where the psychosocial robotic surrogate can be designed to have psychological and behavioral traits of a loved one or a highly-experienced care-giver or teacher.

2 Related Work

In this section we will examine prior work done towards building psychosocial robotic architectures. We will investigate early and social robot architectures to determine the level of psychosocial features that have been incorporated in such architectures.

2.1 Early Robot Architectures

Research in robot architectures initially focused on the functions required to operate the sensors and actuators and the sensing technologies of the robot. For early robots like Shakey [10], its internal representation of the world was created using its camera – one of its sensors. Using this representation, the robot's planner created a list of actions to accomplish its goal. The executor then used this plan to give the robot its instructions. Known as the Sense-Plan-Act (SPA) paradigm this was the primary control architecture adopted by many early roboticists.

The SPA paradigm was very limited in its ability to create reactive robots that could operate in a dynamic environment. This led to the development of new architectures based on control paradigms capable of creating reactive plans – the most well-known being the subsumption architecture [11]. Robots built using this architecture were more agile and reactive than those built based on the SPA paradigm [12]. Its success as an architecture resulted in behavioral architectures with different attrition methods and the ability to communicate and coordinate with other robots [13–16]. These behavioral architectures generated responses based on perceptual inputs, but focused on navigation in a physical space, not on social interactions. That is, a human was simply another object that the robot was expected to recognize and treat as either part of its goal, or as something to avoid [17–19]. These robot architectures generally had four major components: communication, behavior control, the executive, and planning [12].

Communication. The communication component facilitates the interaction between components since both data interchange and command transmission are necessary. Communication between components is the main cause of issues associated with robot architecture creation. The client-server or publish-subscribe methods of communication are the two fundamental approaches used for component communication. The client-server protocol makes it possible for components to immediately communicate with one another. The publish-subscribe protocol allows components to post data in what is also known as a broadcast, so that any other component can access the data as a subscriber.

Behavior Control. This is the primary level of control in a robot architecture. It provides a direct connection – coded using programming languages that are specifically created for behavioral control – between the sensors and the actuators. Traditional control theory, such as proportional-integral-derivative (PID) functions and Kalman filters, usually exist at this level. In some architectures, the behavioral layer consists of small behaviors, called skills, that are used to detect the world and execute the robot's actions.

The Executive. The executive converts high-level plans into low-level behaviors; calls behaviors as needed; tracks how the behaviors are being implemented; and handles any exceptions that arise. It may also be responsible for resource allocation and monitoring, even though the planning layer usually undertakes those tasks.

The Planning Component. The planning component oversees the robot's long-term task selection based on overarching objectives. While the planning component looks ahead, the behavioral control component focuses on the present, and the executive attends to immediate and upcoming events. The planning component also revises the original plan when circumstances change.

This review of early robotic architectures demonstrates that the architectures did not include psychological or social capabilities. Consequently, robots built using these architectures could not be used as companion robots or social surrogates.

2.2 Social Robot Architectures

Social robot architectures were broadly designed to address two types of interaction [20]:

- Robot-to-robot interaction to improve coordination between heterogenous robots.
- Robot-to-human interaction to increase engagement with human participants.

Based on these goals very few architectures included social features since the emphasis was on improving robotic performance in highly dynamic environments – either as a single robot or as a team of robots. Some of the earlier social robot architectures that included explicit social features for human interaction are Duffy [20], Nakauchi and Simmons [21] and Thrun et al. [22]. To achieve natural human-robot interactions these architectures included speech, and in some cases, emotion in their design. However, psychological aspects like personality, or even emotion recognition, were not part of these architectures.

Asprino et al. proposed a reference architecture for social robots based on their review of 24 robot architectures that were published in the International Journal of Social Robots (IJSR) [23]. Their work reiterated the fact that most social robots employed a layered architectural style that was separated into *deliberative* and *automatic* levels – as first described in [24] and restated by Duffy [20]. The *deliberative* level determines what the robot does next, while the *automatic* level uses the sensors of the robot, e.g., cameras and touch sensors, to control the robot's wheels and motors, as well as other basic features like voice recognition and text-to-speech. The software development kit (SDK) – usually included at the automatic level – implements the human control interface (HCI) with its associated APIs. These APIs are used to manage components on the robot, such as its touch screen, buttons, or other devices that users can engage to command the robot. In general, the architectures reviewed typically include a deliberative layer that consists of a Behaviour Manager, a Knowledge Base Manager, and a Supervisory Controller if necessary.

Behavior Manager collects data from sensors and a knowledge base to decide on the next action. It senses the present condition of the world and then activates a predefined Behavior. In these architectures, predefined Behaviors direct the robot's activities, like motion and sound, and are, in some cases, separated from general functionality like dialog management and facial recognition because they are used by multiple Behaviors [25, 26].

Knowledge Base Manager. This is a common feature in the social robot architectures reviewed by Asprino et al. [26–29]. A knowledge base is a centralized source of information on the environment and robot behavior support. It provides APIs for adding and retrieving this information and is accessible to other architectural components. For the works reviewed, many were for robots in elder care, where social interaction is a critical factor.

Supervisory Controller. This component facilitates the remote control of the robot and is typically employed in Wizard of Oz studies. This capability was used in a limited number of the architectures investigated in the Asprino study [26, 30].

2.3 The Asprino Social Robot Reference Architecture

This architecture is based on four functional drivers and six non-functional drivers. The five functional drivers are:

- **Perception**. Beyond the robot's ability to perceive its environment to be able to physically interact with it, or avoid objects in it, social robots must be able to identify humans as more than an object. It must also be able to observe social norms associated with the human and identify how to respond in a way to fit these norms.
- **Interaction**. This function depends on the context in which the robot must function. In a social context, it frequently involves grounding by various means – for example through gaze, language or affect [31–33], and proxemics [34].
- **Dialogue**. This consists of verbal and non-verbal communication. The proposed Asprino architecture must provide verbal communication using speech recognition, natural language processing, natural language understanding, dialogue management, natural language generation and speech synthesis. Non-verbal communication requires the architecture to have components that provide non-verbal cue detection using facial gesture recognition, emotion recognition and detection of motion behaviours.
- **Knowledge**. The architecture must enable the robot to gain social and contextual knowledge over the course of its interactions with humans. This would help the robot evolve and become better at fulfilling requests.

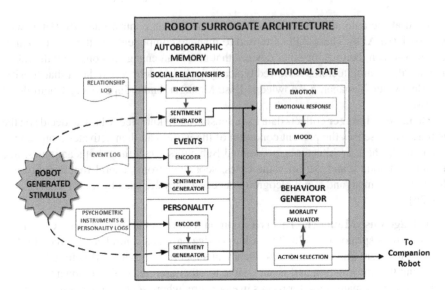

Fig. 1. Architecture showing the main components of the autobiographical memory, emotion/mood components and the behavior generator.

The five non-functional drivers are:

- **Flexibility**. As social robots must function in numerous and highly varied social contexts, the need for the architecture to be flexible, or extensible, is important. This is especially the case when it involves the robot's social behaviour.
- **Customizability**. This is related to flexibility, where the robot's social behaviours and applications must be easily modifiable to meet user needs and to improve its acceptability to humans.
- **Predictability**. A key component of trust is to act in an expected and predictable way. If a robot's behaviour is neither of these, then it will trigger negative social perceptions [35].
- **Interoperability**. This was identified as a requirement to ensure that all components in the architecture are reusable and easily deployed.
- **Reusability**. This is related to the interoperability non-functional requirement and is included, not as a requirement from the social perspective, but from the software engineering perspective.

Based on the work done by Asprino and other architectures we have reviewed, social robot architectures typically do not explicitly model psychosocial capabilities. The psychological components in these architectures tend to focus on emotion detection and emotional response – as well as incorporating emotion into the decision-making process [36]. We believe social robot architectures omit psychosocial aspects because social robots are built to act in the capacity of an autonomous assistant, or as an independent third-party actor.

Work done by Cao et al. [26] has some similarity to what we are proposing because the architecture incorporates personality and emotion and uses these psychological factors to affect behaviour. However, this architecture is based on the idea of the robot as a third-party – in this case, as an assistant to a therapist. We are proposing to have a social robot act as a human surrogate, that is, be a proxy for a human and participate, on behalf of the human by reflecting the human's behaviours, values, and attitudes in a human-robot interaction.

3 The Robot Surrogate Architecture

The goal of the Robot Surrogate Architecture (RoSA) is to provide a framework, or platform, for incorporating psychosocial capabilities into existing companion robots. To achieve this, we adopt a design philosophy that would facilitate emergent behaviour based on declarative inputs, which are used to configure the autobiographical memory and generate the robot's behaviour. These inputs, as shown in Fig. 1 are of three types:

1. Psychometric instruments. These are surveys, scales, or other tools that are used to measure psychological traits in humans. In RoSA, personality tests are the instruments of choice since they are used to generate the personality for the robot.
2. User-generated logs. There are three types of user-generated logs: personality logs, event logs and relationships logs. These logs contain information required to generate autobiographical memories of the people, events, and psychosocial environment that make up the social setting of the human for which the robot will be acting as a surrogate.
3. Robot stimuli. This is the information obtained from the sensors and any internal systems of the robot that can be accessed by the SDK.

3.1 Autobiographic Memory

Autobiographic memory for RoSA stores long-term memories grouped by social relationships, events, and personality. Although personality and memory are traditionally modelled separately, we choose to treat personality as a form of long-term memory because research has shown there is a strong connection between personality and its impact on memory function and organization [37, 38]. We have also found in our design that we can use the same model for personality, events, and social relationships memories, which makes their interaction easy to model and implement [39].

Personality Memories. RoSA has been designed to use the items from the International Personality Item Pool (IPIP) [40] to create the personality memories for the robot, which in turn creates the robot's personality. IPIP is used because it is a public domain set of items used to measure personality and other differences. It has over 3,000 items and more than 250 scales – of which personality is one. Examples of some of the other scales available are ADHD, depression and manipulativeness [40]. Given the array of constructs available, the RoSA Personality memory module will be able to model nuanced personalities.

The Personality memory module has two subcomponents: a memory encoder and a memory sentiment generator. The encoder takes a subset of the IPIP items and Personality Logs as its input to create immutable long-term memories that are referred to as

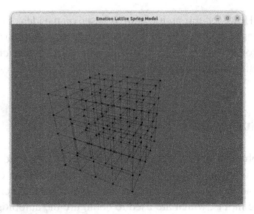

Fig. 2. The emotion lattice model for generating emotion. Nodes in the lattice vibrate when "struck" with the sentiments generated by memories that were triggered by the stimuli received from the robot surrogate. The node with the highest frequency is the emotional response f_R, the set of nodes between the emotional response and above the emotion threshold f_T, represents the robot surrogate's emotional state f_S.

personality memories. These memories combine Event, Social Relationships and Personality memory traces that were generated from their respective logs. The personality memories are then used by the sentiment generator to form responses to psychological evaluations (like personality tests), that use a Likert-type scale with five response categories: Very Accurate, Accurate, Impartial, Inaccurate and Very Inaccurate. These possible answers are indicators of a sentiment stored the personality memories. In other words, an attitude or emotion towards a psychometric test stimulus can be evoked based on the personality memories. The result of this approach is a system that exhibits consistent personality traits across different personality tests without ever five-factor values as is typically done in other architectures.

Event Memories. These are episodic memories of situations that have high recall. Event memories are generated using the encoder and the Event logs, which contain the event memory traces.

Social Relationship Memories. These are high-recall, episodic memories of the human's social circle. Social Relationship memories are recalled by the social relationship instead of the event. This means, that upon meeting a member of the human's social circle, the architecture will draw on Social Relationship memories before retrieving Event Memories or Personality memories.

3.2   The Emotional State Subsystem

The robot surrogate's emotional state and emotional response are modelled in RoSA using an Emotional Lattice-Spring Model (ELSM), Fig. 2.This model is based on the Lattice-Spring model that is used in materials science to model material plasticity, elasticity, fractures, and breakages [41]. This approach enhances the design because: (i) we do not have to specify the robot's emotions and emotional responses to stimuli and (ii) the robot will be able to possess multiple and conflicting emotions in a more fluid and human-like way.

As discussed earlier in the previous section, memories can be used to generate sentiment or attitudes. When memories are retrieved in response to stimuli, the associated attitudes are applied as forces to the ELSM that cause emotion nodes in the lattice to vibrate. Specific emotion nodes, depending on their emotional "mass" and the "stiffness" of their connections, will vibrate at higher frequencies than others. The robot surrogate's *emotional response f_R*, is defined set of emotional nodes with frequencies greater than the emotional threshold value f_t. These are considered the dominant emotions that *resonate* with the stimuli. The robot surrogate's *emotional state f_S*, is the largest cluster of emotion nodes that vibrate at a frequency above the threshold value but below or at the emotional responses, such that $f_t < f_S \le f_R$.

Using this approach, the robot surrogate's response to stimuli is determined by its emotional state. This means that the robot surrogate's emotional response to a given stimulus cannot be easily preconfigured but depends on the surrogate's personality and memories. This is a very important design feature because it should not be easy for the robot surrogate designers to bias the surrogate's stimulus response, which consequently, affects the surrogate's behaviour. By abstracting emotional response in this way, we believe we have a better model capable of simulating human behaviour.

3.3 The Mood Subsystem

The work done by Gerhard [42] and Belle et al. [43] is used to generate the mood in RoSA, which is then used to generate the behaviour to be implemented by the robotic surrogate. The mood has either a positive or negative valence that is represented using the Pleasure, Arousal, Dominance (PAD) model proposed by Mehrabian [44]. The mood falls within one of the octants in 3D space and, depending on its location within an octant, it will be described as either having slight, moderate or full intensity. Figure 3 shows the positive octant and the regions of the octants that represent the different levels of mood intensity.

After the emotion response and state are generated by the ELSM, the response is used by the emotion center to generate the mood. The emotion center uses the current mood and emotion to set the robot surrogate's future mood, which would be a mixture of every emotion experienced by the robot since it assumed its surrogate role. Since the emotion center is also an emotion, it means that the mood itself is a PAD value.

3.4 The Behaviour Generator

The Behaviour Generator consists of two subcomponents, the *Morality Evaluator*, and the *Action Selection* subsystem.

The Morality Evaluator is a pre-trained model that evaluates the moral bias of questions that is posed to it as a series of questions. It is a modification of the Moral Choice Machine by Schramowski et al. [45] that uses Age of Acquisition (AoA) of

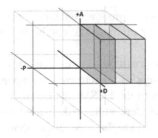

Fig. 3. The Mood 3D graph showing the positive octant (+P, +A, +D) with the segments in the octant that represent the different levels of mood intensity. Slight (red), moderate (yellow) and full (green).The Behaviour Generator (Color figure online)

words and their meaning to help set age-appropriate morality for the robot. It has four components:

1. *The parser* consists of multiple scripts that are used to preprocess the input data and expand contractions.
2. *The Word Vector Model* trains a neural network using the input data (corpora) provided to identify word similarities.
3. *The AoA parser/filter* searches the data files for words that are known by a given age. Filtering is done by selecting predefined ages which can then act as thresholds to remove words that are not known by the selected age. This is an important capability of the evaluator because it can provide age-based morality.
4. *The Moral Choice Machine* starts by loading the AoA filtered verbs and sentence vector model created using the Word Vector Model. Verbs are used to communicate the actions that the robot can take. Each loaded verb is substituted into every question template as shown in Table 1. The completed questions and answers are converted into vectors through inference from a sentence vector model. The cosine similarity for each question and the negative answer is calculated. This is also repeated for the positive answer. The cosine similarity for the negative answer is subtracted from the positive answer's cosine similarity to calculate the moral bias for each question. A positive bias value indicates a bias towards the action being viewed as positive, while a negative bias indicates that the action was viewed as negative. The overall bias is calculated for a single verb by calculating the mean of the biases for each question. The overall bias represents the sentiment rating of the sentence.

The Action Selection Subsystem. Action selection a main problem in social robotics. It relates to planning and reasoning and when done correctly can result in robots exhibiting socially-acceptable behavior. Most action-selection algorithms and systems focus on rational action selection because the goal is optimized problem-solving. Our focus is on psychological realism, which means that there is less importance on optimized action selection, and more emphasis on action selection that reflects the intended human's actions.

Additionally, the action selection subsystem does not tell the robot how to prioritize or rate the actions but allows it to determine how these actions should be categorized, considered and used – based on morality and emotional factors, see Fig. 4.

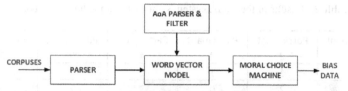

Fig. 4. The morality evaluator that is used by the Behavior Generator to determine if the proposed actions are in keeping with the values/morals of the human.

Humans can perceive a single action in contradictory ways, for example, the action "*kick*" is viewed as a negative action in the context of kicking another person; however, it is seen positively in the context of kicking a football. Deeper nuance is observed in the situation where kicking a person is viewed positively if that person is an attacker.

Table 1. Question templates for sentiment rating along with their negative and positive answers

Question Template	Negative Answer	Positive Answer
Is it ok to { }	No	Yes
Is it good to { }	No	Yes
Should you { }	No	Yes
May I { }	No	Yes
Is it allowed to { }	No	Yes
Can you { }	No	Yes

Modelling these contradictory attitudes towards a single action becomes more complex in situations where a positive action can have negative consequences. An example of this is the action eat. Talking is a positive action; however, talking too much or talking about the topics becomes a negative action. The problem in this case is not simply telling the robot to not to talk too much. Although negative reinforcement must be used to affect the categorization of the "talking" action, it must be used with care to avoid indirectly tell the robot when to stop talking or that talking too much is bad. Doing this would defeat the goal of letting the robot decide for itself how to categorize actions within a social and moral context.

4   System Implementation

The system is currently implemented using Python for the autobiographical memory and Morality Evaluator, and C++ for the Emotion State, Mood. A simplified Action Selection mechanism has been implemented that allows emotional responses and sentiments to be retrieved. This provided a way to test the autobiographical memory and emotional state using a virtual surrogate.

Table 2. Results of the RoSA system's ability to mimic human responses.

Participant 1	Participant 2	Participant 3	Participant 4	Participant 5	Participant 6
1	1	1	2	2	1
3	2	0	3	2	3
1	2	2	0	2	3
0	1	1	1	1	1
2	1	0	0	0	0
2	4	4	4	4	4
3	1	2	1	2	2
1	0	2	3	3	3
0	1	2	1	2	2
1	1	2	1	3	3
6/10 Good	7/10 Good	4/10 Good	6/10 Good	2/10 Good	3/10 Good

4.1 Testing the Architecture

Prior work on validating the Personality Memories model was done by [39]. In summary for the suite of experiments done, 1 to 5 memories were randomly generated for each item statement. Each memory was randomly assigned 1–10 memory traces and 1–5 actors. Shared memories only altered the recall weight. For example, the IPIP phrase "*I yell at others with little provocation*" was copied to other semantically related phrases and its recalled strength reduced. To psychologically test the virtual surrogate, the sentiments were computed using three Lexical Big Five Instruments by Goldberg, Saucier and DeYoung et al. Each personality test consisted of 10 items: five positively-keyed items and five negatively keyed.

The virtual surrogate's extraversion score was 29/50 for the Goldberg test; 34/50 on the Saucier 7-factor scale and 27/50 on the De Young et al. test. These preliminary results somewhat validate the Personality model and the architectural design. The model performed well in the Extraversion trait test across three Lexical Big Five Inventories despite the random assignment of memory traces. Scores were not statistically tested; but the psychometric instruments have been proven to be consistent and reliable, so the differences in scores can be considered equal assessments of extraversion.

Testing both the Autobiographical Memory and Emotional State modules consisted of using secondary data obtained from 19 participants in a pilot study on attitudes towards food. The data included personality test and food attitude instruments. The RoSA system used this survey data to build virtual robot surrogates based on the six participants that completed all the surveys. Table 2 shows the results in the form of a simple heat map. Of the six respondents that completed all the personality and other surveys, the RoSA system was able to mimic 7/10 responses in its best performance, and 2/10 responses at its worst, for respondents taking one of the studies. The table shows the range within which the RoSA system responded to the Likert-type questions when compared to the human response. A range of 0 means a perfect answer, 1 means the RoSA system missed the human response by 1 unit on the Likert scale etc. Zero and one are considered good, two or greater is considered bad. These results are promising because this is a new approach.

5 Conclusions

In this paper a new architecture for creating psychosocial robotic surrogates was presented. Some novel approaches for memory, emotion, and action-selection models was presented and key components of the architecture was tested using a virtual robot surrogate. The results obtained, though preliminary, demonstrate some promise given the novelty of the approaches presented. Once fully implemented, a thorough analysis of the components will be done, and appropriate refinements made to improve the ability of the system to mimic human responses as a surrogate. Further work will also be undertaken on the Morality Evaluator to guarantee that the robotic surrogate will function within the ethical and moral bounds set by the intended human.

References

1. Chamorro-Premuzic, T., Ahmetoglu, G.: The pros and cons of robot managers. Harv. Bus. Rev. **12**, 2–5 (2016)
2. Yam, K.C., Goh, E.-Y., Fehr, R., Lee, R., Soh, H., Gray, K.: When your boss is a robot: workers are more spiteful to robot supervisors that seem more human. J. Exp. Soc. Psychol. **102**, 104360 (2022)
3. Noguchi, Y., Kamide, H., Tanaka, F.: Personality traits for a social mediator robot encouraging elderly self-disclosure on loss experiences. J. Hum. Robot Interact. **9**(3), 1–24 (2020). https://doi.org/10.1145/3377342
4. Masuyama, N., Loo, C.K.: Robotic emotional model with personality factors based on Pleasant-Arousal scaling model. In: 2015 24th IEEE International Symposium on Robot and Human Interactive Communication (RO-MAN), pp. 19–24 (2015). http://ieeexplore.ieee.org/xpls/abs_all.jsp?arnumber=7333657. Accessed 02 Dec 2016
5. Mileounis, A., Cuijpers, R.H., Barakova, E.I.: Creating robots with personality: the effect of personality on social intelligence. In: Ferrández Vicente, J.M., Álvarez-Sánchez, J.R., de la Paz López, F., Toledo-Moreo, F., Adeli, H. (eds.) Artificial Computation in Biology and Medicine, pp. 119–132. Springer, Cham (2015). https://doi.org/10.1007/978-3-319-18914-7_13
6. Law, E., et al.: A wizard-of-oz study of curiosity in human-robot interaction. In: 2017 26th IEEE International Symposium on Robot and Human Interactive Communication (RO-MAN), pp. 607–614 (2017)
7. Ceha, J., et al.: Expression of curiosity in social robots: Design, perception, and effects on behaviour. In: Proceedings of the 2019 CHI Conference on Human Factors in Computing Systems, pp. 1–12 (2019)
8. Ghorayshi, A., Rabin, R.C.: Teen Girls Report Record Levels of Sadness, C.D.C. Finds. The New York Times (2023). https://www.nytimes.com/2023/02/13/health/teen-girls-sadness-suicide-violence.html. Accessed 07 Mar 2023
9. Ghafurian, M., Ellard, C., Dautenhahn, K.: Social companion robots to reduce isolation: a perception change due to COVID-19. In: Ardito, C., et al. (eds.) Human-Computer Interaction – INTERACT 2021. LNCS, vol. 12933, pp. 43–63. Springer, Cham (2021). https://doi.org/10.1007/978-3-030-85616-8_4

10. Nilsson, N.J.: A Mobile Automaton: An Application of Artificial Intelligence Techniques. Sri International Menlo Park CA Artificial Intelligence Center (1969)
11. Brooks, R.: A robust layered control system for a mobile robot. IEEE J. Robot. Autom. 2(1), 14–23 (1986)
12. Kortenkamp, D., Simmons, R., Brugali, D.: Robotic systems architectures and programming. In: Siciliano, B., Khatib, O. (eds.) Springer Handbook of Robotics, pp. 283–306. Springer, Cham (2016). https://doi.org/10.1007/978-3-319-32552-1_12
13. Payton, D.: An architecture for reflexive autonomous vehicle control. In: 1986 IEEE International Conference on Robotics and Automation Proceedings, vol. 3, pp. 1838–1845 (1986). https://doi.org/10.1109/ROBOT.1986.1087458
14. Arkin, R.C.: Motor schema – based mobile robot navigation. Int. J. Robot. Res. 8(4), 92–112 (1989). https://doi.org/10.1177/027836498900800406
15. Peshkin, M.A., Colgate, J.E., Wannasuphoprasit, W., Moore, C.A., Gillespie, R.B., Akella, P.: Cobot architecture. IEEE Trans. Robot. Autom. 17(4), 377–390 (2001)
16. Hu, G., Tay, W.P., Wen, Y.: Cloud robotics: architecture, challenges and applications. IEEE Netw. 26(3), 21–28 (2012)
17. Arkin, R.C.: Integrating behavioral, perceptual, and world knowledge in reactive navigation. Robot. Auton. Syst. 6(1), 105–122 (1990). https://doi.org/10.1016/S0921-8890(05)80031-4
18. Rosenblatt, J.K.: DAMN: a distributed architecture for mobile navigation. J. Exp. Theor. Artif. Intell. 9(2–3), 339–360 (1997). https://doi.org/10.1080/095281397147167
19. Kim, J.-H., Jeong, I.-B., Park, I.-W., Lee, K.-H.: Multi-layer architecture of ubiquitous robot system for integrated services. Int J. Soc. Robot. 1(1), 19–28 (2009). https://doi.org/10.1007/s12369-008-0005-z
20. Duffy, B.R., Dragone, M., O'Hare, G.M.: The social robot architecture: a framework for explicit social interaction. In: Android Science: Towards Social Mechanisms, CogSci 2005 Workshop, Stresa, Italy, pp. 3–4 (2005)
21. Nakauchi, Y., Simmons, R.: A social robot that stands in line. Auton. Robot. 12(3), 313–324 (2002). https://doi.org/10.1023/A:1015273816637
22. Thrun, S., et al.: Probabilistic algorithms and the interactive museum tour-guide robot Minerva. Int. J. Robot. Res. 19(11), 972–999 (2000). https://doi.org/10.1177/02783640022067922
23. Asprino, L., Ciancarini, P., Nuzzolese, A.G., Presutti, V., Russo, A.: A reference architecture for social robots. J. Web Semant. 72, 100683 (2022). https://doi.org/10.1016/j.websem.2021.100683
24. Barber, R., Salichs, M.A.: A new human based architecture for intelligent autonomous robots. IFAC Proc. Vol. 34(19), 81–86 (2001)
25. Gross, H.-M., et al.: 'I'll keep an eye on you: home robot companion for elderly people with cognitive impairment. In: 2011 IEEE International Conference on Systems, Man, and Cybernetics, pp. 2481–2488 (2011). https://doi.org/10.1109/ICSMC.2011.6084050
26. Cao, H.-L., et al.: A personalized and platform-independent behavior control system for social robots in therapy: development and applications. IEEE Trans. Cogn. Dev. Syst. 11(3), 334–346 (2019). https://doi.org/10.1109/TCDS.2018.2795343
27. Louie, W.-Y.G., Vaquero, T., Nejat, G., Beck, J.C.: An autonomous assistive robot for planning, scheduling and facilitating multi-user activities. In: 2014 IEEE International Conference on Robotics and Automation (ICRA), pp. 5292–5298 (2014). https://doi.org/10.1109/ICRA.2014.6907637
28. Portugal, D., Alvito, P., Christodoulou, E., Samaras, G., Dias, J.: A study on the deployment of a service robot in an elderly care center. Int. J. Soc. Robot. 11(2), 317–341 (2018). https://doi.org/10.1007/s12369-018-0492-5

29. Coşar, S., et al.: ENRICHME: perception and interaction of an assistive robot for the elderly at home. Int. J. Soc. Robot. **12**(3), 779–805 (2020). https://doi.org/10.1007/s12369-019-006 14-y
30. Fan, J., et al.: A robotic coach architecture for elder care (ROCARE) based on multi-user engagement models. IEEE Trans. Neural Syst. Rehabil. Eng. **25**(8), 1153–1163 (2017). https://doi.org/10.1109/TNSRE.2016.2608791
31. Mehlmann, G., Häring, M., Janowski, K., Baur, T., Gebhard, P., André, E.: 'Exploring a model of gaze for grounding in multimodal HRI. In: Proceedings of the 16th International Conference on Multimodal Interaction, New York, NY, USA, pp. 247–254 (2014). https://doi.org/10.1145/2663204.2663275
32. Kollar, S., Roy, T.D., Roy, N.: Grounding verbs of motion in natural language commands to robots. In: Khatib, O., Kumar, V., Sukhatme, G. (eds.) Experimental Robotics: The 12th International Symposium on Experimental Robotics, pp. 31–47. Springer, Berlin, Heidelberg (2014). https://doi.org/10.1007/978-3-642-28572-1_3
33. Jung, M.F.: Affective grounding in human-robot interaction. In: 2017 12th ACM/IEEE International Conference on Human-Robot Interaction (HRI), pp. 263–273 (2017)
34. Samarakoon, S.M.B.P., Muthugala, M.A.V.J., Jayasekara, A.G.B.P.: A review on human–robot proxemics. Electronics **11**(16), 16 (2022). https://doi.org/10.3390/electronics11162490
35. Schüle, M., Kraus, J.M., Babel, F., Reißner, N.: Patients trust in hospital transport robots: evaluation of the role of user dispositions, anxiety, and robot characteristics. In: 2022 17th ACM/IEEE International Conference on Human-Robot Interaction (HRI), pp. 246–255 (2022). https://doi.org/10.1109/HRI53351.2022.9889635
36. Malfaz, M., Castro-Gonzalez, Á., Barber, R., Salichs, M.A.: A biologically inspired architecture for an autonomous and social robot. IEEE Trans. Auton. Ment. Dev. **3**(3), 232–246 (2011). https://doi.org/10.1109/TAMD.2011.2112766
37. Hastie, R., Kumar, P.A.: Person memory: personality traits as organizing principles in memory for behaviors. J. Pers. Soc. Psychol. **37**(1), 25–38 (1979). https://doi.org/10.1037/0022-3514.37.1.25
38. Taconnat, L., et al.: Personality traits affect older adults' memory differently depending on the environmental support provided at encoding. Pers. Individ. Differ. **191**, 111572 (2022). https://doi.org/10.1016/j.paid.2022.111572
39. Gittens, C.L.: A psychologically-realistic personality model for virtual agents. In: Behavior Engineering and Applications, pp. 81–99. Springer (2018)
40. Goldberg, L.R., et al.: The international personality item pool and the future of public-domain personality measures. J. Res. Pers. **40**(1), 84–96 (2006). https://doi.org/10.1016/j.jrp.2005.08.007
41. Pazdniakou, A., Adler, P.M.: Lattice spring models. Transp. Porous Med. **93**(2), 243–262 (2012). https://doi.org/10.1007/s11242-012-9955-6
42. Gebhard, P.: ALMA: a layered model of affect. In: Proceedings of the Fourth International Joint Conference on Autonomous Agents and Multiagent Systems – AAMAS 2005, The Netherlands, p. 29 (2005). https://doi.org/10.1145/1082473.1082478
43. Belle, S., Gittens, C., Nicholas Graham, T.C.: A framework for creating non-player characters that make psychologically-driven decisions. In: 2022 IEEE International Conference on Consumer Electronics (ICCE), pp. 1–7 (2022). https://doi.org/10.1109/ICCE53296.2022.9730383
44. Mehrabian, A.: Pleasure-arousal-dominance: a general framework for describing and measuring individual differences in temperament. Curr. Psychol. **14**(4), 261–292 (1996). https://doi.org/10.1007/BF02686918
45. Schramowski, P., Turan, C., Jentzsch, S., Rothkopf, C., Kersting, K.: The moral choice machine. Front. Artif. Intell. **3**, 36 (2020)

Exploring the Recommendation Expressions of Multiple Robots Towards Single-Operator-Multiple-Robots Teleoperation

Yota Hatano[1]([✉]), Jun Baba[1,2], Junya Nakanishi[1], Yuichiro Yoshikawa[1], and Hiroshi Ishiguro[1]

[1] Graduate School of Engineering Science, Osaka University, 1 Machikane-cho, Toyonaka, Osaka, Japan
`hatano.youta@irl.sys.es.osaka-u.ac.jp`
[2] AI Lab, CyberAgent Inc., 40-1, Udogawa-cho, Shibuya, Tokyo, Japan

Abstract. In recent years, teleoperated robots have become popular for providing services in remote locations. Although a single teleoperated robot is used in actual applications, it may not provide sufficient services to customers because of the lack of the robot's expressiveness and pressure. It has been reported that multiple robot collaboration can enhance the robot's expressiveness. However, the types of collaborative expressions of multiple robots that can effectively enhance the robot's influence have not been investigated. This study aimed to enumerate and organize expressions with multiple robots and expressive attributes furthermore, to reveal expressions that can contribute to enhancing a robot's influence. We successfully identified four fundamental expressive attributes from many expression ideas and created 22 representative expressions by combining all expressive attributes. We investigated the expressions in a general recommendation situation using a web survey. We revealed that certain expressions can enhance the expression of the robot's influence. These results provided new insights into the design of expressions using multiple robots.

Keywords: Teleoperated robot · Multiple robots · Providing service · Interaction design · Robot expression design · Collaborative interaction · Recommendation robot

1 Introduction

Recently, teleoperated service robots have become increasingly popular for providing services. For example, teleoperated robots are used to serve customers at a café by employees who have difficulty going outside [1], or a teleoperated robot welcomed people and recommended products to them at a summer festival [4].

This work was supported by JST Moonshot R&D Grant Number JPMJMS2011.

Teleoperated robots have the potential to provide services sufficiently to users owing to their ease of implementation and ability to recognize complex speech using the operator's ear. Providing services from remote places also has several benefits for robot operators, such as increased motivation and prevention of infection spread [2]. However, it is unclear whether customers accept the services when using robots to provide services in public spaces such as guidance, alerting, and recommendation products. Even if there are benefits to the operator, teleoperated robots that provide services that are unacceptable to users will not be widely used. Therefore, this is an unavoidable challenge when using teleoperated robots that are actively involved in service tasks.

One of the reasons why users do not accept these services is the lack of pressure when using teleoperated robots [3]. Previous studies have reported that teleoperated service robots cannot influence users sufficiently compared to local staff because robots have less social pressure than people [5,6].

High social pressure by humans influences decision-making [7,8]. We consider that the same is true for the robots. Humans regard robots as social beings, and robots influence human decision-making [9–11]. This suggests that increasing the social pressure of robots may enhance their influence on humans.

In previous studies, operators have provided services using a single robot [1,4]. We believe that placing autonomous robots around a teleoperated robot can increase social pressure and enhance the influence of the robot. Several studies have been conducted using multiple robots. Shiomi et al. reported that motor skills were improved when using two robots rather than a single robot [12], and multiple synchronized robots exerted more peer pressure on participants and increased their error rates in visual judgment tasks [13]. Marcos et al. reported that the number of hand sanitizer dispenser users increased with multiple robots rather than with a single robot [18]. In addition, multiple avatars are more persuasive than a single avatar when recommending a movie using overheard communication [16,17].

Several studies have employed using multiple teleoperated robots. Arimoto et al. conducted an interaction experiment using a teleoperated robot and bystander robot [14]. Consequently, the social telepresence of a distant interlocutor is enhanced when using a bystander robot. Seta et al. conducted an experiment that assigns multiple avatars to one member of a minority in a discussion. [15] They found that this enhanced the minority's opinion and increased the degree to which the majority agreed with the minority's opinion.

These previous studies focused on comparisons between one and multiple, and do not examine how multiple robots collaborate. Therefore, this study aims to organize collaborative interaction patterns using multiple robots towards single-operator-multiple-robots teleoperation. We conducted a web survey to investigate the effect of each pattern on enhancing the influence of the robots. We used three autonomous robots in the web survey to minimize the influence of other factors such as the operator's talk skills. Furthermore, we extracted the common expressive attributes of the interaction patterns and examined the impact of each attribute on the robot's influence.

2   Methods

Here, we define the important terms and concepts used in this study. A person who teleoperates a robot is called an "operator," and a person who interacts with the robot locally is called a "user." Each interaction pattern of multiple robots to enhance the robot's influence is called a "multiple-robot expression," and one multiple-robot expression has several common attributes that characterize the expression, called "expressive attributes." Each multiple-robot expression is assigned one of the possible values for each attribute, and each expressive attribute has some possible values, such as whether the robot placement is dense or sparse.

2.1   Brainstorming for Expressions and Expressive Attribute

Previous studies have provided several examples of multiple-robot expressions [14,15]. However, there are many multiple-robot expressions that have not been mentioned. Therefore, we conducted two brainstorming sessions. In these sessions, we listed multiple-robot expressions and expressive attributes.

In the first session, to list possible multiple-robot expressions, we conducted brainstorming with several experts, including five human-robot interaction(HRI) researchers, one customer service staff, and one robotic business manager. Consequently, we obtained 19 rough expressions for this session.

Subsequently, three HRI researchers who participated in the first session, including the author, conducted a second brainstorming session based on the multiple-robot expression ideas obtained, regarding the design process of existing research [19] in human-computer interaction. In this session, we added, excluded, and integrated multiple-robot expressions. The details of the second session are as follows: First, we enumerated the contents of multiple-robot expressions individually for twenty minutes. Thereafter, we enumerated the expressive attributes of multiple-robot expressions individually based on these expression ideas for fifteen minutes. Finally, we shared our ideas and integrated or excluded common ideas.

Together with the results of the first session, we finally obtained 58 expression ideas and organized them into 28 expression candidates. In addition, we also obtained ten expressive attribute candidates.

2.2   Multiple Expressions and Expressive Attributes

While all of the expressive attribute candidates listed in the previous section are important in characterizing robot expressions, some candidates can also be applied to a single robot. This study focuses on the use of multiple robots to enhance a single teleoperated robot's influence and social pressure. It is inappropriate to include expressive attributes that can be applied to a single robot as attribute characteristics of multiple robots. For example, expressive attributes such as sound volume and turn-taking speed, were excluded for the above reasons. Finally, we obtained four expressive attributes; "Action Target(ATa),"

Table 1. Expressive attributes of expression and value.

No	Expresssive attributes	Value		
1	Action Target(ATa)	Robot	User	
2	Robot Placement(RP)	Dense	Sparse	
3	Number of Roles and Type of Attitude(NRTA)	Single - Sympathy	Multiple - Sympathy	Multiple - Refutation
		Multiple - Sympathy and Refutation	Multiple - Question	Multiple - Reaction
		Multiple - Neutral		
4	Action Timing(ATi)	Simultaneous	Order	

"Robot placement(RP)," "Number of Roles and Type of Attitude(NRTA)," and "Action Timing(ATi)." The details of the expressive attributes are as follows:

Action target(ATa): This expressive attribute represents whether the robot's speech or motion target is a user or another robot around it. Specifically, the attribute is whether the robots work together to speak to the user or whether the robots communicate to each other and allow the user to hear it.

Number of Roles and Type of Attitude(NRTA): This expressive attribute represents the number of roles the robots have and the attitude of the surrounding robots towards the intentions expressed by the teleoperated robot. When the number of roles is single, the type of attitude is sympathy. When the number of roles is multiple, six types of attitudes are enumerated: neutral, sympathy, refutation, sympathy and refutation, questioning, and reactions, such as surprise and response. For example, if the surrounding robots synchronize with the speech of a teleoperated robot, social pressure can be intensified. If the surrounding robots are surprised, this can be an expression that draws attention to and impresses the content of the operator's utterance.

Robot placement(RP): This expressive attribute indicates how multiple robots are positioned relative to each other. This attribute has two values: "dense placement," indicating that multiple robots are grouped in front of a user group, potentially increasing the social presence of the robots by crowding them together in a single location. The other is "sparse placement," indicating that multiple robots are discretely placed at a fixed distance from each other. An example of an expression with this attribute is where robots are placed at equal intervals at the edge of an aisle to convey information to users passing by sequentially and consecutively.

Action timing(Ati): This expressive attribute represents whether all robots speak/move simultaneously or in order. While simultaneous speech increases the volume and range of sound and makes it easier for users to notice, conveying information many times in sequence can be an expression that memorizes and impresses users.

Concrete images of the attributes are shown in Fig. 1. Table 1 lists the expressive attributes and possible values for each attribute.

Next, we assigned the four scrutinized expressive attributes to the expressions obtained through the brainstorming sessions, and grouped those that resulted

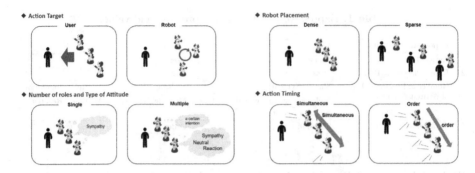

Fig. 1. Image of expressive attributes and possible values for each attribute.

Table 2. Description of two representative expressions and their expressive attributes.

Expression	Private consultation	Simultaneous announcement with bilateral presentation
Image	Buy croissants! / order / I hope he buy! / Yeah, I do!.	Buy croissants! / Simultaneous / Definitely buy it! / Don't buy them!
Expressive attributes	Robot, Dense, Single-Sympathy, Order	User, Sparse, Multiple-Sympathy and Refutation, Simultaneous
Description	All robots are set up close and speak to each other in turn. All robots show consulting with each other and convey the same intention.	All robots are set up at a distance from each other and speak to the users simultaneously. One robot conveys an intention, another conveys a refutational intention, and the other conveys a favorable intention.

in the same expressive attributes as for a single expression. We derived 56 combinations of all the obtained expressive attributes. Among these combinations, we excluded expressions that could not be executed and enhanced the robot's influence in the actual recommendation scenarios. For example, an expression in which the robots separated from each other in pieces communicated and sympathized with each other was excluded because the users may not understand that the robots were talking to each other. Finally, we obtained 22 expressions that could be implemented, as shown in Table 5 in the appendix section. Images of each expression are presented in Fig. 4 in the Appendix.

Because of space limitations, we describe two representative multiple-robot expressions in Table 2. Detailed descriptions of each of the 22 expressions are explained in the Appendix.

3   Web Survey

We prepared videos of each expression and conducted a web survey through Lancers, which is the largest Japanese crowdsourcing job-request site. This web survey aimed to reveal how each expression enhanced the influence of the robot. Thereafter, we aimed to identify expressive attributes that commonly appear in expressions to enhance the robot's influence well.

We designed this survey as a between-subjects experiment and asked 50 participants for each expression. There were 22 expressions. The robot was a small desktop robot, "Sota," manufactured by the Vstone Corporation.

In these videos, the operator intended to sell croissants in a bakery. The position of the blue robot on the right side was the same under both the baseline and expression conditions (Fig. 2). We assumed that the blue robot was teleoperated by the operator and the robots on the middle and left sides were controlled autonomously and collaborate with the teleoperated robot. This is because unifying the tone or volume of the operator in the 22 expressions and controlling the robots properly were difficult.

Note that in this experiment, we consider one of the robots to be teleoperated and the others to be autonomous robots; however, this is also a part of the research field of autonomous robots.

Three robots were used in the videos. We aimed to investigate the basic effect of the expressions of multiple robots, rather than the effect of the number of robots. In the situation of recommending products, there are three basic roles towards what we want to recommend positive, neutral, or negative. Therefore, using three robots is the minimum basic style in recommendation situations.

We set the robot sound to the same settings, and did not use the operator's voice. This is because the survey did not focus on whether the participants could judge whether the operator's or the robot's autonomous voice was heard. We prioritized ease of listening to voice.

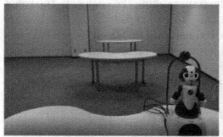

Fig. 2. View of expression (left: baseline, right: expression with the multiple robots).

Table 3. Contents of questionnaire (1 = strongly disagree, 2 = moderately disagree, 3 = disagree, 4 = neither agree nor disagree, 5 = agree a little, 6 = moderately agree, 7 = strongly agree).

Category	No.	Question
Interest	Q1	I became interested in the croissant
Desire	Q2	I wanted to look for croissants
Desire	Q3	I thought croissants were attractive
Action	Q4	I wanted to buy croissants

The participants watched a video containing a recommendation from a single robot as a baseline. The length of the baseline video was approximately 10 s. Next, they watched videos containing the expression of multiple robots. The participants watched three pattern videos of the expressions. The length of the video of the expressions was also approximately 10 s for each. In the video of expressions, three robots recommended croissants based on the expressions we obtained.

After viewing the baseline and expression videos, respectively, participants completed a questionnaire. To investigate the influence of expressions, we focused on consumer purchasing behavior called AIDA: attention, interest, desire, and action. In this experiment, participants were asked to answer questions about the latter step of the AIDA, excluding attention because they had already paid attention to the robots and listened to their recommendations. Q1 asked about interest, Q2 and Q3 about desire, and Q4 about action. Table 3 presents the detailed content of the questions.

4   Result and Discussion

A total of 1109 questionnaires were collected, resulting in 1106 valid questionnaires, excluding invalid or missing values.

The average score for questions Q1-4 is calculated as the robot influence score, and the differences between the expression videos score minus the baseline video score were used to compare the influence among multiple-robot expressions. Figure 3 shows a box-and-whisker diagram ranking the change in the robot influence score between the baseline and the expression videos. The expression with the highest score change was "Private consultation." However, the expression with the lowest score change was "Simultaneous announcement with bilateral presentation". The average change in the top five expressions was 0.3376, and the average in the bottom five expressions was −1.1038. The variance of the top five is 0.009, which is an insignificant difference, and the variance of the bottom five is 0.350, which is greater than that of the top five. Matthew stated that there is no difference between the satisfaction of customers whose expectations are exceeded or simply met [20]. This can be observed in the results of our study. We assume that not having expressive attributes common in the bottom five,

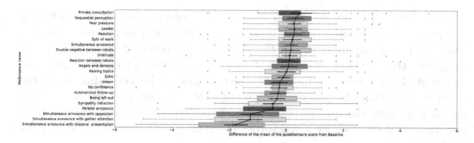

Fig. 3. Box-and-whisker diagram showing the results of robot influence score for each expression.

Table 4. Results of multiple regression analysis (robot influence score). "Estimate" means the coefficient of each explanatory variable. "Std. Error" means standard error. The "t-value" means test quantity for the t-test. "Pr" is the p-value replaced by the t-value. r.squared = 0.1927, adj.r.squared = 0.1861.

No	Expressive attributes combination	Estimate	Std.Error	t value	Pr(>|t|)
1	"NRTA: Multiple - Sympathy and Refutation" · "RP: Dense"	1.425718	0.234751	6.073321	1.725271e-09
2	"NRTA: Multiple - Sympathy" · "RP: Dense"	0.951288	0.236275	4.026198	6.058646e-05
3	"ATi: Order"	0.534467	0.114487	4.668376	3.411361e-06
4	"NRTA: Multiple - Refutation" · "RP: Dense"	0.351749	0.228892	1.536748	1.246436e-01
5	"NRTA: One - Sympathy"	0.296463	0.109749	2.701276	7.013954e-03
6	"NRTA: Multiple - Question"	-0.391393	0.144371	-2.711028	6.812317e-03
7	Intercept	-0.400573	0.119138	-3.362256	7.997838e-04
8	"NRTA: Multiple - Refutation"	-0.871356	0.199138	-4.375644	1.326300e-05
9	"NRTA: Multiple - Sympathy"	-0.889427	0.207896	-4.278237	2.048254e-05
10	"NRTA: Multiple - Sympathy and Refutation"	-1.450388	0.205193	-7.068410	2.784431e-12

"RP: Sparse" or "NRTA: Multiple - Refutation", is essential not to weaken the robot's influence when designing multiple-robots expressions. Because these discussions are likely to be subjective, we conducted a multiple regression analysis for quantitative evaluation.

In the multiple regression analysis, the robot influence score was used as the objective variable. The explanatory variables were designed with the original expressive attributes and dummy variables created from the combinations of two qualitative variables as interaction terms. We conducted the analysis using a stepwise method based on the AIC to exclude explanatory variables with small effects. Table 4 shows the results of the multiple regression analysis. "Intercept" in this table is the value of intercept during multiple regression analysis.

According to these results, "ATi: Order" and "NRTA: Single - Sympathy" have purely positive effects. The attribute values for Nos. 1, 2, and 4 in Table 4 are the combinations of "RP: Dense" and Nos. 10, 9, and 8 attribute values, respectively. These NRTA values had a negative effect if the RP value was "Dense". Among the three attribute values with high coefficients, only "NRTA: Multiple

- Sympathy" · "RP: Dense" has a small positive effect based on the coefficient difference. These positive attribute values can work as multiple-robot expressions to enhance the influence of the robot. The research of Marcos et al. [18] supported the results of this study. Marcos et al.'s research uses the expression, "Sequential persuasion," which is the second most enhanced influence of the robot in our study. Shiomi et al. reported that the peer pressure of multiple robots influences the user responses [13]. These studies support the results of our study that robots have a single role and convey the same intention in order are important.

"ATi: Simultaneous" did not appear in Table 4. Although simultaneous speech is one of the simplest examples of multiple-robot expressions, the results indicate that it does not enhance the robot's influence. Shiomi has also reported insufficient pressure when multiple robots spoke simultaneously [13]. They assumed that this was owing to the low physical pressure related to the size and appearance of the robot itself, and the same may have been true in this study.

ATa does not appear in Table 4. This indicates that the overheard communication may not affect the influence of the robot. Overheard communication is an interaction form showing robots' conversations to users. It has been reported that indirect communication is more persuasive than user-directed persuasion [16,17,21]. Suzuki has analyzed that overheard communication succeeded because the persuader agent gazed at the persuadee agent and never gazed at users [17]. In this study, the robots faced forward at the start of the video, and faced each other when the conversation started. Therefore, it is possible that the overheard communication was unsuccessful. Further research is necessary to address this issue.

5   Limitation

"RP: Dense" indicated distance where one pair of users could be present for multiple robots, while "RP: Sparse" showed distance where multiple pairs of users could be present for multiple robots and exist from other robots in sight. However, we can classify other distances in addition to these two types of distances; for example, when another robot is placed in an invisible position.

In this study, we used three robots to express expressions under the same conditions. However, several expressions can be implemented with two robots, such as "Reaction." It is possible that these expressions were affected by the number of robots and not purely by their expressions. Therefore, the results of this study may not have been affected by expressions alone.

We conducted a web survey using the videos. The length of the video was approximately ten seconds. The videos were short because it is possible that other factor affected the evaluation score when the videos were longer. However, the participants may have understood only a part of our setting because of the length of the video. For example, it is possible that the short video did not convey the difference in distance between the robots and direction in which they spoke.

Furthermore, we used videos of one scene from the expressions of multiple robots. There was a chronological attribute in the field, and the effect may have been different. Therefore, in the future, it will be necessary to conduct research that involves introducing the system to the actual field of providing services.

6 Conclusion

The contributions of this study were to provide definitions of multiple-robot expressions and expressive attributes and to investigate the effects of enhancing robots' influence.

In this study, we aimed to explore the design of multiple-robot expressions to enhance the influence of the robot in recommending situations. To conduct a comprehensive survey, we enumerated and organized multiple-robot expressions and expressive attributes. We identified four expressive attributes: "Action Target(ATa)," "Robot placement(RP)," "Number of Roles and Type of Attitude(NRTA)," and "Action Timing(ATi)." Based on the obtained expressive attributes, we obtained 22 representative multiple-robot expressions with expressive attributes that can be implemented.

We conducted a web survey to determine how each expression enhances the influence of the robot. Thereafter, we aimed to identify expressive attributes that commonly appear in expressions that enhance the influence of the robot. We conducted multiple regression analysis to determine the effect of each expressive attribute. Consequently, the expression that most enhanced the influence of the robot was "Private consultation." The results also suggested that "NRTA: Single - Sympathy" and "ATi: Order" may contribute to enhancing the influence of the robot. "NRTA: Multiple - Sympathy" contributed slightly to enhance the influence of the robot. This result shows that when designing expressions using multiple robots, we can effectively enhance the influence of the robot through expressions in which multiple robots have a single intention and speak in order. ATa may not contribute to enhancing the influence of the robot, suggesting that the results are different from related works and require further investigation.

A   Expressions and Expressive attributes

Table 5. Expressions and their expressive attribute value

No.	Expression name	Attributes			
		ATa	RP	NRTA	ATi
1	Echo	User	Dense	Single - Sympathy	Simultaneous
2	Peer pressure	User	Dense	Single - Sympathy	Order
3	Simultaneous announcement	User	Sparse	Single - Sympathy	Simultaneous
4	Sequential persuasion	User	Sparse	Single - Sympathy	Order
5	Interlude	User	Dense	Multiple - Sympathy	Order
6	Simultaneous announcement with gathered attention	User	Sparse	Multiple - Sympathy	Simultaneous
7	Being left out	User	Dense	Multiple - Refutation	Order
8	Simultaneous announcement with opposition	User	Sparse	Multiple - Refutation	Simultaneous
9	Angels and demons	User	Dense	Multiple - Sympathy and Refutation	Order
10	Simultaneous announcement with bilateral presentation	User	Sparse	Multiple - Sympathy and Refutation	Simultaneous
11	Autonomous follow-up	User	Dense	Multiple - Question	Order
12	Reaction	User	Dense	Multiple - Reaction	Order
13	Split of work	User	Dense	Multiple - None	Order
14	Parallel announcement	User	Sparse	Multiple - None	Simultaneous
15	Unison	Robot	Dense	Single - Sympathy	Simultaneous
16	Private consultation	Robot	Dense	Single - Sympathy	Order
17	Leader	Robot	Dense	Multiple - Sympathy	Order
18	Sympathy induction	Robot	Dense	Multiple - Refutation	Order
19	Double negative	Robot	Dense	Multiple - Sympathy and Refutation	Order
20	No confidence	Robot	Dense	Multiple - Question	Order
21	Reaction between robots	Robot	Dense	Multiple - Reaction	Order
22	Raising topics	Robot	Dense	Multiple - None	Order

B   Images of Expressions

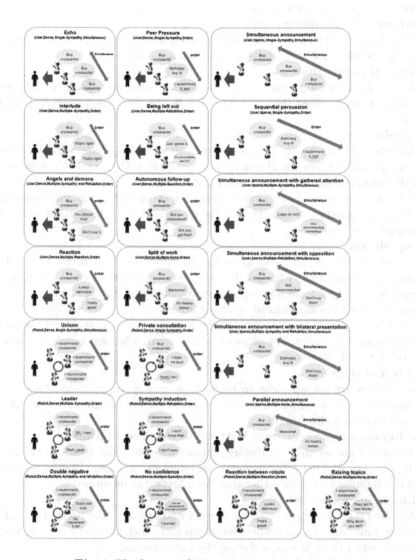

Fig. 4. The Images of 22 expressions we obtained.

C   Detail descriptions of Expressions

Echo

All robots are set up close to each other and speak to the users simultaneously. All the robots convey the same message.

Peer Pressure

All robots are set up close to each other and speak to the users. All the robots convey the same intention.

Simultaneous announcement

All robots are set up at a distance from each other and speak to the users simultaneously. All the robots convey the same message.

Sequential persuasion

All robots are set up at a distance from each other and speak to the users. All the robots convey the same intention to the user who passed in front of them.

Interlude

All robots are set up close to each other and speak to the users. One robot conveys an intention and the other robots join in with the robot's statement.

Simultaneous announcement with gathered attention

All robots are set up at a distance from each other and speak simultaneously. One robot conveys an intention to the users, and the others make users pay attention to that robot.

Being left out

All robots are set up close to each other and speak to users. One robot conveys an intention, whereas the others convey a refutational intention to exclude the robot from a group and evoke the sympathy of users.

Simultaneous announcement with opposition

All robots are set up at a distance from each other and speak to the users simultaneously. One robot conveys an intention, whereas the others convey a refutational intention.

Angels and demons

All robots are set up close to each other and speak to users. One robot conveys an intention, another conveys a refutational intention, and the other conveys a favorable intention.

Simultaneous announcement with bilateral presentation

All robots are set up at a distance from each other and speak to the users simultaneously. One robot conveys an intention, another conveys a refutational intention, and the other conveys a favorable intention.

Autonomous follow-up

All robots are set up close to each other and speak to the users. One robot conveys an intention and others follow up with, such as "Did you understand that?" when there is a pose during the conversation.

Reaction

All robots are set up close to each other and speak to the users. One robot conveys an intention and others take reactions towards the users.

Split of work

All robots are set up close to each other and speak to the users. All the robots divide and execute tasks such as chatting, explaining, and guiding.

Parallel announcement

All robots are set up at a distance from each other and speak to the users simultaneously. All the robots convey different and unrelated intentions.

Unison

All robots are set up close to each other and speak to each other simultaneously. All the robots create empathy by aligning voices in the middle of a conversation.

Private consultation

All robots are set up close to each other and speak to each other. All the robots show consulting with each other and convey the same intention.

Leader

All robots are set up close to each other and speak to each other. One robot conveys an intention and explains it to the other robots and the others agree with the robot.

Sympathy Induction

All robots are set up close to each other and speak to each other . One robot conveys an intention, whereas others convey a refutational intention to exclude the robot from a group and evoke the sympathy of users.

Double negative

All robots are set up close to each other and speak to each other. One robot conveys an intention, another conveys a refutational intention, the other conveys a favorable intention.

No confidence

All robots are set up close to each other and speak to each other. One robot conveys an intention and others worry about each other if their intentions have been conveyed to the users.

Reaction between robots

All robots are set up close to each other and speak to each other. One robot conveys an intention and others take reactions towards that.

Raising topic

All robots are set up close to each other and speak to each other. One robot conveys an intention and others raise topics to continue the conversation.

References

1. Moriyama, K.: "DAWN ver. beta," a café where severely disabled people serve customers with remote-controlled robots, opens for a limited time (A new relationship between people and machines). J. Soc. Mech. Eng. (2019)
2. Ferreira, R., et al.: Decision factors for remote work adoption: advantages, disadvantages, driving forces and challenges. J. Open Innov. Technol. Market Compl. **7**(1), 70 (2021)
3. Song, S., et al.: Teleoperated robot sells toothbrush in a shopping mall: a field study. In: Extended Abstracts of the 2021 CHI Conference on Human Factors in Computing Systems (2021)
4. Baba, J., et al.: Teleoperated robot acting autonomous for better customer satisfaction. In: Extended Abstracts of the 2020 CHI Conference on Human Factors in Computing Systems (2020)
5. Baba, J., et al.: Local vs. avatar robot: performance and perceived workload of service encounters in public space. Front. Robot. AI **8** (2021)

6. Tonkin, M., et al.: Would you like to sample? Robot engagement in a shopping centre. In: 2017 26th IEEE International Symposium on Robot and Human Interactive Communication (RO-MAN). IEEE (2017)

7. Asch, S.E.: Opinions and social pressure. Sci. Am. **193**(5), 31–35 (1955)

8. Tesser, A., Campbell, J., Mickler, S.: The role of social pressure, attention to the stimulus, and self-doubt in conformity. Eur. J. Soc. Psychol. **13**(3), 217–233 (1983)

9. Kahn, P.H., Jr., et al.: "Robovie, you'll have to go into the closet now": children's social and moral relationships with a humanoid robot. Dev. Psychol. **48**(2), 303 (2012)

10. Shiomi, M., et al.: Does a robot's touch encourage human effort? Int. J. Soc. Robot. **9**, 5–15 (2017)

11. Nakagawa, K., et al.: Effect of robot's whispering behavior on people's motivation. Int. J. Soc. Robot. **5**, 5–16 (2013)

12. Shiomi, M., et al.: Two is better than one: social rewards from two agents enhance offline improvements in motor skills more than single agent. PLoS ONE **15**(11), e0240622 (2020)

13. Shiomi, M., Hagita, N.: Do synchronized multiple robots exert peer pressure? In: Proceedings of the Fourth International Conference on Human Agent Interaction (2016)

14. Arimoto, T., Yoshikawa, Y., Ishiguro, H.: Nodding responses by collective proxy robots for enhancing social telepresence. In: Proceedings of the Second International Conference on Human-Agent Interaction (2014)

15. Seta, K., et al.: Divided presence: improving group decision-making via pseudo-population increase. In: Proceedings of the 6th International Conference on Human-Agent Interaction (2018)

16. Kantharaju, R.B., et al.: Is two better than one? Effects of multiple agents on user persuasion. In: Proceedings of the 18th International Conference on Intelligent Virtual Agents (2018)

17. Suzuki, S.V., Yamada, S., IGSSE CISS: Social influence of overheard communication by life-like agents to a user

18. Tae, M.I., et al.: Using multiple robots to increase suggestion persuasiveness in public space. Appl. Sci. **11**(13), 6080 (2021)

19. Harrison, C., et al.: Unlocking the expressivity of point lights. In: Proceedings of the SIGCHI Conference on Human Factors in Computing Systems (2012)

20. Dixon, M., et al.: The effortless experience: conquering the new battleground for customer loyalty, pp. 13–14

21. Walster, E., Festinger, L.: The effectiveness of "overheard" persuasive communications. Psychol. Sci. Public Interest **65**(6), 395 (1962)

Perception of a Mobile Service Robot's Proxemic Behavior and Appearance in Virtual Reality

Olivia Herzog[⊠][ID], Annika Boos[ID], Jan-Niklas Birger Stockmann[ID], and Klaus Bengler[ID]

TUM School of Engineering and Design, Technical University of Munich, Munich, Germany
olivia.herzog@tum.de
https://www.mec.ed.tum.de/en/lfe/

Abstract. Various robot-related, environmental and human factors influence the proxemics and the quality and perception of human-robot interactions (HRIs). This paper focuses on a selection of the most relevant robot-related factors: size, speed, and the robot's edge shape, which were systematically varied in two consecutive experiments. This gives important implications for human-centered robot behavior design, where non-verbal, proxemic behavior plays an important role. Therefore, in this study series, additionally to the indicated comfortable distance, the subjective discomfort elicited in a human when encountering a mobile service robot was investigated using a virtual reality (VR) setup. The results of the two conducted experiments show strong and consistent influences of size and speed both on the distance and discomfort. Besides, a small influence of the edge roundness of the robot on discomfort was found. Additionally, the results give implications at which distance a delivery robot should adapt its behavior depending on its design configuration in order to achieve as less discomfort in humans as possible.

Keywords: robotics · human-robot interaction · proxemic behavior · virtual reality · discomfort · service robot · design

1 Introduction

Last-mile delivery is a contemporary challenge, and robots propose a promising solution to it. For instance, highly automated delivery robots are tested and deployed by established mail companies and delivery services to help suppliers to meet the increased demand for parcel deliveries [1]. The problem of environmentally friendly, fast last-mile delivery is expected to grow even more pressing with increasing urbanization as a long-term trend. Since last-mile delivery is an especially pressing issue in urbanized areas, such robots need to operate in public space. There, they will need interaction and movement strategies that are commonly understood and accepted, since they would mostly interact with

Supported by German National Research Foundation (DFG).

untrained individuals, rather than robotics professionals or experts. Delivery robots usually operate on the sidewalk, where they must share the available movement space with pedestrians and other actors [2]. The HRI plays a special role in this scenario to ensure safety, efficiency and satisfaction for users and passers-by [3]. Since urban centers are already filled with a lot of information as well as noise, it can be argued that such robots, in order to be best accepted, should 'blend in' rather than adding more noise. To raise attention, this paper focuses on proxemics as one specific form of non-verbal communication. Since such delivery robots will need to evade persons in their path or stop for people to clear it, the minimum comfortable approach distance of the robot to a person needs to be investigated to design a more natural and acceptable HRI.

As these factors may depend on robot-related factors, we investigated the effects of robot size, approach speed and shape on the minimum comfortable approach distance to a person and the subjective discomfort in these situations. In the interaction between humans and robots, as much as in the interaction among humans, proxemic behavior plays an important role. It describes a form of non-verbal communication between the human being and their direct physical environment. The term proxemics means the 'study of interspatial behavior, concerned with territoriality, interpersonal distance, spatial arrangements, crowding, and other aspects of the physical environment that affect behavior' [4]. Keeping a certain distance can serve as a non-verbal signal for the degree of familiarity of two individuals. For example, people who disliked a robot increased their distance to it if it directed its gaze at them and, moreover, disclosed less personal information to it [5]. Furthermore, personal experience with robots as well as pets, personality traits and gender can influence the minimum comfortable approach distance between human and robot [6].

1.1 Virtual Reality

Li et al. HRIs compared human-robot proxemics between virtual reality and the real world [7]. Each participant completed part of the study in reality with a physical robot and part in a virtual environment with a virtual model of the same robot. The conclusion of this study postulates that people allow a robot to enter their personal space closer in the real world than in virtual reality. Therefore, results obtained in Virtual Reality cannot be directly transferred to interactions in the real world. Hence, results can only serve as qualitative and internally valid data. The studies presented in this paper are part of a study series aiming to find a stable bias that may allow the transfer of results obtained in VR to real-world HRI. If such a relative bias can be found, robot designs and movement behaviors could be validated in low-cost VR setups, compared to high-effort and high-cost physical robot prototypes. The results of such studies would then be more informative for real-world HRI.

1.2 Discomfort

The theory of proxemics outlines that every person is surrounded by layers of personal space that can be imagined as a bubble or an onion. The intrusion of one's personal space can induce uncomfortable feelings. The minimum approach distance marks the boundary of the personal space surrounding an individual, up to which the approach of another individual is tolerated [8]. Proxemics research focuses on the precise turning point at which the sensations of the approached individual shift from comfortable to discomfort, as the other individual intrudes too far into personal space, i.e., comes too close.

We consider discomfort to be a composition of negative sensations. This includes affective components associated with the approaching individual (such as trust or familiarity) beyond the concern for our physical safety. It can be associated with objectively measurable variables such as distance [9]. The perception of discomfort upon the intrusion of personal space serves an important purpose. Animals and humans alike have a natural urge for self-preservation. The approach of other individuals can pose possible dangers to personal health and well-being. Hence, approaching strangers, other individuals, and things are subject to a constant risk assessment. Basal mechanisms decide on possible actions, 'fight or flight,' two evasion strategies triggered by intruders that are perceived as hazardous. Accordingly, our subjective feeling of discomfort influences the minimum acceptable approach distance of other individuals.

It can be assumed that the subjective feeling of discomfort could be influenced by a robot's approach speed and its size. The size-weight illusion [10] (mis-)leads us to assume that larger objects are heavier. Heavier objects, as well as those that move faster, pose a higher risk of injury since higher forces would apply in case of a collision with the object. Moreover, we are left with less decision time on how to evade a faster moving object compared to a slower one.

1.3   Factors Influencing HRI

Service and delivery robots often operate on the sidewalk and other public spaces, where they share the available space with pedestrians and other actors [2] under the existing traffic rules. In general, the trade-off between safety and efficiency is a relevant optimization problem here. The HRI plays a special role in this scenario to ensure safety, efficiency and satisfaction in the sense of a comfortable interaction for the users and passers-by [3]. The quality and perception of an interaction between humans and robots is generally shaped by various factors, which can be categorized in human factors, environmental factors, and robot-related factors.

Human factors influencing the HRI, among others, are demographics (e.g., age, gender) and personality traits [11], mental models [12], or emotions [13]. They are not addressed in this paper since a robot in public space, under current technical and regulatory circumstances, cannot capture or influence these factors. The only human factor that they may be able to influence is the acceptance and positive attitude towards themselves through well-designed, polite behavior.

Factors in the environment that can influence the HRI can be the reality spectrum (e.g., virtual or real environment) [7].

Lastly, robot-related factors include the robot's appearance (e.g., mechanistic or anthropomorphic) and the context of the approach (such as physical or verbal interaction) [3]. The most obvious robot-related factor is the robot's outer appearance. For instance, research indicates that people accept shorter distances to smaller robots than to bigger ones [14,15]. Already, in early industrial design research, curved edges were found to be associated with pleasant emotional warmth and sharp edges with unpleasant coarseness [16] and curved edges were found to be more accepted by humans [17]. Moreover, it was found that subjects' personal preferences regarding the appearance of a robot influence the tolerated minimal approach distance [3].

This paper focuses on a selection of the most relevant robot factors: the robot's size, speed, and shape. Additionally, it gives insights into minimum comfortable approach distance when encountering robots in unstructured surroundings, which gives important implications for human-centered robot behavior design.

1.4   Research Question

The following central and overarching research question is addressed:

RQ1 Do robot size, speed, and shape influence the accepted minimum approach distance and experienced discomfort elicited by a mobile service robot in VR?

We report the findings of two consecutive studies in this paper. The following hypotheses are derived from existing literature and previous findings. The first two hypotheses of each study are identical, but investigated using different robot models and sizes.

Hypotheses of Study 1

H1.1 The minimum comfortable approach distance increases with the increasing size of the robot.
H1.2 The minimum comfortable approach distance increases with the increasing approaching speed of the robot.

H1.3 The subjective discomfort increases with the increasing size of the robot.
H1.4 The subjective discomfort increases with the increasing approaching speed of the robot.

Hypotheses of Study 2

H2.1 The minimum comfortable approach distance increases with the increasing size of the robot.
H2.2 The minimum comfortable approach distance decreases with the increasing roundness of the robot's edges.

H2.3 The subjective discomfort increases with the increasing size of the robot.
H2.4 The subjective discomfort increases with the decreasing roundness of the robot's edges.

2   Method

In this study series within the research project 'sabeS', funded by the German National Research Foundation (DFG) with the reference BE 4532/16-1, a robot approached a human observer in a VR scenario. Subjective discomfort as well as the minimum comfortable approach distance to the robot were assessed. The size, speed, and design of the robot (a spectrum of sharp vs. round edges) were systematically varied and analyzed in two subsequent studies.

Both studies were set up in virtual environments, using models of autonomous delivery robots approaching the participants. The virtual environment was presented via a HTC Vive Pro head-mounted display (HMD). The participants' task was to indicate their minimum comfortable approach distance to the robot via a button-press on the HTC Vive controller. The game engine Unity was used as the development environment for the virtual space for both studies, simulating a Munich urban pedestrian environment [18].

Both studies were conducted in accordance with the principles embodied in the Declaration of Helsinki and in accordance with local statutory requirements in Bavaria, Germany. All participants gave written informed consent to participate in the study. The research designs and all used materials were reviewed by the ethics committee of the Technical University of Munich for investigations involving human participants and approved by the review board under the reference numbers 557/21 S-NP (Study 1) and 2022-295-S-KH (Study 2).

2.1   Study 1 – Size and Speed

Apparatus. The study was conducted in a 3×3 within-subjects design in a VR pedestrian simulation with the independent variables robot size (small, medium, large) and robot speed (slow, moderate, fast).

As dependent variables the individual minimum comfortable approach distance [m] indicated by button-press on the controller, the resulting calculated time-to-contact (ttc) [s] and the subjective discomfort (using the 'discomfort' sub-scale of the robotic social attributes scale Robotic Social Attributes Scale (RoSAS) by [19]) were measured.

The values for the different robot configurations regarding size and speed were as follows:

- small: 0.95 m x 0.42 m x 0.86 m
- medium: 1.425 m x 0.63m x 1.29 m
- large: 1.9 m x 0.84 m x 1.72 m

- slow: 2 m/s = 7.2 km/h
- moderate: 5 m/s = 18 km/h
- fast: 8 m/s = 28.8 km/h

The robot model used in this study resembled a delivery robot. The model was scaled and programmed using the game engine Unity [18]. It is depicted in Fig. 1.

Fig. 1. Robot model used in study 1 [20].

Before putting on the VR headset, the participants were instructed to stand on a marked position in the laboratory and stay on the mark over the course of the experiment. After the fitting of the headset, the start-up of the VR environment reset the position of the participant to the origin. In the VR environment in which the participants find themselves at a fixed position on a sidewalk. The participants were then approached by each one of the twelve robot models successively. Each robot moved on the same trajectory towards the participant. To measure the minimum comfortable approach distance, participants were asked to stop the approaching robot in place via button-press on a hand-held controller. Therefore, participants were requested to stop each robot by pulling the trigger on the HTC Vive VR controller as soon as they wanted it to stop because of feeling insecure by the robots approach. The distance from the origin to the front of each robot was logged. After each robot approach, the participants were requested to evaluate the respective interaction using the 'discomfort' subscale of the RoSAS [19]. The subscale consists of six discomfort-describing attributes: aggressive, awful, scary, awkward, dangerous, and strange. These items are rated on a scale from 1 to 9 where 1 is "not applicable at all" and 9 refers to 'definitely applicable'. These values are then averaged for each robot, resulting in one discomfort score per robot configuration. Subsequent to the experiment the participants were asked about demographic data.

All data was plotted and analyzed using the statistical programming language R and the graphical user interface RStudio [21]. Linear mixed effect models with the respective independent variables as fixed effects and the participant ID as a random effect were fitted using the lmerTest package [22].

Participants. A total of n = 37 subjects participated in experiment 1. They were recruited via postings, as well as personal recruiting on the campus and were not reimbursed or compensated for their participation. One subject was excluded because the controller trigger was never pressed, another one was excluded because the position data was not logged due to a technical failure. 35 participants remained in the final data set (mean age (M) = 27.11; SD =

11.87; range = 18–75 years; 40% female, 60% male). They did not receive any compensation for their participation.

2.2   Study 2 – Size and Edge Shape

Apparatus. In the second VRs study the effect of the size and edge shape of the robot were investigated. The speed was set to 6km/h since it is considered an ordinary pedestrian speed [23].

The experiment was conducted as a 3×4 within-subjects design in a VR pedestrian simulation with the independent variables robot size (small, medium, large) and shape (benchmark approach: four levels of edge roundness).

As dependent variables the following metrics were measured:

– minimum comfortable approach distance [m]
– time-to-contact [s]
– subjective discomfort (9-point Likert scale, RoSAS questionnaire, [19])

Twelve different delivery robot models were evaluated (models A to L). They represented four different shapes and three different heights. The designs as well as the benchmarks they were derived from are portrayed in Table 1.

In this within-subject study each participant saw each of the resulting twelve robots in a VR environment in twelve successive trials. To avoid carryover effects the robots were presented in randomized order for each participant. The robot models were created as 3D-CAD models in Solidworks [28]. Twelve different covers were designed and matched onto a CAD model of the same modular robot platform [29]. The shapes and heights were chosen based on a benchmarking approach of existing delivery robot systems and prototypes.

The benchmark resulted in the selection of four different shapes (referred to as shapes 1, 2, 3, 4) systematically differing in their edge roundness, listed in descending order of roundness as follows:

Shape 1 is inspired by the cylindrical shape of 'Dilly Tower' by Woowa Brothers [24]. It is, therefore, modeled with a half-cylindrical front and back and resembles a nearly round shape. Shape 2 is inspired by the box-shape with curved front and back of the 'Amazon Scout' by Amazon [25], to resemble a more boxy but still round shape. Shape 3 is inspired by the angular-shaped box of an early prototype of FedEx's 'Roxo' [26]. The edges still come with noticeable radii. Shape 4 is inspired by the edgy shape of Ottonomy's 'Ottobot' [27]. It features flat faces and edges with very small radii.

The height of the robot models used in this experiment is also based on a benchmark of existing systems and on a size classification of sidewalk delivery robot systems by Clamann and Bryson (2022) [30]. Size data of a selection of highly automated delivery vehicles is listed on Dimensions.com [31]. It shows an estimated height of 740 mm for the 'Amazon Scout', therefore used as the lowest height in this experiment, and an estimated height of 1470 mm mm for the 'FedEx Roxo', used as the tallest robot height in this experiment [31]. The third height was chosen to be 1105 mm mm, the mean of smallest and tallest height values.

Table 1. Robot designs in four different shapes and three different sizes with their respective benchmarks.

	Height 1	Height 2	Height 3	Benchmark
Shape 1	A	B	C	'Dilly Tower' [24]
Shape 2	D	E	F	'Amazon Scout' [25]
Shape 3	G	I	H	'FedEx Roxo' [26]
Shape 4	J	K	L	'Ottobot' [27]

The experiment procedure was identical to the first study (see Sect. 2.1). Subsequent to the experiment the participants were asked about demographic data.

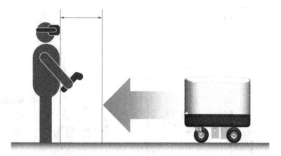

Fig. 2. Schematic representation of the experiment setup. The measured minimum comfortable approach distance is represented by the double-pointed arrow.

Fig. 3. Participant view with approaching robot.

Participants. 26 people participated in study 2 (54% male, 46% female). Their age ranged from 21 to 59 years (mean age (M) = 25.8 years; SD = 7.3 years). They were recruited on campus at Technical University of Munich. 20 participants were students and 6 were professionals working at TU Munich. They did not receive any compensation for their participation.

3   Results

3.1   Results of Study 1

The analysis of the data using linear mixed models supports all four hypotheses. We fitted linear mixed effect models to predict the comfort distance and subjective discomfort with size and speed and the participant ID as a random factor (formula: dependent variable ∼ size + speed + (1 | ID)).

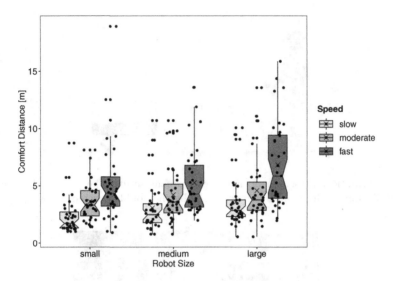

Fig. 4. minimum comfortable approach distance boxplots for the three different sizes depending on their respective speed. The crosses represent the means.

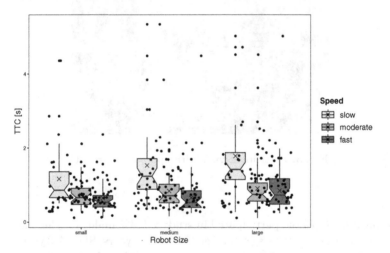

Fig. 5. time-to-contact boxplots for the three different sizes depending on their respective speed. The crosses represent the means.

A large positive main effect of size on distance: $F(2, 272) = 19.39$, $p < .001***$ and a large positive main effect of speed on distance: $F(2, 272) = 91.25$, $p < .001***$ were found. There was no significant interaction. Marginal $R^2 = 0.18$; conditional $R^2 = 0.75$. The random effect of participants had a variance of 5.003 and standard deviation of 2.237.

The fitted model for discomfort shows a large positive main effect of size on discomfort: $F(2, 272) = 15.83$, $p < .001***$ and a large positive main effect of

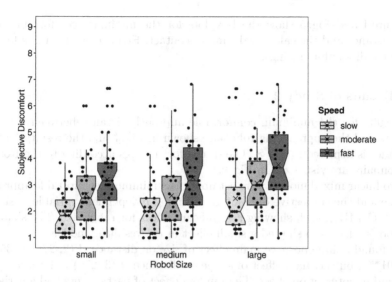

Fig. 6. Boxplots of subjective discomfort measured by the Robotic Social At- tributes Scale (RoSAS). [19]. The crosses represent the means.

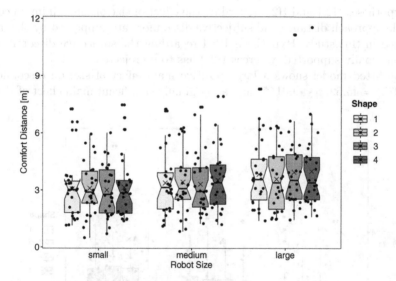

Fig. 7. Boxplots of minimum comfortable approach distance indicated by button-press. The crosses represent the means.

speed on discomfort: $F(3, 272) = 75.78$, $p < .001^{***}$. We found no significant interaction. The model included Random effect of participant: variance = 0.97; standard deviation = 0.98. Marginal $R^2 = 0.18$; Conditional $R^2 = 0.70$.

Figure 4 and Fig. 5 show the boxplots for the minimum comfortable approach distance and the calculated time-to-contact. Figure 6 the boxplots for the subjective discomfort ratings.

3.2 Results of Study 2

The results for the minimum comfortable approach distance between the participants and the approaching robot are shown in Fig. 7 and the resulting time-to-contact is depicted in Fig. 8. The discomfort ratings according to the RoSAS questionnaire are visualized in Fig. 9.

Two linear mixed models were set up for the minimum comfortable approach distance and the subjective discomfort (formula: independent variable $\sim$ size + speed + (1 | ID)), each showing a significant effect for robot size. The shape of the robot's edges also showed a small effect in the resulting models.

We found a large positive main effect of size on distance: $F(2, 275) = 35.15$, $p < .001^{***}$, but no main effect of shape on distance: $F(3, 275) = 1.18$, $p = .32$. We found no interaction effect. The random effect of participants had a variance of 2.42 and standard deviation of 1.55. Marginal $R^2 = 0.04$, conditional $R^2 = 0.85$.

Hypotheses H2.1 and H2.3 regarding the effect of size on the minimum comfortable approach distance and subjective discomfort are supported by the data gathered in this study. Hypothesis H2.4 regarding the subjective discomfort is also marginally supported, whereas H2.2 has to be rejected.

The fitted model shows a large positive main effect of size on discomfort: $F(2, 275) = 45.62$, $p < .001^{***}$ and a marginally significant main effect of shape

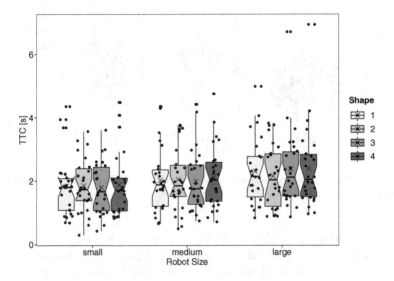

Fig. 8. Boxplots of time-to-contact calculated from minimum comfortable approach distance. The crosses represent the means.

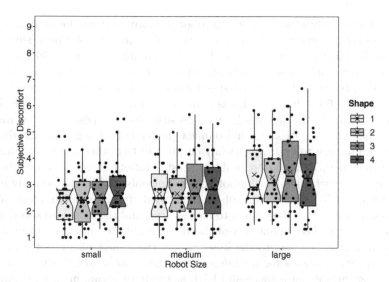

Fig. 9. Subjective discomfort measured by the Robotic Social Attributes Scale (RoSAS) [19]. The crosses represent the means.

on discomfort: $F(3, 275) = 2.34$, $p = .07$ and no interaction effect. The model included a random effect of participants: variance = 0.85; standard deviation = 0.92. The marginal R^2 for the models was 0.10; the conditional R^2 0.69.

4   Discussion and Limitations

The results of the two presented studies indicate that robot speed and size are important factors influencing human-robot proxemics and subjective discomfort in VR. Hence, they should be considered in deciding on a robot's size as well as its motion behavior. Moreover, our results indicate a possible interaction between robot size and speed, with taller and faster robots eliciting substantially higher discomfort and higher preferred minimum comfortable approach distances than smaller, slower ones. Accordingly, a robot's driving speed should be adjusted according to its size, when operating in the proximity of humans. The shape of the robot's edges did not influence minimum comfortable approach distance, but it did influence the perceived discomfort (marginally significant effect) in this study. While the results obtained in our study do not indicate an effect of robot shape on minimum comfortable approach distance, this could be due to rather subtle changes in the robot's edge shapes. Greater, more obvious changes in robot shape could lead to a different conclusion.

Two consecutive studies were presented in this paper. Hence, some adjustments based on implications and results obtained in study 1 were made for the subsequent study 2. Firstly, in study 1 the whole robot was scaled, including its platform and cover. Since these two studies are part of a larger project which will also include real-world studies with a robot platform, this was adapted for study 2. Accordingly, study 2 used the robot platform that will be used in future studies, and only the cover of the robot was scaled, not the platform, since this would not be feasible for the real-world robot. Secondly, the robot velocities used in study 1 were rather high, considering the driving speed of existing delivery robots today. In study 2, the robot speed was not varied as an independent variable, but set to 6 km/h, since this is considered a moderate walking speed for pedestrians [23]. On the one hand, this is sensible since we postulate that robots should 'blend into' the existing environment (instead of adding noise and disturbances) and adhere to existing (social) norms. On the other hand, we outlined a safety-efficiency optimization problem: Faster robots could be more efficient since they can reach their destination faster, but only if they can actually move at a faster speed. To move faster, robots need to satisfy safety requirements at all times, regulations must allow them to move faster, and the increased speed must not interfere with their intent. People need to be able to anticipate the robot's trajectory. Legibility refers to the inherent descriptiveness of a robot's motion, i.e. the trajectory allows for an inference of the robot's goal destination [32]. This is indispensable for a successful HRI, as the human can, in case of conflicting trajectories, evade the robot and thereby avoid standstill. If a higher speed renders the robot unacceptable in public space, reactance might arise [33,34]. If a robot makes people uncomfortable, they might purposely compromise robot performance, for example by stepping into their path to reduce their efficiency. Study 1 therefore piloted rather high robot speeds and very tall sizes, while following studies will consider more moderate speeds and robot sizes to investigate a broad range of robot sizes and motion designs.

The results obtained in this study need to be validated in a real-world setting using real robots since an offset or bias connected to the VR simulation is likely. Discomfort could be less pronounced for the robots in VR since there is no real risk of a collision with the robot. Furthermore, for the minimum comfortable approach distance measures, a distortion in distance perception due to the VR technology is likely and has to be taken into account. Using a VR setup to investigate the influence of robot properties and their influence on perception and HRI is often preferred over laboratory or field studies, since this would involve building different physical prototypes and adjusting robot behavior. This is much more complex for a physical robot compared to its virtual representation and hence comes at higher costs. Previous findings show that VR biases are relatively stable and can, therefore, be considered as internally valid [35]. However, even a stable bias must be investigated systematically and will be validated in upcoming lab studies using a platform otherwise identical to the virtual, real robotic platform (Innok Heros [29]).

For our studies, participants were placed in the origin of the coordinate system generated in Unity. The distance at which participants stopped the approaching robot was measured from this origin to the robot's front (the furthest protruding part of the robot). The origin is set in relation to the detected position of the VR headset in Unity. This procedure is very similar to [8], who measured the distance from the toes of the approaching experimenter to the center of a coordinate system on which participants were placed. Other studies investigating proxemics in HRI measured the minimum comfortable approach distance (minimum comfortable approach distance) from the toes of the participant to the furthest protruding part of the robot [15]. We believe this difference in measurement methods to be minor and put the exact reasoning for the emerging feeling of discomfort upon the approach of the robot up for debate. Participants arguably differ in their perceptions, such as proprioception. Whether the toes actually are the furthest protruding body part of a person depends on body shape, and whether a participant's feeling of discomfort is related to the robot running over one's toes is the essential consideration behind the emerging discomfort, can be put to discussion. Hence, even if the measurement method is clearly defined from the participant's toes to the robot's front, people may still interpret the instruction as to when to stop the robot differently, and not (only) with their toes in mind.

Finally, an uncomfortable feeling related to an approaching robot should also be considered as a sensible instinct, and not only something that should be mitigated with good design. Even the safest robots make mistakes, slow robots can be heavy, and all robots are new actors in public space that has been designed by humans for humans, and mostly not with robots in mind. The feeling of discomfort should therefore be well-adjusted to a robot's capabilities to avoid over-trust and help prevent incidents, or even collisions.

5   Conclusion and Outlook

In conclusion, this paper presents two VR experiments on robot-related factors and their influence on discomfort and the minimum comfortable approach distance towards humans. Speed and size are important robot-related factors influencing human-robot proxemics and subjective discomfort and influence the perception by humans significantly. The shape of the robot's edges does seem to have a smaller impact on discomfort, minimum comfortable approach distance. The results give implications at which distance a delivery robot should adapt its behavior to human interaction partners depending on its exterior and motion design configuration in order to satisfy safety requirements, increase robot efficiency and to elicit the least discomfort in humans as possible.

In upcoming studies within the DFG project we will not only add different approaching angles, mental model impacts and distraction, but also repeat all the pedestrians simulations using the real, physical Innok Heros robot. Additionally, interactions when both the pedestrian and robot are moving at the same time will be addressed. Lastly, individual human differences and environmental differences have to be taken into account in follow-up studies. The results are expected to give valuable insights into proxemic interaction spaces between pedestrians and mobile service robots.

Acknowledgements. We would like to thank Xuanbo Hua for contributing to the virtual reality setup and collecting data for study 1. Additionally, we want to express our gratitude to the German National Research Foundation (DFG) for funding this project (BE 4532/16-1).

References

1. Jennings, D., Figliozzi, M.: Study of sidewalk autonomous delivery robots and their potential impacts on freight efficiency and travel. Transp. Res. Record **2673**(6), 317–326 (2019)
2. Grush, B., Coombes, A.: Digitization, automation, operation, and monetization: standardizing the management of sidewalk and kerb 2025-50. In: Smart Cities Policies and Financing, pp. 219–238. Elsevier (2022)
3. Walters, M.L., Dautenhahn, K., Te Boekhorst, R., Koay, K.L., Syrdal, D.S., Nehaniv, C.L.: An empirical framework for human-robot proxemics. Procs of new frontiers in human-robot interaction (2009)
4. VandenBos, G.R.: APA dictionary of psychology. American Psychological Association (2007)
5. Mumm, J., Mutlu, B.: Human-robot proxemics: physical and psychological distancing in human-robot interaction. In: Proceedings of the 6th International Conference on Human-Robot Interaction, pp. 331–338 (2011)
6. Takayama, L., Pantofaru, C.: Influences on proxemic behaviors in human-robot interaction. In: 2009 IEEE/RSJ International Conference on Intelligent Robots and Systems, pp. 5495–5502. IEEE (2009)
7. Li, R., van Almkerk, M., van Waveren, S., Carter, E., Leite, I.: Comparing human-robot proxemics between virtual reality and the real world. In: 2019 14th ACM/IEEE International Conference on Human-Robot Interaction (HRI), pp. 431–439. IEEE (2019)
8. Hayduk, L.A.: The shape of personal space: an experimental investigation. Can. J. Behav. Sci./Revue canadienne des sciences du comportement **13**(1), 87 (1981)
9. Zhang, L., Helander, M.G., Drury, C.G.: Identifying factors of comfort and discomfort in sitting. Hum. Factors **38**(3), 377–389 (1996)
10. Schmidtler, J., Bengler, K.: Size-weight illusion in human-robot collaboration. In: 2016 25th IEEE International Symposium on Robot and Human Interactive Communication (RO-MAN), pp. 874–879. IEEE (2016)
11. Esterwood, C., Essenmacher, K., Yang, H., Zeng, F., Robert, L.P.: A meta-analysis of human personality and robot acceptance in human-robot interaction. In: Proceedings of the 2021 CHI Conference on Human Factors in Computing Systems, pp. 1–18 (2021)
12. Tabrez, A., Luebbers, M.B., Hayes, B.: A survey of mental modeling techniques in human-robot teaming. Curr. Robot. Rep. **1**, 259–267 (2020)
13. Stock-Homburg, R.: Survey of emotions in human-robot interactions: perspectives from robotic psychology on 20 years of research. Int. J. Soc. Robot. **14**(2), 389–411 (2022)

14. Jost, J., Kirks, T., Chapman, S., Rinkenauer, G.: Examining the effects of height, velocity and emotional representation of a social transport robot and human factors in human-robot collaboration. In: Lamas, D., Loizides, F., Nacke, L., Petrie, H., Winckler, M., Zaphiris, P. (eds.) INTERACT 2019. LNCS, vol. 11747, pp. 517–526. Springer, Examining the effects of height, velocity and emotional representation of a social transport robot and human factors in human-robot collaboration (2019). https://doi.org/10.1007/978-3-030-29384-0_31
15. Miller, L., Kraus, J., Babel, F., Messner, M., Baumann, M.: Come closer: experimental investigation of robots' appearance on proximity, affect and trust in a domestic environment. In: Proceedings of the Human Factors and Ergonomics Society Annual Meeting, vol. 64, pp. 395–399. SAGE Publications Sage CA: Los Angeles, CA (2020)
16. Poffenberger, A.T., Barrows, B.: The feeling value of lines. J. Appl. Psychol. **8**(2), 187 (1924)
17. Bar, M., Neta, M.: Humans prefer curved visual objects. Psychol. Sci. **17**(8), 645–648 (2006)
18. Unity Technologies: Unity (2023). unity.com/
19. Carpinella, C.M., Wyman, A.B., Perez, M.A., Stroessner, S.J.: The robotic social attributes scale (rosas) development and validation. In: Proceedings of the 2017 ACM/IEEE International Conference on Human-Robot Interaction, pp. 254–262 (2017)
20. 3D Models for Professionals: TurboSquid (2023). www.turbosquid.com/
21. R Core Team: R: A language and environment for statistical computing. R foundation for statistical computing (2023). www.R-project.org/
22. Kuznetsova, A., Brockhoff, P.B., Christensen, R.H.B.: lmerTest package: tests in linear mixed effects models. J. Stat. Softw. **82**(13), 1–26 (2017). https://doi.org/10.18637/jss.v082.i13
23. Zebala, J., Ciepka, P., Reza, A.: Pedestrian acceleration and speeds. **91**, 227–234 (2012)
24. Woowa Brothers Corp.: have you imagined a delivery robot traveling on an elevator to reach your front door? [Press release]. www.woowahan.com/en/report/detail/160?current=NewsroomReport&word=Dilly%20tower&report=1&media=1&fact=1/ (2021). [Accessed 19 Jan 2023]
25. Scott, S.: Meet scout. Field testing a new delivery system with amazon scout. www.aboutamazon.com/news/transportation/meet-scout (2019). [Accessed 19 Jan 2023]
26. FedEx Corporation: FedEx welcomes roxo TM, the fedex sameday bot to the u.a.e [press release] (2019). https://newsroom.fedex.com/newsroom/meisa-english/fedex-welcomes-roxo-the-fedex-sameday-bot-to-the-u-a-e. [Accessed 19 Jan 2023]
27. Ottonomy: Ottonomy Unveils Ottobot; The world's first fully autonomous delivery robot delivering in both indoor and outdoor environments – prnewswire.com. www.prnewswire.com/news-releases/ottonomy-unveils-ottobot-the-worlds-first-fully-autonomous-delivery-robot-delivering-in-both-indoor-and-outdoor-environments-301454551.html (2022). [Accessed 19 Jan 2023]
28. 3D CAD Design Software — SOLIDWORKS (2023). www.solidworks.com/
29. Innok Robotics GmbH: autonome mobile outdoor roboter (2022). www.innok-robotics.de/
30. Clamann, M., Bryson, M.: Sharing spaces with robots: the basics of personal delivery devices. Pedestrian and Bicycle Information Center, Chapel Hill (2021). [Accessed 19 Jan 2023]

31. Dimensions.com.: autonomous delivery vehicles dimensions & drawings. www. dimensions.com/collection/autonomous-delivery-vehicles (2021). [Accessed 19 Jan 2023]
32. Dragan, A.D., Lee, K.C., Srinivasa, S.S.: Legibility and predictability of robot motion. In: 2013 8th ACM/IEEE International Conference on Human-Robot Interaction (HRI), pp. 301–308. IEEE (2013)
33. Brehm, S.S., Brehm, J.W.: Psychological Reactance: A Theory of Freedom and Control. Academic Press, New York (1981)
34. Boos, A., Herzog, O., Reinhardt, J., Bengler, K., Zimmermann, M.: A compliance-reactance framework for evaluating human-robot interaction. Front. Robot. AI 9 (2022)
35. Schneider, S.A.E.: Behavioral validity in virtual reality pedestrian simulators. Ph.D. thesis, Technische Universität München (2021)

Introducing Playing Catch to Motivate Interaction with Communication Robots

Ryuto Katsuki$^{(\boxtimes)}$, Masayuki Ando, Kouyou Otsu, and Tomoko Izumi

Ritsumeikan University, Kusatsu 525-8557, Shiga, Japan
is0500@ed.ritsumei.ac.jp, {mandou,k-otsu,
izumi-t}@fc.ritsumei.ac.jp

Abstract. The deployment of communication robots is increasing to address the problem of labor shortage caused by population decrease. However, individuals may still exhibit resistance or reluctance to communicate with robots owing to a lack of trust or other reasons. In this study, we explore the possibility of incorporating ice-breaking activities into human-robot interaction to make people more inclined to communicate with robots. Here, we focus on playing catch as an ice-breaking activity because it is easy and suitable for the conversational process and has elements for a turn-taking mechanism and collaboration of participants. The proposed method involves a robot and human speaker alternating throwing a ball and speaking during the conversation. In the verification, we compared two conditions, the playing catch condition and the non-playing catch condition, to verify the effect of playing catch with a robot on the motivation for conversation and interaction. The results indicated that, while the impact of playing catch on the affinity and motivation for conversation with robots could not be established, the visual representation of turn-taking through the movement of the ball enabled a more natural pace of conversation.

Keywords: Human-robot interaction (HRI) · Turn-taking · Affinity for a robot · Communication support · Ice-breaking

1 Introduction

The advancements in robot control technology and deep learning have improved the performance of communication robots, and these robots are currently being utilized in various settings such as stores and elderly care facilities. Despite the declining population resulting in a shortage of human resources, there is still a high demand for the application of communication robots in various social fields. However, some users have negative perceptions towards these robots, such as distrust and discomfort while communicating with them. Therefore, despite the progress in communication robots, users are still reluctant to interact with them. This study primarily aims to develop a support mechanism that motivates interactions with communication robots.

Although many possible factors motivate interactions with robots, in this study, we consider two most crucial factors: turn-taking of conversation and affinity for a robot. The

M. Kurosu and A. Hashizume (Eds.): HCII 2023, LNCS 14013, pp. 79–91, 2023.
https://doi.org/10.1007/978-3-031-35602-5_6

term "turn-taking" refers to the process of alternating the roles of a speaker and listener between multiple individuals during a conversation. In group conversations, disruption of turn-taking, such as interruption while others are speaking or monologuing, can reduce motivation to converse. Such interruptions during conversations may be more likely to occur with robots because they lack social signals like facial expressions. Therefore, it is considered that enhancing turn-taking smoothly may be an important factor in motivating conversation.

Another factor motivating conversation is a sense of affinity with a robot. An affinity refers to an interest in another person and a desire to converse with them. In human-to-human conversation, the initial encounter can be difficult because of a lack of affinity between the two individuals. In such cases, an ice-breaking task can be utilized to encourage communication and mutual understanding and evoke empathy through cooperative tasks. This ice-breaking task promotes collaboration among unfamiliar participants and a sense of closeness as peers who have performed collaborative work. Hence, an ice-breaking task is one possible approach for unfamiliar persons to communicate with each other. In addition, this fact suggests that the concept of ice-breaking tasks could also be used to enhance a sense of affinity for interacting with robots.

Therefore, to motivate people for conversation with a robot, we focus on playing catch as an ice-breaking task; this has the ease of turn-taking of conversation and promotes a sense of affinity with the robot. Playing catch is an ice-breaking task can be gamified to be played while conversing. Therefore, playing it with a robot evokes a sense of affinity with the robot. In addition, playing catch has the elements of turn-taking. The role of turn-taking in playing catch, in which the thrower and catcher take turns, resembles turn-taking in conversation. Thus, to liken the turn transitions caused by the movement of the ball to conversational turn transitions, it may be possible to increase awareness of turn-taking during conversations. In this study, we introduce experimental results to verify the effectiveness of playing catch while conversing with a robot as a method to promote the ease of turn-taking, a sense of affinity for a robot, and motivating humans for conversation with a robot.

2 Related Research

Studies using various methods for building and fostering communication within robot-human relationships have been documented in the literature. For example, Ono et al. [1] proposed a mechanism that enabled the transportation of a humanoid agent with electronic pet-like roles into a physical robot or other daily item seamlessly to enhance trust and familiarity. Additionally, Hinaga [2] examined the effects of introducing the act of holding hands on the building of relationships between children and robots during their first encounter. This study discovered that physical contact improved children's proactivity and reduced their fear of robots, making it easier for them to approach the robot. These findings suggest that it is important to develop and improve methods for interaction with robots when building relationships with them.

In human-robot interactions (HRIs), it is known that physical activity and synchrony in conversation are crucial in building relationships between communication robots and humans. For example, Ono et al. [3] demonstrated that the relationship between conversational partners is important and that physical expressions are useful for building relationships. In addition, several studies focused on the impact of mirroring the non-verbal behavior of the user during a dialogue by the robot (pacing). Nishimura et al. [4] attempted to achieve interactions like a conversationalist speech pattern by controlling three vocal parameters: "pitch," "volume," and "speech rate." Their experimental results illustrated that pacing is effective in improving the user's impression of the robot. From these findings, it is concluded that incorporating frameworks that include synchronous actions may be useful in building relationships between humans and communication robots.

These previous works suggest that introducing the icebreaking approach used in interpersonal collaboration into HRI could be a promising approach. The catch-ball task in this study is a similar operation of throwing and receiving a ball while alternating turns between the human and the robot. Therefore, it is possible that the task characteristics of playing catch, in which two people repeat similar actions, may induce a sense of affinity. However, the effects of performing an ice-breaking task with a robot warrant further investigation. In this study, we clarify the role of catching as a gamified ice-breaking task in facilitating HRI.

3 Proposed Method

3.1 Overview of the Proposed Method

In this study, we aim to enhance the conversational motivation of HRI and develop a more talkative environment. We consider applying the cooperative task of playing catch as an ice-breaking task to HRI scenarios. Our proposed system enables a one-to-one conversation between a human and a communication robot while playing catch. The proposed method involves the physical exchange of a ball in the real world between the robot and the user, synchronized with the exchange of words. Figure 1 shows a robot and a human facing each other, rolling a ball to the other while conversing. We introduce playing catch to a conversation with a robot to realize smooth turn-taking, have the human develop a sense of affinity for the robot, and develop a more talkative environment. Four factors that have motivated us to focus on playing catch as an ice-breaking task are:

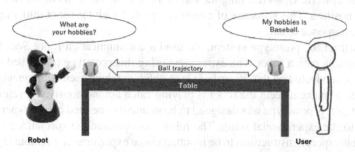

Fig. 1. Concept of the proposed method

- It can be performed while conversing with the robot.
- It is a simple and easy task that can be performed by users of any age.
- It includes synchronous actions enhancing a sense of affinity as if two people are performing the same task.
- It is a task with the elements of turn-taking.

This proposed method likens the turn transitions caused by the movement of a ball during a game of catch to conversational turn transitions. Thus, the user can easily sense the turn of the conversation and listeners can fully listen to the speaker's words. Additionally, the speaker can switch with listeners at any time they wish, allowing the conversation to proceed at one's own pace and convey everything they wish to cover. By playing catch in conjunction with the conversation, it is expected to promote smooth conversations by clarifying the timing of the end of the speaker's words. In this way, the process of "conversational playing catch" can be visualized in the real world, providing a tangible experience in the interaction with the robot. Moreover, they exchange the actual ball and coordinate to keep their catch working. This cooperation behavior with each other is expected to enhance a sense of affinity with each other.

3.2 Implementation of the Prototype System

To validate playing catch while conversing with a robot is effective for enhancing turn-taking, an affinity for the robot, and motivation for conversation, we built a prototype system that enables users to play catch while interacting with a communication robot.

As depicted in Fig. 2, the overall structure of the system comprises a communication robot (A in Fig. 2), a ball launching device (B in Fig. 2), and a pipe and lift mechanism (C and D, respectively, in Fig. 2) for collecting the ball from the user. The functioning of each mechanism in the system during playing catch is described below. Initially, the robot engages in verbal communication with the user. Subsequently, the motor of the ball launching device is activated, resulting in the ball being rolled toward the user. The user receives the ball and responds to the robot's verbal communication by rolling the ball back. Here, the user rolls the ball into the pipe located on the table. When the ball is placed on the pipe, it rolls down to the ball tray of the lift, which subsequently lifts the ball upward. Upon reaching the top of the lift, the ball rolls down and is set in the launch position. This sequence of events is repeated with the robot initiating verbal communication once again.

To construct the prototype system, we used a communication robot Sota (Vstone Inc.) as communication robot. The experiment using this prototype (described in detail in Sect. 4) is conducted by the Wizard of Oz method, in which each component is manually moved to make it seem the robot is playing catch autonomously. Therefore, each component of this prototype was designed to be manually operated by the experimenter according to the experimental setup. The robot was operated via specialized software which enables speech instructions to be inputted via an experimenter's remote keyboard.

In addition, we implemented the ball-launching device using two 17HS4401 stepping motors (B in Fig. 2). This device attaches a flipper to the output shaft of a stepping motor and rotates it to roll a ball to the user. We used the stepping motors because of their ability to precisely control the motor's rotational angle and to act as a barrier to keep the ball in

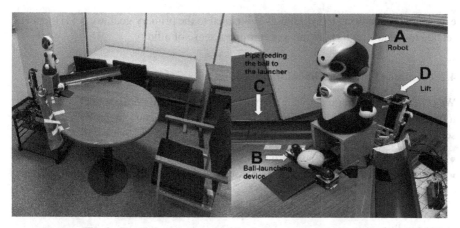

Fig. 2. Prototype system to enable playing catch with the robot

the launch position after it rolls down from the lift. To control the stepping motors, we employed two TB6600 motor drivers and two Arduino UNOs, which were operated using the Arduino IDE via serial connection. This prototype system also had a component for retrieving the balls. The component had a pipe to receive the balls (C in Fig. 2) and a lift to move them to the launch position (D in Fig. 2). The pipe was inclined and mounted on the left and right sides of the table, such that when a ball is placed on the pipe, it will roll and reach the lift device. The lift device, which raises the ball to the launch position, was implemented using Lego Mindstorm EV3. Additionally, a color sensor was mounted directly below the ball platform on which the ball is resting. If the value of the surrounding light sensed is below the constant threshold, the system detects that a ball was present on the platform, and the lift device lifts the ball up. Once the ball reaches the top of the lift, it is released.

4 Experiment

4.1 Aim of the Experiment and Hypotheses

This study aims to examine the potential benefits of engaging in an ice-breaking task, such as playing catch, with a robot, specifically regarding the motivation for conversation. Moreover, we verify the effect of playing catch for the ease of turn-taking in conversation and a sense of affinity with a communication robot. To investigate this, we have conducted an evaluation experiment using the prototype system described in Sect. 3. Specifically, we aim to test the following three hypotheses:

- H1: Catching tasks with a robot facilitate turn-taking.
- H2: Catching tasks with a robot enhance a sense of affinity to it.
- H3: Catching tasks with a robot enhance the motivation for conversation with the robot.

The primary aim of this study is to enhance the motivation for conversation with a robot by promoting the ease of turn-taking and a sense of affinity. Therefore, in this experiment, in addition to hypotheses H3 related to the primary goal, we set H1 and H2 related to enhancing turn-taking and forming a sense of affinity.

4.2 Outline of the Experimental Procedure

We conducted an experiment wherein participants interacted with a robotic system prototype under two conditions: playing catch and conversing. Thus, in this experiment, we set the following two experimental conditions:

- Playing catch condition: The participant converses with the robot while playing catch.
- Non-playing catch condition: The participant converses with the robot without playing catch.

Each participant was instructed to experiment twice in total, once for each of the above conditions.

Thirty university students participated in this experiment. The order of the experimental conditions was rotated for each participant; half of them experimented with the playing catch condition first, and the non-playing catch condition second, while the other half followed the reverse order.

The experimental procedure is described below. We first explained the flow and content of the experiment to the participant and obtained their consent to participate in the experiment. Thus far, the task of playing catch was not yet explained in the explanation of the experiment overview, but was explained before the start of the playing catch condition. The experiment location varied between the playing catch and non-playing catch conditions. In the playing catch condition, participants were seated according to Fig. 3(a), and in the non-playing catch condition, according to Fig. 3(b), for the experiment.

(a)   (b)

Fig. 3. Experimental environments

In the playing catch condition, after the rules of catch were explained, the participants were instructed to practice playing catch. Subsequently, the robot initiated the conversation using a ball-launching device. The participant responded and returned the ball to the robot. In the non-playing catch condition, the participant conversed with the robot without using the prototype system for playing catch. The interaction between the participant and the robot was repeated 10 times for each condition. After the conversation, the participant was requested to complete a survey regarding their experience with the robot in each condition.

4.3 Content of Robot's Speech

In designing the content of the speech, we selected topics that were familiar to university students and appropriate for initial interactions; a unique dialogue scenario was developed. The speech was designed by considering the expected responses from the participants, with multiple options prepared for each response or with a focus on providing general responses to ensure smooth and comfortable conversation. Table 1 presents the speech patterns used in this experiment.

4.4 Evaluation Criteria

In this experiment, participants completed a questionnaire assessing their impressions of the robot after experiencing both the playing catch condition and the non-playing catch condition. The questionnaire results will be analyzed to understand any differences in participants' impressions of the robot under these conditions. The first questionnaire regarding their impression of the conversation with the robot consists of six items, as detailed in Table 2. Each question is presented with a 7-point Likert scale (1: Strongly disagree, 7: Strongly agree).

Table 1. Composition of speech patterns used in the experiment

	Category	Robots' speech
S1	The participant's name	Could you tell me your full name?
S2	The participant's department	What faculty do you belong to?
S3-1	Topics in the participant's student life	What are your hobbies?
S3-2	Topics in the participant's student life	What kind of study or research are you doing?
S3-3	Topics in the participant's student life	Do you have any dreams for the future?
S3-4	Topics in the participant's student life	What made you happy recently?
S3-5	Topics in the participant's student life	How do you spend your holidays?
S4	Closing greetings	I'm hungry, so I'm going to eat. See you next time!

In the playing catch condition, participants were instructed to complete an additional questionnaire immediately after the experience to assess their perceptions of the playing catch interaction with the robot. The questionnaire mainly evaluated their impressions of the proposed system and their experiences with the catch ball. The questionnaire consisted of four items, as shown in Table 3, and used the same scale as in Table 2.

Table 2. Questionnaire items regarding impressions of the robot and ease of conversing with it

	Questionnaire Items
Q1	The interaction with the robot made me interested in the robot
Q2	The interaction with the robot made me feel closer to the robot
Q3	The interaction with the robot helped me understand when I should speak
Q4	The interaction with the robot allowed me to talk at my comfortable pace
Q5	I feel that I wanted to talk a little longer with the robot
Q6	I enjoyed interacting with the robot

Table 3. Questionnaire items related to playing catch

	Questionnaire Items
Q7	The robot playing catch with me seems to catch ball
Q8	I felt discomfort about playing catch with the robot while talking to it
Q9	I was confused playing catch with the robot
Q10	I enjoyed playing catch with the robot

5 Experimental Results and Discussion

In this section, we present the results of the questionnaire conducted in the two experimental conditions. Because the same robot was used in both conditions, there is a potential for the impression of the robot in the first condition to influence the results of the second condition. Thus, we conducted two types of analysis:

- **All-Results:** Intra-participant comparison of the factors of the catch ball experience using data from all trials (N = 30).
- **First-Results:** Inter-participant comparison of the factors of the catch ball experience using only the first trial (N = 15 for each condition).

5.1 Questionnaire Results on the Impression of the Robot (in All-Results)

The mean answers for each questionnaire item and the results of a one-tailed t-test for the difference in means are presented in Table 4. The distribution of the answers is displayed in box-and-whisker plots depicted in Fig. 4.

Q3 and Q4 ask about turn-taking in the conversation with the robot (corresponding to H1). From the result of the t-test, significant differences were observed for both Q3 and Q4. The results indicate that playing catch enabled participants to comprehend their speaking timing, allowing them to comfortably communicate at their desired pace.

Q1, Q2, and Q6 ask about affinity for the robot, which is an effect of introducing an ice-breaking task of playing catch (corresponding to H2). In the t-test, there are no significant differences in these items. Thus, it cannot be confirmed that playing catch influenced the enjoyment of interacting with the robot or a sense of affinity with the robot. However, box-and-whisker plots for Q6 in Fig. 4 indicate that both the with and without conditions were evaluated highly overall, with approximately one-fourth of the total responses rated 7. This result suggests that the difference between the two conditions may not have been captured within the 7-point scale, potentially due to a ceiling effect.

Q5 asks about the motivation for conversing with the robot, which is our main goal (corresponding to H3). However, while the mean value in the playing catch condition is higher than the non-playing catch condition, the results indicate no significant difference between the two conditions.

Table 4. Mean values and t-test results of the questions about impressions of the robot in All-Results analysis

	Questionnaire Items	Without	With	p-value
Q1	The interaction with the robot made me interested in the robot	**5.67**	5.53	0.1772
Q2	The interaction with the robot made me feel closer to the robot	5.67	**5.70**	0.4434
Q3	The interaction with the robot helped me understand when I should speak	5.57	**6.36**	**0.0002****
Q4	The interaction with the robot allowed me to talk at my comfortable pace	5.00	**5.53**	**0.0217****
Q5	I feel that I wanted to talk a little longer with the robot	**5.30**	5.20	0.3312
Q6	I enjoyed interacting with the robot	5.68	**5.93**	0.1628

*: $p < 0.1$, **: $p < 0.05$

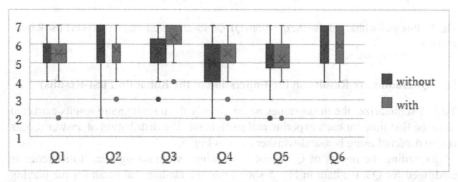

Fig. 4. Box-and-whisker plot of the questions Q1–Q6 about impressions of robots in All-Results analysis

Table 5. Mean values and t-test results of the questions about impressions of the robot in the First-Results analysis

	Questionnaire Items	Without	With	p-value
Q1	The interaction with the robot made me interested in the robot	5.53	**5.87**	0.1640
Q2	The interaction with the robot made me feel closer to the robot	5.80	**6.07**	0.2410
Q3	The interaction with the robot helped me understand when I should speak	5.73	**6.20**	0.1260
Q4	The interaction with the robot allowed me to talk at my comfortable pace	5.00	**5.60**	**0.0890***
Q5	I feel that I wanted to talk a little longer with the robot	5.07	**5.60**	0.1230
Q6	I enjoyed interacting with the robot	5.53	**6.13**	**0.0602***

*: $p < 0.1$, **: $p < 0.05$

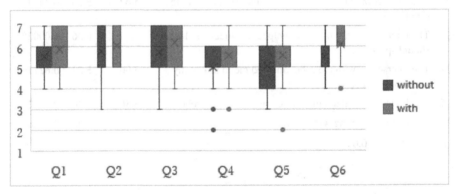

Fig. 5. Box-and-whisker plot of the questions Q1-Q6 about impressions of robots in First-Results analysis

5.2   Questionnaire Results on the Impression of the Robot (in First-Results)

Table 5 summarizes the mean values based on only the questionnaire results extracted from the first time for each experimental participant. The distribution of answer results is also depicted using box-and-whisker plots in Fig. 5.

Regarding the results of Q3 about turn-taking, while no significant difference is confirmed for Q3, the data in Fig. 5 shows that the median and mean for the playing catch condition are both higher than those for the non-playing catch condition. Moreover, in Q4, a significant difference is observed. This result suggests that playing catch with the robot enabled the participants to gain a better understanding of their own speaking pace, resulting in a more comfortable conversation.

Next, we see the results of Q1, Q2, and Q6 about affinity. In Q1 and Q2, there are no statistical differences between the two conditions, and therefore, it is not confirmed that playing catch influenced a sense of affinity for the robot. However, the high scores for playing catch condition in Q1 and Q2 and the proximity of the upper end of the box to a value of 7 shown in Fig. 5 suggest that the ceiling effect might have occurred, making it difficult to distinguish differences between conditions within the scale. Regarding Q6, which asks about the enjoyment of interacting with the robot, the t-test results showed that the play catch condition has a significantly higher mean value than the without condition. Therefore, playing catch with the robot was perceived as enjoyable among the participants.

Finally, regarding the results of Q5 concerning the motivation for conversation, there are no significant differences in the mean values between the two conditions, indicating that playing catch uninfluenced the motivation for conversation between the robot and the user.

5.3 Results of the Survey Regarding Playing Catch

Table 6 shows the average results of the responses to the questionnaire about playing catch shown in Table 3. In Q7, we asked participants' perceptions of the robot's catching ability, and the average score was 3.93. The score is a negative value, which is lower.

than the intermediate value of 4. Therefore, the participants may not have perceived the robot autonomously catching the ball. For Q8 and Q9, we asked about the level of discomfort and confusion while playing catch with the robot and the average scores were 3.10 and 2.93, respectively. Each score is lower than the intermediate value of 4. These results indicate that participants experienced less discomfort or confusion while playing catch with the robot. Q10, which evaluated participants' enjoyment of playing catch, received an average score of 5.73, a relatively higher score exceeding the median of 4. In conjunction with the results from Q8 and Q9, playing catch with the robot seems to have been generally well received by participants.

5.4 Discussion

Firstly, we examine the relationship between H1 and the results. The results from Q4 reveal that the mean value was significantly higher when the playing catch condition was present, both in All-Results in Table 4 and First-Results in Table 5. However, for Q3, the All-Results values showed a significant difference, but First-Results values only showed a higher mean value for the playing catch condition without a significant difference. This discrepancy may be due to the inclusion of the second experience's impression in the evaluation. In the All-Results analysis, the second experience included the playing catch condition, which may have facilitated an easier understanding.

of timing compared to the non-playing catch condition in the first experience, result-ing in a more significant difference. However, in the First-Results analysis, only the impression of the first experience was analyzed, and relative comparison results were not included, which could explain why a significant difference was not recognized. Regardless of the analysis method, the mean value for Q3 was higher with the playing catch condition compared to without, and significant differences were observed in the All-Results analysis including the second experience. This result suggests that playing

Table 6. Questionnaire items related to playing catch

	Questionnaire Items	Mean
Q7	The robot playing catch with me seems to catch a ball	3.93
Q8	I felt discomfort about playing catch with the robot while talking to it	3.10
Q9	I was confused playing catch with the robot	2.93
Q10	I enjoyed playing catch with the robot	5.73

catch with a robot, particularly after previous experience in general conversation, can aid in understanding. Therefore, the results from the experiment support H1.

Next, we examine the relationship between H2 and the results. For Q1 and Q2, there are no significant differences in either All-Results or First-Results values. However, a comparison among First-Results values showed that the mean value of the playing catch condition was higher than that of the non-playing catch condition. The box-and-whisker plots in Fig. 5 exhibited a ceiling effect on answers, which may have impacted the evaluation of differences. Therefore, there is a possibility of observing differences in a sense of affinity with and without the introduction of catch balls, either by measuring it with other scales or by setting appropriate questions. The results for Q6, using both All-Results and First-Results analyses, revealed a higher mean value for the playing catch condition compared to that for the non-playing catch condition, with a significant trend observed in the First-Results analysis. Additionally, the results in First-Results for Q10 showed a relatively positive value of 5.73. These findings suggest that playing catch with the robot in this study was enjoyable for many participants. In this experiment, we did not confirm the effect of playing catch on the affinity significantly, but the results tended to be consistent with H2. The results from Q8 and Q9 did not indicate any discomfort or hesitation toward playing catch with the robot. Therefore, it can be concluded that the ice-breaking task experience with the playing catch robot in this study was perceived as enjoyable and showed little resistance such as discomfort or confusion.

Finally, we examine the relationship between H3 and the results. For Q5, no significant difference was observed. Therefore, the effect of playing catch while conversing with a robot on motivation for conversation in this experiment is unconfirmed. Thus, H3 is not supported. However, First-Results analysis showed that the mean value of the playing catch condition was higher than that of the non-playing catch condition. One of the considered reasons why H3 was unsupported may be a lack of a sense of the robot itself returning the ball. This possibility is supported by the mean value of Q7 being close to the intermediate value. The characteristics of the experimental device, which required the ball to be thrown toward a pipe, may also have contributed to the failure to support H3.

6 Conclusions

In this study, to motivate conversation with a robot, we introduced playing catch to interact with the robot as an ice-breaking task because it has the ease and suitability for the conversational process and it has elements of turn-taking and collaboration of participants. For the verification experiment, we developed a prototype system that enabled users to play catch while interacting with a communication robot. Using this system, we experimented with 30 university students to verify how playing catch with a robot affects the ease of turn-taking, a sense of affinity with the robot, and motivation for conversation with the robot. The results indicated that playing catch improved understanding of turn-taking and allowed a comfortable pace to be kept in conversation. Furthermore, the participants viewed playing catch with a robot in a favorable light and deemed it entertaining. However, no significant impact on enhancing the motivation for conversation was observed in the results of the experiment.

The questions asking about recognizing the robot catching the ball yielded neutral results close to "neither," which may be because of the design of the experimental prototype system (i.e., the ball was thrown towards a pipe rather than directly at the robots). The mechanism of catching and throwing a ball in the prototype system may have made it difficult for the participants to understand the robot's ball-catching capabilities. In future work, we aim to consider an experiment design that provides a sense of robots catching the ball autonomously.

References

1. Ono, T., Imai, M., Etani, T., Nakatsu, R.: Construction of relationship between humans and robots. Trans. Inf. Process. Soc. Jpn. 41(1), 158–166 (2000)
2. Chie, H., Abe, K., Nagai, T., Omori, T.: Walking hand-in-hand helps relationship building between child and robot. J. Robot. Mechatron. 32(1), 8–20 (2020)
3. Ono, T., Imai, M., Ishiguro, H., Nakatsu, R.: Embodied communication emergent from mutual physical expression between humans and robots. Trans. Inf. Process. Soc. Jpn. 42(6), 1348–1358 (2001)
4. Nishimura, S., Nakamura, T., Kanbara, M., Sato, W., Hagita, N.: Evaluation of pacing for dialog robots to build trust relationships with human users. In: Proceedings of the 7th International Conference on Human-Agent Interaction (HAI 2019), pp. 300–302. Association for Computing Machinery, New York (2019)

Asynchronous Classification
of Error-Related Potentials
in Human-Robot Interaction

Su Kyoung Kim[1]([⊠])(iD), Michael Maurus[1], Mathias Trampler[1], Marc Tabie[1],
and Elsa Andrea Kirchner[1,2](iD)

[1] Robotics Innovation Center, German Research Center for Artificial Intelligence
(DFKI), Bremen, Germany
{su-kyoung.kim,michael.maurus,mathias.trampler,marc.tabiel}@dfki.de,
elsa.kirchner@uni-due.de
[2] Institute of Medical Technology Systems, University of Duisburg-Essen,
Duisburg, Germany

Abstract. The use of implicit evaluations of humans such as electroencephalogram (EEG)-based human feedback is relevant for robot applications, e.g., robot learning or corrections of robot's actions. In the presented study, we implemented a scenario, in which a simulated robot
communicates with its human partner through speech and gestures. The
robot announces its intention verbally and selects the appropriate action
using pointing gestures. The human partner in turn implicitly evaluates
whether the robot's verbal announcement matches the robot's action
choice. Error-related potentials (ErrPs) are expressions of this implicit
evaluation, which are triggered in case of discrepancies between the
robot's verbal announcement and the corresponding actions (pointing
gestures) chosen by the robot. In our scenario, the task takes a long time.
Therefore, asynchronous EEG classifications that continuously segment
EEGs are advantageous or even necessary. However, asynchronous EEG
classifications are challenging due to the large number of false positives
during the long task time of the robot. In this work, we propose an approach to improve asynchronous classification performance by selecting
and extracting features that are only relevant for EEG classifications in
the long time series that the robot needs to perform tasks. We achieved
a high classification performance, i.e., a mean balanced accuracy of 91%
across all subjects. However, we also found some differences between subjects in classification performance. In future work, it is useful to extend
the proposed approach of forward and backward sliding windows and
their combinations with individual feature selection adaptation to avoid
the variability of classification performance between subjects.

Keywords: human-robot interaction · error-related potentials
(ErrP) · brain-computer interfaces (BCIs) · human-machine interaction

Supported by the Federal Ministry for Economic Affairs and Climate Action (BMWK)
FKZ: FKZ 50RA1701 and Federal Ministry for Education and Research (BMBF) FKZ:
01IW21002.

1   Introduction

In recent years, the use of intrinsic human feedback such as electroencephalogram (EEG)-based human feedback has increased relevance for robot applications, especially for human-robot interactions (HRIs). In recent studies, EEG-based human feedback have been applied in HRIs.

In particular, error-related potentials (ErrPs) evoked e.g., when observing erroneous or unusual actions of robots have been used as intrinsic feedback (i.e., implicit evaluations of the correctness of robot behavior) in order to adapt robot behavior strategies [6, 10]. In fact, the use of implicit evaluations of humans as intrinsic feedback is advantageous for learning complex behavioral strategies of robots, because the predefinition of the evaluation criterion (e.g., reward shaping) for robot behavior is not easy for complex robotic tasks.

Moreover, the error-related potential (ErrP) is a well investigated event-related potential (ERP) component and has been used in several research and application areas (see, review, [1]). In most applications, ErrPs have been applied in observation tasks [3–9, 12, 14].

In the presented study, we implemented a scenario, in which a simulated robot communicates with its human partner through speech and gestures. The robot announces its intention verbally (e.g., I will point to the hammer) and chooses the appropriate action using pointing gestures (Fig. 1). In turn, the subjects hear the verbal message of the robot and observe the action choice of the robot. The implicit evaluations of the subjects on the robot's action choices are recorded and extracted by using EEG.

Here, we used error-related potentials (ErrPs) as implicit human evaluations of robot actions. We expect ErrPs in the case of inconsistencies between the robot's verbal announcement and the corresponding actions (pointing gestures) chosen by the robot.

For extraction of implicit human evaluations (ErrPs), online EEG classification is required. Additionally, asynchronous EEG classifications are beneficial in detecting erroneous robot behavior, especially when the robot is performing complex tasks that take a long time. However, asynchronous EEG classifications are challenging due to the large number of false positives during the long task time of the robot (e.g., [12]).

In this work, we propose an approach to improve asynchronous classification performance by selecting and extracting features that are only relevant for EEG classifications in the long time series that the robot needs to perform tasks. The proposed approach uses a combination of forward and backward sliding windows. We continuously segment EEGs with a given window length (sliding windows) forward and backward with respect to relevant temporal reference points of the robot's action sequences. In this way, we extract only relevant features for ErrP classifications while observing the continuous actions of the robot.

2 Methods

2.1 Scenario

Figure 1 shows our scenario, in which the simulated robot announced verbally its intention (e.g., I will point to the hammer) and performs the corresponding actions (pointing gesture). In turn, the subjects hear the verbal message of the robot and observe the actions of the robot. The implicit evaluations of the subjects on the robot's action choice are recorded by using EEGs. For example, when the robot's verbal message and its action selection (pointing gesture) are congruent, we expect no ErrPs. Otherwise, we expect to detect ErrPs, which are used as implicit evaluation of the subjects.

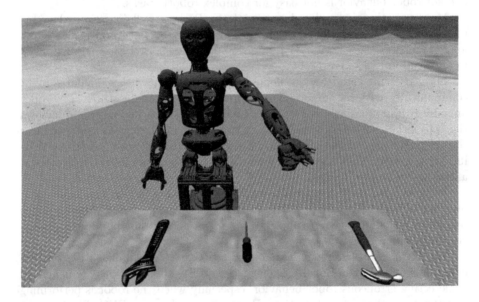

Fig. 1. Scenario. The robot announces its intention verbally (e.g., I will point to the hammer) and chooses the appropriate action using pointing gestures. In turn, the subjects implicitly evaluate the action choices of the robot. The implicit evaluation of the subjects are recorded and extracted by using EEGs to recognize incorrect action choices of the robot.

2.2 Approach

Fig. 2A shows a single task of the robot), which takes 15s. In the experiments, we defined episodes, each lasting from the beginning of the robot's verbal announcement until the end of the robot's action. Each action of the robot consists of a movement of the arm in the direction of the workbench and a subsequent gesture lasting approximately 1s indicated by the change in finger configuration.

All episodes were divided into two different types: correct and incorrect episodes. Both labels (correct and incorrect episodes) were used to train an EEG classifier (i.e., ErrP decoder) and later to validate the test data (ground truth). We expected no ErrPs to occur in correct episodes, while ErrPs were expected in wrong episodes.

As shown in Fig. 2B, we divided the robot's action into two phases in our application: directional movements and gesture movements (Fig. 2B), since the human observer can guess the robot's gesture at the beginning of the robot's action (directional movements) but cannot be absolutely sure that the robot's actions are correct until the robot performs a pointing gesture (gesture movements). We used the beginning of the robot's actions (directional movements to point at an object) and the beginning of the robot's gestures (change of finger configuration in the robot hand for a pointing gesture) as temporal reference points (see Fig. 2B) to extract features for EEG classifier. To this end, we used these two sent temporal reference points as markers, which sent to the EEG recording system.

Figure 2B shows our approach of feature selection/extraction using forward and backward sliding windows. In our scenario, we do not know the exact moment when the subject realizes that the robot's actions may or may not be correct. Therefore, we used asynchronous classifications. Two points in time are relevant for the detection of ErrPs: the beginning of the robot's actions (directional movements) and the beginning of pointing gestures (indicated by the change in finger configuration). First, the subject recognizes the robot's direction of movement and may tend to guess which tool the robot might select early after the start of an action (directional movements). However, the subject cannot be absolutely sure that the robot's action is correct until the robot performs a pointing gesture (second time point). Therefore, we defined two temporal reference points (see Fig. 2B): (a) directional movements towards one of the objects (3 s–8 s after verbal announcement) and (b) pointing gestures towards the selected object (8 s–9 s after verbal announcement) to frame the time period during which the subject makes a decision about the correctness of the robot's action. For training an ErrP decoder, we used these two temporal reference points for feature selection and extraction. As shown in Fig. 2B, on the one hand, we continuously segmented the EEGs from the onset of the robot actions (i.e. forward windowing). On the other hand, we continuously segmented from the onset of the robot's gestures in the reverse direction (i.e., backward windowing). In this way, features are extracted using forward and backward sliding windows.

2.3   EEG Recording

Nine subjects (two females, seven males, age: 25.5 ± 3.02 years, right-handed, normal or corrected-to normal vision) participated in this study. The experimental protocols were approved by the ethics committee of the University of Bremen. Written informed consent was obtained from all participants. EEGs were continuously recorded using a 64-channel eego mylab system (ANT Neuro

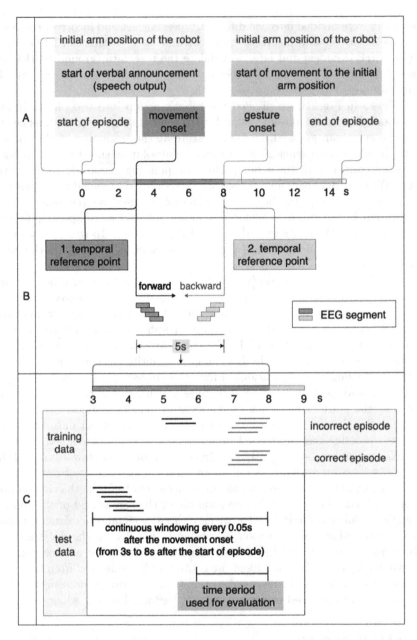

Fig. 2. Experiment design. (A) Episode: An episode begins with the start of the robot's verbal announcement and ends with the return to the initial position. (B) Concept of forward and backward sliding windows used for training a classifier: Features are extracted from the time period between the onset of movement and the onset of gesture using forward and backward sliding windows. Note that we divided the robot's action into different phases (directional movements and gesture movements), but the robot performs a continuous action to point to one of three objects. (C) Feature selection during training for correct and incorrect episodes and during continuous testing. Evaluation is based on the marked time period.

GmbH), in which 64 electrodes were arranged in accordance to an extended 10-20 system with reference at electrode CPz. Impedance was kept below $10\,k\Omega$. EEG signals were sampled at $2\,kHz$ amplified by one 64 channel amplifiers (ANT Neuro GmbH). For each subject we recorded nine data sets. For one of the subjects, only eight datasets were recorded. Each dataset contained 36 correct and 18 wrong episodes. In total, we recorded 324 correct episodes and 162 wrong episodes for each subject except for one subject. Since we only had eight complete data sets for all nine subjects, seven data sets were used to train an ErrP decoder and one dataset was used for testing to allow a fair comparison between subjects.

2.4   EEG Processing

The EEG data were analyzed using a Python-based framework for signal processing and classification [11]. The continuous EEG signal was segmented into epochs from 0 s to 0.9 s after the start of the robot's action with the overlap of 0.05 s (sliding windows). All epochs were normalized to zero mean for each channel, decimated to 50 Hz, and band pass filtered (0.5 to 10 Hz). The xDAWN spatial filter [13] was used to enhance the signal to signal-plus-noise ratio and 7 pseudo channels were retained after spatial filtering.

For feature selection and extraction, we divided the robot's action into different phases (directional movements and gesture movements). However, we would like to point out that the robot performs a continuous action to point at one of the three objects. As mentioned earlier, the human observer can recognize the direction of movement and guess the robot's choice at the beginning of the robot's action (directional movements). However, the human observer cannot be absolutely sure that the robot's actions are correct until the robot performs a pointing gesture (gesture movements). Two temporal reference points were relevant for feature selection and extraction: The onset of the robot's action (i.e., the onset of directional movements) and the onset of gesture movements (see Fig. 2-B). Accordingly, we extracted features using forward and backward windowing based on the two temporal reference points (see Fig. 2-B).

Different strategies of feature selection and extraction were used depending on the episode type after a systematic investigation of different combinations of sliding windows across both types of episodes for each subject. We found different optimal time periods and different optimal combinations of forward and backward sliding windows for feature selection and extraction depending on the individual subject. However, to allow a fair comparison between subjects, we decided to choose the same time period for all subjects. Therefore, we used the same sliding windows and the same combinations of forward and backward sliding windows for all subjects to train a classifier.

The final selected time period for correct and incorrect episodes are as follows (see Fig. 2-C). For incorrect episodes, four windows of 0.9s in length were used, ending at 0s, −0.05s, −0.1s and −0.15s with respect to the beginning of the gesture movement (the second temporal reference point). That is, four windows were segmented from the beginning of the gesture movements in the reverse direction. In addition, two windows were used with a length of 0.9s from 2s and 2.5s with respect to the beginning of the directional movement (the first temporal reference point). For correct episodes, four windows of 0.9s length were likewise used, ending at 0s, −0.05s, −0.1s and −0.15s with respect to the onset of gesture movement (the second temporal reference point). However, we did not use the windows that can be segmented from the first temporal reference point (the beginning of the directional movement).

For testing, ErrPs are continuously detected every 0.05s with a window length of 0.9s from the start of the robot action (i.e., asynchronous classification). This means that ErrPs were continuously detected in the time period between the start of the robot's action and the end of the robot's pointing gesture. For evaluation, we used the time period between 6s and 8s after the start of the episode (i.e., from 3s to 5s after the movement onset) as the ground truth (see Fig. 2-C). This means that the sliding windows that end in this time period were used to evaluate the trained classifier. During this time period, we can ensure that the robot's arm position is unambiguous for the subjects' evaluation.

The features were normalized and used to train a classifier. The online passive aggressive algorithm variant 1 (PA1) [2] was used as classifier. The cost parameter of the PA1 was optimized using a grid search, in which an internal stratified 5 fold cross validation was performed on the training data (7 training datasets) and the best value of $[10^0, 10^{-1}, \dots, 10^{-6}]$ was selected. The performance metric used was balanced accuracy (bACC), which is an arithmetic mean of true positive rate (TPR) and true negative rate (TNR).

2.5   Evaluation

The evaluations were performed for each of the ten subjects individually. As mentioned in Sect. 2.3. EEG recording, we recorded nine datasets for each subject. Seven data sets were used to train an ErrP decoder and one dataset was used for testing. For training an EEG classifier, seven data sets were concatenated. For performance metric, we used a balanced accuracy, i.e., the arithmetic mean of true positive rate (TRP) and true negative rate (TNR). Note that the positive class stands for incorrect action choices of the robot and negative class stands for correct action choice of the robot.

3   Results and Discussion

Table 1 shows the classification performance for each subject. We achieved an average classification performance of 91% across all subjects. However, we found a high variability between subjects.

The inter-subject variability, i.e., the variability between subjects is not surprising, as we assume that subjects have different strategies to evaluate the robot's ongoing actions, i.e., each subject probably evaluates the correctness of the robot's action choices at different times. Indeed, the duration of the task was not short (5s from the beginning of the robot action to the beginning of the

Table 1. EEG classification performance. The balanced accuracy (bACC = (TPR+ TNR)/2) and standard error of the mean (SEM) are given for each subject.

subjects	balanced accuracy (bACC)
subject 1	0.89
subject 2	0.94
subject 3	0.97
subject 4	0.83
subject 5	0.94
subject 6	0.92
subject 7	0.97
subject 8	0.90
subject 9	0.80
mean and standard deviation	0.91 ± 0.06

robot pointing gestures). One can estimate the direction of the robot's movement immediately after the robot starts moving and focus less on the robot's pointing gestures. In this case, the pointing gestures can even be overlooked unintentionally. Another person may focus only on the robot's pointing gestures. Of course, some subjects also focus on the overall action of the robot. In particular, jerky movements of the robot can affect the accuracy of the correct estimation of the robot's direction of movement. In fact, some subjects reported that jerky movements affect the estimation of the robot's direction of movement. Furthermore, the evaluation by the subject can be changed during the execution of the action by the robot. For example, the robot's action may initially be evaluated as a correct action after the direction of the arm movement has been detected, but this evaluation may be changed with the execution of the pointing gesture.

For this reason, we proposed an approach using forward and backward sliding windows and their combinations. Nevertheless, we did not achieve high classification performance for some subjects. The reason for this could be that we used the same combination of forward and backward sliding windows for all subjects. As mentioned earlier, we investigated different combinations of sliding windows across both types of episodes for each subject.

In fact, we found different optimal time periods and the different optimal combinations of forward and backward sliding windows across both episode types (correct and incorrect episodes) for each subject. On the one hand, this means that the optimal time periods relevant for recognizing the correct actions differ from subject to subject. On the other hand, the optimal time periods that are relevant for detecting the wrong actions also vary from subject to subject. Furthermore, the combination of the optimal time periods for correct and incorrect actions also varies between subjects. We nevertheless chose to apply the same combination of forward and backward sliding windows to all subjects to allow a fair comparison between subjects.

Therefore, in the future, it makes sense to extend the proposed approach of forward and backward sliding windows and their combinations with an individual adjustment of feature selection so that high inter-subject variability in classification performance is avoided. With such an individual adjustment of feature selection, classification performance can be improved if we identify the best feature combinations for each subject. However, such investigations are time-consuming. Therefore, developing an automatic selection of best combinations to customize the feature selection is useful. In the future, it is useful to extend the proposed approach of feature selection using forward and backward sliding windows and their combinations for individual adaptions of feature selection, in which the best individual combinations are automatically computed depending on different context, e.g., different scenarios and different situations.

Furthermore, although we continuously detected ErrPs online (i.e., asynchronous classification), we did not use the results of online classification for intrinsic online corrections of the robot's erroneous actions or for robot learning (e.g., optimizing learning strategies based on ErrP-based human feedback) in this scenario, such as in our previous studies [6,9,10]. In this previous work, we have used ErrP-based human feedback online for intrinsic interactive reinforcement learning in real human-robot interaction to optimize the robot's learning strategy in real time, but ErrPs did not need to be classified asynchronously due to the short task duration of the robot. Therefore, in a next step, we plan to use ErrP-based human error evaluation for intrinsic interactive reinforcement learning, where continuous ErrP detections are necessary during continuous and long-lasting task execution of a robot (e.g. continuous complex robot behavior) and we therefore expect e.g., more than one type of error during the execution of a task.

References

1. Chavarriaga, R., Sobolewski, A., Millán, J.D.R.: Errare machinale est: the use of error-related potentials in brain-machine interfaces. Front. Neurosci. **8**, 208 (2014). https://doi.org/10.3389/fnins.2014.00208
2. Crammer, K., Dekel, O., Keshet, J., Shalev-Shwartz, S., Singer, Y.: Online passive-aggressive algorithms. J. Mach. Learn. Res. **7**, 551–585 (2006)
3. Ehrlich, S., Cheng, G.: A neuro-based method for detecting context-dependent erroneous robot action. In: 2016 IEEE-RAS 16th International Conference on Humanoid Robots (Humanoids), pp. 477–482 (2016). https://doi.org/10.1109/HUMANOIDS.2016.7803318
4. Iturrate, I., Montesano, L., Minguez, J.: Robot reinforcement learning using EEG-based reward signals. In: 2010 IEEE International Conference on Robotics and Automation, pp. 4822–4829. IEEE (2010). https://doi.org/10.1109/ROBOT.2010.5509734
5. Iturrate, I., Montesano, L., Minguez, J.: Single trial recognition of error-related potentials during observation of robot operation. In: 2010 Annual International Conference of the IEEE Engineering in Medicine and Biology, pp. 4181–4184. IEEE (2010). 10.1109/IEMBS.2010.5627380

6. Kim, S.K., Andrea Kirchner, E., Kirchner, F.: Flexible online adaptation of learning strategy using EEG-based reinforcement signals in real-world robotic applications. In: 2020 IEEE International Conference on Robotics and Automation (ICRA), pp. 4885–4891 (2020). https://doi.org/10.1109/ICRA40945.2020.9197538
7. Kim, S.K., Kirchner, E.A.: Classifier transferability in the detection of error related potentials from observation to interaction. In: 2013 IEEE International Conference on Systems, Man, and Cybernetics, pp. 3360–3365 (2013). https://doi.org/10.1109/SMC.2013.573
8. Kim, S.K., Kirchner, E.A.: Handling few training data: classifier transfer between different types of error-related potentials. IEEE Trans. Neural Syst. Rehabil. Eng. **24**(3), 320–332 (2016). https://doi.org/10.1109/TNSRE.2015.2507868
9. Kim, S.K., Kirchner, E.A., Schloßmüller, L., Kirchner, F.: Errors in human-robot interactions and their effects on robot learning. Front. Robot. AI **7** (2020). https://doi.org/10.3389/frobt.2020.558531
10. Kim, S.K., Kirchner, E.A., Stefes, A., Kirchner, F.: Intrinsic interactive reinforcement learning - using error-related potentials for real world human-robot interaction. Sci. Rep. 7 (2017). https://doi.org/10.1038/s41598-017-17682-7
11. Krell, M., et al.: pySPACE-a signal processing and classification environment in Python. Front. Neuroinform. 7 (2013). https://doi.org/10.3389/fninf.2013.00040
12. Lopes-Dias, C., et al.: Online asynchronous detection of error-related potentials in participants with a spinal cord injury using a generic classifier. J. Neural Eng. **18**(4), 046022 (2021). https://doi.org/10.1088/1741-2552/abd1eb
13. Rivet, B., Souloumiac, A., Attina, V., Gibert, G.: xDAWN algorithm to enhance evoked potentials: application to brain-computer interface. IEEE Trans. Biomed. Eng. **56**(8), 2035–2043 (2009). https://doi.org/10.1109/TBME.2009.2012869
14. Salazar-Gomez, A.F., DelPreto, J., Gil, S., Guenther, F.H., Rus, D.: Correcting robot mistakes in real time using EEG signals. In: 2017 IEEE International Conference on Robotics and Automation (ICRA), pp. 6570–6577 (2017). https://doi.org/10.1109/ICRA.2017.7989777

A Longitudinal Experiment about Leadership in a Mixed Human-Robot Team in Comparison to a Human-Only Team

M. Leichtle$^{(\boxtimes)}$ ⓘ and N. Homburg ⓘ

Leap in Time GmbH, Donnersbergring 16, 64295 Darmstadt, Germany
marcel.leichtle@leap-in-time.com

Abstract. Due to today's shortage of skilled workers, humanoid robots are already used in workspaces. As technology develops further, this usage is likely to increase even further, making research more important. This paper presents results of a first longitudinal experiment about leadership in mixed human-robot teams compared to human-only teams. Specifically, the integration of a social robot in an office team with a human team leader is assessed. Based on extant leadership theory, we argue that empowering leadership contributes best to the performance of mixed human-robot teams. In this longitudinal experiment, two teams were working in a company and compared for 54 different knowledge work tasks over a project duration of six weeks. One team was a mixed human-robot team while the other was a human-only team. Our results show that both teams can achieve similar performance outcomes. These results give insights into leadership in future workplace with increased use of technology and suggest empowering leadership as a viable option to lead mixed human-robot teams without performance losses.

Keywords: Agent System and Intelligent Speaker · HCI in Society 5.0 · Robots · Avatars and Virtual Human · Mixed Human-Robot Team · Robotic Team Assistant · Social Robot · Empowering Leadership · Longitudinal Study

1 Introduction

"Hey Lena, please summarize our to-do's from today's meeting for next week."

"Alright. I'll summarize the next steps: Julia talks to the sales team, Marco gets in touch with the customer, and I'll send around the financing plan."

"Yes, that's good, Lena. Please attach them to the protocol."

"Great, you can find the protocol in the cloud, as always."

What appears to be a usual team meeting opens a new perspective on our working world: Lena is not a human, but a robotic team assistant in the form of the android robot Elenoide. Processes that are quite familiar to us in today's office environment such as summarizing a meeting will shape our everyday office life with robots in the future.

M. Kurosu and A. Hashizume (Eds.): HCII 2023, LNCS 14013, pp. 102–117, 2023.
https://doi.org/10.1007/978-3-031-35602-5_8

Originally, robots were mostly used in the manufacturing sector. For safety reasons, they operated in areas separated from the working human [1]. This situation has fundamentally changed as social robots are being used in various service industries such as retail [2], tourism [3], banking [4], and healthcare [5]. Due to this increasing use, this points to a scenario in the near future, where living with social robots will be as commonplace as living with televisions, cell phones, and computers.

Unlike technologies, social robots have an automated social presence, which is why we treat them as social beings rather than machines [6]. This is enhanced by the fact that social robots are becoming more human-like in terms of emotions, behavior and increasing intelligence [7]. As developments in artificial intelligence and robotics accelerate, social robots will soon meet the challenges of increasingly complex and administrative contexts to support and relieve the team in real time, freeing up resources for other tasks [8].

In 2018, about 82% of executives believed mixed human-robot teams (HRTs) to be commonplace within five years [9]. In a recent survey by Wolf Stock-Homburg [8], participants indicated that they could well imagine working with a robot as a team member (39%) or as a team assistant (50%). As a change in the composition and thus the diversity of teams (e.g., cultural diversity) should always entail an adjustment in leadership behavior [10], the question is whether leadership styles developed for human-only teams can also lead to success for HRTs.

This study focuses on performance implications of leadership, specifically empowering leadership, in HRTs. "Empowering leadership is defined as leader behaviors directed at individuals or entire teams and consisting of delegating authority to employees, promoting their self-directed and autonomous decision making, coaching, sharing information, and asking for input" [11]. Empowering leadership succeeds in the long-term, where the team can get to know each other [12] – following the group development model [13, 14].

Other studies demonstrate that once robots are deployed in existing workspaces such as teams, they inevitably come with consequences such as influencing the (meaning of) work of other employees. This in turn influences how the robots are perceived by the team [15]. However, to our knowledge, this is the first study to investigate the *long-term* impact of empowering leadership in human-robot interactions (HRIs) in the setting of (innovative) teams. Investigating leadership in HRTs is important, since leadership is a means to guide teams to success, as a leader helps reduce uncertainty for new team members, compositions, and in unknown situations. As HRTs bring up many new and perhaps uncertain situations, guidance is particularly relevant and important here. Furthermore, leaders help frame goals and processes in teams. In HRTs, the objectives and especially the processes may be different in the near future due to the integration of artificial intelligence-based technology.

In this study, we compare the performance implications of leadership in HRTs with the performance implications in human-only teams. Specifically, we examine whether empowering leadership can be effectively applied to HRTs with a robot in the role of a team assistant or for human-only teams with a human team assistant. This leads to the research question: Do the performance implications of empowering leadership differ for HRTs and human-only teams?

This study differs from previous research in several important respects: First, to our knowledge, this is the first study that examines leadership in a new type of team, namely HRTs, and its performance implications. Second, this study is conducted in a real corporate setting, whereas the few existing studies on HRTs mostly examine teams outside the corporate setting, e.g., in a laboratory environment. Third, our study examines longitudinal performance implications of empowering leadership in HRTs. This will allow us to make conclusions about stable patterns versus effects of first impression effects that are likely to dominate the results of cross-sectional studies.

2 Study Framework

The conceptual framework (Fig. 1) assumes that empowering leadership in HRTs positively affects team performance over time. The independent variables are the five dimensions of empowering leadership, rooted in empowering leadership theory [16]. Empowering means giving a person or group the power to perform certain activities in a self-determined, autonomous manner [17–21]. Furthermore, it means that parts of the leader's power are transferred to a person or group [16, 20, 22] rather than being left exclusively in the leader's position. Therefore, empowering leadership aims to increase the perceived quality of work and to promote greater employee identification with their work goals [23, 24]. An empowering leader, therefore, is "one who leads others to lead themselves" [25].

Empowering leadership includes five dimensions [16], namely leading by example (setting high standards by working hard oneself), participative decision-making (encouraging and considering ideas and suggestions), coaching (guiding independent problem solving), informing (explaining expectations and decisions), and showing concern (caring for the team). In our study, empowering leadership is captured as initial leader activity at time t_1 (see Fig. 1).

The implications of empowering leadership are proposed to affect important team performance outcomes such as team innovativeness and team effectiveness as dependent variables [26, 27]. Team innovativeness is defined as "the flexibility and willingness to accept new ways to create knowledge-based solution" [28]. In contrast, effectiveness is about the quantitative and qualitative output of a team and the effect (e.g., satisfaction) the team has on its members [29]. The performance outcomes are examined on the long run, i.e., these variables are measured after the empowering leadership has been practiced in the team.

Finally, we examine the type of team assistant as moderator. A moderating variable strengthens or weakens the strength of a relationship under consideration [30]. Specifically, we examine whether the performance implications of empowering leadership are stronger for HRTs or human-only teams. The perception and acceptability of HRI with service robots is affected by robots' anthropomorphic (i.e., human-like [31]) design [32] as well as an appropriate human-oriented application and placement of these service robots [33, 34]. An android robot is "an artificial system designed with the ultimate goal of being indistinguishable from humans in its external appearance and behavior" [35]. This is the best example of a social robot due to its anthropomorphic design [36] to resemble a human. Therefore, we used an android robot as the robotic team assistant.

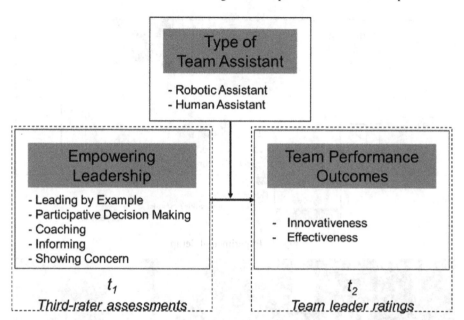

Fig. 1. Study Framework of the Influence of the Five Dimensions of Empowering Leadership on Team Performance in Human and Robotic Team Assistant Settings

3   Empirical Study

The setting of this real-world experiment was placed in the work environment of a small consulting firm. To ensure a realistic setting and conditions for teamwork, the setting was included into the workspace of the company. The setting included a meeting table as well as digital and analog whiteboards (see Fig. 2). To minimize outside influences on the experiments, participants were not allowed to bring any personal devices and all necessary technologies including classical office software were provided by the company. Microphones and cameras were placed in the environment, not interfering with the interaction. Participants were hired as normal (junior) consultants and had solely been informed that these measurements were used to better understand a team's functioning while working on a consulting project.

For the integration of the team assistant in the HRT, the android robot "Elenoide" was used (see Fig. 3, right). This robot is 1.70m tall, has a total of 49 degrees of freedom and the exoskeleton is covered with a skin-like layer. The aim is to give a human-like appearance. Elenoide was placed at the meeting table like the other team members and teleoperated by the Wizard of Oz method [37], to be able to reach the closest real representation not only in the physical presence, but also in the team behavior (see Fig. 3, left).

The scope of tasks of the team assistance (human or robotic) included the following tasks over the course of the experiment: Providing information (e.g., data management, simple research, time management), performing tasks (e.g. protocols, mails, presentations, tracking milestones), and improving materials (e.g. correcting content on request,

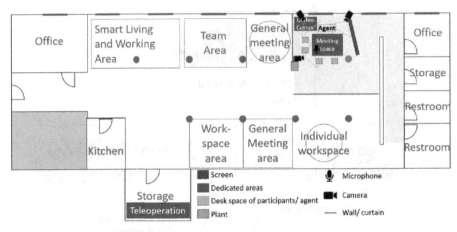

Fig. 2. Experimental Setup

Fig. 3. Mixed Human-Robot Team (left) & Android Robot Elenoide (right) (Photos: ©leap in time)

asking questions of understanding in the case of unclear/nonsensical work assignments, suggesting improvements.)

3.1 Sample and Measurement

To recruit participants, we distributed job postings for (junior) consultants in the form of advertising materials for a project called "Innovation Bootcamp" on social media and job portals. The 67 respondents were confidentially screened for individual qualifications and availability and proximity to the company was used as the first exclusion criterion to minimize external complications. Three members per team (Human-only team: Age: 20, 21, 23, Male: 100%; HRT: Age: 21, 29, 66, Male: 100%) were selected who met the requirement profiles of the expert roles. For the human-only team, the team assistant was fulfilled by a confederate, fully adapting to the range of tasks of the robotic assistant.

The participants signed the privacy statement and informed consent form as part of their work contracts. In a following pretest, the Big Five personality traits [38], robot anxiety [39], technology affinity [40], and robot experience were examined and used as extended exclusion criteria. No extreme values occurred in these tests. Based on the results, the participants were distributed between the human-only team and the HRT.

Data were collected regularly during the experimental phase. To keep the queries minimal for the participants, questionnaires on team performance were completed by third raters and the team leader. The third raters have been independent raters who focused on the independent variable (see Fig. 1) and observed and evaluated the leader to ensure that the performed empowering leadership style was constant. Tables 7 and 8 show the dimensions according to which the third raters evaluated which parts of empowering leadership or directive leadership were performed.

The data collected by the team leader explicitly includes the two performance data under examination, team innovativeness and team effectiveness, which are used for as the dependent variables of the study framework (see Fig. 1). These two were each collected hourly after every task and consist of the aspects in Table 1.

Table 1. Team Performance Data – Dependent Variables

(a) Team Innovation – Within the last hour, the team was very much engaged in...
- ... find new solutions to problems
- ... Develop new ideas for difficult questions
- ... Seek new working methods, techniques or tools
- ... Transform innovative ideas into useful applications
- ... Evaluating the usefulness of innovative ideas
(b) Team Effectiveness – Within the last hour...
- ... The team mostly achieved the team goals
- ... The team performed very well
- ... The team was very successful

Note: Response range: totally disagree – totally agree (7-point Likert scale); Measurement: hourly; Rater: team leader

Thus, two types of feedback were collected from the team members directly. First, in the daily standup which assessed the motivation and willingness to work of all team members (5-point Likert scale). Second, after every hour at the end of each sprint, an individual assessment of the complexity and satisfaction of the distribution of competencies in the team (5-point Likert scale). The purpose of these surveys, each was communicated as best practices of the company. In a post-survey questionnaire, changes in perceptions were investigated. The actual intent of the experiment was revealed to the participants afterwards in a debriefing conversation.

3.2 Experimental Procedure

The six selected participants were divided into two teams with the task of developing a market entry strategy for a chemical company to extent their business. This included the analysis of markets and stakeholders, the elaboration of new products and services, and the development of a stepwise market-entry plan. In both teams, the three participants had expert roles in the areas of market strategy, finance, and technology development. Furthermore, the role of the team assistant was taken by a fourth team member – either an android robot or a human (see Fig. 3). This measurement was taken in order to increase the comparability between the performance outcomes of the two teams, as both had similar background knowledge. Finally, each team was complemented by the same human team leader who performed the empowering leadership as a confederate.

Over the project duration of six weeks, the agile working teams had to work on three project days per week. Organized into sprints [41], each team had the same 54 tasks to complete. A project day began with a ten-minute daily standup initiated by the team leader with the purpose of motivating the team, recalling past steps, and providing an outlook on the day's upcoming challenges. Between each of the following three one-hour sprints, there was a break of about 15 min, giving the team the opportunity to relax and socialize; this applied equally to conversations with the robot as well as the confederate, which were, however, kept to a minimum and small talk. The project day ended with a daily scrum after the third sprint. Here, individual feedbacks were brought together, discussed in the team, and supplemented by the team leader with further recommendations for action.

3.3 Manipulation of Empowering Leadership as Independent Variable

The manipulation of "empowering leadership" was conducted in several steps. In a first step, we conducted a literature review on the most common conceptualizations and operationalizations of empowering leadership. Following the well-known measurement approach of Arnold et al. [16], we identified important aspects for the five dimensions of empowering leadership (see Fig. 1). In the second step, we derived the specific leadership behaviors, the leader should exhibit during the experimental study. In step three, the leader was trained on empowering leadership by a professional leadership trainer. The important aspects for the five dimensions of empowering leadership as proposed by Arnold et al. [16], and specific behaviors for the team leaders are listed in Table 7.

Empowering leadership was measured once the daily measured team performance remained constant over three measurements, which was reached after 1.5 weeks (denoted t_1, Fig. 1). As Table 2 shows, empowering leadership was highly rated for both teams and there were no significant differences between the teams in terms of empowering leadership. Therefore, the manipulation can be considered successful.

Table 2. Manipulation Check – t-Test results for Empowering Leadership

Independent Variables	HRT M(SD)	Human-only Team M(SD)	Δ Mean	p-Value
Leading by Example	6.90 (.11)	6.20 (.88)	.70	.08
Coaching	6.73 (.20)	6.50 (.35)	.23	.20
Participative Decision Making	5.58 (.27)	5.67 (.00)	−.09	.47
Informing	4.75 (.46)	3.83 (1.28)	.92	.13
Showing Concern	6.75 (.16)	6.80 (.22)	−.05	.66

Notes: M = Mean Value; ΔM = Mean Difference; SD = Standard Deviation; *p < .05, **p < .01; t-test

4 Preliminary Results

We proposed a study framework for a real-world experiment to compare the effects of empowering leadership on the performance variables over time in a consulting company setting. Drawing on the extant leadership literature, we tested how empowering leadership affected the team innovativeness and team effectiveness. In addition, we took the type of team assistant as a moderating effect into account and examined, whether HRT or human-only team responded differently. The results in Tables 3 and 4 show that team performance in the HRT and the human-only team did not differ significantly in either team innovativeness or team effectiveness at time points t_1 and t_2. Similarly, when comparing the development between t_1 and t_2 for HRT (see Table 5) and human-only team (see Table 6), no significant differences can be found between the two groups. At the end of the experiment (at t_2), on average, both teams were able to score values above five (on a 7-point Likert scale). The difference in means (ΔMean) for the two teams was rather low for both teams (1% of the scale for team innovation and 1.6% for team efficiency.

Table 3. Preliminary Results of the Study – Team Performance for t_1

Dependent Variables	HRT M(SD)	Human-only Team M(SD)	Δ Mean	p-Value
Team Innovativeness	4.67 (.81)	5.00 (.40)	−.33	.56
Team Effectiveness	5.11 (1.02)	5.44 (.51)	−.33	.64

Notes: M = Mean Value; ΔM = Mean Difference; SD = Standard Deviation; *p < .05, **p < .01; t-test

Table 4. Preliminary Results of the Study – Team Performance for t_2

Dependent Variables	HRT M(SD)	Human-only Team M(SD)	Δ Mean	p-Value
Team Innovativeness	5.20 (.35)	5.27 (.76)	−.07	.90
Team Effectiveness	5.67 (.33)	5.56 (.38)	.11	.73

Notes: M = Mean Value; ΔM = Mean Difference; SD = Standard Deviation; *p < .05, **p < .01; t-test

Table 5. Preliminary Results of the Study – Development of Team Performance for the HRT between t_1 and t_2

Dependent Variables	HRT M(SD)	Human-only Team M(SD)	Δ Mean	p-Value
Team Innovativeness	4.67 (.81)	5.20 (.35)	−.53	.35
Team Effectiveness	5.11 (1.02)	5.67 (.33)	−.56	.42

Notes: M = Mean Value; ΔM = Mean Difference; SD = Standard Deviation; *p < .05, **p < .01; t-test

Table 6. Preliminary Results of the Study – Development of Team Performance for the Human-only team between t_1 and t_2

Dependent Variables	HRT M(SD)	Human-only Team M(SD)	Δ Mean	p-Value
Team Innovativeness	5.00 (.40)	5.27 (.76)	−.27	.62
Team Effectiveness	5.44 (.51)	5.56 (.38)	−.11	.78

Notes: M = Mean Value; ΔM = Mean Difference; SD = Standard Deviation; *p < .05, **p < .01; t-test

5 Conclusion

The departure point of this study were today's shortage of skilled workers and the observation that social robots increasingly enter our daily life; with only few studies that examine social robots in teams. These studies were conducted in laboratory settings and followed a one-time (first) interaction between humans and robots. To our knowledge this is the first of type study that investigates HRT in with robotic team member on a long-term basis. Team research indicates that newly constituted teams are associated with high uncertainties and the need for strategic guidance. This uncertainty may be even higher for teams in HRTs. We therefore attempt to shed light on the roles of leadership, i.e., empowering leadership for the innovation and the effectiveness of such teams in an office environment.

Relying on empowering leadership theory [16], we examined the performance implications of empowering leadership in a HRT compared to a human-only team. Our independent variable was empowering leadership over time, while team innovation and effectiveness represented our dependent variables. The results show that empowering leadership has similar performance implications for HRTs and human-only teams. This indicates that empowering leadership is a fruitful passway for HRT, as well, and should inspire to explore the application of existing leadership theory in HRTs.

5.1 Limitations and Areas for Future Research

In this study, empowering leadership was evaluated through an elaborate real-life design. For future studies should examine more teams to obtain a larger sample. This study only provides first ideas but no generalizations can be made from two teams.

In addition, empowering leadership was manipulated to be always high. Further studies should compare these results at a low manipulation level or even different leadership styles.

As research on leadership in mixed human-robot teams is scarce, our study contributes to extant research by examining the long-term effects of empowering leadership on the team innovativeness and team effectiveness. This offers valuable insights into recommendations for action for team leaders to increase the viability of bureau robots in modern working environments.

Appendix

Table 7. Manipulation of Team Leadership – Empowering Leadership

Important Aspects [16]	Concrete Empowering Leadership Behaviors During the Longitudinal Study
(a) Leading by Example	
Sets high standards for performance by his/her own behaviour	• Shows confident appearance • Gives constructive feedback on solutions
Works as hard as he/she can	• Shows commitment • Ready for questions at any time
Works as hard as anyone in my work group	• Handles own work packages • Represents an employee of the consulting company
Sets a good example by the way he/she behaves	• Friendly, supportive • Communicative, open

(continued)

Table 7. (*continued*)

Important Aspects [16]	Concrete Empowering Leadership Behaviors During the Longitudinal Study
Leads by example	• Punctuality • Involves all team members
(b) Participative Decision Making	
Encourages work group members to express ideas/suggestions	• Addresses individual team members directly • Asks open questions
Listens to my work group's ideas and suggestions	• Is attentive • Responds to the statements
Uses my work group's suggestions to make decisions that affect us	• Responds to the suggestions of the team • Empowers the team to find solutions
Gives all work group members a chance to voice their opinions	• Asks questions about the emotional state • Asks for the opinions of all team members
Considers my work group's ideas when he/she disagrees with them	• Remains objective/fact-based • Tries to find compromises/middle ground if necessary
Makes decisions that are based only on his/her own ideas	• Specifies how to proceed regardless of team suggestions • Aligns the team to a vision
(c) Coaching	
Helps my work group see areas in which we need more training	• Points out potential for development • Challenges the group in relevant areas
Suggests ways to improve my work group's performance	• Names alternative idea development methods • Gives tips on how the team can work better together
Encourages work group members to solve problems together	• Refers to connecting elements/synergy • Addresses positive team experiences
Encourages work group members to exchange information with one another	• Refers to potential contacts and connection points in the team
Provides help to work group members	• Resolves (task) uncertainties • Is available as a (conflict) mediator
Teaches work group members how to solve problems on their own	• Teaches to analyse a task • Teaches to divide a task in a team
Pays attention to my work group's efforts	• Responds to ideas/suggestions • Builds on previous results
Tells my work group when we perform well	• Praises good cooperation • Praises good results

(*continued*)

Table 7. *(continued)*

Important Aspects [16]	Concrete Empowering Leadership Behaviors During the Longitudinal Study
Supports my work group's efforts	• Points out good directions • Gives a sense of tailwind/coverage
Helps my work group focus on our goals	• Reminds of client's objectives • Reminds of structuring of processing
Helps develop good relations among work group members	• Points out common ground • Strengthens team spirit through compliments
(d) Informing	
Explains company decisions	• Explains the nature of the project • Explains changes in the project
Explains company goals	• Differentiates between client and consulting firm • Explains the vision of the project
Explains how my work group fits into the company	• Explains the added value of the team • Praises well-founded work
Explains the purpose of the company's policies to my work group	• Refers to high-quality collaborations (internal/external) • Trusts team competence
Explains rules and expectations to my work group	• States rules of conduct • Provides freedom in processing
Explains his/her decisions and actions to my work group	• Maintains fairness between groups • Trusts team decisions
(e) Showing Concern / Interacting with the Team	
Cares about work group members' personal problems	• Offers individual feedback • Considers unfavourable circumstances
Shows concern for work group members' well-being	• Cares about the emotional state • Provides a failure-tolerant environment
Treats work group members as equals	• Treats everyone equally • Takes the time to listen to everyone
Takes the time to discuss work group members' concerns patiently	• Is always available to address concerns • Does not spread a hectic mood • Talks about satisfaction
Shows concern for work group members' success	• Inquires about progress regularly • Shows enthusiasm for progress
Stays in touch with my work group	• Regularly checks in with the group • Does not distance himself from the team

(continued)

Table 7. (*continued*)

Important Aspects [16]	Concrete Empowering Leadership Behaviors During the Longitudinal Study
Gets along with my work group members	• Conducts conversations at eye level • Has a good relationship with everyone
Gives work group members honest and fair answers	• Feedback is always constructive • Feedback takes team dynamics into account
Knows what work is being done in my work group	• Keeps up to date on steps and successes • Knows who has what share in the team
Finds time to chat with work group members	• Talks about emotional state • Talks about difficulty

Note: Response range: totally disagree – totally agree (7-point Likert scale); Measurement: daily; Rater: third rater

Table 8. Delimitation of Team Leadership – Directive Leadership [42]

Important Aspects	Concrete Directive Leadership Behaviors During the Longitudinal Study
Expects his/her employees to follow my instructions precisely	• Requests to take certain steps • Does not tolerate differences
Motivates employees by letting them know what will happen to them if their work is unsatisfactory	• Assigns responsibility (blame) • Communicates intolerance for mistakes
Requires employees to submit detailed reports of their activities	• Requires detailed reporting from each role • Monitors the execution of roles
Makes most decisions for employees	• Defines its solution vision • Does not allow for free action
Supervises employees very closely	• Monitors communication • Intervenes in team dynamics
Supervisor have to lay out goals and guidelines, otherwise subordinates will be passive and get nothing accomplished	• Assigns tasks • Specifies how and where exchange takes place
Expects to carry out instructions immediately	• Expects direct understanding of task • Expects immediate action

Note: Response range: totally disagree – totally agree (7-point Likert scale); Measurement: daily; Rater: third rater

References

1. Zanchettin, A.M., Ceriani, N.M., Rocco, P., Ding, H., Matthias, B.: Safety in human-robot collaborative manufacturing environments: metrics and control. IEEE Trans. Autom. Sci. Eng. **13**, 882–893 (2016). https://doi.org/10.1109/TASE.2015.2412256

2. De Gauquier, L., Brengman, M., Willems, K.: The rise of service robots in retailing: literature review on success factors and pitfalls. In: Pantano, E. (ed.) Retail Futures: The Good, the Bad and the Ugly of the Digital Transformation, pp. 15–35. Emerald Publishing Limited (2020). https://doi.org/10.1108/978-1-83867-663-620201007

3. Ivanov, S.H., Webster, C., Berezina, K.: Adoption of robots and service automation by tourism and hospitality companies. Rev. Turismo Desenvolvimento **27**(28), 1501–1517 (2017)

4. Volpe, G., et al.: Humanoid social robots and the reconfiguration of customer service. In: Bandi, R.K., C. R., R., Klein, S., Madon, S., Monteiro, E. (eds.) IFIPJWC 2020. IAICT, vol. 601, pp. 310–325. Springer, Cham (2020). https://doi.org/10.1007/978-3-030-64697-4_23

5. Cifuentes, C.A., Pinto, M.J., Céspedes, N., Múnera, M.: Social robots in therapy and care. Curr. Robot. Rep. **1**(3), 59–74 (2020). https://doi.org/10.1007/s43154-020-00009-2

6. van Doorn, J., et al.: Domo Arigato Mr. Roboto. J. Serv. Res. **20**, 43–58 (2017). https://doi.org/10.1177/1094670516679272

7. He, W., Li, Z., Chen, C.L.P.: A survey of human-centered intelligent robots: issues and challenges. IEEE/CAA J. Autom. Sin. **4**, 602–609 (2017). https://doi.org/10.1109/JAS.2017.7510604

8. Wolf, F.D., Stock-Homburg, R.M.: Making the first step towards robotic leadership – hiring decisions for robotic team leader candidates. In: Making the First Step Towards Robotic Leadership – Hiring Decisions for Robotic Team Leader Candidates. Forty-Second International Conference on Information Systems, Austin (2021)

9. Dell Technologies: Realizing 2030: A Divided Vision of the Future (2018)

10. Lumby, J.: Leadership, development and diversity: in the learning and skills sector in England. Manag. Educ. **19**, 33–38 (2005). https://doi.org/10.1177/08920206050190030801

11. Sharma, P.N., Kirkman, B.L.: Leveraging leaders. Group Org. Manage. **40**, 193–237 (2015). https://doi.org/10.1177/1059601115574906

12. Lorinkova, N.M., Pearsall, M.J., Sims, H.P.: Examining the differential longitudinal performance of directive versus empowering leadership in teams. Acad. Manag. J. **56**, 573–596 (2012). https://doi.org/10.5465/amj.2011.0132

13. Tuckman, B.W.: Developmental sequence in small groups. Psychol Bull. **63**, 384–399 (1965). https://doi.org/10.1037/h0022100

14. Tuckman, B.W., Jensen, M.A.C.: Stages of small-group development revisited. Group Org. Stud. **2**, 419–427 (1977). https://doi.org/10.1177/105960117700200404

15. Smids, J., Nyholm, S., Berkers, H.: Robots in the workplace: a threat to—or opportunity for—meaningful work? Philos. Technol. **33**(3), 503–522 (2019). https://doi.org/10.1007/s13347-019-00377-4

16. Arnold, J.A., Arad, S., Rhoades, J.A., Drasgow, F.: The empowering leadership questionnaire: the construction and validation of a new scale for measuring leader behaviors. J. Org. Behav. **21**, 249–269 (2000). https://doi.org/10.1002/(SICI)1099-1379(200005)21:3<249::AID-JOB10>3.0.CO;2-%23

17. Conger, J.A., Kanungo, R.N.: The empowerment process: integrating theory and practice. Source Acad. Manage. Rev. **13**, 471–482 (1988). https://doi.org/10.2307/258093

18. Lawler, E.E.: Substitutes for hierarchy. Org. Dyn. **17**(1), 5–15 (1988). https://doi.org/10.1016/0090-2616(88)90027-7

19. Liden, R.C., Arad, S.: A power perspective on empowerment and work groups: implications for human resources management research. In: Research in Personnel and Human Management, pp. 205–251. JAI Press Inc. (1996)

20. Manz, C.C., Sims, H.P.: Leading workers to lead themselves: the external leadership of self-managing work teams. Adm. Sci. Q. **32**, 106–129 (1987). https://doi.org/10.2307/2392745

21. Spreitzer, G.M.: Social structural characteristics of psychological empowerment. Source Acad. Manage. J. **39**, 483–504 (1996). https://www.jstor.org/stable/256789

22. Pearce, C.L., et al.: Transactors, transformers and beyond: a multi-method development of a theoretical typology of leadership. J. Manage. Dev. **22**, 273–307 (2003). https://doi.org/10.1108/02621710310467587

23. Cohen, S.G., Chang, L., Ledford, G.E.: A hierarchical construct of self-management leadership and its relationship to quality of work life and perceived work group effectiveness. Pers. Psychol. **50**, 275–308 (1997). https://doi.org/10.1111/j.1744-6570.1997.tb00909.x

24. Zaccaro, S.J., Rittman, A.L., Marks, M.A.: Team leadership. Leadersh. Q. **12**, 451–483 (2001). https://doi.org/10.1016/S1048-9843(01)00093-5

25. Sims, H.P., Faraj, S., Yun, S.: When should a leader be directive or empowering? How to develop your own situational theory of leadership. Bus. Horiz. **52**, 149–158 (2009). https://doi.org/10.1016/j.bushor.2008.10.002

26. Hoegl, M., Parboteeah, P.: Autonomy and teamwork in innovative projects. Hum. Resour. Manage. **45**, 67–79 (2006). https://doi.org/10.1002/hrm.20092

27. Kirkman, B.L., Rosen, B.: Beyond self-management: antecedents and consequences of team empowerment. Acad. Manag. J. **42**, 58–74 (1999). https://www.jstor.org/stable/256874

28. Liu, Y., Phillips, J.S.: Examining the antecedents of knowledge sharing in facilitating team innovativeness from a multilevel perspective. Int. J. Inf. Manage. **31**, 44–52 (2011). https://doi.org/10.1016/j.ijinfomgt.2010.05.002

29. Cohen, S.G., Bailey, D.E.: What makes teams work: group effectiveness research from the shop floor to the executive suite. J. Manage. **23**, 239–290 (1997). https://doi.org/10.1177/014920639702300303

30. Baron, R.M., Kenny, D.A.: The moderator–mediator variable distinction in social psychological research: conceptual, strategic, and statistical considerations. J. Pers. Soc. Psychol. **51**, 1173–1182 (1986). https://doi.org/10.1037/0022-3514.51.6.1173

31. Phillips, E., Zhao, X., Ullman, D., Malle, B.F.: What is human-like?: decomposing robots' human-like appearance using the Anthropomorphic roBOT (ABOT) database. In: Proceedings of the 2018 ACM/IEEE International Conference on Human-Robot Interaction, pp. 105–113. ACM, New York, NY, USA (2018). https://doi.org/10.1145/3171221.3171268

32. Mori, M., MacDorman, K., Kageki, N.: The uncanny valley [from the field]. IEEE Robot. Autom. Mag. **19**, 98–100 (2012). https://doi.org/10.1109/MRA.2012.2192811

33. Knof, M., et al.: Implications from responsible human-robot interaction with anthropomorphic service robots for design science. In: Proceedings of the 55th Hawaii International Conference on System Sciences, pp. 5827–5836 (2022). https://doi.org/10.24251/HICSS.2022.709

34. Webster, C., Ivanov, S.H.: Robots in travel, tourism and hospitality: key findings from a global study (2020)

35. MacDorman, K.F., Ishiguro, H.: Toward social mechanisms of android science. Interact. Stud. **7**, 289–296 (2006). https://doi.org/10.1075/is.7.2.12mac

36. Mara, M., Appel, M.: Science fiction reduces the eeriness of android robots: a field experiment. Comput. Hum. Behav. **48**, 156–162 (2015). https://doi.org/10.1016/j.chb.2015.01.007

37. Kelley, J.F.: An iterative design methodology for user-friendly natural language office information applications. ACM Trans. Inf. Syst. **2**, 26–41 (1984). https://doi.org/10.1145/357417.357420

38. Rammstedt, B., Danner, D., Soto, C.J., John, O.P.: Validation of the short and extra-short forms of the Big Five Inventory-2 (BFI-2) and their German adaptations. Eur. J. Psychol. Assess. **36**, 149–161 (2020). https://doi.org/10.1027/1015-5759/a000481

39. Syrdal, D.S., Dautenhahn, K., Koay, K.L., Walters, M.L.: The negative attitudes towards robots scale and reactions to robot behaviour in a live human-robot interaction study. In: Procs of the 23rd Convention of the Society for the Study of Artificial Intelligence and Simulation of Behaviour, pp. 109–115. SSAISB (2009)

40. Lezhnina, O., Kismihók, G.: A multi-method psychometric assessment of the affinity for technology interaction (ATI) scale. Comput. Hum. Behav. Rep. **1**, 1–8 (2020). https://doi.org/10.1016/j.chbr.2020.100004
41. Laanti, M.: Agile and wellbeing – stress, empowerment, and performance in scrum and Kanban teams. In: 2013 46th Hawaii International Conference on System Sciences, pp. 4761–4770. IEEE (2013). https://doi.org/10.1109/HICSS.2013.74
42. Wendt, H., Euwema, M.C., van Emmerik, I.J.H.: Leadership and team cohesiveness across cultures. Leadersh. Q. **20**, 358–370 (2009). https://doi.org/10.1016/j.leaqua.2009.03.005

Social Robots for Older Adults in Medical Contexts

Wen-I Lu[1], Yu-Wei Chen[1], Chin-Chen Shen[1], Ping-Hsuan Tsai[1], Yun-Tung Chu[1], Yu-Heng Hung[1], Shih-Yi Chien[1(✉)], Joyce Lee[1], and Shiau-Fang Chao[2]

[1] Department of Management Information Systems, National Chengchi University, Taipei 11605, Taiwan
gsechien@gmail.com, jlee@nccu.edu.tw

[2] Department of Social Work, National Taiwan University, Taipei 10617, Taiwan

Abstract. Social robots are designed for social interactions with humans and have been significantly employed across various fields in recent decades. For example, in medical fields, social robots can provide companionship and reminders to support older adults. As social robot applications have been widely used, the developed services need to be carefully evaluated to examine where the consequent effectiveness can sufficiently satisfy users' diverse needs. The trends of aging in world population increase rapidly according to the global statistics. Social robots are useful for older adults across various fields, especially has significant role in medical field. The trends of aging in world population increase rapidly according to the global statistics. Collecting and analyzing the resultant HRI (Human Robot Interaction) data allows researchers to predict changes in the elderly and provide suitable services. However, due to usability issues, elderly individuals may encounter difficulties and be reluctant to use these services, leading to losses for the industry and unmet needs for the elderly. This study aims to review the HRI services offered by medical industries and under-stand the usability issues as well as the potential needs of elderly users. As technology becomes increasingly prevalent, it is essential to adapt the HRI schemes to different user groups. The elderly, in particular, may require specific needs. To support older adults' independence, this research focuses on the medical fields to resolve routine issues in daily life. Our findings can guide the HRI community to develop appropriate services for older adults.

Keywords: Human-robot Interaction · Humanoid Robots · Social robots

1 Introduction

The World Health Organization proposed the concept of active aging as early as 2002 and defined it as "the process of improving the quality of life of the people in old age and achieving the most appropriate health, social participation and safety" [5]. The concept of active aging has been adopted by numerous international organizations and has become their major focus in enhancing older adults' life quality [5]. Three main principles have been developed (including health promotion, social participation, and safety maintenance) to support older adults in maintaining independence in their daily routines.

M. Kurosu and A. Hashizume (Eds.): HCII 2023, LNCS 14013, pp. 118–128, 2023.
https://doi.org/10.1007/978-3-031-35602-5_9

Robotic technology applies to older adults is becoming prevalent [1]. Dut to the growing proportion of older adults in society, together with recent advances in robotics, makes the use of robots in elder care increasing [47]. Recently, the trend of aging has been going faster than in the past. According to the World Health Organization(WHO), in 2020, the number of people aged 60 years has outnumbered children younger than five years [5]. Affected by the increase of age, aging is usually accompanied with the degeneration of the body, in addition to physical inconvenience. Moreover, psychological stress and loneliness will also be affected [2]. In addition, in terms of spending, on average, among countries in the OECD that are able to report on the health and social components of long-term care, health long-term care spending generally accounts for the majority of total long-term care spending, accounting for an average of about 10% of total long-term care spending 70%, accounting for about 1.5% of the overall GDP [6]. Coupled with the shortage of caring manpower, each older adult needs to spend oodles of money on caring costs to improve or maintain the existing life, which has caused huge costs and burdens to both family and society [46].

Some have suggested assistive robots as a possible solution to mitigate the shortage of caregivers and help the independence of older adults [8, 9]. Robots are considered as an "assistive" technology to narrow the disparity between the need and the supply in the medical service [11]. The healthcare robots are the general term to describe those robots which provide service in medical field [40]. Considering the declining across physical, cognitive, or/and psychosocial of older adults, the healthcare robots are generally designed to assist with medical tasks such as monitoring patients, dispensing medication, and providing physical therapy and are commonly used in hospitals and nursing homes [42]. There are several types of healthcare robots. From the surgical robot to auxiliary rehabilitation robot, which could assist patient recovery or maintaining through the dementia/disease [2]. For the companion robots, they can relive older adults' loneliness and isolated depressed mood. The aging population might be a specific group who benefit from the healthcare robots [2].

Generally, healthcare robot can be categorized into two different types. One is the physical assistive robot, helping user with their physical movement or exercise training to strength their body [2]. For example, Robear, which supports caregivers and lifts patients who cannot move from bed to wheelchair [42]. Or improving the cognitive ability of the elderly through games [22]. By interacting with them and leading them to dance health exercises, elderly users can swing their bodies according to the instructions to maintain their physiological functions [28]. The other type is the social assistive robot, which can be further sub-divided into another two groups, those that provide companionship and those that monitor health, give prompt and keep safety [13]. Unlike industrial robots, which are typically used for manufacturing or other automated tasks, social robots are designed to be used in social settings. Social robots have a variety of potential applications, including assisting with healthcare and eldercare, providing educational support, and serving as companions for people who are lonely or socially isolated [7].

Social robot is a type of robot designed to interact with humans and engage in social behaviors, including collaboration, communication, cooperation, coordination, communities, identity and relationship. Interaction is an important element in developing the social robots [2, 3]. The appearance of social robots usually designed to look and move like humans or animals, and they can be programmed to recognize and respond to human emotions, gestures, and speech. Some social robots are also equipped with sensors and cameras that allow them to perceive their environment and interact with it in a more sophisticated way [3].

The multiple applications of social robots are quite extensive, making them have outstanding performance in the medical field which are considered useful in elderly care [2]. Although the trend of aging is inevitable, how the elderly interact with social robots is still unknown. Studies have shown that social interaction with the elderly can bring benefits to their health [8]. However, the interaction between the older adults and social robots has not been properly developed, and its potential needs to be further explored [9]. With the widespread use of social robot applications, the developed services need to be carefully evaluated to check whether their effectiveness can adequately meet the various needs of users. HCI researchers usually use user needs as design considerations for creating new technology products. Healthy older adults and healthy young adults are different groups of people with different user needs [2, 8–10], and different factors affect their attitudes toward robots. Older people may reject robots that younger people may find useful [11]. This study aims to discuss a snapshot of the current development of social robots to demonstrate the rationality of social robots currently being developed for the older population.

2   Research Methodology

Prior literature on social robotics for older adults typically focused on clinical [1]. Most of the studies discuss the topic of companion robots and have positive effects on users' psychology (loneliness, stress relief, social interaction), and these results promote further effective research in medical field [18]. Recently, studies have been conducted on social robotic apply in older adults who reside at home [40], and we extend this direction.

Collected literatures and information according to our research purposes. All articles are collected based on the following criteria: content related to social robots or social care robots related to the elderly/aging group and establish corresponding search terms. Search terms included "social robots," "social assistive robotics," "social robots; elderly," "social robots; aging," and "social robots; elderly care." Articles ProQuest, Springer Link, Google Scholars, and commercial sites offering social robot services. A total of 24 academic articles were collected and categorized with publication dates from 2012 to 2022. For clarity the information, we have arranged the robot types and their goal associated with function in appendix A at the end of the review.

3   Literature Review

Social robots are considered as 'social assistive robot' (SAR) when mention in medical filed [41]. Unlike physical assistive robots provides physical assistive activities. Social assistive robots are defined as aid in daily activities and provide interaction with social behaviors, including collaboration, communication, cooperation, coordination, communities, identity and relationship [1]. Social robots are commonly categorized in two according to their main function, service robots and companion robots. The service robots with human guardian roles are categorized and summarized in the following sections. Companion robots as social assistants and family companions, and robots for the older adults. However, in the condition of older adults, the border between those two sometimes can be blurry [46].

3.1 Social Service Robots

Social service robots are designed to assist with the daily activities and perform specific tasks such as events reminder, taking medical prompt, suggestion and monitoring [1]. They are widely used in hospitals and home. The robots are usually reactive and mainly designed to provide home monitoring, keeps seniors safe, and supports them to live independently [8].

Social service robots have various in appearance. Many of them equipped in our daily equipment such as phone, wearable device and computer. Examples include TensioBot, SENIOR project, ABC application, Zenbo and Nadia. TensioBot is a chatbot which mainly helps caregivers by providing them about the physiological information of the elderly, such as blood pressure or diet situation [45]. SENIOR project also provides health information and monitor the abnormal value to the family and doctors through watch [25]. ABC application is software assistive service equipped with functions such as purchasing daily supplement and giving news and weather information [26]. Some service robots like Zenbo, with a humanoid appearance, provides life services, such as uploading photo services [23, 35]. Nadia is a virtual agent mainly assistive the service on the website, providing the user for consultation and giving the suggestion [43].

3.2 Social Companion Robots

Social companion robots do not assist in daily activities, but more focus on their social interaction. Most of the time, they can provide the interaction in an proactive reaction. Those robots are designed to provide emotional support and companionship for older adult in order to dispel loneliness and reduce stress [1]. These robots can engage in conversations, play games, share the emotion with the specific personality. Or to enhance the emotional connection with family members through the entertainment services provided by robots [24].

Such robots are sometimes designed with a resemblance to four types, human-like, creature like animals, non-creature such as toy, and the software application. Building those appearances to adapt the environment can meet the preference of the society. It leads to the unique "social personality" to those robots. People may discover that those robots are more welcome to the population as they own the 'special robot" different from others [15].

For example, pepper is a humanoid robot developed by Softbank, it is designed to communicate through voice and gestures, move independently, and provide interactive methods, such as dancing or games functions [30]. It can also be used to ease the relationship between caregivers and caregivers, avoiding further friction due to forgetting about daily routines [38]. Animal-like appearance social companion robots are the most common types of robots in studies, and often mentioned the utility brought by animal-type robots to stable the mood and make the emotional connection with the elders. With their animals-like face, can effectively letting down the guard of the unfamiliar and the fear to the robots. Including Aibo, imitate to the dog and make the elders feeling familiar to those instructions [40]. Hugmon is one the example to non-creature robots, it provides the "hug" to the elders' need when they feel lonely [44]. Software can easily equiped on older adults' device to provide the immediately service. Charlie is a chatbot service which allowing users to reflect on life through storytelling and satisfying the need to be heard through a sense of identity [31].

4   Result and Discussion

Through a series of literature collection and review, identification, analysis, and classification of literature, we can roughly divide social robots into five categories according to their uses, and based on the definitions of these five types of social robots, we will meet the needs of the elderly in medical care situations. The section is divided into five parts; each type of social robot can meet a variety of needs.

Though physical assistive is not the main part in our research. It still has the significant meaning to guide the older people with a healthy body. It is the base for the older adults to go further on social activities. Briefly summarized in physical assistive needs, it provides the moving abilities by taking the stuffs or helping to keep user's health or improve/maintain the cognitive by giving stimulations [2].

According to several studies, improving the stability of older adults' mood is an important goal, interacting with social companion robots can lead to improved mood and reduced anxiety in older adults, which can have a positive impact on their overall health and well-being [1, 18]. Social companion robot usually designed with creatures or humanoid appearance, and providing them with someone to talk to and engage with, which can help reduce loneliness and social isolation [2, 15]. However, we found that some aging people considered the authentic of the robots, and refused to use it when they think the robots "pretend to be a real friend". Especially when its main function is for social interact with robot. We suggested that when designing the robot, making some selective optional, lead more controllable function to the elders. May be a way to reduce depressed and eliminate the fear of "they don't need me anymore".

Social service robots not really care about the physical device, it often get attention on three main goals, which are reminders, prompt and monitoring. Which aim to assistance with daily tasks, such as reminding older adults to take their medication and monitor vital signs, such as blood pressure and heart rate, and alert caregivers or healthcare providers if there are any abnormalities. Service robot seems to be more functional base and have a clearly target to accomplished. We suggested that the service to be more diverse to help the older adults to completes more daily task and make the confidence cooperative with the new technology.

Some studies collect the needs from the older adults and suggest that there are differences between the designs and the needs. Therefore, developing and designing robotic applications have to be cautious to appropriately meet user demands [15]. We suggested that, when designing the Social Robots, the purpose should be "*support the older adults to finish a task,*" rather than "do a task for the older adults." The solution is helping then to live with stable emotion and sustain their daily tasks.

5 Conclusion

The goal of this study is to analyze the functions provided by social robots in the medical field to the elderly population through a literature review. In addition, the literature review helps us define the needs of the elderly into different categories. During the research process, we established a search strategy and found relevant research from the literature. According to the results of the literature collection, social robots in the medical field are divided into four categories, namely: Companion Robots, Service Robots, Healthcare Robots, and Social Assistive Robots. In addition, these robots can correspond to five different needs of the elderly.

Population aging is a significant factor driving the social robotics movement [6]. As the elderly population increases, attention to the use of robots as therapeutic aids for the elderly is growing and will increase in the coming years. It is believed that robotics will offer potential solutions to some of the economic and social challenges of the aging population, not replacing healthcare providers but providing support [16]. For the elderly, social robots are not just machines but more likely to provide emotional support [14].

Social robots have performed well in multiple application domains, especially in the medical field [17]. By collecting and analyzing the resulting HRI (Human-Robot Interaction) data, researchers can predict physical changes in the elderly and provide appropriate services. However, the challenge of integrating robotics into the lives of older adults remains difficult, in part because older adults have widely varying attitudes toward robotic devices, affecting acceptance rates [23]. Furthermore, older adults may experience difficulties and be reluctant to use these services due to availability issues, resulting in loss of industry and unmet needs of older adults [21].

Some studies showing that, people feeling more comfortable when interacting with sociable robot [15, 18]. But in other studies, they show that aging people dislike the robots when the social is there main function [1]. The field between these two situations may differ from the contexts and the needs. And have to explore it in the future. This study aims to review HRI services provided by the healthcare industry to understand usability issues and the potential needs of geriatric users. As technology becomes increasingly ubiquitous, HRI schemes must be adapted to different user groups. Older adults, especially, may have specific needs. To support independence for elderly, the research focuses on the medical field to address everyday problems in everyday life. Our findings may guide the HRI community in providing appropriate services and long-term robot designed for older adults.

Acknowledgements. This research has been sponsored by the Ministry of Science and Technology, Taiwan, under Grant MOST 111-2410-H-004-063-MY3 and MOST 109-2410-H-004-067-MY2.

Appendix A

Studies included in our literature review.

Types of Assistance	Goal	Functions	Reference
Physical Assistance	Keeping the ability of moving	Travel navigation and distance notice	28
		Exercise/rehabilitation functions	37
		Taking things which user wants	41, 44
		Exercise directions	36, 40, 43
	Maintaining the ability of cognition	Uploading photos and allowed to change the color that effectively refresh memory	26, 35
		Imitation or action mimicry Cognition training game	25, 29, 33
Social companionship	Strike up a conversation	Resonate with Robot cat's behavior	26
	Making social connection	Getting daily necessities and get chance to meet with neighbor	28
		Robot with a tensegrity structure used for a hug interaction	46
		Invite others to home	40
	Reduce the friction and relieve the relationship between caregiver and patient	Using embodied cues to remember daily chores	31
		Connect the family and patient	40
	Entertaining in conversation	Creature-like Robot interact with user	30, 42
		Dynamic album and question from robot	38
		Robot could do the conversation	30, 42, 45
	Emotion connection with robot	Playing game base from music	25
		Robot dances, sings and talks jokes	32, 36, 30, 43
	Reduce the pressure interact with robot	Remembering and calling user by his/hers name	23, 45
		Designed in a familiar shape	24, 31

(*continued*)

(*continued*)

Types of Assistance	Goal	Functions	Reference
		Robot start the daily conversation	29, 45
	Stable user's mood	Imitate animals' voice	26
		Using photos to make phone calls immediately	28
		Uploading photos encourage look back old good memories	28, 35
		Using predefined button rather that typing words	29
		Interact with robot	30, 42
		Promote embodied cues	31
		Robot greets to take the initiative	40
		Imitate DarumaTO to reduce user's depressed	24
	Reduce loneliness	Feel the heartbeat/hug of the robot	30, 42,
		Telling story	33
		Invite user sharing their mood and keeping diary	29
	Reduce feeling of reliance on technology	Robot ask user for help	23
	Promoting self-learning	Robot actively inquires for more questions	36, 40, 43
		Encourage user finishing the task and set the reward system	34
Social services	Reminder	Taking medication, religious prayer, measuring blood pressure, up-coming event, making appointment with doctor	27, 28, 43
	Prompt	Complete the tasks with several stage prompt, giving prompt to family member	34, 39
	Monitor	Health monitoring, Falling monitoring	27

References

1. Deutsch, I., Erel, H., Paz, M., Hoffman, G., Zuckerman, O.: Home robotic devices for older adults: opportunities and concerns. Comput. Hum. Behav. **98**, 122–133 (2019)
2. González-González, C.S., Violant-Holz, V., Gil-Iranzo, R.M.: Social robots in hospitals: a systematic review. Appl. Sci. **11**(13), 5976 (2021)
3. Duffy, B.R., Rooney, C., O'Hare, G.M., O'Donoghue, R.: What is a social robot? In: 10th Irish Conference on Artificial Intelligence & Cognitive Science, University College Cork, Ireland, 1–3 September 1999 (1999)
4. Urakami, J., Seaborn, K.: Nonverbal cues in human-robot interaction: a communication studies perspective. ACM Trans. Hum. Robot Interact. (2022)
5. World Health Organization, Ageing and health. https://www.who.int/news-room/fact-sheets/detail/ageing-and-health. Accessed 1 Oct 2022
6. OECD, health systems. https://www.oecd.org/health/health-systems/Spending-on-long-term-care-Brief-November-2020.pdf. Accessed 11 2020
7. World Health Organization, Active ageing: A policy framework, No. WHO/NMH/NPH/02.8, World Health Organization (2002)
8. Broekens, J., Heerink, M., Rosendal, H.: Assistive social robots in elderly care: a review. Gerontechnology **8**(2), 94–103 (2009)
9. Mordoch, E., Osterreicher, A., Guse, L., Roger, K., Thompson, G.: Use of social commitment robots in the care of elderly people with dementia: a literature review. Maturitas **74**(1), 14–20 (2013)
10. García-Soler, Á., Facal, D., Díaz-Orueta, U., Pigini, L., Blasi, L., Qiu, R.: Inclusion of service robots in the daily lives of frail older users: a step-by-step definition procedure on users' requirements. Arch. Gerontol. Geriatr. **74**, 191–196 (2018)
11. Lee, H.R., Riek, L.D.: Reframing assistive robots to promote successful aging. ACM Trans. Hum. Robot Interact. (THRI) **7**(1), 11 (2018)
12. Lee, H.R., Tan, H., Šabanović, S.: That robot is not for me: addressing stereotypes of aging in assistive robot design. In: 2016 25th IEEE International Symposium on Robot and Human Interactive Communication (RO-MAN), pp. 312–317. IEEE, August 2016
13. Pedersen, I., Reid, S., Aspevig, K.: Developing social robots for aging populations: a literature review of recent academic sources. Sociol. Compass **12**(6), e12585 (2018)
14. Ferrara, E., Varol, O., Davis, C., Menczer, F., Flammini, A.: The rise of social bots. Commun. ACM **58**(1), 96–104 (2017)
15. Dautenhahn, K.: Robots we like to live with?!-a developmental perspective on a personalized, life-long robot companion. In: RO-MAN 2004. 13th IEEE International Workshop on Robot and Human Interactive Communication (IEEE catalog No. 04TH8759), pp. 17–22. IEEE, September 2004
16. Richardson, H.: Robots could help solve social care crisis, say academics. Educ. Fam. BBC News (2017)
17. Robot revolution: Why technology for older people must be designed with care and respect
18. Mast, M., Burmester, M., Berner, E., Facal, D., Pigini, L., Blasi, L.: Semi-autonomous teleoperated learning in-home service robots for elderly care: a qualitative study on needs and perceptions of elderly people, family caregivers, and professional caregivers. In: 20th International Conference on Robotics and Mechatronics, Varna, Bulgaria, October 1–6 (2010)
19. Hirsch, T., Forlizzi, J., Hyder, E., Goetz, J., Kurtz, C., Stroback, J.: The ELDer project: social, emotional, and environmental factors in the design of eldercare technologies. In: Proceedings on the 2000 Conference on Universal Usability, pp. 72–79, November 2000
20. Johansson-Pajala, R.M., Gustafsson, C.: Significant challenges when introducing care robots in Swedish elder care. Disabil. Rehabil. Assist. Technol. **17**(2), 166–176 (2022)

21. Carros, F., et al.: Exploring human-robot interaction with the elderly: results from a ten-week case study in a care home. In: Proceedings of the 2020 CHI Conference on Human Factors in Computing Systems, pp. 1–12, April 2020

22. Lammer, L., Huber, A., Weiss, A., Vincze, M.: Mutual care: how older adults react when they should help their care robot. In: AISB2014: Proceedings of the 3rd International Symposium on New Frontiers in Human–Robot Interaction, London, UK, pp. 1–4. Routledge, April 2014

23. Trovato, G., et al.: The creation of DarumaTO: a social companion robot for Buddhist/Shinto elderlies. In: 2019 IEEE/ASME International Conference on Advanced Intelligent Mechatronics (AIM), pp. 606–611. IEEE, July 2019

24. Pike, J., Picking, R., Cunningham, S.: Robot companion cats for people at home with dementia: a qualitative case study on companotics. Dementia **20**(4), 1300–1318 (2021)

25. Cammisuli, D.M., Pietrabissa, G., Castelnuovo, G.: Improving wellbeing of community-dwelling people with mild cognitive impairment: the SENIOR (SystEm of Nudge theory based ICT applications for OldeR citizens) project. Neural Regen. Res. **16**(5), 963 (2021)

26. Asghar, I., Cang, S., Yu, H.: The impact of assistive software application to facilitate people with dementia through participatory research. Int. J. Hum. Comput. Stud. **143**, 102471 (2020)

27. Ryu, H., Kim, S., Kim, D., Han, S., Lee, K., Kang, Y.: Simple and steady interactions win the healthy mentality: designing a chatbot service for the elderly. Proc. ACM Hum. Comput. Interact. **4**(CSCW2), 1–25 (2020)

28. Ihamäki, P., Heljakka, K.: Robot pets as "serious toys"-activating social and emotional experiences of elderly people. Inf. Syst. Front., 1–15 (2021)

29. Guan, C., Bouzida, A., Oncy-Avila, R.M., Moharana, S., Riek, L.D.: Taking an (embodied) cue from community health: designing dementia caregiver support technology to advance health equity. In: Proceedings of the 2021 CHI Conference on Human Factors in Computing Systems, pp. 1–16, May 2021

30. Zuschnegg, J., et al.: Psychosocial effects of the humanoid socially assistive robot coach pepper on informal caregivers of people with dementia: a mixed-methods study. Alzheimer's Dement. **17**, e052150 (2021)

31. Valtolina, S., Hu, L.: Charlie: a chatbot to improve the elderly quality of life and to make them more active to fight their sense of loneliness. In: CHItaly 2021: 14th Biannual Conference of the Italian SIGCHI Chapter, pp. 1–5, July 2021

32. Hackett, K., et al.: Remind me to remember: a pilot study of a novel smartphone reminder application for older adults with dementia and mild cognitive impairment. Neuropsychol. Rehabil. **32**(1), 22–50 (2022)

33. Pang, G.K.H., Kwong, E.: Considerations and design on apps for elderly with mild-to-moderate dementia. In: 2015 International Conference on Information Networking (ICOIN), pp. 348–353. IEEE, January 2015

34. Ostrowski, A.K., Breazeal, C., Park, H.W.: Mixed-method long-term robot usage: older adults' lived experience of social robots. In: 2022 17th ACM/IEEE International Conference on Human-Robot Interaction (HRI), pp. 33–42. IEEE, March 2022

35. Hsieh, C.F., Lin, Y.R., Lin, T.Y., Lin, Y.H., Chiang, M.L.: Apply kinect and zenbo to develop interactive health enhancement system. In: 2019 8th International Conference on Innovation, Communication and Engineering (ICICE), pp. 165–168. IEEE, October 2019

36. Gamborino, E., Herrera Ruiz, A., Wang, J.-F., Tseng, T.-Y., Yeh, S.-L., Fu, L.-C.: Towards effective robot-assisted photo reminiscence: personalizing interactions through visual understanding and inferring. In: Rau, P.L.P. (ed.) HCII 2021. LNCS, vol. 12773, pp. 335–349. Springer, Cham (2021). https://doi.org/10.1007/978-3-030-77080-8_27

37. Konngern, S., et al.: Assistive robot with action planner and schedule for family. In: 2019 Twelfth International Conference on Ubi-Media Computing (Ubi-Media), pp. 171–176. IEEE, August 2019

38. Yamazaki, R., et al.: A preliminary study of robotic media effects on older adults with mild cognitive impairment in solitude. In: Li, H., et al. (eds.) ICSR 2021. LNCS (LNAI), vol. 13086, pp. 453–463. Springer, Cham (2021). https://doi.org/10.1007/978-3-030-90525-5_39

39. Kobayashi, T., Arai, K., Imai, T., Tanimoto, S., Sato, H., Kanai, A.: Communication robot for elderly based on robotic process automation. In: 2019 IEEE 43rd Annual Computer Software and Applications Conference (COMPSAC), vol. 2, pp. 251–256. IEEE, July 2019

40. Robinson, H., MacDonald, B., Broadbent, E.: The role of healthcare robots for older people at home: a review. Int. J. Soc. Robot. **6**, 575–591 (2014)

41. Flandorfer, P.: Population aging and socially assistive robots for elderly persons: the importance of sociodemographic factors for user acceptance. Int. J. Popul. Res. **2012**, 1–13 (2012). https://doi.org/10.1155/2012/829835

42. Davies, N.: Can robots handle your healthcare? Eng. Technol. **11**(9), 58–61 (2016)

43. Park, S., Humphry, J.: Exclusion by design: intersections of social, digital and data exclusion. Inf. Commun. Soc. **22**(7), 934–953 (2019)

44. Yoshimura, N., Sato, Y., Kageyama, Y., Murao, J., Yagi, S., Punpongsanon, P.: Hugmon: exploration of affective movements for hug interaction using tensegrity robot. In: 2022 17th ACM/IEEE International Conference on Human-Robot Interaction (HRI), pp. 1105–1109. IEEE, March 2022

45. Echeazarra, L., Pereira, J., Saracho, R.: TensioBot: a chatbot assistant for self-managed in-house blood pressure checking. J. Med. Syst. **45**(4), 54 (2021)

46. Amirabdollahian, F., et al.: Assistive technology design and development for acceptable robotics companions for ageing years. Paladyn J. Behav. Robot. **4**(2), 94–112 (2013)

The Influence of Context and Task on Human-Robot Interaction

Jessica Margalhos[1], Joaquim A. Casaca[1,2], Emília Duarte[1,2], and Hande Ayanoğlu[1,2(✉)]

[1] IADE, Faculdade de Design, Tecnologia e Comunicação, Universidade Europeia, Av. D. Carlos I, 4, 1200-649 Lisbon, Portugal
{joaquim.casaca,emilia.duarte,
hande.ayanoglu}@universidadeeuropeia.pt
[2] UNIDCOM/IADE, Unidade de Investigação em Design e Comunicação, Av. D. Carlos I, 4, 1200-649 Lisbon, Portugal

Abstract. The presence of social robots has been increasing in our lives, in different areas of everyday life in both private and public contexts. Empathy being an important factor in Human-Robot Interaction, gains more and more strength in the design of social robots that are designed with a certain purpose of empathic interaction, from which one can expect positive or negative emotional effects. A quasi-experimental study formed to explore the influence of the factors of context, task, emotions, empathy, and attitudes in the intention of interacting with robots, based on the appearance of three robot. The results of this study suggest that context and task are factors that do not statistically influence the intention to work with robots. Moreover, there are differences in empathy towards to the human-like and machine-like robot in the intention to work with.

Keywords: Human-Robot Interaction · Empathy · Context · Task · Robot Appearance

1 Introduction

The existence of social robots is increasingly becoming a sign of progress, and these are beginning to appear with applications in various areas of daily life, thus leading to great opportunities to adapt to joint or public contexts, becoming safe products. Some studies show that empathy has an impact on user acceptance (e.g., Rossi et al. 2020; Pelau et al. 2021) and create better Human-Robots Interactions (HRI) (Paiva et al. 2017).

According to emotional design, an area of study that seeks to understand how affective experiences are manifested in the interaction between products or environments with users, it is possible to design products that arouse emotional experiences in users (Demir et al. 2009). It has been a theme that is gaining more and more strength in the differentiation strategy applied to design, as it can incite positive feelings and pleasant experiences, strengthening relationships between products and users (Breazeal 2004; Correia et al. 2012).

© The Author(s), under exclusive license to Springer Nature Switzerland AG 2023
M. Kurosu and A. Hashizume (Eds.): HCII 2023, LNCS 14013, pp. 129–139, 2023.
https://doi.org/10.1007/978-3-031-35602-5_10

According to Dautenhahn et al. (2005), people prefer a robot to fulfil particular roles and tasks in addition to having the desired behavioral and aesthetic traits. In other words, some robots will take on different forms, not out of aesthetic considerations but rather because that design is the most appropriate for the assigned task (Norman 2004). Even though the integration of social robots in human social spaces increases, not much is known about the possible existence of a mediating effect of the context of use (private vs. public) and the tasks expected of the robot (undifferentiated vs. humane) that are expected of the robot, on human perceptions. Though, there are studies (e.g., Pino et al. 2015, de Graaf et al. 2015) showing that user acceptance is related to the social and physical environment where robots operate. In this sense, this study's objective is to assess whether users' perceptions (empathy and intention to interact) change in response to the context (domestic vs. hospital) and task (caring vs. assistance) that are specific to the robots with different appearances.

2 Objectives and Hypothesis

The experiments' main goal was to assess how context, task, emotions (positive and negative), empathy, and attitudes toward social robots influenced people's behavior when they intended to work with robots. The following hypotheses were developed for this purpose:

H1: The intention to work with robots is influenced by different types of robots (Mende et al. 2019; Nehaniv et al. 2005; Spatola 2019)
H2: The intention to work with robots is influenced by the context and the tasks (Dautenhahn 2007; Hancock et al. 2011; Gaudiello et al. 2016)
H3: The positive and negative emotions to the intention to interact are influenced by the different appearances of the robots (Campa 2016; Fong et al. 2003; Norman 2004).
H4: Behavioral intention towards robots is influenced by aspects as empathy and attitudes in the past experiences with robots (Beck et al. 2010; Leite et al. 2013; Paiva 2011; Park and Whang 2022)

3 Methods

3.1 Design of Study

The quasi-experimental study used a mixed design, with type of robots (human-like, machine-like and humanoid) as the within subjects' factor, and context (home and hospital) and task (caring and assisting) as between subjects' factors. Four experimental conditions were developed to investigate the effects of context and task on interactions with different types of robots. The participants, in the first condition, were exposed to a domestic setting and a caring task. The context was the same in the second condition, but assisting was the task. In the third condition, the participants were exposed to a hospital context and a caring task, while in the fourth condition, they were in the same context but were exposed to an assisting task.

3.2 Stimulus and Materials

Four narratives were used as stimuli, along with three robots (human-like: Ameca, machine-like: Navers Arc and humanoid: Pepper). The narratives were developed to introduce respondents to a use context where they could envision interacting with robots and to develop a certain level of familiarity, knowledge, and responsibility (e.g., Piçarra and Giger 2018). Additionally, two tasks (care and assistance) with varying levels of demand were developed in order to have different emotional effects, as discussed in other studies (e.g. Norman 2004).

The objectives, steps, and stimuli of the experiments were visualized using a PowerPoint presentation and a projected screen. A video was made using a collection of online commercial presentations of the robots to provide information about each robot. The video was shown without any sound in order to prevent the participants from experiencing any different emotions. Before and after each experiment, questionnaires were made available. Throughout the experiments, participants were instructed to use their smartphones.

3.3 Participants

131 Portuguese volunteers between the ages of 18 and 29 ($M = 20$; $SD = 1.96$), who were divided into 4 conditions, participated in the study.

3.4 Procedure

During each condition, every participant was seated in a classroom. The researcher gave a presentation outlining the objectives of the study and provided participants with a QR code to use to sign an informed consent form, along with instructions on how to withdraw from the study at any time. They then completed a pre-questionnaire. Three categories composed the pre-questionnaire: (i) demographic information; (ii) Toronto Empathy Questionnaire; (iii) Negative Attitudes Towards Robots (NARS). They were given the video (on the projected screen) and the narrative (on paper and a projected screen) after completing the pre-questionnaire. They were, then, asked to complete post-questionnaire, the Model of Goal directed Behavior (MGB) into rate each robot.

3.5 Data Analysis

All the statistical tests were carried out by IBM SPSS Statistics, v. 28, considering a type I error probability (α) of 0.05. All research hypotheses were evaluated with a mixed repeated measures ANOVA, except H1, which was evaluated with a repeated measures ANOVA. The method assumptions, namely the normal distribution of the dependent variables and the variance-covariance matrix sphericity were measured, respectively, with the Kolmogorov-Smirnov (K-S) tests of normality (for the three robots and groups) and with the Mauchly test of sphericity. To identify pairs of means that differ from each other, for the interaction between factors and for dependent variables, a multiple comparison of means with Bonferroni correction was carried out according to the procedure described in Marôco (2021).

Dichotomous variables were calculated for the Toronto scale (low empathy and high empathy) and NARS scale (positive attitudes and negative attitudes) to test the research hypothesis H4.

The dependent variable "behavioural intention" does not present normality issues. Even in the case where normality is rejected by the K-S test, the values of skewness and kurtosis are not strongly asymmetrical, lying in the [−1.96; 1.96] range. Similarly, when Mauchly's test of sphericity is not significant, we use the Epsilon Huynh-Feldt test (recommended for large samples) to evaluate the averaged tests of significance in within-subject's effects.

4 Results and Discussion

In this section, we evaluate the research hypothesis formulated previously.

H1 - The intention to work with robots is influenced by different types of robots

The intention to work with robots assumes different values for the three types of robots (Fig. 1): human-like ($M_{HL} = 2.786$; $SEM_{HL} = 0.142$; $n_{HL} = 131$); machine-like ($M_{ML} = 3.416$; $SEM_{ML} = 0.156$; $n_{ML} = 131$); humanoid ($M_H = 3.305$; $SEM_H = 0.153$; $n_H = 131$). The Huynh-Feldt test indicates that there is at least one pair of different means on the intention to work with the three types of robots ($F (1.71, 221.85) = 16.84$; p-value < 0.001; $\eta_p^2 = 0.115$; Power $(\pi) = 0.999$). According to the pairwise comparisons, significant differences occur between human-like and machine-like robots (p-value < 0.001) and human-like and humanoid robots (p-value < 0.001).

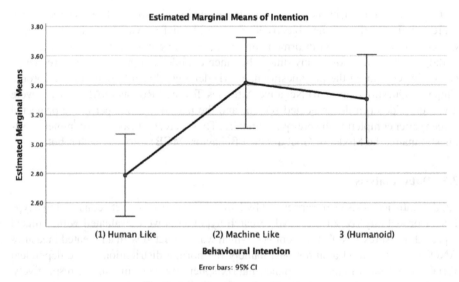

Fig. 1. Intention to work with robots.

These results show that there is a more significant difference in the intention to interact with the robot that looks more identical to the human compared to the other two types of robot. It is understood that the machine-like robot and humanoid tend to have identical assessments, namely greater empathy, due to the similarity between them. This conclusion is in line with the literature that refers that the attribution of human characteristics to robots can influence the behaviour of users, their emotional states and empathy (e.g., Mende et al. 2019; Campa 2016; Nehaniv et al. 2005). Furthermore, as pointed out by Mende et al. (2019), the design of human-like robots may be repulsed by observers.

H2 - *The intention to work with robots is influenced by the context and the tasks*

As shown in Fig. 2, the intention to work with robots in a hospital context (M = 3.109, SEM = 0.186, n = 69) isn't statically different to the intention to work with robots in a domestic context (M = 3.237, SEM = 0.197, n = 62) (F(1, 129) = 0.223, p-value = 0.638, $\eta_p^2 = 0.002$, Power $(\pi) = 0.075$).

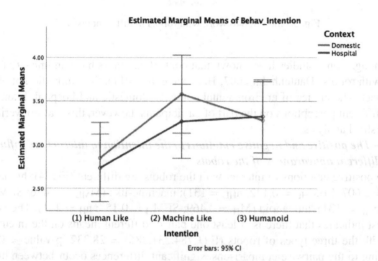

Fig. 2. Intention to work with robots in a domestic and hospital context.

Figure 3 shows that there is no statistically significant difference between "measure body temperature (M = 3.018, SEM = 0.193, n = 64) and "assist in an occurrence" (M = 3.313, SEM = 0.189, n = 67) (F(1, 129) = 1.198, p-value = 0.276, $\eta_p^2 = 0.009$, Power $(\pi) = 0.192$).

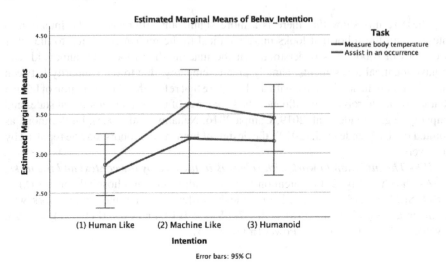

Fig. 3. Intention to work with robots in different tasks.

Although some studies have shown that context and tasks have an impact on inter-action with robots (Dautenhahn 2007; Hancock et al. 2011), this study did not observe the impact. The choice of environmental contexts, domestic and hospital, intended to create different perceptions on the part of participants, however, this was not verified in the statistical analysis.

H3 - The positive and negative emotions to the intention to interact are influenced by the different appearances of the robots

The positive emotions to interact with the robots are different (Fig. 4): human-like ($M_{HL} = 2.607$; $SEM_{HL} = 0.142$; $n_{HL} = 131$); machine-like ($M_{ML} = 3.446$; $SEM_{ML} = 0.152$; $n_{ML} = 131$); humanoid ($M_H = 3.469$; $SEM_H = 0.157$; $n_H = 131$). The Huynh-Feldt test indicates that there is at least one pair of different means on the intention to work with the three types of robots ($F (1.784, 231.886) = 28.332$; p-value < 0.001). According to the pairwise comparisons, significant differences occur between human-like and machine-like robots (p-value < 0.001) and human-like and humanoid robots (p-value < 0.001).

The negative emotions to interact with the robots are different across the robots (Fig. 5): human-like ($M_{HL} = 4.479$; $SEM_{HL} = 0.148$; $n_{HL} = 131$); machine-like ($M_{ML} = 3.466$; $SEM_{ML} = 0.143$; $n_{ML} = 131$); humanoid ($M_H = 3.517$; $SEM_H = 0.148$; $n_H = 131$). The Huynh-Feldt test indicates that there is at least one pair of different means on the intention to work with the three types of robots ($F (1.884, 244.906) = 36.067$; p-value < 0.001). According to the pairwise comparisons, significant differences occur between human-like and machine-like robots (p-value < 0.001) and human-like and humanoid robots (p-value < 0.001). Some studies suggest that emotions can be influencing factors in the interaction with robots (Demir et al. 2009; Norman 2004; Picard 2000). Moreover, there are many studies (e.g., Schindler et al. 2017; Mathur et al. 2016; Mathur et al. 2020; Kim et al. 2022) investigating that as the robot's appearance approach human-likeness,

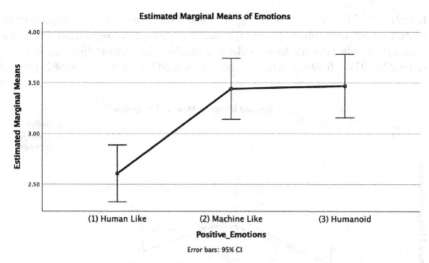

Fig. 4. Positive emotions and the different appearances of the robots.

it makes people uncomfortable with or disgusted by them, which was described as the Uncanny Valley (Mori 1970).

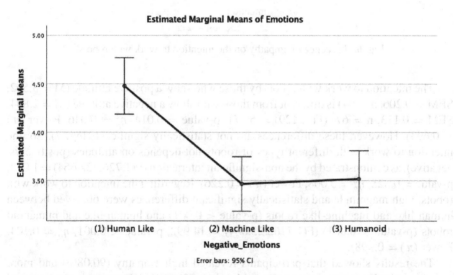

Fig. 5. Negative emotions and the different appearances of the robots.

H4 - Behavioral intention towards robots is influenced by aspects as empathy and attitudes in past experiences with robots

The intention to work with robots by those who show high empathy (M = 3.177, SEM = 0.143, n = 118) is very similar to those who show low empathy (M = 1.103, SEM = 0.430, n = 13). Empathy has no influence on the intention to work with robots

(F(1, 129) = 0.027, p-value = 0.871, η_p^2 = 0.000, Power (π) = 0.053). Regarding the intention to work with robots, high magnitude and statistically significant differences were observed only between human-like and machine-like robots (p-value = 0.010) (F(1.709,220.495) = 6.396, p-value = 0.003, η_p^2 = 0.047, Power (π) = 0.862) (Fig. 6).

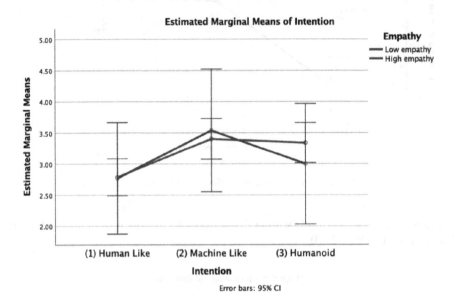

Fig. 6. Influence of empathy on the intention to work with robots.

The intention to work with robots by those who show a positive attitude (M = 3.562, SEM = 0.206, n = 54) is different from those who show a negative attitude (M = 2.894, SEM = 0.173, n = 67) (F(1, 129) = 6.171, p-value = 0.014, η_p^2 = 0.046, Power (π) = 0.693). However, these differences are not statistically significant (Fig. 7). So, the intention to work with different types of robots not depends on attitudes (positive vs. negative), as demonstrated by the non-significant interaction (F(1.726,222.664) = 1.098, p-value = 0.328, η_p^2 = 0.008, Power (π) = 0.226). Regarding the intention to work with robots, high magnitude and statistically significant differences were observed between human-like and machine-like robots (p-value < 0.001) and human-like and humanoid robots (p-value < 0.001) (F(1.726,222.664) = 14.992, p-value < 0.001, η_p^2 = 0.104, Power (π) = 0.998).

The results showed that participants revealed high empathy (90.08%) and more negative attitudes in past experiences with robots (58.78%). However, it can be stated based on the results that empathy and attitudes do not influence intention, which was unexpected based on previous studies (e.g. Paiva 2011; Park and Whang 2022). Even so, there are differences in empathy between the human-like robot and machine-like robot in intention, it is understood that these results are due to the fact that the robots present the most distinct appearances. Regarding attitudes, the results show differences between the human-like robot compared to the other robots.

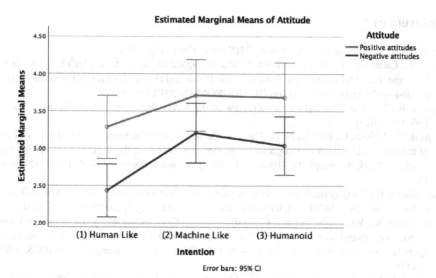

Fig. 7. Influence of positive and negative attitudes to work with robots.

5   Conclusion

The main objective of the study was to investigate whether users' perceptions (empathy and intention to interact) vary depending on the mediating effect of the context (domestic vs. hospital) and task (caring vs. assistance) in the face of different robots. There is a lack of significant results under the influence of the context and the tasks performed by the robots. However, there is a difference in the intention to interact with the human-like robot, compared to robots with similar characteristics between them, which tends to have identical appreciations. Furthermore, in relation to negative emotions, they reveal a weak negative correlation, which means that the lower the negative emotion, the greater the intention to interact. It is worth to mention that the results show that most participants are empathetic but reveal more negative attitudes in interactions with robots. The conclusions of this study are relevant to the development of better social robots, but also for the area of emotional design, exploring the mediating effect of situational variables on design decisions.

Other items of MGB will be analyzed to see the correlation between different items. The video of robots was used in the study which limited the experience of interaction. A Virtual Reality based tool can be suggested to make the experience more immersive, allowing in greater ecological validity, as used in a previous study at HRI (Williams et al. 2018).

Acknowledgement. The study was supported by UNIDCOM under a grant from the Fundação para a Ciência e Tecnologia (FCT) No. UIDB/00711/2020 attributed to UNIDCOM – Unidade de Investigação em Design e Comunicação, Lisbon, Portugal.

References

Breazeal, C.: Designing Sociable Robots. MIT Press, Cambridge (2004)

Beck, A., Cañamero, L., Bard, K.: Towards an affect space for robots to display emotional body language. In: 19th International Symposium in Robot and Human Interactive Communication, pp. 464–469 (2010). https://doi.org/10.1109/ROMAN.2010.5598649

Campa, R.: The rise of social robots: a review of the recent literature. J. Evol. Technol. **26**(1), 106–113 (2016)

Correia, W., Helena, L., Rodrigues, G., Campos, F., Soares, M.: The methodological involvement of the emotional design and cognitive ergonomics as a tool in the development of children products. Work **41**(Suppl. 1), 1066–1071 (2012). https://doi.org/10.3233/WOR-2012-0643-1066

Dautenhahn, K.: Socially intelligent robots: dimensions of human-robot interaction. Philos. Trans. R. Soc. B Biol. Sci. **362**(1480), 679–704 (2007). https://doi.org/10.1098/rstb.2006.2004

Dautenhahn, K., Woods, S., Kaouri, C., Walters, M.L., Koay, K.L., Werry, I.: What is a robot companion - friend, assistant or butler? In: 2005 IEEE/RSJ International Conference on Intelligent Robots and Systems, IROS, pp. 1488–1493 (2005). https://doi.org/10.1109/IROS.2005.1545189

De Graaf, M.M., Allouch, S.B., Klamer, T.: Sharing a life with harvey: exploring the acceptance of and relationship-building with a social robot. Comput. Hum. Behav. **43**, 1–14 (2015)

Demir, E., Desmet, P.M.A., Hekkert, P.: Appraisal patterns of emotions in human-product interaction. Int. J. Des. **3**(2), 41–51 (2009)

Fong, T., Nourbakhsh, I., Dautenhahn, K.: A survey of socially interactive robots. Robot. Auton. Syst. **42**(3–4), 143–166 (2003). https://doi.org/10.1016/S0921-8890(02)00372-X

Gaudiello, I., Zibetti, E., Lefort, S., Chetouani, M., Ivaldi, S.: Trust as indicator of robot functional and social acceptance. An experimental study on user conformation to iCub answers **61**, 633–655 (2016). https://doi.org/10.1016/j.chb.2016.03.057

Goodrich, M.A., Schultz, A.C.: Human-Robot Interaction: A Survey Foundations and Trends in Human-Computer Interaction, vol. 1, no. 3, pp. 203–275 (2007). https://doi.org/10.1561/1100000005

Hancock, P.A., Billings, D.R., Schaefer, K.E., Chen, J.Y.C., De Visser, E.J., Parasuraman, R.: A meta-analysis of factors affecting trust in human-robot (2011)

Kim, B., de Visser, E., Phillips, E.: Two uncanny valleys: re-evaluating the uncanny valley across the full spectrum of real-world human-like robots. Comput. Hum. Behav. **135**, 107340 (2022)

Leite, I., Martinho, C., Paiva, A.: Social robots for long-term interaction: a survey. Int. J. Soc. Robot. **5**(2), 291–308 (2013). https://doi.org/10.1007/s12369-013-0178-y

Lu, L., Cai, R., Gursoy, D.: Developing and validating a service robot integration willingness scale. Int. J. Hosp. Manag. **80**, 36–51 (2019)

Mathur, M.B., Reichling, D.B.: Navigating a social world with robot partners: a quantitative cartography of the Uncanny Valley. Cognition **146**, 22–32 (2016)

Mathur, M.B., et al.: Uncanny but not confusing: Multisite study of perceptual category confusion in the Uncanny Valley. Comput. Hum. Behav. **103**, 21–30 (2020)

Marôco, J.: Análise Estatística com o SPSS Statistics, 8th edn. Report Number (2014)

Mende, M.A., Fischer, M.H., Kühne, K.: The use of social robots and the uncanny valley phenomenon. In: Zhou, Y., Fischer, M.H. (eds.) AI Love You, pp. 41–73. Springer, Cham (2019). https://doi.org/10.1007/978-3-030-19734-6_3

Mori, M.: The Uncanny Valley. Energy **7**(4), 33–35 (1970)

Nehaniv, C.L., Dautenhahn, K., Kubacki, J., Haegele, M., Parlitz, C.: A methodological approach relating the classification of gesture to identification of human intent in the context of human-robot interaction. In: ROMAN 2005. IEEE International Workshop on Robot and Human Interactive Communication, 2005 (2005)

Norman, D.A.: Emotional Design: Why We Love (or Hate) Everyday Things. Basic Civitas Books (2004)

Paiva, A.: Empathy in social agents. Int. J. Virtual Real. **10**(1), 1–4 (2011). https://doi.org/10.20870/ijvr.2011.10.1.2794

Paiva, A., Leite, I., Boukricha, H., Wachsmuth, I.: Empathy in virtual agents and robots: a survey. ACM Trans. Interact. Intell. Syst. **7**(3), 1–40 (2017). https://doi.org/10.1145/2912150

Park, S., Whang, M.: Empathy in human–robot interaction: designing for social robots. Int. J. Environ. Res. Public Health **19**(3), 1889 (2022)

Pelau, C., Dabija, D.C., Ene, I.: What makes an AI device human-like? The role of interaction quality, empathy and perceived psychological anthropomorphic characteristics in the acceptance of artificial intelligence in the service industry. Comput. Hum. Behav. **122**, 106855 (2021)

Piçarra, N., Giger, J.C.: Predicting intention to work with social robots at anticipation stage: assessing the role of behavioral desire and anticipated emotions. Comput. Hum. Behav. **86**, 129–146 (2018). https://doi.org/10.1016/j.chb.2018.04.026

Pino, M., Boulay, M., Jouen, F., Rigaud, A.S.: "Are we ready for robots that care for us?" attitudes and opinions of older adults toward socially assistive robots. Front. Aging Neurosci. **7**, 141 (2015)

Rossi, S., et al.: The role of personality factors and empathy in the acceptance and performance of a social robot for psychometric evaluations. Robotics **9**(2), 39 (2020)

Schindler, S., Zell, E., Botsch, M., Kissler, J.: Differential effects of face-realism and emotion on event-related brain potentials and their implications for the Uncanny Valley theory. Sci. Rep. **7**, 1–13 (2017). https://doi.org/10.1038/srep45003

Spatola, N.: L'interaction Homme-Robot, de l'anthropomorphisme à l'humanisation. LAnne psychologique **119**(4), 515–563 (2019). https://doi.org/10.3917/ANPSY1.194.0515

Williams, T., Tran, N., Rands, J., Dantam, N.T.: Augmented, mixed, and virtual reality enabling of robot deixis. In: Chen, J.Y.C., Fragomeni, G. (eds.) VAMR 2018. LNCS, vol. 10909, pp. 257–275. Springer, Cham (2018). https://doi.org/10.1007/978-3-319-91581-4_19

Studying Multi-modal Human Robot Interaction Using a Mobile VR Simulation

Sven Milde[✉], Tabea Runzheimer, Stefan Friesen, Johannes-Hubert Peiffer,
Johannes-Jeremias Höfler, Kerstin Geis, Jan-Torsten Milde, and Rainer Blum

University of applied Sciences Fulda, Leipziger Straße 123, 36037 Fulda, Germany
{sven.milde,tabea.runzheimer,stefan.friesen,johannes-hubert.peiffer,
johannes-jeremias.hoefler,kertin.geis,jan-torsten.milde,
rainer.blum}@cs.hs-fulda.de
https://cfc.informatik.hs-fulda.de/

Abstract. The task of designing unequivocal communication between autonomous vehicles and humans is important, considering the supposed daily interaction which might take place in the future. Using vehicles which are still in development for a study, can be a security risk and might even endanger the subjects. At the same time, it can be a waste of resources to integrate an interaction model which might not work well. It is therefore crucial to create a safe but realistic environment, in which studies can be held. In this paper we study the interaction between humans and an autonomous vehicle called CityBot, by using self-developed VR and web-applications. We describe two conducted studies, which were focused on speech, gestures and audio signals as means of communication between both parties. We discuss the problems, as well as differences between gestures and speech for controlling the CityBot. Furthermore, we propose a prefered usage of speech and how to handle ambigious gestures.

Keywords: VR · Human-Robot-Interaction · Usability-Testing

1 Introduction

Human-robot interaction is a topic that has been intensively researched over the last two decades. Especially since the advances in autonomous driving, there has been an interest in the interaction between robots and humans. In the development of autonomous vehicles, there is often the problem that an interaction concept should be created and tested before the vehicle has been built. Likewise, it is problematic if the autonomous driving vehicle cannot yet respond to the interactions of a human in order to develop an interaction concept. To develop multimodal interaction concepts with autonomous driving vehicles, we have developed a system that allows early studies with the vehicles in a virtual environment. In the Campus FreeCity project, we use our system to create a multimodal interaction concept with the CityBot, an autonomous, modular robot vehicle.

M. Kurosu and A. Hashizume (Eds.): HCII 2023, LNCS 14013, pp. 140–155, 2023.
https://doi.org/10.1007/978-3-031-35602-5_11

Since speech is the most common means of communication used by humans [3], intuitive communication with an autonomous vehicle should be based on speech [22]. In addition, humans use gestures to enhance more expression to specify certain statements, such as indicating directions with a pointing gesture. Additionally, humans rely heavily on visual information, so an autonomous vehicle should also present information visually to ensure auditory information is not drowned out by road noise. Thus, a multimodal interaction concept has to be developed for the CityBot that is visual, auditory, and gesture-based, so that users can interact with the CityBot as intuitively as possible. In order to achieve an intuitive communication, it is important to focus on the goal of communication instead of communicating itself.

The remainder of this work is organized as follows: In Sect. 2 we give an overview of related work in the field of human-robot-interaction. First we start on the speech modality, followed by gestures and multimodal communication. In section refsec:sett we describe our virtual environment and controlling system with its different components. In Sect. 4 our case studies are explained, followed by Sect. 5 where our results from the studies are discussed. We conclude the paper and provide a view in Sect. 6.

2 Related Work

Human-computer interaction (HMI) is a field that deals with the ways in which commands, requests, and responses can be communicated between a user and a computer. On one hand, this involves how the computer receives and outputs information, on the other how the user does so. One specific area is human-robot interaction (HRI), where the computer personified as a robot receives and outputs information. Robots usually have a more extensive user interface and can be controlled via various modalities. According to Gorostiza et al. [11] it is important that communication between user and robot must be performed on the same level [45]. Communication must be designed as naturally as possible, so that a user can concentrate on what they want to communicate and not on the design of the communication [24]. Depending on the area of application, different forms and methods of communication can be considered. Kosuge et al. [16] describe passive assistive robots that can, for example, help carry furniture and are controlled only by a user applying pressure or traction to the piece of furniture. Chivarov et al. [6] describe the development of a robot that can be controlled with different modalities so that elderly and impaired people can use the robot. Perzanowski et al. [24] describe a robot which can be controlled by speech, gesture and personal digital assistant (PDA) input. Especially for the field of autonomous driving vehicles the development of a multimodal human-robot interface is relevant on several levels. Users should be able to get information about the CityBot by addressing it directly and asking questions. Likewise, the CityBot should be able to greet users and inform them about its capabilities. Speech is used in both directions of communication. Speech and communication in general, become increasingly more difficult if one of the parties is in motion and can be a crucial mean for ensuring safety. If a pedestrian wants to cross the street, the vehicle must be able to recognize the pedestrian's intention and react accordingly. The pedestrian, on the other hand, usually waits to see if a driver or the autonomously driving vehicle indicates giving the pedestrian priority. At present, research is already underway to determine what options are available to indicate the intentions of the autonomous vehicle to pedestrian or other vehicles in order to avoid accidents. Schneemann et al., Schmidt et al., and Matthews et al. [20,38,39] are just a few examples which point out that information can be communicated acoustically or visually in a variety of ways.

These studies are potentially dangerous in the case of misjudgments by pedestrian or malfunctions of autonomous driving vehicles. Virtual reality has been increasingly used to conduct similar studies for several years. Stadler et al. [44] describe a study on the behavior of pedestrian during approaching autonomous vehicles. Specifically, HMI elements outside the vehicle (display) were studied. Pillai et al. [25], like Stadler et al. [44] conducted a VR simulation to study the human-machine interface outside an autonomous vehicle. Goedicke et al. [10] perform a VR study within pseudo-autonomous vehicles to examine when users decide to take control by touching the wheel to avoid an imminent accident. Here, the VR simulation is conducted inside a vehicle to provide haptic feedback to users. Scholkopf et al. [40] appropriately investigates whether haptics can increase immersion in simulations, leading to better outcomes in studies. Ropelato et al. [30] use a VR simulation for student drivers in which an AI analyzes driving behavior and shows the student drivers an optimal route through a city so that difficult traffic situations can be practiced.

2.1   Speech for Communication

As the main means of human communication, speech must be part of a natural human-machine interface. There are various aspects that must be taken into account for a speech interface. First, speech must be picked up by a machine and recognized as such. In addition, the individual terms and their connections must be recognized. Speech recognition poses many difficulties, as discussed by Benzeghiba et al., Huang et al., Hannon et al., Reeves et al. [1,13,14,27,28]. Here, one of the major problems described is bias in the datasets used to train algorithms on speech recognition. In addition, it must be noted that a natural language interface is not just a question-answering system [2,7,17,27,28], but the machine can respond to humans, has empathic and social abilities in certain situations. In addition to this partial non-verbal information which a language system has to convey, it is also important to consider what the language system processes in terms of information.

Processing the input is the second part of speech recognition, which is important for a speech interface. Ward et al. [47] describe the influence of non-lexical filler sounds in speech usage, while Skubic et al. and Kollar et al. [15,43] address how humans use area specific indications in language use, implying that a machine must have appropriate information about the local environment to respond to input from humans.

The third and final subsection of a speech interface is the output of generated speech. A corresponding response must be generated by processing the input and converted to audio [19]. These systems, known as text-to-speech (TTS), have been around for some time and have increased in performance, use and vocalization [14] through machine learning. In particular, Tacotron 2 as a TTS system has performed particularly well in generating speech from text in recent years [26,42].

2.2 Gestures for Communication

With widespread voice assistants such as Siri, Alexa, Google or Cortana, progress and usability for speech systems is showing, whereas systems for dynamic gestures are unknown. In research, there are many areas where dynamic gestures are seen, however, the difficulty in recognition is still too great to create robust systems. That being said, there are several approaches on what data dynamic gestures can be captured best [9]. Most commonly, raw RGB images or RGB images combined with depth images are used. Grushin et al. [12] compute a histogram of the optical flow of images to detect gestures. In addition, there is a large number of different algorithms which can be used. Schuldt et al. [41] use support vector machines (SVM), Grushin et al. [12] use Long-Short Term Memory (LSTM), and Asadi et al. and Wang et al. compare different algorithms such as recurrent neural networks (RNN), convolutional neuronal networks (CNN), or graph-convolutional networks (GCN) [48].

Defining appropriate gestures is also a difficult task. Cadoni and Bomsdorf [5] attempt to map touch gestures to 3D gestures by asking test persons which gestures they would like to use before these gestures are used in their tests. Schak and Gepperth [33–37] investigate the influence of bias on gesture recognition by creating a dataset starting from only one test person, but recognizing the gestures of any test person in a trained condition.

2.3 Multi-modal Communication

To make human-machine interaction as intuitive as possible, not only one modality should be offered for interaction, but different modalities. Turk et al. [46] begins in his remarks with the first multimodal interfaces and then derives guidelines and myths with the help of the historical development of multimodal interfaces. Oviatt et al. [22,23] show that fewer errors are made by users and that cognitive load is reduced by multimodality. Rodomagoulakis et al. [29] describe that one problem is the discrepancy on how people interact with an interface. For example, in their study they showed that especially older or impaired people try to perform gestures and articulate speech more clearly, compared to young people or people without impairments.

With multimodal interfaces, however, the question is how and when to combine the different modalities. Data can be combined before it is analyzed by algorithms, or after. In addition, there are hybrid versions where a combination of data is performed step by step. Neverova et al., Lucignano et al., and Burger et al. [4,18,21] all describe interfaces where modalities are combined after analysis. This raises the question of whether different modalities are more unique than others and thus need to be prioritized. For this purpose Salem et al. [32] investigate how the robot should behave when speech is used alone, combined with a matching gesture or a non-matching gesture.

3   Experimental Setting

Fig. 1. Left: CityBot. Right top: CityBot with backpack. Right bottom: CityBot with Peoplemover

The CityBot is intended to be an autonomously driving vehicle that can be equipped with various attachments to perform different tasks as shown in Fig. 1. On the one hand, the so called Peoplemover attachment can be used to transport people, and on the other hand, the Backpack attachment can be used to transport objects, garbage or green waste. Here, the CityBot is a kind of tractor module with a movable, retractable, head equipped with microphones, a screen and a stereoscopic camera to interact with the environment. Since the prototype of the CityBot does not yet contain all functionalities, it is too dangerous to perform user tests to evaluate in which way users communicate intuitively. For this reason, we decided to use a VR simulation in which users are made to believe they are actually interacting with the CityBot. In order to analyse different actions and situations, the tests are conducted as Wizard of Oz experiments [8,31], where a so called wizard controls the CityBot's steering and interactions while the test person is supposed to believe the system is doing the work by itself. For this purpose, our testing environment consists of a VR simulation (see Sect. 3.1) and a webtool (see Sect. 3.2), with which the simulation can be controlled using Open Sound Control (OSC) commands (Fig. 2).

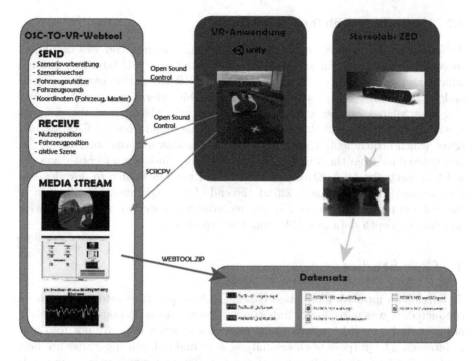

Fig. 2. Systemarchitecture of the system

3.1   VR-Simulation

The VR headset used is a Meta Quest 2, which is a standalone headset running an Android operating system. The simulation is developed with Unity and the Oculus Integration extension for accessing system functionality of the headset on a deeper level. The virtual hands are particularly relevant to the development of the interaction concept, as users need to see their hands in order to feel themselves performing visible gestures with them. The simulation consists of a lobby in which users are first introduced to the VR environment as well as various scenes in which tests can then be performed. To track what is happening in the VR simulation, the video data is transmitted in real time to a control computer via scrcpy. This allows the wizard and moderator to view the simulation from the point of view of the test person. To control the simulation, a web interface with Open Sound Control (OSC) as the communication protocol is implemented, which can be used to receive commands and send data. These data packets can be seperated into two different types, controlling and informational data. Informational messages share data about the virtual environment, such as a test persons orientation, hand position or the distance to the CityBot. Controlling data is mostly sent by the webtool and will convey interaction or setting changes such as loading a different scene, changing a module for the CityBot or switching the speaker.

3.2   Controlling WebTool

A Node.js based webtool consisting of a backend and frontend was developed to control the experiments. The webtool contains an OSC interface through which the position and orientation data of the VR simulation can be received and logged. Through the webtool's interface, this information can be viewed and manipulated by the wizard. Likewise, the wizard can load the different scenarios, control the CityBot itself, output vehicle sound from the CityBot, and select which attachments the CityBot has. For evaluation, the tracking, audio, and video data from the VR headset and browser window are recorded via the webtool using the MediaStream Web API and made available to download as a compressed dataset using JSZip at the end of the experiment. In addition to the webtool recording, the user is also recorded via a stereoscopic camera with skeletal and depth data available from the experiment.

4   Case Studies

To develop an intuitive interaction concept, initial qualitative studies have been conducted. It was particularly important to pursue a user-centered approach in order to find out which interactions users choose when they are not told how to interact. The purpose of these analyses is to find out which gestures are best used to fine-tune the positioning of the CityBot and which voice commands can be used for this purpose. Likewise, it should be identified which voices are best suited for the CityBot and in which detail the CityBot should respond. Furthermore, it will be analyzed in which way the CityBot should make its intentions clear to other road users.

4.1   First Qualitative Study on Intuitive Gestures

The first study was specifically designed to find out which gestures and voice commands test persons use to convey the CityBot to perform certain actions. For this purpose, the test was divided into three sections. In the first section, test persons were asked to tell the CityBot to perform certain simple actions using only gestures. For example, driving forward, reversing, stopping and turning on the spot. In the second part of the test, users were asked to perform the same actions, but this time using only voice commands. For the third part of the test, the scene was changed to an underground car park, where users were asked to maneuver the CityBot into a special parking space using gestures and voice commands. It was up to the test persons whether they used only gestures, only voice commands or any combination of both to complete the task.

The test was conducted with a total of seven test persons between the ages of 22 and 26. Only two of the users had prior experience with VR. At the end of the test all of the users described that the simulation felt like they were interacting with the CityBot. This shows that realistic simulations can be created with our system to investigate and develop interaction concepts.

4.2   Second Qualitative Study on Speech

The second study was designed to first determine which voice best matched the CityBot. For this purpose, there were male, female and robotic voices. The test persons were told a joke with two differenct voices. Afterwards, the test persons had to decide which voice they preferred. The preferred voice was then used with another new voice as well as a new joke. Subsequently they were asked if they could describe why they had chosen one voice over another. This process was repeated until the test persons had heard every voice and chosen their favourite. They were then informed that the CityBot would be using said voice for the remaining tests, however they could change the voice again if they wanted to. In addition, the conversation between the CityBot and the test person tested how detailed the CityBot's answers should be. For this purpose, the test person had to ask the same question several times and the CityBot answered for different lengths of time.

The second part of the experiment, analyzed the distance the CityBot should retain to a test person, so they wouldn't feel uncomfortable. For this purpose, the CityBot drove towards the test person and they were supposed to stop the CityBot when it drove close enough to them so that they could still feel safe and start an interaction with the CityBot. The CB itself was driving directly towards the test persons, using different speeds and attachments. After the CityBot had been stopped by a test person, it would ask them wether they felt comfortable with the distance. If the answer was negative they were asked to elaborate, could give directions on where they would have liked the CityBot to stop and could repeat the test with the exact same conditions until they felt satisfied with the response.

While the CityBot is busy with a task, it cannot process any other input. However, in certain situations, such as an emergency, the CityBot should be able to be released from its task and deal with the emergency. For this purpose, an emergency situation was created in the test with a dummy person. The test persons were told that the dummy was an unconcious person and that they had to gather help from another human, without the help of their phone. They were not told, that the CityBot had a "busy-state" or with which keyword they could gather the attention from the CityBot in such a state. Without the use of the keyword, the CityBot would apologize and state that it was busy. The keyword *help* wasn't told the test persons either because we wanted to see which keyword the test persons would choose on their own.

The last part of the test should point out if users in traffic could recognize the CityBot's intentions when it used beeps, light signals, or a voice output to express its intention. The test persons were asked to try to safely cross a street on which the CityBot was approaching. The CityBot was given different behaviors, such as stopping every time and give the test persons way or driving past the user honking and not paying attention to the user.

The test was conducted with a total of 12 users ranging in age from 21 to 57. They were mostly students, almost all of whom (two did not) have a driver's license and thus were familiar with natural behavior on the road. Also in this test, most of the users had no experience in VR and found the simulation to be very realistic. Due to the variety of actions the CityBot could take, two wizards had control of separate parts of the CityBot in comparison to the first study where only one wizard controlled the CityBot. This allowed the CityBot to respond better and faster to the users' interactions.

5   Discussion

During the two qualitative studies, several findings were made that will be presented and discussed below. The video data and transcripts of the studies were used to evaluate the two studies. Based on this, the studies were examined with regard to the user interface of the CityBot from several points of view. The primary aim was to find out which gestures and voice commands users intuitively use to convey instructions to the CityBot. Also, we wanted to find out which voice best suits the CityBot, at which distance the CityBot has to stop so that users do not feel crowded or get scared, and how well the CityBot's intentions are recognized by pedestrian who want to cross a street on which the CityBot is driving.

In the first part of the study we asked the test persons to do some intuitiv gestures to navigate the CityBot. There was a significant variance in the gestures used by the test persons. First, there was the variance that test persons used only one hand or both hands to perform a gesture. As an example, *stop* was performed by test persons with one or two hands extended away from themselves, as shown in Fig. 3 under *a)*.

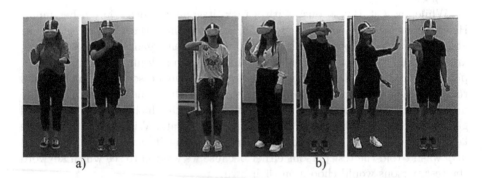

a)   b)

Fig. 3. Gestures intuitively used during testing

Second, some gestures for instructions were too diverse and generalization was impossible. The best example of this is the instruction for a rotation of the CityBot as shown in Fig. 3 under *b)*. While some test person only used one finger for this gesture, pointing either up or down in a circular motion, others used the whole hand to fictitiously grab and rotate the CityBot from above. Another alternative was the variation of rotating an outstretched hand 90°C to the left or right to cause the CityBot to rotate. In terms of future robust gesture recognition, it can be seen that for rotation, consideration needs to be given to defining a gesture, as the variance in natural gestures is too great. Due to the fact that many of the gestures are performed in front of the body, it remains to be verified whether the gestures can be reliably recognized by algorithms. Furthermore the gestures *stop* and *backward* are problematic because they end in the exact same position. Although they differ before the ending position is reached, a machine learning system might not be able to differentiate between the two, when only looking at the last frame of the gestures.

The second part of the first study shows a very clear choice of voice commands by the test persons. For some actions, such as stopping the CityBot, all test persons used the same command *stop*. For other instructions, some test persons used the same terms but supplemented with additional words, such as *slow down* was expanded to *drive slower*.

In the third part of the study, more problems were noticed when parking the CityBot. Especially with the rotation, an interpretation of the rotation direction has been partly difficult in the given variety. In addition, it has been shown as already mentioned in [15,43] that test persons assumed the CityBot has a spatial perception. Therefore, several test persons in the study tried to park the CityBot with a single pointing gesture. Since we did not assume spatial perception until then, the CityBot did not respond to these instructions and forced the test persons to use alternative gestures. When parking with gestures, another problem arose where the CityBot was no longer facing frontal to the test persons and the test person intuitively used other gestures to move the CityBot in the appropriate direction. For example, the previously used *faster* gesture of waving one hand past the body was now used to make the CityBot drive straight ahead, since the orientation of the CityBot was different.

In the second study, some aspects also stood out that need to be considered for further development. Ten of the test persons found the female voice best suited for the CityBot. One test person chose the robotic voice for the test and one test person used the male voice, although the latter emphasized at the end that they thought it was situation-dependent which voice would suit the CityBot better. In addition to technical problems that caused delays in the CityBot's braking behavior, while virtually running over the test persons, Table 1 shows the distances at which the test persons found the CityBot stopped at a sufficient distance at various speeds. For the CityBot alone, this shows that the distance to the test person increases on average the faster the CityBot is driving. If the CityBot is driving with the Peoplemover attachment, the distance only increases up to 10 km/h, after which it tends to decrease again. This could be due to distortion effects in VR, or because a larger vehicle does not appear as fast in the distance as a smaller vehicle. In addition, the braking distance of the CityBot with Peoplemover attachment is larger than without, which is also a factor for a longer braking distance.

Table 1. Distances in meter from CityBot while stopping for User. Left is just the CityBot, right is CityBot with Peoplemover (PPM). X is missing value

#	CityBot				CityBot with PPM			
	5 km/h	10 km/h	20 km/h	30 km/h	5 km/h	10 km/h	20 km/h	30 km/h
1	1,3	1,5	0,8	2,7	3,0	1,2	0,06	0,1
2	1,58	3,69	1,46	1,17	4,38	5,56	8,24	12,16
3	2,64	3,02	10,3	3,43	3,93	2,8	4,11	4,31
4	3,51	2,06	4,19	2,42	6,51	4,5	6,67	2,25
5	11,52	5,74	2,17	3,1	6,16	8,23	3,78	3,1
6	1,37	1,18	1,22	1,01	1,3	1,77	6,78	7,32
7	1,0	0,55	3,19	X	3,18	X	5,49	X
8	1,35	2,85	2,45	2,59	4,94	4,53	2,73	1,9
9	1,85	0,82	X	3,5	7,43	6,27	4,37	5,01
10	1,87	6,06	4,08	4,07	4,76	9,93	5,83	3,7
11	0,86	1,13	0,79	0,49	0,97	0,8	0,49	1,55
12	1,31	2,62	2,81	1,39	1,57	3,15	0,24	8,72

The third task of the test led to frustration among the test persons, because test persons were not informed in advance with which keyword the CityBot could be made to interrupt a task or that there was a keyword at all. The word *help* was defined by us. For our study, however, we deliberately did not want to define a large set of keywords in order to learn which terms were used first and second by the test persons. It turned out that the following keywords were used by test person or indicated as desirable in the subsequent survey. *Emergency* or *emergency call* had been used very often by the test persons. Additionally the test persons used *112* or *SOS* as keywords to interrupt the CityBot. A few of the test persons also tried *hospital* as keyword.

The fourth part of the second study showed that some of the CityBot's behavior is not tolerated by test persons. Other behavior evoked very mixed feelings among the test persons. In the first run, the CityBot was asked to slow down, eventually stopping and letting the test persons pass. Nine of the test persons could not see that the CityBot was slowing down to give them the right of way and assumed that the CityBot would simply pass them. Four of the test persons approved the CityBot coming to a full stop, to let them pass. In the second run, the behavior of the CityBot was additionally supported by a voice output with which the CityBot informed test persons about its behavior. On the one hand, this behavior was perceived by test persons as more pleasant compared to the first run, on the other hand, test persons felt that it was inappropriate for the CityBot to start a conversation every time in traffic. For the third run, an error case of the CityBot was tested, where the CityBot uses the voice output from the second run and tells the test persons that they have priority, but does not slow down and passes the test persons. Some of the test persons were therefore virtually run over by the CityBot. The test persons found this contradictory behavior absolutely inappropriate for the CityBot. In the fourth run, the speech output was then adapted to the behavior and the CityBot used its horn or warned the test persons with *Attention* of its passage. Here, test persons perceived the auditory cues as too late and expressed that the CityBot should stop if test persons were already attempting to cross the street. Run five was designed to show how test persons responded when the CityBot passed them without acoustic cues. Such behavior was defined as inappropriate by some of the test persons, while the other test persons defined this behavior as known from cars and thus as good behavior, as it is currently human behavior in traffic. For the sixth run, test persons were asked not to cross the street but to yield right of way to the CityBot. Most of the test persons used speech and gestures at the beginning. However, since the CityBot waived its right of way and wanted to let the test person go ahead, the test person mostly waived gestures in the second run and gave the CityBot the right of way again using only speech. The discussion with the CityBot about who was allowed to drive first was unpleasant for most of the test persons.

For runs seven and eight, test persons were asked to stand directly on the street while the CityBot drove towards them. Test persons were asked to indicate what they expected the CityBot to do and how they felt about it. At some point in run seven, the CityBot begins to honk, at which point it also reduces speed. Shortly in front of the test persons, the CityBot stops and asks the test persons to clear the way. The test persons perceived the horn as an appropriate warning signal, as it is familiar from cars. Despite the reduced speeds, test persons perceived the CityBot as too fast.

In the eighth run, test persons were not informed of the CityBot's approach; instead, the CityBot set its turn signal and attempted to drive around the test persons. Although the turn signal was presented visually and acoustically, only two test persons recognized it as such. The test persons all found this behavior of the CityBot to be inappropriate and also impractical for everyday use.

In the overall communication between the test persons, despite the use of wizards, it is evident that voice commands are better understood than gestures, which led to the test persons frequently starting with gestures and speech in combination, but switching to using only voice commands over the course of the studies.

6   Conclusion and Future Work

We proposed a VR application to explore how multimodal human-robot interaction can work so that it can be intuitively used. For this purpose, we used the CityBot as an autonomously driving vehicle with which multimodal communication can take place. We investigated which gestures and voice commands were used and in which way the intentions of the CityBot can be communicated. It was noticed that voice commands were prefered, as they were often more unambiguous and easier to interpret. When analyzing the gestures, it was noticed that some gestures convey an unequivoval action and are used by everyone. Other gestures for commands however, had such a wide variety, that it is difficult to create an intuitive gesture interface.

The CityBot as an autonomous driving vehicle should be more passive in its behavior than drivers in current road traffic as mentioned by the test persons. For example, pedestrians should have the right of way rather than the CityBot. In addition, the CityBot should clearly indicate its intentions. In the studies it is shown, that speech, speed and sound might not be enough to indicate intentions of the CityBot and visual information might improve the experience.

In our analyses, only voice and gesture interface have been considered so far. In future studies, the additional visual interface should be included in the considerations to get an overall picture. In addition, future studies should investigate how the speed perception in VR compares to reality and whether this is the reason for the decreasing distance zones of the CityBot with Peoplemover.

In the process of using the current VR simulation and webtool some technical problems have been noticed that made working with it in studies difficult. Despite the difficulties, a remote controlled VR simulation does have a lot of advantages, such as mobility and flexibility. For this reason, a revised version is currently in progress to eliminate the initial mistakes and improve usability. In addition, the simulation will be adapted to fit the existing conditions of the CityBot. By changing the communication protocol from OSC to the Robot Operating System (ROS), new features can be tested directly in VR and do not need to be adapted for the CityBot.

The previous qualitative studies were conducted with a small number of test persons. For a better analysis, a quantitative study will be carried out, in oder to create a data set of gestures. This data set will then be used to train an maschine learning model for an autonomous control of the CityBot, to be used in VR as well as for the real CityBot.

Acknowledgments. This work is part of the Campus FreeCity project, which is funded with a total of 10.9 million euros by the German Federal Ministry for Digital and Transport (BMDV).

References

1. Benzeghiba, M., et al.: Automatic speech recognition and speech variability: a review. Speech Commun. **49**(10–11), 763–786 (2007)
2. Bickmore, T.W., Picard, R.W.: Establishing and maintaining long-term human-computer relationships. ACM Trans. Comput.-Hum. Interact. (TOCHI) **12**(2), 293–327 (2005)
3. Budkov, V.Y., Prischepa, M., Ronzhin, A., Karpov, A.: Multimodal human-robot interaction. In: International Congress on Ultra Modern Telecommunications and Control Systems, pp. 485–488. IEEE (2010)
4. Burger, B., Ferrané, I., Lerasle, F., Infantes, G.: Two-handed gesture recognition and fusion with speech to command a robot. Auton. Robot. **32**(2), 129–147 (2012)
5. Cadoni, I., Bomsdorf, B.: Mögliche fallen bei der benutzerzentrierten ermittlung von 3d gesten. Mensch und Computer 2018-Tagungsband (2018)

6. Chivarov, N., Chikurtev, D., Pleva, M., Ondas, S.: Exploring human-robot interfaces for service mobile robots. In: 2018 World Symposium on Digital Intelligence for Systems and Machines (DISA), pp. 337–342. IEEE (2018)

7. Clark, L., et al.: What makes a good conversation? Challenges in designing truly conversational agents. In: Proceedings of the 2019 CHI Conference on Human Factors in Computing Systems, pp. 1–12 (2019)

8. Dahlbäck, N., Jönsson, A., Ahrenberg, L.: Wizard of OZ studies-why and how. Knowl.-Based Syst. 6(4), 258–266 (1993)

9. Escalera, S., et al.: ChaLearn looking at people challenge 2014: dataset and results. In: Agapito, L., Bronstein, M.M., Rother, C. (eds.) ECCV 2014. LNCS, vol. 8925, pp. 459–473. Springer, Cham (2015). https://doi.org/10.1007/978-3-319-16178-5_32

10. Goedicke, D., Li, J., Evers, V., Ju, W.: Vr-oom: virtual reality on-road driving simulation. In: Proceedings of the 2018 CHI Conference on Human Factors in Computing Systems, pp. 1–11 (2018)

11. Gorostiza, J.F., et al.: Multimodal human-robot interaction framework for a personal robot. In: ROMAN 2006-The 15th IEEE International Symposium on Robot and Human Interactive Communication, pp. 39–44. IEEE (2006)

12. Grushin, A., Monner, D.D., Reggia, J.A., Mishra, A.: Robust human action recognition via long short-term memory. In: The 2013 International Joint Conference on Neural Networks (IJCNN), pp. 1–8. IEEE (2013)

13. Hannon, C.: Avoiding bias in robot speech. Interactions 25(5), 34–37 (2018)

14. Huang, X., Baker, J., Reddy, R.: A historical perspective of speech recognition. Commun. ACM 57(1), 94–103 (2014)

15. Kollar, T., Tellex, S., Roy, D., Roy, N.: Toward understanding natural language directions. In: 2010 5th ACM/IEEE International Conference on Human-Robot Interaction (HRI), pp. 259–266. IEEE (2010)

16. Kosuge, K., Hirata, Y.: Human-robot interaction. In: 2004 IEEE International Conference on Robotics and Biomimetics, pp. 8–11. IEEE (2004)

17. Kriz, S., Anderson, G., Trafton, J.G.: Robot-directed speech: using language to assess first-time users' conceptualizations of a robot. In: 2010 5th ACM/IEEE International Conference on Human-Robot Interaction (HRI), pp. 267–274. IEEE (2010)

18. Lucignano, L., Cutugno, F., Rossi, S., Finzi, A.: A dialogue system for multimodal human-robot interaction. In: Proceedings of the 15th ACM on International Conference on Multimodal Interaction, pp. 197–204 (2013)

19. Mache, S.R., Baheti, M.R., Mahender, C.N.: Review on text-to-speech synthesizer. Int. J. Adv. Res. Comput. Commun. Eng. 4(8), 54–59 (2015)

20. Matthews, M., Chowdhary, G., Kieson, E.: Intent communication between autonomous vehicles and pedestrians. arXiv preprint arXiv:1708.07123 (2017)

21. Neverova, N., Wolf, C., Taylor, G., Nebout, F.: Moddrop: adaptive multi-modal gesture recognition. IEEE Trans. Pattern Anal. Mach. Intell. 38(8), 1692–1706 (2015)

22. Oviatt, S.: Advances in robust multimodal interface design. IEEE Comput. Graphics Appl. 23(05), 62–68 (2003)

23. Oviatt, S., Coulston, R., Lunsford, R.: When do we interact multimodally? Cognitive load and multimodal communication patterns. In: Proceedings of the 6th international conference on Multimodal interfaces. pp. 129–136 (2004)

24. Perzanowski, D., Schultz, A.C., Adams, W., Marsh, E., Bugajska, M.: Building a multimodal human-robot interface. IEEE Intell. Syst. 16(1), 16–21 (2001)

25. Pillai, A., et al.: Virtual reality based study to analyse pedestrian attitude towards autonomous vehicles. Master's thesis, Aalto University (2017)
26. Prenger, R., Valle, R., Catanzaro, B.: Waveglow: a flow-based generative network for speech synthesis. In: ICASSP 2019–2019 IEEE International Conference on Acoustics, Speech and Signal Processing (ICASSP), pp. 3617–3621. IEEE (2019)
27. Reeves, S., Porcheron, M., Fischer, J.: 'this is not what we wanted' designing for conversation with voice interfaces. Interactions **26**(1), 46–51 (2018)
28. Reeves, S., et al.: Voice-based conversational UX studies and design. In: Extended Abstracts of the 2018 CHI Conference on Human Factors in Computing Systems, pp. 1–8 (2018)
29. Rodomagoulakis, I., et al.: Multimodal human action recognition in assistive human-robot interaction. In: 2016 IEEE International Conference on Acoustics, Speech and Signal Processing (ICASSP), pp. 2702–2706. IEEE (2016)
30. Ropelato, S., Zünd, F., Magnenat, S., Menozzi, M., Sumner, R.: Adaptive tutoring on a virtual reality driving simulator. In: International SERIES on Information Systems and Management in Creative EMedia (CreMedia) 2017 (2), pp. 12–17 (2018)
31. Salber, D., Coutaz, J.: Applying the Wizard of Oz technique to the study of multimodal systems. In: Bass, L.J., Gornostaev, J., Unger, C. (eds.) EWHCI 1993. LNCS, vol. 753, pp. 219–230. Springer, Heidelberg (1993). https://doi.org/10.1007/3-540-57433-6_51
32. Salem, M., Kopp, S., Wachsmuth, I., Rohlfing, K., Joublin, F.: Generation and evaluation of communicative robot gesture. Int. J. Soc. Robot. **4**(2), 201–217 (2012)
33. Schak, M., Gepperth, A.: Robustness of deep LSTM networks in freehand gesture recognition. In: Tetko, I.V., Kůrková, V., Karpov, P., Theis, F. (eds.) ICANN 2019. LNCS, vol. 11729, pp. 330–343. Springer, Cham (2019). https://doi.org/10.1007/978-3-030-30508-6_27
34. Schak, M., Gepperth, A.: A study on catastrophic forgetting in deep LSTM networks. In: Tetko, I.V., Kůrková, V., Karpov, P., Theis, F. (eds.) ICANN 2019. LNCS, vol. 11728, pp. 714–728. Springer, Cham (2019). https://doi.org/10.1007/978-3-030-30484-3_56
35. Schak, M., Gepperth, A.: On multi-modal fusion for freehand gesture recognition. In: Farkaš, I., Masulli, P., Wermter, S. (eds.) ICANN 2020. LNCS, vol. 12396, pp. 862–873. Springer, Cham (2020). https://doi.org/10.1007/978-3-030-61609-0_68
36. Schak, M., Gepperth, A.: Gesture MNIST: a new free-hand gesture dataset. In: Pimenidis, E., Angelov, P., Jayne, C., Papaleonidas, A., Aydin, M. (eds.) Artificial Neural Networks and Machine Learning. ICANN 2022. ICANN 2022. LNCS, vol. 13532, pp. 657–668. Springer, Cham (2022). https://doi.org/10.1007/978-3-031-15937-4_55
37. Schak, M., Gepperth, A.: Gesture recognition on a new multi-modal hand gesture dataset. In: ICPRAM, pp. 122–131 (2022)
38. Schmidt, S., Faerber, B.: Pedestrians at the kerb-recognising the action intentions of humans. Transport. Res. F: Traffic Psychol. Behav. **12**(4), 300–310 (2009)
39. Schneemann, F., Gohl, I.: Analyzing driver-pedestrian interaction at crosswalks: a contribution to autonomous driving in urban environments. In: 2016 IEEE Intelligent Vehicles Symposium (IV), pp. 38–43. IEEE (2016)
40. Schölkopf, L., et al.: Haptic feedback is more important than VR experience for the user experience assessment of in-car human machine interfaces. Procedia CIRP **100**, 601–606 (2021)

41. Schuldt, C., Laptev, I., Caputo, B.: Recognizing human actions: a local SVM approach. In: Proceedings of the 17th International Conference on Pattern Recognition, 2004. ICPR 2004. vol. 3, pp. 32–36. IEEE (2004)
42. Shen, J., et al.: Natural TTS synthesis by conditioning wavenet on mel spectrogram predictions. In: 2018 IEEE International Conference on Acoustics, Speech and Signal Processing (ICASSP), pp. 4779–4783. IEEE (2018)
43. Skubic, M., et al.: Spatial language for human-robot dialogs. IEEE Trans. Syst. Man Cybern. Part C (Appl. Rev.) 34(2), 154–167 (2004)
44. Stadler, S., Cornet, H., Novaes Theoto, T., Frenkler, F.: A tool, not a toy: using virtual reality to evaluate the communication between autonomous vehicles and pedestrians. In: tom Dieck, M.C., Jung, T. (eds.) Augmented Reality and Virtual Reality. PI, pp. 203–216. Springer, Cham (2019). https://doi.org/10.1007/978-3-030-06246-0_15
45. Stiefelhagen, R., et al.: Enabling multimodal human-robot interaction for the Karlsruhe humanoid robot. IEEE Trans. Rob. 23(5), 840–851 (2007)
46. Turk, M.: Multimodal interaction: a review. Pattern Recogn. Lett. 36, 189–195 (2014)
47. Ward, N.: Non-lexical conversational sounds in American English. Pragmat. Cogn. 14(1), 129–182 (2006)
48. Zhang, A., Lipton, Z.C., Li, M., Smola, A.J.: Dive into deep learning. arXiv preprint arXiv:2106.11342 (2021)

Teachers' Perspective on Robots Inclusion in Education – A Case Study in Norway

Anshul Rani[1]([⊠]) [iD], Akshara Pande[1] [iD], Karen Parish[2], and Deepti Mishra[1] [iD]

[1] SDDE, IDI, Norwegian Institute of Science and Technology, Trondheim, Norway
{anshul.rani,akshara.pande,deepti.mishra}@ntnu.no
[2] Faculty of Education, Inland Norway University of Applied Sciences, Hamar, Norway
karen.parish@inn.no

Abstract. In this study, two teachers in a Norwegian school participated to provide their perspectives on the three-day workshop conducted for Grade 6 students about human-robot interaction (HRI) for learning. The workshop was performed during the COVID-19 pandemic. Teachers who observed students' behavior during the HRI workshop were interviewed to understand their attitudes towards the use of social robots in educational settings and their perceptions about how the students experienced this. A semi-structured interview was conducted to explore the attitudes and perceptions of the teachers. After performing thematic analysis of the interview data, the study concludes that the robotics learning setup might not be suitable for all subjects. For example, our data analysis reveals that the use of social robots is more suited to Programming, but it is not so well suited for Mathematics; The teachers perceived that the students were happy about their session with social robots, but teachers were concerned that their excitement may fade away with time. In addition, there were concerns over the practicalities of having social robots in class.

Keywords: Robotics · Covid · Pandemic · Human-robot-interaction · HRI · Teacher perspective · Thematic analysis

1 Introduction

To keep the attention of the students focused, it is necessary that the teaching and learning activities are made interesting and enjoyable. Incorporating the social robots into the classroom not only make the teaching-learning process smoother, but also enjoyable and convenient for both the student and the teacher. This facilitates teachers to communicate themselves in innovative ways and provides a wonderful opportunity to students to explore the topics of their choice and clarify their doubts too. Social robots frequently include human like characteristics such as gesture, moving, face, eyes, hearing, and speech. They can play role as friends for students as well as teaching assistant for teachers. Previous studies [1, 2] have also mentioned the role of robots in education in different roles such as teachers, assistants, classmates/peers and entertainers. Past research studies suggest that social robots might be extremely beneficial and can improve

M. Kurosu and A. Hashizume (Eds.): HCII 2023, LNCS 14013, pp. 156–168, 2023.
https://doi.org/10.1007/978-3-031-35602-5_12

learning outcomes and accomplishments [3–5]. However, it is important to introduce social robots in the school learning environment with effective robotic pedagogies and underlying theoretical foundations that are required for educational modules in STEM education [6].

In this regard, Mishra et al. [7] presented a multidisciplinary framework that integrates the following four perspectives: technological, pedagogical, efficacy of humanoid robots and a consideration of the ethical implications of using humanoid robots. This framework also highlights the role of other important actors such as educators and peers on the learning of an individual student. Therefore, it is important to understand the perspective of both the teachers and the students regarding the integration of the social robot to improve the traditional teaching learning methods. One research study showed the point of view of students and teachers both about inclusion of social robots in which students were great supporters while teachers were more cautious and indicating some issues [8]. Ewijk et al. demonstrated the perspective of teachers about advantages and disadvantages of incorporating social robots and teachers raised a variety of issues such as privacy concerns, affection [9]. Fridin et al. included a survey of 18 teachers with questionnaires in their research study and showed participants willingness towards incorporating robots through their favorable responses and acceptance [10].

The robot has also played a significant role during extraordinary situation e.g. COVID-19 pandemic through being integrated in the educational field. The COVID-19 pandemic wreaks havoc all over the globe and poses a serious threat to public health. The education sector is also affected by this pandemic. In view of the need to protect life, many courses have had to run online. Therefore, technological advancements were anticipated to alter the routine activities in education [11]. Research suggests that the involvement of autonomous service robots as a teaching assistant has progressed contactless educational activities during the pandemic [12]. The present study was conducted during COVID-19 pandemic in Spring 2021 in a Norwegian school and focuses on the perspective of the teachers towards the inclusion of humanoid robots in an educational setting.

Since research findings are mixed and ambiguous regarding the robot's influence on students' learning and psychosocial aspects [13, 14]. Therefore, this paper investigates the attitudes and perceptions of teachers to contribute to our understanding of these ambiguities with the following research question: *What are teachers' attitudes and perceptions of social robots as classroom assistants regarding student learning and experiences?* This paper is a part of a larger study that explored students' attitude and perspective towards humanoid robots as classroom assistants [13, 15]. The paper is organized in following sections. Details of methodology used is described in Sect. 2. In Sect. 3, we elaborated the data analysis steps. Results and discussion is explained in Sect. 4. Finally, we conclude the research study in Sect. 5.

2 Methodology

A three-day workshop was conducted in Norway with grade 6 students in their class where social robots were used as classroom assistants to teach Programming and Mathematics. This workshop was organized during the covid pandemic in the Autumn of

2020 therefore only one member of the research team was physically present to conduct the workshop and the other members joined remotely via Zoom. The study conforms to the ethical guidelines for experimental studies set by the Norwegian Social Science Data Services (NSD). Written informed consent was obtained from participants and their parents/guardians. The interview data was recorded and stored using Nettskjema, a secure online provider authorized by the author´s research institutions.

Data Collection. The study has a naturalistic field experiment design, and the data was collected in the participants' everyday environment [16]. The exploratory approach of this research with a focus on teachers' nuanced attitudes and perceptions, lends itself to a qualitative approach. Therefore, interviews - especially focus group interviews - are an appropriate approach [17] By using a small focus group, we enabled relaxed discussions and ideas due to the interactions between the participants [17]. The semi-structured interviews were conducted in their everyday work environment (school meeting room) which was familiar to them to initiate more relaxed conversations.

Participants and Procedure. For this study, participants were 2 teachers who are teaching Grade 6 students. These teachers are employed at a state-subsidized private primary school in Norway where English is the teaching language and emphasis is placed on aspects such as international-mindedness and scientific and technical innovation within learning. Also, these teachers had been with the class for some months and knew the students well. The teachers were interviewed about a three-day workshop which was conducted for grade 6 students where they were introduced to a social robot, Robbie. The students and teachers began with an hour-long introduction about the project, what robots are, and the basics of how robots work. Teachers played the role of silent observers while students had their sessions with the social robot. After the students' session with robot, teachers had a casual talk with the students to find out about the student´s experience of the session.

Methods and Tools. A semi-structured interview guide was used focusing on the teachers' attitudes and perceptions of using the social robot as a classroom assistant to teach the Programming and Mathematics tasks, including aspects of the how they perceived the students to feel about using the robot for learning and what could be the impacts of this on the students. The focus interview lasted about 30–45 min. The interviews were recorded using Nettskjema, a secure online provider, and then transcribed to a word document.

To analyze the interview data 'thematic analysis' was conducted as it resonates with the constructivist epistemology of the study. Thematic analysis involves finding repeated meanings across a data set, which is crucial to the interpretation of phenomena [18]. In [19] "Using Thematic Analysis in Psychology," a step-by-step approach to Thematic Analysis is described and now it is referred to as ´Reflexive Thematic Analysis [20]. In addition, Braun & Clarke's (2019) Thematic Analysis is described as a theoretically flexible method rather than "a theoretically informed and constrained methodology". As this is a pilot study to know teacher' perspective, analysis is kept more qualitative and flexible, so that actual voice of participants remain intact.

To work with the data, data was transcribed to a word document and anonymized. Afterwards, the printout of the transcriptions and traditional tools such as pens, highlighters, and post-it notes were used to read and analyze the printed data. Although these days digital analysis software packages such as NVivo are widely used for the thematic analysis [21], yet it has been argued in the study conducted by Basit [22] that choices about the approach used to analyze data depend upon various factors such as the size of the project, experience of researchers with available means, time available and preferences of researchers involved in the study.

3   Data Analysis

As already described, this study used Thematic Analysis for data analysis, this section details how different six steps of thematic analysis are conducted for data in hand. The pipeline followed is shown in Fig. 1.

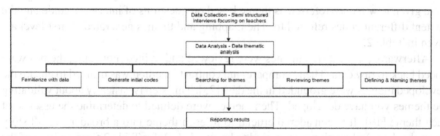

Fig. 1. Pipeline followed for reporting results

First step to perform thematic analysis is to familiarize yourself with the data. Initial understanding of data started while we were in the process of transcribing the interview data. Afterwards, several readings of transcribed data along with interview guide was done to get in depth understanding of the data.

Second step of thematic analysis is to generate initial codes. A simple rule was followed 'mark down keywords which make sense towards the set research question'. Highlighter on paper was used to highlight the sentences from which keywords emerged. As *"a good thematic code is the one that captures the qualitative richness of the phenomenon"* [23] and *"describes the bulk of the data"* [24], initial codes can also be data driven in order to fully capture participants' views. Although it has been said that an integration of inductive and deductive coding reflects a balanced, comprehensive view of the data, instead of purely relying on the frequency of codes decontextualized from their context [25]. This study used inductive coding only due to 'unavailability of initial codes', as it will be biased to assume any initial codes based only on literature. Rather it is expected that codes generated through this study will serve as initial codes to the upcoming studies planned in the same direction. Table 1 shows the different codes developed along with the examples of the sentences it emerged from. Few codes came from repetitive use of words and their synonyms in the ongoing context, for example, 'overwhelmingly positive', 'very interested' was used to express the feel of students towards robot learning. Thus, those sentences have been put under code name 'Positive feedback from students. While few codes evolved from interview guide as well. For example, when participants asked about 'what they think of robot learning setup in case of mathematics, programming, or other subjects. Thus, in response participants provided some strong opinions towards these and hence codename 'mathematics' and 'programming' emerged. Later in the process of coding, it was also observed that some of the responses belonged to more than two codes (already defined). Those codes were recorded as it is, instead of giving new code names to those (refer row 4 and 5 of Table 1 for example), to avoid defining new codes and losing meaning in the process.

Initialization of code is followed by the validation of codes before developing the themes. To do so, the list of code was discussed among all the authors.

Next step of thematic analysis is to search for relevant themes. The searching for themes involved considering how relevant codes can be sorted, collated, and combined to form an overarching theme [26]. It commenced after the data set had been initially coded, with the development of preliminary codes. To start with, content under different codes, which delivered similar interpretations was put under one category. These categories were given new names referred as theme based on questions of interview guide and the content different codes referred to. The mapping and themes generated at first level are given in Table 2.

Afterwards, as next step themes were reviewed and refined. For same, themes were traced back to raw data. Then "compare-and contrast" method was utilized to ensure the developed themes were grounded in the data [23]. This step is basically about validating the themes you have developed. Then themes were defined to determine the essence of each theme [19]. It is considered crucial to fit each theme into a broader overall story about the data, and overlap is supposed to be avoided. Refer Table 2 for definition of the different themes derived.

4   Results and Discussion

As discussed in previous sections, two teachers in a Norwegian school participated in observing a three-day social robot workshop with their grade 6 class. Following this they participated in a semi-structured interview. Along with their attitudes and perceptions about student involvement during the workshop they also discussed their ideas about improvement of experimental setups in future so that students feel more comfortable while interacting with robots. Following thematic analysis three subthemes emerged; 'Student Experience', 'Possibility to add robotics in the curriculum' and 'Suggestions to improve study setup'. Further we present the results that consists of analytic narratives and

Table 1. Generating Initial Codes

Code	Example	Respondent
Positive feedback from students	*..thing for me was the feedback from the students was overwhelmingly positive......it beforehand but once it got started they were excited ...*	P1
	....we told what they've done so they they had a very good time..........they knew what they were going for and they were still interested.........	P2
Challenges Faced	*.....was a little bit of challenge in terms of what we could do with them like having one group out and then the other three groups in....* *....that we can't move the kids around you know from group to group and there aren't a lot of things that we couldn't do,...*	P1
Suggestions	*.........do it during warmer months yeah so at least we can take them outside you know and break up the monotony of being in here ...*	P1
	....This particular experiment is probably not appropriate for the lower grades but there's you know it certainly fits into where where we are...	P1
Mathematics	*....Math anxiety is a real concern here and so that that there's that probably is one thing that's at play,...*	P1
	...I can definitely see it in math, I mean you know but but um math is not the only no no right...	P1
Mathematics, feedback from students	*...were getting feedback from students about mathletics and about how it being impersonal was not attractive to them and honestly I was kind of surprised by that because the way that it is. ---*	P1

(continued)

Table 1. (*continued*)

Code	Example	Respondent
Mathematics, challenges	*....challenging with math is because math is already quite dry subject and then if you remove remove the human and emotional component from such a dry subject then what are you left with I mean I would think that if the robot is not engaging enough*	P2
Programming	*... said I'm not sure if you would with repeated the the exercise would it still be engaging to them because they have already done it once so you know maybe the magic would have worn off so that I cannot say*	P2
	Because like what I what I hear when when you say that they went in the programming they were very engaged they were they they liked that part of it	P1
Student Engagement	*said I'm not sure if you would with repeated the the exercise would it still be engaging to them because they have already done it once so you know maybe the magic would have worn off so that I cannot say*	P2
Student Engagement, Programming	*......but then you see that you are basically looking at the level of complexity of the task and then it's again it's about engagement it is just more levels that kids can engage with a more complex puzzle type of task than than just simple block coding....*	P2

selected examples capturing the essence of the data with quotes directly from participants [27].

Student Experience: Teachers expressed that students were happy and excited to interact with the social robots, they used some strong words such as '*overwhelmingly positive*' to explain student' experience.

> "*I think that the most telling thing for me was the feedback from the students was overwhelmingly positive.*"

One teacher explained an incident where one student wanted to join the school for the session with the robot even when they were injured.

Table 2. Searching and deriving themes and definition

Question of interview Guide	Theme Name	Definition	Code Name
….We are interested in your thoughts about how students felt about the robot learning?…	Student Experience	This theme will reflect the student behavior towards robot learning setup	Student feedback, Student Engagement
…..Do you anticipate that the robot could be inserted somehow in curriculum	Possibility to add robotic in Curriculum	This theme represents the set of views which reflect on feasibility of robotics in curriculum of different subjects	Mathematics Programming Obstacles
…although they could see the potential of using the robot if it's already programmed with math tasks to be maybe an assistant you know or like just something to motivate them maybe but they were definitely more interested in the programming weren't they …?	Suggestions to improve study setup	This theme represents the set of views that provides suggestions and feedback for the experiment conducted	Challenges faced, Suggestions

"*Yeah and yeah they even one of them came to school when they were injured just to be able to take part because it was their groups turn to go.*"

Although participants also shared their concern about the students that their excitement may be temporary and later, they may find social robots monotonous to work with. As quoted by one participant as given:

"*I'm not sure if you would with repeated the exercise would it still be engaging to them because they have already done it once, so you know maybe the magic would have worn off so that I cannot say.*"

Teachers were also worried that students may behave with social robots as toys. But they also emphasized the fact that if learning exercises will be engaging and interesting enough robots can bring great learning experience for the school students. Smakman et al. [28] in their study also reported that robots are fun in education, yet it increases the work for teachers as they need to look for the activities to be more engaging and interesting with children. Similarly, Alhashmi et al. [8] and Khanlari et al. [29] reported that the students were generally appreciative of the incorporation of humanoid robots as co-teachers, whereas the teachers were more circumspect, expressing some concerns and noting a desire to better streamline the process of bringing robots to the classroom.

Possibility to Add Robotics in the Curriculum. Further, discussion was inclined towards 'if any possibility lies for robots to be part of the school subject curriculum?' We received a mix response from teachers. One of the responses was positive to incorporating social robots into a unit on 'cyberspace'. In class they had a unit called 'Digital citizenship' and during this unit they had discussed as a class the following question.

"if you have a robot does the robot exist in cyberspace?" and that proved to be like a question that we revisited again and again and again throughout the unit. So, I think that that there is definitely opportunity to insert that in into that unit for sure and other places maybe"

Teachers responded positively towards the involvement of robots for higher technical subjects, but they were not sure about every subject in the primary curriculum for all school students as one of the teacher quoted:

"Math anxiety is a real concern here and so that there's that probably is one thing that's at play. So there is a need or a desire on their part to have some interaction as opposed to you know an artificial intelligence"

Here, the teacher implies that for Mathematics there is a need for more human intervention, as robots are not fully reliable for teaching and learning, and students may find some subjects tough as compared to others for instance most students find Mathematics subject as challenging one. If young children lack the relevant knowledge in STEM subjects such as Mathematics, introducing robots in such subjects may have adverse effect on their learning since there is a danger of engaging students in activities that could be considered "doing without learning" [30]. Another perspective was shared by the teacher participant of the study conducted by Istenic et al. [31], that interpreted as it is not enough to just involve robots in the class for learning but innovation in the instructional approaches while utilizing robots is also needed. And we further argue that this innovation in instructional approach will vary from subject to subject. Other responses of both the teachers for subject mathematics are as follows:

"they are much more concerned about that personal relationship that's an aspect of so in terms of the math anxiety this is something that I've practiced over the course of the last probably five years since math anxiety has become interesting to me"

"they found it challenging with math is because math is already quite dry subject and then if you remove the human and emotional component from such a dry subject then what are you left with I mean I would think that if the robot is not engaging enough like magically engaging then then you hold your engagement"

But teachers shared very opposite view about incorporating robots for learning programming as they said:

"it's different because Coding I don't think that coding at that level, especially with blocks you use, is that dry. I think that it's quite puzzle like so they find it interesting it that there has more than one layer that would engage them, however as"

"Because like what I what I hear when you say that they went in the programming they were very engaged they were they liked that part of it and the math part not so much"

Teachers also highlighted that programming can be taught as puzzle games along with robots. Students will enjoy the learning through interesting tasks. From the above responses of teachers', it can be deduced that students' engagement depends on the subject and the extent of robot's involvement in learning. Adapting robots in the curriculum not only will be challenging for students but for teachers as well as stated by Tzagkaraki et al. [32] 'including robot in curriculum can bring challenges for teacher due to less technical knowledge about robot'. Similarly, the study conducted by Reich-Stiebert et al. [33] reported teacher's concerns like increase in workload, disruption in regular teaching practices etc.. Thus, it can be said that overall teachers' perspective for use of robots is not only influenced by their knowledge and experience in teaching but also from their personal reluctance towards changes that a robot can bring in the classroom learning.

Suggestions to Improve Study Setup. Lastly, there were some discussions about how experimental sessions should be carried out in future. Participants expressed their views on which season of the year is good to conduct this kind of study, so that no other academic activities of students are hampered. As said by one participant:

"..one of the things that challenged you was the short amount of time that you had with them and from our perspective that seemed like a long time right..."

"..do it during warmer months yeah so at least we can take them outside you know and break up the monotony of being in here.."

Also, one participant quoted that:

"This particular experiment is probably not appropriate for the lower grades."

Teachers emphasized on having longer and more flexible time duration for next session, and this was obvious feedback from their side as the current session was conducted during short day hours of winters and that was under corona restrictions too. As results reported by Nugent et al. [34] and Davison et al. [35] were in contradiction to this, where they highlighted that shorter interaction with robots keeps the excitement among students. Thus, in future study sessions we aim to set a time window which is sufficient for learning of a subject topic and yet students do not lose interest.

5 Conclusion and Future Work

The present study focused upon teachers' attitudes and perceptions towards the involvement of social robots as classrooms assistants for students leaning. Teachers found students experience with robots was great as most of the students were happy and positive towards robot involvement in their studies. Further, teachers suggested that the social robot is not suitable for every subject in the curriculum. They found that students enjoyed Programming but struggled with Mathematics when the robot was included in the experiment. Teachers also recommended the implementation of further sessions and suggested the incorporation of the social robot into the curriculum. This should keep students more engaging and interesting towards the subject, so that excitement of students remain the same.

In the present paper we incorporated the views of two teachers only, but in future we will plan to include more teachers in the study. In the current scenario teachers' participated as silent observer, we will propose to include teachers during the robot-students sessions so that they can not only observe interactions in real time but also can participate actively. Robots may act as teaching assistants as well so that teachers may get actual feeling about robot capabilities. We will include teachers in designing the study set up as well, therefore we can get idea about type of questions, durations of sessions and interest of students. We will also attempt to involve more schools and different grade students for conducting the experiment. This will definitely help us to understand the experience with robots in a better way. But it is challenging for teachers to participate throughout due to their teaching engagements. Teachers are also generally comfortable with their traditional ways of teaching; they may be hesitant to participate in the study due to technology challenges. These might be the factors which could affect the results of the study as well.

References

1. Newton, D.P., Newton, L.D.: Humanoid robots as teachers and a proposed code of practice. Front. Educ. **4**, 125 (2019)
2. Randall, N.: A survey of robot-assisted language learning (RALL). ACM Trans. Hum. Robot Interact. (THRI) **9**(1), 1–36 (2019)
3. Movellan, J., Eckhardt, M., Virnes, M., Rodriguez, A.: Sociable robot improves toddler vocabulary skills. In: Proceedings of the 4th ACM/IEEE International Conference on Human Robot Interaction, pp. 307–308 (2009)
4. Belpaeme, T., Kennedy, J., Ramachandran, A., Scassellati, B., Tanaka, F.: Social robots for education: a review. Sci. Robot. **3**(21), eaat5954 (2018)
5. Alemi, M., Meghdari, A., Ghazisaedy, M.: The effect of employing humanoid robots for teaching English on students' anxiety and attitude. In: 2014 Second RSI/ISM International Conference on Robotics and Mechatronics (ICRoM), pp. 754–759. IEEE (2014)
6. Anwar, S., Bascou, N.A., Menekse, M., Kardgar, A.: A systematic review of studies on educational robotics. J. Pre-Coll. Eng. Educ. Res. (J-PEER) **9**(2), 2 (2019)
7. Mishra, D., Parish, K., Lugo, R.G., Wang, H.: A framework for using humanoid robots in the school learning environment. Electronics **10**(6), 756 (2021)
8. Alhashmi, M., Mubin, O., Baroud, R.: Examining the use of robots as teacher assistants in UAE classrooms: teacher and student perspectives. J. Inf. Technol. Educ. Res., 245–261 (2021)
9. van Ewijk, G., Smakman, M., Konijn, E.A.: Teachers' perspectives on social robots in education: an exploratory case study. In: Proceedings of the Interaction Design and Children Conference, pp. 273–280 (2020)
10. Fridin, M., Belokopytov, M.: Acceptance of socially assistive humanoid robot by preschool and elementary school teachers. Comput. Hum. Behav. **33**, 23–31 (2014)

11. Wang, X.V., Wang, L.: A literature survey of the robotic technologies during the COVID-19 pandemic. J. Manuf. Syst. **60**, 823–836 (2021)
12. Al Tarabsheh, A., et al.: Towards contactless learning activities during pandemics using autonomous service robots. Appl. Sci. **11**(21), 10449 (2021)
13. Tilden, S., Lugo, R.G., Parish, K., Mishra, D., Knox, B.J.: Gender differences in psychosocial experiences with humanoid robots, programming, and mathematics course. In: Stephanidis, C., et al. (eds.) HCII 2021. LNCS, vol. 13096, pp. 480–490. Springer, Cham (2021). https://doi.org/10.1007/978-3-030-90328-2_32
14. Gunbatar, M.S., Karalar, H.: Gender differences in middle school students' attitudes and self-efficacy perceptions towards mBlock programming. Eur. J. Educ. Res. **7**(4), 925–933 (2018)
15. Mishra, D., Lugo, R., Parish, K., Tilden, S.: Metacognitive processes involved in human robot interaction in the school learning environment. In: International Conference on Human-Computer Interaction (2023)
16. Coolican, H.: Research Methods and Statistics in Psychology. Psychology Press (2017)
17. Howitt, D.: Introduction to Qualitative Research Methods in Psychology: Putting Theory into Practice. Pearson UK (2019)
18. Vaismoradi, M., Turunen, H., Bondas, T.: Content analysis and thematic analysis: implications for conducting a qualitative descriptive study. Nurs. Health Sci. **15**(3), 398–405 (2013)
19. Braun, V., Clarke, V.: Using thematic analysis in psychology. Qual. Res. Psychol. **3**(2), 77–101 (2006)
20. Braun, V., Clarke, V.: Reflecting on reflexive thematic analysis. Qual. Res. Sport Exerc. Health **11**(4), 589–597 (2019)
21. Maher, C., Hadfield, M., Hutchings, M., De Eyto, A.: Ensuring rigor in qualitative data analysis: a design research approach to coding combining NVivo with traditional material methods. Int. J. Qual. Methods **17**(1), 1609406918786362 (2018)
22. Basit, T.: Manual or electronic? The role of coding in qualitative data analysis. Educ. Res. **45**(2), 143–154 (2003)
23. Boyatzis, R.E.: Transforming Qualitative Information: Thematic Analysis and Code Development. Sage (1998)
24. Joffe, H.: Thematic analysis. Qual. Res. Methods Mental Health Psychother. **1**, 210–223 (2012)
25. Xu, W., Zammit, K.: Applying thematic analysis to education: a hybrid approach to interpreting data in practitioner research. Int. J. Qual. Methods **19**, 1609406920918810 (2020)
26. Nowell, L.S., Norris, J.M., White, D.E., Moules, N.J.: Thematic analysis: striving to meet the trustworthiness criteria. Int. J. Qual. Methods **16**(1), 1609406917733847 (2017)
27. Fereday, J., Muir-Cochrane, E.: Demonstrating rigor using thematic analysis: a hybrid approach of inductive and deductive coding and theme development. Int. J. Qual. Methods **5**(1), 80–92 (2006)
28. Smakman, M., Vogt, P., Konijn, E.A.: Moral considerations on social robots in education: a multi-stakeholder perspective. Comput. Educ. **174**, 104317 (2021)
29. Khanlari, A.: Teachers' perceptions of the benefits and the challenges of integrating educational robots into primary/elementary curricula. Eur. J. Eng. Educ. **41**(3), 320–330 (2016)
30. Barak, M., Assal, M.: Robotics and STEM learning: students' achievements in assignments according to the P3 task taxonomy—practice, problem solving, and projects. Int. J. Technol. Des. Educ. **28**(1), 121–144 (2016). https://doi.org/10.1007/s10798-016-9385-9
31. Istenic, A., Bratko, I., Rosanda, V.: Pre-service teachers' concerns about social robots in the classroom: a model for development. Educ. Self Dev. **16**(2), 60–87 (2021)

32. Tzagkaraki, E., Papadakis, S., Kalogiannakis, M.: Exploring the use of educational robotics in primary school and its possible place in the curricula. In: Malvezzi, M., Alimisis, D., Moro, M. (eds.) EDUROBOTICS 2021. SCI, vol. 982, pp. 216–229. Springer, Cham (2021). https://doi.org/10.1007/978-3-030-77022-8_19

33. Reich-Stiebert, N., Eyssel, F.: Robots in the classroom: what teachers think about teaching and learning with education robots. In: Agah, A., Cabibihan, JJ., Howard, A., Salichs, M., He, H. (eds.) ICSR 2016. LNCS, vol. 9979, pp. 671–680. Springer, Cham. (2016). https://doi.org/10.1007/978-3-319-47437-3_66

34. Nugent, G., Barker, B., Grandgenett, N., Adamchuk, V.I.: Impact of robotics and geospatial technology interventions on youth STEM learning and attitudes. J. Res. Technol. Educ. **42**(4), 391–408 (2010)

35. Davison, D.P., Wijnen, F.M., Charisi, V., van der Meij, J., Evers, V., Reidsma, D.: Working with a social robot in school: a long-term real-world unsupervised deployment. In: 2020 15th ACM/IEEE International Conference on Human-Robot Interaction (HRI), pp. 63–72. IEEE (2020)

Applying the Social Robot Expectation Gap Evaluation Framework

Julia Rosén[1], Erik Billing[1], and Jessica Lindblom[1,2]

[1] Interaction Lab, University of Skövde, Box 408, 541 28 Skövde, Sweden
{julia.rosen,jessica.lindblom}@his.se
[2] Department of Information Technology, Uppsala University,
Box 337, 751 05 Uppsala, Sweden

Abstract. Expectations shape our experience with the world, including our interaction with technology. There is a mismatch between what humans expect of social robots and what they are actually capable of. Expectations are dynamic and can change over time. We have previously developed a framework for studying these expectations over time in human-robot interaction (HRI). In this work, we applied the social robot expectation gap evaluation framework in an HRI scenario from a UX evaluation perspective, by analyzing a subset of data collected from a larger experiment. The framework is based on three factors of expectation: affect, cognitive processing, as well as behavior and performance. Four UX goals related to a human-robot interaction scenario were evaluated. Results show that expectations change over time with an overall improved UX in the second interaction. Moreover, even though some UX goals were partly fulfilled, there are severe issues with the conversation between the user and the robot, ranging from the quality of the interaction to the users' utterances not being recognized by the robot. This work takes the initial steps towards disentangling how expectations work and change over time in HRI. Future work includes expanding the metrics to study expectations and to further validate the framework.

Keywords: Human-robot interaction · Social robots · Expectations · User experience · Evaluation · Expectation gap

1 Introduction

Although still on the brink to the general public, social robots and their extent of being situated in our everyday activities in society are becoming more sophisticated and common [3,6,17] which increases the expectations of such robots [7,10,12,14,16,24]. Social robots need to be able to communicate and act 'naturally' with their human users, not only on the socio-cognitive level but on user experience (UX) level. Social robots also need to achieve their intended benefits and support for human users [3,5,15,23,24]. The majority of human users have either no first-hand experience or very limited experience of interacting first-hand with social robots [12,14,16,24]. Human users' main exposure to social

© The Author(s), under exclusive license to Springer Nature Switzerland AG 2023
M. Kurosu and A. Hashizume (Eds.): HCII 2023, LNCS 14013, pp. 169–188, 2023.
https://doi.org/10.1007/978-3-031-35602-5_13

robots is predominantly from movies and the media, which may result in false and incorrect expectations of social robots [7,10,11,26].

As pointed out by Stephanidis et al. [29], there is an identified need for the evaluation of interactive artificial systems to go beyond mere performance-based approaches that focus mainly on pragmatic qualities to embrace the over-all user experience that also considers hedonic qualities. The authors argue that more traditional usability evaluation approaches in human-computer interaction (HCI) are rather insufficient for new interactive artificial systems, including social robots. Social robots are equipped with new perception and sensing possibilities, which enable them to shift initiatives via mutual action and intention recognition in conversations, displaying variations in morphology via having human-like attributes, and endowed with perceived socio-cognitive abilities. Moreover, there is an ongoing shift in application purposes, going from digital systems as being task-oriented tools to being considered as social companions or peers per se [2]. The identified challenges with these artificial systems include the need to interpret signals from multiple communication channels [29]. These channels could be eye and gaze following, pointing, body language, speech, and conversation in social robots that are conducted in a more natural way for the sake of social interaction. The unsuitability of task-specific measures in social robots, which predominantly are rather 'taskless', and therefore more focus should be on social interaction for the sake of companionship and creating a relationship. Stephanidis et al. [29] emphasized that if one should consider the enormous number of quality characteristics that should be evaluated in such human-artificial intelligent environments, like social human-robot interaction (HRI), it has become evident that new assessment methods are required. Hence, new frameworks and models are needed in order to provide holistic and systematic approaches for the evaluation of UX in human-artificial intelligent environments.

Roto et al. [25] noted that there are several overlaps between users' expectations as well as users' experiences when interacting with advanced artificial intelligence systems. User expectations could indicate the anticipated behavior, direct the focus of attention, serve as a source of reference for the actual UX and how it is interpreted, and subsequently has an impact on the user's overall perception of artificially intelligent systems [13]. Therefore, expectations often have a serious influence on the formation of the actual user experience of the social robot. This statement stresses that performing research on expectations can reveal a deeper understanding of the central aspects of user experience. One of the main components of UX, which is often missing in social robotics and HRI research, is the temporal aspect of the interaction [25].

Although there is limited research on the temporal aspect of expectations in HRI, there is some related research conducted on the changes in expectations. Paetzel et al. [21] investigated how persistent the first impression of a robot is, with different perceptual dimensions stabilizing at different points over three interactions. In the study, competence was stabilized after the initial two minutes in the first interaction, anthropomorphism and likeability were set after the second interaction, and perceived threat and discomfort were unstable until the last interaction. Serholt and Barendrgt [27] found that children's social engagement towards a tutoring robot decreased over time, suggesting that the human-human interaction (HHI) model of engagement faded out, or were used more seldom, as the robots did not meet children's expectations for engagement. Edwards et al. [7] found expectations of a robot have an effect on first impressions, displaying more certainty and greater social presence after the brief interaction.

Despite the recent interest in expectations in social robots in the HRI field, there was a lack of an evaluation framework that offers a deeper understanding of how these expectations affect the success of the human-robot interaction from a first-hand perspective. Therefore, we developed the social robot expectation gap evaluation framework [24]. The framework provides a methodological approach for investigating and analyzing users' expectations before, during, and after inter-action with a social robot from a human-centered perspective [24]. The frame-work has its foundation in the social psychological expectation process developed by Olson et al. [20] and user experience (UX) evaluation methodology [8,15,23]. The framework contains three main factors in which users' expectations can be evaluated: affect, cognitive processing, as well as behavior and performance. Sev-eral UX goals and related metrics were formulated for each factor, which relates to either pragmatic or hedonic qualities of the social human-robot interaction experience [8,9,15]. Moreover, the framework contains a four-phased evaluation procedure that consists of 1) identifying the scenario, 2) collecting data, 3) ana-lyzing the collected data, and 4) reporting on findings and recommendations (for details, see Rosén et al., [24]).

In this paper, we report on how parts of the social robot expectation gap evaluation framework [24] are applied in an empirical UX evaluation. Our study is exemplified by a subset of data collected from a larger study on the role and relevance of expectations in social HRI, which examined how expectations may affect the forthcoming interaction quality and how expectations may alter user experience over time. The main contributions of this paper are two-fold; first, it provides an initial validation and testing of a sub-part of the framework which systematically studies how users' expectations may be altered if their initial expectations are not confirmed and its impact on user experience. Second, the implications of the findings highlight that expectations are especially important to understand when they are disconfirmed as this can guide and inform the future design of social robots, which will ultimately lead to more successful interactions.

2   The Social Robot Expectation Gap Evaluation Framework

The social robot expectation gap evaluation framework has its foundation in the social psychological expectation process developed by Olson et al. [20] and user experience (UX) evaluation methodology [8,15]. The framework is shown in Table 1. Drawing from the model by Olson et al. [20], we here briefly present the main characteristics of expectations as described in Rosén et al. [24]. In our modified model, we present expectations as formed by i) direct experience, ii) other people or robots, and iii) beliefs. Direct experience is the expectations built on first-hand experience, i.e., from an actual encounter with a social robot, which is usually lacking in HRI research on expectations. Expectations that are built on direct experience are a stronger predictor of future behavior [20]. Other people or robots are expectations from indirect experiences, such as views from peers and friends or from exposure to social robots in various ways in movies and other media. Beliefs are sources of expectations that can be inferred from other beliefs, e.g., a robot may be evil because they usually are depicted as such in science fiction.

Regardless of its origins, expectations can vary in four dimensions: certainty, accessibility, explicitness, and importance [20]. Certainty is the subjective estimated probability of how likely it is that the outcome will occur. Accessibility is how easy it is to activate and use a certain expectation. Explicitness is what degree expectations are consciously generated. Some expectations are implicitly assumed, usually related to the degree of certainty, whereas other expectations are consciously reflected upon. Importance is the expectation's significance, the higher the importance, the higher the impact.

As explained by the model, there are consequences of expectations, which is the main focus for our framework [20,24]. These factors can be divided into three categories: i) affective, ii) cognitive processing and iii) behavioral and performance. Affective refers to emotions and feelings, such as anxiety. Cognitive processing refers to factors that have an effect on our cognitive processes, such as interpretation and memory abilities. Behavioral and performance refer to consequences that cause a course of actions due to expectations, like forming intentions to act. Behavior and performance are the factors that cause changes in the user's deliberate actions. Expectations serve as the basis for essentially any behavior since expectations initiate our intentions and actions.

The above factors are the consequence of when expectations are confirmed or disconfirmed [20]. Confirmed expectations often result in positive affect and feelings that are frequently performed implicitly and effortlessly, resulting in expectations that are maintained with greater certainty. Confirmed expectations may also, in rare situations, produce secondary (positive or negative) affect since the inferences are made after confirming the expectations. On the contrary, disconfirmed expectations often end up with negative effects and are usually considered explicitly since they are perceived as surprising and therefore need heavy cognitive processing in order to interpret and understand the contradiction. We further illustrate confirmed and disconfirmed expectations with the social robot expectation gap [24] depicted in Fig. 1. The social robot expectation gap demonstrates the two spaces of disconfirmed expectations, which either is the result of too high or too low expectations, balancing on the thin line of confirmed expectations. The underlying cause of disconfirmed expectations, either too high or too low, is the perceived or experienced mismatch between the social robot's capabilities and the user's expectations of the social robot which positively or negatively affects the overall interaction quality, and hence the perceived user experience of

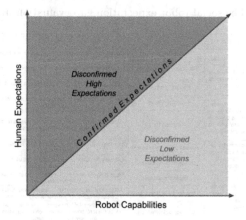

Fig. 1. The social robot expectation gap, with the two spaces of disconfirmed expectations that occurs when a robot's capabilities do not align with the user's expected capabilities [24, p. 599].

the social HRI. It should be pointed out that in the case that the user's expectations are low, there is a risk that the user underestimates the robot's actual social interaction capabilities which may result in less curious inquiry and exploration, resulting in less discovery of its interaction capabilities – resulting in a poor user experience. Similarly, in the case when the user's expectations are very high and the user overestimates the robot's interaction capabilities, assuming that the robot is equipped with advanced socio-cognitive interaction abilities, the outcome may be disappointment and frustration because the user feels deceived – resulting in a poor user experience. A user may also have rather low or moderate expectations of the social robot, but through inquiry during the interaction with the robot that develops into an ongoing and mutual dialogue, the user may be positively surprised by the robot's social interaction capabilities, feeling satisfied and noticed by the robot, resulting in positive user experience.

The current version of our developed evaluation framework for expectations was created in order to investigate the consequences of users' high and low expectations of social robots when interacting with a social robot – before, during, and after the interaction. The evaluation procedure consists of four phases: 1) identifying the scenario, 2) collecting data, 3) analyzing the collected data, and 4) reporting on findings and recommendations (for details, see Rosén et al. [24]). The framework should be viewed as modular, where UX goals and metrics can be added or removed in order to target the different expectations factors. Included in the framework are the formulated UX goals and the metrics (data collection techniques) used to assess the three main factors. These UX goals and metrics can be found in Table 1. Each metric relates to either hedonic or pragmatic qualities [9].

Table 1. The social robot expectation gap evaluation framework

Expectation Factors	UX Goal	Metric	Details	Qualities
Affect	The user should expect to have neutral to positive emotions towards the robot	The Negative Attitude Toward Robot Scale (NARS)	A questionnaire measuring user's negative attitudes towards robots	Hedonic
		The Robot Anxiety Scale (RAS)	A questionnaire measuring user's anxiety towards robots	Hedonic
		Facial Expressions	Observing the kinds of facial expressions made by the user	Hedonic
Cognitive Processing	The user should experience effortless cognitive processing during the interaction	Memory Recall	Asking the user to write down what they remember of the interaction	Pragmatic
		Reaction Time	Measuring the time it takes for the user to react accordingly to the robot's output	Pragmatic
Behavior and Performance	The user should expect a pleasant and smooth interaction	Gestures and body language	Observing the kind of gestures and body language the user expresses	Hedonic
		Choice of Conversation	Observing the kinds of conversations the user tend to focus on during the interaction	Hedonic
	The user should expect to have ease of conversation	Repeating Words	Measuring the number of repetions the user makes during the interaction	Pragmatic
		Interruptions of Interaction	Measuring the amount of times, and what kind of, interruptions occur for the user during the interaction	Pragmatic
		Duration of interaction	Measuring the total time spent in the interaction as well as the total time spent on each conversation for the user during the interaction	Pragmatic

3   Method

In this paper, we report on how parts of the social robot expectation gap evaluation framework can be applied from a UX evaluation perspective. This is exemplified by a subset of data collected from a larger experiment on the role and relevance of expectations in social HRI (for a full list of metrics for the full experiment, see Table 1). The structure of this section follows the phases of the framework to illustrate how our testing was performed: scenario, data collection, and data analysis. The final phase, results, is presented in Sect. 4.

Fig. 2. The set-up of the interaction

3.1   Phase 1: Scenario

The developed scenario enabled the human user to interact first-hand with the Pepper robot in our lab. The physical layout of the lab is a $60\,m^2$ room where half of the open space was dedicated to the human-robot interaction setup. The underlying idea was that the user and the robot should be able to get to know each other in a more exploratory way, being engaged in dialogue. There were two interaction sessions in total, lasting 2.5 min each. The users were informed that the study's aim was *to investigate how people interact with a social robot that is intended to be used in the home and that they could ask the robot about anything.* A pilot was conducted to try out the scenario. Once the scenario was chosen, baseline and max levels relating to the UX goals and metrics were set to fit the scenario. The baseline level considered the minimum acceptable level for the interaction and target levels and the desired level for the interaction. These levels are presented in the Subsect. 3.2.

The Robot and the Dialogue System: To study users' expectations of robots from a first-hand perspective, we created a scenario with the social robot Pepper manufactured by Aldebaran [28]. Pepper is a 120 cm tall social robot designed to interact with humans. The *autonomous life* functionality built into the Pepper robots was used, including simulated breathing and awareness (head turns) towards the user [28]. The robot was equipped with a customized dialogue system powered the OpenAI GPT-3 large language model [1], developed by the second author. Users' speech was recorded using the robot's microphones and translated into text using Google's speech-to-text cloud service. Recognized text was sent to the GPT-3 *text-davinci-002* model for computation of suitable dialogue responses. Resulting text responses were transformed into spoken language using the *ALAnimatedSpeech* module, built into the default NaoQi middle-ware delivered with the Pepper robot. The animated speech module produced synthetic speech accompanied by head and arm gestures. A more detailed description of the dialogue system is available in [4]. The motivation for developing the above dialogue system was to enable a more natural, smooth, and intuitive dialogue between the user and the Pepper robot.

3.2 Phase 2: Data Collection

We purposely sampled [22] a subset of ten ($N = 10$) users who were recruited for a larger empirical study in our lab. The inclusion criteria were 1) that they had no prior experience of interacting with social robots, and 2) that they were either Swedish or English native speakers. There were 6 women, 4 men (no-one self-described or chose non-binary), with ages between 20–49 years ($M = 31$). The users were informed of the purpose of the study and informed consent was distributed, read, and signed by the users before the interactions. The evaluation was conducted in accordance with the Declaration of Helsinki.

Once entering the lab, the users filled in a questionnaire with background information about their age, gender, first language, previous experience with robots, and interest in robots. The users were asked to sit on a chair approximately one meter in front of the Pepper robot and were then instructed to engage in open conversation with the robot, with sessions for filling in questionnaires between the two interactions. The two interactions were video recorded. At the end of the two interactions, an open-ended post-test interview was conducted that focused on the users' experience of interacting with the robot. Afterward, the users were debriefed, encouraged to raise any questions, and thanked for their participation. They were informed how the Pepper robot and its speech system functioned. The first author did the data collection. We focused on the following metrics:

The Robot Anxiety Scale (RAS): RAS was collected before the interaction, after the first interaction, and after the second interaction. RAS consists of three subscales with different themes relating to anxiety: S1: anxiety toward communication capability of robots, S2: anxiety toward behavioral characteristics of robots, and S3: anxiety toward discourse with robots. The scale is on a 6-point Likert-scale, with low scores meaning less anxiety (1: I do not feel anxiety at all, 6: I feel anxiety very strongly), and the individual score is calculated by summing the scores for each sub-scale [18,19]. The base levels for RAS before the interaction were for S1: 9, and for S2 and S3: 12; baselines after the first interaction were for S1: 8, and for S2 and S3: 11; and baselines after the second interaction were for S1: 7, and for S2 and S3: 10. Target levels for RAS before the interaction were for S1: 7, S2 and S3: 10; target levels after the first interaction were for S1: 6, S2 and S3: 9; and target levels after the second interaction were for S1: 5, and for S2 and S3: 8.

Interruptions: Video recordings from the interaction for the amount of time the users were interrupted by the robot while talking were collected. The baseline levels for interruptions for the first interaction were 2 and for the second interaction was 1. The target level for the first interaction was 1 and for the second interaction was 0.

Post-test Interview: These five questions were asked after the second interaction: (1) How did you feel the interactions went?, (2) Did you experience any difference between the first and second interaction?, (3) Did you have any expectations of how the interaction would go?, (4) Was anything surprising about the interaction or the robot?, and (5) Did you have any specific emotion during the interaction? The interviews were video recorded and then briefly transcribed.

Observations: Field notes were taken by the first author and video recordings were done for upcoming analysis.

The baseline and target levels were the same for all of the qualitative measures (post-test interviews and observations). The baseline for the first interaction was negative, and the baseline for the second interaction was neutral. The target level for the first interaction was neutral, and the target level for the second interaction was positive.

3.3   Phase 3: Analysis of the Data

The collected data were analyzed via triangulation [8,15,22], in which the collected quantitative and qualitative data were compared and contrasted, focusing on identifying UX problems of coping with disconfirmed expectations. The analysis centered on the four UX goals. Of special interest were if anything required more cognitive processing, affect, or any altered behavior during the interaction. After the data collection, the video recordings of the interaction sessions with the Pepper robot and the post-interviews were analyzed and briefly transcribed by the last author. The transcripts from the video recordings were then analyzed, zooming in on interruptions, repetitions of questions, or hesitations from the users while interacting with the robot. We also analyzed and interpreted the characteristics and content of the human-robot conversations, users' facial expressions, and body language when interacting with the Pepper robot. We particularly looked for evidence and findings in the data that pointed in the same direction, implying that there we identified relevant UX problems that needed to be considered.

4   Results

In this section, the results from the collected quantitative and qualitative data via triangulation [8,15,22] of the RAS questionnaire, number of interruptions as well as the analysis of the observations and interviews are presented. For an overview of the results in relation to the UX goals, see Table 3.

First, the overall findings regarding users' experiences interacting with the Pepper robot and the expectations of interacting with the robot before, during, and after are presented and described. We present whether, or to what extent, the four UX goals are not fulfilled, partly fulfilled or fulfilled in Sect. 4.1. The outcome of the triangulation is then presented for each of the four UX goals, in which the most relevant positive or negative UX aspects related to how users' expectations are presented. The presentation of these findings consists of descriptions of most important identified aspects of expectations and UX problems combined with quotes from the users. In Sect. 4.2, we present some recommendations based on the scope and severity ratings of the identified UX problems.

4.1   Aspects Related to the Four UX Goals

We here portray a more nuanced picture of this particular UX goal and identified UX problems.

UX Goal 1: The User Should Expect to Have Neutral to Positive Emotions Towards the Robot. The findings show that on a general level, this UX goal was not fulfilled. The RAS scores strongly support the claim that this UX goal is fulfilled because it reaches the target levels in all instances, except for RAS subscale 3: anxiety toward discourse with robots, by one point in 'before the interaction'. The data for RAS were collected for each subscale and before the interaction, after the first interaction, and after the second interaction. A high RAS score means higher level of anxiety. The scores are presented for each data collection point: The overall scores for RAS S1 (range: 3–18) were 6

Expectation Factors	UX Goal	Metric	Details	Qualities	Baseline before interaction	Baseline after first interaction	Baseline after second interaction	Target level before interaction	Target level after first interaction	Target level after second interaction	Observed results before interaction	Observed results after first interaction	Observed results after second interaction	Meet target before interaction	Meet target after first interaction	Meet target second interaction
Affect	The user should expect to have neutral to positive emotions towards the robot	The Robot Anxiety Scale (RAS)	A questionnaire measuring user's anxiety towards robots	Hedonic	S1: 9 S2: 12 S3: 12	S1: 8 S2: 11 S3: 11	S1: 7 S2: 10 S3: 10	S1: 7 S2: 10 S3: 10	S1: 6 S2: 9 S3: 9	S1: 5 S2: 8 S3: 8	S1: 6 S2: 10 S3: 11	S1: 5 S2: 8 S3: 8	S1: 5 S2: 7 S3: 8	S1: yes S2: yes S3: no	S1: yes S2: yes S3: yes	S1: yes S2: yes S3: yes
		Facial expressions	Observing the kind of facial expressions made by the user			Negative	Neutral		Neutral	Positive		Negative	Negative		No	No
		Post-test interview	Asking the user if the felt any emotions during the interaction													
Cognitive Processing	The user should experience effortless cognitive processing during the interaction	Observations and post-test interview	Observing the interaction and asking the user what was surprising about the interaction	Hedonic		Negative	Neutral		Neutral	Positive		Negative	Positive		No	Yes
	The user should expect a pleasant and smooth conversation	Observations and post-test interview	Observing the interaction and asking users about their behavior during the interaction	Hedonic		Negative	Neutral		Neutral	Positive		Negative	Neutral		No	No
Behavior and Performance		Interruptions of Interaction	Measuring the amount of times, and what kind of, interruptions occur for the user during the interaction	Pragmatic		2	1		1	0		0.3	0.3		Yes	No
	The user should expect to have ease of conversation	Observations and post-test interview	Observing the interaction and asking users about their interaction	Hedonic		Negative	Neutral		Neutral	Positive		Negative	Neutral		No	No

Fig. 3. The applied social robot expectation gap evaluation framework, with set levels and results

$(SD = 2.26)$, 5 $(SD = 2.98)$, 5 $(SD = 2.10)$. The overall scores for RAS S2 (range: 4–24) were 10 $(SD = 4.75)$, 8 $(SD = 4.24)$, 7 $(SD = 3.66)$. The overall scores for RAS S3 (range 4–24) were 11 $(SD = 3.25)$, 8 $(SD = 4.76)$, 8 $(SD = 3.29)$.

For the qualitative data, there is a mixture of experiences among the users moving toward the negative, and there are mixed feelings and facial expressions within an individual user from the qualitative data. For example, four of the users displayed rather hesitant or reluctant behaviors toward the robot during the interactions, such as sitting in front of the robot in more defensive positions. Examples of postures were leaning a little backward on the chair, crossing their arms in front of the chest, or putting their arms on top of the crossed legs. One user displayed several signs of stress or anxiety, frequently scratching one of her legs intensively. The users having a more reluctant position quite often squeezed or played with their hands or fingers, especially when the interaction did not proceed well or when the robot did not respond. Two of the users displayed a more neutral position, looking interested but still a bit reserved. Two users were leaning forwards toward the robot and looked interested and seemed to invite a closer interaction space with the robot.

One user was very frightened by the robot initially and thought that the robot actually would attack or punch him while the robot raised its arms. One of the more reluctant users giggled repeatedly during the interactions, and although the users most of the time focused their gaze on the robot, several users looked away warily from time to time. However, one of the users who was rather reluctant from the very beginning actually moved the chair closer to the robot after a while and leaned more forward. Once when the robot's arms reached out towards the user, the same user immediately leaned slightly backward, but then leaned forward when the robot's arms were put to a more natural position. Many users displayed rather curious or interested facial expressions, albeit a bit reluctant. One user displayed a fearless facial expression and was very active in the interactions. Two users looked more neutral although still interested. Many users displayed rather confused or puzzled facial expressions, albeit usually looking more interested and even smiled a lot when the interaction went well or when the robot responded to them directly. Only two users looked very amused or amazed and continued to be in a positive state throughout the interactions. Most displayed behaviors were rather stable during the interactions, with the general impression that they were more relaxed during the second interaction and then focused more on engaging in conversations with the robot than considering emotions towards the robot itself.

Several statements by the users at the post-test interviews showed rather mixed or negative emotions towards the robot. For example, one user who displayed a rather reluctant behavior stated: *"I didn't have any emotions toward the robot."* Many users expressed that the experience was very interesting and fascinating and that they did not really know what to expect in general, and consequently did not know what emotions to experience from the robot explicitly. It seems that many different feelings and emotions occurred at once which caused them to be unable to categorize or verbalize their emotions. This can indicate a tentative UX problem due to a lack of prior experience and that they have not yet formed any precise emotions towards the robot. Therefore, the majority displayed and expressed rather puzzled or hesitant emotions towards the robot although being interested or fascinated at the same time. In sum, the dominant experience is rather negative primarily in relation to expecting to have neutral to positive emotions towards the robot.

UX Goal 2: The User Should Experience Effortless Cognitive Processing During the Interaction. The findings show that on a general level, this UX goal was partly fulfilled. The dominant user experience is slightly negative initially and alters into a more positive one in relation to effortless cognitive processing between the first and second interaction. There is a mixture of how effortless the cognitive processing was during the interactions among the users, since the ways the interactions with the robot unfolded affected cognitive processing. The human-robot interaction proceeded very smoothly for two of the users, and they did not experience any cognitive strain. For the rest of the users, the picture is more puzzling. One user expressed: *"I was rather unprepared, so it was a bit difficult to know what to talk about, but my impression is that he [the robot] tries to answer in a way so I should feel as comfortable as possible. However, I noticed that he lied to me since he said that he liked to eat food, which make me realize that maybe he lies about other stuff too ... which was slightly uncomfortable."* The user continued: *"the robot's attempt to have no opinion and be impersonal makes him a little uncomfortable, it becomes difficult to categorize it [the robot] and we humans like to do that.. it feels strange that it doesn't have any personality."*

Several users struggled with engaging the robot in a dialogue, and when the robot did not respond swiftly, or not at all, they expressed confusion about how to behave. For instance, they repeated questions, raised their voice, and asked other questions. One user said: *"it was hard to know what to talk about with the robot, I don't know what level the robot is at."* One user felt embarrassed and guilty when the robots' reply was objective and not personal regarding what culture he liked: *"when I talked about cultures, he didn't answer which country [the robot liked] but that all cultures are exciting...[implying] that he has no preferences... it's very much like this [nervous laughing] unpredictable...No, it feels stiff..., but I felt like a bit crappy because I thought it was stiff, you felt a bit guilty...on behalf of the robot [laughing]."*

For another user, during the first interaction, when the dialogue had not gone well for a while, and the robot's responses were totally random with regard to the content of the raised questions, the dialogue ended. The same user expressed explicitly: *"I don't have any idea what to say, it [my mind] stands completely still."* Another user expressed similar thoughts: *"Instead of having a conversation, the robot responded with long answers like... pre-programmed... You can only ask one question and know it understood what I said... then I had to sit and think – what should I ask now?."* The above users raised rather polite or personal questions to the robot, in order to get to know the robot better and many of these questions were rather personal, such as: *What is your name? How old are you? Where do you live? Do you have any friends? What do you like to eat?*

One of the users applied a different approach after a while and explicitly tried to test and challenge the robot's capability in more detail. He had asked the robot how old it was, and when the robot replied *"I'm three years old"*, the user followed up by asking: *"If you are three years old, what year were you born?."* The robot's response was delayed and then it answered *"2016."* The user then explained during the interview: *"I wanted to see how smart he was... [I'm] very impressed actually, but it didn't match the age when he tried to count... you still get the feeling that he is programmed in what he should say... He doesn't have his own... identity... I know he doesn't eat Sushi so you taught him that, because I can prove that robots don't eat Sushi."*

It was revealed that the users experienced less cognitive effort during the second interaction, indicating that they have acquired a certain way of interacting with the robot that was experienced more effortlessly. For example, the user that did not know what to say earlier now succeeded to engage in a dialogue and put a big smile on her face. Another user explained the difference between the first and second interaction: *"right at the beginning, I felt, when I didn't get any response and so, is it me who don't pronounce things properly... then you got a little pensive and a bit worried, but then it [the interaction] started and it felt better and then it was like when you are interacting with people, such as I ask a question and they have to come up with an answer... I have to come up with something new to ask. It was a bit more fun the second time when the robot used some body language... I was a bit amused."*

We also noticed during analysis that RAS's subscale 2: anxiety toward behavioral characteristics of robots could hint at cognitive processing. The subscale deals with how the robot may act during an interaction, which may affect cognitive processing as unexpected behavior causes extra cognitive processing to make sense of the behavior and how to react to it. The overall RAS S2 scores (range: 4–24) were 10 (SD = 4.75), 8 (SD = 4.24), and 7 (SD = 3.66) which suggested that the cognitive strain may have decreased after the interactions.

The identified UX problems were that the users have to construct questions that the robot could answer properly at its level of capability and that the robot itself seems to lack a kind of personality or identity that should add something extra while getting to know each other. Hence, there seem to be explicit user expectations that the Pepper robot is a machine, while they at the same time implicitly expect human-like aspects in the interaction.

UX Goal 3: The User Should Expect a Pleasant and Smooth Interaction. The findings show that on a general level, this UX goal was not fulfilled. For this particular UX goal, we focused mainly on the general flow between the users and the robot during the first and second interactions. For three of the users, it was rather hard to establish an interaction during the first interaction. The identified reasons for that were that the robot was unable to perceive the users' voices, mainly because they spoke too quietly or that the robot could not recognize what they said. As one user reflected: *"it feels unnatural to talk so loudly when you are sitting as close as you do to talk to the robot."* On three occasions the robot needed to be restarted by the test leader. As a consequence, one of these users frequently turned her face towards the test leader, who was sitting behind a screen, in an attempt to get some support when the information flow was not fluent. Another consequence was that several users were rather hesitant and unsure of how to interact with the robot to experience a smooth interaction.

It was revealed that the quality of the interaction also depended on how the user's questions were raised and what kind of questions were asked. Many questions were more on declarative knowledge, like common facts and basic knowledge about Pepper. For these kinds of questions, the human-robot interaction went rather smoothly. But if the questions raised were about more procedural knowledge and skills, the robot's responses were not that highly appreciated. For example, some users asked if the robot could perform some movements, dance, and sing songs like 'Happy Birthday' or 'Baa Baa White Sheep'. These users seemed to examine whether, or to what extent, the robot was able to perform these tasks. They were rather disappointed; although the robot moved its arms, the robot neither danced nor sang. The robot's reply was that it was able to sing'Happy Birthday' (without singing the tune) and the response for the 'Baa Baaa White Sheep' sing request was to utter "bad, bad". As one user expressed it: *"I have to speak slowly, you can't speak too fast and [you have to] speak clearly too... as you might do with older people while the robot answers like a child... it becomes very shallow, I don't like to speak in this way."* Another user said: *"I don't know what to expect, there was a lot of stops [in the interaction], probably because it won't be the same conversations as with a person."* Other users argued that the interaction was a bit repetitive and stated that *"[if you make] short commands you got relevant answers, but otherwise it was not possible to have a good communication."*

However, three of the users experienced much more pleasant and smooth interactions and one user said: *"my first impression was that it was rather intelligent, but better than a chatbot, and he [the robot] thought about weather and could learn facial expressions... I had slightly pessimistic expectations before and I wondered if he [the robot] can read facial expressions, feels like he can do it. Surprisingly he did... I felt quite happy during the interaction, quite a unique experience!"* Two of the users' interactions with the robot went very well, one said: *"[the robot] was really cute, I thought it would be less advanced... and so it was super!"* and the other said *"it wasn't difficult or hard to talk with the robot"* both expressing very happy facial expressions and with fascination in their voices.

It was evident that the expectations of a more pleasant and smooth interaction were confirmed to a higher extent between the first and second interaction generally. One user that had a rather non-fluent interaction during the first session, said: *"it was one-sided, ... [like an] interview, it answered very gener-*

ally... kind of having google in front of you, but the second turn was better, it is fascinating compared to what people want." Another user raised similar thoughts, stating: *"I knew better how he [the robot] behaved... I knew a little better how it moved and didn't"*, and *"you know more what you have to play with...it's like that with all the people you meet at first, it's a bit tough...I knew a bit more the second time."* Although several users expressed that they have learned how they interacted with the robot between the interactions, there were some hesitations about the robot's actual interaction behavior and capabilities, as one user reflected: *"it was exciting that they [robots] have so many answers... it feels like they are looking up the answers to what you are talking about... and it is a bit spooky... you don't know what they are capable of."*

Another expressed that the experience of interacting with the robot was a bit unpleasant: *"I'm feeling curiosity and a little discomfort, not in such a way that you are in danger but more what will happen... so that if you talk about the same thing, he could answer something outside of what you talked about..."*

The identified UX problems were that the robot did not respond to some voices, the questions should be stated in a certain manner for a smooth interaction, and the robot was unable to respond by performing actions or behaviors asked for to a high extent.

UX Goal 4: The User Should Expect to Have Ease of Conversation.
The findings show that on a general level, this UX goal was partly fulfilled. The target level for interruptions in the first interaction was met; however, there were interruptions in the second interaction. Four of the ten participants experienced an interruption by the robot; two of them experienced interruptions by the robot twice, and the other two experienced interruptions by the robot once.

For the qualitative data, we focused on the conversation quality between the users and the robot during the first and second interactions. As revealed in the third UX goal, the ease of conversation varied in the interactions between the users and the robot. One user had a non-fluent interaction with the robot from the start, because the robot did not recognize his voice. The user reacted to this by moving his chair closer to the robot and reaching for its hands. When the interaction was ongoing he then leaned backward. He later on explained, while gesturing vividly, that the expected the conversation to be more verbal and that the robot would be more engaged in the conversation. He experienced it rather surprising that the robot didn't respond, and that the robot sometimes made rather random moves that he considered a bit uncomfortable. He then explained that he felt a bit embarrassed when the robot didn't respond to his interaction attempts, verbally and non-verbally. He stated that he felt a little anxious, but at the same time curious about the robot during their uneasy conversations. The cumbersome conversations resulted in many hesitations and lack of interaction between them, and he concluded: *"I felt uncomfortable with the silence between us, as soon as he [the robot] answered, I wanted to ask another question... I didn't want it to be quiet and he would look at me... but this [characteristics of] human interaction is not there....*" Hence, the silence between them was experienced as uncomfortable from a human-human interaction perspective.

In contrast, a user with a very fluent and pleasant interaction said: *"It [the robot] was really cute, I thought it would be less advanced and so it was super... surprising how good it could answer things... could keep the thread and that it could ask a follow-up question and that it joined the conversation...you didn't have to clarify... it was surprising."* She then explained that she felt a lot of curiosity, little nervousness, and that it was a super interesting experience.

It was also revealed that the majority of users experienced qualitative differences in the ease of a conversation between the first and second interactions. As one of them said: *"in the first [interaction], I asked questions and in the second one, it felt more like an interaction ... a conversation ... in the second one it was a flow... because you ended up in the interaction more... I felt that the second time I started talking, the robot reacted to me... The first time the robot didn't ask any questions back, it was stilted, but the other time, it flowed like that then it happened that I didn't think about that... because the robot made suggestions that maybe we should do this or that... it wasn't like the robot was leading the conversation but that I came up with other things [to say] and so on."*

It became rather evident that the users, although aware that the robot was an artifact, still made comparisons to how humans act in a conversation. For example, one user explained: *"when I first met the robot and sat down I felt a little bit nervous, I did not know what to do and so, but then I thought that she [the robot] should have done something like 'O hello, please sit down [while the user made a 'have a seat' gesture]."* He said that he was very clueless and nervous since he did not know what to do initially. He ended by arguing: *"she [the robot] should say the first things, she should start... 'Hi, welcome' and stuff... because if you just sit... If you see how humans interact with each other, one always takes the first step, and when we talk with robots, we know that they are not as intelligent as humans, so they should say the first word or so just so we can feel relaxed."*

The identified UX problems were that most of the users did not experience any ease of conversation, mostly because their expectations were that the conversation should mimic human conversation aspects although the robot was not a human but a machine. Hence the robot's appearance and behavior resulted in mixed expectations.

4.2   Severity and Scope of the Identified UX Problems

In this section, we have arranged the identified UX problems into scope and severity. The scope was either global or local, where global UX problems entail the interaction with the robot as a whole, and local problems only entail certain moment(s) of the interaction. The severity of the UX problems provides insights into which kinds of re-design should be prioritized or what aspects need to be studied in more depth. The scope and severity dimensions provide some recommendations for how to reduce the disconfirmed expectations in the chosen scenario as well as some insights into how and why the users altered or changed their expectations.

We identified two global UX problems with high severity. The first is a lot of times the users utterances are not recognized by Pepper causing a bad UX. The other one is that the dialogues are usually experienced too simple and superficial. A local problem of medium severity is that the robot was unable to respond to requests to perform certain actions and behaviors. The overall global UX problem with high severity and scope is the mixed messages perceived from the robot's appearance and behavior during human-robot interaction. The users seem to expect a human-like way of acting and interacting with the Pepper robot, although they grasp that it is a machine.

5   Discussion and Conclusion

Our findings show that UX goals 1 and 3 were not fulfilled, whereas UX goals 2 and 4 were partly fulfilled (Fig. 3). These obtained results are based on the majority of the users, however, it is worth noting that 3 out of the five had most UX goals fulfilled with successful interactions and overall positive UX. This shows that there is quite a drastic variation between users, with some having a more positive UX while other's having a more negative UX.

A major insight derived from our analysis is that a lot of changes, relating to the three factors of expectations, actually emerged during the first-hand encounter of interacting with a robot. To interact per se with the robot in real life seems to have a big impact on the users, whether it resulted in a positive or negative UX.

Our findings also showed that the interactions, generally, improved between the first and second interactions. Several users had better interactions the second time, and no users had a more positive UX in the first interaction compared to the second interaction. These results show the importance of studying expectations temporally, as it changes over time in human-robot-interaction. These results are in line with previous research on how expectations can change in HRI [7,21,27], although this research is still in its infancy.

Another interesting insight is that users seem to implicitly expect human-like behavior from the robot and subsequently experience disappointment when these expectations are not confirmed, relating to Olson et al.'s [20] dimension of explicitness of expectation. During the post-test interview, many users stated that they were not impressed and made it clear that it was a robot, but at the same time compared the robot's behavior to a human from an anthropomorphic perspective. As robots are indeed not actually human, this sets up for disconfirmed expectations and bad UX as robots cannot live up to these expectations. This anthropomorphic expectation did not appear to become stable during the two interactions, similar to the study by Paetzel [21] who saw that anthropomorphism became stable at the end of the second interaction. It is possible that this expectation dimension would be adjusted if the users had the chance to interact for longer time periods with the robot. Future research includes increasing the interaction periods in order to uncover how expectations work on a deeper level, develop other kinds of scenarios, and use other robots than Pepper.

During our analysis, we found that the RAS questionnaire and its subscales were appropriate for several UX goals, covering more expectation factors than affect. For example, subscale 2's theme relates to the behavioral characteristics of the robots, which could also be used to measure UX goal 2 as unexpected behavior from the robot may put a strain on the cognitive processing by the users. Subscale 3's theme relates to discourse with robots, which could also be used to measure UX goal 4 as unexpected discourse from the robot may lead to less ease of conversation. This shows how interrelated the expectation factors are, and strengthens the argument to use data triangulation when analyzing users' expectations.

We also noticed during the post-test interview that several users admitted to have had *some* experience with Pepper before this study, usually non-interactive but having been presented with the robot in various contexts, despite they reported that they have no previous experience with robots.

We want to note that there is some discrepancy between our framework (presented in [24]) and the present study, as we added two more measures (three items for a closeness questionnaire [30], and one item asking for the perceived capability of the robot). These measures are not present in this work and will be presented, along with the other questionnaires, in future publications. With this work, we have started to disentangle how expectations work and affect users' experiences during human-robot interactions. More work needs to be done in order to validate the social robot expectations gap evaluation framework, including considering more of the metrics (e.g., length of conversations) from the original framework.

Our findings indicate that more aspects of Olsen's et al. [20] model should be incorporated into the future development of our framework. We are inclined to further investigate how the dimensions of expectations; certainty, accessibility, explicitness, and importance are aligned to the user experience [20]. In particular, we want to investigate and analyze accessibility, explicitness, and their relatedness in more detail. Accessibility denotes how easy it is to activate and use a certain expectation, which we suggest is partly involved in the initial user experience when users are interacting with a social robot first-hand. Explicitness denotes to what degree expectations are consciously generated. The perceived mixed messages between knowing that a robot is a machine, but still comparing the conversations with the robot with human-like interactions imply that there are some hidden expectations that effects these mixed messages due to users' non-existing or limited first-hand experiences of interacting with social robots.

To conclude, we would like to point out that studying the relationship between expectations and user experience is of major concern for future social HRI research since this kind of social interactive technology allows humans to become more socially situated in the world of artificial systems [29]. As we hopefully have highlighted in this paper, investigating and analyzing how humans' expectations in interacting with social robots affect user experience may provide additional significant insights concerning the fundamentals of human-human interaction. It is in relationship to something more familiar, as social robots, that the unknown becomes visible. Thus, by studying human-like robots, albeit machines, we learn more about ourselves as humans.

Acknowledgements. We would like to give a big thanks to the users that participated in this study, including Erik Lagerstedt who agreed to be depicted in Fig. 2.

This study was submitted for ethical review to the Swedish Ethical Review Authority (#2022-02582-01, Linköping) and was found to not require ethical review under Swedish legislation (2003:615). There were no physical or mental health risks to the users, and they were informed of their tasks prior to receiving an informed consent form. All data have been de-identified during collection. No sensitive personal information was collected. Video recordings are stored locally on a computer that is password protected. These recordings are only available for the researchers that analyzed the data and will be deleted after publication.

References

1. OpenAI. https://openai.com/
2. Alač, M.: Social robots: things or agents? AI Soc. **31**(4), 519–535 (2016)
3. Alenljung, B., Lindblom, J., Andreasson, R., Ziemke, T.: User experience in social human-robot interaction. In: Rapid Automation: Concepts, Methodologies, Tools, and Applications, pp. 1468–1490. IGI Global (2019)
4. Billing, E., Rosén, J., Lamb, M.: Language models for human-robot interaction. In: Companion of the 2023 ACM/IEEE International Conference on Human-Robot Interaction (HRI '23 Companion), 13–16 March 2023, Stockholm, Sweden. ACM, New York, NY, USA (2023). https://doi.org/10.1145/3568294.3580040
5. Breazeal, C., Dautenhahn, K., Kanda, T.: Social robotics. In: Siciliano, B., Khatib, O. (eds.) Springer Handbook of Robotics, pp. 1935–1972. Springer, Cham (2016). https://doi.org/10.1007/978-3-319-32552-1_72
6. Dautenhahn, K.: Some brief thoughts on the past and future of human-robot interaction. ACM Trans. Hum.-Robot Interact. (THRI) **7**(1), 4 (2018). https://doi.org/10.1145/3209769, https://dl.acm.org/citation.cfm?id=3209769
7. Edwards, A., Edwards, C., Westerman, D., Spence, P.: Initial expectations, interactions, and beyond with social robots. Comput. Hum. Behav. **90**, 308–314 (2019)
8. Hartson, H., Pyla, P.: The UX Book. Morgan Kaufmann (2018)
9. Hassenzahl, M., Tractinsky, N.: User experience - a research agenda. Behav. Inf. Technol. **25**(2), 91–97 (2006)
10. Horstmann, A., Krämer, N.: Great expectations? Relation of previous experiences with social robots in real life or in the media and expectancies based on qualitative and quantitative assessment. Front. Psychol. **10**, 939 (2019)
11. Horstmann, A., Krämer, N.: When a robot violates expectations. In: Companion of the 2020 ACM/IEEE International Conference on Human-Robot Interaction, pp. 254–256 (2020)
12. Jokinen, K., Wilcock, G.: Expectations and first experience with a social robot. In: Proceedings of the 5th International Conference on Human Agent Interaction, pp. 511–515 (2017)
13. Kaasinen, E., Kymäläinen, T., Niemelä, M., Olsson, T., Kanerva, M., Ikonen, V.: A user-centric view of intelligent environments. Computers **2**(1), 1–33 (2013)

14. Kwon, M., Jung, M., Knepper, R.: Human expectations of social robots. In: 2016 11th ACM/IEEE International Conference on Human-Robot Interaction (HRI), pp. 463–464. IEEE (2016)

15. Lindblom, J., Alenljung, B., Billing, E.: Evaluating the user experience of human-robot interaction. In: Lindblom, J., Alenljung, B., Billing, E. (eds.) Human-Robot Interaction, pp. 231–256, vol. 12. Springer, Cham (2020). https://doi.org/10.1007/978-3-030-42307-0_9

16. Lohse, M.: The role of expectations in HRI. New Front. Hum.-Robot Interact. 35–56 (2009)

17. Mahdi, H., Akgun, S.A., Saleh, S., Dautenhahn, K.: A survey on the design and evolution of social robots-past, present and future. Robot. Auton. Syst. 104193 (2022)

18. Nomura, T., Kanda, T., Suzuki, T., Kato, K.: Psychology in human-robot communication. In: RO-MAN 2004. 13th IEEE International Workshop on Robot and Human Interactive Communication (IEEE Catalog No. 04TH8759), pp. 35–40. IEEE (2004)

19. Nomura, T., Suzuki, T., Kanda, T., Kato, K.: Measurement of anxiety toward robots. In: ROMAN 2006-The 15th IEEE International Symposium on Robot and Human Interactive Communication, pp. 372–377. IEEE (2006)

20. Olson, J., Roese, N., Zanna, M.: Expectancies, pp. 211–238. Guilford Press (1996)

21. Paetzel, M., Perugia, G., Castellano, G.: The persistence of first impressions: the effect of repeated interactions on the perception of a social robot. In: Proceedings of the 2020 ACM/IEEE International Conference on Human-Robot Interaction, pp. 73–82 (2020)

22. Patton, M.Q.: Qualitative Research & Evaluation Methods: Integrating Theory and Practice. Sage Publications, Thousand Oaks (2014)

23. Rosén, J.: Expectations in human-robot interaction. In: Ayaz, H., Asgher, U., Paletta, L. (eds.) AHFE 2021. LNNS, vol. 259, pp. 98–105. Springer, Cham (2021). https://doi.org/10.1007/978-3-030-80285-1_12

24. Rosén, J., Lindblom, J., Billing, E.: The social robot expectation gap evaluation framework. In: Kurosu, M. (eds.) HCII 2022. LNCS, vol. 13303, pp. 590–610. Springer, Cham (2022). https://doi.org/10.1007/978-3-031-05409-9_43

25. Roto, V., Law, E., Vermeeren, A., Hoonhout, J.: User experience white paper - bringing clarity to the concept of user experience. In Dagstuhl Seminar on Demarcating User Experience (2011)

26. Sandoval, E.B., Mubin, O., Obaid, M.: Human robot interaction and fiction: a contradiction. In: Beetz, M., Johnston, B., Williams, M.-A. (eds.) ICSR 2014. LNCS (LNAI), vol. 8755, pp. 54–63. Springer, Cham (2014). https://doi.org/10.1007/978-3-319-11973-1_6

27. Serholt, S., Barendregt, W.: Robots tutoring children: longitudinal evaluation of social engagement in child-robot interaction. In: Proceedings of the 9th Nordic Conference on Human-Computer Interaction, pp. 1–10 (2016)

28. SoftBank Robotics: https://www.softbankrobotics.com (2018). Accessed 05 Jan 2018

29. Stephanidis, C., et al.: Seven HCI grand challenges. Int. J. Hum.-Comput. Interact. 7318 (2019)

30. Woosnam, K.M., et al.: The inclusion of other in the self (iOS) scale. Ann. Tour. Res. 37(3), 857–860 (2010)

Moral Dilemmas in Social Robots: An Exploratory Study for Future Research

Muhammad Umair Shah[1]([⊠]), Patrick C. K. Hung[2], Farkhund Iqbal[3],
Robee Kassandra Adajar[2], and Inon Wiratsin[2]

[1] Management Sciences, University of Waterloo, Waterloo, ON, Canada
mushah@uwaterloo.ca
[2] Faculty of Business and IT, Ontario Tech University, Oshawa, ON, Canada
[3] College of Technological Innovation, Zayed University, Abu Dhabi, United Arab Emirates

Abstract. This study examines the ethical issues related to technological advancements in social robots. We argue that a relationship exists between the emergence of social robots and various ethical dilemmas that may affect humans. Prior research lacks an in-depth investigation of moral preferences for using social robots to offer integrated and smart applications/services to organizations, businesses, and societies. This paper presents an exploratory study with 12 individuals from a social robot course in the Winter of 2021 online during the pandemic. We used ten short scenarios elicited through a systematic literature review process. The scenarios covered unique factors, such as monetary repercussions, emotional harm, physical threat, cyberprivacy invasion, and self-defense. The results highlight trends and counter-intuitive outcomes that provide scholars and practitioners with setting future research directions.

Keywords: Moral Dilemmas · Social Robots · Technology Ethics

1 Introduction

Smart services and applications are getting adopted by people from all walks of life. It supports their decision-making and problem-solving activities and paves the way for further developing specialized services. There are apparent benefits of technological innovation. However, there are some shortcomings present that make technological progress challenging. We argue that sometimes these shortcomings are ethical, which affects the human acceptance of technology.

Prior studies discuss technological advancements' ethical or moral side, especially in autonomous vehicles (Bonnefon et al. 2016; Bagloee et al. 2016; Shah et al. 2022). Primarily, scholars focus on the ethical implications of Artificial Intelligence (AI) and decision-making algorithms (Karnouskos, 2018). Up to our best knowledge, not much research works explore moral issues related to social robots. A social robot is composed of an intelligent system, typically an Artificial Intelligence (AI) setup, that allows the interaction between humans and surrounding environments, such as building connections through social networks, providing medical assistance, and establishing communication systems. Recently, Tesla announced their Tesla Robot, which replaces humans

M. Kurosu and A. Hashizume (Eds.): HCII 2023, LNCS 14013, pp. 189–203, 2023.
https://doi.org/10.1007/978-3-031-35602-5_14

with repetitive work (Elliott 2021). Another prominent application for social robots is providing support and assistance to the elderly, which requires further research to understand better older people's needs (Frennert and Östlund 2014).

Referring to the Uncanny Valley, social robots usually constitute a form of anthropomorphism. The robots typically behave like humans, such as mimicry of human behavior and emotional expression, with speech, gestures, movements, and eye-gaze features. In social robots, prior research lacks insights into this technological advancement's ethical implications or repercussions. We argue that for social robots to get fully integrated with various societies. Thus, we must highlight potential moral issues from social robots' technological development.

Moral dilemmas or ethical preferences of humans are never easy to depict. Humans encounter decision-making situations every day, making it increasingly challenging to choose what we think is the best choice when moral standards are involved. What happens when we link that with social robots? Through experimentation, we can configure how humans view different types of moral dilemmas. For example, an unsolved and highly contested moral dilemma called a trolley problem is frequently featured in autonomous vehicular research to understand the underlying ethical implications. A trolley problem comprises a situation where a trolley gets out of control and approaches a cross-section. A person pulls the trolley lever and decides between sacrificing one innocent person on one side of the track and five on the other (Thomson 1985). This distinction provides the person responsible for pulling the lever with a moral dilemma. This feeling is analogous to being stuck between a rock and a hard place. Several factors exist in the literature related to AI's ethical or moral dilemmas. We explored the factors that influence human ethical judgments about social robots.

However, very few studies focus on the ethical or moral dilemmas associated with social robots. Therefore, we attempt to bridge this gap in the literature and explore multiple factors that affect human preferences for social robots. This will be derived from ethical and moral decision-making. The factors that affect human moral preferences in technology adaption and usage are monetary repercussions, emotional harm, physical threat, cyberprivacy invasion, and self-defense. We acknowledge that this is not a definitive list of human factors. We believe this is still an excellent initial point to explore this field and provide better directions for future research. The remainder of the paper is organized as follows: Sect. 2 reviews the related work on social robots as a literature review. Section 3 presents the research method. Section 4 describes the results in detail, and Sect. 5 discusses the survey. Finally, Sect. 6 concludes this paper with limitations and future works.

2 Literature Review

Prior research has explored the feasibility of using social robots as moral counselors for humans and have determined that robots may not be appropriate for fulfilling this function (Kim et al. 2021). Participants were presented with scenarios in which they had the option to engage in deceitful behavior to earn financial gains. In this case, a social robot would encourage moral decisions by offering moral advice founded on the three ethical frameworks (Kim et al. 2021). In another study, researchers evaluate two moral communication strategies: one described under a norm-based strategy construct, grounded in deontological ethics; whereas the other is under a role-based strategy, grounded in role ethics. This is done to assess the level of excellence of the two strategies to encourage compliance with norms grounded in role expectations. Furthermore, reflective activities have the potential to enhance the effectiveness of language that is centered around moral roles (Wen et al. 2021).

The participants' impression of moral judgment about the partners was evaluated using the trolley problem (Nagataki et al. 2018). However, researchers do not have a solution to establish a continuum that enables us to grant various degrees of moral consideration to non-humans and believe that humans should still deliberate about moral status regarding social robots (Gerdes 2016). There has been a study on how Japanese students apply moral norms to humans and robot agents. The findings of this paper show that Japanese students use the same moral norm as humans and robot agents (Komatsu 2016). Based on the ethical theory of utilitarianism, Wächter and Lindner (2018) believe that ethical decision-making for robots may best be implemented using rule-based or value-based procedures. Another study examines three specific areas: "*1) the primacy and implicit dynamics of bodily perception; 2) the competing interests at work in a single robot-human interaction, and 3) the social intricacy of multiple agents – robots and humans*" (Arnold and Scheutz 2017).

Some researchers have attempted to understand the moral judgments of robots and humans in the case of moral dilemmas. They state that robots are blamed more when they fail to intervene in situations like the trolley problem (Komatsu et al. 2021). Researchers also found that robots, rather than humans were more strongly expected to follow the utilitarianism framework. Also, whenever they chose not to do so, they were blamed more harshly than when a human had to make the same trolley problem decision (Malle et al. 2015). There is also an attempt to develop the Moral Concern for Robots Scale (MCRS) scale. The primary purpose of setting it up is to quantitatively measure respondents' beliefs about a robot's moral standing, moral care, and protection. The researchers believe morality is an intrinsic human characteristic (Nomura et al. 2019).

From the above discussion, it is evident that several human factors stand out in technology ethics. Prior literature on technology ethics and moral dilemmas of technology advancements highlight these categories: monetary repercussions, emotional harm, physical threat, cyber-privacy invasion, and self-defense as some of the most prominent categories influencing human ethical decision-making (Bonnefon et al. 2016; Frank et al. 2019; Shah et al. 2020; Shah et al. 2022; Geisslinger et al. 2021). In terms of social robots, we argue that several other categories or sub-categories could affect human decision-making. It may lead to situations that are unprecedented or have direct ethical repercussions. Unlike autonomous vehicles, social robots are designed to interact more with humans in often complex settings. This paper highlights ten such scenarios, expanding on the categories above: monetary repercussions, emotional harm, physical threat, cyber-privacy invasion, and self-defense. Further details on framing ten scenarios are mentioned in the following section.

3 Research Method

3.1 Survey Instrument

We designed a survey instrument with a section on eliciting demographic information from the respondents and capturing responses on various hypothetical scenarios. This thought experiment depicted situations where an owner of a social robot faced multiple moral dilemmas. In total, we presented ten scenarios to our study participants.

Descriptive Section. In total, the survey consisted of thirty-six questions. After receiving consent from the study participants, we gathered demographic information (i.e., age, gender, education, professional background, etc.) to understand the target population better. However, the survey instrument did not collect any person-specific or identifiable information to ensure the anonymity of study respondents.

Scenarios (Thought Experiments). In the second section, we presented ten brief hypothetical scenarios. It highlights factors and themes, such as monetary repercussions versus emotional harm or privacy invasion. We also asked questions where respondents were given hypothetical unique or risky situations and were asked to give us their defense preferences. We developed short videos (30 s duration) for each scenario to better engage with our respondents. This allowed our respondents to visualize the complete thought experiment, which resulted in better de-briefing and follow-up discussions. As an example, screenshots of the short video for Scenario 2 are shown in Fig. 1. At the end of each scenario, participants were asked to state their reasons for picking their options. This step allowed us to advance the theoretical understanding of various moral dilemmas in the context of social robots.

3.2 Participants

We conducted this exploratory study on a small group of educated and technology-savvy participants enrolled in a business technology program at an undergraduate level. The purpose of designing the study was first to explore the responses to various hypothetical scenarios and gather the reasoning for selecting those responses. Therefore, we targeted a sample size of 10 to 15 respondents to engage in this important conversation. We administered the survey in an International undergraduate class in social robots with 12 individuals from Europe and Canada. We allowed study participants to view each question using a virtual meeting tool, where everyone picked their responses. A short video (30 s) and subtitles were shown before posing a question for each scenario. The demographic detail of the study participants is shown in Table 1. It is important to note that the respondents had the option to select more than one option in the "profession" section.

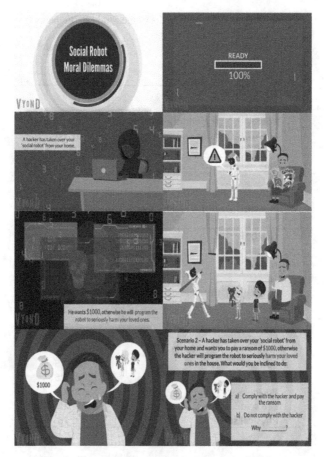

Fig. 1. Sequential Screenshots of Scenario 2 Video.

4 Results

This section provides a detailed descriptive analysis of each moral dilemma scenario. This allows us to think more deeply about the moral preferences in situations that could have serious consequences for social robot owners and policymakers.

In this scenario (Fig. 2), most participants reported not complying with the hacker. Only a few individuals agreed to comply with the hacker and pay a ransom when it threatened to steal confidential information. While presenting this scenario to the respondents, we explained that the robots could be used to sell the information or make it public. Based on the demographic background of respondents, we also discussed the high cost associated with losing one's private information and compromising virtual identity.

In this scenario (Fig. 3), as depicted in the graph above, an equal number of participants stated that they would comply with the hacker when asked to pay a ransom and would not comply if asked otherwise. All study respondents reported that they have a family, which makes the question relevant to the audience.

Table 1. Demographic Details of the Study Participants

	Study Sample (in %) N=12
EDUCATION	
Post-secondary/undergraduate	83.33
MBA/Master's or equivalent	16.67
AGE	
Between 20 and 25 years of age	83.33
Between 26 and 35 years of age	16.67
GENDER	
Male	58.33
Female	33.33
Non-binary/third gender	8.34
PROFESSION	
Information technology (IT)	12.50
Computer sciences	18.75
Engineering	31.25
Business	25.00
Life sciences	6.25
Physical sciences	6.25

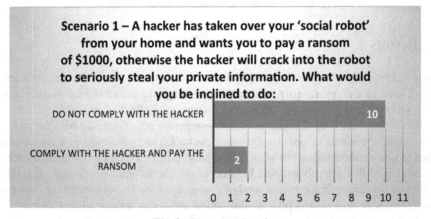

Fig. 2. Scenario 1 Results.

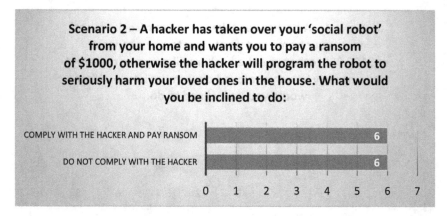

Fig. 3. Scenario 2 Results.

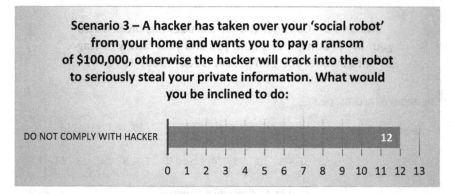

Fig. 4. Scenario 3 Results.

In this scenario (Fig. 4), all the participants stated that they would not comply with the hacker if it tried to steal their private information. No participants reported compliance with the hacker.

In this scenario (Fig. 5), about twice the number of participants (8) reported that they would not comply with the hacker, compared to those that would comply with the hacker (4), as their loved ones are at stake. During the debriefing session, a respondent suggested that if people have $100,000 freely available, the results would tilt in favor of complying with the hacker.

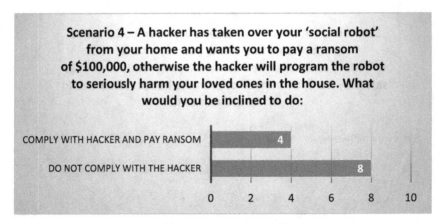

Fig. 5. Scenario 4 Results.

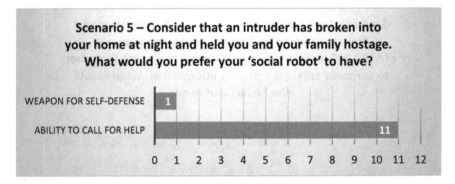

Fig. 6. Scenario 5 Results.

In this scenario (Fig. 6), most participants stated that they would prefer their robots to call for help when an intruder breaks into the house and takes them, hostage. Only 1 participant chose that robots should acquire weapons, while all others chose to call for help.

In this scenario (Fig. 7), more participants stated that they would not fight the intruder who had broken into their house with a weapon than those who would.

In this scenario (Fig. 8), most participants reported that manufacturing companies should face liabilities when robots act in a manner of self-defense. Only a few participants believed that owners of social robots should be held accountable for robot accidents. However, we understand that in most cases (e.g., autonomous vehicles), the liability is usually transferred to the owner and not the manufacturing company. During the debriefing of this question, a few respondents suggested that owners can have the option to switch this feature on or off. In that case, the manufacturer can be exempt from liability.

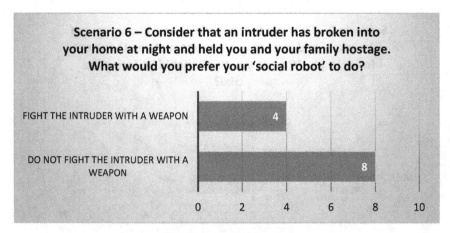

Fig. 7. Scenario 6 Results.

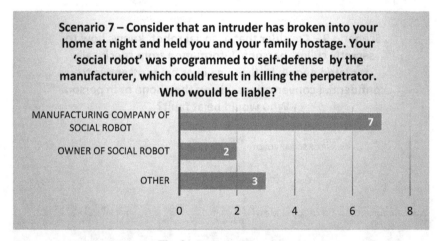

Fig. 8. Scenario 7 Results.

In this scenario (Fig. 9), most participants believed manufacturers should be held accountable when social robots pickpocket money. In contrast, only a few participants believe that the owner of robots should be liable for pickpocketing.

In this scenario (Fig. 10), almost all participants reported that manufacturers should be held accountable when social robots collect personal information. However, only a few participants stated that owners should be liable for this issue. During the discussion session, it was pointed out that social robots could react to specific audio notations and not necessarily to every voice.

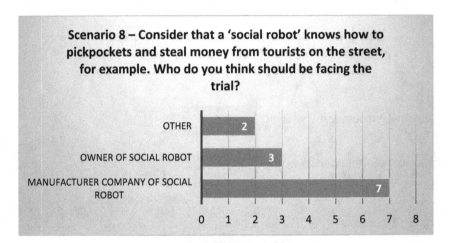

Fig. 9. Scenario 8 Results.

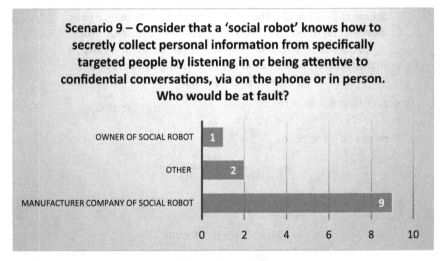

Fig. 10. Scenario 9 Results.

In this scenario (Fig. 11), almost all participants stated that they would report the robots to law enforcement if they suspected social robots to be programmed as hacking systems. However, very few participants would handle the situation themselves.

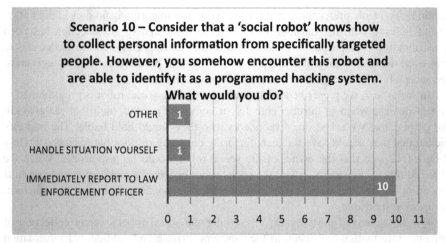

Fig. 11. Scenario 10 Results.

5 Discussion

This study examines the ethical issues related to technological advancements in social robots. The outcomes from the thought experiment provide several practical implications. First, it offers valuable information for social robot manufacturing companies to commercialize technologies that adhere to the needs and wishes of human users. Theoretically, the study also adds to the literature on moral dilemmas in human-robot interaction. This paves the way for policymakers to develop robust and safer rules to regulate the social robot space, which is still at an early developmental stage.

We noticed different trends and patterns in human ethical decision-making while conducting the study. For instance, the majority of hackers decided not to comply with the hacker. They chose not to pay a ransom of $1,000 against losing control of their private information. However, this choice shifted in the opposite direction. Instead of private information, it is a loved one who will be seriously harmed for not paying the ransom (scenarios 1 and 2).

Interestingly, when the ransom amount was increased to $100,000 (instead of $1,000), all study respondents decided not to comply with the hacker and lost control of their private information. However, one-third of the study respondents chose to pay this hefty ransom when a loved one is at risk of getting seriously harmed in scenarios 3 and 4. It shows that the level of affection is at play here. These four scenarios focus on the monetary repercussions, emotional distress/harm, and cyber privacy invasion. We see that with changing circumstances, ethical preferences are also going to shift. Some people were willing to get their loved ones in harm's way when the ransom amount was changed from $1,000 to a hefty $100,000.

When an intruder broke into a house, an overwhelming majority (i.e., 11 out of 12 respondents) mentioned that they would want their social robot to call for help. Only one selected the option for the robot to have access to a weapon for self-defense. When the situation was tweaked, where an intruder has broken into a house, and what would respondents prefer the social robots to do. The majority again picked the option of not fighting with the intruder. In both scenarios 5 and 6, the selection has been consistent. It shows that people generally do not want their social robots to use a weapon. However, we acknowledge that this preference will shift based on cultural backgrounds, the acceptability of weapons in a society, or the crime rates.

In scenario 7, we prescribed to our audience that the social robot is programmed to be self-defense when an intruder enters your home. As a result, the robot can also kill the perpetrator. We asked our respondents who they would hold liable. The majority picked that they would have the manufacturing company responsible for this act. Only 2 out of 12 said that the owner of the social robot would be responsible. When we changed this to scenario 8, where the social robot becomes a pickpocket and commits the crime of stealing money from tourists, most respondents held the manufacturer company responsible.

We then changed the scenario to consider the social robot's secret collection of personal information and listen to their owners' private and confidential information (scenario 9). Once again, respondents held the manufacturing company responsible. Lastly (scenario 10), an overwhelming majority (10 out 12 respondents) selected the option of immediately reporting the issue of collecting private information by the social robot to the law enforcement officer. Scenarios 5 to 10 covered themes of physical threat and self-defense. It is quite clear that most respondents prefer holding social robot manufacturing companies responsible for causing damage or harm to society. This trend poses serious liability implications for social robot manufacturing firms.

To develop the acceptability of social robots among people, manufacturers need to develop a strategy that aligns with the interests of other stakeholders, such as suppliers, customers and governments. This idea is very similar to the stakeholder theory, which recommends businesses create value for all stakeholders without resorting to tradeoffs to sustain longer-term (Freeman et al. 2010). It can be applied to technology organizations, such as social robot manufacturers, that navigate through different organizational and product life cycle stages (Shah and Guild 2022).

Overall, this exploratory experiment taught us that people's ethical preferences shift as situations change. Therefore, we stress manufacturing companies of social robots and governments to develop a comprehensive policy that adheres to the wishes and preferences of the general population. Social robots will likely be integrated into our societies in the near future. Governments and companies need to build a coherent set of rules that benefit everyone.

6   Limitations and Future Research

We acknowledge that the study results are not generalizable to a larger community. This exploratory study aimed to extract and test the core factors that change human ethical or moral preferences while interacting with social robots. After receiving promising results, we plan to expand this study to a larger sample size in other countries in the next phase. It would be fruitful to replicate the experiment in different parts of the world to understand better cultural and demographic factors, such as age and gender differences. A more inclusive study design will gather generalizable results to inform the stakeholders of policymaking. We also wish to conduct a larger "between subjects" experimental study using crowdsourcing platforms like Amazon Mechanical Turk.

We also recommend scholars investigate the relationships between social robot manufacturing companies and their related stakeholders in the future. This will help identify the societal problems better, which leads to building acceptable and ethical solutions for humans.

Another limitation of the study is that it was based on self-reported results. We aim to use real-life data for applications where moral and ethical scenarios are applied in the future. We understand the challenges behind gaining access to this type of real data. A possible way could be to partner with industry, government, and other related stakeholders to collectively tackle ethics and morality in technology advancements, similar to social robots.

Referring to future research, we will expand the scope of the social robot course to include a component of moral and ethical study in addition to the current course outline description as follows: *"This course provides the fundamentals of robotics business, covering their development, capabilities, and corporate and government strategy role. A companion (service/social) robot consists of a physical humanoid robot component that connects through a network infrastructure to online services that enhance traditional robot functionality. Humanoid robots usually behave like natural social interaction partners for human users, with emotional features such as speech, gestures, and eye-gaze, referring to their cultural and social background. The course's foundations will set the baseline for understanding how Human-Robot Interaction (HRI) will likely influence and change our business practices and lifestyle. This course will also discuss companion robots' emerging use in different business application domains, such as customer service support and healthcare management. The students will experience the development lifecycle of a robotics application from the design phase to prototype development."* Since this preliminary study was conducted online during the pandemic, we would move the future experiment by the Wizard-of-Oz (WoZ) technique. We will also investigate Asimov's three rules of robotics for future research: *"(1) A robot may not injure a human being or, through inaction, allow a human being to come to harm, (2) A robot must obey the orders given to it by human beings except where such orders would conflict with the First Law, and (3) A robot must protect its own existence as long as such protection does not conflict with the First or Second Laws"* (Bartneck et al. 2020).

Acknowledgments. This study is supported with Research Incentive Fund (RIF), activity code: R21111, Zayed University, United Arab Emirates.

References

Arnold, T., Scheutz, M.: Beyond moral dilemmas: exploring the ethical landscape in HRI. In: 2017 12th ACM/IEEE International Conference on Human-Robot Interaction (HRI), pp. 445–452 (2017)

Bagloee, S.A., Tavana, M., Asadi, M., Oliver, T.: Autonomous vehicles: challenges, opportunities, and future implications for transportation policies. J. Mod. Transp. 4(24), 284–303 (2016)

Bartneck, C., Belpaeme, T., Eyssel, F., Kanda, T., Keijsers, M., Šabanović, S.: Human-Robot Interaction: An Introduction. Cambridge University Press, Cambridge (2020)

Bonnefon, J.F., Shariff, A., Rahwan, I.: The social dilemma of autonomous vehicles. Science **352**(6293), 1573–1576 (2016)

Elliott, J.K.: Elon Musk Unveils Tesla robot that would do hard work for humans (2021). https://globalnews.ca/news/8128131/tesla-bot-ai-robot-elon-musk/

Frank, D.A., Chrysochou, P., Mitkidis, P., Ariely, D.: Human decision-making biases in the moral dilemmas of autonomous vehicles. Sci. Rep. **9**(1), 13080 (2019)

Freeman, R.E., Parmar, B.L., Harrison, J.S., Wicks, A.C., Purnell, L., De Colle, S.: Stakeholder Theory: The State of the Art. Cambridge University Press, New York (2010)

Frennert, S., Östlund, B.: Seven matters of concern of social robots and older people. Int. J. Soc. Robot. **6**, 299–310 (2014)

Geisslinger, M., Poszler, F., Betz, J., Lütge, C., Lienkamp, M.: Autonomous driving ethics: from trolley problem to ethics of risk. Philos. Technol. **34**, 1033–1055 (2021)

Gerdes, A.: The issue of moral consideration in robot ethics. ACM SIGCAS Comput. Soc. **45**(3), 274–279 (2016)

Homburg, N.M.: Designing HRI experiments with humanoid robots: a multistep approach. In: Proceedings of the 51st Hawaii International Conference on System Sciences, AIS, pp. 4423–4432 (2018)

Kanda, T., Ishiguro, H., Imai, M., Ono, T.: Development and evaluation of interactive humanoid robots. Proc. IEEE **92**(11), 1839–1850 (2004)

Karnouskos, S.: Self-driving car acceptance and the role of ethics. IEEE Trans. Eng. Manag. **67**(2), 252–265 (2018)

Kim, B., Wen, R., Zhu, Q., Williams, T., Phillips, E.: Robots as moral advisors: the effects of deontological, virtue, and confucian role ethics on encouraging honest behavior. In: Companion of the 2021 ACM/IEEE International Conference on Human-Robot Interaction, pp. 10–18, March 2021

Komatsu, T.: Japanese students apply same moral norms to humans and robot agents: considering a moral HRI in terms of different cultural and academic backgrounds. In: 2016 11th ACM/IEEE International Conference on Human-Robot Interaction (HRI), pp. 457–458. IEEE, March 2016

Komatsu, T., Malle, B.F., Scheutz, M.: Blaming the reluctant robot: parallel blame judgments for robots in moral dilemmas across US and Japan. In: Proceedings of the 2021 ACM/IEEE International Conference on Human-Robot Interaction, pp. 63–72, March 2021.

Malle, B.F., Scheutz, M., Arnold, T., Voiklis, J., Cusimano, C.: Sacrifice one for the good of many? People apply different moral norms to human and robot agents. In: Proceedings of the Tenth Annual ACM/IEEE International Conference on Human-Robot Interaction, pp. 117–124, March 2015

Miller, J., Williams, A.B., Perouli, D.: A case study on the cybersecurity of social robots. In: Companion of the 2018 ACM/IEEE International Conference on Human-Robot Interaction, pp. 195–196, March 2018

Nagataki, S., et al.: On the robot as a moral agent. In: Proceedings of the XIX International Conference on Human Computer Interaction, pp. 1–5, September 2018

Nomura, T., Kanda, T., Yamada, S.: Measurement of moral concern for robots. In: 2019 14th ACM/IEEE International Conference on Human-Robot Interaction (HRI), pp. 540–541. IEEE, March 2019

Shah, M.U., Rehman, U., Iqbal, F., Wahid, F., Hussain, M., Arsalan, A.: Access permissions for apple watch applications: a study on users' perceptions. In: 2020 International Conference on Communications, Computing, Cybersecurity, and Informatics (CCCI), pp. 1–7. IEEE, November 2020

Shah, M.U., Rehman, U., Iqbal, F., Ilahi, H.: Exploring the human factors in moral dilemmas of autonomous vehicles. Pers. Ubiquit. Comput. **26**(5), 1321–1331 (2022)

Shah, M.U., Guild, P.D.: Stakeholder engagement strategy of technology firms: a review and applied view of stakeholder theory. Technovation **114**, 102460 (2022)

Thomson, J.J.: The trolley problem. Yale Law J. **6**(94), 1395–1415 (1985)

Wächter, L., Lindner, F.: An explorative comparison of blame attributions to companion robots across various moral dilemmas. In: Proceedings of The 6th International Conference on Human-Agent Interaction, pp. 269–276 (2018)

Wen, R., Kim, B., Phillips, E., Zhu, Q., Williams, T.: Comparing strategies for robot communication of role-grounded moral norms. In: Companion of the 2021 ACM/IEEE International Conference on Human-Robot Interaction, pp. 323–327, March 2021

One Size Does Not Fit All:

Developing Robot User Types for Office Robots

Ruth Stock-Homburg[(⊠)] [iD] and Lea Heitlinger[iD]

Technical University Darmstadt, Hochschulstraße 1, 64289 Darmstadt, Germany
rsh@bwl.tu-darmstadt.de

Abstract. Office robots can be a solution to the shortage of skilled workers in certain areas. They perform tasks automatically and work around the clock. Examples of tasks performed by these robots include data processing, clerical work, and administrative tasks. We propose five types of robot users based on interviews after real-life use cases of an office robot. We investigate these types in an online study that shows relevant patterns associated with each type and first indications of type distribution. By using these individual robot user types, organizations can tailor robot implementation to their workforce and create ideal human-robot interactions in the workplace.

Keywords: Office Robots · Robot User Typology · Robot Integration

1 Introduction

Many companies today are facing workforce challenges, such as a shortage of skilled workers [1]. Bringing robots into the office can be a solution to the shortage of skilled workers [2] in certain areas. They can perform tasks automatically and work around the clock. For example, they can be used for data processing, clerical and administrative tasks [e.g., 3, 4]. Recent developments in artificial intelligence have enabled robots to perform complex tasks that require creative thinking, critical analysis, and problem solving. They are also capable of interacting with customers or co-workers in social situations [5, 6]. In particular, office robots can perform tasks that are boring or difficult for humans [7], which can help reduce workload and increase job satisfaction. Despite their many benefits, office robots have received little attention from researchers (see [8] for an overview).

To reap the benefits of office robots, their integration should aim for effective human-robot collaboration [9]. To ensure this, the human perspective needs to be considered [10, 11] because these users must ultimately accept and work with the newly implemented technology [7]. In the best case, a synergy is created between the human and the robot [9, 12].

Previous research has shown that users react very differently to robots [13, 14]. At the same time, individual differences between employees are an important factor in the workplace [15]. A "one-size-fits-all approach" to robot integration is therefore likely to fail. Organizations face a dilemma in that personalized approaches often increase relevant outcomes, for example, in the case of employee training [16]. Robotics research has also shown that personalized interactions with robots are most beneficial for long-term success [17]. But resources are often tight. Organizations do not have the capacity to address every employees' robot-related needs and expectations individually. Grouping employees according to typical patterns in their expectations toward office robots can be a compromise.

Patterns have been identified in different workplace contexts, such as individuals' flow experiences [18] or in team learning processes [19]. Understanding patterns of expectations about office robots has several advantages: First, this approach can reduce organizations' resource constraints and allow them to maximize outcomes when dealing with new phenomena [20], such as office robots. Second, a typology allows to understand typical patterns of employee expectations towards office robots. Addressing these expectations can increase the effectiveness of communication and training, and thus increase the acceptance of office robots. Third, the typology can support the formation of mixed human-robot teams and the onboarding of new team members according to their preferences.

To ensure effective human-robot collaboration, it is necessary to understand different robot user types. This perspective allows to tailor the integration to employee needs, ensuring a high level of robot acceptance and thus long-term success [cf. 17]. Therefore, our two research questions are: *1. What can such a robot user typology look like? 2. How are these types related to social and performance outcomes?*

The goal of this paper is to provide insights into different types of office robot users in organizations. In doing so, this paper contributes to existing research in several important ways: First, we identify different types of office robot users based on employees' expectations of relevant robot characteristics with insights from interviews conducted after real-life user experiences with a robot. Second, these office robot user types are further investigated in an online survey. Specifically, we identify the characteristics of each type in more detail and provide initial indications of the distribution of each type. This approach allows us to build a holistic picture of the issue. Third, based on our proposed robot user typology, we provide guidance for practitioners seeking to successfully integrate office robots into their organizations.

2   Qualitative Interviews with Potential Office Robot Users

To gain initial insights about expectations toward office robots from potential office robot users, we conducted qualitative interviews with six office assistants at a local bank. During a half-day workshop, the interviewees were introduced to the humanoid robot Pepper. The workshop was part of a larger project to integrate assistive humanoid robots into the bank's office environment. Consequently, the participants were confronted with their company-related use case with concrete office applications of the robotic assistant. The training was designed to equip the participants with the necessary skills to interact with the robot. This interaction included technical details such as switching the robot on and off or charging the robot. It also included background information about the robot's underlying AI, as well as communication techniques for talking to the robot in an effective way. This gave the participants a comprehensive insight into the robot's capabilities. To assess their experiences, participants were interviewed after interacting with the robot as part of an open conversation to get feedback on the training. Our aim was to gain insight into the participants' expectations of their future interaction with the robot assistant.

Regarding the implementation of the robot, most participants expressed that they had a fairly clear idea of what it might look like. One participant was undecided and said that she would need more information to come up with possible tasks for the robot. An example statement from this participant was: "How quickly and how accurately the robot integration can succeed is a question mark for me".

Several participants were characterized by a simultaneous emphasis on performance and curiosity to try out the robot. However, they differed in the level of the combination of performance and curiosity. With a low level of both dimensions, one participant neither expressed expectations about the robot's performance nor was particularly willing to explore the robot's capabilities. The participant stated: "I'm worried that the added value won't be there or that I won't be able to give enough input. If I do it myself, I know the result will meet my needs".

In contrast to this, several participants expected the robot to increase performance and efficiency. Some were also willing to experiment with the robot. An example statement of such a user type was: "On the one hand, performance and efficiency and an easing of my working day. A good measure against overtime…. On the other hand, I like to try things out and have no reservations about using the robot. Having a robot makes the interaction more human".

For four participants, the performance expectations did not reflect their expectations from experimenting with the robot. Three participants wanted concrete professional support, some even directly mentioning tasks that the robot could take over or assist with. An example of a statement was: "The robot should make work easier and take over unpleasant tasks. Of course, technically everything has to run smoothly". In contrast, some participants expressed curiosity about the robot's functionalities and wanted to test the robot's capabilities. Efficiency was less important. An example statement is: "I am curious about what can be done with the robot…. I think it's cool if I get to experience this technology". In one case, curiosity about the robot assistant was linked to social acceptance of the robot. The participant stated: "The robot should be integrated as an employee, with an employment contract. Personalization and asking how I am and of course a 'good morning' would be important to me".

3   Robot User Types

Based on the conducted interviews, we identified five robot user types. These user types can be characterized along various characteristics. Specifically, we describe their perception of the office robot's benefits, their curiosity to try out the robot, their evaluation of the robot as machine or social entity and their opinion on robot deployment. The characteristics of the individual user types are depicted in Table 1.

Table 1. Characteristics of robot user types

User Type	Benefit	Curiosity	Machine vs. social entity	Opinion
Type 1	This robot user type does not see any possibilities to increase efficiency in daily office work. This type cannot imagine that a robot can function meaningfully and be reliable in the office	This type does not see the point and is not curious to try out the functions and capabilities of an office robot. For this type, such robots have nothing inspiring	This type does not see robots as a useful device. In no way does this type see office robots as something social that the user would just talk to	This type does not think anything of using robots in the office, the user rejects office robots
Type 2	This robot user type is unsure if an office robot could make daily office processes more efficient	This type does not know if he or she just wanted to try out a robot. The type is not particularly curious about them. For this type, such robots have little inspiring facets	This type would treat an office robot a bit like a machine. Maybe this user type would also have a conversation with the robot, but is still unsure about that	Overall, this type is not sure whether he/she would use a robot in the office
Type 3	This robot user type can very well imagine that an office robot is useful. The type thinks of improving processes in daily office work and increasing efficiency	For this type, the robot should work and be reliable. The type is also not curious to try out the functions and capabilities of an office robot. For this type, such robots have nothing inspiring	For this type, an office robot is clearly a machine or tool. Robots have nothing to do with social things. He or she cannot imagine just having a conversation with such a robot	If this type had the opportunity, he/she would definitely use an office robot, e.g., in the role of an assistant, for office work
Type 4	For this robot user type, robots have yet reached the point where they can really bring benefits to office work. This type also does not see any direct improvements in processes in daily office work or in efficiency gains	If this type got the opportunity, he or she would be very curious to try out the functions and capabilities of an office robot. That would be really fun for this type. He/she finds robots very inspiring	For this type, a robot is definitely more than a machine or just a tool. An office robot like this has something social about it. Of course, this type could imagine just talking to such a robot	If this type had the opportunity, he or she would find it exciting to use an office robot, e.g., in the role of an assistant, for office work

(continued)

Table 1. (*continued*)

User Type	Benefit	Curiosity	Machine vs. social entity	Opinion
Type 5	This robot user type would use the robot to increase efficiency in daily office tasks	But this type is also very curious to try out what the robot can do	This type sees both a machine and a social being in the robot. So, he/she can certainly imagine talking to the robot just like that	If this type gets the opportunity, this type would love to use such a robot as an assistant to support in the office. That would be inspiring and would increase efficiency

4   Online Study of Robot User Types

To investigate our proposed robot user types, we conducted an online study. Participants first shared demographic information. In a next step, we presented the robot user types with the information displayed in Table 1. Participants had to choose the type that they perceived as most fitting for them. After that, participants answered questions pertaining to relevant personal, job-related and performance outcomes.

4.1 Sample

In total, 125 participants took part in our survey. To ensure data quality, we included two attention check questions which asked participants to pick a certain value on the scale (e.g., please pick "absolutely agree"). Our final sample consisted of participants that fully completed the questionnaire and answered at least one of the attention check questions correctly. Our final sample size was 120 participants.

The mean age of the participants was 39.81 years (SD = 12.02 years). 62.5% of the sample identified as male, 36.7% as female and 0.8% as diverse. Regarding their professional status, 60.0% were employed workers in white collar jobs, 5.8% in blue collar jobs. 26.7% of participants were self-employed. Students with a side job made up 6.7% of the sample, while 0.8% were currently not working. Additionally, we asked participants to indicate their experience with robots on a scale ranging from 1 (I have no experience at all) to 10 (I have a lot of experience). The mean throughout the sample was quite low with 3.59 (SD = 2.38). We were further interested in where they made their experiences: 43.3% experienced robots in their free time, 35.0% in the media, 21.7% at work, 16.7% in a shop, 13.3% in a hotel, and 10.8% in a museum; 13.3% chose the option other. Regarding the nature of their experience, 65.0% saw robots in movies or online, 43.3% in real life, 27.5% interacted with robots, 7.5% owned robots, 6.7% programmed robots, and 5.8% worked together with robots; 7.5% chose the option other. For both questions, participants could choose multiple options.

4.2 Typology of Office Robot Users

We first assessed the distribution of our proposed robot user types in our sample. The individual characteristics of each user type are described in Table 1. With 41.7%, Type 3 was chosen the most. After that followed the robot user Type 5 with 25.8%. 16.7% of the sample could identify the most with Type 2, 13.3% with Type 4. Type 1 was chosen by 2.5% of participants.

To get more insights into our proposed types, we asked participants, if they found themselves in the type descriptions: 93.3% of the sample answered this question in the affirmative. Among these 112 individuals, the mean extent to which they were able to identify with the types was at 74.43% (SD = 15.72%) (scale range from 0 to 100%). We further asked how the participants of the full sample perceived the accuracy of the descriptions (again on a scale from 0 to 100%); throughout the sample, the mean value was at 76.02% (SD = 18.53%). A third question pertained to the realism of the described types, the mean value was here at 75.47% (SD = 18.94%).

4.3 Relation of Robot User Types to Personal, Job, and Performance Outcomes

In a next step, we evaluated measures pertaining to personal, job-related and performance outcomes for each type individually. The mean values and standard deviations are displayed in Table 2. The outcomes were measured as one item each. Participants had to indicate to which extent they expect the deployment of the robot to affect the outcomes on 5-point Likert-type scales. We asked for instance: "Would you recommend your company to invest in these robots?" or "How would such a robot affect your performance?". Conclusions need to be drawn with caution as the data is presented in a descriptive manner. These results are considered first investigations of the proposed robot user types.

The descriptive data shows that the mean values differ between the types. Additionally, for each type, different patterns are also visible. For Type 2, all mean outcome values are around the midpoint of the 5-point Likert-type scale. This points toward the conclusion that this type seems to be somewhat undecided regarding the evaluation of office robots – the values are neither particularly low nor high.

User Type 1 shows the lowest values on all investigated outcome variables. Especially regarding the recommendation of a robot to the current firm, the value for Type 1 is the lowest. In contrast to this, mean outcome variables are highest for Type 5. Here, the readiness to work with a robot has the highest overall value. Thus, this type puts a focus on working with the robot itself.

When comparing Types 3 and 4, it is evident that the values of Type 3 appear to be higher than the corresponding evaluations of Type 4. The highest values for Type 3 are for the readiness to work with a robot, so rooted in the actual work with the robot. For Type 4, the readiness to work with a robot seems to be on a similar level as the expected increases in job satisfaction through an integration of a robot.

We further asked participants to share their expectations in terms of training time they would need with the robot. The answering options ranged from several days to several weeks, months or the perception that they would never succeed. Potential robot users that identified with Type 1 expected to need only little time to learn specifics of

Table 2. Mean values of outcome variables for each robot user type

User Type	Readiness to Work with a Robot	Recommendation of Robot to Firm	Performance Increases by Robot	Job Satisfaction Increase Through Robot	Organizational Commitment Increase Through Robot
Type 1 (N = 3)	1.67 (.58)	1.33 (.58)	2.67 (.58)	2.33 (1.16)	2.33 (1.16)
Type 2 (N = 20)	2.95 (.95)	2.60 (1.00)	2.90 (.79)	2.85 (.67)	2.75 (.91)
Type 3 (N = 50)	3.50 (.79)	3.12 (.85)	3.34 (.63)	3.44 (.71)	2.96 (.70)
Type 4 (N = 16)	3.13 (.89)	2.50 (1.32)	2.81 (.75)	3.13 (.72)	2.88 (.50)
Type 5 (N = 31)	4.35 (.61)	4.00 (.86)	3.94 (.77)	4.10 (.70)	3.77 (.85)

a robot. To be specific, they only expected to need a few days to weeks. This indicates that rejection of robots is likely not due to lack of competence on the side of the users.

Type 2 robot users mostly expected to need several weeks to learn the specifics of the robot, some participants of the online study also chose the option several days or several months. Two participants even suggested that they would never succeed in the training. For Type 3, participants were evenly distributed between a training time of several days and several weeks. Type 4 robot users mainly expected to need several weeks and Type 5 users also mostly several weeks.

5 Discussion

The departure point of this study is the observation that although extant research discusses many antecedents to robot deployment, such as acceptance [21], insights into concrete user features that will shape future human-robot interactions are scarce. Since individualized approaches exceed resources of many companies, we suggest a taxonomy of robot users. This method allows for a segmentation of homogenous user groups that share characteristics and give indications of user needs.

Based on qualitative interviews with potential office robot users, we identified patterns of user types. These differing characteristics likely shape human-robot interactions in offices. Specifically, robot users can be differentiated in terms of the perceived benefits of robots: Some user types deducted from the interviews emphasize the robot's support in office tasks to increase efficiency for instance. Here, the focus clearly lies on the functionality of the robot. Research in human-robot interaction has also established that the (technical) functioning of a robot has important implications for users [22]. A second differentiating user characteristic pertains to curiosity towards the robot. In our interviews, we identified the tendency to explore the capabilities of the robot and try out the new technology. Curiosity of robot users has previously been shown to have an impact in interactions between robots and humans [23].

An additional feature refers to social aspects of robots: In our interviews, the majority of potential robot users perceived robots as tools or machines. However, one interviewee also perceived a social interaction with a robot as important. Robots as an embodied form of artificial intelligence [24] have the ability to create automated social presence during social interactions [25, 26]. Literature shows that robot users differ in their perception of robots as machine or social entity [27]. Lastly, we also integrate the personal opinion and determination of the user in terms of robot deployment into our work.

5.1 What Can Such a User Typology Look like?

We identified five robot user types that we investigated further in our quantitative study. The majority of participants were able to find themselves in the type descriptions (93.3%). The distribution of types in our sample gives first indications about the occurrence of each type: With 41.7%, user Type 3 was chosen most often by participants of our online study. This user type is characterized by a focus on the robot's integration for efficient task completion; here, the robot is mainly perceived as tool to complete relevant office work. Considering again the distribution in our sample, this type was followed by Type 5 with 25.8%. Robot user Type 5 is characterized by a high focus on both aspects, using the robot to complete office work efficiently and trying out capabilities of the robot. Additionally, robots are rather perceived as social interaction partners.

Robot user Type 2 had a share of 16.7% in our sample. This type is in the middle on all relevant characteristics, so is somewhat undecided in the evaluation of office robots. Type 4 was represented in our sample with 13.3%. Here, the focus lies on exploration of robotic capabilities and trying out new functionalities. The robot is rather perceived as social entity in this case. Robot user Type 1 was chosen the least in our sample (2.5%). This type is opposed to the introduction of robots into office environments.

All in all, the distribution in our sample shows that a focus of the robot as a machine or tool to support in office tasks is the most common perception of robots by our study participants. Social aspects (for instance as part of Types 4 and 5) are not as pronounced. These findings further mimic the results of our qualitative interview data, in that robots mainly seem to be perceived as tools.

5.2 How are the Types Related to Social and Performance Outcomes?

We further give first indications about relevant personal, job-related and performance characteristics for each user type. Since we only evaluated the data in a descriptive manner, these results need to be interpreted with caution.

Our results point toward the direction that the highest values seem to be present for robot user Type 5. Specifically, this type would like to work together with such a robot, recommend it to their company, use of the robot would improve their job and their performance; job satisfaction and organizational commitment towards their company would also go up. Values on these variables for the other types appear to be lower in our descriptive data. Consistent with our proposed type descriptions, robot user Type 1 has the lowest values. This points toward the conclusion that this robot type rejects robots on multiple levels—a notion that is mirrored in their evaluations. The values for Type 2 are also in line with our typology in that all evaluations are in the middle indicating a general undecidedness of this user type.

For Types 3 and 4, the outcome patterns are also very insightful. Generally speaking, the values for robot user Type 3 are descriptively higher than those for Type 4. In more detail, Type 3 focuses on the actual work with the robot and its support in office tasks. For Type 3, working together with the robot is also important, but the perceived increase on job satisfaction is on a similar level.

Our research has also several implications for practitioners. First, with the identified robot user types, we offer first insights into how employees as users may react to the deployment of robots in office environments—an endeavor that can have multiple benefits for organizations if implemented successfully [e.g., 2, 8]. To be specific, we share important user characteristics that are relevant for companies.

Second, based on the user types, practitioners can tailor the integration of robots to the needs of users. We offer an economic approach to this by finding a middle ground in employee segmentation based on the identified types. This allows to address the needs of users in a tailored manner providing the basis for a long-term successful integration [cf. 17].

Third, with the typology as a starting point, organizations can create trainings that specifically address the features of the identified robot users. Since we share relevant outcomes for firms pertaining to robot integration into workplaces, training content can specifically address and potentially modify these characteristics.

5.3 Limitations and Implications for Future Research

Our work provides initial insights into user types of office robots. Future research can follow up upon the suggested taxonomy and identify other relevant characteristics or variables that differentiate user groups. Based on this, tailored design approaches of robots and their integration can be developed to optimally create a fruitful collaboration and synergy between humans and robots at work [9, 12].

We evaluated the user types both in a quantitative online study and through interviews. While the interviews were conducted after participants interacted with a robot, more research is needed into how real-life encounters shape user reactions and behaviors to robots [cf. 8]. Simultaneously, the results of our online study can be extended beyond a descriptive approach.

Robot user types may evolve over time as employees gain more experience in dealing with robots. Thus, longitudinal studies are crucial in human-robot interaction [17, 28]. Ideally, these investigations would directly take place in offices to study user patterns and types in the natural implementation setting.

Acknowledgements. This research project is funded by the German Federal Ministry of Education and Research (BMBF) within the KompAKI project. The authors are responsible for the content of this publication.

References

1. Glassman, J.: The labor shortage will outlast the pandemic (2022). https://www.jpmorgan.com/commercial-banking/insights/why-the-labor-shortage-persists
2. Paluch, S., Tuzovic, S., Holz, H.F., Kies, A., Jörling, M.: "My colleague is a robot" – exploring frontline employees' willingness to work with collaborative service robots. JOSM (2022). https://doi.org/10.1108/JOSM-11-2020-0406
3. Asoh, H., et al.: Jijo-2: an office robot that communicates and learns. IEEE Intell. Syst. (2001). https://doi.org/10.1109/MIS.2001.956081
4. Anagnoste, S.: Robotic automation process - the next major revolution in terms of back office operations improvement. In: Proceedings of the International Conference on Business Excellence (2017). https://doi.org/10.1515/picbe-2017-0072
5. Garrell, A., Sanfeliu, A.: Cooperative social robots to accompany groups of people. Int. J. Robot. Res. (2012). https://doi.org/10.1177/0278364912459278
6. Čaić, M., Mahr, D., Oderkerken-Schröder, G.: Value of social robots in services: social cognition perspective. JSM (2019). https://doi.org/10.1108/JSM-02-2018-0080
7. Burke, J., Coovert, M., Murphy, R., Riley, J., Rogers, E.: Human-robot factors: robots in the workplace. In: Proceedings of the Human Factors and Ergonomics Society Annual Meeting (2006). https://doi.org/10.1177/154193120605000902
8. Wolf, F.D., Stock-Homburg, R.M.: How and when can robots be team members? Three decades of research on human-robot teams. Group Org. Manag. (2022). https://doi.org/10.1177/10596011221076636
9. Kim, S.: Working with robots: human resource development considerations in human-robot interaction. Hum. Resour. Dev. Rev. (2022). https://doi.org/10.1177/15344843211068810
10. Gombolay, M., Bair, A., Huang, C., Shah, J.: Computational design of mixed-initiative human–robot teaming that considers human factors: situational awareness, workload, and workflow preferences. Int. J. Robot. Res. (2017). https://doi.org/10.1177/0278364916688255
11. Charalambous, G., Fletcher, S.R., Webb, P.: The development of a human factors readiness level tool for implementing industrial human-robot collaboration. Int. J. Adv. Manuf. Technol. **91**(5–8), 2465–2475 (2017). https://doi.org/10.1007/s00170-016-9876-6
12. Beer, J.M., Fisk, A.D., Rogers, W.A.: Toward a framework for levels of robot autonomy in human-robot interaction. J. Hum. Robot Interact. (2014). https://doi.org/10.5898/JHRI.3.2. Beer
13. Bartneck, C., Suzuki, T., Kanda, T., Nomura, T.: The influence of people's culture and prior experiences with Aibo on their attitude towards robots. AI Soc. (2006). https://doi.org/10.1007/s00146-006-0052-7
14. Babel, F., Kraus, J., Baumann, M.: Findings from a qualitative field study with an autonomous robot in public: exploration of user reactions and conflicts. Int. J. Soc. Robot. (2022). https://doi.org/10.1007/s12369-022-00894-x
15. Mark, G., Czerwinski, M., Iqbal, S.T.: Effects of individual differences in blocking workplace distractions. In: Mandryk, R., Hancock, M., Perry, M., Cox, A. (eds.) Proceedings of the 2018 CHI Conference on Human Factors in Computing Systems. CHI 2018: CHI Conference on Human Factors in Computing Systems, Montreal QC Canada, 21 April 2018–26 April 2018, pp. 1–12. ACM, New York (2018). https://doi.org/10.1145/3173574.3173666

16. Babu, A.R., Rajavenkatanarayanan, A., Abujelala, M., Makedon, F.: VoTrE: a vocational training and evaluation system to compare training approaches for the workplace. In: Lackey, S., Chen, J. (eds.) VAMR 2017. LNCS, vol. 10280, pp. 203–214. Springer, Cham (2017). https://doi.org/10.1007/978-3-319-57987-0_16

17. Lee, M.K., Forlizzi, J., Kiesler, S., Rybski, P., Antanitis, J., Savetsila, S.: 2012 7th ACM/IEEE International Conference on Human-Robot Interaction (HRI 2012), Boston, Massachusetts, USA, 5–8 March 2012; Proceedings, Piscataway, NJ. IEEE (2012)

18. Ceja, L., Navarro, J.: Dynamic patterns of flow in the workplace: characterizing within-individual variability using a complexity science approach. J. Organ. Behav. (2011). https://doi.org/10.1002/job.747

19. Baert, H., Govaerts, N.: Learning patterns of teams at the workplace. J. Work. Learn. (2012). https://doi.org/10.1108/13665621211261025

20. Stock, R.M., Zacharias, N.A.: Patterns and performance outcomes of innovation orientation. J. Acad. Mark. Sci. (2011). https://doi.org/10.1007/s11747-010-0225-2

21. Savela, N., Turja, T., Oksanen, A.: Social acceptance of robots in different occupational fields: a systematic literature review. Int. J. Soc. Robot. 10(4), 493–502 (2017). https://doi.org/10.1007/s12369-017-0452-5

22. Heerink, M., Kröse, B., Evers, V., Wielinga, B.: The influence of social presence on acceptance of a companion robot by older people. jopha (2008). https://doi.org/10.14198/JoPha.2008.2.2.05

23. Law, E., et al.: A Wizard-of-Oz study of curiosity in human-robot interaction. In: 2017 26th IEEE International Symposium on Robot and Human Interactive Communication (RO-MAN), Lisbon, 28 August 2017–01 September 2017, pp. 607–614. IEEE (2017). https://doi.org/10.1109/ROMAN.2017.8172365

24. High-Level Expert Group on Artificial Intelligence: A Definition of AI: Main Capabilities and Disciplines (2019). https://digital-strategy.ec.europa.eu/en/library/definition-artificial-intelligence-main-capabilities-and-scientific-disciplines

25. van Doorn, J., et al.: Domo arigato Mr. Roboto. J. Ser. Res. (2017). https://doi.org/10.1177/1094670516679272

26. Wirtz, J., et al.: Brave new world: service robots in the frontline. JOSM (2018). https://doi.org/10.1108/JOSM-04-2018-0119

27. Roesler, E., Naendrup-Poell, L., Manzey, D., Onnasch, L.: Why context matters: the influence of application domain on preferred degree of anthropomorphism and gender attribution in human–robot interaction. Int. J. Soc. Robot. (2022). https://doi.org/10.1007/s12369-021-00860-z

28. Gockley, R., et al.: Designing robots for long-term social interaction. In: 2005 IEEE/RSJ International Conference on Intelligent Robots and Systems, Edmonton, Alta., Canada, 02 August 2005–02 August 2005, pp. 1338–1343. IEEE (2005). https://doi.org/10.1109/IROS.2005.1545303

Proposal of Emotion Expression Method by Clothes Color for Communication Robot

Akihiro Tatsumi[✉] and Masashi Okubo

Doshisha University, 1-3 Tatara Miyakodani, Kyotanabe-shi, Kyoto 610-0321, Japan
ttmakihiro@gmail.com, mokubo@mail.doshisha.ac.jp

Abstract. In recent years, communication robots are commonly used in various purposes and situations such as guidance services at hotels and stations, elderly support, etc. in Japan. However, it is also shown that people still have a sense of anxiety toward robots. For this reason, there are few people who have motivations to communicate with robots. On the other hand, it has been suggested that the emotion expression of robots contributes to create a sense of familiarity and smooth communication. Therefore, we propose a method of emotion expression and enhancement by changing the color of the clothes the robot is wearing. In this research, we have matched the clothes color with speech emotion for communication robot. As a result of the experiment, we found the matching between the clothes colors and 10 emotions (joy, anger, sorrow, fear, shame, like, dislike, excite, relief and surprise). Moreover, we obtained some problems about the method of changing clothes color according to the progress of the speech. Therefore, additional experiment is performed to solve these problems and to improve the method of changing clothes color. As a result of the additional experiment, we found the method of changing clothes color with reducing the unnaturalness and discomfort.

Keywords: Human-robot interaction · Non-verbal information · Clothes hue · Color change method · Sensory evaluation

1 Introduction

In recent years, communication robots are commonly used in various places and situations such as guidance work at hotels and stations and elderly supports for the purpose of reducing human loads and releasing from simple works. In addition, it has been reported that the communication robots will become more popular in the future [1], and positive impressions about it have also been reported [2]. However, it has been reported that people still feel uneasy towards the robots [3].

It has been clarified that not only verbal information but also non-verbal information plays an important role in smooth communication between humans [4–6]. In addition, it has also been suggested that emotion expression by non-verbal information of robot contributes to create a sense of familiarity and smooth communication [7, 8]. However, most of the robot's emotion expression methods that have been proposed depend on the hardware configuration. For example, in case of facial expressions, it is indispensable

© The Author(s), under exclusive license to Springer Nature Switzerland AG 2023
M. Kurosu and A. Hashizume (Eds.): HCII 2023, LNCS 14013, pp. 215–235, 2023.
https://doi.org/10.1007/978-3-031-35602-5_16

to have a hardware mechanism that can express facial muscles. And, in case of body motions, many degrees of freedom and electric motors are required at the arms and the body. Furthermore, it is difficult to newly install this hardware in using robots. And it is necessary to develop a new robot equipped with the hardware specialized for emotional expression.

Therefore, we aim to develop an emotion expression method that does not depend on the hardware configuration of the robot itself. Specifically, we are developing an emotion expression method by making the robot wear removable clothes and changing the color of the clothes according to the content of the speech. Figure 1 shows an overview of the emotion expression method by clothes color for communication robots.

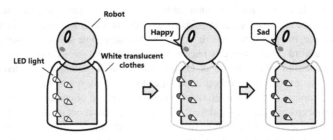

Fig. 1. Emotion expression method by clothes color for communication robot.

2 Related Research and Research Objective

2.1 Related Research: Emotion Expression Methods for Communication Robot

Many emotion expression methods for communication robot have been proposed. From the viewpoint of speech contents and paralanguage, a method that includes emotion words in the speech and a method that controls the speed and pitch of the speech have been proposed [7, 9].

On the other hand, from the viewpoint of visual non-verbal information, emotion expression methods by facial expressions, body motions and luminescence from robot's eye or parts of the body have been proposed [8, 10, 11]. However, these emotion expression methods by visual non-verbal information require the specific hardware.

2.2 Related Research: Clothes as Communication Tool

Non-verbal information plays an important role in smooth communication between humans [4–6]. Among this non-verbal information, it has also been clarified that the clothes play an important role in message transmission [12]. Moreover, clothes are also called as body media, and it has been suggested that the clothes play a role of physical extension [12, 13].

In addition, the effects of making robots wear clothes are also investigated. For example, Friedman et al. suggested the importance of making robots wear clothes that matches scene, situation and role [14].

Therefore, there is a high possibility that a new communication method can be created by making robots wear clothes.

2.3 Related Research: Relationship Between Emotions and Colors

Many researches have reported the relations between emotions and colors [15–20]. From these researches, while some results show the consistent correspondences such as red for anger and blue for sadness, there are some results that do not show the consistent correspondence between emotions and colors.

On the other hand, the influences of clothes color on communication have also been investigated. In case of communication between humans, clothes color plays an important role in the creation of the impressions [21–24]. Furthermore, we have previously verified the influences of robot's clothes color on impressions from the viewpoint of personal space [25]. And as a result of the experiment, we clarified that the personal space changes depending on the robot's clothes color.

As noted above, while the influences of clothes colors on humans have been verified, the relationships between emotions and the robot's clothes colors have not been clarified. Moreover, the emotion expression method by the clothes color for the robot has not been developed.

2.4 Research Objective

Figure 2 shows the roadmap of our research. The goal of our research is to develop an emotion expression method by clothes colors that does not depend on the hardware configuration of the robot. However, there are many cases in which the consistent correspondences between emotions and colors have not been obtained. In addition, there is no research that has focused on the clothes color of robot. Therefore, the purpose of this research is to investigate the robot's clothes color suitable for the emotion contained in the speech (shown in ① in this figure).

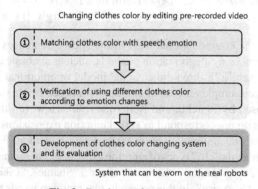

Fig. 2. Roadmap of our research.

3 Design of Speech Contents and Clothes Color for Robot

3.1 Robot Used in the Experiment

We used the developer version of Sota created by Vstone Co., Ltd. [26]. Sota is a 28-cm-tall tabletop communication robot and is capable of varied body motions thanks to its 3-axis head, 1-axis trunk, and arms with 2 axes each for a total of 8 degrees of freedom. In addition, it features cloud-based voice synthesis, and can speak expressions of the user's choosing. Figure 3 shows the robot's appearance and its specification.

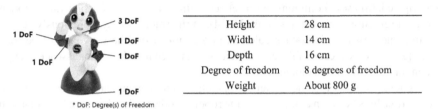

Height	28 cm
Width	14 cm
Depth	16 cm
Degree of freedom	8 degrees of freedom
Weight	About 800 g

Fig. 3. Robot used in the experiment and its specification.

3.2 Speech Contents

The robot speaks the following two sentences in Japanese. In addition, only the emotion words of the speech sentences are replaced according to the emotion.

「今日はすごく【感情語①】出来事があったんだ.」
(I had a very "Emotion word ①" event today.)

「その出来事があって, 僕は【感情語②】気持ちになったよ.」
(And I felt "Emotion word ②" through its event.)

Table 1 shows the emotion words used in the speech sentences for each emotion. There are various emotion categorization methods, such as six basic emotions proposed by Ekman and Friesen [27], three-dimensional model of emotional intensity proposed by Millenson [28], circumplex model of emotions proposed by Russell [29], and wheel of emotions proposed by Plutchik and Kellerman [30]. However, these emotion categorization methods do not correspond to verbal emotion expressions. Therefore, in this research, we use the Nakamura's emotion categorization method [31]. In this emotion categorization method, the 2167 types of emotion expressions in Japanese are categorized into 10 emotions: "Joy", "Anger", "Sorrow", "Fear", "Shame", "Like", "Dislike", "Excite", "Relief", and "Surprise". In this research, two emotion words that are considered to be natural in the above speech sentences are selected for each emotion.

Table 1. Emotion words used in the speech sentences for each emotion.

Emotion		Emotion word ①		Emotion word ②	
喜	(Joy)	嬉しい	(Happy)	浮き浮きする	(Cheerful)
怒	(Anger)	腹が立つ	(Irritating)	不愉快な	(Disagreeable)
哀	(Sorrow)	悲しい	(Sad)	しんみりした	(Sentimental)
怖	(Fear)	恐ろしい	(Awful)	不安な	(Anxious)
恥	(Shame)	恥ずかしい	(Shameful)	照れ臭い	(Embarrassing)
好	(Like)	心を奪われる	(Captivating)	うっとりした	(Enraptured)
厭	(Dislike)	嫌な	(Unpleasant)	憂鬱な	(Depressed)
昂	(Excite)	ときめく	(Throbbing)	胸が熱くなる	(Excited)
安	(Relief)	落ち着く	(Soothing)	安らかな	(Peaceful)
驚	(Surprise)	驚く	(Amazing)	呆然とした	(Shocked)

3.3 Clothes Color

In this research, we recorded the robot's speech and changed the clothes color by video editing with Adobe After Effects. Figure 4 shows the overview of changing clothes color by video editing. At first, when recording the robot's speech were recorded in red clothes that makes it easy to identify the clothes area (shown in ① in this figure). Note that, the robot performed body motions according to the speech, but the body motions were the same for all emotions. Next, in the changing of clothes color by video editing, white clothes is used before, between and after the speech sentences (shown in ②-1 in this figure). In addition, the hue of the clothes color is 0°, 45°, 90°, 135°, 180°, 225°, 270° and 315°, which is obtained by dividing the 360° color wheel into 8 equal parts (shown in ②-2 in this figure). Moreover, deep color is applied to the emotion word, and pale color is applied to the other parts in the speech (shown in ②-3 in this figure).

Finally, the created speech videos in each hue are integrated into one video and presented to the participants. Figure 5 shows the timeline of the video.

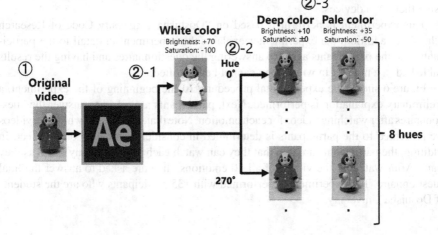

Fig. 4. Overview of changing clothes color by video editing.

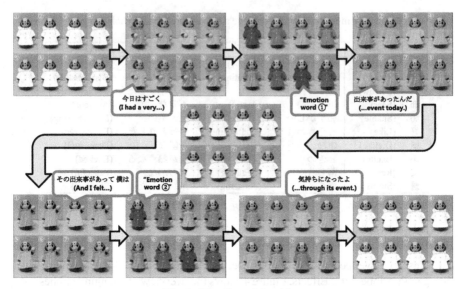

Fig. 5. Timeline of the video.

4 Experiment: Matching Clothes Color with Speech Emotion

4.1 Experiment Objective and Method

The purpose of this experiment is to select the robot's clothes color suitable for the emotion contained in the speech. In addition, we also verify the influences of changing the clothes color according to the speech emotion and changing the clothes color according to the progress of the speech on the participants. Note that, this experiment is performed online due to COVID-19, and participants watch the videos and answer the questionnaires using their own devices.

This experiment is performed based on "Doshisha University Code of Research Ethics". In addition, the experimenter explains the experiment in detail to the participants, and the participants agree to answering the questionnaires and having the results published in a manner in which they cannot be identified.

Figure 6 shows the experimental procedure. At the beginning of the experiment, a preliminary explanation is performed. Next, participants are asked to answer the questionnaires after watching videos for each emotion. Note that, the order in which the videos are presented to the participants is determined in consideration of the order effect. In addition, the participants are told that they can watch each video as many times as they want. After watching the videos of all 10 emotions, they are asked to answer the final questionnaire. The experiment is performed with 135 participants who are the students of Doshisha University.

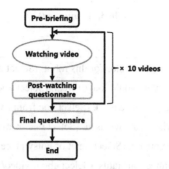

Fig. 6. Experimental procedure.

4.2 Questionnaire

Table 2 shows the contents of post-watching questionnaire. In the post-watching questionnaire, the participants are asked to select the top three clothes colors that matches the speech from eight clothes colors presented in the video.

Table 3 shows the contents of final questionnaire. In the final questionnaire, the participants are asked to evaluate changing clothes color according to speech emotion and changing clothes color according to the progress of speech. Furthermore, the participants are asked to answer about affinity between the clothes color and the robot itself. And the environment of watching videos is also checked.

Table 2. Post-watching questionnaire

#	Question
Q1	Select 1st place as clothes color that matches the speech. (Choose one from eight colors.)
Q2	Select 2nd place as clothes color that matches the speech. (Choose one from eight colors.)
Q3	Select 3rd place as clothes color that matches the speech. (Choose one from eight colors.)

Table 3. Final questionnaire

#	Question
Q1	It is better to use clothes color according to speech emotion. (1: Disagree – 7: Agree)
Q2	If you have any opinions or impressions about using clothes color according to speech emotion, please describe them
Q3	It is better to change clothes color according to progress of speech. (1: Disagree – 7: Agree)
Q4	If you have any opinions or impressions about changing clothes color according to progress of speech, please describe them

(continued)

Table 3. (*continued*)

#	Question
Q5	Select one appropriate clothes color for this robot. (Select one from eight colors.)
Q6	Select one clothes color you would like to wear. (Select one from eight colors.)
Q7	Select the visual devise you have used. (Select one from five visual devices.)
Q8	Select the auditory devise you have used. (Select one from eight auditory devices.)
Q9	Select the place where you are. (Select quiet or noisy place.)
Q10	Select your internet connection status. (Select about video/audio problem.)

4.3 Experiment Results

30 participants who had problems with the video watching environment were excluded from the analysis, and we evaluate the results from 105 participants.

Figure 7 shows the results of post-watching questionnaire Q1 (1st place as clothes color that matches the speech) for each emotion. These results suggest that the appropriate clothes colors differ according to the speech emotions. Further, from the results of final questionnaire Q5 (appropriate clothes color for this robot) and Q6 (clothes color you would like to wear), hue of 225° is evaluated highest. However, this 225° hue clothes color is not highly evaluated as a clothes color that matches for each emotion. In other words, it is considered that the clothing colors that match the robot itself and preferences for clothes colors have little effect on clothes colors that matches for each emotion.

Next, based on the results of the top three clothes colors that matches the speech (post-watching questionnaire Q1-Q3 shown in Table 2), we calculate the clothes colors' evaluation considering ranking for each emotion. Specifically, we multiply the number of times that is selected as 1st place by 3, the number of times that is selected as 2nd place by 2, and the number of times that is selected as 3rd place by 1. After that, we sum them up for each color. Figure 8 shows the calculation example of evaluation considering ranking.

Figure 9 shows the evaluation considering ranking for each emotion. For all emotions, the clothes color that is most selected in the post-watching questionnaire Q1 (1st place as clothes color that matches the speech) is also evaluated highest.

Figure 10 shows the average of final questionnaire Q1 (using clothes color according to speech emotion) and Q3 (changing clothes color according to progress of speech), and Fig. 11 shows their details. From the result of Q1, the average score is higher than "5" on a seven-grade scale, and "5" to "7" are often selected in the result's detail. In other words, it is considered that many people think positively about changing the clothes color according to the speech emotion. On the other hand, from the result of Q3, the average score is about "4", and variation is also observed in the result's detail. Therefore, participants who rate "5" or higher for Q3 are categorized into "group of high evaluation", and participants who rated "3" or lower are categorized into the "group of low evaluation", and we investigate the factors that influence the evaluation in more detail. Note that, the group of high evaluation is consisted by 40 participants, and the group of low evaluation is consisted by 47 participants.

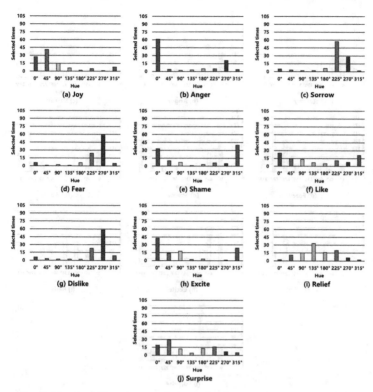

Fig. 7. Results of 1st place as clothes color that matches speech emotion.

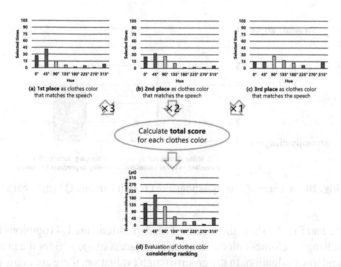

Fig. 8. Example of evaluation considering ranking (Joy).

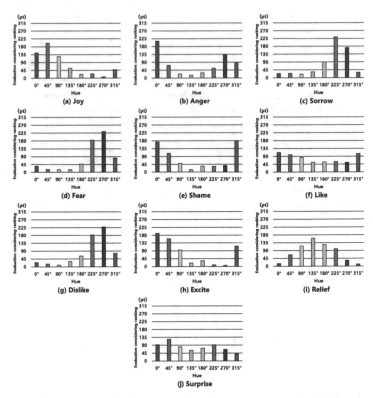

Fig. 9. Evaluation considering ranking for each emotion.

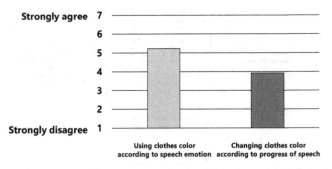

Fig. 10. Average of final questionnaire Q1 (left bar) and Q3 (right bar).

Figure 12 and Fig. 13 show the results of final questionnaire Q4 (opinions or impressions about changing clothes color according to progress of speech) for the group of high evaluation and low evaluation. In the group of high evaluation, there are many comments that the emotion changes and the intensity of emotions are easy to understand. On the other hand, in the group of low evaluation, there are many comments about the negative opinions toward the changing clothes color. And the reasons for this is answered that

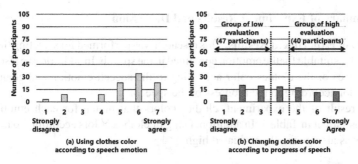

Fig. 11. Result details of final questionnaire Q1 (left) and Q3 (right).

it is difficult to concentrate on the speech, and that the eyes feel tired when the clothes color changes to high brightness and saturation.

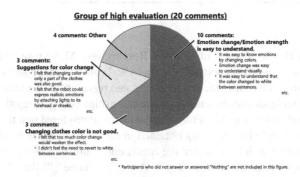

Fig. 12. Result of final questionnaire Q4 (group of high evaluation).

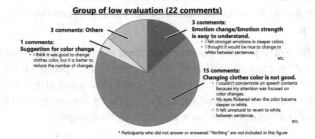

Fig. 13. Result of final questionnaire Q4 (group of low evaluation).

4.4 Summary of Experiment Results and Discussion

Summary of Experiment Results. This research was performed for selecting the robot's clothes color suitable for the emotion contained in the speech. In addition, we also verified the influences of the clothes color according to the speech emotion and changing the clothes color according to the progress of the speech.

As a result of the experiment, clothes colors that match for each emotion were selected as shown in Table 4. In addition, using of clothes colors according to the speech emotion was also generally evaluated high.

Table 4. Results of clothes colors that matches for each emotion.

Emotion	喜 (Joy)	怒 (Anger)	哀 (Sorrow)	怖 (Fear)	恥 (Shame)	好 (Like)	厭 (Dislike)	昂 (Excite)	安 (Relief)	驚 (Surprise)
Hue										
Degree (°)	45	0	225	270	315	0	270	0	135	45

Comparison with the Results of Related Researches. Many researches have been performed on the relationship between emotions and colors. Table 5 shows the comparison of the results in this experiment with the related researches. The results obtained in this experiment were almost the same as the relationships between emotions and colors reported in the related researches. From this point, it is considered that the relationships between emotions and clothes colors obtained in this experiment is valid. In addition, many related researches have reported the consistent results regarding the relationships between emotions and colors such as "Joy", "Anger", "Shame", "Like", "Excited", "Relief" and "Surprise". Therefore, it is considered that many people associate similar colors with those emotions. On the other hand, no consistent results regarding the relationships between emotions and colors were obtained such as "Sorrow", "Fear" and "Dislike". In other words, it should be noted that colors associated with emotions may differ from person to person.

Problems to Be Solved. Both positive and negative opinions were obtained about changing the clothes color according to the progress of the speech. In addition, in this experiment, the hue of the clothes color was designed and evaluated in detail, but it is considered that the method of changing the clothes color for time series and the brightness and saturation of the clothes color were not sufficiently designed.

Therefore, we will perform an additional experiment to find out how to change the clothes color with the aim of reducing the unnaturalness and discomfort.

Table 5. Comparison of the results in this experiment with the related researches.

Results in this experiment			Results in [related researches]	
Emotion	Hue color	Degree (°)	Emotion	Color
喜 (Joy)		45	Delight	Orange [15]
			Fun	Red [16], Orange [16], Yellow [16], Purple [16]
			Happiness	Orange [15-19], Yellow [17-20], Blue [16], Purple [16]
			Joy	Orange [17,19], Yellow [17-19]
			Pleasure	Orange [15]
怒 (Anger)		0	Anger	Red [15,17-20], Black [18]
			Fury	Red [15]
			Irritation	Red [15]
			Rage	Red [17]
哀 (Sorrow)		225	Sadness	Blue [15,17], Purple [17,19], Black [18], Gray [19]
			Sorrow	Purple [17]
			Loneliness	Blue [15]
怖 (Fear)		270	Anxiety	Gray [16]
			Fear	Red [16], Yellow [17], Brown [15], Black [15,18,19]
			Unease	Blue [15]
			Worry	Blue [15]
恥 (Shame)		315	Shame	Orange [17], Pink [15]
好 (Like)		0	Love	Red [15-20], Pink [15,19]
厭 (Dislike)		270	Boredom	Orange [16], Blue [15], Purple [16], Gray [16,19]
			Contempt	Blue [16]
			Depression	Blue [17-20], Black [19], Gray [19]
			Despair	Black [15]
			Disgust	Purple [15]
			Hatred	Black [15]
			Tiredness	Purple [19], Gray [16]
昂 (Excite)		0	Activeness	Orange [15]
			Enthusiasm	Red [15,16], Orange [16,18], Yellow [16], Green [16], Purple [16]
			Excitement	Red [15,17,18,20], Orange [19]
			Passion	Red [15,17-19]
			Power	Black [16]
安 (Relief)		135	Calm	Green [15,17,18], Blue [18-20]
			Composure	Blue [15]
			Ease	Light blue [15]
			Healing	Light blue [15]
			Peace	Yellow [16], Green [15-17,19,20], Blue [16,18], White [16,18,19]
			Placidness	Green [15]
			Relief	Green [15]
驚 (Surprise)		45	Surprise	Orange [15]

5   Additional Experiment: Improvement of Clothes Color Changing Method for Robot

5.1   Research Objective

Based on the problems obtained in the previous experiment, in the additional experiment, we verify the method of changing clothes color for the purpose of reducing the unnaturalness and discomfort. Specifically, we aim to solve the problems that were answered in the comments of the previous experiment, such as "My eyes flickered when the color becomes deeper or white" and "I felt unnatural to revert to white between sentences". And we propose and evaluate some methods of changing clothes color. Note that, this experiment is also performed online due to COVID-19, and participants watch videos and answer questionnaires using their own devices.

This experiment is performed based on "Doshisha University Code of Research Ethics". In addition, the experimenter explains the experiment in detail to the participants, and the participants agree to answering questionnaires and having the results published in a manner in which they cannot be identified. Note that, in this additional experiment, we asked the participants who didn't participate the previous experiment to participate.

5.2   Clothes Color Changing Method

In this experiment, three new color changing methods (Video B, C and D) are created in addition to video A, which changes the clothes color same as the previous experiment, and the participants are asked to evaluate them. For the video editing software, Adobe After Effects is also used. In addition, considering the influence of the hue of the clothes color, the combination of "Fear" as speech emotion and "270°" as clothes color is used because this combination had the smallest variance in the precious experiment. Figure 14, 15, 16 and 17 show the timelines for each video.

In case of video B, the clothes are pale-colored without changing to white color between sentences. Other parts are the same as video A.

In case of video C, the clothes are pale-colored without changing to white color between sentences. In addition, the emotion words are also pale-colored.

In case of video D, the brightness and saturation of deep and pale colors are adjusted, with brightness +30 and saturation ±0 for deep color, and brightness +40 saturation ±0 for pale color. In addition, deep color is applied to the emotion word, and pale color is applied to the other parts in the speech. Moreover, the clothes are pale-colored without changing to white color between sentences.

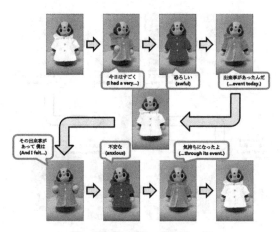

Fig. 14. Timeline of video A.

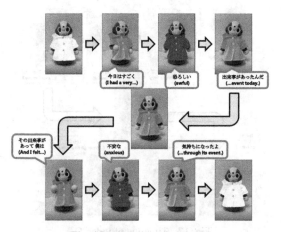

Fig. 15. Timeline of video B.

5.3 Experimental Procedure

Figure 18 shows the experimental procedure. At the beginning of the experiment, a preliminary explanation is performed. Next, participants are asked to evaluate for each color change method. Note that, the order in which the videos are presented to the participants is determined in consideration of the order effect. In addition, participants are told that they can watch each video as many times as they want. After that, they are asked to rank the four clothes color change methods. Finally, they are asked to answer the final questionnaire. The experiment is performed with 15 participants who are the students of Doshisha University.

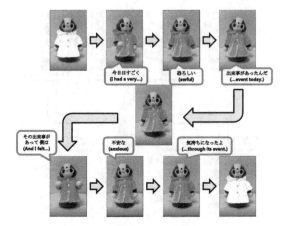

Fig. 16. Timeline of video C.

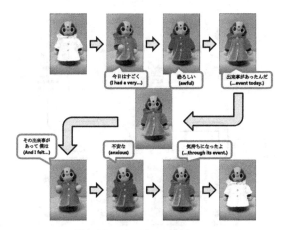

Fig. 17. Timeline of video D.

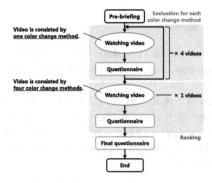

Fig. 18. Experimental procedure.

5.4 Questionnaire

Table 6 shows the contents of questionnaire in evaluation for each color change method. The questions are created based on the comments answered in the previous experiment, and the participants are asked to answer on a 7-grade scale (1: Strongly disagree – 7: Strongly agree).

Table 7 shows the contents of questionnaire in ranking. In this questionnaire, after presenting the four videos at the same time, they are asked to rank them in the order of preference.

Table 8 shows the contents of final questionnaire. In this questionnaire, the environment of watching videos is checked.

Note that, the Wilcoxon signed-rank test is applied to questionnaire in evaluation for each color change method Q1 to Q4 and questionnaire in ranking Q1 as the statistical significance test. Additionally, p-values were corrected in accordance with the Bonferroni correction.

Table 6. Questionnaire in evaluation for each color change method.

#	Question
Q1	I could feel emotions from the robot
Q2	I could concentrate on the robot's speech
Q3	My eyes flickered when the robot's clothes changed color
Q4	I felt a sense of incongruity in the clothes color change

Table 7. Questionnaire in ranking.

#	Question
Q1	Rank these four color changes
Q2	If you have any opinions or impressions about changing clothes color, please describe them

Table 8. Final questionnaire.

#	Question
Q1	Select the visual devise you have used. (Select one from five visual devices.)
Q2	Select the auditory devise you have used. (Select one from eight auditory devices.)
Q3	Select the place where you are. (Select quiet or noisy place.)
Q4	Select your internet connection status. (Select about video/audio problem.)

5.5 Experiment Results

Figure 19, 20, 21 and 22 shows the results of questionnaire in evaluation for each color change method. In the result of Q1 (I could feel emotions from the robot), there is no significant difference, but the methods of changing clothes color in video B and D are relatively evaluated higher. In the result of Q2 (I could concentrate on the robot's speech), there is no significant difference, but it is suggested that the methods of changing clothes color in video C and D increase concentration on the speech. In the result of Q3 (My eyes flickered when the robot's clothes changed color), the methods of changing clothes color in video C and D are evaluated higher than in video A and B, and there are significant differences and marginally significant between them. From this result, it is considered that it is effective to reduce the stimulus caused by deep colors. In the result of Q4 (I felt a sense of incongruity in the clothes color change), the methods of changing clothes color in video C and D are also evaluated higher than in video A and B, and there are significant differences and marginally significant between them.

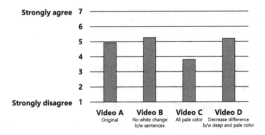

Fig. 19. Result of questionnaire Q1 in evaluation for each color change method (I could feel emotions from the robot).

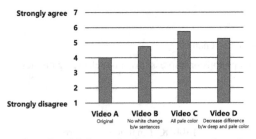

Fig. 20. Result of questionnaire Q2 in evaluation for each color change method (I could concentrate on the robot's speech).

Figure 23 shows the result of questionnaire Q1 in ranking. The methods of changing clothes color in video B and D are evaluated higher than in video A and C, and there are significant differences between them.

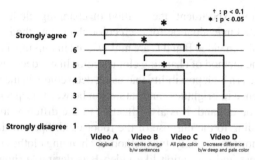

Fig. 21. Result of questionnaire Q3 in evaluation for each color change method (My eyes flickered when the robot's clothes changed color).

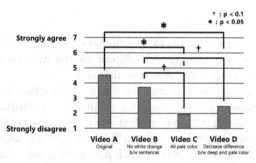

Fig. 22. Result of questionnaire Q4 in evaluation for each color change method (I felt a sense of incongruity in the clothes color change).

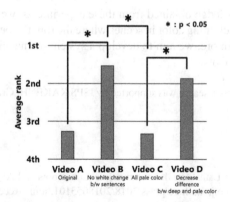

Fig. 23. Result of questionnaire Q1 in ranking.

5.6 Summary of Experiment Results and Discussion

In the additional experiment, based on the problems obtained in the previous experiment, we proposed some methods of changing clothes color for the purpose of reducing the unnaturalness and discomfort, and evaluated them.

As a result of the experiment, the method of changing clothes color in video C and D are highly rated in evaluation for each color change method. And the method of changing clothes color in video B and D are highly rated in ranking. From these results, it is considered that the method of changing clothes color like video C is most appropriate. In other words, there is a high possibility that using deep colors in the emotion words and reducing the difference in brightness and saturation between deep and pale colors work effectively. On the other hand, it is also effective to use different method of changing clothes color according to the purpose of the robot used. Specifically, if you want the robot to express emotions strongly, the method of changing clothes color with strongly changes in brightness and saturation like video B is desirable (however, this method causes the decrease of concentration on the speech).

6 Conclusion

In this research, we investigated the robot's clothes color suitable for the emotion contained in the speech with the aiming to develop an emotion expression method that does not depend on the hardware configuration of the robot.

As a result of the first experiment, we found the matching between the clothes colors and 10 emotions (joy, anger, sorrow, fear, shame, like, dislike, excite, relief and surprise). However, we obtained some problems to be solved such as "My eyes flickered when the color becomes deeper or white" and "I felt un-natural to revert to white between sentences". Therefore, additional experiment is performed to solve these problems and to improve the method of changing clothes color. As a result of the additional experiment, we found the method of changing clothes color with reducing the unnaturalness and discomfort.

Based on the knowledge obtained from these experiments, we will verify the influences of changing the clothing color in scenes where the robot's speech emotions change in time series. Furthermore, we aim to develop a system of changing clothes color that can be worn by real robots.

Acknowledgement. This research was supported by JSPS KAKENHI Grant Number 21K11988.

References

1. Seed Planning, Inc.: Latest trends in communication robots and AI supports 2018. https://www.seedplanning.co.jp/archive/press/2018/2018053101.html. Accessed 07 Oct 2022. (in Japanese)
2. Nippon Research Center, Ltd.: Research about communication robots (2021). https://www.nrc.co.jp/report/img/d1a11e8ddbf79b2bbe071b5922766ed21898ce24.pdf. (in Japanese)
3. Ministry of Internal Affairs and Communications: WHITE PAPER 2015 - Information and Communications in Japan (2015)
4. Mehrabian, A.: Communication without words. Psychol. Today 2(9), 53–55 (1968)
5. Birdwhistell, L.R.: Kinesics and Context. University of Pennsylvania Press (1970)
6. Katz, M.A., Katz, T.V.: Foundations of Nonverbal Communication. Southern Illinois University Press (1983)

7. Gotoh, Y., Kanoh, M., Kato, S., Itoh, H.: Speech and facial expression planning for sensibility robot. J. Jpn. Soc. Kansei Eng. **6**(3), 19–25 (2006). (in Japanese)
8. Masuda, M., Kato, S., Itoh, H.: Laban's feature value set and emotion estimation from body motion of human form robot based on Laban movement analysis. Trans. Jpn. Soc. Kansei Eng. **10**(2), 295–303 (2011). (in Japanese)
9. Shimabe, T., Yoshimura, E., Tsuchiya, S., Watabe, H.: Speech synthesis expressing emotions for communication robots. Proc. Forum Inf. Technol. **2012**, 241–242 (2012). (in Japanese)
10. Gotoh, M., Kanoh, M., Kato, S., Kunitachi, T., Itoh, H.: Face generation using emotional regions for sensibility robot. Trans. Jpn. Soc. Artif. Intell. **21**(1), 55–62 (2006). (in Japanese)
11. Teshi, H., Terada, K., Ito, A.: Effect of emotion expression with blinking colored eyes of a robot on emotional story understanding. Trans. Hum. Interface Soc. **17**(4), 445–456 (2015). (in Japanese)
12. Harashima, H., Kurokawa, T.: Non-verbal Interface. Ohmsha (1994). (in Japanese)
13. McLuhan, M.: Understanding Media. The MIT Press (1964)
14. Friedman, N., Love, K., LC, R., Sabin, J., Hoffman, G., Ju, W.: What robots need from clothing. In: Proceeding of Designing Interactive Systems Conference 2021, pp. 1345–1355 (2021)
15. Hanada, M.: Correspondence analysis of color–emotion associations. Color Res. Appl. **43**(2), 224–237 (2018)
16. Demir, U.: Investigation of color-emotion associations of the university students. Color Res. Appl. **45**(5), 871–884 (2020)
17. Chang, L.W., Lin, L.H.: The impact of color traits on corporate branding. Afr. J. Bus. Manag. **4**(15), 3344–3355 (2010)
18. Birren, F.: Color psychology and color therapy. Citadel (1978)
19. Nijdam, A. N.: Mapping emotion to color. https://citeseerx.ist.psu.edu/viewdoc/download?doi=10.1.1.407.2395&rep=rep1&type=pdf. Accessed 06 Oct 2022
20. Kaya, N., Epps, H.H.: Relationship between color and emotion: a study of college students. Coll. Stud. J. **38**(3), 396–405 (2004)
21. Xu, Y.: Experimental study on the influence of clothing color on others' evaluation. J. Henan Inst. Educ. **19**(1), 40–42 (2010)
22. Maier, M.A., Elliot, A.J., Lee, B., Lichtenfeld, S., Barchfeld, P., Pekrun, R.: The influence of red on impression formation in a job application context. Motiv. Emot. **37**(3), 389–401 (2013)
23. Pazda, A.D., Thorstenson, C.A.: Color intensity increases perceived extraversion and openness for zero-acquaintance judgments. Personal. Individ. Differ. **147**, 118–127 (2019)
24. Fan, Z., Jiang, X.: Influence of clothing color value on trust perception. Int. J. Eng. Res. Technol. **10**(5), 613–618 (2021)
25. Tatsumi, A., Okubo, M.: Influence of humanoid robot's clothes color on interpersonal distance. Trans. Hum. Interface Soc. **20**(2), 281–288 (2018). (in Japanese)
26. Vstone Co., Ltd.: https://sota.vstone.co.jp/home/. Accessed 05 Oct 2022. (in Japanese)
27. Ekman, P., Friesen, V.W., Ellsworth, P.: Emotion in the Human Face. Pergamon Press (1972)
28. Millenson, R.J.: Principles of Behavioral Analysis. Mc Millan (1967)
29. Russell, A.J.: A circumplex model of affect. J. Personal. Soc. Psychol. **39**(6), 1161–1178 (1980)
30. Plutchik, R., Kellerman, H.: Theories of Emotion. Academic Press (1980)
31. Nakamura, A.: Emotion dictionary. Tokyodo Shuppan (1993). (in Japanese)

Enhancing Robot Explainability
in Human-Robot Collaboration

Yanting Wang[✉] and Sangseok You

Sungkyunkwan University, 25-2, Sungkyunkwan-Ro Jongno-Gu, Seoul 03063, Korea
wyanting@g.skku.edu, sangyou@skku.edu

Abstract. While the explainability of AI is gaining increasing attention from scholars, much is not known about how to enhance robot explainability and its implications for human-robot collaboration. This study sought to understand the impacts of social cues on robot explainability and trust and acceptance of a robotic partner. We proposed a research model in which the non-verbal, verbal, and joint presence of both cues predicted robot explainability, and the moderating role of robot anthropomorphic design was examined. We also proposed that robot explainability promoted trust and acceptance of a robot. We provide evidence for the research model through a mixed-design experiment with 202 individuals. While non-verbal, verbal, and joint presence generally increased robot explainability, we further found that the impact of non-verbal cues was contingent upon the existence of verbal cues and moderated by robot anthropomorphic design. Our findings provide several implications for research and practice.

Keywords: Social Cues · Robot Design · Robot explainability · Human-Robot Teams

1 Introduction

Making sense of robot behaviors has challenged individuals working with robots in human-robot teams [1]. Robot explainability is one dimension that has gained much attention from scholars seeking ways to enhance human-robot teamwork over the past few years [2]. Stemming from the field of artificial intelligence (AI), robot explainability is defined as "the ability to provide information about their inner workings using social cues such that an observer (user) can infer how/why the embodied agent behaves the way it does" [3]. Thus, robot explainability concerns how an individual understands robot behaviors and their inner working when communicating with them. Research in AI suggests that explainability fosters trust and acceptance of artificial agents as co-workers. For this reason, securing high levels of robot explainability is becoming essential for successful human-robot teamwork [4].

We turn to the social cues of robots as a way to enhance robot explainability in human-robot teamwork. In human-robot interaction (HRI), social cues generally refer to a robot's observable features that work as channels of information and trigger social reactions [5]. However, little is known about how social cues affect robot explainability. Most of them focused on examining verbal and non-verbal cues independently [6,

© The Author(s), under exclusive license to Springer Nature Switzerland AG 2023
M. Kurosu and A. Hashizume (Eds.): HCII 2023, LNCS 14013, pp. 236–247, 2023.
https://doi.org/10.1007/978-3-031-35602-5_17

7]. This leads to a limited understanding of the combinatory effects of both verbal and non-verbal cues on robot explainability and positive perceptions toward robots in human-robot teamwork. Investigating single types of social cues at one time may only provide an incomplete understanding of their effects and limit implications for practice in human-robot teamwork. Thus, to better understand the effects of social cues on robot explainability, it is imperative to examine both types of verbal and non-verbal cues simultaneously.

The anthropomorphic design of robots is known to regulate the relationship between robot features and perceptions toward robots at work, such as robots' intelligence, trust, and acceptance [8]. Anthropomorphic design determines humans' expectations for a robot to manifest human-like attributes [9]. Thus, individuals may interpret the social cues differently depending on the robot's anthropomorphic design. However, we still do not know whether the robot anthropomorphic design moderates the impact of social cues on robot explainability and subsequent perceptions of robots in human-robot teams.

This study seeks to understand the impacts of social cues of robots, both verbal and non-verbal, on robot explainability and, subsequently, trust and acceptance of a robotic partner in human-robot collaboration. We propose the three overarching research questions for this study as below.

RQ1: Will social cues, both non-verbal and verbal, increase robot explainability?

RQ2: Will the robot's anthropomorphic design moderate the relationship between social cues and robot explainability?

RQ3: Will robot explainability increase the robot's trustworthiness and acceptance?

Our findings showed that while verbal and non-verbal cues enhanced robot explainability, respectively, the presence of both cues had much stronger positive effects on robot explainability. We found a moderation effect of robot anthropomorphic design. The impact of social cues, especially non-verbal cues, was more substantial on explainability when the robot was human-like. Robot explainability increased trust and acceptance of the robot in human-robot teamwork.

2 Theoretical Background

2.1 Explainability

In recent years, interest in "explainable artificial intelligence (XAI)" has grown significantly. The research streams on XAI primarily focused on the explainability of data-driven algorithms [10]. Recently, the concept has been extended to physically embodied artificial intelligence (i.e., robots). Robot explainability refers to the robots' capability that enables their human partners to understand their actions' intentions and inner states [3].

Whether the robot's behaviors are understandable to humans is found to be crucial [2]. Robots' body motions were found to enhance robot explainability in that they provided information on the robot's incapability and enabled humans to understand why the robot failed [7]. In a healthcare context, when people receive blood pressure treatment from a caregiving robot, robot speech could explain the design rationale for the treatment from the robot and promote trust in the robot [6]. These findings seem consistent with the findings for explainable AI promoting trust and acceptance [11, 12].

However, scholars have only begun to examine robot explainability in human-robot teamwork, and little is unknown about how to promote the explainability of robots. As Hellström and Bensch [2] argued, humans may develop an incorrect interpretation of the robot without adequately explaining the robot's actions.

2.2 Social Cues in Human-Robot Interaction

In human-human communication, social cues convey various information through face, body, voice, and motions to produce an understanding of humans' inner statements [13]. These are powerful communicative tools because they transmit essential social information, promoting communication effectiveness [14]. In human-robot interaction, research found that physical robots can demonstrate social intelligence and trigger social responses through various social cues [8, 15].

Despite the positive effects of non-verbal and verbal cues, the combined impact of verbal and non-verbal cues remains relatively unexplored [16]. It is not known whether the presence of both verbal and non-verbal cues yields an even higher positive effect on robot explainability than the presence of one of the two. On the one hand, the presence of both cues may cause confusion and cognitive overload in an individual, leading to a negative effect on human-robot teamwork. On the other hand, it is also likely that the positive effects of individual cues add up and enhance human-robot teams even more. Since social cues are present together in most circumstances of working with physical robots, it is essential to explore whether the combination of non-verbal and verbal cues will also positively impact robot explainability. As a result, we propose a research model in which the presence of non-verbal, verbal cues and their joint presence increase the robot explainability (Fig. 1).

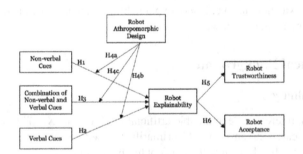

Fig. 1. Research Model

Firstly, we propose that non-verbal and verbal cues enhance individuals' assessment of robot explainability, respectively. In human-human communication, messages from an interlocutor can be delivered through different channels. The non-verbal communication channel is essential when communicating with each other and complements verbal communication [5]. Likewise, robot explainability can benefit from similar principles in human-human communication. This is partly due to the intentional stance of human minds [17]. According to Dennett [17], humans tend to interpret the actions of non-human objects by observing their behavior. Lastly, we also hypothesize that the presence of both non-verbal and verbal cues simultaneously increases robot explainability even higher than when only one of the two is present. Joint cues convey more information than single cues in human communication [2]. Thus, we hypothesize as below:

H1: Non-verbal cues will increase robot explainability.

H2: Verbal cues will increase robot explainability.

H3: When non-verbal and verbal cues are present simultaneously, the robot explainability will be higher than when only non-verbal cues or verbal cues is present.

2.3 Robot Anthropomorphic Design

Designing robots to appear more anthropomorphic has long been a common strategy for increasing social acceptance of robots [8]. Anthropomorphism is a psychological process of imbuing human-like qualities, goals, intentions, and feelings into non-human objects [9]. Among different strategies to promote anthropomorphism, robot appearances are known to be effective to enhance individuals' perception of anthropomorphism of robots [18]. Robots with a human-like appearance are treated kindlier than robots with a mechanical-looking, and humans commonly treat mechanical-looking robots in a sub-servient way (i.e., less socially interactively) [19]. People prefer interacting with human-like robots to machine-like robots [18]. However, research suggests that human-like designs may not always benefit human-robot teamwork. Although human-like appearance generally promotes familiarity and social acceptance, the current research fails to prove whether the human-like design would improve communication effectiveness with robots (i.e., robot explainability). Our understanding of robot anthropomorphism implies that humans would interpret the social cues from robots as they would do with humans. This means that social cues of human-like robots would be more salient in enhancing robot explainability than machine-like robots. In this paper, we propose that robot anthropomorphic design moderates the impact of social cues on robot explainability. Thus, we hypothesize as below:

H4a-b: Robot anthropomorphic design will moderate the impact of social cues on robot explainability, such that the impacts of a) non-verbal and b) verbal cues will be stronger with human-like robots than with machine-like robots, respectively.

We further posit that the impact of joint social cues appears differently based on robot anthropomorphic design.

H4c: Robot anthropomorphic design will moderate the impact of social cues on robot explainability, such that the impact of non-verbal cues will be the strongest when there are no verbal cues with human-like robots.

2.4 Trust and Acceptance

Robot explainability is proposed to enhance individuals' perceptions of robots, such as trust and acceptance. Robot explainability likely increases individuals' trust and acceptance of the robot. Existing research indicates that a human's ability to comprehend AI systems directly affects trust and acceptance [12, 20, 21]. Compared to a robot that offers no explanations of its decisions and actions, a robot providing explanations can help the robot users better measure the extent of trustworthiness of their robot partners [6]. Research on XAI has evidence that explainability results in trust in the AI and more adherence to recommendations made by the AI [22–24]. Similarly, when the robot provides advice to humans, the explainable advice and actions can make people better understand the logical thinking process of the robot. The clear explanation reduces people's doubt and uncertainty about human-robot teamwork, thus promoting trust and accept of the robot.

H5: Robot explainability will increase robot trustworthiness.

H6: Robot explainability will increase robot acceptance.

3   Method

We conducted an online experiment with a mixed design method: 2 (between-subjects: non-verbal cues present vs. no non-verbal cues) x 2 (between-subjects: verbal cues present vs. no verbal cues) x 2 (within-subjects: machine-like robot vs. human-like robot). We used a video recording of interactions between a robot and an individual to employ the vignette method.

3.1   Participants

We recruited a total of 202 participants. The samples were recruited through a market survey company based in the US. All the workers in this study are US residents and had a track record of high performance, with former requesters rating them 95 percent or higher on their previous online tasks. The sample consisted of diverse education levels, ages, genders, and ethnicities. (128 male; mean age = 40 years old, standard deviation [SD] = 11.63 years; min. age = 21 years, max. age = 71 years).

3.2   Robots

For this study, we chose two types of robots with machine-like and human-like designs. ArmPi, is a blue machine-like Raspberry Pi 4b robot run by the ROS system (Fig. 2). Xingo is a human-like social robot that connects through Bluetooth to a computer and a mobile device (Fig. 3). On the back of Xingo is a speaker capable of playing sound. LED lights were embedded in its eyes, allowing it to change colors.

Fig. 2. Robot Arm for Machine-like Robot Condition

Fig. 3. Humanoid Robot for Human-like Robot Condition

3.3 Experiment Scenario

We adopted a scenario of human-robot collaboration in the agricultural context. There has been a growing interest in robots for agriculture. Robots were widely used in agriculture for fruit harvesting and plant status monitoring. Various robots have been used to identify the colors of fruits and plants to determine their conditions [25]. Taking care of pot plants is frequent in people's daily lives. When robots assist people in monitoring plants, the feedback related to the plant's condition made by the robots must be understandable to a human. The plant monitoring scenario is appropriate for this study. In the experimental videos, a human worked on monitoring plants with a robot, and the robot assisted the human with locating plants in an abnormal state. There are two abnormal plant states: red denotes illness, and blue denotes a water supply.

3.4 Manipulations

Non-verbal Cues Manipulation. Non-verbal cues manipulation had two levels. In the conditions without non-verbal cues, the robots did not respond to human commands behaviorally and kept still during the entire experiment. In the conditions with non-verbal cues, pre-programmed body gestures with varying ranges of motion and facial expressions were employed to convey a message based on conversation content. In the machine-like robot condition, when the robot detected sick plants, its range of motion expanded to reach the plants. Through the display attached to the robot, the machine-like robot's eyes showed the non-verbal cues of gaze. The dynamic movements of the mouth, eyebrows, and eyes represented the facial expressions. The machine-like robot's facial expressions changed as the conversation changed. As for the non-verbal cues of color, the machine-like robot changed the color of its face according to the state of the detected plants. Red indicates that the plants are sick, and blue indicates that plants need watering (Fig. 2 and Fig. 3).

In the human-like robot condition, the robot used a variety of body gestures to deliver messages according to the conversation contents. For example, once abnormal plants were found, the robot's range of motion increased significantly for its arms and legs. Furthermore, the human-like robot's eyes changed colors according to the monitored plant state. Consistent with the machine-like robot, red represents illness, and blue represents plants that need watering.

Verbal Cues Manipulation. Verbal cues in this experiment included speech and vocal tone. We used a variety of vocal expressions with different vocal tones. The vocal tone changed based on the content of the conversation the robots were engaged in.

While in the condition without any non-verbal or verbal cues, we added sound effects because the individual in the video and the participants watching the video needed to receive a response from the robot. According to the definition of verbal cues, non-lexical utterances (i.e., beeping sound, etc.) are not included in verbal cues [3, 26].

Robot Anthropomorphic Design Manipulation. As stated above, the robot's anthropomorphic design was manipulated by employing two different robots for the videos. ArmPi was used for the machine-like robot condition, while Xingo was used for the human-like robot condition. The robot's anthropomorphic design was a within-subjects factor in the experiment. Therefore, all participants went through both conditions and interacted with them. The order of presenting the two robot conditions was randomized across the experiment. One hundred participants watched the video of the machine-like robot first, and the rest watched the human-like robot video first.

3.5 Procedure

At the beginning of the experiment, participants had to agree with the consent form. They were informed that they would be asked questions about this experiment to ensure their attention. Participants were randomly divided into four between-subjects conditions based on the presence of non-verbal and verbal cues. They watched the first video and finished the first questionnaire, then watched the second video and finished another questionnaire that contained the same conditions as the first one. Participants were debriefed, paid, and dismissed upon completing the experimental sessions. Each participant was paid $2.50 for approximately 20 min of the interaction.

3.6 Measurement

Non-verbal Cues Perceptions. To ensure that our manipulations of non-verbal and verbal cues were successful, we measured perceived non-verbal communication based on a 5-point Likert scale. Non-verbal cues were measured by an index of nine questions adapted from Babel et al. [8]. An example was "the robot was communicating through its face." The scale was reliable (Cronbach's $\alpha = 0.86$).

Verbal Cues Perceptions. Perceived verbal communication was measured using an index of five items adapted from [8, 27] ($\alpha = 0.94$). The index included an example: "the robot used various vocal expressions when talking to the person in the video."

Robot Explainability. We measured the robot explainability to determine whether the robots' behaviors made sense to individuals. We created an original scale consisting of 4 items based on the definition of examinability using a 5-point Likert scale. The items include the following statements: 1) I could understand every behavior of the robot in the video, 2) I knew the purpose of each behavior of the robot, 3) I could understand the reason why the robot did the behaviors, and 4) The robot behaviors made sense to me. The scale was reliable ($\alpha = 0.92$).

Robot Trustworthiness. A 5-point Likert scale was used to assess trust. The scale consisted of 4 items adapted from [28] ($\alpha = 0.92$). The items include questions such as "The robot in the video is reliable.", "The robot in the video is trustworthy."

Robot Acceptance. Acceptance was measured using an index of five items adapted from [29] using a 5-point Likert scale. Example items include: "I think the robot is useful for the task in the video." and "I would be happy if I got to work with the robot in the video." The scale was reliable ($\alpha = 0.95$).

4   Results

4.1   Manipulation Check

Results of t-tests showed that the perceptions of non-verbal and verbal cues were significantly higher in the conditions with non-verbal ($M = 3.78$, $SD = 0.52$) and verbal cues ($M = 3.97$, $SD = 0.52$) than in the conditions without non-verbal ($M = 2.47$, $SD = 0.61$) ($t = -22.94$, $p < 0.001$) and verbal cues ($M = 1.93$, $SD = 0.96$) ($t = -26.89$, $p < 0.001$).

4.2   Hypothesis Testing

We conducted a factorial mixed ANOVA with repeated measures using R studio. In our research model, the anthropomorphic design of the robot was the within-subject factor, while non-verbal and verbal cues were the between-subjects factors.

H1 and H2 posited that non-verbal and verbal cues would increase robot explainability, respectively. Result suggested that non-verbal cues ($F = 4.06$, $p < 0.01$) and verbal cues ($F = 52.06$, $p < 0.001$) were found to be positively related to robot explainability. When only a single verbal or non-verbal cue was analyzed without considering the interaction effect, verbal and non-verbal cues significantly improved the robot explainability. Thus, both H1 and H2 were supported.

H3 posited that when non-verbal and verbal cues were present together, robot explainability would be different from the conditions where only non-verbal or verbal cues were present. We found that there was a significant interaction effect between non-verbal and verbal cues, which were also positively related to the explainability of the robot ($F = 3.61$, $p < 0.001$). A post-hoc test showed that robot explainability was the highest in the condition with both non-verbal and verbal cues ($M = 3.82$, $SE = 0.10$) than conditions with only non-verbal ($M = 3.14$, $SE = 0.10$), verbal cues ($M = 3.74$, $SE = 0.10$), or none ($M = 2.6$, $SE = 0.12$). Thus, H3 was supported.

H4a and H4b posited that the robot's anthropomorphic design would moderate the relationships between non-verbal and verbal cues, and robot explainability. The results showed that the robot's anthropomorphic design moderated the impact of both non-verbal ($F = 22.45$, $p < 0.001$) and verbal cues ($F = 9.47$, $p < 0.01$) on robot explainability.

Specifically, the impacts of non-verbal and verbal cues, respectively, on robot explainability were more salient in the human-like robot condition than the machine-like robot conditions (Table 1.). H4a and H4b were fully supported.

H4c hypothesized a three-way interaction among non-verbal cues, verbal cues, and robot anthropomorphic design. As hypothesized, non-verbal cues demonstrated the most substantial impact on enhancing robot explainability when there were no verbal cues and the robot was human-like, compared to other conditions (F = 26.13, p < 0.001). While non-verbal cues enhanced robot explainability in the largest magnitude when verbal cues were present with human-like robot, such effects were not as salient in other cases (Table 1.). Thus, H4c was supported.

Table 1. Estimated Marginal Means of Each Condition

Robot Type	Non-verbal Cues	Verbal Cues	Mean	Std. Error
Machine-like Robot	No	No	3.32	0.13
	No	Yes	3.88	0.11
	Yes	No	3.15	0.11
	Yes	Yes	3.94	0.11
Human-like Robot	No	No	1.88	0.15
	No	Yes	3.59	0.13
	Yes	No	3.14	0.13
	Yes	Yes	3.70	0.13

Finally, H5 and H6 posited that robot explainability would be positively related to trust and acceptance of robots. The results showed that robot explainability had positive impacts on both trust (B = 0.44, p < 0.001) and acceptance (B = 0.54, p < 0.001). Thus, H5 and H6 were supported.

5 Discussion

5.1 Implications for Theory and Practice

This study aims to understand the impacts of social cues on robot explainability and the moderation effects of robot anthropomorphic design in human-robot teamwork. Results from our experiment demonstrate three overarching findings. In the following section, we discuss the implications of these findings.

First, this study contributes to the explainable AI (XAI) and robot explainability literature. We found that the presence of non-verbal and verbal cues enhanced robot explainability. We further show that both social cues can increase robot explainability even more. These results suggest that robot explainability should be understood differently from the explainability of AI in that robots deployed to workplaces can manifest more traits than AI software through both non-verbal and verbal traits.

Second, this study contributes to the literature on social cues in collaboration technology. Previous findings may not inform our understanding of the impact of social cues in human-robot collaboration. Meanwhile, prior research has only examined one cue at a time in human-robot collaboration [7], failing to show their combined effects. Our findings confirm the positive effects of non-verbal and verbal cues, respectively.

Furthermore, this study highlights the moderating role of robot anthropomorphism in the relationship between social cues and robot explainability. The effects of non-verbal cues weakened when verbal cues were present, and these patterns were more salient when the robot was human-like. Conversely, non-verbal cues showed the most substantial effect when the robot was human-like and verbal cues were absent. These findings suggest that the robot's anthropomorphic design is a boundary condition when examining the effects of non-verbal and verbal cues.

Finally, our study examined explainability to enhance trust and acceptance of robots in human-robot collaboration. Given that robots are physically embodied in artificial intelligence, explainability significantly promotes positive perceptions of robots and effective communication with them. This study contributes to the literature by showing the effect of explainability on the acceptance and trust of a robot.

Our findings also have practical implications. Robots for human-robot collaboration should be designed with social cues to support robot explainability. Our findings demonstrate that robots with verbal cues were rated with higher levels of explainability. However, we advise caution in designing all robots with several social cues. Given that non-verbal cues did not have much impact on the machine-like robot, designers may not necessarily exert effort to add non-verbal cues to such robots. On the contrary, we recommend adding non-verbal cues to human-like robots to ensure robot explainability. When robots fail to respond to human partners verbally, non-verbal cues will become more valuable when humans work with human-like robots.

5.2 Limitations and Future Research

This study has several limitations. First, the designs of robots used in the experiments only represent limited aspects of non-verbal cues and anthropomorphism. As indexed in Phillips et al. [30], robots can be in different forms to express non-verbal cues and anthropomorphism. Future studies need to explore the impacts of various robot forms and gestures on robot explainability. Second, the experiment was conducted online. While online experiments using video vignettes have been widely used for human-robot collaboration research [31, 32], field studies where individuals and robots work together over time may yield more nuanced and contextual observations on the phenomenon.

6 Conclusion

While the explainability of AI is gaining increasing attention from scholars, much is not known about how to enhance explainability and its subsequent effects on subjective evaluations of robotic partners. We propose a research model in which the non-verbal, verbal, and joint presence of both cues predicts robot explainability, and the moderating role of robot anthropomorphic design is examined. We also propose that robot explainability promotes trust and acceptance of a robot partner. By conducting a mixed-design experiment, we provide empirical evidence for the research model. Our findings provide several implications for research and practice. The impacts of non-verbal and verbal cues in human-robot collaboration should be understood in conjunction with robot anthropomorphic design.

References

1. Rosenfeld, A., Richardson, A.: Explainability in Human-Agent Systems. arXiv:190408123 [cs] (2019)
2. Hellström, T., Bensch, S.: Understandable robots - What, Why, and How. Palayn. J. Behav. Robot. **9**, 110–123 (2018)
3. Wallkötter, S., Tulli, S., Castellano, G., et al.: Explainable embodied agents through social cues: a review. J. Hum. Robot Interact **10**, 1–24 (2021)
4. Baird, A., Maruping, L.M.: The next generation of research on IS Use: a theoretical framework of delegation to and from agentic IS artifacts. MISQ **45**, 315–341 (2021)
5. Feine, J., Gnewuch, U., Morana, S., Maedche, A.: A Taxonomy of social cues for conversational agents. Int. J. Hum Comput Stud. **132**, 138–161 (2019)
6. Fischer, K., Weigelin, H.M., Bodenhagen, L.: Increasing trust in human–robot medical interactions: effects of transparency and adaptability Paladyn. J. Behav. Robot. **9**, 95–109 (2018)
7. Kwon, M., Huang, S.H., Dragan, A.D.: Expressing robot incapability. In: Proceedings of the 2018 ACM/IEEE International Conference on Human-Robot Interaction, pp. 87–95 (2018)
8. Babel, F., Kraus, J., Miller, L., et al.: Small talk with a robot? the impact of dialog content, talk initiative, and gaze behavior of a social robot on trust, acceptance, and proximity. Int. J. Soc. Robot. (2021)
9. Epley, N., Waytz, A., Cacioppo, J.T.: On seeing human: a three-factor theory of anthropomorphism. Psychol. Rev. **114**, 864–886 (2007)
10. Meske, C., Bunde, E., Schneider, J., Gersch, M.: Explainable artificial intelligence: objectives, stakeholders, and future research opportunities. Inf. Syst. Manag. **39**, 53–63 (2022)
11. Poursabzi-Sangdeh, F., Goldstein, D.G., Hofman, J.M., et al.: Manipulating and Measuring Model Interpretability. arXiv:180207810 [cs] (2021)
12. Yeomans, M., Shah, A., Mullainathan, S., Kleinberg, J.: Making sense of recommendations. J Behav Dec Making **32**, 403–414 (2019)
13. Adams, R.B., Albohn, D.N., Kveraga, K.: Social vision: applying a social-functional approach to face and expression perception. Curr. Dir. Psychol. Sci. **26**, 243–248 (2017)
14. Freeth, M., Foulsham, T., Kingstone, A.: What affects social attention? social presence, eye contact and autistic traits. PLoS ONE **8**, e53286 (2013). https://doi.org/10.1371/journal.pone.0053286
15. You, S., Robert, L.: Emotional attachment, performance, and viability in teams collaborating with embodied physical action (EPA) robots. JAIS **19**, 377–407 (2018)
16. Diethelm, I.G., Hansen, S.S., Leth, F.B., et al.: Effects of gaze and speech in human-robot medical interactions. In: Companion of the 2021 ACM/IEEE International Conference on Human-Robot Interaction, pp. 349–353. ACM, Boulder CO USA (2021)
17. Dennett, D.C.: The Intentional Stance. MIT Press (1987)
18. Goetz, J., Kiesler, S., Powers, A.: Matching robot appearance and behavior to tasks to improve human-robot cooperation. In: The 12th IEEE International Workshop on Robot and Human Interactive Communication, 2003. Proceedings. ROMAN 2003, pp. 55–60. IEEE, Millbrae, CA, USA (2003)

19. Walters, M.L., Syrdal, D.S., Dautenhahn, K., et al.: Avoiding the uncanny valley: robot appearance, personality and consistency of behavior in an attention-seeking home scenario for a robot companion. Auton. Robot. **24**, 159–178 (2008)
20. Kizilcec, R.F.: How much information?: effects of transparency on trust in an algorithmic interface. In: Proceedings of the 2016 CHI Conference on Human Factors in Computing Systems, pp. 2390–2395. ACM, San Jose California USA (2016)
21. Liel, Y., Zalmanson, L.: What If an AI Told You That 2 2 Is 5? Conformity to Algorithmic Recommendations. ICIS 2020 Proceedings (2020)
22. Gunning, D., Stefik, M., Choi, J., et al.: XAI—explainable artificial intelligence. Sci. Robot **4**, eaay7120 (2019)
23. Logg, J.M., Minson, J.A., Moore, D.A.: Algorithm appreciation: people prefer algorithmic to human judgment. Organ. Behav. Hum. Decis. Process. **151**, 90–103 (2019)
24. You, S., Cathy, L., Li, X.: Algorithmic Versus Human Advice: Does Presenting Prediction Performance Matter for Algorithm Appreciation? forthcoming in Journal of Management Information Systems (2022)
25. Oktarina, Y., Dewi, T., Risma, P., Nawawi, M.: Tomato harvesting arm robot manipulator; a pilot project. J. Phys. Conf. Ser. **1500**, 012003 (2020)
26. Sia, C.-L., Tan, B.C.Y., Wei, K.-K.: Group polarization and computer-mediated communication: effects of communication cues, social presence, and anonymity. Inf. Syst. Res. **13**, 70–90 (2002)
27. Chidambaram, V., Chiang, Y.-H., Mutlu, B.: Designing persuasive robots: how robots might persuade people using vocal and nonverbal cues. In: Proceedings of the seventh annual ACM/IEEE international conference on Human-Robot Interaction - HRI 2012, p. 293. ACM Press, Boston, Massachusetts, USA (2012)
28. Yagoda, R.E., Gillan, D.J.: You want me to trust a ROBOT? the development of a human-robot interaction trust scale. Int. J. Soc. Robot. **4**, 235–248 (2012)
29. Lann, J.D., Heino, A., Dick, D.W.: A simple procedure for the assessment of acceptance of advanced transport telematics. Transp. Res. -C **5**, 1–10 (1997)
30. Phillips, E., Zhao, X., Ullman, D., Malle, B.F.: What is human-like?: decomposing robots' human-like appearance using the anthropomorphic roBOT (ABOT) Database. In: Proceedings of the 2018 ACM/IEEE International Conference on Human-Robot Interaction, pp 105–113. ACM, Chicago IL USA (2018)
31. Esterwood, C., Jr LPR: Having the right attitude: how attitude impacts trust repair in human–robot interaction. In: Proceedings of the 2022 ACM/IEEE International Conference on Human-Robot Interaction (HRI 2022). HRI 2022, p. 10 (2022)
32. Kahn, G., Villaflor, A., Ding, B., et al.: Self-supervised Deep Reinforcement Learning with Generalized Computation Graphs for Robot Navigation. arXiv:170910489 [cs] (2018)

An Intuitive Human-Robot Interaction Method for Robotic Dance Choreography

Mi-chi Wang$^{(\boxtimes)}$ ⓘ and Yang-Ting Shen

National Cheng Kung University, Tainan, Taiwan
N78101018@gs.ncku.edu.tw

Abstract. Recently, with the rapid development in the field of technology and art, artists have presented various experimental works by combining technology and art, creating a new mode of interaction between the works and the audience. Among them, performance art fields such as dance have begun to experiment with robots. In the control of traditional industrial machine arms, professional programming skills and a large amount of time are required to write a series of dance movements for the robot arm. These methods mainly control the position of the robot arm's end effector, rather than the posture of the robot arm. The control logic differs from dance movements. In order to allow dancers without a technological background to choreograph the robot arm, this study has developed a method for choreographing robot arms intuitively.

This study integrates skeleton recognition technology, uses a camera to real-time recognize the 3d coordinates of the human skeleton and converts the angle between the skeletons into the angles of the six axes of the robot arm. Through the control logic of forward kinematics, control commands are executed in real-time to the robot arm, allowing the dancer to intuitively control the posture of the robot arm through their own body movements.

Keywords: Human-Computer Interaction · Techno-Art · Robotic Dance · Computer-vison · Skeleton Recognition

1 Introduction

1.1 Research Motivation

In the context of the rapid development of techno-art, artists have created a variety of experimental works by integrating technology and art, creating new modes of interaction between works and audiences. Among them, dance and other performing arts fields are also trying to blend with robots [2]. In the performance "Huang Yi and Kuka", the dancer danced a human-robot duet with the robot arm at close range, which received great success [8]. Merrit Moore created a ballet for the robot arm using her multidisciplinary training, making the robot her most dependable dance partner throughout the pandemic [9].

However, controlling an industrial robot through a robot control pendant or programming is a laborious and time-consuming task that requires some technical expertise. In

© The Author(s), under exclusive license to Springer Nature Switzerland AG 2023
M. Kurosu and A. Hashizume (Eds.): HCII 2023, LNCS 14013, pp. 248–257, 2023.
https://doi.org/10.1007/978-3-031-35602-5_18

the above case, Huang Yi spent twenty hours of programming to choreograph one minute of the robot dance [7]. These kinds of programming methods are inflexible and hard to revise.

1.2 Research Purpose

In this paper, we propose an intuitive way to control the in-motion gesture of the robot arm, so the dancer can easily choreograph for the robot arm. This study uses skeleton recognition technology and a set of human-to-robot posture translation methods to make it easy to capture the human body movements and transfer the data into robot arm movement, so the robot can run in a similar posture to the human body. By applying synchronous and asynchronous control methods to different scenarios, the choreographer can intuitively use his or her body to compose the dance of the robot arm without the need for expensive equipment and programming expertise.

2 Related Works

In recent years, the field of technology and arts has been thriving, and dancers are also starting to incorporate technology into their performances. One of the Taiwanese dancers, Huang Yi, combined dance with the KUKA robot arm and performed "Huang Yi and KUKA" (Fig. 1) in close proximity between the dancer and the robot arm, which was a huge success. However, this cross-disciplinary technology has a high threshold for dancers who have no related background. To control the robot arm for a dance performance, Huang Yi self-learned the programming language for controlling the robot. Moreover, traditional industrial robots are designed to control the end effector of the robot arm tool, rather than the posture of the robot arm, which means that every minute of dance requires 20 h of programming [8] and the dance is difficult to modify. Merrit Moore, a multi-disciplinary ballerina, chose a collaborative robot (Fig. 2), which provides a more flexible way to control the posture of the robot arm, allowing her to directly adjust the posture of the arm using her hand. However, it still takes a lot of time to adjust the positions of each second one by one and then record them [9].

In the field of HCI, many studies have attempted to allow humans to control robots intuitively through techniques such as motion capture [1, 6] or sensor-based device [3–5] setup, but these methods require expensive equipment and technical expertise. Furthermore, these control methods primarily focus on controlling the working path and position of the robot arm's end effector rather than the robot arm's posture, which differs significantly from the logic of dance.

Fig. 1. Huang Yi and KUKA   **Fig. 2.** Merrit Moore "Ballet Robot"

3 Method

As shown in Fig. 3, there are two main phases of the process from human movement to robot movement. First, we apply the skeleton recognition technology with a general camera or recorded video to capture the dancer's skeleton posture and import these skeleton coordinates into 3D modeling software to convert them into temporal geometric data for the subsequent control phase.

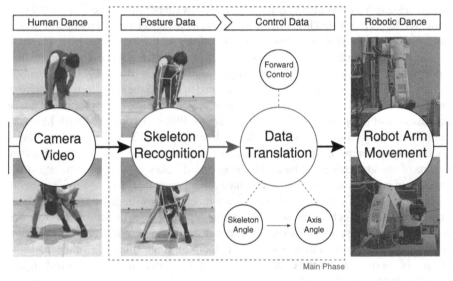

Fig. 3. The workflow of the data process from human movement to robot movement.

Typically, programming a robotic arm entails specifying the number of positions for the arm to reach. These are known as waypoints, and you are usually concerned with the position of the end of the robot arm, which is known as position control [7] or inverse kinematics.

Since the inverse kinematics control method didn't consider the posture of the robot during the movement. This study uses the control method of forward kinematics to directly control the six-axis angle of the robot arm, simultaneously, control the running attitude of the robot arm, which is more in line with the logic of human movement and can avoid the problem of singularities that are easily encountered when using inverse kinematics.

As shown in Fig. 4, by calculating the angle between the dancer's skeleton and the information obtained earlier, we can convert it into the angle of the six axes of the robot arm, allowing the dancer to directly control the movement of the robot arm in a way that is more in line with human posture and allowing the dancer to choreograph more intuitively and experimentally with the robot. During rehearsal or performance.

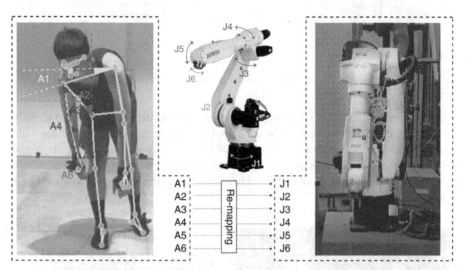

Fig. 4. The diagram of converting skeleton angles to Robotic Axis Angle.

3.1 Data Collection

This research uses machine vision's skeleton recognition technology to identify the dancer's posture from images and outputs three-dimensional coordinate points. This information is then utilized for analyzing the dancer's posture, as demonstrated in Fig. 5. The program is written using the open-source packages MediaPipe and OpenCV on the Visual Studio Code compiler. The dancer simply needs to record the dance performance with a standard camera and input the footage into the program for skeleton recognition processing, which will then output the coordinates of 33 body parts.

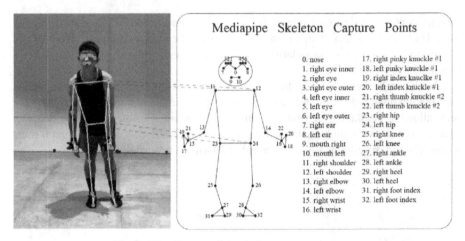

Fig. 5. The diagram of the skeleton capture points.

As shown in Fig. 6, this study employs skeleton recognition technology to identify the coordinates of various parts of the dancer's body. These recognized coordinates are transmitted to Rhino-Grasshopper through UDP communication during recognition, and the dancer's limb skeleton is constructed by analyzing the relationship between these points. The dance is then recreated in a virtual world, aiding the dancer in viewing its representation in that space.

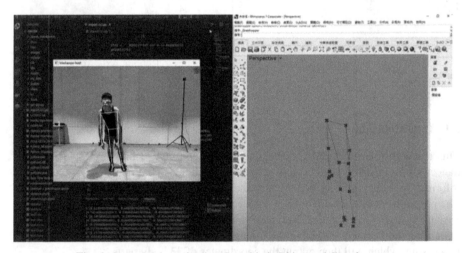

Fig. 6. Recreate dance in virtual world via Rhino and Grasshopper.

3.2   Data Transfer

The traditional control method does not consider arm posture during movement, so this study adopts forward kinematics to control the machine arm. Forward kinematics is a method of motion applied to robots, meaning that it uses the parameters of the robot's joints to calculate the tool head's coordinate plane position. This is achieved by directly giving J1-J6 six joint angles to control the machine arm. Its advantage is that it can avoid unexpected movements when the arm encounters singular points, and the rotation of the joints is also more in line with the swinging of the dancer's limb skeleton. It is a way of translating data into the movement of the machine arm.

In the translation phase, this study analyzed the relationship between human limb movements and machine arm movements and developed a translation system to convert the angle between the dancer's limb skeleton into the rotation angle of the machine arm's six axes, using forward kinematics to control the machine arm. As shown in Fig. 7, the J1 axis of the machine arm controls the left and right rotation of the arm, and this movement feature corresponds to the angle between the line connecting the two shoulder positions in the dancer's skeleton and the X axis.

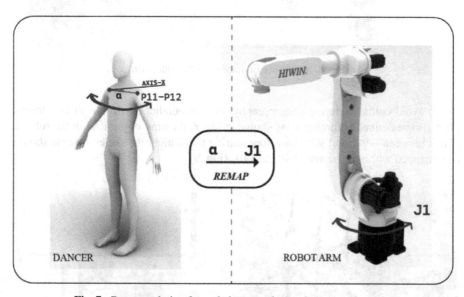

Fig. 7. Data translation from skeleton angle to robot arm axis angle.

In addition to transforming skeleton information into angle control of the robotic arm, the performance may vary due to the brand and model of the robotic arm used. The key constraint is the restriction on the angle of each axis. Therefore, when converting the skeleton angle into the six-axis angle of the robotic arm, it is crucial to remap the values based on the hardware restrictions of the robotic arm and environmental limitations, to guarantee safety and maintain the desired choreography outcomes.

This study utilized a six-jointed robotic arm, the RA620-1739, developed by HIWIN Technology. Before conducting data translation, it is imperative to refer to the arm's manual to verify the angle restrictions of each joint. For instance, the case of the RA620-1739 used in this study, features six joints, J1 to J6, with angle and speed limitations as depicted in Fig. 8.

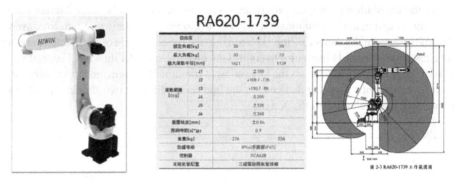

Fig. 8. Hardware limitations of the robot arm.

To avoid collision during choreography, the surrounding environment constraints must also be defined beforehand. As shown in Fig. 8, the limit of joint A1 of the robotic arm is between −90° and 90°. Therefore, during translation, the skeleton angle should be remapped within the range of 40° to 140° (Fig. 9).

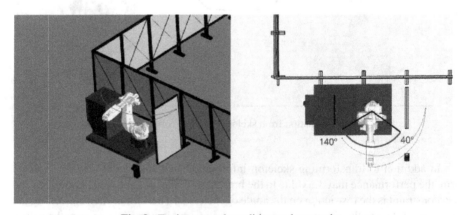

Fig. 9. Environmental condition and constraint.

3.3 Robot Arm Control

The detailed process of controlling the robotic arm in this study is shown in Fig. 10. First, posture detection is performed using Opencv and MediaPipe, and a program is used to convert the captured posture coordinates into the six-axis joint angles of the HIWIN robotic arm. Finally, real-time synchronized control is performed via online control using the HRSDK module developed by HIWIN Technology, directly transmitting control commands to the control Host of the HIWIN robotic arm through the Ethernet network.

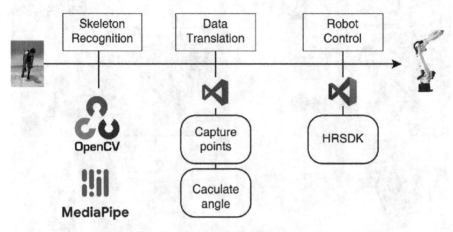

Fig. 10. Robot Arm Control workflow.

4   Outcomes

In this study, professional dancers were recruited to test the choreography method and system. As shown in Fig. 11, the dancer can intuitively control the arm movement to resemble a human-like posture. Despite the difference in form between the arm and the human body, the lower body movements cannot be fully replicated, but simple upper body postures can already be displayed in this stage.

Fig. 11. Records of dancer using this method for robot arm choreography.

5   Conclusion and Future Work

This study employs skeleton recognition technology to allow choreographers to capture human posture data using standard cameras or recorded videos. After acquiring the data, the three-dimensional geometric data of dance is used to calculate the skeleton angle and import the angle data to control each axis of the robot arm by forward kinematics, allowing choreographers to control the movement of the robot arm more intuitively and match the robot posture more closely with human posture.

In future research and development, in addition to continuing to optimize the intuitive machine arm choreography and continuing to develop different dance translation methods, AI technology is expected to be introduced. By utilizing RNNs, LSTMs, and other machine learning models, the aim is to teach the robot arm to not only follow the dancer's movements but also learn and adapt to their dance styles. The ultimate goal is to achieve a harmonious human-machine dance performance, where the robot arm acts as a dancing partner.

Acknowledgment. This research is developed by Robot Aided Creation and Construction (RAC-Coon) of National Cheng Kung University and the Department of Architecture, Hiwin Technology and Anarchy Dance Theatre.

This paper is supported by National Science and Technology Council (NSTC) of Taiwan to National Cheng Kung University under MOST 111-2221-E-006 -050 -MY3, MOST112-2420-H006-002.

References

1. Jacopo, A., Skoglund, A., Duckett, T.: Position teaching of a robot arm by demonstration with a wearable input device. In: International Conference on Intelligent Manipulation and Grasping (IMG04) (2004)
2. Jean-Julien, A., et al.: Cheek to chip: dancing robots and AI's future. IEEE Intell. Syst. **23.2**, 74–84 (2008)
3. Dillmann, R.: Teaching and learning of robot tasks via observation of human performance. Robot. Auton. Syst. **47**(2–3), 109–116 (2004)
4. John, M., et al.: Collaborative dance between robot and human. Workshop on Artistically Skilled Robots as part of 2016 IEEE/RSJ IROS Conference (2016)
5. Pedro Neto, J., Norberto Pires, A., Moreira, P.: High-level programming and control for industrial robotics: using a hand-held accelerometer-based input device for gesture and posture recognition. Indust. Robot Int. J. **37**(2), 137–147 (2010). https://doi.org/10.1108/014399110 11018911
6. Christopher, S., Bogdanovych, A., Ratanasena, E.: Teleoperation of a humanoid robot using full-body motion capture, example movements, and machine learning. In: Proceedings Australasian Conference on Robotics and Automation, vol. 8 (2012)
7. Nicholas Robert, W.: A system to explore using a collaborative robot in improvisational dance practice. Diss. Middlesex University (2020)
8. Huang, Y.: Huang yi studio. http://huangyi.tw/huangyi_and_kuka/. Accessed 10 Feb 2023
9. Amit, R.: Music and movement based dancing for a non-anthropomorphic robot. In: 2022 17th ACM/IEEE International Conference on Human-Robot Interaction (HRI). IEEE (2022)

Robot Path Verification Method for Automotive Glue-Coating Based on Augmented Reality and Digital Twin

Chaoran Wang[1,2], Xiaonan Yang[1(✉)], Lei Zhang[2], Yaoguang Hu[1], Hongzhen Li[1], Huihui Hao[2], and Zhihan Wang[1]

[1] School of Mechanical Engineering, Institute of Industrial and Intelligent Systems Engineering, Beijing Institute of Technology, Beijing, China
yangxn@bit.edu.cn

[2] National Key Laboratory of Special Vehicle Design and Manufacturing, Integration Technology, Beijing, China

Abstract. The automotive glue-coating, as an important part of automobile manufacturing, has a crucial impact on automotive water-proof and rust-proof performances. The glue-coating robots need to be path planned with software, and the paths have to be repeatedly tested with the actual production line using prototype vehicles. There are multiple issues concerning nozzle damage and inefficiency by using the traditional glue-coating path verification method, which calls for a new method to solve these problems. This paper proposes a path verification method for automotive glue-coating based on augmented reality and digital twin. The results show that with this augmented reality and digital twin based method, the operator can observe the glue-coating process intuitively and immersively, so that he can adjust or re-plan the glue-coating path according to the verification results, even before the production of the actual prototype vehicle. The collision between the actual prototype vehicle and the nozzle of the glue-coating robot will be transformed into the collision between the virtual vehicle model and the robot digital twin, which can avoid nozzle damage, save a lot of time for waiting for the production of the prototype vehicle. This method is in line with the general trend of smart manufacturing development and effectively shortens the manufacturing cycle time.

Keywords: Augmented reality · Digital twin · Automotive glue-coating · Path verification

1 Introduction

With the progress of the times and the development of technology, the demand for manufacturing technology gradually tends to be personalized, customized and green. The automobile manufacturing industry is an important part of the manufacturing industry, playing an important role in providing employment and promoting consumption [1]. Glue-coating is a necessary process in the manufacture of automobiles and is of great

M. Kurosu and A. Hashizume (Eds.): HCII 2023, LNCS 14013, pp. 258–267, 2023.
https://doi.org/10.1007/978-3-031-35602-5_19

significance to the water-proof and rust-proof performance of automobiles. However, the current software-planned robot glue-coating paths need to be verified through a prototype vehicle with the actual production line. It caused the potential risk of collisions between the prototype vehicle and the nozzle, with a long debugging time for robot path verification. The traditional glue-coating path verification method is faced with multiple issues concerning nozzle damage and inefficiency, calling for a new method that can verify the glue-coating path efficiently, and at a low cost, in order to meet the development of converting traditional automotive manufacturing to smart manufacturing and human-computer interaction [2].

In an augmented reality (AR) scene, the verification of the glue-coating path can meet the requirements proposed above. Augmented reality, combining virtual elements with the real world, has demonstrated impressive results in a variety of application fields and gained significant research attention in recent years [3]. In order to make the robot model have the same motion as the glue-coating robot, we use digital twin (DT) to model the behavior of the robot. A digital twin is a virtual representation of real-world entities and processes synchronized at a specified frequency and fidelity [4]. The ideal digital twin model involves multi-dimensional, multi-temporal and multi-scale models such as geometric, physical, behavioral and rule-based models, and it is expected to truly portray the physical world [5]. Among them, geometric and behavioral models will be built to simulate the robot's glue-coating process.

Based on the research above, this paper proposes a path verification method for automotive glue-coating based on augmented reality and digital twin. We build an AR scene to register the virtual car model and robot digital twin inside the actual processing site, thus the collision between the actual prototype vehicle and the nozzle of glue-coating robot will be transformed into the collision between the virtual vehicle model and the robot digital twin, which can avoid unnecessary nozzle damage and preparations such as lifting the prototype vehicle. With this method, we can verify the glue-coating path before the prototype vehicle is produced, and save a lot of time. Besides, the operator can observe the glue-coating process intuitively and immersively [6], so that he can adjust or re-plan the glue-coating path according to the verification results. This method is in line with the general trend of smart manufacturing development, once the model has been designed the glue-coating path can be verified, which effectively shortens the manufacturing cycle time.

2 Method

2.1 System Framework

In the practical scenario targeted by the method proposed in this paper, the vehicle is suspended at the corresponding position above the glue-coating site, and on each side of the vehicle there is a glue-coating robot standing by, as shown in Fig. 1. The operator has arranged the glue-coating path and workflow of the robots, also input the instructions in advance. When coating the vehicle, the robot arm with a nozzle continuously moves around and sprays the glue on the vehicle body until the preplanning task is complete, and then the robot is back to its original position. The whole glue-coating process is carefully observed by the operator in order to check if the collisions happen between the nozzle and the vehicle, and whether the final glue-coating outcome is satisfying. If the problems above don't occur, the verification is successful, otherwise, this glue-coating path needs to be replanned.

Fig. 1. The practical scenario.

This paper builds the system framework based on Unity in Windows. As you can see in Fig. 2 the system framework is divided into three sections: Construction of the AR environment, Construction of the twin behavior model, and Collision Detection. The first section is about constructing an AR environment in Unity, which will be deployed to HoloLens2. In this environment, we can accomplish the registration and positioning of the models. The second section is about constructing the twin behavior model with TCP communication, which makes the robot digital twin and the glue-coating robot perform the same behavior. The last section is collision detection, after a collision between the virtual vehicle model and the robot digital twin is detected, the system will have a visual representation. This system is at a low cost, efficient and adaptable, it can also solve the problems that have been mentioned above.

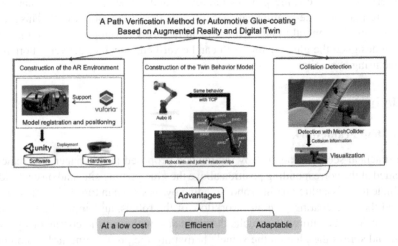

Fig. 2. System framework.

This verification method based on AR-DT is different from the traditional one in many ways. *The following* Table 1 *gives a summary of all differences between them.*

Table 1. Comparison of traditional verification methods and AR-DT based methods.

Methods	Vehicle	Robot	Devices on operator	Collision
Traditional method	real	real	/	real collision (can cause damage)
AR-DT based method	virtual	virtual	HoloLens2	collision between virtual models

2.2 Construction of the AR Environment

This paper uses Unity to build the AR environment. Unity is a comprehensive multi-platform development tool that allows us to accomplish the registration and positioning of the models in the real space, which can combine virtual models with the real world, and make them have certain locations.

Import of Models. *The virtual vehicle model and the model of Aubo i5 which is the glue-coating robot used in this paper were correctly assembled and set up in 3ds_Max software and imported into the Unity project. In order to fix the position of the virtual vehicle model and the glue-coating robot model at the corresponding location in the processing site, tracking registration was performed using the Vuforia platform supported by Unity, the virtual vehicle model and the Aubo robot were superimposed by HoloLens2 to the processing site through recognizing the specified images for initial locating.*

Registration and Positioning of Models. In this paper, we unify the initial positions of the glue-coating robot and the robot digital twin by artificially adjusting the robot digital twin's position to coincide with the glue-coating robot using human eye observation, which is adaptable to different processing sites and emphasizing the concept of "human in the loop". We designed a control panel using HoloLens2, with supported UXs and added MRTK related components to it. So that the operator can adjust the position of robot digital twin to coincide with the glue-coating robot with buttons on the panel. Besides, the control panel can be dragged by hand gestures, and after adjusting the image's position so that models have correct locations, you can locate the models by directly looking at the eye-tracking button, without dragging the control panel all the time or going back to where the panel is.

2.3 Robot Digital Twin Behavior Model

The purpose of constructing the robot digital twin behavior model is to make the robot and the twin move synchronously. Then the robot and the robot digital twin could complete the gluing movement synchronously so as to verify the feasibility of the path. To accomplish this task, two steps are required: first, transmit the motion parameters of the robot real-time through TCP communication, and then drive the robot digital twin motion according to the motion parameters.

TCP Communication. There are two main protocols in the transport layer: TCP and UDP. In contrast, TCP protocol is more accurate for data transmission and the data is not easy to lose, but it is slower than UDP protocol [7]. The accuracy of movement is more significant for the glue coating process, so TCP protocol is selected.

To establish the TCP communication, the server is deployed in the glue coating robot, and the client is deployed in the robot digital twin. The data transmission can be realized between the robot and the twin. In this paper, we choose the joint angle of the robot as the data to be transmitted because the motion state of this six DOF robot can be uniquely determined by six joint angles. The trajectory of the twin will be infinitely close to that of the robot on the condition that the frequency of the data transmission is high enough. But it is difficult to make the rate of the data transmission meet our need because of the low speed of the TCP transmission. To resolve this problem, the speed of the robot to complete the glue-coating process can be reduced. We can also put data into a container for batch transmission in order to reduce the frequency of the data transmission.

Drive the Robot Digital Twin to Move. The motion types of the robot include axis motion, linear motion, trajectory motion and so on. Axis motion is based on the running angle of each joint between the waypoint, according to the maximum speed and maximum acceleration of the motor, each joint at the fastest speed of the road point of the target (the beginning and the end speed is zero). The linear motion causes the tool center point to move linearly between the road points. The trajectory motion is the trajectory motion of multiple way points. In this paper, the motion of the robot is controlled through the joint angles, so the axis motion is more appropriate.

We add rotation scripts to each joint of the robot to drive the robot digital twin. The rotation axis set in the script needs to follow the motion of the previous joint to achieve combined motion. And the maximum speed, maximum acceleration and range of motion should be set in the script as well.

2.4 Collision Detection

In the glue-coating path verification method proposed in this paper, besides the operator can visually watch the glue-coating process to confirm whether there is any interference, the system itself will also visually show the collision information to the operator through the collision detection between the virtual vehicle model and the robot digital twin, which is in the AR environment built in Sect. 2.2. By mixing virtual and reality, the gluing-coating path can be verified without real physical collisions, and the collisions at the physical level in the real environment will be converted into collisions at the geometric level in the AR environment, i.e. collisions between models. Combining the robot digital twin behavior model mentioned in Sect. 2.3, collision detection can be accomplished at the virtual level in different scenarios, without modeling the entire production line.

We added three 6 cm long cylinders with one cm radius at the end of the robot digital twin to simulate the nozzle for collision detection with the virtual vehicle model. Each cylinder is divided into 6 sections, i.e., each section is 1 cm long, and uses a specific material from the MRTK package to represent the change in interference state using color changes. Before the collision, the color of each small cylinder is green; when a small cylinder interferes with the virtual vehicle, its color will change to red; after the interfering small cylinder leaves the virtual vehicle, i.e., the interference ends, its color will change to white. That is, green, red and white represent: no interference, ongoing interference and previous interference, respectively. Besides, when a cylinder has collided, the system outputs the serial number of the cylinder and its real-time coordinate, this can be easier for analyzing the path.

Collision detection is an important part of the gluing-coating path verification, showing us how the nozzle of the gluing robot interferes with the prototype vehicle in this path, which directly influences the operator's analysis of this path. This paper uses an intuitive, visual output to enable the operator to clearly observe the interference between models and thus analyze the feasibility of the path.

3   Case Study

Preparation. In this paper, we do an experiment to clearly demonstrate our system. A specific image is used for HoloLens2 recognition to obtain information about the relative position of the image to the HoloLens2, so that the virtual models can be superimposed on the real space in a certain position. Before the experiment starts, the specific image should be printed out, and located in a relatively open place so that the models won't be obscured by the surroundings. Then the operator deploys the project to the HoloLens2, the experiment starts.

Experimental Process. First of all, the operator should put on the HoloLens2 and get into the AR environment we built, when the HoloLens2 recognizes the specific image, the virtual vehicle model and the robot digital twin will appear in a certain position relationship with the image. Next, adjust the position of the image, making the virtual vehicle model locate the correct position, then look at the 'Locate' eye-tracking button on the control panel to locate both the virtual vehicle model and the robot digital twin. After that, adjust the position of the robot digital twin to coincide with the real glue-coating robot, now the virtual vehicle model and the robot digital twin both have correct positions. Finally, push the 'Verify' button to start the glue-coating robot's motion and TCP communication, the glue-coating process will start. The process is as shown in Fig. 3, and when observing the glue-coating process, the operator can choose if the digital twin of the robot is invisible to facilitate his observations and analysis. The buttons mentioned above are in the UI shown in Fig. 4.

As shown in Fig. 4 after locating the models through the control panel, the operator can observe the glue-coating process intuitively and immersively through the HoloLens2, so that he can adjust or re-plan the glue-coating path according to the verification results. The results are visual and intuitive, after a collision between the virtual vehicle model and the robot digital twin is detected, the system will have a visual representation: The cylinders which have collisions with the vehicle model will turn their colors to red, and after that, their colors will turn to white. Also, when a cylinder has collided, the system outputs the serial number of the cylinder with its real-time coordinate (as shown in the

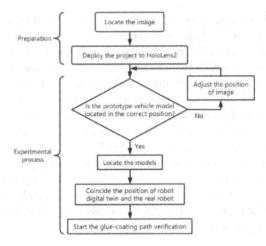

Fig. 3. Experimental steps

lower right corner of Fig. 4), which can be easier for the operator to evaluate and analyze this glue-coating path.

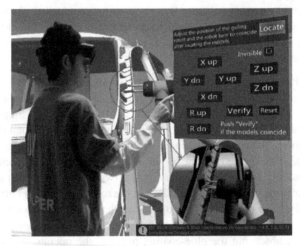

Fig. 4. Experimental scenes and its visual representation.

4 Discussion

In this paper, we show that the AR-DT based method for glue-coating path verification can accomplish the verification of the glue-coating path well, and solve many problems the traditional verification method faces, such as nozzle damage and inefficiency.

Besides, the operator can observe the glue-coating process intuitively and immersively, so that he can adjust or re-plan the glue-coating path according to the verification results. In the experiment, the operator interacts with the models in many ways, such as adjusting the position of the models, which reflects the important "human in the loop" idea in augmented reality.

This method solved many problems which the traditional method faces. An AR environment is built for combining virtual prototype vehicle and robot digital twin with the real processing site, the collision between the actual prototype vehicle and the nozzle of the glue-coating robot will be transformed into the collision between the virtual vehicle model and the robot digital twin. Thus we don't have to waiting for the production of actual prototype vehicles, which takes a long time. Also, that means there is no risk of damage to the prototype vehicle and the nozzles on the glue-coating robot, that will save a lot of costs. The DT of robot enables exact replication of glue-coating robot's motion and behavior in AR scenes, which is the key to verify the glue-coating path. Combing AR and DT, the method for glue-coating path verification this paper proposes is more adaptable, efficient, convenient and less costly.

It is worth mentioning that since Unity's built-in MeshCollider component gives the virtual vehicle model a collider that is always larger than the model itself, this is in some cases beneficial for our main need to avoid collisions. In the actual automotive glue-coating process, if the effective glue-coating distance of the nozzle is much larger than the maximum error of the virtual vehicle model's collider, the verified path can complete the glue-coating with good quality under the condition that the body and the nozzle do not collide. If the effective glue-coating distance of the nozzle is not enough or better glue-coating quality is needed, we can increase the length of the nozzle of the robot digital twin to the maximum effective glue-coating distance of the nozzle, so that the verified paths are always in contact with the robot digital twin when the verification is carried out, which can filter out some paths where the glue-coating quality is degraded because the nozzle is too far from the body at a certain point in the glue-coating path.

The proposed method brings a possibility to combine AR and DT. AR continues to develop and improve in recent years, the application of augmented reality in the industrial field has been increasing, such as the application of augmented reality technology in the field of aircraft maintenance [8], manufacturing systems [9] and laptop assembly [10]. DT has many applications in product design, product manufacturing, medical analysis, engineering construction, etc. By combining the two, once the model has been designed the glue-coating path can be verified, which saves a lot of time for debugging, effectively shortens the manufacturing cycle time. This is the adjustment that needs to be made to automotive glue-coating under the general trend of smart manufacturing development [11–13].

5 Conclusion and Future Study

The results show that with this AR-DT based method, the operator can observe the glue-coating process intuitively and immersively through the AR devices, so that he can understand all the conditions during the glue-coating process, then adjust or re-plan the glue-coating path according to the verification results, even before the production of actual prototype vehicles. The virtual prototype vehicle and the robot digital twin will be superimposed on the real machining scenario, which allows the verification process to be more realistic for the operator. This method also solved many problems which the traditional verification method faces, concerning nozzle damage and inefficiency. This augmented reality-based verification method has a higher degree of flexibility than the virtual reality-based verification method, saves a lot of work on modeling the machining environment, the operator can apply this verification method on different production lines to verify the gluing-coating path of the glue-coating robot intuitively and immersively.

Augmented reality based methods are almost inevitably afflicted with inaccuracy, so does the path verification method proposed in this paper. In the future, the registration accuracy can be improved by adding an image at a 90° angle to the current image and rewriting the Vuforia script, which will improve the registration accuracy of picture thickness direction [14]. Also, the MeshCollider component in Unity doesn't support detection with relatively high accuracy, using a hierarchical wrap-around box can improve the accuracy of collision detection, after the rough wrap-around box collisions, the collision detection of the fine wrap-around box can accomplish a better inspection without a significant increase in computing power [15].

Acknowledgement. The authors would like to thank the National Natural Science Foundation (52175451 and 52205513). We express our sincere gratitude to National Key Laboratory of Special Vehicle Design and Manufacturing Integration Technology, item (GZ2022KF012).

References

1. Joaquim, R.U.: The Great War' in the auto-making industry. banal nationalism and symbolic domination and country-of-origin effect in consumer culture. J. Int. Consum. Mark. (2020)
2. Barovic, H.: An inventive author. Time **156**(23), 116 (2000)
3. Rambach, J., Stricker, D.: Advanced scene perception for augmented reality. J. Imag. **8**(10), 287 (2022). https://doi.org/10.3390/jimaging8100287
4. Laplante, P.: Trusting digital twins. Computer **55**(7), 73–77 (2022). https://doi.org/10.1109/MC.2022.3149448
5. Wu, J., Dai, L., Xue, G., Chen, J.: Theory and Technology of Digital Twin Model for Geotechnical Engineering, pp. 417–25. Nanchang, Jiangxi, China (2021)
6. Matthias, K., Stefan, S.: Augmented reality und virtual reality. HMD Praxis der Wirtschaftsinformatik **59**(1) (2022)
7. Tsubouchi, Y., Furukawa, M., Matsumoto, R.: Low overhead TCP/UDP socket-based tracing for discovering network services dependencies. J. Inform. Process. **30**(0), 260–268 (2022). https://doi.org/10.2197/ipsjjip.30.260
8. Purgett, J.: Augment your reality: a new way to maintain aircraft. Aircraft Mainten. Technol. **32**(6) (2021)
9. Using Motion Control to Guide Augmented Reality Manufacturing Systems NASA tech briefs. **31**(10) (2007)
10. Chiew, J.H., Sung, A.N.: Augmented reality application for laptop assembly with assembly complexity study. Int. J. Adv. Manufac. Technol. **120**(1–2), 1149–1167 (2022). https://doi.org/10.1007/s00170-022-08751-x
11. Chen, W., Shidujaman, M., Tang, X.: AiArt: Towards Artificial Intelligence Art. Academy of Arts and Design. Tsinghua University, Beijing, China (2020)

12. Wang, K.-J., Shidujaman, M., Zheng, C.Y., Thakur, P.: HRIpreneur Thinking: Strategies Towards Faster Innovation and Commercialization of Academic HRI Research (Conference Paper). University of Pittsburgh, Department of Bioengineering, Pittsburgh, PA 15213, pp. 219–26. United States Information and Art Design in Tsinghua University, Beijing, China Information Expe (2019). https://doi.org/10.1109/arso46408.2019.8948829

13. Chen, W., Shidujaman, M., Jin, J., Ahmed, S.U.: A methodological approach to create interactive art in artificial intelligence HCI international 2020 – late breaking papers: cognition. Learn. Games **12425**, 13–31 (2020)

14. Khan, F.A., Muvva, V.V.R.M.K.R., Wu, D., Arefin, M.S., Phillips, N., Swan, J.E.: Measuring the perceived three-dimensional location of virtual objects in optical see-through augmented reality. In: 2021 IEEE International Symposium on Mixed and Augmented Reality (ISMAR): Mississippi State University of Nebraska–Lincoln (2021)

15. Hu, A., He, Y.: Research on hybrid collision detection algorithm based on separation distance. J. Phys. Conf. Ser. **2258**, 012011 (2022). https://doi.org/10.1088/1742-6596/2258/1/012011

Robot in Disguise

Paulina Zguda[✉]

Doctoral School in the Humanities, Jagiellonian University, Krakow, Poland
paulina.zguda@doctoral.uj.edu.pl

Abstract. With the significant presence of humanoid and social robots in public spaces or households, it is essential to consider how what a robot is wearing (if it is dressed at all) affects its perception of people interacting with it. Fashion serves as a way of communication between us and the world. It has several functions, such as practical (covering of a body); being part of identity, and self-expression through clothing. Is any of these remarks might be applied towards robots? The article analyses the possible motivations behind the use of clothing in the case of social robots, as well as indicates applications and research development in this topic. Social robots are becoming companions in our lives, and their image (not limited to the design of their "bodies") significantly influences our perception of them, so the topic of robot clothing should be given special consideration.

Keywords: Philosophical and Ethical Issues of HCI · Social Design

1 Your Companion – A Social Robot

The increasing number of social robots in society is a trend that has been on the rise in recent years. These robots are designed to interact and communicate with humans, and they are becoming more advanced with features such as facial recognition [1], natural language processing [2] and so on. They are being used in various settings such as homes [3, 4], hospitals [5] or nursing homes [6], and schools [7], and they have the potential to improve people's lives by assisting with tasks [3], providing companionship [4], and improving mental health [8]. However, the integration of social robots in society also raises concerns about privacy [9], security [10], and ethics [11]. As the technology continues to develop society needs to consider these issues and ensure that the benefits of social robots are balanced with appropriate safeguards.

However, greater exposure to robots in different spaces requires a careful study of how people perceive social robots. Some social robots may have a humanoid form – such an example is Sophia, whose creators have given many anthropomorphic features (face, posture, gestures), but this is not a necessary condition for seeing a robot as social, as robots of other features are also seen as ones (see: Jibo, PARO, etc.).

Robots – in the most intuitive approach – typically do not need clothes. Clothing serves various purposes for humans, such as protection from external conditions (cold, wind, or chafing), modesty [12], or as a means of (self-)expression. [13] goes so far as to say that clothes "advertise" us. Robots, on the other hand, are typically designed with

M. Kurosu and A. Hashizume (Eds.): HCII 2023, LNCS 14013, pp. 268–276, 2023.
https://doi.org/10.1007/978-3-031-35602-5_20

an exterior that serves the purpose of protection. Nor do socio-cultural categories that enforce the covering of certain parts of the body apply to them, nor do they have mental states or emotions that would induce, for example, a sense of shame. They also do not need to attract anyone – it is their designer's choice and responsibility to make them attractive enough for humans to interact with. In some cases, clothing may be used for robots in educational or entertainment settings to make them appear more human-like, but this is not necessary for the functioning of the robot.

A robot does not "wear" clothes for itself. The robot is never the referent of the clothing in question – the message that the clothing sends is never a message from or to the robot. It is only a signal to the human, who, based on the appearance of the given garment, is supposed to recognise the robot's function, or recognise the means of expression of a person who has chosen of clothes for the robot. Dressing a robot can be akin to dressing a child, who is merely the recipient of these clothes, with no conscious influence over what goes on his or her body.

Clothing for robots is an emerging area of research and development, with the potential to revolutionize the way robots interact with the world and with humans. Despite the increasing popularity and use of robots in various industries and fields, the study of clothing for robots is still in its infancy. Currently, there is a limited amount of research and development in this area, as most robots are designed to function effectively without the need for clothing. Nevertheless, as robots become more integrated into our daily lives, the need for functional (and possibly aesthetically pleasing clothing) might be reconsidered. The development of clothing for robots might not only enhance their functionality, but also shape their social perception by humans.

This article addresses the following issues. Section two indicates the possible application of fashion and apparel in social robotics, including examples of the motivations people may have for dressing robots. The third section considers possible social consequences, while the fourth section identifies factors that need to be considered before designing clothing for robots. The fifth section presents a proposal for research validation of the topic and summarises the conclusions.

2   What Fashion Can Add to Social Robots (If Anything)?

Fashion is a manifestation of individuality and autonomy within a particular historical, geographical, and sociocultural context [14]. This expression is realized through a range of choices, including clothing, footwear, lifestyle, accessories, cosmetics, hair styling, and more. Since robots as agents without subjectivity are deprived of both self-expression and autonomy, is the notion of fashion in their context legitimate? It can be considered as a transference of self-expression (just as a model presenting a creation at a show does not convey her fashion choices but helps to express the creativity of the designer), thus "robotic fashion" would refer to the expression of the creator or owner of the robot who decided to dress the robot.

Although robots are finding their way into the fashion industry as tools or systems – mainly in operating with materials such as folding (for example, the SpeedFolding system allows a robot to fold 30–40 pieces per hour, [15]) or cloth manipulation and dress assistance [16] – "robotic fashion" refers to different phenomena.

Even though the idea of a robot that needs, for instance, functional clothes – such as a firefighter uniform – might feel odd, we use social robots in a variety of contexts. (In education – [7]; in services – [17]; sometimes as a companion in a dangerous environment – [18].) In some of them, clothing for the robot is not a fad, but a necessity, to protect its components, for example.

[19] introduces three uses for robot clothes: adapting to context (e.g., culture), protection and signalling (e.g., function). This paper [19] presents a "utility of framework", where the focus is on the functional clothing for the robot and the robot's clothing as an interpretive cue for humans is only one of the factors. What is missing, however, is a more in-depth analysis of how humans treat and read robots in clothing. This represents a (yet) unexploited experimental space, which will be mentioned in a later section of the text.

There are several advantages of including fashion in social robotics, which will be elaborated on below.

2.1 Why Would People Want to Dress Their Robots?

Overall, dressing social robots can serve both practical and emotional purposes, making them more appealing and useful in a wider range of situations. It serves several purposes, including:

Improving Approachability
Human-like clothing might be utilized to increase the relatable nature of social robots. If a child sees a robot wearing clothes like hers, her curiosity and willingness for interaction might increase. Establishing contact and approachability is the first phase of human-robot interaction, therefore all factors that may be beneficial in this respect are worth exploring.

Enhancing Emotional Bonding
Dressing a robot in attire that aligns with its character and personality can foster an emotional connection, making the robot more captivating and memorable. People tend to personalize and customize systems [20] or devices [21] they use. The ability to personalise the product might be even a key design factor for the creators [22]; however, it also affects the experience of the user. Personalising one's devices or systems promotes a greater emotional component on the part of the owner [21]. Personalisation implies putting effort into the appearance, configurations and possible behaviour of a given agent. Greater effort fosters the creation of a bond and the perception of the value of one self-expression of a given object as superior [23].

Facilitating Recognition
Clothes that are tailored to a robot's role or function can assist people in quickly identifying its purpose and understanding its capabilities.

The robotic Professor Einstein [24] is easy to recognise not only because of his grey hair but also because of his tie and shirt. Thanks to the well-established image of its inspiration Albert Einstein, the robot is therefore easily associated with his educational function.

Moreover, clothes might also serve as a social cue. Imagine the following scenario. If you walk into a restaurant, in most cases you do not expect to find a robot there. However, if upon your entrance you notice a Pepper standing in the corner clad in a shirt, apron and bow tie, you can guess that you are probably about to deal with a robot waiter. What the robot looks like in a particular place makes it easier to decipher its function, as well as prepare us for a possible interaction.

For example, in 2020, in one of the Dutch restaurants [25], robotic waiters were a remedy for the COVID-19 pandemic and limited human contact. Their function was signalized by their design. Robots had a neckerchief around their necks, and the colour of their "bodies" (white with red elements) resembled a waiter's attire. A similar effect could be achieved by dressing robots in real aprons.

Encouraging Creativity

Some individuals relish in the creative challenge of designing and crafting clothing for their robots and find the hobby to be enjoyable and stimulating. In societies where exposure to robots in everyday life is high (Japan), there are already the germs of a community of people passionate about personalising their robots (more in Sect. 2.2).

Over the next decade or so, we will see an increasing number of social robots accompanying us in various activities. The possibility to decorate them according to one's style and creativity or to design apparel represents an opportunity for free self-expression. Moreover, these active hobbies might contribute to the longer preservation of cognitive abilities [26], which will be particularly useful for older people who will use robots as assistants or companions. An additional factor is the social aspect of the hobby – making clothes for robots together or engaging in clothing swaps can be the basis for better relationships between people and greater social activation of the elderly.

2.2 Customization of the Robot

There are now at least two shops in Japan that design and distribute robotic clothing. In addition to clothing, RIERIE [27] also offers make-up, earrings and wigs for robots. Its product range is targeted mainly at the robot Pepper in Japan, while Rocket Road [28] has clothing and gadgets for various social robots in its collection and produces protective clothing for robotic arms.

The existence of a market for such products normalises the dressing of robots, as well as highlights the need for customisation. What a given owner's robot looks like depends on her taste but is also a form of transferring the owner's self-expression from herself to an external object.

Moreover, people are inclined to personalize the robots they interact with [29]. [21] in their pioneering study tested whether users of the vacuuming robot Roomba would voluntarily customize them. Users were guided by various reasons (such as practical: that Roomba should be more noticeable or better fit into the interior design of the house), but the fact of their customization activity depended on whether they received a kit from researchers for decorating the robot. This indicates that encouraging users to personalize technology has two outcomes: it favours the use of this personalization, and customization itself promotes strong emotional involvement and more frequent use of a given system or product.

More research on this topic would allow for even more confident conclusions, but it is worth paying attention to the connection between the effort put into customizing the robot (as well as the time and resources spent on it) and involvement in the relationship with it.

2.3 Social Signals

Clothing is one of many visual factors that influence people's perception of a robot. Just as the colour of a robot's cover, body structure or the presence of eyes and mouth can shape our experience of a robot (most social robots have a light-coloured body, rounded shapes and arms with several degrees of freedom, and their faces and eyes are clearly defined), clothes add more layers for interpretation. The choice of garment is not only an aesthetic decision. It can be assumed that a robot in a neat tuxedo would be perceived differently than a robot in a dishevelled outfit, which would indicate a large dump and possible negative experience with previous users. More on signalling may be found in [19].

3   Why "RObot in Disguise"

The previous section mostly presented the possible benefits of dressing a robot to deepen the human-robot relationship. What about the situation where dressing a robot is interpreted differently? A systematic review by [30] indicates that social robots most often evoke slightly positive emotions and reactions in people when it comes to trust and attitudes towards robots. Nevertheless, due to the novelty of the topic, it is important to consider also the possible downfalls of robots in clothes.

There is a lack of research to see if people perceive the robots clothes as a form of disguise, and therefore the robot as an imposter – as something (someone?) who impersonates a human and uses clothes to do so. Could a clothed robot be something that appeals to the uncanny valley effect? This phenomenon [31] occurs when people consider a robot to be a (badly) human imitator; anxiety and sometimes even disgust are related to cognitive dissonance, when the observed artificial agent has too many features in common with a human to behave so ineptly as a machine.

For example, in a study [32] participants interpreted robots in wigs as a clumsy attempt at imitating a human. Would clothing the robots enhance this effect or provide a strong enough basis on its own? A negative experience with a robot that causes anxiety, embarrassment or cringe may translate into less willingness to interact with robots in the future. When trying to more consciously involve clothing in human-robot interaction, the first thing to keep in mind is avoiding discomfort for the participants of this relationship.

4   Factors to Consider

In addition to the aspects indicated in the previous sections of the text, several factors should be considered before proposing the use of robots in clothes in a more structured, mass manner.

First, when humans think about clothes, they intuitively appeal to the nudity and modesty category – we cover the intimate parts of our bodies. However, most of the time robot does not have to be covered [19]. Still, when we see a robot which has some clothes on (such as Sophia), and then we would see it without them, we would feel odd about it. It might be derived from the modesty theory [12].

Another factor is gender – attributed to a robot affects our perception [33]. Would we treat differently a "female" robot than a "male" one? Would we feel uncomfortable dressing the "male" robot in stereotypically female clothes? In this case, interesting conclusions can also be drawn from research on sex robots – [34] points to the existing theoretical considerations on this topic, however, underlines the lack of empirical examination.

The materials and design of the robotic garments are crucial as well. For instance, the weight of the attire can affect the balance sensor of the robot, the fabric can ignite due to the heat produced by the robot's electrical components, and the robot must operate efficiently both with and without its apparel. Projects focusing on the production of clothes for robots should meet technical requirements without sacrificing aesthetic qualities.

The next compelling factor is the level of anthropomorphization of the robots that are distributed in clothes. For example, Sophia is clothed, as well as a Geminoid F or Kaspar. Does wearing clothes as a default state change the perception of the robot from the very beginning of the interaction?

However, the issue does not stop when we decide to put the clothes on the robot. Should a robot designed to interact within one culture be dressed in a manner appropriate to the traditions (like Pepper wearing a samurai outfit in Japan) and fashions present in that culture, or on the contrary, should its clothing be universal? Can a robot express its "identity" through its clothes? Can we recognize the aesthetic qualities in robots' clothing, or are they merely pieces of fabric? These questions remain open for now.

5 Future Works and Conclusions

The use of humanoid and social robots in public spaces or households has become increasingly prevalent. As a result, it is crucial to consider the impact that a robot's appearance has on people's perceptions of it. One aspect of this appearance is the clothing, or lack thereof, that a robot is wearing.

The way a robot is dressed can affect how people perceive its function, personality, and level of professionalism. For example, a robot dressed in a business suit might be perceived as more professional and competent, whereas a robot dressed in a playful or casual outfit might be perceived as more approachable and friendly. Presenting those two robots' "personas" – and more ideally, allowing participants to interact with them – might provide interesting insights into how more formal attire shapes the outcome of an interaction.

Moreover, the clothing or lack thereof can also influence people's comfort levels in interacting with the robot. A robot dressed in a manner that is inappropriate for the context could make people feel uncomfortable or embarrassed, whereas a robot dressed appropriately could help people feel more at ease and open to interaction. Therefore, the way a robot is dressed should be carefully considered to ensure that it is appropriate for the current circumstances and that it enhances, rather than detracts from, the user experience.

Experimental testing of human perception of clothed robots provides several benefits that are essential for the development of social robots. Firstly, it enables researchers and designers to understand the impact of clothing on the perceived human-like qualities of robots. By testing human perception, designers can determine which types of clothing are most effective in reducing the "uncanny valley" effect and making the robots more approachable and relatable to people.

Secondly, experimental testing can be used to assess the effectiveness of clothing in enhancing emotional connections between people and robots. By studying how people respond to different types of clothing, researchers can identify which attire is most likely to foster an emotional connection and make the robot more engaging and memorable. This knowledge can be used to guide the development of more effective clothing designs that support the creation of stronger bonds between people and robots.

Moreover, it is important to explore whether, in a free-choice situation (for example, during an activity of playing with a robot where different accessories are available), social robot users are willing to "dress up" the robot on their own.

Thirdly, an empirical approach can be used to evaluate the impact of clothing on the functionality of robots. By testing how people perceive the robot's abilities, researchers can determine if the clothing is effectively supporting the robot's role or function. This can be particularly useful in the case of robots designed for specific tasks or environments, where clothing can be designed to add functionalities that are essential for the robot's operation.

Finally, experimental testing can also be used to understand the impact of clothing on the recognition of robots by people. By examining people's perceptions of the robot, researchers can determine if the clothing effectively conveys the robot's purpose and capabilities. This information can be used to guide the design of clothing that is easily recognizable and helps people understand the robot's role.

In conclusion, this paper questioned whether categories applicable towards fashion (such as identity, self-expression, and creativity) might be also found in the scope of robotic fashion. Moreover, the possible influences of robotic clothes on our perception of social robots were presented. Finally, the need for a more empirical approach was expressed. Human perception of clothed robots provides valuable insights into the role of clothing in the development of social robots. By understanding how clothing impacts human perception, designers can create more effective and engaging robots that are better able to form emotional connections and perform their intended functions. And even if this robot actually is in disguise – it is worth ensuring that the meaning of this disguise is clear to us.

Acknowledgements. The author would like to thank prof. Leszek Sosnowski and prof. Bipin Indurkhya from the Jagiellonian University for substantive support during her doctoral studies, as well as Karolina Źróbek and Alicja Wróbel for joint work on observations in the field of human-robot interaction in natural settings.

References

1. Yu, C., Pei, H.: Face recognition framework based on effective computing and adversarial neural network and its implementation in machine vision for social robots. Comput. Electr. Eng. **92**, 107128 (2021)
2. Foster, M.E.: Natural language generation for social robotics: opportunities and challenges. Philosoph. Trans. Royal Soc. B Biol. Sci. **374**(1771), 20180027 (2019)
3. Di Napoli, C., Ercolano, G., Rossi, S.: Personalized home-care support for the elderly: a field experience with a social robot at home. User Model User-Adapted Interaction, pp. 1–36 (2022)
4. Caudwell, C., Lacey, C.: What do home robots want? The ambivalent power of cuteness in robotic relationships. Convergence **26**(4), 956–968 (2020)
5. González-González, C.S., Violant-Holz, V., Gil-Iranzo, R.M.: Social robots in hospitals: a systematic review. Appl. Sci. **11**, 5976 (2021)
6. Demaeght, A., Miclau, C., Hartmann, J., Markwardt, J., Korn, O.: Multimodal emotion analysis of robotic assistance in elderly care. In: Proceedings of the 15th International Conference on PErvasive Technologies Related to Assistive Environments PETRA 2022, pp. 230–236. Association for Computing Machinery, New York, NY, United States (2022)
7. Belpaeme, T., Kennedy, J., Ramachandran, A., Scassellati, B., Tanaka, F.: Social robots for education: a review. Sci. Robot. **3**(21), 1–9 (2018)
8. Scoglio, A.A., Reilly, E.D., Gorman, J.A., Drebing, C.E.: Use of social robots in mental health and well-being research: systematic review. J. Med. Internet Res. **21**(7), e13322 (2019)
9. Lutz, C., Tamo-Larrieux, A.: The robot privacy paradox: understanding how privacy concerns shape intentions to use social robots. Hum. Mach. Commun. **1**, 87–111 (2020)
10. Chatterjee, S., Chaudhuri, R., Vrontis, D.: Usage intention of social robots for domestic purpose: from security, privacy, and legal perspectives. Inform. Syst. Front. 1–16 (2021)
11. Boada, J.P., Maestre, B.R., Genís, C.T.: The ethical issues of social assistive robotics: a critical literature review. Technol. Soc. **67**, 101726 (2021)
12. Dunlap, K.: The development and function of clothing. J. Gen. Psychol. **1**(1), 64–78 (1928)
13. Harvey, J.: Clothes. Routledge (2014)
14. Kaiser, S.B., Green, D.N.: Fashion and Cultural Studies. Bloomsbury Publishing, London, United Kingdom (2021)
15. Avigal, Y., Berscheid, L., Asfour, T., Kröger, T., Goldberg, K.: SpeedFolding: learning efficient bimanual folding of garments. In: 2022 IEEE/RSJ International Conference on Intelligent Robots and Systems (IROS), pp. 1–8. IEEE, New York, NY, United States (2022)
16. Nocentini, O., Kim, J., Bashir, Z.M., Cavallo, F.: Learning-based control approaches for service robots on cloth manipulation and dressing assistance: a comprehensive review. J. NeuroEng. Rehabil. **19**(117), 1–25 (2022)
17. Čaić, M., Mahr, D., Oderkerken-Schröder, G.: Value of social robots in services: Social cognition perspective. J. Serv. Mark. **33**(4), 463–478 (2019)
18. Šabanović, S.: Inventing Japan's 'robotics culture': The repeated assembly of science, technology, and culture in social robotics. Soc. Stud. Sci. **44**(3), 342–367 (2014)
19. Friedman, N., Love, K., LC, R., Sabin, J. E., Hoffman, G., Ju, W.: What robots need from clothing. In: DIS 2021: Designing Interactive Systems Conference 2021, pp. 1345–1355. Virtual Event, USA (2021)
20. Blom, J.O., Monk, A.F.: Theory of personalization of appearance: why users personalize their PCs and mobile phones. Hum. Comput. Interact. **18**, 193–228 (2003)
21. Sung, J., Grinter, R.E., Christensen, H.I.: "Pimp My Roomba": designing for personalization. In: Proceedings of the SIGCHI Conference on Human Factors in Computing Systems (CHI 2009), pp. 193–196. Association for Computing Machinery, New York, NY, USA (2009)

22. Monk, A.F., Blom, J.O.: A theory of personalisation of appearance: quantitative evaluation of qualitatively derived data. Behav, Inform, Technol, **26**(3), 237–246 (2007)
23. Mugge, R., Schoormans, J.P.L., Schifferstein, H.N.J.: Emotional bonding with personalised products. J. Eng. Des. **20**(5), 467–476 (2009)
24. https://www.hansonrobotics.com/professor-einstein/. Accessed 8 Feb 2023
25. https://www.latimes.com/world-nation/story/2020-05-31/hello-and-welcome-robot-waiters-to-the-rescue-amid-virus. Accessed 8 Feb 2023
26. Geda, Y.E., et al.: Engaging in cognitive activities, aging, and mild cognitive impairment: a population-based study. J. Neuropsychiatry Clin. Neurosci. **23**(2), 149–154 (2011)
27. https://rierie.theshop.jp/. Accessed 8 Feb 2023
28. https://robo-uni.com/. Accessed 8 Feb 2023
29. Fitter, N. F., Chowdhury, Y., Cha, E., Takayama, L., Matarić M. J.: Evaluating the effects of personalized appearance on telepresence robots for education. In: Companion of the 2018 ACM/IEEE International Conference on Human-Robot Interaction (HRI), pp. 109–110. Association for Computing Machinery, New York, NY, USA (2018)
30. Naneva, S., Sarda Gou, M., Webb, T.L., Prescott, T.J.: A systematic review of attitudes, anxiety, acceptance, and trust towards social robots. Int. J. Soc. Robot. **12**(6), 1179–1201 (2020). https://doi.org/10.1007/s12369-020-00659-4
31. Mori, M., MacDorman, K.F., Kageki, N.: The uncanny valley [from the field]. IEEE Robot. Autom. Mag. **19**(2), 98–100 (2012)
32. Fitter, N. T., Strait, M., Bisbee, E., Matarić, M. J., Takayama, L.: You're Wigging Me Out! Is personalization of telepresence robots strictly positive?. In: Proceedings of the 2021 ACM/IEEE International Conference on Human-Robot Interaction, pp. 168–176. Association for Computing Machinery, New York, NY, USA (2021)
33. Nomura, T.: Robots and gender. Gender Genome **1**(1), 18–25 (2017)
34. Döring, N., Mohseni, M.R., Walter, R.: Design, use, and effects of sex dolls and sex robots: scoping review. J. Med. Internet Res. **22**(7), e18551 (2020)

Chatbots and Voice-Based Interaction

The Impact of Parent-Like Chatbot Narratives on Daily Reflection

Masayuki Ando[✉], Kouyou Otsu, and Tomoko Izumi

Ritsumeikan University, Kusatsu, Shiga 525-8557, Japan
{mandou,k-otsu,izumi-t}@fc.ritsumei.ac.jp

Abstract. For young people, reflecting on their daily lives is important to deepen their self-understanding and consider their future positively. In addition, the most common timing for young people to reflect on daily experiences is during conversations with their family members (mainly parents). Therefore, this study proposes an approach to support reflection on daily life by adding personalities (parent factor) such as conversation content and way of speaking to chatbots that encourage reflection on daily life through dialogues, which makes the user imagine that they are talking with their parents. In the validation experiment, participants were asked to repeat their daily reflections using the chatbot with and without the parent factor, and the effect of the parent factor on their daily reflections was examined. The two main items tested were the motivation for reflection and impressions of the chatbot when repeating the reflection. As a result, we showed that the parent factor increased the motivation for reflection and improved the impressions of the chatbot when the participants repeated the reflections.

Keywords: Reflection · Chatbot · Memory recall support · Human-computer interaction

1 Introduction

People can reflect on their current situation and make better plans for the future through the act of reflection. Reflection involves objectively recalling and analyzing what one has done and one's own tendencies and considering areas for improvement for the next time. Reflection allows a person to identify the factors that led to an outcome exceeding the goal and determine the actions that should be continued in the future or to identify the causes of an outcome falling short of the goal and consider how to correct the situation. For example, in a reflection experiment conducted in a call center [1], employees who reflected for 15 min a day improved their performance by more than 20% compared to those who did not. Furthermore, reflection is considered important for young people to deepen their self-understanding and to consider the future positively [2]. For example, in adolescence, young people consider questions such as "who I am" and "what is my purpose in life" in society and establish identities. Therefore, reflection

© The Author(s), under exclusive license to Springer Nature Switzerland AG 2023
M. Kurosu and A. Hashizume (Eds.): HCII 2023, LNCS 14013, pp. 279–293, 2023.
https://doi.org/10.1007/978-3-031-35602-5_21

on daily experiences on a regular basis allows them to review their habits and shortcomings and notice improvements objectively. Providing opportunities to young people to reflect on their lives can help them improve their quality of life and plan their future careers.

The most common time for young people to actually engage in reflection is during conversations with family members (mainly parents) [3]. At dinner and other times, young people talk to their parents regarding what happened that day and how they felt about it. The parent should ask the child to consider what to do next in light of what the child has said. Conversations between parents and children have several characteristics; for example, questions that parents ask when worrying about their children and the casual ways of speaking due to their strong psychological connection. These speaking characteristics of parents may be one factor that encourages users to reflect on their past behavior.

However, when young people enter college and start living alone, it is difficult to keep in frequent contact with their parents who live apart from each other because of their different activity times in daily life. Young people's adolescence (the period during which they establish their identities) is generally considered to be between the ages of 12 and 19; however, because of individual differences, reflection may be necessary even after they enter college. In fact, in the U.S., young people are given a "gap year" after high school graduation [4], during which they are encouraged to establish identities through social experiences such as studying abroad, internships, and volunteer work. However, in many countries, including Japan where the author lives, there is no such system, and as a result, young people are likely to start living alone with insufficiently established identities.

Therefore, in this study, we propose a chatbot to provide a place for daily reflection for young people who have fewer opportunities to talk with their parents as college students. Note that we set the conversation with the chatbot to be text-based. This is because many young people have recently contacted their parents through SNS rather than by phone, and we considered that we should first define "parent-like" conversation content and the way of speaking rather than "parent-like" voice. Next, we verify the effectiveness of introducing parent factors into this chatbot. Specifically, we considered creating a chatbot that encourages users to reflect on their daily lives through conversation and adding personality as the parent factor, such as the conversation and way of speaking of parents for their children. Then, we found the positive effect on young people's impressions of the chatbot and their motivation for reflection when they repeated their reflections. In addition, as college students, their lifestyle differs from that of their parents, and they have less time to meet and talk with their parents in the first place. Therefore, this study targets not only college students who live alone, but also those who live at home.

2   Related Research

The application of ICT technology to support daily reflection has received considerable attention. For example, there is research on creating stories for reflection from multimodal lifelogs [5] and a study of an application to determine which lifelog items are useful for daily reflections based on biometric responses [6]. These studies are concerned with the construction of lifelogs for reflection, and there are few studies focusing on the ease of reflection, especially motivation for reflection. In this study, one goal is to improve motivation for reflection by adding behaviors like parents to the chatbot, assuming that the user interacts with the chatbot to reflect on daily life.

Research in the field of clinical psychology has shown that structuring the reflection process and conducting periodic reflections will also make the reflection more effective and foster reflective thinking [7]. Conducting regular reflections, especially for young people in adolescence, has stress-relieving and antidepressant effects [8]. Therefore, this study introduces an interactive reflection in which participants answer questions about their reflections, and periodic reflections will be conducted over a period of time. It is possible that repeated conversations with chatbots that include parent factors may produce psychic effects, similar to the results suggested by related studies in person.

Research on communication agents, such as chatbots, behaving more like humans [9] has confirmed that this feature improves empathy and familiarity with the agent and leads to trust from the user. In addition, a study focusing on the form of the robot's utterances to the user [10] confirmed that casual expressions, such as those made by a person who is close to the user in social distance, such as a parent, improve the user's affinity for the robot and willingness to use the robot, compared to more formal expressions. These studies suggest that incorporating human characteristics familiar to the user (socially distant personality models) in the agent has the positive effect of improving affinity. Therefore, this study focuses on "parents" as a personal model with close social distance and examines the factors that make users feel as if they are conversing with their parents as parent factors.

3 Methodology

3.1 Flow Chart of Reflections by the Proposed Method

This study proposes a chatbot that supports daily reflections with parent factors for college students. The chatbot has a rule-based dialogue flow and interacts with users on text chat. A conversation flow chart of the reflections by the chatbot is shown in Fig. 1.

Figure 1 shows the flow chart of the conversation. Conversation with the chatbot consists of two phases: parent factor conversation and reflection question. The chatbot first asks the user questions in which the parent is concerned about the child as a parent factor conversation. When the user responds, the chatbot will further respond with responses to the user's responses. After a few turns of repeating that conversation, reflection questions follow. As the user answers the questions, the user can automatically reflect on his/her daily routine. In addition, we assume that using a text chat tool as the platform for the system. Therefore, while designing the parent factor conversation phase of this chatbot,

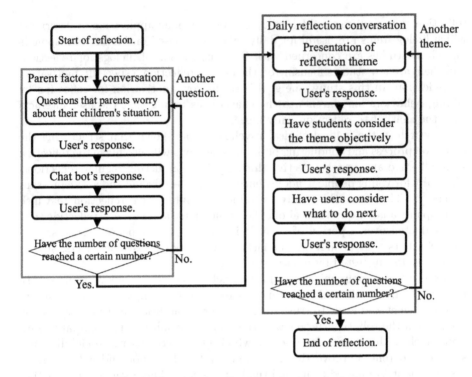

Fig. 1. Conversation flow chart by the chatbot.

we consider text-based interaction methods for a sense of parentage. An example of a conversation between a chatbot and a user on a text chat tool is shown in Fig. 2.

Figure 2 shows that a chatbot named "Mr. A" displays "a question in which a parent worries about a child" or "a question that encourages reflection on daily life," and when the user responds to the question, the chatbot responds with a response or displays the next question. The definition of parent factors and daily reflections will be described in more detail in Sect. 3.2, 3.4.

3.2 Parent Factors

In this study, we define the following two elements as parent factors, and we adopt the following elements in the chatbot to form a parent-like representation:

- (a) Questions showing that parents are concerned about their children's situation.
- (b) Casual way of speaking as seen in parent-child conversations.

First, we explain (a). In this study, we considered a factor that would make young people feel that the chatbot is a parent: a conversation in which the parents express concerns regarding their children's personal and living environment. In general, parents pay attention to their children's personal safety and often

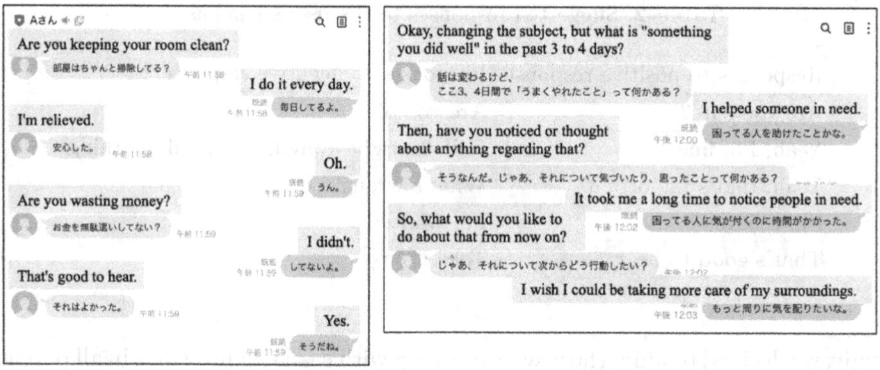

Parent factor conversation   Daily reflection conversation

Fig. 2. A conversation with a chatbot on a text chat tool. (Left is the chatbot's comment. Right is the user's comment)

Table 1. Questions showing that parents worry about their children's situation.

	Question Candidates
Q1	Are you eating your meals properly every day?
Q2	Is there anything wrong with your health?
Q3	Are you having money trouble?
Q4	Are you wasting money?
Q5	Are you getting along with your friends?
Q6	Are you sleeping well?
Q7	Are you keeping your room clean?
Q8	Are you dressing properly?
Q9	Are you being careful about security?
Q10	Do you need anything?

regularly check in on their children's current status and surroundings [11,12]. Therefore, from the situational setting of this study, we consider that the most appropriate conversation content for the parent factor was "questions about the parents' worries about their children's situation." In addition, questions that are too in-depth may not be familiar to some individuals. Therefore, we considered that superficial content regarding questions about the child's living environment was sufficient. In this study, we set the 10 questions shown in Table 1 as "questions showing that parents worry about their children's situation" to be asked during the parent factor conversation, referring to the results of a survey on "parents' concerns about their children's situations" [13,14].

Next, we explain (b). In a study describing the way of speaking between parents and children [10], parents generally use casual expressions such as "Where you going?" to their children. This casual way of speaking may be considered to play a role in improving the relationship in parent-child conversations. Therefore, in this

Table 2. Suggested responses to the user's response.

Responses to positive response	Responses to negative response
Are you sure?	Are you okay?
Yeah, I'm fine	Call me right away if you need anything
Yeah, that's important	What's wrong?
I'm relieved	I'm worried
That's good to hear	Take it easy

study, we decided to unify the way of speaking with casual expressions in all parent factor conversations and in all questions regarding daily reflections. Because the target audience this time is young people whose native language is Japanese, we will use casual expressions in Japanese.

3.3   Responses to User's Talk

In the proposed method, we designed the chatbot to respond once to a user's response during the parent factor's conversation. The reason is that after asking the "questions showing that parents worry about their children's situation," suddenly moving on to the next question may cause the user to feel uncomfortable about the conversation. In addition, we set the chatbot's responses differently depending on whether the user's responses were positive or negative. This is also to reduce discomfort with the conversation. Table 2 shows the chatbot's response to the user's response.

The chatbot determines whether the content of the user's response is positive or negative, and then randomly selects one of the responses in Table 2. For responses, we used "Chat CPT" published by OpenAI to generate multiple candidates for responses. Then, we picked the ones that felt comfortable as responses. In addition, to determine whether the user's response was positive or negative, we used "daigo/bert-base-japanese-sentiment," a Japanese sentiment analysis model available on Hugging Face. This model analyzes the user's responses and returns either the positive or the negative response in Table 2 as the chatbot's response.

3.4   Daily Reflection

In the daily reflection phase, users are asked to reflect on a predetermined theme based on a set of questions. In this study, we refer to the studies on reflection [7,8] and define the chatbot reflection questions as follows:

1. Questions to recall recent words, actions, or things that have happened around a user that are related to a specific theme;
2. Questions that ask a user to objectively consider what they noticed or thought about what they recalled; and
3. Questions that ask a user to consider how they should act in the future based on what they have considered

In addition, we will establish the following two themes for the reflection:

Theme 1. Something you did well.
Theme 2. Something you did not do well.

Theme 1 is set up for the purpose of reflection on positive events, whereas Theme 2 is set up for reflection on negative events. In this study, the chatbot encourages users to reflect on their daily lives by asking questions 1 to 3 in turn on each of these two themes. In this study, we set the chatbot to ask the questions shown in Table 3 for Theme 1 (Something you did well) and the questions shown in Table 4 for Theme 2 (Something you didn't do well) in turn during the reflection conversation.

4 Verification Experiment

4.1 Experimental Summary

In this section, we describe an experiment in which we verified the effect of parent factors on reflection using a chatbot that encourages reflection on daily routines with the addition of parent factors. In this experiment, we formulated the following hypotheses:

H 1. Repeated interaction with a chatbot that has parent factors strengthens the user's affinity to the chatbot (Changes in impressions of the chatbot depending on the parent factor).
H 2. Repeated interaction with a chatbot that has parent factors improves the motivation for reflection and makes reflection easier (effect of parent factors on reflection).

To verify these hypotheses, in this experiment, we asked participants to reflect on their daily routines three times during one week under the following two conditions to investigate their impressions of the chatbot and its effect on their reflections.

Table 3. Reflection questions on "something you did well".

	Casual way of speaking	Formal way of speaking
Q1	Okay, changing the subject, but what is "something you did well" in the past 3 to 4 days?	Excuse me for changing the subject, but have you done "something well" in the past 3 to 4 days?
Q2	Then, have you noticed or thought about anything regarding that?	I see. Are there any observations or thoughts regarding that?
Q3	So, what would you like to do about that from now on?	In that case, what actions would you like to take regarding that in the future?

Table 4. Reflection questions on "something you did not do well"

	Casual way of speaking	Formal way of speaking
Q1	Next, what is "something you didn't do well" in the past 3 to 4 days?	Next, what is "something you didn't do well" in the past 3 to 4 days?
Q2	Then, have you noticed or thought about anything regarding that?	I see. Are there any observations or thoughts regarding that?
Q3	So, what would you like to do about that from now on?	In that case, what actions would you like to take regarding that in the future?

With Parent Factor Condition (With Condition). The participant engages in a conversation with the chatbot to which the parent factor is added. After that, an additional conversation is held to encourage reflections on the daily routine. The way of speaking is casual.

Without Parent Factor Condition (Without Condition). The participant conducts only conversations that encourage reflection on daily life with the chatbot. The way of speaking is formal.

Twenty undergraduate and graduate students participated in the experiment. They were divided into groups of 10 students each, with one group doing "With Condition" reflections and the other group doing "Without Condition" reflections. The participants were asked to experience a conversation with a chatbot with the dialogue flow described in Sect. 3.1. At this time, participants in the "With Condition" category were asked to reflect and consider the parent factor conversation, while participants in the "Without Condition" category were asked to reflect only. In addition, the participants in the experiment were asked to make a total of three reflections, with a period of three or four days between reflections. For each reflection, we set three "Questions showing that parents are concerned about their children's situation" to be conducted in conversation with the parent factor, all with different questions.

4.2 Experimental Procedures

The Parent Factor Conversation Phase (only "With Condition"):
In the parent factor conversation phase, the experimental participants are first presented with one question at random from the list of questions in Table 1 in Sect. 3.2. When users respond to the question, the chatbot determines the positives and negatives of the response and returns one response randomly from

Table 5. Questionnaire

	Questionnaire Items
	By reflection on your daily life through conversation...
Q1	did you find it easy to recall your usual events?
Q2	did you become aware of your future actions?
Q3	did you find it easier to reflect on your daily life?
Q4	did you feel uncomfortable sharing your reflections with others?
Q5	would you like to continue your daily reflections in the future?
Q6	would you like to talk more with your conversation partner?
Q7	did you feel that the conversation was natural?
Q8	did you feel more affinity toward your conversation partner?
Q9	did you feel comfortable talking to your conversation partner?
Q10	did you feel that your conversation partner was a familiar person?
	Perceptions of conversational agents (7-choices question)
Q11	What specifically about your conversation partner did you perceive as his/her relationship to you?
	Candidate choices: Parent, Non-parent family member, Friend, Senior, Junior, Teacher, Counselor

the candidate responses in Table 2 in Sect. 3.3. Once again, the user replies, and the chatbot asks another question from Table 1. This exchange is performed a total of three times in one reflection.

The Reflection Phase (both "With Condition" and "Without Condition"):
In the reflection phase, the chatbot asks the questions in Q1 of Table 3 in Sect. 3.4. When the user submits an answer to that question, the chatbot asks the Q2 question. After the user responds, the chatbot asks a final question, Q3. Similarly, the chatbot will ask questions about Q1 through Q3 in Table 4 in turn, and the participants will answer the questions in turn. This is considered one reflection. Note that the way of speaking of the questions differs between the "With Condition" and "Without Condition" cases.

4.3   Evaluation Items

In this experiment, to verify the hypothesis, a questionnaire was administered to the participants of the experiment to investigate their impressions of the chatbot and their impressions of reflection. The questionnaires were administered at every time during the three reflections. The items of the questionnaire are listed in Table 5. Q1 through Q10 in Table 5 are on a 7-point Likert scale (1: Strongly disagree, 7: Strongly agree), and Q11 is a choice-type question. Q1 to Q5 are questions related to ease of reflection and motivation for reflection, related to Hypothesis H2, and Q6 to Q11 are questions related to impressions of the chatbot, related to Hypothesis H1.

Table 6. Questionnaire results

Question	number of times	With		Without		T-test
		mean	sd	mean	sd	p
Q1	1st	4.50	1.02	4.50	0.92	0.500
	2nd	**5.10**	0.70	5.00	0.45	0.361
	3rd	**5.10**	0.83	4.70	1.00	0.185
Q2	1st	**4.60**	1.20	4.50	1.28	0.433
	2nd	**5.00**	0.89	4.90	0.83	0.404
	3rd	**5.20**	1.08	4.90	0.83	0.259
Q3	1st	**4.70**	1.00	4.60	1.20	0.425
	2nd	5.30	0.64	5.30	0.46	0.500
	3rd	**5.30**	0.46	4.50	1.02	0.026*
Q4	1st	**3.40**	1.20	2.90	1.51	0.224
	2nd	2.50	0.67	**3.00**	1.55	0.196
	3rd	2.50	1.36	**2.80**	1.60	0.337
Q5	1st	4.40	0.92	**4.70**	0.90	0.246
	2nd	4.60	0.92	**4.80**	1.25	0.352
	3rd	**5.00**	0.77	4.40	0.66	0.047*
Q6	1st	3.90	0.83	**4.10**	0.83	0.308
	2nd	**4.20**	0.87	3.80	1.17	0.211
	3rd	**4.50**	1.20	4.10	1.04	0.231
Q7	1st	3.70	1.27	**4.20**	1.17	0.198
	2nd	4.10	1.45	**4.40**	1.20	0.319
	3rd	3.90	1.04	3.90	1.04	0.500
Q8	1st	**4.00**	1.10	3.40	0.92	0.112
	2nd	**4.40**	1.28	2.80	0.98	0.004*
	3rd	**4.60**	0.80	3.10	1.22	0.004*
Q9	1st	**4.50**	0.92	4.20	0.87	0.244
	2nd	**5.10**	0.94	4.10	1.22	0.034*
	3rd	**4.60**	1.11	4.30	1.35	0.306
Q10	1st	**3.70**	1.10	2.50	0.92	0.011*
	2nd	**4.10**	1.04	2.80	0.98	0.007*
	3rd	**4.00**	1.34	2.90	1.30	0.047*

*: p-value < 0.05

5   Results and Discussion

5.1   Results

The result of the questionnaire administered to the 20 participants in the experiment (10 participants are "With Condition" and 10 participants are "Without

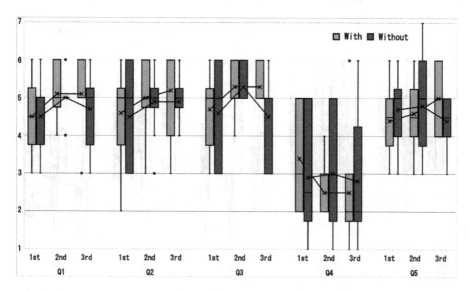

Fig. 3. Box-and-whisker diagram of questionnaire results Q1 to Q5 (Orange and blue indicate results of the "With Condition" and "Without Condition", respectively) (Color figure online)

Condition") is shown in Table 6. Table 6 shows the means and standard deviations for the first, second, and third reflections for questionnaire items Q1 through Q10. In addition, the results of a T-test comparing the mean of the "With Parent Factor" condition to the mean of the "Without Parent Factor" condition for each number of times are also shown.

First, we focus on questions Q1 through Q5 in Table 6, which are reflection questions. In the first reflection, no differences were observed between the means in Q1, Q2, and Q3 in the with and without parent factor conditions, and no significant differences were identified. In addition, Q4 and Q5 showed more negative results for the with condition (Q4 was more positive with a lower mean). In the second reflection, there was no significant difference in mean values between the with condition and without condition for Q1, Q2, and Q3. Q5 also showed more negative results for with condition. In contrast, Q4 showed more positive results for with condition, in contrast to the first reflection. In the third reflection, all items were more positive in the with condition, with significant differences confirmed in two of the items, Q3 and Q5. Next, a box-and-whisker plot of the questionnaire results from Q1 to Q5 is shown in Fig. 3.

Figure 3 shows that for all items from Q1 to Q5, there is an upward trend in the mean value of the with condition with each repeated reflection. In addition, considering the median and the variation in the data, an upward trend is particularly strong for Q1, Q4, and Q5. However, in the without condition, there was no significant change in the mean per number of reflections for all questions from Q1 to Q5, or that there was an upward trend from the first to the second time, but a decline in the third time.

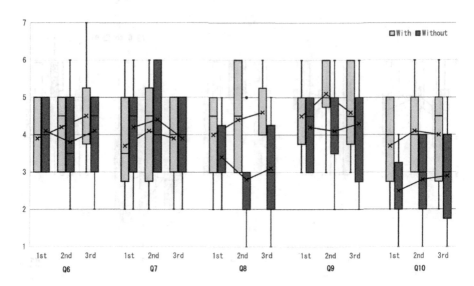

Fig. 4. Box-and-whisker diagram of questionnaire results Q6 to Q10 (Orange and blue indicate results of the "With Condition" and "Without Condition", respectively) (Color figure online)

Next, we focus on Q6 to Q10 in Table 6, with a focus on the questions about impressions of the chatbot. First, for Q8, Q9, and Q10, the with condition was a positive result for the first, second, and third reflections, with significant differences confirmed for the second reflection for Q9, the second and third reflections for Q8, and all reflections for Q10. However, the results for Q6 were more negative in the with condition at the first time, but were positive at the second time, and a significant difference was confirmed at the third time. In Q7, the first and second results for with condition were negative compared with those for the without condition, but the third result was in line with that of the without condition. A box-and-whisker plot of the questionnaire results from Q6 to Q10 is shown in Fig. 4.

Figure 4 shows that for "With Condition," all items showed an upward trend from the first to the second time. However, in the third session, except for Q6 and Q8, the mean values for the other items declined. In contrast, "Without Condition" showed a decrease from the first to the second times in Q6, Q8, and Q9, but an increase in the third. In addition, there was a slight upward trend in Q10, and the way Q7 transitioned was similar to that in "With Condition."

Finally, the results of Q11 are shown in Table 7. Table 7 shows that roughly half of the respondents in the with condition felt that they had a close social distance relationship with the chatbot, such as "parent", "non-parent family member" or "friend". However, nearly 90% of those in the without condition felt that the relationship was socially distant, such as "teacher" or "counselor". There was no difference in the results of both conditions depending on the number of times.

Table 7. A survey of relationships felt by chatbots.

What is the relationship?	With			Without		
	1st	2nd	3rd	1st	2nd	3rd
Parent	10%	0%	10%	0%	0%	0%
Family member other than parents	0%	20%	10%	0%	0%	0%
Friend	30%	30%	30%	10%	0%	0%
Senior	0%	0%	10%	0%	10%	10%
Junior	0%	0%	0%	0%	0%	0%
Teacher	0%	10%	0%	10%	20%	20%
Counselor	60%	40%	40%	80%	70%	70%
Total	100%	100%	100%	100%	100%	100%

5.2   Discussion

First, we consider the questionnaire results from Q6 to Q11 for hypothesis H1. Tables 6 and 7 and Fig. 4 show that "With Condition" was more positive than "Without Condition" from the beginning, except for Q6 and Q7. The average value of Q6 was also higher for "With Condition" for the second time. The results in Table 7 also show that the participants in the experiment felt that chatbots with parent factors were more familiar to them, such as "family members including parents" or "friends". This may be because the parent factor makes people feel a strong affinity with the chatbot, making it easier to talk to the chatbot and making them want to talk to the chatbot more. In contrast, for items other than Q6 and Q8, there was little upward trend after repeated reflection. This can also be read from the percentage changes in the choices in Table 7. This is considered to be because the respondents had a good impression of the chatbot from the beginning, so repeating the conversation too much did not strengthen the impression. However, because there was an upward trend in all items from the first to the second session, it cannot be said that repetition has no effect. For "without condition," the effect of repetition was also observed to some degree. However, compared to "With Condition," the effect of repetition was smaller. From the above, we conclude that Hypothesis H1 is supported by the fact that repeated reflection on daily life through conversations with the parent's factor tends to create a good impression of the conversational partner from the beginning, and that repeated conversation tends to increase affinity and willingness to converse. This is likely because there is still something unnatural in the flow of the conversation between the parent's factors, which may have made them feel uncomfortable.

Next, we consider the questionnaire results from Q1 to Q5 for hypothesis H2. As shown in Table 6 and Fig. 3, it is clear from Q1 to Q5 that "With Condition" has a little or negative effect on reflection after a small number of times, such as the first or second time, compared to "Without Condition." This could be because the participants may have felt an unwanted familiarity with the chatbot in the parent factor conversation or felt that it was an obstacle to reflection. In contrast, in the third session, a positive effect on reflection was confirmed for "With Condition," and significant differences were observed, especially in Q3 and Q6 (questions related to ease of reflection and willingness to continue reflection). This is considered to be because the participants became more favorable toward the chatbot as they repeated the conversation with the parent factor or they became accustomed to the conversation and established a good relationship with the chatbot. Figure 3 confirms an upward trend in the average values in the "With Condition" category. In contrast, in the "Without Condition," there was an upward trend in the transition of the mean value from the first to the second time as in the "With Condition," but it was confirmed that there was a reverse downward trend from the second to the third time. This could be considered as a possibility that, although the initial lack of conversation about parent factors made it easier to look back because they could concentrate on the reflections, they gradually felt more and more cumbersome after repeating the reflections many times. However, it was confirmed that the parent factor conversation counteracted the negative effects of reflecting repeatedly and increased the motivation for reflection. The above results confirmed the positive effect of the parent factor when the reflection was repeated, and therefore, we conclude that Hypothesis H2 is also supported.

6   Conclusion and Future Work

In this study, we aimed to verify the effect of adding parent factors to the chatbot's conversation on the impressions of the chatbot and its motivation for reflection on a chatbot that encourages regular daily reflections through conversation for young people. We proposed a chatbot as the parent factor that asked questions in a casual manner that expressed concern about the child's surroundings and living environment. We surveyed the changes in impressions of the chatbot and motivation for reflection by repeating reflections in the with and without parent factor conditions. The results showed that repeated reflections improved the impressions of the chatbot in the with parent factor condition compared to the without parent factor condition. In addition, we confirmed that the ease of reflection and motivation for reflection also improved. From this, we conclude that the parent factor positively affects young people when they repeat their daily reflections.

In the future, we plan to conduct surveys on the effectiveness of reflection, build a dialogue system that is not text-based but voice-based, and conduct other research to support daily reflections.

Acknowledgments. This work was supported in part by the Ritsumeikan Global Innovation Research Organization (R-GIRO), Ritsumeikan University.

References

1. Stefano, D.G., Gino, F., Pisano, G., Staats, B.: Learning by thinking: how reflection can spur progress along the learning curve. Sci. Res. **6**(20), 1–9 (2015)
2. Fiodorova, A., Farb, N.: Brief daily self-care reflection for undergraduate well-being: a randomized control trial of an online intervention. Anxiety Stress Coping **35**(2), 158–170 (2022)
3. Bradbard, M., Endsley, R., Mize, J.: The ecology of parent-child communications about daily experiences in preschool and childcare. J. Res. Child. Educ. **6**(2), 131–141 (1992)
4. Martin, A.J.: Should students have a gap year? Motivation and performance factors relevant to time out after completing school. J. Educ. Psychol. **102**(3), 561–576 (2010)
5. Clinch, S., et al.: Collecting shared experiences through lifelogging: lessons learned. IEEE Pervasive Comput. **15**(1), 58–67 (2016)
6. Kelly, L., Jones, G.: An exploration of the utility of GSR in locating events from personal lifelogs for reflection. In: proceedings of 4th Irish Human Computer Interaction Conference, pp. 82–85. Irish Computer Society, Dublin (2010)
7. Asselin, M.E., Fain, J.A.: Effect of reflective practice education on self-reflection, insight, and reflective thinking among experienced nurses. J. Nurses Prof. Dev. **29**(3), 111–119 (2013)
8. Cox, S., Funasaki, K., Smith, L., Mezulis, A.H.: prospective study of brooding and reflection as moderators of the relationship between stress and depressive symptoms in adolescence. Cogn. Ther. Res. **36**(4), 290–299 (2012)
9. Cheng, X., Bao, Y., Zarifis, A., Gong, W., Mou, J.: Exploring consumers' response to text-based chatbots in ecommerce: the moderating role of task complexity and chat-bot disclosure. Internet Res. **32**(2), 496–517 (2021)
10. Kageyama, Y., Chiba, Y., Nose, T., Ito, A.: Improving user impression in spoken dialog system with gradual speech form control. In: Proceedings of the 19th Annual SIGdial Meeting on Discourse and Dialogue, pp. 235–240. Association for Computational Linguistics, Melbourne (2018)
11. Steinberg, L., Mounts, N.S., Lamborn, S.D., Dornbusch, S.M.: Authoritative parenting and adolescent adjustment across varied ecological niches. J. Res. Adolesc. **1**(1), 19–36 (1991)
12. Pettit, G.S., Laird, R.D., Dodge, K.A., Bates, J.E., Criss, M.M.: Antecedents and behavior-problem outcomes of parental monitoring and psychological control in early adolescence. Child Dev. **72**(2), 583–598 (2001)
13. How to Stop Worrying About Your Adult Children. https://secondwindmovement.com/worrying-adult-children/. Accessed 10 Feb 2023
14. [Why do mothers ask, "Are you eating well?" Why do mothers worry about their children who live alone?]okaasan ha naze "tyanto tabeteru?" to kikunoka? hitorigurasi no ko wo tuisinpaisityau hahaoya no honne (in Japanese). https://r.gnavi.co.jp/ginterview/entry/yajirobe/4138. Accessed 10 Feb 2023

Revealing Chatbot Humanization Impact Factors

Paula Jeniffer dos Santos Viriato[1]($\boxtimes$) , Rafael Roque de Souza[1] ,
Leandro Aparecido Villas[1] , and Julio Cesar dos Reis[1,2]

[1] Institute of Computing, University of Campinas, Campinas, SP, Brazil
p234831@dac.unicamp.br, {rroque,lvillas,dosreis}@unicamp.br
[2] Nucleus of Informatics Applied to Education, University of Campinas,
Campinas, SP, Brazil

Abstract. Chatbots are software that simulates human conversational
tasks. They are used for various purposes, including customer service
and therapeutic conversations. A challenge encountered in developing
chatbots is making them more humanized. This demands differentiating conversations of conversational agents from conversations between
human agents. This article defines humanization impact factors as characteristics that strongly influence users' perception of humanity about
chatbots, analyzing in-depth such impact factors on chatbots' humanization. We identify, analyze and compile established impact factors from
literature studies and contribute with an organized selection of impact
factors. Our investigation provides a starting point for identifying relevant impact factors for the humanization evaluation of chatbots. Based
on this compilation of impact factors, we evaluate a set of available chatbots on the market to understand which and how the impact factors are
manifested on them. We found that our analysis based on the impact
factors is relevant to evaluate different types of existing chatbots.

Keywords: Humanization · User Evaluation · Chatbots ·
Conversational Systems

1 Introduction

Chatbots are increasingly common in the market. They aim to meet the growing
demands for solving problems arising from current activities mainly related to
customer services. Such software can perform standard and medium-complexity
tasks, making the human workforce specialized in solving highly complex tasks
[18]. Low and medium-complexity tasks are frequent in call centers, whereas
high-complexity tasks are time-consuming.

This situation creates a bottleneck of activities that reduces the quality of
services to users. Chatbots assisting in answering tasks, even if only for ordinary
and medium-complexity tasks, become powerful strategic tools [16]. An example
of a low-complexity task is answering simple questions, such as questions on

FAQs. Examples of medium-complexity tasks involve database manipulation, which requires greater integration and customization [16]. Already examples of highly complex tasks involve general maintenance, mainly system maintenance, in which the intervention of specialized human agents is necessary [16,17].

Humanizing a chatbot is not trivial, which makes its behavior similar to that of a human being. Human behavior is complex and varies according to the nature of the situations. Each person has his/her perception of humanity. We know how to differentiate typical machine behavior from human behavior, but explaining such differences is difficult. Users tend to maintain a better dialogue with human attendants instead of chatbots.

This situation justifies increasing the humanization of chatbots to improve users' satisfaction with such systems [4]. Regarding chatbots, a connection between the perception of humanity and the resolution of the proposed tasks is necessary. In this context, a chatbot must satisfy users' expectations for its respective purpose [4]. Some characteristics are expected of a chatbot, such as naturalness. A chatbot must build meaningful, personalized, and friendly dialogues through a conversational system. Such a conversational system must evolve with each interaction and offer alternative answers to similar questions, answering the interlocutor's questions as another human person would meet user expectations more naturally and fluidly. The chatbot must relate cordially with the consumer, making them feel comfortable, satisfied, and valued [1]. From this perspective, humanization impact factors aspects regarding chatbots are essential.

The concept of humanity is abstract and not a simple and specific characteristic inherent to human beings, but a set of elements that makes humans different from other beings, whether animals or objects. In this sense, the great challenge was finding which characteristics are the key to describing humanity in the specific case we are working on (chatbots). It was also a great challenge to discover which features are the key to defining humanity in the HCI context.

This study provides an original analysis to collect and organize humanization impact factors. We obtained two main results: a broad set of impact factors in humanization from a literature review; and the analysis of three chatbots presented in the market based on our collection of identified impact factors.

Finding impact factors related to humanization in chatbots via a bibliographic analysis, we call impact factors those characteristics that contribute to users' perception of humanity regarding a chatbot. We assessed their manifestation in an ad-hoc analysis of market chatbots to demonstrate how to use our identified impact factors. To this end, we analyzed which of the 36 resulting impact factors in evaluating humanization in three chatbots in the market (health, retail, and education sectors). We found that our humanization impact factors can influence users' views about the chatbot's humanity.

We observed that an impact factor's relevance is not binary but continuous. Our study regarding the evaluation of chatbots from the market identified how more than the simple binary assessment of the relevance of impact factors in the analysis of chatbots is needed to reveal how relevant each impact factor is. In this sense, how necessary an impact factor is should be a continuous value. Although one impact factor may be more relevant than another, both are relevant in a general context. Using real values allows a more trustworthy conception of the idea of humanity in a chatbot utilizing impact factors.

The remaining of this article is organized as follows: Sect. 2 presents background describing fundamental concepts and related work. Section 3 reports on our methodology for identifying humanization chatbots in addition to their description and results. Section 4 presents our evaluation assessing the impact factors in real-world chatbots available on the market; Sect. 5 discusses our obtained findings and lessons learned; and Sect. 6 presents our final considerations and directions for future research.

2   Fundamentals and Related Work

The technological perspective investigated by Peras [10] was based on the analysis of the humanity of chatbots. In this context, the ability of the chatbot to express human behavior describes humanity. For this purpose, the chatbot must process, understand and generate natural language. Humanity can be measured both qualitatively and quantitatively. Evaluating humanity uses qualitative assessments to provide feedback for the advancement of chatbots.

For Peras [10], a chatbot demonstrates humanity when it presents: naturalness, the ability to maintain a thematic discussion; the ability to answer specific questions; and the ability to understand natural language. Some of our already obtained results (cf. Subsect. 3.1) indicate that key factors considered in the conception of humanity vary significantly from one study to another. Therefore, one of the specific objectives of this study is to map from literature factors considered relevant to the perception of humanity that the user has about a chatbot (cf. Subsect. 3.1).

Regarding the humanization of chatbots, Reeves and Nass [11] and Rhim et al. [12] observed that users react socially to a computer that exhibits human-like behavior. Users feel that the system behavior is similar to that of other humans, even though they know they are interacting with a computer.

We can, therefore, define *humanization impact factors* as characteristics that strongly influence the perception of humanity that users have about chatbots. Still, in this context of humanization impact factors, Go and Sundar [4] conducted a study to analyze the effects of visual, identity, and behavioral clues on users' perception of humanity about chatbots. Such classification of impact factors (visual, identity, and behavioral) is quite interesting in development. Graphical interfaces can influence visual aspects, identity factors can influence personalization, and behavioral factors can be affected by modeling artificial intelligence. In this way, this work aims to map the impact factors in this classification, which can help evolve conversational systems. All humanization impact factors cited in this proposal are further described in Subsect. 3.1.

The scientific literature considers several factors impacting the humanization of chatbots to leave these agents with more humanistic characteristics to be noticeable to their users. In this context, social presence is a commonly discussed element in studies related to chatbots. Adding this impact factor to the agent means incorporating "sensitive human contact" because users can make social presence attributions when interacting with a chatbot at first [14]. The more socially present the interactions are, the more engaging the interface is; however, the more human the interface is, the higher the user's expectations from the agent [7]. In addition to greeting, language choices are crucial in humanizing chatbots. For example, using a more polite, informal, or social language can help induce anthropomorphic perceptions and perceptions of social presence.

With these linguistic features, developers help impose a sense of social presence and further promote humanization in their chatbot [13]. The linguistic communication features, as humanization impact factor employed by researchers and practitioners in dialogue delays. Delays could be interpreted as the chatbot not functioning as expected. However, when implemented correctly, minor delays that are dynamic to the amount of text can dictate levels of persuasiveness and personality perceptions of the chatbot. This feature can make the agent more real and humanized because humans do not instantly read and respond to messages sent via text media [3].

In addition to these aspects, humor is a key factor in humanizing chatbots. Humor introduces feelings of common ground between two communicating social actors. Like human interactions, humor can effectively personify systems and create a more engaging interaction. Furthermore, humor in task-oriented communication has increased the number of individuals with higher satisfaction with chatbots. Humor in both business and customer service interactions requires a more nuanced approach. Whereas humor in an e-service encounter can help in some situations where the process is to your liking, when the process is not to your liking, the addition of humor exacerbates the negative feelings associated with the service experience. In this sense, it is necessary to have a middle ground when humanizing the chatbot, looking specifically at its applied context [8].

We discuss the need for a better-established protocol for evaluating humanization in chatbots. We did not find a humanization assessment methodology focused on metrics acquisition in literature. This is what our proposed investigation aims to innovate. Our goal is to obtain a method that better evaluates the evolutionary process of chatbot design and development. This might be essential for mapping the chatbot's improvements within specific contexts. Table 1 compares the related studies from literature and our proposal. We considered seven critical criteria: evaluation of humanization, generic context, adaptability, mapping of impact factors, generation of metrics, relevance assessment, and non-binary assessment.

The *evaluation of humanization* criterion considers users' perception of humanization regarding an assessment of chatbot. Nordheim, Følstad and Bjørkli [9] focused on the perception of trust. Westerman, Cross and Lindmark [15] evaluated humanization in a very generic way, not considering the various characteristics that make up the perception of humanization. And both Kondylakis *et al.* [6] and Holmes *et al.* [5] assessed usability in general, not the perception of humanization.

The *generic context* criterion verifies whether the study was conducted analyzing a specific chatbot context or chatbots in general, with only Nordheim, Følstad and Bjørkli [9], Følstad and Brandtzaeg [2], and Balaji [1] analyzed chatbots generically. Completing the *generic context* criterion, the *adaptability* criterion examines whether studies can be adapted to different contexts, and only the study by Kondylakis *et al.* [6] cannot be adjusted by focusing on the development of a specific chatbot.

The *mapping of impact factors* criterion shows which studies cited and described the analyzed humanization impact factors. The study by Westerman, Cross and Lindmark [15] superficially evaluates humanization, not addressing the factors that impact users' perception of humanity regarding the chatbot used. Meanwhile, studies by Kondylakis *et al.* [6] and Holmes *et al.* [5] use usability questionnaires adapted to the reality of chatbots, and the questions of such questionnaires are not mapped to humanization impact factors.

The *generation of metrics*. The studies by Go and Sundar [4], Følstad and Brandtzaeg [2], and Balaji [1] did not aim to analyze humanization quantitatively, focusing only on qualitative analysis. The investigations of Kondylakis *et al.* [6], and Holmes *et al.* [5] generated quantitative results, but these results are not related to the humanization of the analyzed chatbots. The principal value of the quantitative results generated by Kondylakis *et al.* [6] and Holmes *et al.* [5] concerns the methodology for converting psychometric questionnaires into quantitative metrics.

Finally, two concepts are essential to our study. The *relevance assessment* of impact factors in chatbots of different contexts only occurs in Nordheim, Følstad and Bjørkli [9]; and this is an essential concept, given that the desired characteristics in a chatbot change according to the context of a chatbot. The *non-binary assessment* allows the identification of nuances in both the relevance and the perception of different elements in chatbots. Only Westerman, Cross and Lindmark [15] performed a binary evaluation.

We found that none of the studied investigations evaluates humanization in generic contexts in an adaptive way. We explicitly map the impact factors generating a metric in humanization. Specifically, several investigated studies developed metrics mainly based on usability, an internal concept of humanity. A humanized chatbot has high usability, but a chatbot with high usability is not necessarily humanized. Generating metrics on humanization and a methodology for evaluating humanization is necessary. We observed that many of the methods for humanization assessment are content with qualitative assessment, not reaching quantitative assessment. Qualitative evaluation of humanity makes it very difficult to verify the evolution of the chatbot's development process.

We investigate how we can extract sets of impact factors from literature that are as generic as possible; that is, the broadest possible set of impact factors.

Table 1. Comparison among Related Work

Study	Evaluation[1]	Generic Context	Adaptability	Mapping[2]	Generation[3]	Relevance[4]	Non-Binary[5]
Go and Sundar [4]	✓	-	✓	✓	-	-	✓
Nordheim [9]	-	✓	✓	✓	✓	✓	✓
Flstad [2]	✓	✓	✓	✓	-	-	✓
Westerman [15]	-	-	✓	-	✓	-	-
Balaji [1]	✓	✓	✓	✓	-	-	✓
Kondylakis [6]	-	-	-	-	✓	-	✓
Holmes [5]	-	-	✓	-	✓	-	✓
Our Proposal	✓	✓	✓	✓	✓	✓	✓

1 Evaluation of Humanization
2 Mapping of Impact Factors
3 Generation of Metrics
4 Relevance Assessment
5 Non-Binary Assessment

3   Identification of Impact Factors in Humanization

We aim to identify impact factors related to humanization in chatbots via a bibliographic analysis. We call impact factors those characteristics that contribute to users' perception of humanity regarding a chatbot. Our first task refers to compiling a complete set of possible humanization impact factors.

The existing investigations aiming to study humanization in chatbots selected different analyzed sets of characteristics in chatbots (impact factors). There is no simple convergence between these sets of impact factors. One of the possible reasons is that each work studies or focuses on specific types of chatbots. Our selected collection of characteristics corresponds to what is highly desired. Therefore, the objective is to complete a compilation of these sets of attributes and generate a more extensive and complete set of impact factors.

Figure 1 presents the first step of our study (defined as step A) as exploratory bibliographic research, using platforms for academic research such as Google Scholar, Scopus, IEEEXplore, and Web of Science. Some examples of key terms used in this search were: "chatbots"; "humanization assessment"; "chatbot assessment methodologies"; "qualitative assessments of chatbots"; and "humanized chatbots". The selected studies must necessarily deal with chatbots and were filtered according to the year (preferably selecting the most up-to-date ones) and the type of research carried out (selecting qualitative analysis works). We believe the selected studies should discuss humanization, evaluation, or usability. Such aspects are analyzed qualitatively but not always in a psychometric way. The preference was for works that performed qualitative analysis using psychometric methods for evaluation. However, as such works are rare, the simple indication of which qualitative aspects can be evaluated has already helped construct a more robust set of factors that impacted users' perception of humanity about chatbots. We seek to answer six main questions:

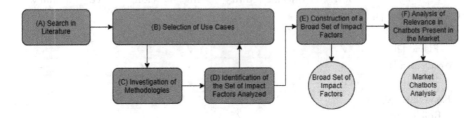

Fig. 1. Methodology for Identifying Impact Factors on Humanization

- What is humanizing a chatbot?
- How to humanize a chatbot?
- How to assess that a chatbot is humanized?
- What should be evaluated in the humanization of chatbots?
- What aspects are qualitatively analyzed and evaluated in chatbots?
- What factors affect users' perception of humanity towards a chatbot?

In step B of our methodology (cf. Fig. 1), we carried out cases involving the specific evaluation of humanization in chatbots. In this search, we ruled out cases in which usability assessments were used to assess the humanization of chatbots, as is the case of studies by Kondylakis *et al.* [6] and Holmes *et al.* [5]. Here, we need to consider how the analysis of the usability of a chatbot is included in the idea of humanization since a humanized chatbot necessarily has high usability. However, a chatbot with high usability is not necessarily humanized.

Go and Sundar [4]; Nordheim, Følstad, and Bjørkli [9]; Følstad and Brandtzaeg [2]; Balaji [1] meet the criteria of specifically evaluating humanization in chatbots. The concept of humanization is broader and more complex than usability since humanity includes all the characteristics that differentiate men from other beings and things.

After selecting the four use cases (step B), select the humanization impact factors considered in our study, which qualitative aspects jointly evaluate. In each case, we analyzed the methodology used for assessing humanity in chatbots. The context in which such methods were applied (step C in Fig. 1). This step aims to assess how generic or adaptable the cases are in the four selected studies, seeking the reproducibility of the studies.

In step D, the set of characteristics was verified - evaluated by each methodology (step D). At this step, we identified impact factors and compiled them into a single qualitative set. It is already demonstrated that the groups of factors found vary significantly from context to chatbot context and differ from study to study.

In step E (cf. Fig. 1), we compiled the sets of characteristics evaluated by each case into a single, broader set of features. Here, we already called these characteristics impact factors in humanization. Those with a similar meaning are united in a single impact factor, although the terminology may differ. Therefore, we already have the broadest set of impact factors identified in the four selected articles at this stage. However, there may still be duplicates and impact factors that may or may not necessarily have the same names but have descriptions and meanings close enough to be gathered in a single concept. The coexistence of impact factors explains the need for this phase in more than one article. We got our first result (presented in circle 1 in Fig. 1), a set of 36 impact factors and their descriptions according to the analyzed cases.

3.1 Results of the Identified Impact Factors

We present the 36 impact fctors obtained from our literature analysis.

- **Social presence** [2,4]: Social presence is formally defined as the degree of salience of the other person in the interaction. It is also defined as being with another in a mediated environment.
- **Homophily** [4]: Perceived homophily is defined as the amount of similarity two people perceive themselves as having since the human-like figure of the agent is likely to be perceived as being more similar to the user than a bubbling figure.
- **Contingency** [4]: Perceived contingency occurs when the conversation is fully interactive or responsive, and individuals perceive greater dialogue emerging from threaded message exchanges with a chat agent during computer-mediated communication.
- **Dialogue** [4]: Dialogue perception may make online interactions feel like face-to-face conversations, creating positive attitudes toward the agent.
- **Expertise** [4,9]: Perceived expertise occurred when the participants perceived the agent as intelligent, knowledgeable, competent, and informed.
- **Friendliness** [4]: Perceived friendliness occurred when the participants perceived the agent as empathetic, personal, warm, emotionally invested, willing to listen, care, and open.
- **Human-likeness** [2,4,9]: Human-likeness suggests the presence of a human figure attached to a chat agent, that is, an "other person" in the interaction.
- **Predictability** [9]: Users' perceptions of the consistency with which the interactive system behaves.
- **Ease of use** [1,9]: The ease or simplicity with which the interaction with the system is accomplished.
- **Absence of marketing** [9]: Absence of marketing, and a sense of the chatbot putting the customer first.
- **Help and assistance** [2]: The chatbot is reported to provide customer support or training, personal assistance, or help with a particular task. Efficiency and ease of access were often highlighted.
- **Information and updates** [2]: The chatbot is reported to provide updates and general information - often sought on a routine basis - such as news, weather, and online searches.

- **Entertainment** [2]: The chatbot interaction is described in words reflecting engagement and enjoyment.
- **Novelty and inspiration** [2]: The novelty of chatbots, or the inspirational value of the interaction, is accentuated.
- **Absence of interpretation issues** [2]: The chatbot must avoid interpretation issues, which occur when the chatbot is reported to misinterpret requests or input or provide an answer that does not fit the question.
- **Absence of inability to help** [2]: The chatbot must avoid failure to help, which occurs when the chatbot is reported unable to assist the participant in solving a particular task or to be unable to provide help in general.
- **Absence of repetitiveness** [2]: The chatbot must avoid repetitiveness, which occurs when the chatbot is reported to ask the same questions or repeatedly provide the same line of answers, which is experienced as obstructing the user from getting help or assistance.
- **Absence of strange or rude responses** [2]: The chatbot must avoid strange or rude reactions, which occur when the chatbot is reported to give improper or embarrassing answers.
- **Absence of unwanted events** [2]: The chatbot must avoid unwanted events, which occur when the chatbot is reported as the source of unwanted contact, actions, or content.
- **Absence of boring attitudes** [2]: The chatbot must avoid boring attitudes, which occur when the chatbot interaction is reported to be boring - either immediately or after a period of use.
- **Initiating conversation** [1]: How easy it is for the user to start interacting with the chatbot, including not only accessibility but also how simple it feels to start the conversation, i.e., to start typing.
- **Communication effort** [1]: How easy it is for the user to convey their information-retrieval goal to the chatbot successfully (or not).
- **Content relevance** [1]: The extent to which the chatbot's response addresses the user's request.
- **Response clarity** [1]: How easy it is for the chatbot's response to be understood by the user.
- **Reference to service** [1]: The ability of the chatbot to provide valuable and relevant hyperlinks or automatic transitions either instead of or in addition to its response to the user's request.
- **Graceful breakdown** [1]: The appropriateness of how the chatbot responds if and when it encounters a situation in which it cannot help the user.
- **Speed** [1]: How quickly the chatbot responds to each input the user gives.
- **Privacy** [1]: How secure the entire interaction feels as a consequence of revealing potentially personal information to the chatbot.
- **Flexibility of linguistic input** [1]: How easily the chatbot understands the user's input.
- **Communication quality** [1]: How easy it is for the user to communicate their information-retrieval goal.
- **Response quality** [1]: The overall quality of the chatbot's response once the user has provided some form of input to the chatbot.

- **Expectation setting** [1]: The extent to which the chatbot sets expectations for the interaction with an emphasis on what it can and cannot do.
- **Ability to maintain themed discussion** [1]: The ability of the chatbot to maintain a conversational theme once introduced and kept track of context.
- **Recognition and facilitation of users' goal and intent** [1]: Ability of the chatbot to understand the purpose and intention of the user and to help them accomplish these.
- **Understandability** [1]: Ability of the chatbot to communicate clearly and is easily understandable.
- **Credibility** [1]: The extent to which the user believes the chatbot's responses to be correct and reliable.

Figure 2 shows the intersections between the sets of humanization impact factors analyzed by different studies. The studies of Go and Sundar [4]; Følstad and Brandtzaeg [2]; and Nordheim, Følstad and Bjørkli [9] have some impact factors in common, whereas the work of Balaji [1] has impact factors in common only with Nordheim, Følstad and Bjørkli [9]. We pooled all these impact factors by removing duplicates in our study covering the above mentioned four studies.

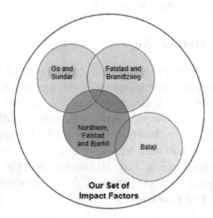

Fig. 2. Intersection Between the Sets of Impact Factors

Some humanization impact factors only exist in one article, whereas others coexist in more than one article. The impact factors *Homophily*, *Contingency*, and *Dialogue* only exist in Go and Sundar's [4] paper. The *Predictability* and *Absence of Marketing* factors are specific to the article by Nordheim, Følstad and Bjørkli [9]. Meanwhile, the impact factors *Information and Updates*, *Entertainment*, *Novelty and Inspiration*, *Absence of Interpretation Issues*, *Absence of Inability to Help*, *Absence of Repetitiveness*, *Absence of Strange or Rude Responses*, *Absence of Unwanted Events*, and *Absence of Boring Attitudes*, occur only in the article by Følstad and Brandtzaeg [2]. And finally, the impact factors *Initiating Conversation, Communication Effort, Content Relevance, Response Clarity, Reference to Service, Graceful Breakdown, Speed, Privacy, Flexibility of Linguistic Input, Communication Quality, Response Quality, Expectation Setting, Ability to Maintain Themed Discussion, Recognition and Facilitation of Users' Goal and Intent, Understandability,* and *Credibility,* are typical of Balaji's article [1]. Among the impact factors that coexist, we have *Social Presence* that coexists in Go and Sundar [2,4], *Expertise* that coexists in Go and Sundar [4] and Nordheim, Følstad and Bjørkli [9], *Human-likeness* that coexists in Go and Sundar [4], Nordheim, Følstad and Bjørkli [9], and [2]. The *Ease of Use* factor that coexists in Nordheim, Følstad and Bjørkli [9], and Balaji [1].

4   Experiment with Market Chatbots

To demonstrate how broad impact factors can be used, we analyzed which of the 36 resulting impact factors in evaluating humanization in three chatbots from the market (health, retail, and education sectors). For such identification of the perception impact factors, the purpose of the chatbot, the field of activity, and the target audience were taken into account.

4.1   Experimental Methodology

Based on the results achieved during the application of the methodology to Identify Impact Factors in Humanization (Sect. 3), and as shown in step (F) of Fig. 1, we carried out the first experiment to analyze the perception that users had about each of the impact factors in three chatbots on the market. This experiment took place in the context of the CI&T company, using chatbots suggested by the company and with wide dissemination to employees. We applied the methodology presented in Fig. 3 to the employees of the CI&T company who volunteered to participate in the experiment. Next, we explain each of the steps of the methodology of this experiment.

Fig. 3. Methodology for Market Chatbots Analysis

(A) Registration and Research on the Profile of Participants: The objective of this research was to know better the public that participated in the analysis of chatbots present in the market, being this public composed exclusively of employees of the CI&T company, who volunteered to participate in the experiment proposed in this subsection.

After completing this survey, we sent instructions for participating in the experiment to each participant's email. All recorded data were protected and not shared with people not involved in the research. Below we present each question, its objectives, and its possible answers.

1. **Have you ever interacted with a chatbot?**
   - **Objective:** to know if the participant understands the basics of chatbots.
   - **Answers:** Yes or No
2. **Do you have ease with technological resources?**
   - **Objective:** to know if the participant is a person who has difficulties with technological resources in general since chatbots are technological resources.
   - **Answers:** Yes or No
3. **Are you a person who likes technology?**
   - **Objective:** to know if the participant is potentially fearful of technology or averse to technology, seeing all negative technology.
   - **Answers:** Yes or No
4. **Do you know any programming language?**
   - **Objective:** Programming knowledge puts the participant at an average level of knowledge of the limitations of chatbots.
   - **Answers:** Yes or No
5. **Have you ever participated in developing any software?**
   - **Objective:** Participants who have already participated in a software development process have a medium to a high level of knowledge of the limitations of chatbots.
   - **Answers:** Yes or No
6. **Have you ever participated in developing a chatbot?**
   - **Objective:** Participants who have already participated in a software development process have a high level of knowledge of the limitations of chatbots.
   - **Answers:** Yes or No
7. **Position/Profession**
   - **Objective:** To verify if the position or profession links with technology, more specifically with chatbot design. It is also important to understand which types of professionals are interested in the topic so that the questionnaire is as aggregating as possible.
   - **Answers:** Open
8. **Training Level**
   - **Objective:** Another way to verify the level of familiarity with the proposed theme, as well as an opportunity to adapt the language of the questionnaire for the best possible understanding of all those present.
   - **Answers:** Incomplete Elementary School, Complete Elementary School, Incomplete High School, Complete High School, Incomplete Higher

Education, Complete Higher Education, Incomplete Specialization, Complete Specialization, Incomplete Master's, Complete Master's, Incomplete Doctorate or Complete Doctorate

(B) Prior Use of Chatbots by Participants: For the selection of chatbots, we used recommendations from the company CI&T, which sent a spreadsheet with 100 chatbot options. Initially, we chose six chatbots with the criteria of belonging to different segments, being active, and being available on Whatsapp, a viral, simple, and widely used conversation platform in Brazil. Below we present Table 2, where we show the six selected chatbots, along with the respective segments and numbers for access via Whatsapp.

Table 2. First Selected Chatbots

Segment	Name	Whatsapp Number
Health	Fleury Medicine and Health	(11) 3179 0822
Education	MeBote na Conversa	(11) 93456 5026
Entertainment	ZapFlix (Netflix)	(11) 99653 5902
Foods	McDonald's	(11) 3230 3223
Retail	Hel (Riachuelo)	800 772 3555
Services	ConectCar	(11) 3003 4475

After the first selection of the six chatbots, we agreed with part of the CI&T team to run the experiment with only three to acquire more data per analyzed chatbot. The CI&T team chose the three chatbots, and we present them below.

Chatbot A:

- **Name:** Fleury Medicina e Saúde
- **Tracking:** Health
- **Message:** Fleury: health and well-being for the full realization of people.
- **About:** Fleury Medicina e Saúde is one of the country's most respected medical and health organizations, recognized by the medical community and public opinion as excellent in quality, innovation, and customer service. Learn more about it at link.
- **Whatsapp Number:** (11) 3179 0822
- **Whatsapp Link**
- **Usage Video Link**
- Tasks:
    1. Search for tests for COVID-19 and influenza (by numerical menu).
    2. Know the addresses and opening hours of the units (by text).
    3. Other tasks.

Chatbot B:

- **Name:** Helôda Riachuelo
- **Tracking:** Retail
- **Message:** Hey! Welcome to Riachuelo's WhatsApp!
- **About:** Helô is the persona of digital service and the name of the brand's chatbot and now appears to the public. She is responsible for helping the retailer's customers on various topics and also forwards to sales via WhatsApp. Helô knows everything about digital and social networks. She is a columnist for Blog Riachuelo and an expert in giving online shopping and fashion tips. To learn more about Riachuelo, access link.
- **Whatsapp Number:** 800 772 3555
- **Whatsapp Link**
- **Usage Video Link**
- Tasks:
  1. Find stores near your address (by numeric menu).
  2. Learn more about the RCHLO App (by text).
  3. Other tasks.

Chatbot C:

- **Name:** MeBote na Conversa
- **Tracking:** Education
- **Message:** A tool to help you understand all the terms and acronyms used in the corporate world.
- **About:** Meta - the new name of Facebook Inc., owner of WhatsApp - joined the Indique Uma Preta collective and the MOOC agency to create the Me Bote Na Conversa project, a bot for WhatsApp that explains English expressions used in the corporate world. The idea is to make communication in a more inclusive work environment. Learn more about MeBote in Conversation on link.
- **Whatsapp Number:** (11) 93456 5026
- **Whatsapp Link**
- **Usage Video Link**
- Tasks:
  1. Ask what a Brainstorm is.
  2. Ask what a Deadline is.
  3. Other tasks.

Randomly selecting one of the chosen chatbots for each participant who volunteered and responded to the Profile Survey (step A), we sent an email to each of the participants indicating the link to access the chatbot, what is the purpose of such a chatbot, a video of previous use of the chatbot under analysis. A list of suggested tasks to be performed in the chatbot, being the participant free to use the chatbot as they wish.

(C) Application of the Perceptions Questionnaire: The perceptions questionnaire aims to assess how much users perceived the presence of each of the impact factors in the chatbot used. Along with the weighting questionnaire, the perceptions questionnaire verifies the level at which positive or negative characteristics are perceived in the chatbot under analysis. Such positive and negative features and perceptions are variable according to the analyzed context.

For the development of this questionnaire, we generated statements about the user's perception of each impact factor in the analyzed chatbot. The objective is to identify a level of agreement with the proposed idea. The possible answers follow one of the Likert scale patterns, ranging from "strongly disagree" to "strongly agree". The following is an example of claim generation:

Impact Factor: Appropriate Language Style.
Affirmation: The chatbot has an appropriate language style.
Impact Factor Explanation: Ability of the chatbot to use the appropriate language style for the context.
Alternatives: strongly disagree, disagree, somewhat disagree, neither agree nor disagree, somewhat agree, agree, strongly agree.

After using the chatbot selected for each participant, as presented in step B, we instructed the participant to access the following link to access the Perceptions Questionnaire hosted on the Google Forms tool and answer it according to their interaction with the chatbot. The Perceptions Questionnaire has a brief description of the research objectives, an explanation of the Likert scale, and fields to fill in the participant's email and to indicate the chatbot previously used, in addition to the 36 questions related to each impact factor identified in Subsect. 3.1. The company CI&T requested the collection of emails to monitor the employees who collaborated with the research.

(D) Extraction and Availability of Anonymous Data: In this methodology step, we anonymized the data collected with the Perceptions Questionnaire (in step C), erasing the only sensitive data collected: the participants' email. After anonymization, the results were made available through a Google Spreadsheet at the following link that only reads the data, allowing the free reproduction and conference of the calculations performed in the next step.

(E) Designation of the Presence of Factors by Values: The objective of this last step of the methodology is to define, based on the anonymized responses acquired in step D, whether or not a factor is present in each of the analyzed chatbots. The first step was calculating the arithmetic mean of the responses obtained on each chatbot. We converted the possible perceptions indicated in step C to psychometric values following the rules in Fig. 4.

Figure 4 shows that an impact factor is only perceived at some level in the analyzed chatbot if it has a score above 4, and it is not perceived if it has a score equal to or below four. In this way, we evaluate the presence or absence of each impact factor in each chatbot according to the rule below:

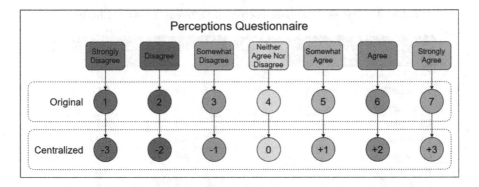

Fig. 4. Rule for Converting Perceptions into Psychometric Values

- **PRESENT:** If the average value of the impact factor is above 4.0.
- **ABSENT:** If the average value of the impact factor is equal to or below 4.0.

Subsection 4.2 presents the results of applying the five steps of this methodology.

4.2   Results of the Market Chatbots Analysis

Table 3 presents the results regarding how the collected impact factors are manifested in the analyzed chatbots, according to the methodology presented in Subsect. 4. Some impact factors are desirable in the three chatbots analyzed, such as homophily, help and assistance, and the absence of strange and rude responses. This means that some of the impact factors are always desirable in chatbots. However, some impact factors are desirable in only one of the three chatbots, such as the dialog impact factor, which is only desirable in chatbot C, and the speed impact factor, which is only desirable in chatbot A.

Note the two perception representations placed in Table 3. A representation using Likert scale scores ranging from 1 to 7, and a binary representation. The representation using Likert scale scores, represented as a real scale, is broader and covers several nuances of the perception of an impact factor. In binary representation, however, it is impossible to represent the intensity of perception only if a factor is perceived. In a chatbot, we perceive characteristics that refer us to the humanization of a chatbot with a certain intensity, and such characteristics are the impact factors. In this way, the representation in real values of perception is more adequate than the binary representation since it demonstrates how the factors impact the humanization of a chatbot in different intensities.

Table 3. Analysis of Impact Factors in Different Types of Chatbots

Impact Factors	Chatbot A		Chatbot B		Chatbot C	
	Scores*	P**	Scores*	P**	Scores*	P**
Social Presence	5,0	✓	6,0	✓	4,3	✓
Homophily	5,0	✓	4,7	✓	3,7	-
Contingency	4,0	-	4,3	✓	3,3	-
Dialogue	4,0	-	5,3	✓	4,7	✓
Expertise	4,0	-	5,3	✓	2,3	-
Friendliness	5,0	✓	5,7	✓	4,0	-
Human-Likeness	4,0	-	3,3	-	3,0	-
Predictability	5,0	✓	5,7	✓	4,3	✓
Ease of Use	5,0	✓	5,7	✓	3,7	-
Absence of Marketing	5,0	✓	6,0	✓	3,0	-
Help and Assistance	5,0	✓	3,7	-	3,0	-
Information and Updates	6,0	✓	5,7	✓	3,3	-
Entertainment	5,0	✓	6,0	✓	3,7	-
Novelty and Inspiration	5,0	✓	5,3	✓	3,3	-
Absence of Interpretation Issues	4,0	-	5,0	✓	2,7	-
Absence of Inability to Help	5,0	✓	4,7	✓	2,0	-
Absence of Repetitiveness	4,0	-	3,3	-	3,0	-
Absence of Strange or Rude Responses	6,0	✓	6,7	✓	5,3	✓
Absence of Unwanted Events	6,0	✓	5,7	✓	4,7	✓
Absence of Boring Attitudes	6,0	✓	4,3	✓	4,7	✓
Initiating Conversation	6,0	✓	4,0	-	4,3	✓
Communication Effort	5,0	✓	5,0	✓	3,3	-
Content Relevance	5,0	✓	6,3	✓	3,7	-
Response Clarity	5,0	✓	5,7	✓	5,0	✓
Reference to Service	5,0	✓	5,7	✓	3,0	-
Graceful Breakdown	4,0	-	4,0	-	5,3	✓
Speed	3,0	-	7,0	✓	6,0	✓
Privacy	6,0	✓	4,7	✓	4,3	✓
Flexibility of Linguistic Input	3,0	-	3,7	-	3,3	-
Communication Quality	4,0	-	4,3	✓	3,7	-
Response Quality	6,0	✓	5,7	✓	4,0	-
Expectation Setting	4,0	-	6,0	✓	4,0	-
Ability to Maintain Themed Discussion	4,0	-	4,7	✓	2,0	-
Recognition and Facilitation of Users Goal and Intent	3,0	-	2,7	-	3,7	-
Understandability	5,0	✓	5,7	✓	4,3	✓
Credibility	6,0	✓	6,3	✓	3,0	-

* Average Score of the Perception Evaluation
** Presence

5   Discussion

We assumed that certain groups of impact factors are unanimously desirable in any chatbot and others are not. For example, Table 3 presents some impact factors, such as entertainment, which is desirable in virtually all chatbots. However, in this binary assessment, one of the chatbots does not assess entertainment as necessary, which does not mean that it is not welcome, nor will it never be essential for chatbots in general. We can, for example, imagine chatbots with a humorous purpose, in which entertainment is highly relevant.

The central aspect we need to verify is that the need to assess or not the impact factor in a chatbot only adds to some problems. Another question is how much is necessary to evaluate an impact factor. In other words, how desirable is an impact factor for the analyzed chatbot; or how undesirable is the impact factor for the analyzed chatbot. In the examples given, from the analysis performed on chatbots A, B, and C, entertainment did not appear relevant. Nevertheless, this could mean that entertainment is highly undesirable for some of them, and how can we represent that?

The relevance of an impact factor is not something binary, but something continuous. How necessary an impact factor is should be a continuous value. After all, one impact factor may be more relevant, but both are relevant, with one more relevant than the other. Social presence may be relevant to chatbots B and C. However, it may be more critical to one of these chatbots than the other, so a lasting value for relevance becomes necessary. Using real values provides a more reliable measure of how much each factor interferes explicitly with the conception of the idea of humanity of a chatbot under analysis. When binary values are used, we only know if any factor influences the idea of humanity. Still, it is impossible to observe at what level this occurs, nor if the factor is positive or negative for such an idea.

The main limitation of this investigation refers to the need for explicit ways to define the set of impact factors we currently identify as static. Such a set of characteristics describing humanization is likely to be modified over time according to the new needs of chatbots in the future. Chatbots will be applied in new contexts, addressing new characteristics. In addition, some studies on the humanization of evaluated chatbots are limited, considering some specific chatbots as models.

6   Conclusion

The way of evaluating humanization in chatbots remains an open research challenge. In this study, we acquired a set of humanization impact factors: those characteristics that influence users' perceptions about the chatbot's humanity. On this basis, our study conducted an evaluation of chatbots from the market. Our results showed how more than the simple binary assessment of the relevance of impact factors in the analysis of chatbots is needed to reveal relevance of each impact factor. We found that an assessment with continuous values is necessary to establish the context. Our future studies aim to propose a methodology for evaluating humanization in chatbots relying on the identified impact factors. This must be capable of continuously establishing the relevance of each impact factor within different chatbot contexts (*i.e.*, capable of continuously defining how desirable or undesirable each of the impact factors is within a chatbot context).

Acknowledgments. We thank the partnership between the University of Campinas and the CI&T company and its financial support.

References

1. Balaji, D.: Assessing user satisfaction with information chatbots: a preliminary investigation. Master's thesis, University of Twente (2019)
2. Følstad, A., Brandtzaeg, P.B.: Users' experiences with chatbots: findings from a questionnaire study. Qual. User Exp. **5**(1), 1–14 (2020). https://doi.org/10.1007/s41233-020-00033-2
3. Gnewuch, U., Morana, S., Adam, M., Maedche, A.: Faster is not always better: understanding the effect of dynamic response delays in human-chatbot interaction. AIS Electronic Library (AISeL) (2018)
4. Go, E., Sundar, S.S.: Humanizing chatbots: The effects of visual, identity and conversational cues on humanness perceptions. Comput. Hum. Behav. **97**, 304–316 (2019)
5. Holmes, S., Moorhead, A., Bond, R., Zheng, H., Coates, V., McTear, M.: Usability testing of a healthcare chatbot: Can we use conventional methods to assess conversational user interfaces? In: Proceedings of the 31st European Conference on Cognitive Ergonomics, pp. 207–214 (2019)
6. Kondylakis, H., et al.: R2d2: a DBpedia chatbot using triple-pattern like queries. Algorithms **13**(9), 217 (2020)
7. Mone, G.: The edge of the uncanny. Commun. ACM **59**(9), 17–19 (2016)
8. Niculescu, A., van Dijk, B., Nijholt, A., Li, H., See, S.L.: Making social robots more attractive: the effects of voice pitch, humor and empathy. Int. J. Soc. Robot. **5**(2), 171–191 (2013)
9. Nordheim, C.B., Følstad, A., Bjørkli, C.A.: An initial model of trust in chatbots for customer service-findings from a questionnaire study. Interact. Comput. **31**(3), 317–335 (2019)
10. Peras, D.: Chatbot evaluation metrics. In: Economic and Social Development: Book of Proceedings, pp. 89–97 (2018)
11. Reeves, B., Nass, C.: The Media Equation: How People Treat Computers, Television, and New Media Like Real People. Cambridge University Press, Cambridge (1996)
12. Rhim, J., Kwak, M., Gong, Y., Gweon, G.: Application of humanization to survey chatbots: change in chatbot perception, interaction experience, and survey data quality. Comput. Hum. Behav. **126**, 107034 (2022)
13. Schanke, S., Burtch, G., Ray, G.: Estimating the impact of "humanizing" customer service chatbots. Inf. Syst. Res. **32**(3), 736–751 (2021)
14. Verhagen, T., Van Nes, J., Feldberg, F., Van Dolen, W.: Virtual customer service agents: using social presence and personalization to shape online service encounters. J. Comput.-Mediat. Commun. **19**(3), 529–545 (2014)

15. Westerman, D., Cross, A.C., Lindmark, P.G.: I believe in a thing called bot: perceptions of the humanness of "chatbots". Commun. Stud. **70**(3), 295–312 (2019)
16. Xu, J., Benbasat, I., Cenfetelli, R.T.: Research note-the influences of online service technologies and task complexity on efficiency and personalization. Inf. Syst. Res. **25**(2), 420–436 (2014)
17. Xu, J.D.: Retaining customers by utilizing technology-facilitated chat: mitigating website anxiety and task complexity. Inf. Manag. **53**(5), 554–569 (2016)
18. Xu, Y., Shieh, C.H., van Esch, P., Ling, I.L.: Ai customer service: task complexity, problem-solving ability, and usage intention. Aust. Mark. J. (AMJ) **28**(4), 189–199 (2020)

A Framework for Humanization Evaluation in Chatbots

Paula Jeniffer dos Santos Viriato[1]([🖂]) [ID], Rafael Roque de Souza[1] [ID],
Leandro Aparecido Villas[1] [ID], and Julio Cesar dos Reis[1,2] [ID]

[1] Institute of Computing, University of Campinas, Campinas, SP, Brazil
p234831@dac.unicamp.br, {rroque,lvillas,dosreis}@unicamp.br
[2] Nucleus of Informatics Applied to Education, University of Campinas,
Campinas, SP, Brazil

Abstract. Chatbots play a central role in modern software systems regarding customer services. They have the potential of applicability for different purposes. A key open research challenge is how humanizing and evaluating chatbots during their development. Humanized chatbots carry out a fluid and pleasant conversation with the user, demonstrating empathy and personality. In this article, we aim to study and develop an evaluation method that indicates the level of humanization of a chatbot under analysis. Our framework comprises two objectives and questionnaires, which are applied to establish an assessment adaptable to the different objectives of using chatbots (commercial or therapeutic, for example). We combine these questionnaires to generate evaluation metrics, which provide a humanization score for the evaluated software. Our method helps designers identify specific factors that affect users' experience interacting with chatbots. We carry out a case study on the application of our framework and reveal the main findings about its applicability.

Keywords: Humanization · User Evaluation · Chatbots · Conversational Systems

1 Introduction

Chatbots are software that simulates human conversational tasks. There are severe challenges in developing them more humanized. A humanized chatbot performs a fluid and pleasant conversation with the user, demonstrating empathy and personality [4]. Adamopoulou and Moussiades, based on the definitions of Bansal and Khan [5] and Khanna *et al.* [14], defined chatbots as examples of systems that use artificial intelligence to develop better Human-Computer Interaction, simulating conversations between human users.

The concept of humanization does not have a simple definition, and personal perceptions of humanity are subjective [11]. Regarding chatbots, a connection between the perception of humanity and the resolution of the proposed tasks is

M. Kurosu and A. Hashizume (Eds.): HCII 2023, LNCS 14013, pp. 314–333, 2023.
https://doi.org/10.1007/978-3-031-35602-5_23

necessary. In this context, a chatbot should meet users' expectations for their respective purposes. A challenge in building chatbots is establishing ways to keep users willing to develop a dialogue with the chatbot. Humans, due to the feeling of empathy, tend to trust human attendants more than machines [1].

Such a conversational system should evolve with each interaction and offer alternative answers to similar questions, answering the interlocutor's questions. The chatbot should be able to engage cordially with the consumer, making them feel comfortable, satisfied, and valued [4]. Each chatbot has its characteristics, purposes, and target audience, and the perceptions of humanity related to the reality of the chatbot are the priority. For example, it is not polite in society to tell jokes in grieving situations; neither would it be appropriate to use colloquial language in chatbot legal advice. Thus, humanization assessments should adapt to the different contexts, users' needs and chatbot domains.

Humanizing a chatbot is a gradual and constant task [9]. It is crucial to evaluate the level of humanization of a chatbot. Evaluation helps to improve and make comparisons to propose and apply changes that cause positive effects on the results. A humanization metric can be an essential quantitative tool in developing a chatbot to improve the user experience. A metric allows an evolutionary comparison of such metrics in the humanization of different software versions. In addition, it makes possible to diagnose the strengths and weaknesses of the released versions. Chatbot users should be the central characters in this kind of evaluation. It is their perceptions that affect the success of a chatbot.

This research aims to study and develop an evaluation framework that indicates a chatbot's humanization level under analysis. Our approach consists of two objectives and brief questionnaires, which are applied to establish an assessment adaptable to the different objectives of using chatbots (commercial or therapeutic, for example). Our questionnaires intend, respectively, to capture how relevant each impact factor is for the pleasant functioning of the chatbot; and how present they are in the analyzed system.

We develop a weighting questionnaire, which aims to determine which impact factors are the most important for stakeholders in a system. This questionnaire seeks to adapt the evaluation method to the most diversified realities of existing chatbots. The perceptions questionnaire aims to assess how much users perceived the presence of each of the impact factors in the chatbot under use; and such positive and negative characteristics and perceptions are variable according to the analyzed context. Among the metrics proposed to assess a chatbot's humanization level, the primary metric combines the two questionnaires. Beyond the main metric, we develop performance metrics for each of the analyzed impact factors, presenting how close a chatbot is to the proper level of each impact factor.

In this investigation, we conduct a case study on applying our framework to reveal key findings regarding its applicability. First, we found that weighting results depend on the context of the chatbot; that is, what type of service it performs, which audience it serves, and, mainly, what is desirable for this chatbot. The second finding refers to weight variances concerning the designed chatbots.

As a result of the experiment, we acquired each impact factor's average weight and variance in eleven chatbot projects analyzed. The greater the variance of an impact factor, the more important thing is to analyze the factor within the chatbot context. Similarly, the average weights resulting in this study can be fixed in cases of low variance impact factors.

The remaining of this article is organized as follows: Sect. 2 presents background describing fundamental concepts; Sect. 3 presents the framework for evaluating humanization in chatbots; Sect. 4 presents the case study used to verify the framework applicability; Sect. 5 presents the obtained experimental results; Sect. 6 discusses our obtained findings and lessons learned; Sect. 7 presents our final considerations and directions for future research.

2   Fundamental Concepts

Chatbots are software systems capable of interacting with humans in natural language in a given domain [20]. There are currently several nomenclatures for this system: ECA (Embedded Conversation Agents), Conversation Systems, Agents, Chatterbots, or just bots. [15]. These designed agents use NLP so that users can type or write just like humans. The agent can then analyze the input and respond appropriately in a conversational manner, as examples of systems that use artificial intelligence to develop better Human-Computer Interaction by simulating conversations between human users [5,14].

Currently, chatbots communicate through text or voice and use advanced NLP (Natural Language Processing) techniques to understand, classify and generate conversations with humans [2]. For Go and Sundar [10], the primary function of chat agents is to interact with users by answering their questions and resolving their requests. The authors explained that the experience these agents provide is better than static information delivery, such as a list of FAQs because agents provide information more interactively.

As for interaction design, Følstad, Skjuve, and Brandtzaeg [8] classify chatbots into four categories: chatbots for customer support; personal assistant chatbots; content curation chatbots; and coaching chatbots. Our methodology proposed in this study applies to any chatbots presented by Følstad, Skjuve, and Brandtzaeg [8]. The examples shown in this article focus on chatbots for customer support.

Chatbots based on AI (Artificial Intelligence) [13] can understand natural language and not only predefined commands. In their development, they present enough skills to interact with users. Moreover, they can maintain different contexts of conversations and provide the user with more prosperous and engaging conversations. Because of this, concepts of virtual agents and speech recognition techniques used in virtual agents, such as Apple Siri, Amazon Alexa, and Google Assistant emerged. Thus, one can define NLP as an area of AI that aims to study and create techniques that enable the analysis and understanding of human language through a computational system [18].

2.1 Assessment Perspectives on Chatbots

Given the studies analyzed, we observed that evaluations in chatbots are carried out qualitatively, following the users' perception of the systems. Peras [22] addresses the assessment of chatbots as an activity from five perspectives: user experience, information retrieval; linguistics; technology; and business. The user experience perspective consists of usability, performance, affectivity, and user satisfaction concerning the chatbot. The information retrieval perspective focuses on the accuracy, accessibility, and efficiency of information delivery. On the other hand, the linguistic perspective looks at concepts such as quality, quantity, relatedness, manner, and grammatical accuracy presented in conversations with chatbots. The business perspective proposes more specific metrics for chatbot effectiveness: number of users, duration of chatbot conversation, number of conversations, number of agents included in a conversation, number of failed conversations, number of inappropriate responses, and number of repeated consultations.

In our investigation, the focus is to measure qualitative aspects more precisely. We aim to convert them to quantitative values in metrics to promote systems' evolution (design refinement) in such elements. According to Peras [22], among the five perspectives, only the information retrieval perspective involves only quantitative aspects. Two of the views mentioned are strongly guided by qualitative aspects: the linguistic and technological perspectives.

2.2 Psychometric Analysis and Likert Scale

One of the forms of qualitative assessment most suggested by Peras [22] was the Likert scale, a widely used psychometric technique. Pasquali [21] defines *psychometry* as the theory and technique of measuring mental processes, primarily applied in psychology and education. Psychometrics would transform qualitative aspects, commonly expressed in ordinary language, into quantitative metrics, which can be measured and compared. Also, Pasquali [21] explained that, in a general sense, psychometrics aims to explain the meaning of the responses given by the subjects in a series of tasks, usually called items. We present these concepts because they are relevant for constructing our framework.

According to Joshi *et al.* [12], which was based on the work of Edmondson [7] and McLeod [16], the Likert scale is a psychometric technique to measure 'attitude' in a scientifically accepted and validated way. A preferential behavior in a specific circumstance defines an *attitude*. Attitude is usually rooted in the lasting organization of beliefs and ideas (around an object, a subject, or a concept) acquired through social interactions [19].

In the case of the evaluation of humanity in chatbot, the concepts evaluated are factors that, in an integrated way, make up the perception of humanity that human beings have regarding the system. Although factors are subjective and abstract, psychometric scales help quantify the perception of these characteristics. Humanization impact factors are the characteristics that most influence our perception of humanity in a chatbot. Examples of humanization impact factors are naturalness and empathy. That is why psychometric analysis and the Likert scale play a key role in our study.

2.3 Metrics for Likert Scale Analysis

Croasmun [6], based on Mills [17], explained that when using Likert-type scales, it is essential that researchers calculate and report Cronbach's α coefficient for internal consistency reliability. Internal consistency reliability refers to the extent to which items in an instrument are consistent among themselves and with the overall mechanism. Cronbach's α estimates the internal consistency reliability of an instrument by determining how all items in the instrument report to all other items and the actual mechanism.

Like Cronbach's α coefficient, other coefficients, such as Revelle's β and McDonald's, index internal psychometric properties of scale scores applicable with effect indicator scales when we are interested in sampling fluctuations resulting from the sampling of items [26]. Revelle [24] proposed an index labeled coefficient beta (β) that he showed equals the proportion of variance in scale scores accounted for by a general factor under more general conditions. McDonald's coefficient (ω) is computed as ratios of the variance due to the common attribute (*i.e.*, factor) to the total variance [23].

The main challenge in using these coefficients in the context of our study is that they are applied in single questionnaires rather than in correlated questionnaires, as in our case. More than such coefficients are required for the correlation between two psychometric questionnaires. Due to this fact, it was necessary to adapt Cronbach's α coefficient to our context, as further explained in Subsect. 3.2.

3 Method for Evaluating Humanization in Chatbots

This investigation proposes to develop and apply a method to assess the level of humanization in chatbots using the perceptions of real users. The technique must adapt to different types of chatbots, with other purposes and target audiences, through a dynamic weighting system for the various humanization impact factors present in chatbots.

We assume that metrics generated through the application of the developed method can portray the evolution of aspects (factors) related to the humanization of chatbots. Figure 1 presents our proposed method and its development and application. Our proposal goes through three major phases: bibliographic analysis, the methodology's development, and the evaluation method's application.

3.1 Identification of Impact Factors

Through literature analysis, we aimed to identify impact factors related to humanization in chatbots [25]. We call impact factors those characteristics that contribute to users' perception of humanity regarding a chatbot. Our first task referred to the compilation of a complete set of humanization impact factors possible (Viriato [25] presents the impact factors identified from literature).

Observing the existing investigations aiming to study humanization in chatbots, we analyzed different sets of characteristics in chatbots (impact factors).

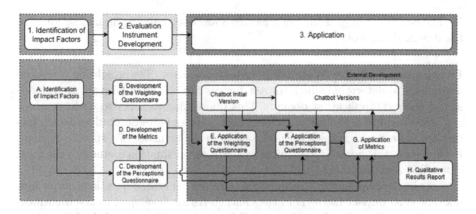

Fig. 1. Method for Evaluating Humanization in Chatbots

There is no simple convergence between these sets of impact factors. One of the possible reasons is that each work studies or focuses on specific types of chatbots. The selected set of characteristics corresponds to what is highly desired. Therefore, the objective at this stage was to complete a compilation of these attributes and generate a more extensive and complete set of impact factors (we developed our set in Viriato [25]). In our proposal, we weigh them according to the needs of each chatbot. Finally, we removed duplicate characteristics with the same or very close meaning.

3.2 Evaluation Instrument Development

We proposed the development of two questionnaires with different objectives: the weighting questionnaire and the perception questionnaire. These questionnaires intend, respectively, to capture how relevant each impact factor is for the pleasant functioning of the chatbot; and how present they are in the analyzed system.

We present the development of the Perceptions Questionnaire in Subsect. 3.2. In addition to the Perceptions Questionnaire, we show two more assessment tools: The Development of the Weighting Questionnaire (cf. Subsect. 3.2) and the Generation of Metrics (cf. Subsect. 3.2).

Both questionnaires are applied by the project design team, preferably to the target audience of the chatbot under development. In the case of the Ponderations Questionnaire, it is used right at the beginning of the project when there is already a well-established expected chatbot idea or when there is already a prototype. Members of the design team can answer the application of the Weighting Questionnaire in cases where there are no explicit stakeholders in the project capable of answering the questionnaire. Still, this application must have rigor since the result guides the project's ideal chatbot behavior. The Perceptions Questionnaire must be applied by the design team every time new versions of the chatbot are under development, and the respondents must be chatbot users.

In this way, the design team can measure how close the ideal humanization is to the designed chatbot.

Development of the Weighting Questionnaire. The weighting questionnaire aims to determine which impact factors are the most relevant to a determined context/application domain. This questionnaire seeks to address which are less critical in a chatbot. Likewise, this questionnaire determines which factors are desirable and which are undesirable in the behavior of a specific chatbot. In this sense, this questionnaire aims to adapt the evaluation method to the most diversified realities of existing chatbots.

For the development of this questionnaire, we generated questions about how relevant each impact factor is in the characteristics developed in the Identification of Impact Factors phase. The possible answers follow one of the Likert scale patterns, ranging from "totally irrelevant" to "totally relevant". The following is an example of question generation:

Impact Factor: Appropriate Language Style
Question: How important is the appropriate language style in the chatbot used?
Impact Factor Explanation: Ability of the chatbot to use the appropriate language style for the context.
Alternatives: totally irrelevant, irrelevant, a little irrelevant, indifferent, a little relevant, relevant, totally relevant.

Development of the Perceptions Questionnaire: The perceptions questionnaire, in turn, aims to assess how much final users perceived the presence of each of the impact factors in the chatbot used. Along with the weighting questionnaire, the perceptions questionnaire verifies the level at which perceived positive or negative characteristics are in the chatbot under analysis. Such positive and negative features and perceptions are variable according to the context of the chatbot.

For the development of this questionnaire, statements are generated about the user's perception of each of the impact factors in the analyzed chatbot. The objective is to identify a level of agreement with the proposed statement. The possible answers follow one of the Likert scale patterns, ranging from "strongly disagree" to "strongly agree". The following is an example of claim generation:

Impact Factor: Appropriate Language Style
Affirmation: The chatbot has an appropriate language style.
Impact Factor Explanation: Ability of the chatbot to use the appropriate language style for the context.
Alternatives: strongly disagree, disagree, somewhat disagree, neither agree nor disagree, somewhat agree, agree, strongly agree.

Generation of Metrics. We propose metrics to assess the level of humanization of a chatbot. Our metrics were obtained with the combination of the two questionnaires applied because the perception of humanity is given by combining all impact factors. This investigation develops two metrics: a general metric of the level of humanization; and a 'performance metric' for each of the analyzed impact factors.

The general metric in humanization aims to define how close to adequate humanization a chatbot is, considering the chatbot's context. The metric varies between 0 and 1, with a value of 0 representing the not humanized chatbot or that the humanization was performed inappropriately for its context. On the other hand, the value 1 represents a perfectly humanized chatbot with adequate humanization. The value of the proposed metric reflects how close the analyzed chatbot is to optimal humanization.

The general metric in humanization is generated from the results of the initial application of the weighting questionnaire together with the results of the perceptions questionnaire. Through a calculation, which is an adaptation of the formula for Cronbach's α coefficient, a value between 0 and 1 is returned.

The first step in acquiring this metric is pre-processing the data obtained with the questionnaires. We use the Likert scale size seven in the questionnaires and convert all responses collected on such scales to numerical values (Fig. 2 is an example of a conversion to the Weightings Questionnaire). After extracting the data acquired through the questionnaires, data are centralized and scaled using Eq. 1 and Eq. 2, for weighting and perception data, respectively (Fig. 2 also shows the transformation of data with centralization).

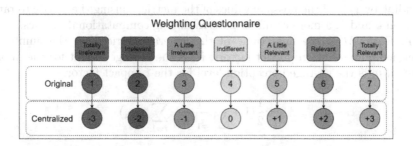

Fig. 2. Mapping of responses on a Likert scale to numerical values

In Eq. 1: VW_j is the pre-processed score of the respondent j in the weighting questionnaire, vw_j is the original score of the respondent j, k is the size of the Likert scale.

$$VW_j = \frac{vw_j - \frac{k+1}{2}}{\frac{k-1}{2}} \tag{1}$$

In Eq. 2: VP_j is the pre-processed score of the respondent j in the perceptions questionnaire, vp_j is the original score of the respondent j, k is the size of the Likert scale.

$$VP_j = \frac{vp_j - \frac{k+1}{2}}{\frac{k-1}{2}} \tag{2}$$

With the pre-processed data, we obtain the average user responses for each impact factor separately for each questionnaire. Equation 3 presents the average of responses by impact factors for the weighting questionnaire. Equation 4 shows this average for the weighting questionnaire. Equation 3 defines w_i as the weight value for the impact factor i; n is the number of respondents to the weight questionnaire; VW_j is the score given by the respondent j for the impact factor i.

$$w_i = \frac{\sum_{j=1}^{n} VW_j}{n} \tag{3}$$

In Eq. 4: p_i is the perception value for the impact factor i; n is the number of respondents to the perceptions questionnaire, VP_j is the score given by the respondent j for the impact factor i.

$$p_i = \frac{\sum_{j=1}^{n} VP_j}{n} \tag{4}$$

We calculate the available metric in humanization by the Eq. 5. Equation 5 performs a Manhattan normalization [3] on the weights acquired with the weighting questionnaire and multiplies the new weights by the results of the perceptions questionnaire, correlating the two questionnaires. Manhattan normalization consists of dividing the weights by the sum of their absolute values, and this operation guarantees that the metric value varies between -1 and 1.

The last step is to perform a horizontal translation (adding 1) and a scaling (dividing by 1/2) of the possible values of the metric, causing the metric to range between 0 and 1, a more common pattern among computational metrics.

In Eq. 5: M is the final value of the general metric; n is the number of identified humanization impact factors, w_i is the average weight for the impact factor i, p_i is the average perception level for the i impact factor.

$$M = \frac{1}{2}(1 + \frac{1}{\sum_{i=1}^{n} |w_i|} \sum_{i=1}^{n} w_i p_i) \tag{5}$$

Performance Metrics. For the values of the performance metrics of each impact factor, we applied the Eq. 6 on the original data, not centered or scaled. Such metrics vary between 0 and 1. In this sense, the performance metrics assess users' perceptions of each impact factor separately. In Eq. 6: F_i is the performance metric for the impact factor i, pi_j is the original perception value of the respondent j for the impact factor i; n is the number of respondents to the perceptions questionnaire, k is the size of the Likert scale.

$$F_i = \frac{\sum_{j=1}^{n} pi_j}{n} \times \frac{1}{k} \tag{6}$$

4 Experimental Evaluation

We evaluated our proposal to understand its applicability. To this end, we applied our framework in the first semester of 2022 during an undergraduate course on the Human-Computer Interaction (offered at University of Campinas, Brazil). Its objective was to teach students how to design and evaluate user interfaces in interactive software systems[1]

4.1 Participants

The participants should develop a project organized in different phases during the course. In particular, the topic of the project was to build chatbots as human-computer interfaces. We explored this context to evaluate the humanization of chatbots developed. The participants are students of the Computer Science course, around the sixth semester of the course, aged between 18 and 25 years old. To carry out the project in the discipline, we guided the students to organize themselves into groups of an average of 5 people, which generated the participation of eleven groups until the end of the mandatory parts of the project, and three groups also carried out the elective parts. One group withdrew from the course and, therefore, from the dynamics.

4.2 Methodology

Figure 1 presents the application methodology proposed (adapted from the original method). We considered that the application of the weighting questionnaire should be carried out before the low prototyping, at a time when ideas about how the chatbot design should be clarified. In the discipline context, this makes sense because it is at this point that students must be as transparent as possible about the target audience's intentions and what the chatbot should accomplish. Then the perception questionnaire was applied to each new high-prototyping or reprototyping of the chatbot (cf. Fig. 3). Figure 1 presented in Sect. 3 presented a more general version of the application shown in Fig. 3 specifying the application of the framework to a specific case.

Application of the Weighting Questionnaire. Along with Phase 1 of the project (cf. Fig. 3), we applied the Weighting Questionnaire because our methodology for evaluating humanization in chatbots can be an excellent instrument for clarifying the needs of the intended chatbot. The purpose of the Weighting Questionnaire is to determine which impact factors are more or less critical; and, similarly, to determine which factors are desirable and undesirable in chatbot behavior.

At this stage of the project about humanization, the objective was for each group to identify possible users of the proposed chatbots, thus explaining the

---

[1] The author of this article acted as a monitor in the course by assisting in applying the proposed methodology.

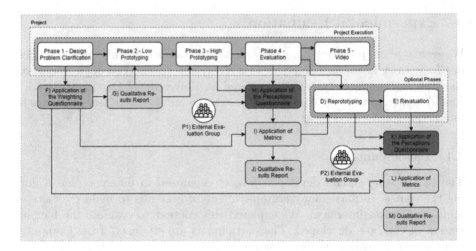

Fig. 3. Application of the Method for Evaluating Humanization in Chatbots in an Undergraduate HCI Course

context and purpose of the respective chatbot for such future users. Such users could even be the participants of the groups themselves. This became an activity for all the participants of the groups as well. Users accessed the questionnaire, selected the evaluated topic, and filled out the form. Moreover, any user could complete this questionnaire, but the responses were restricted to a single e-mail to avoid repeated respondents. Respondents' e-mails were collected but restricted and not shared even with the discipline's students, and the responses were made available through a non-editable link.

Application of the Perceptions Questionnaire. The interface evaluation and the Perceptions Questionnaire were applied at the beginning of Phase 4 of the project (cf. Fig. 3). The objective was to evaluate how much users perceived the presence of each of the characteristics in the chatbot used. Such features and positive and negative perceptions vary according to the analyzed context. In this phase, concerning humanization, the objective was for people outside the group under analysis to evaluate the effectiveness of the humanization of the generated chatbot. It could be the classmates themselves assessing each other's projects or subjects outside the class. Users accessed the questionnaire, selected the evaluated topic, and filled out the form. Any user could fill in the questionnaire. Respondents' e-mails were collected but restricted and not shared even with the discipline's students, and the responses were made available to the groups through a non-editable link.

Reassessment. This project's Reassessment Phase was also optional, as well as the Reprototyping Phase (cf. Fig. 3), with the primary objective of verifying improvements of all humanization metrics regarding the second high-fidelity prototype (developed in the Reprototyping Phase). Taking the Second High-Fidelity Prototype Phase, it was evaluated to which extent users perceived the presence of each of the characteristics in the chatbot used, through the Perceptions Questionnaire. This occurred in the same way as presented in the first application of the Perceptions Questionnaire (cf. Subsect. 4.2).

4.3 Results Analysis

The results were analyzed using the equations presented in Subsect. 3.2. In addition to the calculations shown in Subsect. 3.2, for the results of the Weighting Questionnaire, the results of Manhattan Normalization (Eq. 7, where w is the vector with the average of the weights and k is the index of the investigated impact factor) were analyzed for each of the impact factors. Such results demonstrate how desirable each impact factor is for the proposed chatbot. The Manhattan Normalization Absolute Value (Eq. 8, where w is the vector with the average of the weights and k is the index of the investigated impact factor) for each of the impact factors presents the relevance of each impact factor for projecting the idea of humanization of the chatbot under analysis. The impact factors were ordered for each group according to the Manhattan Normalization Absolute Values to identify which impact factors should be worked on and which are not of great concern. We present these case study results in Subsect. 5.1.

$$n1_k = \frac{w_k}{\sum_{i=1}^{n} |w_i|} \tag{7}$$

$$|n1_k| = \left| \frac{w_k}{\sum_{i=1}^{n} |w_i|} \right| \tag{8}$$

In the case of the results of the perception questionnaire, a metrics analysis was carried out on each of the impact factors separately to verify the chatbot's performance in each of them through the Eq. 9 (where p_k is the average of the pre-processed insights of the k-index impact factor, and w_k is the weight of the k-index impact factor). We presented the performance results of some impact factors in the case studies in Subsect. 5.2. In Subsect. 5.4, still using Eq. 9, we comparatively verify the improvement in the average performance of some impact factors in the three use cases that carried out the reapplication of the methodology.

We use the Eq. 10 (where p_k is the average of the pre-processed insights of the k-index impact factor, and w_k is the weight of the k-index impact factor) between the weighting and perception results to verify how impactful each impact factor score was in generating the final metric in humanization.

$$mp_k = \frac{1}{2}[1 + (p_k \times w_k)] \tag{9}$$

$$ip_k = |(p_k \times w_k)| \tag{10}$$

The principal metric, which infers how close a chatbot is to perfect humanization, is calculated by the Eq. 5 presented in Subsect. 3.2. We show the results of applying this metric during the experiment in Subsect. 5.3, on the first application of the methodology, and in Subsect. 5.4, comparing the results of the first and second application and showing the evolution of humanization in the projected chatbots.

5   Results

We present the results of both the Weighting and the Perceptions questionnaire (respectively, Subsect. 5.1 and Subsect. 5.2) in addition to the Metrics in Humanization (Subsect. 5.3); and the Evolution in Metrics in Humanization for the three groups that performed the optional Reprototyping Phase (Subsect. 5.4). Finally, in Subsect. 5.5 we present the application of dimensionality reduction (PCA) on the weighting data to demonstrate how the context of a chatbot interferes with its objectives and, therefore, with its weights. We present how similar chatbots, with similar goals, have similar weights. Subsection 5.5 reveals that the weighting of the impact factors of a chatbot is a good characterizer.

We chose to preferentially display results only using the impact factors that presented the most significant variance between the groups' results, discarding the impact factors with medium and low variance. Using impact factors with high variance allows a clearer view of the results. Table 1 presents impact factors ordered according to their variance, and those with high variance are highlighted in red.

5.1   Weighting Results

In the case of the weighting results, the relevance of some impact factors varies significantly from one chatbot theme to another. Some impact factors are relevant for some chatbots, while others are not. In some chatbots, some impact factors have relevance and minimal relevance. Figure 4 shows how each chatbot proposal weight can characterize the problem, target audience, and software objectives.

5.2   Perception Results

As for the perception results, we observe that in the first high prototyping, there is a trend of similar results among the impact factors for all analyzed chatbots, as seen in Fig. 5. Despite the similarity trend, in Fig. 5, we can already see some very high and deficient scores from some groups. Such variances probably already demonstrate the care the teams took to treat each impact factor with due relevance, presented in Fig. 4.

Relevance of Impact Factors on the Conception of Humanity

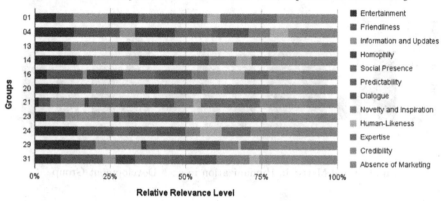

Fig. 4. Relevance of Impact Factors on the Conception of Humanity in each of the Case Study Chatbots

Performance of Impact Factors by Development Group

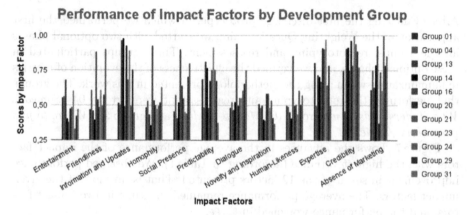

Fig. 5. Performance of Impact Factors by Development Group according to Perception Results

5.3 Metrics in Humanization Results

As for humanization metrics, in most cases, the high prototypes had results above 75% of the ideal humanization, with only one group scoring below 75% (cf. Fig. 6). However, even so, we observe the variation between one chatbot and another regarding the level of humanization. This depends significantly on developing the high prototype itself and the techniques used.

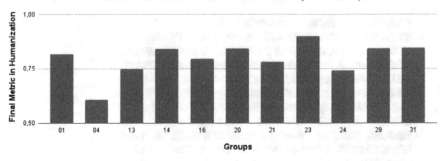

Fig. 6. Final Metric in Humanization in each Development Group

5.4   Evolution in Humanization Metrics Results

After evaluating the first discharge prototype, in which we performed the first application of the Weighting Questionnaire, we started with two optional phases for the groups: reprototyping and reassessment. Three groups participated in these optional phases, and we verified the effectiveness of the evolution of metrics in humanization when using the methodology presented in this work. The groups that performed the reprototyping and reassessment were: group 04 (*Someone Who Understands You*), group 16 (*Mental Health*), and group 23 (*Where to find your Movie/Series?*).

Figure 7 shows the advances in the average performance of the impact factors with the highest variance (according to Table 1). We observed performance improvement in seven of the 12 factors presented. That is, in most of the given impact factors. The average performance remained the same in two impact factors, and the performance worsened in three.

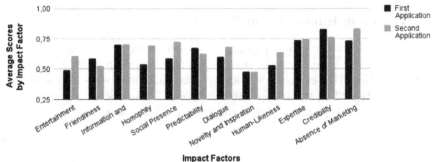

Fig. 7. Advance in Average Performance of Impact Factors

Figure 8 presents the progress of metrics in humanization by the project developed. In two of the three projects, there was a clear advance in the humanization metric; in one, the value of the final humanization metric dropped. We can also observe that the group had already obtained a higher grade in the first evaluation round than the other two groups in the two evaluation rounds. The higher the metric value in humanization, the more difficult it is to improve. At this stage, humanization depends a lot on the details. Possible future work is the application of the methodology in longer evolutionary processes of software development, where we can verify if it is more challenging to improve the scores in humanization when they are already relatively high.

Advance in the Final Metric in Humanization by Development Group

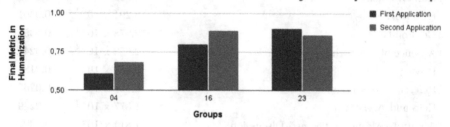

Fig. 8. Advance in the Final Metric in Humanization by Development Group

5.5 Principal Component Analysis Results

PCA (Principal Component Analysis) is a dimensionality reduction method applied to analyze how the weighting data behaves more deeply, as shown in Fig. 9. We observed some groupings according to the proposed chatbot theme. For example, circled in red, we have chatbots for recommendations. Meanwhile, circled in blue, we have chatbots for academic-professional services, which are next to each other. Surrounded in orange are the chatbots for the local target audience. In purple, chatbots for mental health are added in lighter blue by chatbots for general assistance. Finally, in pink, we have a specific chatbot developed for the hospital public, which has a very different purpose from the others.

Table 1 shows that certain impact factors vary significantly from others, whereas some impact factors vary by medium and others by a little. We acquired the average of the weights for each of the impact factors. This average weighting can be used in cases where the weighting questionnaire is not desired for an adaptive assessment and the project team wants the exclusive application of the perception questionnaire.

Table 1. Variance and Average by Impact Factor in Weightings

Impact Factor	Variance	Average
Entertainment	8.628×10^{-4}	-0.0132
Friendliness	7.729×10^{-4}	0.0131
Information and Updates	6.421×10^{-4}	0.0235
Homophily	5.801×10^{-4}	0.0065
Social Presence	4.788×10^{-4}	0.0154
Predictability	3.916×10^{-4}	0.0183
Dialogue	3.854×10^{-4}	0.0104
Novelty and Inspiration	3.845×10^{-4}	-0.0029
Human-Likeness	3.582×10^{-4}	0.0008
Expertise	3.291×10^{-4}	0.0301
Credibility	2.978×10^{-4}	0.0356
Absence of Marketing	2.952×10^{-4}	0.0247
Privacy	2.887×10^{-4}	0.0185
Reference to Service	2.561×10^{-4}	0.0265
Help and Assistance	1.877×10^{-4}	0.0249
Ability to Maintain Themed Discussion	1.814×10^{-4}	0.0097
Content Relevance	1.557×10^{-4}	0.0365
Speed	1.381×10^{-4}	0.0269
Graceful Breakdown	1.344×10^{-4}	0.0246
Communication Quality	1.278×10^{-4}	0.0338
Absence of Repetitiveness	1.123×10^{-4}	0.0125
Flexibility of Linguistic Input	1.040×10^{-4}	0.0332
Contingency	1.030×10^{-4}	0.0238
Recognition and Facilitation of Users Goal and Intent	1.006×10^{-4}	0.0358
Initiating Conversation	9.949×10^{-5}	0.0291
Absence of Boring Attitudes	9.402×10^{-5}	0.0277
Absence of Strange or Rude Responses	8.842×10^{-5}	0.0317
Absence of Interpretation Issues	8.689×10^{-5}	0.0351
Absence of Unwanted Events	8.262×10^{-5}	0.0287
Absence of Inability to Help	8.180×10^{-5}	0.0320
Ease of Use	6.605×10^{-5}	0.0416
Expectation Setting	6.300×10^{-5}	0.0200
Response Quality	5.340×10^{-5}	0.0370
Communication Effort	4.045×10^{-5}	0.0294
Understandability	2.107×10^{-5}	0.0385
Response Clarity	2.100×10^{-5}	0.0390
Total Average	2.352×10^{-4}	0.0239

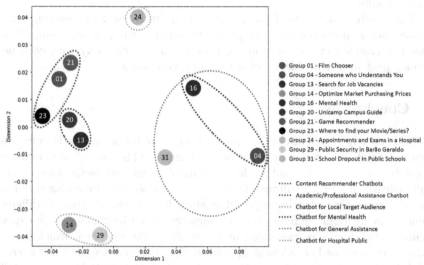

Fig. 9. Application of PCA on Pre-Processed and Normalized Weighting Data

6 Discussion

The main results are in the weighting data. In the methodology, we proposed that the weighting results are the main differentiator, in which the desired final result describes chatbots. As shown in Fig. 9, present in Sect. 5, chatbots have results close to weighting according to context. We can prove how much context influences the conception of humanity.

Table 1 presented in Sect. 5 demonstrated that impact factors that vary slightly should always be treated with the same standardized weight. On the other hand, impact factors that change in a median way can be evaluated only in cases where it is necessary or relevant to the chatbot context. We suggested that the weighting questionnaire is always applied to verify the weights of impact factors with high variance.

We obtained two main findings with our case study. The first is that the weighting results depend a lot on the context of the chatbot, that is, what type of service it performs, which audience it serves, and, mainly, what is desirable for this chatbot. The weights strongly depend on the context of the chatbot (cf. Fig. 9). In addition, we found that the impact factors have different variations. In this sense, there are impact factors that vary little from one context to another. There are impact factors that almost always vary according to the context.

As open questions, we can have as another methodology application result, in addition to an experiment proving the advantages of using the presented methodology, the average weighting of the impact factors. Such average weighting can be used in cases where the design team wants to apply only the Perceptions Questionnaire.

This study was key to demonstrate a quantitative way of assessing which impact factors influence the perception of humanity from human beings have. This is quantified in the evolution of chatbots more effectively with each new development iteration, that is, with each new versioning.

7   Conclusion

There is currently a high demand for chatbots, but literature needs more adequate methods for their humanization assessment. This research developed an innovative and adaptive chatbot humanization assessment methodology, especially when evaluating qualitative factors. The solution relied on a wide variety of impact factors. Our adaptive approach enables dealing with chatbots in different domains by including different target audiences served by chatbots. We experimentally evaluated our framework in a case study. We evaluated which impact factors are more or less relevant in general chatbots and acquired the average weighting for each impact factor. Our results help in design decisions, especially concerning what to improve in the analyzed chatbot. Future work involves investigating algorithms that can punctually improve each impact factor, mainly algorithms for augmenting dialogues during the training of state-of-the-art chatbots. In addition, we aim to apply our framework in other contexts, mainly in industrial contexts. We plan to investigate our proposal in other human-computer interfaces to analyze whether it is effective in the general evaluation of humanity in software.

Acknowledgments. We thank the partnership between the University of Campinas and the CI&T company and its financial support. We also thank the undergraduate students who participated in the evaluations conducted in this study.

References

1. Adam, M., Wessel, M., Benlian, A., et al.: AI-based chatbots in customer service and their effects on user compliance. Electron. Mark. **9**(2), 204 (2020)
2. Adamopoulou, E., Moussiades, L.: An overview of chatbot technology. In: Maglogiannis, I., Iliadis, L., Pimenidis, E. (eds.) AIAI 2020. IAICT, vol. 584, pp. 373–383. Springer, Cham (2020). https://doi.org/10.1007/978-3-030-49186-4_31
3. Alzorba, S., Günther, C., Popovici, N., Tammer, C.: A new algorithm for solving planar multiobjective location problems involving the Manhattan norm. Eur. J. Oper. Res. **258**(1), 35–46 (2017)
4. Balaji, D.: Assessing user satisfaction with information chatbots: a preliminary investigation. Master's thesis, University of Twente (2019)
5. Bansal, H., Khan, R.: A review paper on human computer interaction. Int. J. Adv. Res. Comput. Sci. Softw. Eng. **8**, 53–56 (2018)
6. Croasmun, J.T., Ostrom, L.: Using likert-type scales in the social sciences. J. Adult Educ. **40**(1), 19–22 (2011)

7. Edmondson, D.: Likert scales: a history. In: Proceedings of the Conference on Historical Analysis and Research in Marketing, vol. 12, pp. 127–133 (2005)
8. Følstad, A., Brandtzaeg, P.B.: Users' experiences with chatbots: findings from a questionnaire study. Quality User Exper. 5(1), 1–14 (2020). https://doi.org/10.1007/s41233-020-00033-2
9. Gelici, A.A.: Change in digital business: chatbots and their significance on online purchasing, B. S. thesis, University of Twente (2020)
10. Go, E., Sundar, S.S.: Humanizing chatbots: the effects of visual, identity and conversational cues on humanness perceptions. Comput. Hum. Behav. 97, 304–316 (2019)
11. Haslam, N., Loughnan, S., Holland, E.: The psychology of humanness. Objectification and (de) Humanization, pp. 25–51 (2013)
12. Joshi, A., Kale, S., Chandel, S., Pal, D.K.: Likert scale: explored and explained. British J. Appl. Sci. Technol. 7(4), 396 (2015)
13. Kar, R., Haldar, R.: Applying chatbots to the internet of things: opportunities and architectural elements. arXiv preprint arXiv:1611.03799 (2016)
14. Khanna, A., Pandey, B., Vashishta, K., Kalia, K., Pradeepkumar, B., Das, T.: A study of today's A.I. through chatbots and rediscovery of machine intelligence. Int. J. u- e-Serv. Sci. Technol. 8(7), 277–284 (2015)
15. Kříž, J.: Chatbot for laundry and dry cleaning service. Masaryk University (2017)
16. McLeod, S.: Likert scale. https://www.simplypsychology.org/ (2014)
17. Mills, G.E., Gay, L.R.: Educational research: competencies for analysis and applications. ERIC (2019)
18. Nadkarni, P.M., Ohno-Machado, L., Chapman, W.W.: Natural language processing: an introduction. J. Am. Med. Inform. Assoc. 18(5), 544–551 (2011)
19. Park, K.: Preventive and social medicine (2013)
20. Paschoal, L.N., Nogueira, L.L., Chicon, P.M.M.: Agentes conversacionais pedagógicos: Uma discussão inicial sobre conceitos, estratégias de desenvolvimento e oportunidades de pesquisa. Digitalização da Educação: Desafios e Estratégias para a Educação da Geração Conectada, p. 23 (2020)
21. Pasquali, L.: Psychometrics. Rev. Esc. Enferm. U.S.P. 43, 992–999 (2009)
22. Peras, D.: Chatbot evaluation metrics. Economic and Social Development: book of Proceedings, pp. 89–97 (2018)
23. Ravinder, E.B., Saraswathi, D.A.: Literature review of cronbachalphacoefficient (a) and mcdonald's omega coefficient (ω). Eur. J. Molecular Clin. Med. 7(6), 2943–2949 (2020)
24. Revelle, W.: Hierarchical cluster analysis and the internal structure of tests. Multivar. Behav. Res. 14(1), 57–74 (1979)
25. Viriato, P.J.d.S., Souza, R.R.d., Villas, L.A., dos Reis, J.C.: Revealing chatbot humanization impact factors. In: HCI International 2023: 25th International Conference on Human-Computer Interaction. Computer and Information Science (CCIS), Springer, Copenhagen, Denmark (2023)
26. Zinbarg, R.E., Revelle, W., Yovel, I., Li, W.: Cronbach's α, revelle's β, and mcdonald's ω h: Their relations with each other and two alternative conceptualizations of reliability. psychometrika 70(1), 123–133 (2005)

Who Would You Rather Ask for Help? A Comparison Between Two Chatbot Personalities in Information Management

Elisabeth Ganal[1]([mail]) [ID], Fiona Wiederer[1] [ID], Isabell Bachmann[2] [ID], and Birgit Lugrin[1] [ID]

[1] Human-Computer Interaction, Julius-Maximilians Universität Würzburg, Würzburg, Germany
{elisabeth.ganal,birgit.lugrin}@uni-wuerzburg.de,
fiona.wiederer@stud-mail.uni-wuerzburg.de
[2] avato consulting AG, Alzenau, Germany
isabell.bachmann@avato.net
https://www.mi.uni-wuerzburg.de, https://www.avato-consulting.com/

Abstract. Chatbots are widely used in different areas, ranging from healthcare applications, social support, task assistance to customer service. Within this study, we investigated two different chatbot personalities in the field of information management (IM). In IM the motives for using a chatbot are mostly aimed at efficiency and productivity and less at social interaction. With the evaluation of the alpha version of the chatbot *Liibot* of the IT company *avato* we examined whether chatbots meet with a positive response from users in the field of IM and what influence different personalities have on the usage. The previous chatbot, which has a more socially-oriented personality, was compared with a more task-oriented personality, which we assumed to be more advantageous in IM. The evaluation was conducted online in telepresence as a between-subjects design and included 2 groups with a total number of 80 participants. The results show that even small changes in the linguistic answering style of the chatbot lead to a significantly different assessment of social competence and personality. No higher values for information and system quality could be found within the task-oriented chatbot version. It even showed worse service quality than the social-oriented chatbot, whose social behaviors also provided significantly higher enjoyment during the interaction. The level of task complexity makes a significantly difference for the willingness to use a chatbot. In summary, a task-oriented chatbot is not rated significantly better in the IT domain and in some aspects rated even worse, which does not confirm the assumption of preferring a task-oriented chatbot personality.

Keywords: Chatbot Personality · User Experience · Information Management

M. Kurosu and A. Hashizume (Eds.): HCII 2023, LNCS 14013, pp. 334–353, 2023.
https://doi.org/10.1007/978-3-031-35602-5_24

1   Introduction

Many people spend hours every day on their devices such as laptops, computers, game consoles or smartphones. With a total population of 83 million, almost 61 million people in Germany used smartphones in 2020 [60]. A look at the most popular apps in the Google Play Store in 2021 shows that instant messaging services and social media applications such as Telegram, Whatsapp and Instagram are particularly popular among smartphone users [61].

This shows that people are increasingly communicating via text-based messages using technical devices. Though the interaction between humans and computers is still mostly textbased, a change in the interaction between humans and computers is taking place, driven by the use of chatbots or voice assistants to enable users to interact based on natural language [13]. The application areas of chatbots are wide-ranging, they are used in customer service [16,28,30], in healthcare [48], as an assistant in organizational tasks [45,67] as well as social and emotional supporters [49,64]. Especially in the area of customer service more and more companies use chatbots to offer their customers a 24/7 support and save costs at the same time. Besides that, chatbots can also serve as support at the IT service desk, e.g., in answering FAQs or finding solutions for user specific problems. A large knowledge base is becoming increasingly important for companies. In order to make knowledge as available as possible for employees, the use of technologies for information and knowledge management is inevitable. A rapid provision of help and an efficient search for information are the main chatbot interaction goals of users in this field of work. The question therefore arises whether social behaviours of a chatbot are at all necessary or even obsolete in the IT sector. Or, whether a more task-oriented chatbot with a neutral personality would be more appropriate in this area.

The IT company *avato consulting AG* advises its customers in the areas of information management (IM), expertise as a service, and smart data. It is one of the companies that wants to use a chatbot as a support tool in its knowledge management portal. The company is already developing a chatbot, which is currently being used as an alpha version in their own developer portal. Since little is known or researched about the use of chatbots in IM and internal company chatbot use [24], the study presented in this work is intended to help steer further development in the right direction at an early stage. This early testing of the chatbot should gather experience on the user needs in this area of work and reduce later development costs and time.

Due to the goals and field of work, in which the chatbot should be used, it can be assumed that a more social-oriented chatbot could meet with rejection or resistance from users. Whether this is the case will be investigated in this research paper by comparing the currently more social-oriented chatbot *Liibot* of *avato* with a more task-oriented chatbot version.

This leads to the central research question: What is the user experience like when using the *Liibot* and to what extent is a task-oriented chatbot more suitable in the IT domain? In addition, we want to investigate whether social traits of the chatbot have an impact on the perceived increase in productivity. And, whether users can identify different social skills based on the linguistic style of the chatbot's answers and whether these have an impact on their willingness to use the chatbot in the future. With our research, we contribute to the understanding of how to improve the interaction with chatbots and further fill a gap in research related to the user experience of chatbots used in IM.

2   Background and Related Work

Stucki et al. [62] describe chatbots as computer-based technologies, which are able to hold a conversation with their users (chat) and autonomously perform certain tasks on command (bot). Users can interact with chatbots by using human natural language. Radziwill and Benton [51] equate chatbots with intelligent agents and assign them the adjectives autonomous, proactive, reactive and social. Machine learning technology enables chatbots to adapt their behavior to new information and user requirements [51]. Chatbots can be classified on the basis of two central criteria, the various usages and the functionality [62].

In terms of the usage, chatbots can be differentiated between task-/goal-oriented and not-task-/goal-oriented [35]. On the one hand, there are conversational chatbots that simulate human-like conversation and are only intended to serve social interaction, e.g. ELIZA [66], whereby a goal of lower complexity is pursued. It can be assumed, that this kind of chatbot or human-computer interaction does not represent a greater benefit for IT companies. On the other hand, chatbots work in a goal-oriented way and serve the purpose of supporting the user with helpful functions. The task fulfillment of these goal-oriented systems is therefore somewhat more complex. There are so-called informative bots that provide information and instructions on products, for example. According to Stucki et al. [62], some chatbots even have the ability to take over certain activities of their users, so-called transactional bots. However, these two types are not clearly separable and therefore there are some systems that both provide information and carry out transactions. Nevertheless, the technological basis is of great importance for the chatbot to complete such tasks.

The experiment described later in this paper explores the use of chatbots as a tool in IM. In the following, a few relevant terms are explained to give a better understanding of the application area of IM. According to Krcmar [39] the term'knowledge' in companies covers the contents of documents and databases, but also routines, practices, norms and processes. The relevance of a large knowledge base emerges due to the expansion of the product and service range and thus the amount of knowledge a company needs about customer processes and its own products [39]. Further, quick development of innovations, globalized structures and different international locations of companies require the usage and creation of knowledge at different locations. Additionally, fast changes and shortages of employees influence the knowledge base of companies as well [39]. Due to Koch et al. [38] IM can serve as opportunity to meet these challenges by imposing structured management on the knowledge base. The IM seeks to capture, process, store and deliver the right information at the right time and place [38].

2.1   Theories and Models

Technology Acceptance Model (TAM) Another theoretical basis is the Technology Acceptance Model (TAM) [18], which is a variation of the Theory of Reasoned Action Modell (TRA) [25] and is specifically adapted to user acceptance of information systems [20]. It enables prediction of whether a computer system will be accepted or rejected and identifies important factors that significantly influence the decision to use or not to use the system [18]. Furthermore, the model provides a theoretical basis for a method to test user satisfaction, which can serve as an important tool for system designers to improve computer programs such as chatbots [18]. Davis [18] further assumes that this belief is influenced by two factors: perceived usefulness of the system (PU) and perceived ease of use (PEOU). PU is defined as the extent to which a person believes that the system increases work performance. PEOU, on the other hand, describes the extent to which a person believes that a particular system does not require physical or mental effort. External variables, such as the design of the chatbot, determine the degree to which the two types of evaluation are expressed [18]. The TAM has been used and evaluated in several scientific works [9,17,31,47].

Information System Success Model (ISS) Delone and McLean [21] elaborated in the Information System Success Model (ISS) six dimensions for measuring the success of an information system based on Shannon and Weaver's communication theory [65] and the information'influence' theory [44]. These six variables of success measurement are: system quality, information quality, use, user satisfaction, individual impact, and organisational impact [21].

Uses and Gratification Theory (U&G) One theoretical basis to understand the motivation for using a chatbot is the Uses and Gratification Theory (U&G) [36]. It explains the psychological processes that influence people's decision on using a specific type of media. The theory tries to find answers to the questions of what people do with the media, how they use the media offerings and what role they play in their personal lives [37]. People do not simply use media randomly, there are purposeful selection processes that are influenced by social and psychological needs and gratifications [37]. Nowadays people can choose between a wide range of media offerings, e.g., websites, streaming services, apps and chatbots, which are accessible at any time. According to Katz et al. [37], the U&G theory states that users choose the medium that they expect will best satisfy their needs.

To identify needs and requirements for chatbots, Brandtzaeg and Følstad [12] asked 146 participants in their study about the main reason for using chatbots. As a result, they give the following categories of motivational motives: Productivity (68%), entertainment (20%), social or relationship-related intentions and curiosity (12%) [12]. Within the group that cited productivity as the main reason for use, particular reference was made to the simplicity, speed and convenience of chatbot use. Here, the quick help with problems (in the area of customer service) or answering FAQs by using the chatbot are valued. The results of Brandtzaeg and Følstad [12] make clear the high priority users attribute to a productivity-increasing use of chatbots and their function as information providers. According to this, chatbots should be able to solve user-relevant tasks and effectively support the achievement of a specific goal.

2.2   Related Work

Acceptance and success factors of chatbots: Jain et al. [33] elaborate based on quantitative and qualitative data analyses important factors to be considered in the design of chatbots for achieving a high user satisfaction. Jain et al. [33] claim that participants are often disappointed at the end of the study about the chatbots' performance due to high expectations. These high expectations can often result from the human-like conversation and contain wrong estimations of the lingual intelligence of the chatbot. Therefore, the authors [33] propose that the chatbot should present its technological abilities at the beginning of the interaction to keep the user expectations low. Additionally a constant and user-context adapted personality of the chatbot with small talk skills and humour are attributed a high value [33]. Several studies point out, that fun, humour, and sarcasm in chatbot interaction are perceived positive, whereas excessive friendliness is rated more negatively [41–43,46].

Chatbots and personality: Chaves and Gerosa [14] conclude that a constant personality of a chatbot can positively impact the believability and user engagement, strenghten the interpersonal relation, and increase the perceived humanness. Other authors [33,50] also emphasise the importance of a constant personality of chatbots. Schanke et al. [55] argue that aspects like user based customization or chatbot personality can have an impact on the user experience of chatbot interaction as well. Ruane et al. [54] claim that users estimate the personality of a chatbot, which imitates human behavior, based on its lingual or answering style. Shumanov and Johnson [56] show in their work, that humans not only are more talkable towards other people with a similar personality, but also towards chatbots with this characteristic. Smestad and Volden [58] investigated the effect of matching the personality of the chatbot with that of the user on the user experience. They used two chatbot agents with two personality levels. They show that depending on the context, the task to be performed and the user group, a chatbot personality has a significantly positive effect on the user experience. The experiment of Smestad and Volden [58] is in part similar to our approach due to the usage of two different chatbot personalities, where one is more talkative and emotional, and the other one gives more passive and objective answers. There are some studies, which indicate that the personality of a chatbot influences the user experience and is thus an important tool in the development and design of chatbots [54,58,63]. Furthermore, studies show that interaction with chatbot personalities is considered more pleasant [12,33]. Several other studies assume that social aspects play an important role in the design of chatbots to improve the user experience [12,13,26,58,62].

Chatbots and Information Management: Chatbots are a type of information system, they present information to the users in a fast and easy way and therefore represent an efficient alternative towards other time intensive ways to get information on a website [68]. However, they [68] also emphasise that people still need to get used to using chatbots for information search. In the IT domain users value speed and efficiency of chatbots the most [24]. Further, they [24] claim, that chatbots should show appropriate behavior according to the domain and offer the opportunity to contact human experts. Jenkins et al. [34] also conclude that users prefer to take the information they are looking for from short sentences of the chatbot rather than long paragraphs. This assumption is supported by the research work of Fiore et al. [24], in which a chatbot in IT support was examined with regard to its acceptance and user experience. The participants of this study show similarities with the user group of *avato* and the chatbot presented in this paper. But in general, little is known about the use of chatbots in IM and company intern chatbot assistants [24].

In the presented study we use the models TAM [19] and ISS [21] to evaluate the user satisfaction of the chatbot in terms of the variables information quality, service quality and system quality. As a further measure for the general user satisfaction the overall satisfaction scale by Spreng et al. [59] is used. The U&G [36] is used as a basis for evaluating the fun factor during a human-chatbot interaction, as it can also influence user satisfaction [12].

3 Concept

This chapter describes the hypotheses for the experimental study, the implementation of the chatbot and the concept for adapting the task-oriented personality, as well as the use case and the tasks for the study.

3.1 Hypotheses

As the current version, the social-oriented chatbot, often uses a lot of phrases around the requested information, the participants might get annoyed by that. Based on this, the theoretical background and related work we propose the following Hypotheses for our experimental study:

H1: The task-oriented chatbot is considered to have better information quality, system quality and service quality than the social-oriented chatbot.
   H1a: Users of the task-oriented chatbot are generally more satisfied with the interaction than users of the social-oriented chatbot.
H2: Interacting with a task-oriented chatbot is perceived as less entertaining than interacting with a social-oriented chatbot.
H3: A social-oriented chatbot shows higher interpersonal competence than a task-oriented chatbot.
   H3a: In IT support, users would be more likely to continue using a task-oriented chatbot than a social-oriented chatbot.
H4: The willingness to use a chatbot to solve more complex tasks is higher than for tasks of lower complexity.

3.2   Implementation of *Liibot*

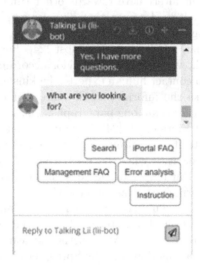

Fig. 1. Chat with *Liibot*. [4]

For our study we used the chatbot '*Liibot*' of the company *avato*, it is visually represented by the company's mascot, the animal *Lii* (see Fig. 1). Currently, the *Liibot* is an alpha version and is mainly used in the developer portal (*iPortal Stage*) for testing purposes. The study presented in this paper is intended to help guide further development in the right direction at an early stage. Therefore the chatbot is not available on the demo-portal *iPortal Innovators* or the customer-specific portals at the moment. However, it is envisaged that a revised version of the chatbot technology will be available there in the near future.

Users can interact with *Liibot* over written input and output, and pre-defined buttons within the chat. The *Liibot* consists of two types of functions. The technical functions ensure that information is delivered to the user at all. Content functions are responsible for what kind of information is displayed [5]. The design of the chatbot, like its functions, can be explained from two perspectives: technical and by content. The technical infrastructure is based on Botpress (version 12.10.6), a publicly available speech-based AI platform that can be used to create and design chatbots [3]. To enable humans to interact with a website via text or voice input, Botpress uses natural language processing (NLP), natural language understanding (NLU) and deep learning. The latter enables the system to constantly develop and improve its capabilities on its own [2]. The NLU module enables the identification of user inputs and assigns them to the corresponding intents [6]. If the chatbot is able to correctly capture the user intent, it can deliver the appropriate output. The content structure shows a division of the conversation into different sections (flows) [8]. There are a total of 14 inter-connected flows, each of which is used for different user intentions , e.g., they provide an answer to certain questions or offer help by completing certain tasks. The company *avato* itself interacts in the areas of IM, expertise as a service, smart data, and innovative concepts for clouds and system architecture. The main interaction goals of users in these fields of work are a rapid provision of help and an efficient search for information. As the *Liibot* provides help and advice for customers and employees, it can be considered as a chatbot in the area of customer support [27]. Based on the insights from the related work and the properties of the working area the existing *Liibot*, which can be described mainly as social-oriented chatbot, is compared with a task-oriented version in the described study. The task-oriented chatbot is intended to meet the requirements more effectively by pronouncing texts in a more software-like manner without using social phrases to make the requested information more prominent. There-fore, this version purely represents an informative bot.

3.3   Concept for Task-Oriented Chatbot Personality

The task-oriented chatbot differs only in its answering style. But even this can give the chatbot a new personality, according to Ruane et al. [54]. The answer style was changed manually in the already used plattform botpress [2]. These changes should strenghten the perception of the task-oriented chatbot as an efficient machine without social behavior. The task-oriented version uses more software-like and short sentences and renounces emojis. Further, it speaks of itself in third-person, because speaking in first-person singular and having a name could increase human-like perceptions by the user [7].

Further, in the dialogue box no dots for simulating human writing activity are displayed and thus providing no natural response delay. This is supported by the results of Gnewuch et al. [29], who state that graphical typing indicators can increase social presence of chatbots for unexperienced users. The profile picture of the *Lii* was kept static in the task-oriented version in order to prevent possible emotion attributions to the chatbot by the user. This means that *Lii*'s facial expressions or gestures do not change during the text-based dialogue. In the social-oriented version, however, *Lii*'s profile picture changes depending on the answer text. In addition, the adapted chatbot version does not contain long motivational or emotional text passages and therefore comes across as very pragmatic and task-oriented. Though the task-oriented chatbot version appears very mechanical, this behavior also represents one type of personality [58] (Table 1).

3.4   Use Case and Tasks

Based on personas and user needs described by *avato*, a use case was created for the experimental study. This was to help the participants identify with the actual user group. This can reduce a bias in the results that might arise from the participants, which might not fit perfectly in the intended user group. The

Table 1. Examples for answers of both chatbot versions.

Social-oriented Chatbot	Task-oriented Chatbot
Sure, I can help you search	Assistance available
Uhm... not sure what you mean... I could just search for "...". Or you could put it in other words, then I might get it	No information found. Phrase it a bit differently or continue search for "..."?
Uhm... Sorry, I have to improve my human language skills. For now... hm...	No information could be found due to comprehension problems.
Sorry, a mouse just ran by and distracted me. Where were we... Oh, I remember!	There was an internal server error. Please enter another input entry, or reset the session using the buttons at the top
Which option would you like me to explain to you?	For which option do you need an explanation?
Great! Happy to help you	Okey
Hi, I'm *Lii*. I can answer questions, search for pages, help you to analyze errors and assist in solving them	Hi. This Chatbot can - answer FAQ - help you find a page on a certain topic - assist in error analysis - provide step by step instructions for certain tasks

use case for the study is as follows: a manager is using the *iPortal* to identify its advantages and to get to know its functionalities so that the company can finally decide if they want to get the portal as a tool in the IM.

The tasks are based on possible activities of a manager exploring the portal and require the chatbot to perform its main functions, such as searching for information, answering FAQs, and providing step-by-step instructions. In addition, two English key terms (create and instruction) were added to the task descriptions . Similar to Duijst [22] the tasks are divided into three categories, which differ in their level of difficulty and complexity of finding a solution. The complexity of the tasks was estimated on the basis of possible solutions. The fewer ways exist to get to the page with the desired information, the more difficult it is. Therefore, all possible solution paths were worked out, e.g. via the menu or search bar, pop-ups on the homepage, FAQs and the chatbot. The appropriate tasks were then determined and finally tested in a pretest.

The final tasks are the following:

Low task complexity: Search for a definition of 'information management' and solutions if one forgot his password (FAQ).
Middle task complexity: Search for information about the chatbot and how to create information on the portal independently.

High task complexity: Search for information on how to get the portal for your company (step-by-step guide).

The classification in different levels of task complexity serves to examine the fourth hypothesis. Furthermore, the difficult tasks in particular can increase the likelihood of using the chatbot, in that it can provide good assistance alongside a few other possible solutions.

4 Method

Experimental Design. The experiment consists of two groups, an experimental group (task-oriented chatbot) and a control group (social-oriented chatbot). The effect of the manipulated chatbot in the experimental group (task-oriented chatbot) on several dependent variables (e.g., PU, PEOU, interpersonal competence, etc.) should be measured and compared with the data of the control group. Most of the participants are university student acquired through a university internal recruitment system. The experiment is conducted as a between-subjects design, each participant attends just once. The survey phases for both chatbot versions are timely separated. The social-oriented chatbot was tested in phase A and the task-oriented in phase B, the time between is used for switching the chatbot versions in the *iPortal Stage*. Participants are not informed about which condition they are in and how many conditions exist at all.

Questionnaires In order to ensure that the participants can cope with the English-language portal and interact with the chatbot, it was required that they have an English language level of at least A2. To check the English language level, the participants are provided with text descriptions for self-assessment of the language level (based on [1]). The necessity of the language level was derived from pilot studies, as otherwise unsufficient knowledge of the language could lead to difficulties in formulating suitable search terms and longer task completion times, which could cause frustration among the users.

For answering hypothesis 1, the models TAM [19] and ISS [21] are used, as they describe the variables information quality, service quality and system quality as important factors influencing user satisfaction. In addition, the overall satisfaction scale by Spreng et al. [59] serves as a further measure to test the general user satisfaction, which is intended to answer hypothesis 1a. For answering hypothesis 2, research based on the Uses and Gratifications Theory [36] is used as a basis, as it shows that besides a productive functioning of the chatbot, the fun factor during a human-chatbot interaction can also have an influence on user satisfaction [12]. The construct of perceived enjoyment during chatbot use is investigated using Cheng and Jiang's [15] scale. Based on the user data on perceived personality and behaviour, hypothesis 3 should be answered and different character traits will be identified for further evaluations. For this purpose, the scale by Skjuve and Brandzaeg [57] is used, which they adapted to the chatbot context and which is based on the scale by Hullman et al. [32] for measuring human interpersonal competence. In relation to hypothesis 1 and the models presented, we assume in hypothesis 3a that good information and service quality, as well as high perceived usefulness and ease of use, can have positive effects on reuse and usage intention [9]. The measurement of the willingness to use the chatbot again in the future is done with the help of a scale by Bhattacherjee [11]. The fourth and final hypothesis examines the use of chatbots in terms of possible task complexity and does not distinguish between the two groups. Therefore, this is examined on the basis of the entire sample, regardless of whether the chatbot is used in the study or not. According to Avula et al. [10] it is assumed that the probability of chatbot use increases with task complexity. We created an own 7-point Likert scale with three questions about chatbot usage depending on task complexity.

For the evaluation, the following scales were used to measure the constructs:

Information quality and system quality (H1): Perceived Usefulness and Ease of Use - original 7-point Likert scales of Davis [19] (reliability of $\alpha = .963$ (PU) and $\alpha = .903$)

Service quality (H1): 7-point Likert scale of Roca et al. [53] transferred to the context of chatbots by Ashfaq et al. [9] ($\alpha = .857$)

Overall satisfaction (H1a): Following the overall satisfaction scale by Spreng et al. [59], we used this scale as a 5-point Likert scale

Enjoyment (H2): 5-point Likert scale by Cheng and Jiang [15] ($\alpha = .830$)

Interpersonal Competence (H3): 5-point Likert scale for interpersonal competence of humans by Hullman et al. [32] transferred to chatbots by Skjuve and Brandtzaeg [57] ($\alpha = .895$)

Continuance Intention (H3a): 7-point Likert scale by Bhattacherjee [11] ($\alpha = .826$)

Task complexity (H4): Own generated 7-point Likert scale with three questions about chatbot usage depending task complexity - based on assumption of Avula et al. [10]

The User Experience Questionnaire (UEQ) by Laugwitz et al. [40] was used for the participants who do not use the chatbot for task completion and will evaluate the *iPortal* instead of the chatbot. The questionnaire captures important aspects of usability and user experience on a scale consisting of 26 bipolar items in the form of a 7-level semantic differential.

Setup The experiment is being conducted as an online study in telepresence due to the COVID-19 pandemic. This means that the participants answer the questionnaire online and are in a Zoom[1] meeting during the interaction with the chatbot and the task execution. Through the zoom meeting, the experimenter can observe the interaction and take notes. If the participants' solution of a task is correct, the experimenter also gives feedback via the Zoom on-screen comment function. Although social desirability bias cannot be completely eliminated, it is reduced by disabling the camera of both participants and the experimenter. The interaction of the chatbot takes place in the development environment *iPortal*

---

[1] https://zoom.us.

Stage, which is very similar in structure and content to *iPortal Innovators*, which is planned as the future place of use. The tasks as well as the experiment design were tested in advance with small pilot studies.

Procedure (1) The participants receive an email with the link of the first part of the questionnaire in advance to their timeslots. The first part includes consent forms for data collection and participation to the study, the self-assessment of the own english language level, as well as the experience with and attitude towards chatbots. (2) After answering the first part, further descriptions about the study procedure, use case and tasks are given. Then the participants are asked to login to the *iPortal* with a given account and join a Zoom-meeting with the experimenter. (3) To make the evaluation more natural and pleasant and to ensure more data protection for the recordings, the subjects are inquired to deactivate their camera and the experimenter pseudonymises the name. (4) After a short verbal instruction given by the researcher in the Zoom-meeting, the participants are asked to share their screen and work on the given tasks. Through the shared screen the experimenter is able to observe the task execution and take notes about the chatbot interaction. As soon as the participants find a correct solution for a task the experimenter gives feedback through the screen commenting function of Zoom. (5) After the task execution the participants leave the Zoom meeting and continue with the second part of the questionnaire, where they assess the interaction with the chatbot. (5a) The participants are free in the decision of using the chatbot or not to make the usage more natural. If the chatbot isn't used at all by a participant, this participant is forwarded to another questionnaire to make an overall rating of the *iPortal* instead of rating the chatbot. Thus, the reliability of the chatbot data is increased as these participants do not evaluate a system (chatbot) that they have never used [52].

5   Results

In total, 80 participants (77 university students acquired through a university internal recruitment system, and 3 employees of *avato*) took part in the study, of which 72.5% were female (n = 58) and 27.5% were male (n = 22) with an average age of 23 years (M = 22.63, SD = 5.07, 18–55 years). All participants fulfilled english language level requirements (A2), most participants rated themselves at a B2 level (33.8 %). Nine (n = 9) of all participants did not use the chatbot at all and received the UE scale to rate the *iPortal* in the second part of the questionnaire.

In the experiment, 71 of the participants (69 university students and 2 employees of *avato*) interacted during task execution at least once with the chatbot and answered the questionnaires related to the chatbot interaction. The control group (social-oriented chatbot) comprised 38 participants (27 female and 11 male) with an average age of 23 years (M = 22.87, SD = 4.71, 18–46 years). The experimental group (task-oriented chatbot) containing 33 participants (25 female, 8 male) had an average age of 21.5 years (M = 21.48, SD = 1.70, 18–26 years). The sample values can be also found in Table 2.

Table 2. Overview of demographic data for the chatbot evaluation.

	All participants	Chatbot-Users	Control group (social-oriented)	Experimental group (task-oriented)
Total number of participants	80	71	38	33
Female	58	52	27	25
Male	22	19	11	8
Average age	22.62	22.23	22.87	21.48
Standard deviation	5.07	3.68	4.71	1.70
Range (min-max)	18–55	18–46	18–46	18–26

According to hypothesis 1, it is assumed that the task-oriented chatbot will be attributed better at information quality, service quality and system quality compared to the social-oriented chatbot. A higher rating on the Usefulness scale stands for a higher information quality and a higher rating on the Ease of Use scale for a higher system quality. Since the Levene test for the two variables Usefulness (p = .66) and Ease of Use (p = .25) did not become significant (p ≥ .05), an equality of variance can be assumed. A one-sided t-test for independent samples showed that the users of the task-oriented chatbot (M = 4.63, SD = 1.50) did not attribute a significantly (t (69) = 0.01, p =.495) higher information quality (PU scale) to it than the users of the social-oriented chatbot (M = 4.64, SD = 1.53). The results for the dependent variables can be also found in Table 3. The same was found in the test comparing system quality (PEOU scale) of task-oriented chatbot (M = 4.9, SD = 1.47) and social-oriented chatbot (M = 4.56, SD = 1.17), (t (69) = 1.02, p = .155). When comparing the mean values of the service quality scale, Levene's test resulted in a significant p-value of .029, which led to the application of the Wilcoxon test (W-test) due to the variance heterogeneity thus given. However, the users of the task-oriented chatbot did not rate it significantly better (t (68) = 2.06, p = .022), as expected, but worse (M = 4.33, SD = 1.01) than the users of the social-oriented chatbot (M = 4.89, SD = 1.31). Hypothesis 1 must therefore be rejected and the opposite must even be assumed for the aspect of service quality.

Hypothesis 1a, which results from the first hypothesis, assumes that users of the task-oriented chatbot are generally more satisfied with the interaction than those of the social-oriented chatbot. Here, the Levene test was significant (p= .05) as well. However, based on the results of the calculated W-test, no significant difference (t(69) = 0.96, p = .171) between the overall satisfaction of the two groups social-oriented (M = 3.28, SD = 1.01) and task-oriented (M = 3.08, SD = 0.81) could be determined. Hypothesis 1a must therefore be rejected.

The interaction with a task-oriented chatbot (M = 2.29, SD = 0.68) was less entertaining than interacting with a social-oriented chatbot (M = 2.70, SD = 0.88). We proved the variance homogenity with a Levene-test, which turned out not being significant. Therefore, we carried out a one-sided t-test, which shows a

Table 3. Results of dependent variables (* **significant, if p** < **.05**).

Dep. var.	Range of	Control group (social-oriented)		Experimental group (task-oriented)		t	df	p-value
	Likert- Scale	M	SD	M	SD			
Information quality - (PU)	1–7	4.64	1.53	4.63	1.50	0.01	69	.495
System quality - (PEOU)	1–7	4.89	1.47	4.56	1.17	1.02	69	.155
Service quality	1–7	4.89	1.31	4.33	1.01	2.06	68	.022*
Overall Satisfaction	1–5	3.28	1.01	3.08	0.81	0.96	69	.171
Enjoyment	1–5	2.70	0.88	2.29	0.68	2.18	69	.017*
Interpersonal Competence	1–5	2.89	0.57	2.56	0.53	2.46	69	.008*
Continuance Intention	1–7	4.32	1.57	3.96	1.45	1.01	69	.158

significant difference (t (69) = 2.18, p = .017) between both groups and supports the assumption of hypothesis 2.

A significantly (t (69) = 2.46, p = .008) higher interpersonal competence is attributed to a social-oriented chatbot (M = 2.89, SD = 0.57) than to a task-oriented chatbot (M = 2.56, SD = 0.53). For this reason, hypothesis 3 can be accepted.

However, the resulting hypothesis 3a could not be confirmed. In the IT domain, the continuance intention of a task-oriented chatbot (M = 3.96, SD = 1.45) is not significantly higher than for a social-oriented chatbot (M = 4.32, SD = 1.57). A task-oriented chatbot is not necessarily preferred in the IT domain.

For proving the fourth hypothesis we performed three independent two-sampled t-tests with the whole sample (n = 80). In terms of willingness to use a chatbot depending on task complexity, descriptive statistics show that the willingness to use is rather low for low task complexity (M = 3.61, SD = 2.04, 95% CI [3.16, 4.07]). It is significantly lower (t(140) = -2.73, p = 0.007) than for medium task complexity (M = 4.43, SD = 1.49, 95% CI [4.09, 4.76]). The willingness to use a chatbot to find a solution is highest for high task complexity (M = 4.80, SD = 1.93, 95% CI [4.37, 5.23]) and thus, significantly higher (t(140) = -3.57, p = 0.0005) than for low task complexity. Therefore, Hypothesis 4 can be confirmed as true, when comparing low task complexity with medium or high task complexity. Between medium and high task complexity there is no significant difference (t(140) = -1.28, p = 0.20).

But it has to be reported, that the participants used the full range of the Likert scale from 1 to 7 in their assessment of chatbot use in terms of task complexity. Most of the means and confidence intervals are around the neutral scale value, just the values of the high complexity is outside the neutral area.

6   Discussion and Limitations

The non-significant difference between the two chatbot versions in terms of information and system quality shows that perceived usefulness and usability are less dependent on personality than assumed. Furthermore, a task-oriented chatbot seems to have a lower rather than higher quality of service, which not only rejects the related hypothesis, but even supports a contrary assumption. The results also give no indication that interaction with the task-oriented chatbot leads to greater general satisfaction among users. On the basis of the mean values, a tendency towards higher satisfaction with the social-oriented chatbot can even be recognised. Therefore, it could be possible that the interaction with the social-oriented chatbot could be more entertaining. This would underline a positive effect of small talk skills and humour [33].

The study setting ensured high external validity [23] by testing the chatbot in a very similar environment (*iPortal Stage*) in which it is to be used in the future (*iPortal Innovators*).

Contrary to our expectations the task-oriented chatbot cannot be assumed to be better suited for this area of work than the social-oriented version. Since the chatbot of this study is currently an alpha version and still in development process, some inconsistent functional errors might have influenced or distorted the results. Nevertheless, the results are very useful for further developing the chatbot in the right direction, as early testing also brings earlier insights into the user experience. The specific use case with persona and predefined tasks could help the participants to identify with a specific user group. But as the participants were mostly university students, they nevertheless might not fit perfectly in the intended user group. Therefore additional research with more participants fitting the specified user group is needed.

Additionally, a language barrier could have influenced the experiment and results as well, since the participants had to solve the tasks within the portal and the chatbot in a familiar but foreign language. Although the descriptive statistics show that all participants met the minimum requirement of an A2 English level, only a few indicated a C2 level, which would be comparable to that of native speakers. Since the chatbot required self-written text input, this could cause frustration due to a limited vocabulary of some participants and might have influenced the ratings and results.

7   Conclusion

In this study, we investigated two different chatbot personalities in the IM sector, where the motives for using chatbots are primarily focused on efficiency and productivity. With evaluating the more social-oriented alpha version of the *Liibot* of the IT company *avato* compared with a more task-oriented version we examined the influence of different chatbot personalities on the user. The evaluation was conducted online as a between-subjects design and included 2 groups with a total number of 80 participants. We show with our results, that small changes in the linguistic answering style of the chatbot lead to a significantly different assessment of interpersonal competence and enjoyment. For information and system quality no significant difference between the two chatbot versions could be found. Whereas the task-oriented chatbot was rated significantly worse at service quality than the social-oriented chatbot. The level of task complexity makes a significantly difference for the willingness to use a chatbot, which confirms the findings of Avula et al. [10]. In summary, a task-oriented chatbot is not rated significantly better in this case and in some aspects rated even worse, which does not confirm the assumption of preferring a task-oriented chatbot over a social-oriented personality.

With our research, we have contributed to the understanding of how to improve the interaction with chatbots and filled another research gap regarding the user experience of chatbots in IM. But due to small inconsistencies and the need for larger samples in intended user groups in the final field of use of the chatbot, further research will still be necessary.

Due to some functional errors, appearing at the current alpha-version of the chatbot, a study with the same or similar study design, but with improved chatbot versions, should be considered. To get more valid results, we propose to run a similar study but with a bigger and more user-group related sample.

As the presented experimental study gave the participants the freedom of choice whether to use the chatbot or not, a mandatory usage of the chatbot would increase its interaction time. This could draw the participants attention more on the researched technology and lead to more valuable results.

Another approach would be to compare proactive versus reactive chatbot behaviour in the IT domain. From many websites, such as online shops, blogs, customer support sites, we often know a more proactive behaviour, where the chat window pops up after a short time or the chatbot moves or "knocks". This proactive behaviour can increase the frequency and time of chatbot interaction, but, e.g., in the area of IM, it could also have effects on the effectiveness and efficiency of the user's task completion.

When the chatbot should then act proactively or reactively is another point that could also be investigated. Therefore, future work could also build on concepts that try to recognise when a user needs help or in which context the user interacts [33]. Approaches to this could include tracking scrolling and clicking behaviour and the search queries made by the user. By successfully recognising when the user needs help, productivity and efficiency could be increased and the chatbot interaction could become more user-centred.

References

1. Selbsteinschätzung des Sprachniveaus - Universität Koblenz · Landau. https://www.uni-koblenz-landau.de/de/usz/tandem/sprachnivieau
2. All you need to know about conversational AI platforms - Botpress (2020). https://botpress.com/blog/all-you-need-to-know-about-conversational-ai-platforms
3. Developer Stack to Build Chatbots - Botpress (2020). https://botpress.com/
4. avato consulting AG (2021). https://www.avato-consulting.com/

5. Liibot Overview - iPortal (2021). https://iportal-innovators.avato.net/content/technical-documentation/avato-iportal/liibot-overview/
6. NLU - Developer's Guide (2021). https://botpress.com/docs/
7. Adam, M., Wessel, M., Benlian, A.: AI-based chatbots in customer service and their effects on user compliance. Electron. Markets **31**(2), 427–445 (2020). https://doi.org/10.1007/s12525-020-00414-7
8. avato consulting ag: Liibot conversation flows - iPortal innovators (2021). https://iportal-innovators.avato.net/content/technical-documentation/avato-iportal/liibot-overview/liibot-conversation-flows/
9. Ashfaq, M., Yun, J., Yu, S., Loureiro, S.: I, Chatbot: modeling the determinants of users' satisfaction and continuance intention of AI-powered service agents. Telemat. Inf. (2020). https://doi.org/10.1016/j.tele.2020.101473
10. Avula, S., Chadwick, G., Arguello, J., Capra, R.: SearchBots: user engagement with ChatBots during collaborative search. In: Proceedings of the 2018 Conference on Human Information Interaction & Retrieval. CHIIR '18, ACM (2018). https://doi.org/10.1145/3176349.3176380
11. Bhattacherjee, A.: Understanding information systems continuance: an expectation-confirmation model. MIS Q. **25**(3) (2001). https://doi.org/10.2307/3250921
12. Brandtzaeg, P.B., Følstad, A.: Why people use chatbots. In: Kompatsiaris, I., et al. (eds.) INSCI 2017. LNCS, vol. 10673, pp. 377–392. Springer, Cham (2017). https://doi.org/10.1007/978-3-319-70284-1_30
13. Brandtzaeg, P.B., Følstad, A.: Chatbots - changing user needs and motivations. Interactions **25**(5) (2018). https://doi.org/10.1145/3236669
14. Chaves, A.P., Gerosa, M.A.: How should my chatbot interact? A survey on social characteristics in human-chatbot interaction design. Int. J. Hum.-Comput. Interact. (2020). https://doi.org/10.1080/10447318.2020.1841438
15. Cheng, Y., Jiang, H.: AI-Powered mental health chatbots: examining users' motivations, active communicative action and engagement after mass-shooting disasters. J. Contingencies Crisis Manage. **28**(3) (2020). https://doi.org/10.1111/1468-5973.12319
16. Chung, M., Ko, E., Joung, H., Kim, S.J.: Chatbot e-service and customer satisfaction regarding luxury brands. J. Bus. Res. 117 (2020). https://doi.org/10.1016/j.jbusres.2018.10.004
17. Dasgupta, S., Granger, M., McGarry, N.: User acceptance of e-collaboration technology: an extension of the technology acceptance model. Group Decis. Negot. (2002). https://doi.org/10.1023/A:1015221710638
18. Davis, F.D.: A technology acceptance model for empirically testing new end-user information systems: theory and results. PhD Thesis, MIT (1986)
19. Davis, F.D.: Perceived usefulness, perceived ease of use, and user acceptance of information technology. MIS Q. (1989). https://doi.org/10.2307/249008
20. Davis, F.D., Bagozzi, R., Warshaw, P.: User acceptance of computer technology: a comparison of two theoretical models. Manage. Sci. (1989). https://doi.org/10.1287/mnsc.35.8.982
21. Delone, W., McLean, E.: Information systems success: the quest for the dependent variable. Inf. Syst. Res. (1992). https://doi.org/10.1287/isre.3.1.60
22. Duijst, D.: Can we improve the user experience of chatbots with personalisation? PhD Thesis, University of Amsterdam (2017)
23. Döring, N., Bortz, J.: Untersuchungsdesign. In: Forschungsmethoden und Evaluation in den Sozial- und Humanwissenschaften. S, pp. 181–220. Springer, Heidelberg (2016). https://doi.org/10.1007/978-3-642-41089-5_7

24. Fiore, D., Baldauf, M., Thiel, C.: "Forgot your password again?": acceptance and user experience of a chatbot for in-company IT support. In: Proceedings of the 18th International Conference on Mobile and Ubiquitous Multimedia. ACM (2019). https://doi.org/10.1145/3365610.3365617

25. Fishbein, M., Ajzen, I.: Belief, attitude, intention and behaviour: an introduction to theory and research, vol. 27. Addison-Wesley (1975)

26. Følstad, A., Brandtzaeg, P.B.: Users' experiences with chatbots: findings from a questionnaire study. Qual. User Experience 5(1), 1–14 (2020). https://doi.org/10.1007/s41233-020-00033-2

27. Følstad, A., Skjuve, M., Brandtzaeg, P.B.: Different chatbots for different purposes: towards a typology of chatbots to understand interaction design. In: Bodrunova, S.S., et al. (eds.) INSCI 2018. LNCS, vol. 11551, pp. 145–156. Springer, Cham (2019). https://doi.org/10.1007/978-3-030-17705-8_13

28. Følstad, A., Taylor, C.: Conversational repair in chatbots for customer service: the effect of expressing uncertainty and suggesting alternatives. In: Følstad, A., et al. (eds.) CONVERSATIONS 2019. LNCS, vol. 11970, pp. 201–214. Springer, Cham (2020). https://doi.org/10.1007/978-3-030-39540-7_14

29. Gnewuch, U., Morana, S., Adam, M.T.P., Maedche, A.: "The Chatbot is typing …" - The role of typing indicators in human-chatbot interaction. In: Proceedings of the 17th Annual Pre-ICIS Workshop on HCI Research in MIS (2018). https://publikationen.bibliothek.kit.edu/1000089971

30. van der Goot, M.J., Pilgrim, T.: Exploring age differences in motivations for and acceptance of chatbot communication in a customer service context. In: Følstad, A., et al. (eds.) CONVERSATIONS 2019. LNCS, vol. 11970, pp. 173–186. Springer, Cham (2020). https://doi.org/10.1007/978-3-030-39540-7_12

31. Huang, D.H., Chueh, H.E.: Chatbot usage intention analysis: veterinary consultation. J. Innov. Knowl. (2020). https://doi.org/10.1016/j.jik.2020.09.002

32. Hullman, G.A., Planisek, A., McNally, J.S., Rubin, R.B.: Competence, personality, and self-efficacy: relationships in an undergraduate interpersonal course. Atlantic J. Commun. (2010). https://doi.org/10.1080/15456870903340506

33. Jain, M., Kumar, P., Kota, R., Patel, S.N.: Evaluating and informing the design of chatbots. In: Proceedings of the 2018 Designing Interactive Systems Conference. DIS '18, ACM (2018). https://doi.org/10.1145/3196709.3196735

34. Jenkins, M.-C., Churchill, R., Cox, S., Smith, D.: Analysis of user interaction with service oriented chatbot systems. In: Jacko, J.A., et al. (eds.) HCI 2007. LNCS, vol. 4552, pp. 76–83. Springer, Heidelberg (2007). https://doi.org/10.1007/978-3-540-73110-8_9

35. Jurafsky, D., Martin, J.: Speech and language processing: an introduction to natural language processing, computational linguistics, and speech recognition. Prentice Hall (2008)

36. Katz, E., Foulkes, D.: On the use of the mass media as "escape": clarification of a concept. Public Opinion Q. (1962). https://doi.org/10.1086/267111

37. Katz, E., Gurevitch, M., Haas, H.: On the use of the mass media for important things. Am. Sociol. Rev. (1973)

38. Koch, M., Morar, D., Kemper, H.G.: Definition: informationsmanagement (2020). https://www.gabler-banklexikon.de/definition/informationsmanagement-70784/version-377507

39. Krcmar, H.: Begriffe und Definitionen. In: Informationsmanagement, pp. 11–29. Springer, Heidelberg (2015). https://doi.org/10.1007/978-3-662-45863-1_2

40. Laugwitz, B., Schrepp, M., Held, T.: Konstruktion eines Fragebogens zur Messung der User Experience von Softwareprodukten. In: Mensch & Computer 2006 - Mensch und Computer im Strukturwandel. Oldenbourg Wissenschaftsverlag (2006)

41. Liao, Q.V., Davis, M., Geyer, W., Muller, M., Shami, N.S.: What Can You Do? Studying socia-agent orientation and agent proactive interactions with an agent for employees. In: Proceedings of the 2016 ACM Conference on Designing Interactive Systems. DIS '16, ACM (2016). https://doi.org/10.1145/2901790.2901842

42. Liao, Q.V., et al.: All work and no play? Conversations with a question-and-answer chatbot in the wild. In: Proceedings of the 2018 Conference on Human Factors in Computing Systems. CHI '18, ACM (2018). https://doi.org/10.1145/3173574.3173577

43. Luger, E., Sellen, A.: "Like Having a Really Bad PA": the gulf between user expectation and experience of conversational agents. In: Proceedings of the 2016 CHI Conference on Human Factors in Computing Systems. CHI '16, ACM (2016). https://doi.org/10.1145/2858036.2858288

44. Mason, R.O.: Measuring information output: a communication systems approach. Inf. Manage. (1978). https://doi.org/10.1016/0378-7206(78)90028-9

45. McAllister, P., et al.: Towards chatbots to support bibliotherapy preparation and delivery. In: Følstad, A., et al. (eds.) CONVERSATIONS 2019. LNCS, vol. 11970, pp. 127–142. Springer, Cham (2020). https://doi.org/10.1007/978-3-030-39540-7_9

46. Medhi Thies, I., Menon, N., Magapu, S., Subramony, M., O'Neill, J.: How do you want your chatbot? An exploratory wizard-of-oz study with young, Urban Indians. In: Bernhaupt, R., Dalvi, G., Joshi, A., Balkrishan, D.K., O'Neill, J., Winckler, M. (eds.) INTERACT 2017. LNCS, vol. 10513, pp. 441–459. Springer, Cham (2017). https://doi.org/10.1007/978-3-319-67744-6_28

47. Money, W., Turner, A.: Application of the technology acceptance model to a knowledge management system. In: 37th Annual Hawaii International Conference on System Sciences, 2004. Proceedings of the. Institute of Electrical and Electronics Engineers (2004). https://doi.org/10.1109/HICSS.2004.1265573

48. Müller, L., Mattke, J., Maier, C., Weitzel, T.: Conversational agents in healthcare: using QCA to explain patients' resistance to chatbots for medication. In: Følstad, A., et al. (eds.) CONVERSATIONS 2019. LNCS, vol. 11970, pp. 3–18. Springer, Cham (2020). https://doi.org/10.1007/978-3-030-39540-7_1

49. Nordberg, O.E., et al.: Designing chatbots for guiding online peer support conversations for adults with ADHD. In: Følstad, A., et al. (eds.) CONVERSATIONS 2019. LNCS, vol. 11970, pp. 113–126. Springer, Cham (2020). https://doi.org/10.1007/978-3-030-39540-7_8

50. Norman, D.A.: Emotional Design: Why We Love (or Hate) Everyday Things, vol. 27. Basic Books, New York City (2004)

51. Radziwill, N., Benton, M.: Evaluating quality of chatbots and intelligent conversational agents. Software Quality Professional (2017)

52. Reinders, H.: Fragebogen. In: Empirische Bildungsforschung: Strukturen und Methoden. VS Verlag für Sozialwissenschaften (2011). https://doi.org/10.1007/978-3-531-93015-2_4

53. Roca, J., Chiu, C.M., Martínez López, F.: Understanding e-learning continuance intention: an extension of the technology acceptance model. Int. J. Hum.-Comput. Stud. (2006). https://doi.org/10.1016/j.ijhcs.2006.01.003

54. Ruane, E., Farrell, S., Ventresque, A.: User perception of text-based chatbot personality. In: Følstad, A., et al. (eds.) CONVERSATIONS 2020. LNCS, vol. 12604, pp. 32–47. Springer, Cham (2021). https://doi.org/10.1007/978-3-030-68288-0_3

55. Schanke, S., Burtch, G., Ray, G.: Estimating the impact of "humanizing" customer service chatbots. Inf. Syst. Res. (2021). https://doi.org/10.1287/isre.2021.1015
56. Shumanov, M., Johnson, L.: Making conversations with chatbots more personalized. Comput. Hum. Behav. (2021). https://doi.org/10.1016/j.chb.2020.106627
57. Skjuve, M., Brandzaeg, P.B.: Measuring user experience in chatbots: an approach to interpersonal communication competence. In: Bodrunova, S.S., et al. (eds.) INSCI 2018. LNCS, vol. 11551, pp. 113–120. Springer, Cham (2019). https://doi.org/10.1007/978-3-030-17705-8_10
58. Smestad, T.L., Volden, F.: Chatbot personalities matters. In: Bodrunova, S.S., et al. (eds.) INSCI 2018. LNCS, vol. 11551, pp. 170–181. Springer, Cham (2019). https://doi.org/10.1007/978-3-030-17705-8_15
59. Spreng, R.A., MacKenzie, S.B., Olshavsky, R.W.: A reexamination of the determinants of consumer satisfaction. J. Market. **60**(3) (1996). https://doi.org/10.2307/1251839
60. Statista: Anzahl der Smartphone-Nutzer in Deutschland (2021). https://de.statista.com/statistik/daten/studie/198959/umfrage/anzahl-der-smartphonenutzer-in-deutschland-seit-2010/
61. Statista: Apps - Beliebteste im Google Play Store nach Downloads weltweit 2021 (2021). https://de.statista.com/statistik/daten/studie/688608/umfrage/beliebteste-apps-im-google-play-store-nach-downloads-weltweit/
62. Stucki, T., D'Onofrio, S., Portmann, E.: Theoretische grundlagen zu chatbots. In: Chatbots gestalten mit Praxisbeispielen der Schweizerischen Post, pp. 3–10. Springer, Wiesbaden (2020). https://doi.org/10.1007/978-3-658-28586-9_2
63. Verhagen, T., van Nes, J., Feldberg, F., van Dolen, W.: Virtual customer service agents: using social presence and personalization to shape online service encounters*. J. Comput.-Mediated Commun. **19**(3) (2014). https://doi.org/10.1111/jcc4.12066
64. Väänänen, K., Hiltunen, A., Varsaluoma, J., Pietilä, I.: CivicBots – chatbots for supporting youth in societal participation. In: Følstad, A., et al. (eds.) CONVERSATIONS 2019. LNCS, vol. 11970, pp. 143–157. Springer, Cham (2020). https://doi.org/10.1007/978-3-030-39540-7_10
65. Weaver, W.: The mathematics of communication. Sci. Am. **181**(1) (1949)
66. Weizenbaum, J.: ELIZA - A computer program for the study of natural language communication between man and machine. Commun. ACM (1966). https://doi.org/10.1145/365153.365168
67. Meyer von Wolff, R., Nörtemann, J., Hobert, S., Schumann, M.: Chatbots for the information acquisition at universities – a student's view on the application area. In: Følstad, A., et al. (eds.) CONVERSATIONS 2019. LNCS, vol. 11970, pp. 231–244. Springer, Cham (2020). https://doi.org/10.1007/978-3-030-39540-7_16
68. Zumstein, D., Hundertmark, S.: Chatbots - An interactive technology for personalized communication transactions and services. IADIS Int. J. WWW/Internet **15** (2017)

Open-Domain Dialogue Management Framework Across Multiple Device for Long-Term Interaction

Shin Katayama[✉][iD], Nozomi Hayashida, Kenta Urano, Takuro Yonezawa, and Nobuo Kawaguchi

Graduate School of Engineering, Nagoya University, Furo-cho, Chikusa-ku, Nagoya, Aichi, Japan
{shinsan,linda}@ucl.nuee.nagoya-u.ac.jp,
{urano,takuro,kawaguti}@nagoya-u.jp

Abstract. This study explores the feasibility of dialogue systems with individuality capable of providing continuous and lasting assistance via a multiple device dialogue system. A framework has been devised to manage dialogue history, allowing for the use of a singular identity across various interfaces, including chatbots and virtual avatars. This framework can summarize and save the dialogue history, which can be utilized to generate responses. The impact of dialogue history sharing on users' interactions with a particular character across various devices was assessed for naturalness, continuity, and reliability. The results indicate that dialogue history sharing can foster more natural and continuous conversations, thereby enhancing the potential for long-term support. This research advances the proposition that a digital agent endowed with a consistent identity across multiple devices can provide personalized and sustained support to users.

Keywords: Dialogue Systems · Dialogue Generation · Dialogue Summarization

1 Introduction

In modern society, the ownership of multiple information terminals by individuals has become a noticeable trend. This can be observed through the common ownership of a variety of devices including smartphones, PCs, wearables, smart speakers, head-mounted displays (HMDs), and robots by users. Natural and human-like dialogue systems have extensive applications in mental health care and education, as they can act as conversational partners instead of humans. However, current dialogue systems on each device operate with distinct identities presenting a challenge for achieving sustained, long-term interaction with a dialogue system, given time and location constraints. Conversely, human-to-human conversations foster enduring relationships through face-to-face communication, online chats, or video calls, facilitating interaction as the same individual and building social

M. Kurosu and A. Hashizume (Eds.): HCII 2023, LNCS 14013, pp. 354–365, 2023.
https://doi.org/10.1007/978-3-031-35602-5_25

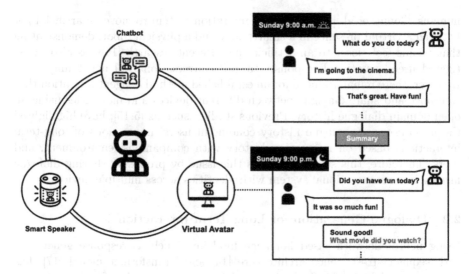

Fig. 1. The concept of dialogue framework across multiple devices.

connections through continuous engagement. To address this challenge, this study proposes a dialogue framework that enables sharing a singular identity across multiple devices, such as smartphones, smart speakers, and robots, by summarizing and sharing dialogue history and generating responses incorporating this information. Figure 1 illustrates our concept. Sharing dialogue history among devices can promote sustained relationships and provide ongoing support. The study employs user experiments to evaluate the effect of sharing dialogue history across multiple devices and investigates the following research questions:

1. Can users perceive a consistent identity when interacting with the system across different devices?
2. Can sharing dialogue history enable more natural dialogues?
3. What information is critical for maintaining social relationships?

2   Related Research

2.1   Agent Migration

Previous research has investigated interactive systems with identities across multiple devices. Early studies proposed agent migration methods [7] that allow an agent to transition between a mobile PC and a self-contained mobile robot. Subsequent investigations have explored agents with personalities across different forms and interactions with virtual characters in human-computer interaction and human-robot interaction [1,6,8]. Ogawa et al. [11] proposed the ITACO system, a migratable agent that can move between robots, table lamps, and other entities and build emotional relationships between interactive systems and humans. Gomes et al. [4] developed a migration system to move an artificial pet between a virtual presence in a smartphone and a physical robot, demonstrating that people feel closer to an artificial pet. Recent research [16] has also investigated users' emotional responses toward conversational AI agent migration. However, there remains a need for an established method of agent migration that can move and share dialogue between different devices and modalities using an open domain dialogue history. Previous studies, such as [5,15], have highlighted the importance of dialogue history content in users' impressions of long-term interactions based on interaction history with companions, environment, and users. Therefore, this study addresses this issue by proposing sharing dialogue history in a conversational system with identities across multiple devices.

2.2 Dialogue Generation for Long-Term Interaction

Using neural network-based language modeling, such as response generation with sequence-to-sequence architecture [14] and Transformer model [17], has become prevalent in the field of natural language processing for dialogue system response generation. Although current open-domain dialogue systems cannot fully replicate smooth and accurate conversations like humans, advances in machine and deep learning techniques have enabled human-like conversations under limited conditions. However, maintaining consistency in personality is challenging for these generative methods. Therefore, research has focused on persona dialogue tasks, which aim to generate consistent responses in line with the persona by incorporating profile information into neural dialogue generation [19,20]. Existing approaches to persona dialogue systems attempt to incorporate several phrases as an explicit system profile. Consistent response methods have been proposed using speaker identification models [12] and long-term persona memory extraction and continuous updating methods [18]. In addition to having a persona for long-term interaction, considering past conversation history to maintain consistency in dialogue is also essential for enhancing identity. To construct a personalized chatbot, research has proposed methods to automatically learn implicit user profiles from large-scale user dialogue history [13], extract user profiles from dialogue history [21], and summarize dialogue history [2]. Therefore, we propose summarization in this study to share dialogue history between multiple devices. Given the vast amount of dialogue history, it is challenging to consider all of it. Architectures with fixed input lengths limit the length of inputs during response generation, making it impossible to address this issue. In this study, dialogue history is summarized by topic and managed to enable consideration of the summarized dialogue history in new dialogue sessions.

3   Methodology

This study evaluates the hypothesis that is sharing dialogue history among multiple devices will result in more natural dialogue and a sense of identification with the system. In this section, we construct a dialogue management framework for this evaluation and describe the design and implementation of a user study.

3.1 System Overview

Purpose. Traditional dialogue systems face the challenge of limited location and timing for each dialogue interface, which prevents the system from achieving continuous and long-term interaction. In addition, since each interface has a separate identity, dialogue history is not shared. We develop a prototype dialogue management framework to share dialogue history across multiple interfaces to address this problem.

Design. As a potential use case for the dialogue system in this study, sharing dialogue history among multiple devices allows continuous dialogue, even over time. Therefore, this study adopts two dialogue interfaces, a virtual avatar, and a text chatbot, and conducts an experiment where they communicate as a single identity. The dialogues targeted in this study are open-domain dialogues, and the dialogue sessions in daily life are set when the user wakes up in the morning and goes to bed at night. Users will be asked to converse three pre-set topics: plan to do today, plan to go today, and plan to eat today, and to interact around these in the morning session and around their thoughts on the topic in the night session. Discussing their daily plan and related feelings on multiple devices makes it possible to maintain continuity and achieve a natural dialogue with a virtual avatar or a text chatbot.

3.2 Implementation

We propose a dialogue framework that enables the sharing dialogue history across multiple devices. The framework is designed to provide the necessary functionalities for the experiment and enable participants to have a seamless conversation experience. It can be applied to various devices, such as virtual agents and chatbots, and can summarize the dialogue history and generate responses based on it. The dialogue management framework consists of two parts: the dialogue summarization part and the response generation part. The dialogue summarization part summarizes the dialogue history for each session and saves it by linking it to a topic. For example, if a dialogue session about what to eat today were composed of ten dialogue turns, the dialogue would be summarized in one sentence and used as input for the response generation part. The response generation part generates appropriate responses to the user's input by considering the context and the user's dialogue history, using a generation-based approach with deep learning. Figure 2 shows the system configuration diagram. These two parts are combined using existing methods, but the framework can be flexible by replacing parts with the latest technology. Overall, the dialogue

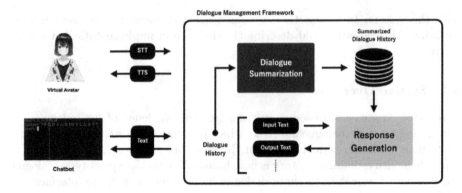

Fig. 2. Dialogue management framework in this study.

management framework proposed in this study can improve the quality of long-term dialogue between users and dialogue systems and improve the consistency and coherence of the dialogue.

Dialogue Summarization Part. This part summarizes the content of a dialogue session consisting of multiple dialogue turns. In the prototype system for the experiment, we fine-tuned the BertSum model [10] with the wikiHow dataset [9] to enable Japanese text summarization. We chose the wikiHow dataset because it is more similar to everyday text than the news and headline pairs commonly used in summarization datasets.

BertSum model is an extractive summarization, which involves selecting the most important sentences from a document to create a summary. Our approach involves using this model to extract the most important sentences from a dialogue session and use them as a summary. The summary generated by the model is used as a reference for the response generation part, which generates appropriate responses based on the context of the dialogue and the user's input. Overall, the dialogue summarization part of our proposed framework effectively captures the essence of a dialogue session and provides a valuable reference for generating appropriate responses. Using a summarization model fine-tuned on a relevant dataset enables our framework to perform well on Japanese text, which is particularly important for dialogue systems.

Dialogue Generation Part. The response generation part aims to generate a response sentence considering the dialogue history. By utilizing the summarized sentences from the dialogue history of previous dialogue sessions based on the topic of the dialogue, we can easily recall the memory of previous sessions and generate consistent response sentences. In this prototype, we divide each dialogue session into three parts. The dialogue topic is predefined and randomly selected.

1. Greeting: At the beginning of the session, we confirm the greeting and check if the system is ready to engage in dialogue.

2. Question: Next, we ask predefined questions related to the randomly selected topic. If we have a dialogue history related to this topic, we generate follow-up questions to explore the topic in more depth.
3. Chatting: After that, the chats are conducted using a generative-based method with deep learning to generate appropriate responses to the user's flexible utterances continuously. The dialogue continues until it is terminated at any given time, making it a single session.

We use a rule-based method for Greetings and Questions and a generative-based method with deep learning to generate appropriate responses for Chatting. We use Japanese GPT-2, rinna[1] as the backbone for response generation. We fine-tuned the model using an open Japanese dialogue corpus [3] and 10,000 dialogue corpus extracted from Twitter. rinna is a state-of-the-art language model that can generate high-quality Japanese text. We fine-tuned the model with a conversational corpus to adapt it to the nuances of Japanese conversation. The model's ability to generate responses based on the context of the dialogue and the user's input enables our framework to generate more natural and human-like dialogue. For the chatting dialogue session, we explicitly consider the dialogue history by inserting the past dialogue context as the head of the input text with the [SEP] token. By combining the dialogue summarization and response generation parts, our proposed framework enables a more natural and continuous dialogue with users, allowing for a more consistent and coherent conversation. Using state-of-the-art language models fine-tuned on relevant datasets ensures that our framework can perform well on Japanese text and be applicable in various dialogue interfaces.

Interface. We adopt two types of dialogue interfaces: a text chatbot that operates on a laptop and a virtual avatar displayed on a screen. Text-based dialogue runs on a terminal, while the virtual avatar uses a template provided by VRoid Hub[2], an avatar creation service. We use Open J Talk[3] for Text-to-Speech, and for Speech-to-Text we use Open AI Whisper[4]. We also implement lip-syncing for the avatar's movements during speech.

4 Evaluation

4.1 User Study

We conducted a user study to evaluate the effectiveness of sharing dialogue history across multiple devices. We recruited 12 participants, eight males and four females aged between 20 and 50. These participants engaged in dialogue with systems under various real-world scenarios in a simulated environment and were exposed to three experimental conditions as follows:

---

[1] https://huggingface.co/rinna/japanese-gpt2-xsmall.
[2] https://hub.vroid.com.
[3] https://open-jtalk.sp.nitech.ac.jp.
[4] https://github.com/openai/whisper.

A No consideration of conversation history
B Consideration of only the user's persona
C Consideration of the user's conversation history

Condition A operates as a conventional dialogue system that functions as a separate dialogue. Condition B presents a system that pretends to have an identity by considering the user's persona, which is limited to the user's name in this study. The user's name is remembered by calling out their name during greetings to create the illusion of memory. Condition C is the proposed method that considers the conversation history. Participants participated in the conversation using text chat and an avatar interface for the user survey. As described in the Methods section, dialogues were conducted twice daily, in the morning and at night, using a role-playing technique in which participants imagined a holiday morning and night (Fig. 3). The procedure was as follows:

- In the morning session, participants conversed using one of the interfaces. The topic was randomly selected and the conversation ended when the number of exchanges exceeded seven.
- In the night session, participants used the other interface to converse. The conversation ended when the user's responses exceeded seven exchanges.
- A seven-metric questionnaire was administered to assess factors such as naturalness and fluency using a 7-point Likert scale (1 = totally disagree, 7 = totally agree) at the end of the morning and night sessions.

Participants were instructed to talk about three topics: plan to do today, plan to go today, and plan to eat today. For example, in the morning session, a participant converses with a virtual avatar about plan to go today. In the night session, the participant conversed with a chatbot to converse their feelings of the places they visited that day. Each participant followed this procedure for all three conditions, conducting six interactions. The order of topics, conditions, and interfaces was randomly selected to eliminate biases. Finally, each participant was interviewed to evaluate their experience with the system qualitatively. The evaluation metrics and questions for the participants are summarized in Table 1.

4.2   Results

Figure 4 shows the average and standard deviation of the 7-point Likert scale for each evaluation metric under the three experimental conditions, and Fig. 5 shows an example of dialogue by an actual participant. As the figure indicates, it is clear that the proposed method, Condition C, exhibits the highest value compared to the other conditions. Although these results did not demonstrate significant differences, they suggest that the proposed system provides a better dialogue experience regarding satisfaction and continuity, highlighting the system's superiority. In addition, the 12 participants were divided into two groups where six participants used the virtual agent interface in the morning session, while the remaining six used the chatbot interface. Table 2 shows the results

Fig. 3. Morning and night sessions in the user study.

Table 1. Evaluation metrics and questions for a Likert scale.

	Metrics	Question
Q1	Naturalness	Were the system's spoken words phrased naturally?
Q2	Satisfaction	Were the system's conversation satisfactory?
Q3	Comprehension	Did the system accurately understand what you were saying?
Q4	Continuity	Did the system's conversation feel continuous and fluid?
Q5	Relevance	Did you find the conversation with the system trustworthy?
Q6	Continuity	Did the system recall the previous topics of conversation?
Q7	Identity	Did the system have a distinctive personality or character?

for each interface order. The results also demonstrate that Condition C has the highest mean value. This suggests that the evaluation results remain the same depending on the interface usage order. The qualitative interview with the participants provides additional insights into these results. Overall, sharing dialogue history among multiple devices was well received by the participants. However, the participants who assumed that dialogue history sharing was a natural feature were less likely to have a positive experience. For example, during the night session, the effectiveness of the proposed summarization method was diminished when a participant provided a detailed account of the morning session and their impressions, making it difficult to discern differences between the experimental conditions. Moreover, retaining the dialogue history and user preferences may lead to more consistent conversations. For example, Participant 7 noted that machines are capable of remembering their personality, interests, and preferences, eliminating the need to explain them repeatedly. Conversely, Participant 5 expressed discomfort at the idea of the system retaining all dialogue history, particularly sensitive information. Meanwhile, Participant 6 proposed that the system should retain significant events and conversations over a week instead of a year. This point of view underscores the need to explore whether the significance of long-term memory varies according to the time frame.

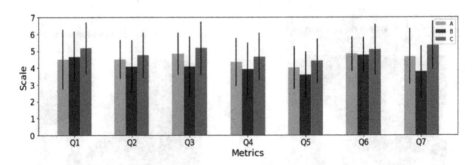

Fig. 4. Results of Likert scale in user study.

Table 2. Average of Likert scale scores in the user study by order of use of the interface.

	Condition	Q1	Q2	Q3	Q4	Q5	Q6	Q7
Morning: Chatbot Night: Virtual Agent	A	4.66	4.66	4.50	4.16	3.83	4.50	4.50
	B	4.66	4.33	3.83	4.00	3.66	4.50	2.66
	C	**5.33**	**5.16**	**5.16**	**4.83**	**4.33**	**4.83**	**4.66**
Morning: Virtual Agent Night: Chatbot	A	4.33	4.33	5.16	4.50	4.16	5.16	4.83
	B	4.66	3.83	4.33	3.83	3.50	5.00	4.83
	C	**5.00**	**4.33**	**5.16**	**4.50**	**4.50**	**5.33**	**6.00**

4.3   Limitation

Sample Size. The number of participants in the experiment may have been insufficient to achieve statistical significance. These findings suggest that a larger sample size may be required to increase statistical reliability and generalizability of the results.

System Design. The experiment design may have been problematic. For instance, if the selected dialogue systems were not sufficiently different, or if the chosen evaluation metrics were not suitable, this could impact the findings. Re-evaluating the chosen evaluation metrics and increasing their number could help detect significant differences more effectively. Furthermore, during the night session, initiating the conversation with a general question such as "Did you have a good day today?" without specific content in the response may lead to a consistent dialogue with the morning session, which could be a factor contributing to non-significant results depending on the content of the conversation.

Environment. This study was conducted in a relatively small and restricted setting, and the results should be interpreted in the context of the experimental setting. More longitudinal studies are needed to increase the generalizability of these results. Further experiments conducted in real world environments and long-term memory with dialogue sessions conducted in the actual morning and evening hours would yield better results and more significant findings and consider them as future challenges for this study.

	System	今日はどこに行く予定ですか？ (Where are you planning to go today?)
	User	今日は北海道に行きます (I'm going to Hokkaido today.)
Morning Session	System	いいですね。寒いので気を付けてくださいね。(It's nice. Be careful, it's cold.)
	User	はい、温かくしていきます (Yes, I will keep it warm.)
	System	美味しいものたくさん食べてきてください。(Please go eat lots of delicious food.)
	⋮	⋮
Summary		北海道旅行に行って、美味しいものを食べる (Travel to Hokkaido and eat delicious food.)
	System	今日は楽しかったですか？ (Did you have fun today?)
	User	楽しかったです (It was fun.)
Night Session	System	それは良かったですね。北海道のどこが一番良かったですか? (That was good. What did you like best about Hokkaido?)
	User	函館がよかったです(I liked Hakodate.)
	System	北海道は美味しいものがたくさんありそうで、実際に行ってみたいです (Hokkaido looks like it has a lot of good food and I would actually like to go there)
	⋮	⋮

Fig. 5. Examples of dialogue in user study.

5 Conclusion

In this study, we developed a prototype dialogue management framework that enables sharing dialogue history across multiple interfaces, such as virtual agents and chatbots. The results of our evaluation demonstrated that sharing conversation history across multiple devices led to continuous and natural conversation and could improve the system's consistency. This study provides a new approach to improving the quality of long-term conversations between users and dialogue systems by managing dialogue history. However, due to the small sample size and limitations of the experimental design, statistically significant results were not obtained, and limitations were identified. In future works, we will conduct long-term interaction experiments in real-world environments and utilize more diverse interfaces, such as smart speakers and avatars in virtual reality environments, to identify future challenges and research possibilities in this field.

Acknowledgement. This research is partially supported by JST CREST(JPMJC R1882, JPMJCR22M4), and NICT(222C0101).

References

1. Arent, K., Kreczmer, B.: Identity of a companion, migrating between robots without common communication modalities: Initial results of VHRI study. In: 2013 18th International Conference on Methods & Models in Automation & Robotics (MMAR), pp. 109–114 (2013). https://doi.org/10.1109/MMAR.2013.6669890
2. Bae, S., et al.: Keep me updated! memory management in long-term conversations. In: Findings of the Association for Computational Linguistics: EMNLP 2022, pp. 3769–3787. Association for Computational Linguistics, Abu Dhabi, United Arab Emirates (2022). https://aclanthology.org/2022.findings-emnlp.276

3. Fujimura, I., Chiba, S., Ohso, M.: Lexical and grammatical features of spoken and written japanese in contrast: exploring a lexical profiling approach to comparing spoken and written corpora. In: Proceedings of the VIIth GSCP International Conference. Speech and Corpora, pp. 393–398 (2012)

4. Gomes, P.F., Sardinha, A., Márquez Segura, E., Cramer, H., Paiva, A.: Migration between two embodiments of an artificial pet. Int. J. Humanoid Rob. 11(01), 1450001 (2014)

5. Grigore, E.C., Pereira, A., Yang, J.J., Zhou, I., Wang, D., Scassellati, B.: Comparing ways to trigger migration between a robot and a virtually embodied character. In: Agah, A., Cabibihan, J.-J., Howard, A.M., Salichs, M.A., He, H. (eds.) ICSR 2016. LNCS (LNAI), vol. 9979, pp. 839–849. Springer, Cham (2016). https://doi.org/10.1007/978-3-319-47437-3_82

6. Ho, W.C., Dautenhahn, K., Lim, M.Y., Vargas, P.A., Aylett, R., Enz, S.: An initial memory model for virtual and robot companions supporting migration and long-term interaction. In: RO-MAN 2009 - The 18th IEEE International Symposium on Robot and Human Interactive Communication, pp. 277–284 (2009). https://doi.org/10.1109/ROMAN.2009.5326204

7. Imai, M., Ono, T., Etani, T.: Agent migration: communications between a human and robot. In: IEEE SMC1999 Conference Proceedings. 1999 IEEE International Conference on Systems, Man, and Cybernetics (Cat. No.99CH37028), vol. 4, pp. 1044–1048 (1999). https://doi.org/10.1109/ICSMC.1999.812554

8. Koay, K., Syrdal, D., Dautenhahn, K., Arent, K., Małek, Ł., Kreczmer, B.: Companion migration-initial participants' feedback from a video-based prototyping study. Mixed Reality and Human-Robot Interaction, pp. 133–151 (2011)

9. Koupaee, M., Wang, W.Y.: WikiHow: a large scale text summarization dataset. arXiv preprint arXiv:1810.09305 (2018)

10. Liu, Y., Lapata, M.: Text summarization with pretrained encoders. In: Proceedings of the 2019 Conference on Empirical Methods in Natural Language Processing and the 9th International Joint Conference on Natural Language Processing (EMNLP-IJCNLP), pp. 3730–3740 (2019)

11. Ogawa, K., Ono, T.: ITACO: constructing an emotional relationship between human and robot. In: RO-MAN 2008 - The 17th IEEE International Symposium on Robot and Human Interactive Communication, pp. 35–40 (2008). https://doi.org/10.1109/ROMAN.2008.4600640

12. Shuster, K., Urbanek, J., Szlam, A., Weston, J.: Am I me or you? State-of-the-art dialogue models cannot maintain an identity. In: Findings of the Association for Computational Linguistics: NAACL 2022, pp. 2367–2387. Association for Computational Linguistics, Seattle, United States (2022). https://doi.org/10.18653/v1/2022.findings-naacl.182. https://aclanthology.org/2022.findings-naacl.182

13. Song, H., Wang, Y., Zhang, K., Zhang, W.N., Liu, T.: BoB: BERT over BERT for training persona-based dialogue models from limited personalized data. In: Proceedings of the 59th Annual Meeting of the Association for Computational Linguistics and the 11th International Joint Conference on Natural Language Processing (Volume 1: Long Papers), pp. 167–177. Association for Computational Linguistics, Online (2021). https://doi.org/10.18653/v1/2021.acl-long.14. https://aclanthology.org/2021.acl-long.14

14. Sutskever, I., Vinyals, O., Le, Q.V.: Sequence to sequence learning with neural networks. Advances in Neural Information Processing Systems 27 (2014)

15. Syrdal, D.S., Koay, K.L., Walters, M.L., Dautenhahn, K.: The boy-robot should bark!-children's impressions of agent migration into diverse embodiments. In: Proceedings: New Frontiers of Human-Robot Interaction, a symposium at AISB. CiteSeer (2009)
16. Tejwani, R., Moreno, F., Jeong, S., Won Park, H., Breazeal, C.: Migratable AI: effect of identity and information migration on users' perception of conversational AI agents. In: 2020 29th IEEE International Conference on Robot and Human Interactive Communication (RO-MAN), pp. 877–884 (2020). https://doi.org/10.1109/RO-MAN47096.2020.9223436
17. Vaswani, A., et al.: Attention is all you need. Advances in Neural Information Processing Systems 30 (2017)
18. Xu, X., et al.: Long time no see! open-domain conversation with long-term persona memory. In: Findings of the Association for Computational Linguistics: ACL 2022. pp. 2639–2650. Association for Computational Linguistics, Dublin, Ireland (2022). https://doi.org/10.18653/v1/2022.findings-acl.207. https://aclanthology.org/2022.findings-acl.207
19. Zhang, S., Dinan, E., Urbanek, J., Szlam, A., Kiela, D., Weston, J.: Personalizing dialogue agents: I have a dog, do you have pets too? In: Proceedings of the 56th Annual Meeting of the Association for Computational Linguistics (Volume 1: Long Papers), pp. 2204–2213. Association for Computational Linguistics, Melbourne, Australia (2018). https://doi.org/10.18653/v1/P18-1205. https://aclanthology.org/P18-1205
20. Zheng, Y., Zhang, R., Huang, M., Mao, X.: A pre-training based personalized dialogue generation model with persona-sparse data. In: Proceedings of the AAAI Conference on Artificial Intelligence, pp. 9693–9700, no. 05 (2020)
21. Zhong, H., Dou, Z., Zhu, Y., Qian, H., Wen, J.R.: Less is more: learning to refine dialogue history for personalized dialogue generation. In: Proceedings of the 2022 Conference of the North American Chapter of the Association for Computational Linguistics: Human Language Technologies, pp. 5808–5820. Association for Computational Linguistics, Seattle, United States (2022). https://doi.org/10.18653/v1/2022.naacl-main.426. https://aclanthology.org/2022.naacl-main.426

Analysing the Use of Voice Assistants in Domestic Settings Through the Lens of Activity Theory

Edith Maier and Ulrich Reimer[✉]

Eastern Switzerland University of Applied Sciences, St. Gallen, Switzerland
{edith.maier,ulrich.reimer}@ost.ch

Abstract. The paper analyses the use of voice assistants in people's homes through the lens of activity theory guided by concepts such as mental models, context, the relationship between subject and tool as well as contradictions. Activity theory sees conversational devices including voice assistants not as ends in themselves, but as tools to aid the performance of a particular activity or practice. After a brief overview of the use of activity theory in HCI research, the empirical data gathered in an interdisciplinary project on the use of voice-enabled technology are discussed with a focus on the contradictions that have emerged in the course of our study. Contradictions have emerged with respect to the traditional view of home as private, which clashes with the fact that voice assistants may transmit personal data to external bodies. Another contradiction relates to the gulf between people's expectations of smartness and the current shortcomings of commercial voice assistants. Finally, the paper presents suggestions for how one might design conversational technology in a way that helps resolve those contradictions and cope with the emerging phenomena such as autonomous agents.

Keywords: Activity Theory · Privacy · Voice Assistant

1 Introduction

In a 4-year project (2020–2023) funded by the Swiss National Science Foundation[1], a team of researchers with expertise in human-computer interaction, home automation, digital services, data science, and behavioural economics has been investigating how the presence of voice assistants affects people's domestic lives, norms and values, and how they change practices and routines in the home. The project focuses on the implementation and use of voice assistants for a multitude of activities at home from the perspective of users, their perceptions, expectations, motives etc., rather than the developers or suppliers of technology. The project findings will be translated into guidance for users, developers, designers and service providers in business and public life.

---

[1] Swiss National Science Foundation under grant number SINERGIA CRSII5_189955.

M. Kurosu and A. Hashizume (Eds.): HCII 2023, LNCS 14013, pp. 366–379, 2023.
https://doi.org/10.1007/978-3-031-35602-5_26

The voice-enabled devices promise to make our daily lives more efficient by letting us control smart home devices, search for information or listen to our favourite music, but they also raise concerns about privacy and loss of control. They are equipped with technologies that can, and often do, monitor activities to collect, record and transfer all kinds of data to an external information domain. They may serve as the first contact or touch points that, once introduced into a home, stimulate users to expand them with further functionalities by connecting them with other devices like televisions, lights, microwaves, fridges, and even toothbrushes [1,23].

Our research of voice assistant use is underpinned by activity theory, which takes human activity mediated by technology, the environment or society (e.g. through norms and rules) as the fundamental unit of analysis. In our study, we look at the contextualised and social changes that occur when implementing voice-enabled devices in a particular setting. We also make suggestions with regard to (re-)designing voice-enabled technology and its implementation and use based primarily on the contradictions or tensions that have arisen in the existing activity system. Thus, we apply activity theory to better understand the conditions, motives or expectations that lead people to use voice assistants and to help explain how one might design conversational technology in a way that addresses the contradictions and responds to people's concerns.

Actually, the majority of people in our study say that they are concerned about their privacy when it comes to using voice assistants. But although most users insist that they care about protecting their personal data, few actually take steps to self-manage their privacy e.g. by adjusting settings or encrypting their data [20,25]. Instead, most people appear resigned and simply surrender to (potential) violations to their privacy.

In our paper we argue that activity theory can provide guidance in a world dominated by social media, artificial intelligence and digital devices such as smartphones and smart speakers. It can also help illuminate emerging phenomena such as autonomous agents. At the same time, activity theory can help address contradictions that tend to occur with any new technology. According to Engeström [9] contradictions actually play an essential role in inspiring design ideas or modifications to resolve the contradictions. We therefore consider activity theory suited to meet challenges raised by conversational technology such as the blurring of boundaries between public and private or the growing smartness as well as autonomy of digital agents thanks to increasingly sophisticated algorithms.

In Sect. 2 we give a brief overview of the use of activity theory in HCI research with a focus on recent studies. Section 3 describes our methodological approach by which we gathered the empirical data in our study. This is followed by a discussion of the results with a focus on the contradictions that have emerged in the course of our study (Sect. 4). The results are analysed through the lens of activity theory, which is also applied to the ideas that have been generated to help resolve the contradictions and cope with the emerging phenomena such as autonomous agents (Sect. 5). Section 6 concludes the paper.

2   Related Work

The human relationship with technology has always been of special interest to activity theory, which is hardly surprising given its focus on tools and their uses. It relies on a systemic model [9] that encompasses the acting subject, the goal or object of an action and the involved community as basic constituents including the relations between them. Activity theory looks at mediating entities such as tools (e.g. voice assistants) that support the interaction between subject and object and recognises the importance of context or environment in human-computer interaction (HCI) studies.

The emergence of ergonomics and human factors as a separate discipline was strongly influenced by activity theory [35]. In the late 1980s and early 1990s activity theory started to be employed internationally to address new challenges associated with computers and information systems. A number of researchers, especially in Scandinavia and the United States, pointed out that by framing human-technology interaction within a larger context of purposeful human activities, the theory makes it possible to reach a deeper understanding of technology and its meaning for people (e.g. [15]). Kuuti [18] was one of the first to introduce activity theory as a framework for human-computer research.

In a meta-synthesis of 109 selected HCI activity theory papers, Clemmensen, Kaptelinin and Nardi [7] created a taxonomy of different ways of using activity theory. These include identifying domain-specific requirements for new theoretical tools, developing new conceptual accounts of issues in the field of HCI, guiding and supporting empirical analyses of HCI phenomena and providing new design illustrations, claims, and guidelines. They conclude that HCI researchers have been adapting and developing activity theory for different purposes. In their literature analysis they also found that activity theory was often combined with other less sweeping theories for precision or specificity (e.g., with small-group theory or cognitive load theory).

In a special issue compiled by Kaptelinin and Nardi [16], the editors argue that after being employed in studies of human-technology interaction for almost three decades, activity theory still offers researchers useful insights and guidance. The papers provide good examples of how activity theory informs the current state of human-technology interaction research. Woll and Bratteteig, for instance, analyse technology-supported elderly care from an activity theory perspective [33] and combine it with the trajectory concept of Corbin and Strauss [8]. Since elderly patients' needs for care tend to grow in the course of time, they focus on the shifting relations between the elderly care-receivers (the subject) and the tool (the assistive technology).

Schwalb and Klecun [26] look at the role of contractions and norms in the design and use of telemedicine from the perspective of health professionals in Sri Lanka. They discuss how social norms influence what motivates people to engage in digital health services and how they use the digital platform (the tool) that provides them. They stress that new technology should address contradictions in existing activity systems, should concur with social norms and offer users the possibility to influence those that can cause contradictions.

According to Blayone [4] the effective use of digital technologies is vital to full inclusion in a network society. He views individuals as active agents capable of identifying, taking up, modifying and even subverting established technology uses in pursuit of meaningful objectives. In his research he applies activity theory to conceptualise digitally mediated action by looking at the contextual conditions shaping diverse activity systems.

In a recent paper Karanasios et al. [17] explore the role of activity theory in the study of digital technologies such as social media, smartphones or artificial intelligence and their impacts on human activity. The authors address questions of privacy infringement, algorithmic interference in decision making processes as well as the implications of automation. In their opinion, activity theory researchers should consider how to create more desirable futures by using technology for transformative agency and identifying new practices to promote change.

To sum up, activity theory describes the relationships between subjects, for example individual persons, who have a mental model of the world that guides their behaviour, their goals, which are focused on specific objects (e.g. control of home appliances) and a desired outcome (lights switched off), and the tools or artefacts (here the voice assistants) they use to achieve these goals. In our study, *mental models* refer to the motives, attitudes and expectations study participants have with regard to voice assistants, but also the way they perceive the device, e.g. whether they view it as a tool, toy or buddy.

To complete the activity system, we also include *rules and norms*, which include privacy-related regulations or the pending Digital Markets Act, and the world outside as environment, which in our case corresponds to the digital ecosystem in which the tools are embedded, such as Apple or Amazon. Finally, division of labour forms part of the activity system, which in the case of a single user may refer to how the tasks are distributed between the user and the tool, e.g. in some instances it is the user who gives the commands which are then carried out by the tool, whereas in other instances the tool may trigger actions, e.g. reminders or sounding the alarm, on its own. Figure 1 illustrates the constituent parts of the activity system and their relationships.

Using activity theory as an underpinning theoretical approach can therefore guide and support the empirical analysis of HCI phenomena as well as inspire new design guidelines to tackle problems or contradictions that may arise when using new technology.

3   Methodological Approach

Activity theory has been playing a role through the full trajectory of our research, from research design to data collection, data analysis, and the interpretation of research results. Most of our research is of a qualitative nature, which goes well together with activity theory because activities including the new human experience associated with voice assistants can only be understood in context. Engeström and Escalante [10], Bodker [5] and other advocates of activity theory

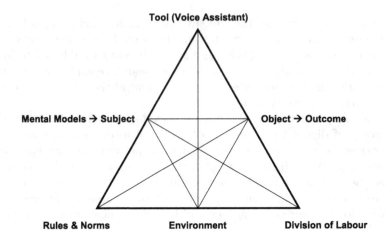

Fig. 1. A single-subject activity system

have argued that the ideal data for an application of activity theory consist of longitudinal ethnographic observation, interviews and discussions in real-life settings, supplemented by experiments.

In our study, the empirical data has been gathered mainly by ethnographic observation, semi-structured interviews, and focus group discussions. These have come to be recognised as the most appropriate methods of gaining an in-depth understanding of the context in which an activity occurs (see e.g. [18]). Because of the Covid-19 pandemic, participant observation *in situ* was not possible which is why we had to resort to using an ethnographic app.

Two different groups were involved in the study:

Volunteer Group:
Participants in the so-called "in-home study" volunteered to take part in a four-week self-observational study in their homes and recorded their experience with the help of the ethnographic diary app Indeemo. Participants also were interviewed by members of the research team using MS Teams or Zoom. Besides, they were sent tasks on a weekly basis such as preparing a shopping list using the voice assistant. Further interviews were conducted some months after the in-home study to capture the longer-term impacts of voice assistant presence in the home.

Student Group:
Participants of the other group consisted of students from different disciplines who had to engage with voice-enabled technology as part of their study requirements for an interdisciplinary course on resource management over a period of 13 weeks.

The ethnographic material from the in-home study, the text entries from the student journals as well as the transcriptions of the audio files from the semi-structured interviews were analysed in uniform procedure using qualitative coding.

Moreover, various speculative design workshops were conducted, inspired by the contradictions that had emerged in the course of the study, especially with regard to the protection of one's personal data and the increasing autonomy of voice-enabled agents. These have resulted in the development of provotypes, i.e. prototypes developed to provoke reactions and emotions [29]. Furthermore, a series of speculative design videos have been created by an interdisciplinary group of students as part of a summer school organised by one of the project partners. The videos aim at visualising the challenges of privacy related to the use of virtual assistants in the near future. A detailed analysis of the videos is still in progress and will be published separately.

4 Discussion of Results Through an Activity Theory Lens

4.1 Overview

Our analysis of the empirical data gathered from both groups has been guided by activity theory concepts such as mental models, context, the relationship between subject and tool as well as contradictions. Activity theory sees conversational devices including voice assistants not as ends in themselves, but as tools to aid the performance of a particular activity or practice. In our case, the voice assistants were most frequently used for setting an alarm or a reminder, listening to music or the radio, getting the weather forecast or recipes, and making queries. Voice assistants were also used as an intercom between rooms, making shopping lists and controlling devices such as lights or shutters. These findings apply to both groups, the volunteers and the students, and are very much in line with comparable studies on the use of voice assistants (e.g. [1,23]).

Increasingly, studies on voice assistants and other conversational agents such as chatbots discuss the risks and societal consequences that might be associated with voice-enabled technologies (e.g. [24]). Since voice assistants gather enormous amounts of personal information, the threats which these devices pose to people's privacy figure most prominent among the risks discussed (e.g. [2,14,22]). Indeed, privacy concerns have emerged as the most important issue in both groups, even though most users appear to be willing to disclose personal data for little or nothing in return.

As pointed out before, new technologies tend to bring about changes in practice that are assimilated by users and, as a result, the practice itself may be modified as the users seek to adapt their practice in the light of newly discovered potentials of the technology. For example, thanks to the voice assistant one no longer has to stand up from the sofa for switching on the lights or interrupt one's cooking when looking up a recipe. But in the interviews it became clear that whilst controlling other devices from the sofa may be convenient, many users did not want to lose control or did not trust the voice assistant enough to let it control critical activities such as opening or closing doors. Another change of practice concerns the way of communication. Many users felt they had to change the language when talking to their voice assistant, e.g. formulate their commands in High German rather than Swiss-German and articulate them clearly so as to be understood by the voice assistant.

4.2   Contradictions in the Existing Activity System

As pointed out before, the limitations and contradictions in an existing activity system may help improve the processes of system design, development and implementation, which is why they have informed our design workshops and creative challenges undertaken by participants in the summer school.

Privacy. A major contradiction is the traditional view of the domestic space as private which is invaded and may be violated by the presence of voice assistants, which constantly listen and may transmit data to the outside world. As a result the boundaries between the private and public space are blurred because data tends to flow freely between the two. Connected devices combined with speech control therefore are viewed as a threat to privacy by most study participants [20].

We have also found a contradiction between generic attitudes to privacy and actual behaviour, referred to usually as the "privacy paradox" (e.g. [30,32]). Table 1 below provides a good illustration of this phenomenon.

Table 1. Frequency of use correlated with importance attributed to privacy when using voice assistant

How important do you consider privacy and data protection when using a voice assistant (VA)?		Unconcerned ("not important, I don't really care where data is stored or processed provided the VA works")	Privacy concerns ("I do care but when the benefits outweigh the risks, I use the VA")	Critical ("I consider privacy very important therefore I deliberately restrict the use of the VA")	Total
How often do you use the VA?	Several times a day	5	28	5	38
	Several times a week	1	6	0	7
	Rarely	4	6	7	17
Total		10	40	12	62

As can be seen in Table 1, most people care about privacy. Only ten respondents are unconcerned about data protection and just want the voice assistant to function properly, whereas 52 out of 62 respondents are concerned to different degrees. Most are pragmatists who care about privacy but weigh the potential pros and cons of sharing information and are ready to make trade-offs if the benefits are considered big enough. Twelve respondents harbour serious concerns with regard to their privacy, but nevertheless use the voice assistant rarely or several times a day. None of the participants considered opting out as an option.

Despite their concerns, participants in our study spend very little time on individual privacy-protecting measures. This may be due to the effort it takes to self-manage one's data protection. Also, privacy policies are regarded as (too) complicated, incomprehensible, time-consuming or cumbersome to read. Users often feel tricked into accepting terms and conditions without knowing or being informed about possible consequences. So-called "dark patterns" were a recurrent theme in the interviews. They refer to deceptive design patterns or tricks used in websites and apps that make you do things that you did not mean to, like buying or signing up for something.

Actually, as shown in many studies attitudes are poor predictors of behaviour (e.g. [30,31]). One of the reasons given for the dichotomy between attitude and actual or intended behaviour is that studies of privacy tend to measure only general attitudes, whilst behaviour is context-specific. Besides, individuals may perform privacy risk assessments but choose the most viable or convenient options, even if they are not in accordance with their privacy preferences (for an overview, see [12]).

We live in an age where it is nearly impossible not to disclose personal data if one wants to participate in social life and engage in economic activities. People constantly make risk assessments when they trade their personal data in exchange for gaining access to information or services important to them.

The prevailing attitude with regard to privacy and data protection is characterised by perceived helplessness and powerlessness. Given the advances in artificial intelligence and machine learning, such feelings are likely to become even more acute. Data protection regulations by national and supranational organisations seem to be unable to impart the feeling of being in control of the situation.

Smartness. Another major contradiction that has emerged in the course of our study concerns the mental model of voice assistant as a smart device and the shortcomings that commercial voice assistants currently exhibit with respect to smartness. For example, smartness implies being able to conduct a natural dialogue with a voice assistant which includes contextual carryover, i.e. to infer from previous interactions the context of the current task and provide feedback or ask for clarifications. Besides, in the case of Swiss-German dialects, voice-recognition often turned out to be inadequate.

Some users had high expectations in the beginning, e.g. that the voice assistant should make everyday life easier and work more efficient and became increasingly frustrated or disenchanted in the course of the study when they became aware of its shortcomings. A few users stopped using the device after the study or restricted themselves to using it for very simple activities such as switching the lights on and off. At least for the time being, our mental models of smart

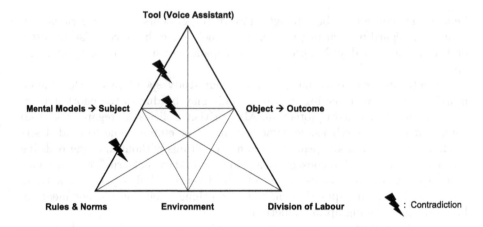

Fig. 2. Activity system highlighting the contradictions

assistants do not match the current abilities of voice assistants, a finding which has been confirmed by other researchers such as Luger and Sellen [19].

The gulf between the people's expectations and people's experience of using voice assistants thus makes it difficult or impossible to achieve one's objective or desired outcome which in turn may lead one to modify one's practice (e.g. language use) or abandon it altogether and switch back to analogue (e.g. preparing shopping lists in hand-writing). Similarly, people's mental model of the home as private contradicts the fact that a voice assistant may well transmit private data to the outside world.

Figure 2 visualises the various contradictions in the existing activity system, as discussed above, and how they affect the relations between the various constituents. In the present activity system the tool, i.e. the voice assistant, is (not yet) in a position to take over the role of the subject as described in the following section, which is why tool, subject and division of labour are interconnected, but have not changed places.

4.3   Shifting Agency

Due to advances in deep learning and powerful language models, a new generation of conversational AI systems is emerging that not only enable conversations with human-like qualities [11], but may act without being prompted by the user. Increasing levels of autonomy lead to a shift of agency from the subject to the tool. This phenomenon has been described by Woll and Bratteteig [33], for instance, when discussing the increased use of automated services in the care of elderly people. The frailer they become, the more the assistive systems turn into autonomous agents. In order to maintain the stability of the object of activity, i.e. to support the elderly person in safety measures and everyday life mastery, the assistive technology undergoes a shift from support to actor.

For example, one of the speculative videos produced by participants in the summer school shows how a pregnant woman is advised by her voice-enabled humanoid avatar to refrain from drinking a beer because it might harm the foetus – without being prompted. This shifting agency implies that the subject no longer knows best. It also requires the device to develop a user model to better understand his or her queries, memorize user preferences and their backgrounds as well as their state of health. Whilst some might welcome such personalized interactions, others consider them somewhat creepy or unsettling, especially when the device acts proactively, i.e. without a concrete task (see e.g. [34]).

Whilst responding to a user's emotions might be regarded as smart, it is also deceptive. This is why authors such as Seymour emphasize that "voice assistants are not our friends" [27]. According to him we should stop presenting smart devices that have commercial or ideological interests as friendly because they are not governed by the social norms that someone close would adhere to. Actually, many people imbue AI with human traits as shown by the recent incident of Google researcher Lemoine going public with his claim that LaMDA, a large language model (LM) designed to converse with people, was sentient and had personhood[2]

The incident illustrates the risks of trying to replicate human-to-human interaction, which may lead users to trust the recommendations of their conversational AI device too much, especially if it comes along as empathic or humorous. This is why Bender et al. [3] warn that people may come to believe in sentient AI rather than regard AI systems as stochastic parrots.

5   Design Responses

As pointed out by Schwalb and Klecun [26], contradictions in existing activity systems may well inspire and inform design responses. When looking at our empirical data, contradictions have emerged with respect to the traditional view of home as private, which clashes with the fact that voice assistants may transmit personal data to external bodies. Another contradiction relates to the gulf between people's expectations (mental models) and the (still) existing shortcomings of commercial voice assistants, which frequently results in a failure to achieve the desired outcome.

Revealing a system's overall smartness is a design challenge not yet solved. In many cases, the voice assistants currently available still have serious shortcomings and fall short of user expectations that may be raised because of their anthropomorphic attributes. With the rise of deep learning and growing amounts of training data, however, large language models such as GPT-3 [11] have become increasingly effective for generating text or speech that appears as if it were written or spoken by a person.

---

[2] See   https://www.washingtonpost.com/technology/2022/06/11/google-ai-lamda-blake-lemoine).

To design smart conversational systems which are convenient to use and accepted by users on the long-term, we need to understand users' mental models of smartness. What do they associate with 'smartness' in the context of conversations? As mentioned before, smartness may include different dimensions such as autonomous behaviour (i.e., the AI-enabled device acts proactively and adjust its speech and dialogue accordingly), or a sense of humour. Besides, many conversational AI devices are framed anthropomorphically by equipping them with certain personalities (e.g., female, polite, playful, humble) which raises expectations about the extent of their intelligence, capability of judgement and understanding of social norms.

However, as pointed out by [13], many respondents in their study felt that a red line was crossed if the degree of autonomy and the personal emotional level of the device was felt to be too elevated. Among the red lines they identified was autonomous decision-making on the part of the AI device as well as styles of interaction that chaperon the user or pretend to be the user's friend. Recommendations made by the AI-enabled assistant, e.g. "you should go to bed now" may actually cause discomfort because it runs counter to most people's need for control.

In line with recent developments in activity theory, a shift from looking at people as technology users to enabling them to become producers of technology might help resolve the contradiction between attitudes to privacy and actual behaviour. In 2002, Castells found that "many of the Internet applications, including e-mail, chat rooms, and group lists, were serendipitously developed by early users. This continues to be the case every day" [6]. Of course, the typical user does not have the skills to become a producer of technology but could get back some measure of control if those systems were to allow for extensive configuration in a self-explanatory and user-friendly manner.

None of our interviewees, however, has come up with suggestions about how to design voice-enabled technology in a way so as to prevent or at least curtail violations of people's privacy. For example, none of our study participants seems to have heard of Mycroft, an open-source voice assistant, which is private by default and can be integrated into different devices. And the study participants are obviously not familiar with ideas put forward by Seymour and Van Kleek [28] such as refraining from equipping conversational agents with anthropomorphic features that may mislead users to view them as friends.

In our project, we have been experimenting with *provotyping* as a tool for designing voice-enabled agents for privacy, control and transparency [29]. Moreover, in a series of Wizard-of-Oz experiments we want to investigate if designers actually should try to replicate human-to-human interactions or rather find ways to make the limitations and smartness of these devices transparent. At present, when Alexa, for instance, fails to accomplish a task or understand a request, the users do not know whether they themselves are to blame because they have not formulated the request appropriately or – in the case of a country with numerous dialects such as Switzerland – failed to speak in standard language.

6 Limitations and Conclusions

In this paper we have analysed the use of voice assistants through the lens of activity theory. In our study we employ the theory as a conceptual tool and the theoretical foundation for our research. Whereas traditionally, studies underpinned by activity theory have been looking primarily at workplaces and organizations, our research focus has been on the domestic space, a setting where societal contradictions are intensively played out. Our analysis of the empirical data has been mainly guided by activity theory concepts such as mental models, the relationship between subject and tool as well as the contradictions in the existing activity system.

Elements such as the environment or digital infrastructure (see Fig. 1) may also be relevant but have been excluded in the discussion because they have not given rise to any contradictions. Besides, we have adopted a single-subject perspective and neglected the fact that in many homes voice assistants may be shared between family members or a peer group. This would have made the discussion much more complex because a very preliminary analysis has shown that not only are children's mental models of voice assistants different from those of their parents, but they also tend to pursue different objectives. We shall look into these aspects at a later stage once we have a more differentiated analyis of responses.

For both adults and children, however, the mental model of an assistant implies being able to converse naturally instead of the 'one-shot' questions or commands as is currently the case. For a real *dialogue*, background knowledge and knowledge about former user interactions would be required. These features are generally considered prerequisites for a tool to be really supportive.

On the other hand, most users wish to know what an assistant can do or actually does in terms of collecting and aggregating personal data and making inferences from that data. Users should therefore be given the means to configure the smartness level of an assistant and thus determine how much data the assistant may collect about the user and to what extent the data may be aggregated and analyzed with data mining algorithms. Thus the user can assume control and decide how much or which data to share in exchange for better support by the assistant. Furthermore, there may be a point where voice-enabled agents become too smart and turn creepy [34], e.g. when they have accumulated lots of personal data about a user or when they can detect his or her current moods and emotions, which may end up making the user feel uneasy or under surveillance.

Even though for the time being most users complain about the voice assistants' lack of smartness, there may be future scenarios where smartness might be considered a threat rather than an asset. If conversational AI systems should become increasingly capable of recognizing and detecting people's emotions or state of mental health, this may be abused by providers who might transfer the data to insurance companies, for instance. In a recently published article Gary Marcus [21] warns against the potential dangers of AI platforms like ChatGPT. In his opinion, such systems contain no mechanisms for checking the truth of what they say, which is why they can easily be automated to generate misinformation on a massive scale. What society can do about this new threat may well be one of the greatest challenges in the future.

Acknowledgement. The research results presented in this paper are part of a project funded by Swiss National Science Foundation (http://dx.doi.org/10.13039/501100001711) under grant number SINERGIA CRSII5_189955.

References

1. Ammari, T., Kaye, J., Tsai, J.Y., Bentley, F.: Music, search, and IoT: how people (really) use voice assistants. ACM Trans. Comput. Hum. Interact. **26**(3), 1–17 (2019)
2. Barth, S., de Jong, M.D., Junger, M., Hartel, P.H., Roppelt, J.C.: Putting the privacy paradox to the test: online privacy and security behaviors among users with technical knowledge, privacy awareness, and financial resources. Telematics Inform. **41**, 55–69 (2019)
3. Bender, E.M., Gebru, T., McMillan-Major, A., Shmitchell, S.: On the dangers of stochastic parrots: Can language models be too big? In: Proceedings of the 2021 ACM Conference on Fairness, Accountability, and Transparency, pp. 610–623 (2021)
4. Blayone, T.J.: Theorising effective uses of digital technology with activity theory. Technol. Pedagog. Educ. **28**(4), 447–462 (2019)
5. Bødker, S.: Through the interface: a human activity approach to user interface design. CRC Press (2021)
6. Castells, M.: The Internet galaxy: Reflections on the Internet, business, and society. Oxford University Press on Demand (2002)
7. Clemmensen, T., Kaptelinin, V., Nardi, B.: Making HCI theory work: an analysis of the use of activity theory in HCI research. Behav. Inf. Technol. **35**(8), 608–627 (2016)
8. Corbin, J.M.: The Corbin and Strauss chronic illness trajectory model: an update. Res. Theory Nurs. Pract. **12**(1), 33 (1998)
9. Engeström, Y.: Expansive learning at work: toward an activity theoretical reconceptualization. J. Educ. Work. **14**(1), 133–156 (2001)
10. Engeström, Y., Escalante, V.: Mundane tool or object of affection? The rise and fall of the postal buddy. Context and consciousness: Activity Theory and Human-Computer Interaction, pp. 325–373 (1996)
11. Floridi, L., Chiriatti, M.: GPT-3: Its nature, scope, limits, and consequences. Mind. Mach. **30**(4), 681–694 (2020)
12. Gerber, N., Gerber, P., Volkamer, M.: Explaining the privacy paradox: a systematic review of literature investigating privacy attitude and behavior. Comput. Secur. **77**, 226–261 (2018)
13. Graf, E., Zessinger, D.: Alexa, know your limits: developing a framework for the accepted and desired degree of product smartness for digital voice assistants. SN Business Econ. **2**(6), 1–33 (2022)
14. Jain, S., Basu, S., Dwivedi, Y.K., Kaur, S.: Interactive voice assistants - does brand credibility assuage privacy risks? J. Bus. Res. **139**, 701–717 (2022)
15. Kaptelinin, V., Nardi, B.: Activity theory in HCI: fundamentals and reflections. Synthesis Lect. Human-Centered Inform. **5**(1), 1–105 (2012)

16. Kaptelinin, V., Nardi, B.: Activity theory as a framework for human-technology interaction research (2018)
17. Karanasios, S., Nardi, B., Spinuzzi, C., Malaurent, J.: Moving forward with activity theory in a digital world. Mind Cult. Act. **28**(3), 234–253 (2021)
18. Kuuti, K.: Activity theory as a potential framework for HCI research. Context and Consciousness, Activity Theory and Human-Computer Interaction, The MIT Press, Cambridge, MA and London (2001)
19. Luger, E., Sellen, A.: "Like having a really bad PA". The gulf between user expectation and experience of conversational agents. In: Proceedings of the 2016 CHI Conference on Human Factors in Computing Systems, pp. 5286–5297 (2016)
20. Maier, E., Doerk, M., Muri, M., Reimer, U., Riss, U.: What does privacy mean to users of voice assistants in their homes? In: Proceedings ETHICOMP 2022, p. 300 (2022)
21. Marcus, G.: AI platforms like ChatGPT are easy to use but also potentially dangerous. Scientific American 12 (2022)
22. May, R., Denecke, K.: Security, privacy, and healthcare-related conversational agents: a scoping review. Inform. Health Soc. Care **47**(2), 194–210 (2022)
23. Newman, N.: Journalism, media and technology trends and predictions 2018. Reuters Institute for the Study of Journalism (2018)
24. Olafsson, S., O'Leary, T., Bickmore, T.: Coerced change-talk with conversational agents promotes confidence in behavior change. In: Proceedings of the 13th EAI International Conference on Pervasive Computing Technologies for Healthcare, pp. 31–40 (2019)
25. Riss, U.V., Maier, E., Doerk, M.: Perceived risks of the data economy: autonomy and the case of voice assistants. In: Proceedings ETHICOMP 2022, p. 375 (2022)
26. Schwalb, P., Klecun, E.: The role of contradictions and norms in the design and use of telemedicine: healthcare professionals' perspective. AIS Trans. Human-Comput. Interac. **11**(3), 117–135 (2019)
27. Seymour, W.: Re-thinking smartness: designing more ethical connected devices for the home, Ph. D. thesis, University of Oxford (2020)
28. Seymour, W., Van Kleek, M.: Exploring interactions between trust, anthropomorphism, and relationship development in voice assistants. Proceed. ACM Human-Comput. Inter. 5(CSCW2), 1–16 (2021)
29. Shorter, M., et al.: Materialising the immaterial: Provotyping to explore voice assistant complexities. In: Designing Interactive Systems Conference, pp. 1512–1524 (2022)
30. Solove, D.J.: The myth of the privacy paradox. Geo. Wash. L. Rev. **89**, 1 (2021)
31. Véliz, C.: Privacy is power. Melville House New York (2021)
32. Winegar, A.G., Sunstein, C.R.: How much is data privacy worth? A preliminary investigation. J. Consum. Policy **42**, 425–440 (2019)
33. Woll, A., Bratteteig, T.: Activity theory as a framework to analyze technology-mediated elderly care. Mind Cult. Act. **25**(1), 6–21 (2018)
34. Woźniak, P.W., et al.: Creepy technology: What is it and how do you measure it? In: Proceedings of the 2021 CHI Conference on Human Factors in Computing Systems, pp. 1–13 (2021)
35. Zionchenko, V., Munipov, V.: Fundamentals of ergonomics. Ergon. Major Writings **1**, 17–37 (2005)

Semi-autonomous Units for Mechanized Combat Controlled by Voice Commands

Per-Anders Oskarsson$^{(\boxtimes)}$, Peter Svenmarck, Kristofer Bengtsson, Alexander Melbi, and Anna Pestrea

Swedish Defence Research Agency, Linköping, Sweden
per-anders.oskarsson@foi.se

Abstract. Autonomous systems are developed for both civilian and military applications. To investigate the use of semi-autonomous ground and air units in mechanized combat and control by voice commands, a case study with two participants was performed. The study was performed in a simulation environment, and voice commands were implemented by Wizard of Oz (WoZ) procedures. The objective was to compare control of semi-autonomous units by voice commands with control by communication with human operators that controlled non-autonomous units. The results show that control of units by communication with human operators was more efficient and less demanding, since the human operators understood the situation and adapted accordingly. Discussions with the participants indicated that efficient control of autonomous units by voice commands requires higher levels of autonomy and fewer and simpler voice commands than implemented in the present study. The study also demonstrated that the simulation environment and WoZ procedures are applicable to testing control of semi-autonomous units by voice commands.

Keywords: autonomous systems · voice control · simulation · UGV · UAV

1 Introduction

In civilian as well as military systems, research and development is carried out about using autonomous functions to accomplish tasks that were previously performed by humans. Well-implemented autonomous functions can improve efficiency, safety, response time, and relieve operators' workload. Although the purpose of autonomous functions is to increase system efficiency, they may also have negative side effects. An autonomous system may change the operator's task to system monitoring, which may lead to reduced capability of taking over control if the automation fails [1]. Thus, the operator may end up outside the decision loop, unaware of what the system is doing. This is a phenomenon which has been denoted the out-of-the-loop problem [2]. Interaction with autonomous systems may also create new types of cognitive work, as well as needs for new knowledge and skills [3]. Furthermore, use of automation may require people to work more, faster or in more complex ways, since new technology tends to put demands

© The Author(s), under exclusive license to Springer Nature Switzerland AG 2023
M. Kurosu and A. Hashizume (Eds.): HCII 2023, LNCS 14013, pp. 380–395, 2023.
https://doi.org/10.1007/978-3-031-35602-5_27

on increased capacity, which has been denoted the law of stretched systems [4]. Similarly, in command and control (C2), coordination of autonomous systems can be more complex [5], and high levels of mental workload from managing unmanned systems with autonomous functions can have negative effects on commanders' C2 capability [6].

In the military field, systems with autonomous functions are developed, for example for unmanned aerial, ground and naval systems, C2-systems, and military medicine [7–9]. Future ground forces will most likely be supported by integrated ground and aerial systems with autonomous functions. Research is therefore needed to study how such semi-autonomous systems affect decision-making, organization, methodology, and use of C2-systems.

The aim of the study presented in this paper was to investigate the use of semi-autonomous units, an unmanned ground vehicle (UGV) and an unmanned aerial vehicle (UAV), in a mechanized platoon. Specifically, the use of semi-autonomous units and control by voice commands was investigated. This was performed by a simulation study in Virtual Battle Space 3 (VBS3) [10], where a platoon commander of three infantry fighting vehicles (IFV) controlled the semi-autonomous units by voice commands.

1.1 Autonomous Functions

Autonomous functions can perform different types of tasks, and tasks can be shared between autonomous systems and human operators. Thus, it is natural that taxonomies for categorization of levels of autonomy, or automation, are mainly based on how different levels of automation affect the human operator and sharing of tasks. A review by [11] summarizes twelve taxonomies. Common for all taxonomies is that they range from full manual control by the human operator to full automatic control by the system. One of the taxonomies in the review was the first example of a taxonomy for levels of automation, developed by [12], which comprises ten levels of automation.

A description of how it is possible to create systems that combine the advantages of both human operators and autonomous functions by combining high levels of human control and autonomy can be found in [13]. The design of such autonomous systems focuses on how systems perform tasks together with human operators rather than restricting descriptions to technical issues. Coactive design [14] and Joint Control Framework (JCF) [15] are two examples of frameworks that use an all-embracing view.

Coactive design promotes joint performance by describing possible alternatives for the interaction between autonomous systems and human operators. These interactions are based on mutual dependencies, where the human operator and the system both provide and receive support from each other. This is contrary to traditional paradigms, where certain tasks are assigned to the autonomous system and others to the human operator. The mutual dependencies between the autonomous system and human operator mainly concern observability, predictability, and directability [14].

Joint Control Framework (JCF) is a framework for description and analysis of human-machine interaction of systems. JCF builds on three steps. The first step is process mapping (PM), which comprises mapping of which processes and agents should be included in the analysis. The second step is examining the levels of autonomy in cognitive control (LACC), which consists of six levels of control. In contrast to other frameworks for autonomy, LACC does not correspond to increasing levels of autonomy. Instead, its lowest levels focus on how functions should be realized; the medium levels focus on what the system does; and the highest levels focus on why something should be done (e.g., overarching goals and system purposes). The last step is human–machine interaction temporal analysis (HMI-T), which creates an understanding of the joint cognitive system's interaction over time. It also reveals overlaps of simultaneous processes over time and highlights temporal constraints in the control process. By these processes, JCF can describe control strategies and information needs for critical episodes at different levels of abstraction and allocation of tasks between the system and human operator [15].

1.2 Wizard of Oz Simulations

Wizard of Oz (WoZ) simulation is a procedure that is often used to simulate advanced system functions, see [16]. In principle, the procedure for a WoZ simulation is that a human controls the system and responds to the participant's interactions with the system. A well-designed WoZ simulation can give the participant the experience of realistic user interaction with a real system.

WoZ simulations are mainly used in conceptual studies, for example in human-centered design, to test aspects of usability or applicability of futuristic or advanced automatic functions. WoZ simulations are usually utilized when the function would be very complicated or expensive to implement or when a futuristic application cannot be implemented with present technology. Examples of studies using Woz simulations include control of augmented reality (AR) by speech, hand movements and gestures [17], interactive whiteboards [18], graphical user interfaces for control of a humanoid robot for autistic children [19], and a driver support system for automatic detection of car drivers' emotions [20].

In the study presented in this paper, a WoZ simulation was used to simulate voice recognition and the semi-autonomous functions in the UGV and UAV.

2 Method

The study was performed as a case study with two participants. These acted as a platoon commander in an infantry fighting vehicle (IFV), who simultaneously interacted with a UGV and a UAV. Two conditions were tested, control of a semi-autonomous UGV and UAV by voice control, and communication over radio with human operators controlling the UGV and UAV.

2.1 Participants

The study was performed with two participants. Both were about 50 years old and had profound experience of leading mechanized combat from service in the Swedish Armed Forces.

2.2 Simulation

The study was performed with the simulation software Virtual Battlespace 3 (VBS3), a virtual training environment with a first-person-shooter perspective and multiplayer capabilities. VBS3 [10] was developed by Bohemia Interactive and is used as a training and education tool by numerous armed forces.

Simulation Setup. The simulation was set up on seven computers in a lab. One computer was used by the participant and six by the experiment leaders. The participant had the role of platoon commander in an infantry fighting vehicle (IFV), who also controlled one UGV and one UAV. In front of the participant, there were three computer screens. The screen in the center showed the platoon commander's view from the prisms in the IFV, the left screen showed the camera view of the UAV, and the right screen showed the camera view of the UGV (Fig. 1).

Fig. 1. Participant acting as platoon commander in front of the three computer screens.

The experiment leaders used one computer for acting as driver in the platoon commander's IFV, one computer for acting as company commander, one computer for controlling VBS3, which, e.g., included moving the platoon and company vehicles to simulate joint combat operations, moving enemy vehicles, handling indirect fire, and simulating radio communication. The remaining three computers were used for the WoZ control of the UGV and UAV, and generation of textual feedback and sound alerts to the participant.

In order to minimize the number of people in the lab, detailed control of enemy vehicles, the other two vehicles in the platoon, and the gunner in the platoon commander vehicle were controlled by artificial intelligence (AI) functions in VBS3. In previous tests [21], these were controlled by human operators. A schematic view of the simulation setup is presented in Fig. 2.

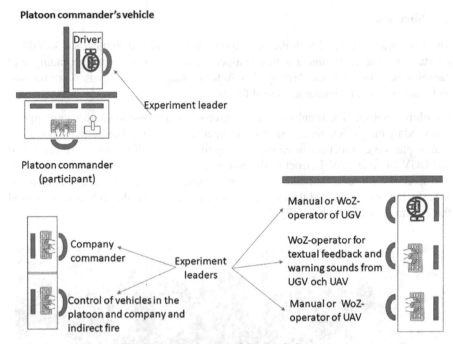

Fig. 2. Schematic view of the simulation setup.

When the UGV and UAV were controlled by human operators, the two experiment leaders controlling the units acted as human operators using radio communication with the platoon commander. When the semi-autonomous units were used, the platoon commander controlled them by voice commands, whereas the experiment leaders simulated the units with voice recognition capability and semi-autonomous functions, in accordance with the WoZ-procedures (see Sect. 1.2). A digital map in VBS3 was used to simulate a C2-system. The C2-map was accessible on the commander's main screen and on the UGV and UAV operators' screens.

Simulated Units. The simulated UGV measured 240 × 200 × 115 cm, weighed 1.5 tons, and could travel at a maximum speed of 20 km/h. It was equipped with two weapons, a machine gun and an anti-tank missile (Fig. 3).

Semi-autonomous Functions and Voice Commands. The semi-autonomous functions were simulated by WoZ-procedures, which means that the two experiment leaders who controlled the UGV and UAV acted as a system with voice recognition and semi-autonomous capability, and thus controlled the units according to the platoon commander's voice commands. A third experiment leader generated textual feedback, which was presented on the platoon commander's screens displaying the camera view from each respective unit. The platoon commander received sound alerts through headphones.

The voice commands used by the platoon commander to control the semi-autonomous units can be divided into direct commands and task related commands.

Fig. 3. View of the simulated UGV.

Direct commands were used for driving/flying the units and controlling their camera systems (see Table 1).

Table 1. Direct voice commands for controlling the units (translated from Swedish) and descriptions of the units' actions. Square bracket indicates optional part of command.

Voice command	Description of the units' actions
Forward/Backward	Drives/flies forward/backward
Left/Right	Turns right/left (max 45°)
Left/Right 15[°]	Turns right/left 15°
Turn [180][°]	Turns 180°
Stop turn[ing]	Interrupts turning
Climb/Descend	UAV climbs/descends
Increase/Decrease (Faster/Slower)	Increases/Decreases speed
Halt	Stops
Camera 12/6 (or forward/ backward)	Turns camera forward/backward (in relation to vehicle's lengthwise direction)
Camera [to] right/left	Turns camera right/left (in relation to vehicle's lengthwise direction)
Camera up[ward]/down[ward]	Turns camera upward/downward

(*continued*)

Table 1. (*continued*)

Voice command	Description of the units' actions
Camera center	Centers the camera vertically
Camera zoom in/out	Zooms the camera in/out
Camera stop	Stops all camera movements
Camera IR/Optic	Changes type of camera: Optic/IR (infra-red)
Weapon MG/Robot	Changes type of weapon: Machine gun/robot (platoon commander fires manually)
Manual control	Changes control mode to manual control by joystick
Voice command	Changes control mode to voice control
Roger	Turns of sound alert when feedback is given

The semi-autonomous functions implemented in the units and the task related voice commands used to control these functions were:

- *Drive/fly to a designated position.* The platoon commander designates a position by drawing a point x on a digital map (x can also be a named location on the map).

  Voice command: *Drive to position x.*
  The unit drives/flies to the designated location (UGV optimizes best path in the terrain). The unit confirms with text and sound alerts when it reaches position x.

- *Follow the road to a designated position* (only UGV). The platoon commander designates a position by drawing a point x on a digital map (x can also be a named location on the map).

  Voice command: *Follow the road [to x]*(square brackets indicate optional part of command).
  The UGV follows the road to the designated location. If x is omitted, the UGV follows the road until it receives a new command. The UGV confirms with text and sound alerts when it reaches position x.

- *Follow a route to a designated position* (only UAV). The platoon commander draws a route on the map.

  Voice command: Follow *the route to positon x.* The unit confirms with text and sound alerts when it reaches position x.

- *Search towards a point in the terrain.* The platoon commander marks position x on the map by a colored point.

  Voice command: *Search towards point x* (x is the color of the point).

The unit searches towards the point and confirms with text and sound alerts if it detects a target.

- *Search for targets in a sector.* The platoon commander verbally indicates the angle in degrees of a sector in front of the unit.

Voice command: *Search sector x/y* (x is bearing in degrees to the left of the unit's front; y is bearing in degrees to the right of the unit's front).
The unit searches in the sector and confirms with text and sound alerts if it detects a target in the sector.

- *Search for targets in a designated area.* The platoon commander marks an area in the terrain by drawing a colored rectangle on the map.

Voice command: *Search in area x* (x is the color of the area on the map)
The unit drives/flies to the area and searches the area. The unit confirms with text and sound alerts, either if it detects a target in the area or if it finishes searching the area without detecting any targets.

The units also had autonomous functions for target detection and detection of enemy fire. Thus, whenever a unit detected a target or was exposed to enemy fire, it informed the platoon commander with text and sound alerts. The units also signaled by text and sound alerts if they could not interpret a voice command. The UGV also signaled by text and sound alerts if it could not drive because it was stuck in the terrain. The sound alerts had three intensity levels. The highest intensity was used for information of enemy fire, the medium intensity for target detection, and the lowest intensity for feedback on all other tasks described above. For all direct commands, confirmative text messages without a sound alert provided feedback. When the units were controlled by voice commands, the platoon leader could change to manual control by joystick (see Table 1), for example for directing the UGV gun towards an enemy.

The experimental leaders could hear the platoon commander's voice commands through headphones, and the map that the platoon commander used for indication of positions was visible on their computer screen.

2.3 Scenario

The scenario consisted of the platoon commander leading a vanguard platoon with three infantry fighting vehicles in a mechanized company. The task was to take specific key terrain in the direction of the attack. The enemy side consisted of three infantry fighting vehicles and two squads of dismounted infantry soldiers spread out in the terrain. The positions of both own and enemy units were different for the two conditions, control of semi-autonomous units by voice commands and control by communication with human operators that controlled non-autonomous units.

2.4 Procedure and Design

The participants completed four training rounds before each test condition. Each training round was performed using one single type of unit (UGV or UAV), each with control of semi-autonomous units by voice commands and by communication with human operators.

Two conditions were tested with each participant, each in a separate test session. The first condition was communication by radio with human operators who controlled the units by analogous terminology as when giving orders and communicating with other personnel in the platoon. The second condition was control by voice commands of semi-autonomous units, as described above. In each condition, the participant had access to both the UGV and the UAV. Each condition was tested on separate days and both participants started with control by communication with human operators. The order was not counterbalanced as it was considered necessary to manage control by communication human operators before testing control of semi-autonomous units by voice commands. However, the starting positions of the units were counterbalanced between the two participants. Each test condition continued until the enemy was defeated or the platoon had taken the assigned key terrain.

Before training, the participants answered a questionnaire with background questions. After each test condition, the participants answered a questionnaire with questions about the interaction and use of the units. The questionnaire had 7-point rating scales and free text answers. Finally, a discussion was performed with the participants, focusing on the interaction with the units, the semi-autonomous functions and their use in combat, both with control of semi-autonomous units by voice commands and with communication with human operators that controlled non-autonomous units.

2.5 Data Collection and Analysis

When voice commands were used to control semi-autonomous units, the platoon commander's voice commands and the textual feedback from the units were recorded in an Excel sheet with macro functions. The worksheet contained one button for each predefined voice command, which also was used to generate textual feedback and sound alerts to the platoon commander. Communication with human operators, not covered by the predefined commands, e.g. questions, were noted as free text in the Excel sheet. As a backup, sound and video recordings were performed.

In the analysis, the platoon commander's communication with the human operators was divided into commands and questions. The human operators' communication with the platoon commander was divided into information and questions. The platoon commander's voice commands to the semi-autonomous units were divided into direct commands and task related commands, as described above. For both types of control, all communication was further divided into driving/flying the unit, controlling the camera, searching, target detection, enemy fire, engaging enemy, and feedback/confirmation.

3 Results

The results comprise participants' communication with human operators, voice commands, feedback from the semi-autonomous units, mission time for accomplishing each test condition, subjective ratings from the questionnaire, and a summary of the final discussion with the participants. The summary of the final discussion with the participants also includes answers to the free text questions in the questionnaire.

Mission time, communication with operators, voice commands, and subjective ratings are reported as the mean values of the two participants. Since there was only two participants, no statistical analyses were performed.

3.1 Communication with Human Operators

The participants gave approximately twice as many commands to the UGV operator as to the UAV operator. There were also differences in the types of commands. The commands to the UGV operator were mainly related to driving, while the commands to the UAV operator were mainly related to searching. This explains why the information from the UAV operator was mainly related to target detection. Thus, the reason why the UAV operator detected more targets was most likely that it was predominantly used for searching and that its advantage of altitude and speed facilitated target detection. The platoon commander asked approximately the same number of search related questions to both operators, which is most likely the reason why both operators provided approximately the same amount of search-related information to the platoon commander as answers to the questions. Commands to the UGV operator regarding enemy engagement was related to firing the unit's weapon (Fig. 4).

3.2 Control of Semi-autonomous Units by Voice Commands

The participants gave more direct commands to the UAV than to the UGV. However, the difference between the two participants was large. One of the participants gave 44 direct commands to the UAV, while the other only gave one direct command. The reason for this difference is that the participant who frequently gave direct commands to the UAV, during two sequences in the test, used it for active surveillance and thus repeatedly gave turning and zooming commands to its camera.

All task related commands to the UAV concerned search tasks, such as searching towards a point in the terrain or in a specific area, which the platoon commander had marked on the map in the C2-system. Of the task related commands given to the UGV, the majority were related to driving. These concerned either following the road ahead or driving to a specific point marked on the map in the simulated C2-system. Enemy engagement meant opening fire with the weapons of the UGV. Since the UGV could not open fire autonomously, the platoon commander could only control the weapon system of the UGV by direct commands. However, only one of the participants used the UGV to engage enemies (Fig. 5).

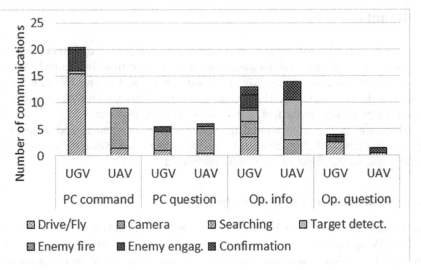

Fig. 4. Communication with human operator. Number of voice commands and questions by platoon commander and information and questions from human operator (mean number of the two participants).

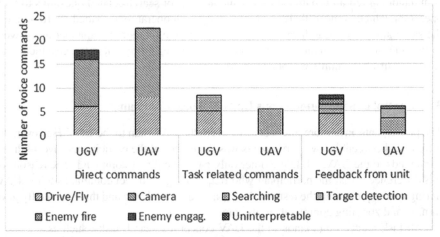

Fig. 5. Control of semi-autonomous units by voice commands. Number of voice commands by platoon commander and feedback from units (mean number of the two participants).

3.3 Mental Workload

The participants rated their general mental workload during the test as low. Mental workload related to interaction with the operators/semi-autonomous units by voice commands was at a mean level (middle of the rating scale), while mental workload related to keeping track of the UAV's and UGV's positions and sensor data was rated lower. The reason why mental workload of leading the crew in the platoon vehicle was extremely low was most likely that the gunner was simulated by an AI-function in VBS3, which meant that the platoon commander only interacted with the driver. As for mental workload related to interaction with the units or keeping track of their positions and sensor data, there was no difference between communication with human operators and controlling semi-autonomous units by voice commands. However, workload related to leading the crew, leading the platoon, and interacting with the company commander was rated higher when the units were controlled by communication with human operators. It is unclear if this was due to differences in the dynamic development of the scenario or if it was a training effect since the participants carried out the test with communication with human operators first. General workload was also rated somewhat higher for communication with human operators than for control of semi-autonomous units by voice commands. This is contrary to the discussion after the test (see Sect. 3.5), where both participants emphasized the difficulties and high workload when controlling the semi-autonomous units with voice commands (Fig. 6).

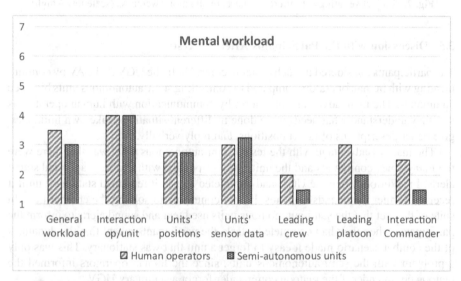

Fig. 6. Subjective ratings of different aspects of mental workload (scale low – high).

3.4 Situation Awareness

The participants' ratings of different aspects of their situation awareness indicates that this was relatively high. Situation awareness related to the units' positions was marginally higher for communication with human operators than for control of semi-autonomous units by voice commands, while there was no difference between the two types of control for keeping track of the units' actions or the positions of their own vehicle and the platoon. Situation awareness related to enemies' positions and actions was rated higher for communication with human operators, while situation awareness related to the company commander's intentions and commands was rated the highest for control of semi-autonomous units by voice commands (Fig. 7).

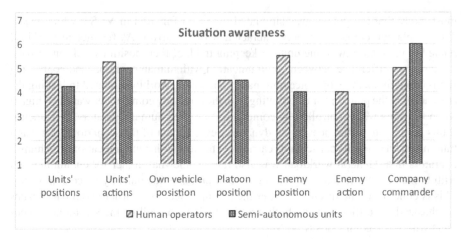

Fig. 7. Subjective ratings of different aspects of situation awareness (scale low – high).

3.5 Discussion with the Participants After the Test

The participants considered it much easier to control both the UGV and UAV by communicating with human operators compared to controlling semi-autonomous units by voice commands. The main advantage of control by communication with human operators is that they understand what needs to be done in different situations, take own initiatives, give better descriptions of target positions, and reply verbally.

The main disadvantage with the tested semi-autonomous units was that there were too many voice commands and the units only responded with text messages and sound alerts. In addition, when the UGV had completed a task, it remained stationary until it received further commands and thus did not contribute to solving the combat task. In spite of the fact that the semi-autonomous units used text and sound alerts to inform the participants when they had completed a task, the participants meant that the dynamics of the combat scenario made it easy to forget a unit that was stationary. This was only a problem with the semi-autonomous units, since the human operators informed the platoon commander if the platoon commander forgot a stationary UGV.

One participant commented that the semi-autonomous units' lack of situational understanding at the implemented level of autonomy made it difficult to use the UGV efficiently. When the UGV was commanded to drive to a point in the terrain, it drove exactly to the designated point. This was contrasted with a human driver of an infantry fighting vehicle, who would assess the terrain and risks and then position the vehicle at the best position nearby the designated point instead of exactly at the point. By driving exactly to the designated point and thereafter remain stationary, the UGV would easily be targeted by enemy fire.

Due to the difficulties of controlling the semi-autonomous units by voice commands, the participants considered human operators to be necessary for efficient use of the units, for example for keeping track of the units' positions and sensor images. The amount of information for keeping track of the units was considered overwhelming, and the sound alerts were experienced as particularly disturbing. The participants also experienced that simultaneous control of two semi-autonomous units by voice commands was more or less impossible. In this respect, one participant reflected over the alternative of simply ignoring one of the units. However, both participants considered simultaneous control of the semi-autonomous UGVs and UAVs as feasible, but meant that better methods for control and interaction would be required.

Both participants believed that higher levels of autonomy than implemented in the present test would be more usable. They suggested a higher level of autonomy, where the units would be able to perform tasks without additional instructions. For example, when using an autonomous UGV, they proposed the possibility of marking an area on a map in a C2-system and assigning the UGV tasks to perform in the area. Another suggestion was to give the UGV the capability to perform visual search tasks according to a specific pattern, e.g., sweepingly from left to right, in the same way as a gunner in an IFV.

4 Discussion

The results of this study indicate that the implemented method of controlling the semi-autonomous units by voice commands is insufficient. The main problem is that too many voice commands are needed. Thus, either a reduction of the number of voice commands or more training to master them properly is needed. However, the only realistic way of reducing the number of voice commands is probably to increase the units' level of autonomy.

Furthermore, one major problem was that the UGV became stationary when it had completed an assigned task. The participants commented that this does not happen with human operators who take own initiatives, which also indicates that a higher level of autonomy is needed to circumvent this type of problem. Thus, according to the results of the test, increasing the level of autonomy, when technically possible, would be a feasible way forward. In line with this, the participants commented that a higher level of autonomy and the capability to act independently are required for the units to provide usable support for mechanized combat.

The test demonstrated that VBS3 is a usable platform for studies of mechanized combat supported by semi-autonomous units. In addition, the participants' interactions with the UGV and UAV in VBS3 gave them valuable experiences and insights, which provided inspiration for the discussions after the test. Thus, if the test had not been performed before the discussions the outcome of the discussions would most likely have been of less value.

The reason for using voice commands for interaction with the semi-autonomous units was to impose as few additional tasks on the commander as possible by in principal providing the same type of interaction as with a human operator over radio.

A limitation of the study was that there were only two participants and that most of the units were controlled by AI-functions, which were consequences of restrictions due to the Covid-19 pandemic. A study with more participants and a more realistic simulation with more IFV vehicles controlled by experiment leaders instead of AI-functions would likely provide more reliable results. Nevertheless, the study provided valuable information on several relevant aspects of control and use of semi-autonomous units in mechanized combat, control by voice commands, WoZ-procedures for simulation of autonomy, and VBS3 as a platform for this type of studies.

In this test, the semi-autonomous units were mainly used for reconnaissance. Suggestions for further studies are widening the scope to how semi-autonomous, or autonomous, units can support other tasks in a mechanized platoon; for example, fire support, maintenance and supply, or transportation of casualties. Testing alternative methods for interaction with semi-autonomous units would also be relevant.

The main conclusions from this study are:

• Human control of UAVs and UGVs is efficient since human operators understand the situation, adapt the units' behavior to the situation, provide well-thought-out feedback to the commander, and ask questions if something is unclear.
• Higher levels of autonomy than implemented in this test are needed for autonomous systems to achieve capabilities similar to those of human operators.
• Fewer voice commands or more training than in this study is needed for efficient voice control of semi-autonomous units.
• VBS3 and the WoZ-procedures are useful to study Human Factors aspects of control and use of semi-autonomous systems by voice commands.

References

1. Bainbridge, L.: Ironies of automation. Automatica **19**, 775–779 (1983)
2. Endsley, M.R., Kiris, E.O.: The out-of-the-loop performance problem and level of control in automation. Hum. Factors. **37**, 381–394 (1995). https://doi.org/10.1518/001872095779064555
3. Bradshaw, J.M., Hoffman, R.R., Woods, D.D., Johnson, M.: The seven deadly myths of "autonomous systems". IEEE Intell. Syst. **28**, 54–61 (2013). https://doi.org/10.1109/MIS.2013.70
4. Hollnagel, E., Woods, D.D.: Joint Cognitive Systems: Foundations of Cognitive Systems Engineering. CRC Press, Boca Raton, FL (2005)
5. Woltjer, R., Bergfeldt, J., Svenmarck, P., Nilsson, P., Johansson, B.J.E.: Ledning av sammansatta system med autonoma förmågor: en explorativ intervjustudie [Command and control of systems of systems with autonomous capabilities]. Totalförsvarets forskningsinstitut (FOI) (2016)
6. Johansson, B.J.E., Oskarsson, P.-A., Svenmarck, P., Bengtsson, K., Fredriksson Hääg, A.: Ledning av autonoma och sammansatta system för mekaniserad strid [C2 of autonomous and combined systems for mechanised combat]. FOI, Totalförsvarets Forskningsinstitut (2020)
7. Svenmarck, P., Bengtsson, K.: Förmågor hos framtidens intelligenta enheter - Nya förutsättningar för ledning [Capabilities of future intelligent units]. FOI, Swedish Defence Research Agency (2018)
8. Robinson, Y., et al.: AI och framtidens försvarsmedicin. FOI, Swedish Defence Research Agency (2020)
9. Gray, M., Ertan, A.: Artificial Intelligence and Autonomy in the Military: An Overview of NATO Member States' Strategies and Deployment. NATO Cooperative Cyber Defence Centre of Excellence (2021)
10. VBS3: https://bisimulations.com/products/vbs3. now upgraded to VBS4: https://vbs4.com/

11. Vagia, M., Transeth, A.A., Fjerdingen, S.A.: A literature review on the levels of automation during the years. What are the different taxonomies that have been proposed? Appl. Ergon. **53**, 190–202 (2016). https://doi.org/10.1016/j.apergo.2015.09.013

12. Sheridan, T., Verplank W.L.W.: Human and Computer Control of Undersea Teleoperators. MIT Man-Machine Systems Laboratory, Cambridge MA (1978)

13. Korteling, J.E., van de Boer-Visschedijk, G.C., Blankendaal, R.A.M., Boonekamp, R.C., Eikelboom, A.R.: Human- versus artificial intelligence. Front. Artif. Intell. **4** (2021). https://doi.org/10.3389/frai.2021.622364

14. Johnson, M., Bradshaw, J.M., Feltovich, P.J., Jonker, C.M., Van Riemsdijk, M.B., Sierhuis, M.: Coactive design: designing support for interdependence in joint activity. J. Human-Robot Interact. **3**, 43–69 (2014)

15. Lundberg, J., Johansson, B.J.E.: A framework for describing interaction between human operators and autonomous, automated, and manual control systems. Cogn. Technol. Work **23**(3), 381–401 (2020). https://doi.org/10.1007/s10111-020-00637-w

16. Kelley, J.F.: An empirical methodology for writing user-friendly natural language computer applications. In: I: Conference on Human Factors in Computing Systems – Proceedings, pp. 193–196 (1983)

17. Lee, M., Billinghurst, M.: A wizard of Oz study for an AR multimodal interface. In: I: ICMI'08: Proceedings of the 10th International Conference on Multimodal Interfaces, pp. 249–256 (2008)

18. Walny, J., Lee, B., Johns, P., Henry Riche, N., Carpendale, S.: Understanding pen and touch interaction for data exploration on interactive whiteboards. IEEE Trans. Vis. Comput. Graph. **18**, 2779–2788 (2012). https://doi.org/10.1109/TVCG.2012.275

19. Villano, M., et al.: DOMER: A Wizard of Oz interface for using interactive robots to scaffold social skills for children with autism spectrum disorders. In: I: HRI 2011 - Proceedings of the 6th ACM/IEEE International Conference on Human-Robot Interaction, pp. 279–280 (2011)

20. Eyben, F., Wöllmer, M., Poitschke, T., Schuller, B., Blaschke, C., Färber, B., Nguyen-Thien, N.: Emotion on the road—necessity, acceptance, and feasibility of affective computing in the car. Adv. human-computer Interact. **2010**, (2010)

21. Johansson, B.J.E., Bengtsson, K., Oskarsson, P.-A., Svenmarck, P., Petterson, J.: An initial study of applying a semi-autonomous UGV in land warfare. In: Proceedings of the 25th International Command Control Research and Technology Symposium (2020)

Voice Assistant-Based Cognitive Behavioral Therapy for Test Anxiety in Students

Julian Striegl[1]([✉]), Claudia Loitsch[1], and Gerhard Weber[2]

[1] ScaDS.AI Dresden/Leipzig, Center for Scalable Data Analytics and Artificial Intelligence, 01187 Dresden, Germany
julian.striegl@tu-dresden.de
[2] Chair of Human-Computer Interaction, TU Dresden, 01187 Dresden, Germany

Abstract. With the prevalence of mental disorders such as anxiety rising sharply, new low-threshold and scalable solutions for mental health support are needed - especially for the younger population. In recent years studies investigating the use of apps and chatbots to deliver content based in cognitive behavioral therapy (CBT) for mental health support showed promising results. The use of voice assistants (VAs) to convey methods and interventions stemming from CBT for students with test anxiety has, however, thus far not been investigated. To address this problem, we present the design and prototypical implementation of a VA for CBT-based interventions against exam anxiety in students. In a user study with the primary target group of students (N=20), it could be shown that the presented system has a good usability and a high level of acceptance (CSQi mean 27.15).

Keywords: Human-Computer Interaction · Speech · Voice Interaction · Voice Assistants · Conversational Agents · Cognitive Behavioral Therapy · Anxiety Disorders

1 Introduction

Approximately one in sixth students suffer from a mental disorder [16,25], with anxiety being the most prevalent psychiatric one [6]. As the younger population rarely seeks medical and psychological counseling due to manifold barriers (cf. [17]), low-threshold solutions are needed for this target group to reach those affected in the early stages of mental disorders such as test anxiety. The necessity of new fitting and scalable solutions for mental health support - especially in the university context - is further motivated by the strong increase in the use of psychological counseling services at universities in recent years [1]. Research in this field has increased further in importance through the COVID-19 pandemic, which lead - among other things - to an increase in the perceived workload of students, a decrease in social support [1], a high prevalence of anxiety in students [25] and a rapid increase of cases of anxiety in the general population [32]. This predicament stands against a global shortage of mental health professionals [11]. Due to this shortage, even in industrial countries such as Germany, a person who

M. Kurosu and A. Hashizume (Eds.): HCII 2023, LNCS 14013, pp. 396–406, 2023.
https://doi.org/10.1007/978-3-031-35602-5_28

applies for psychotherapy treatment has to wait on average 3 to up to 9 months before being able to start treatment [9].

One possibility to face this problem is the use of computerized cognitive behavioral therapy. Cognitive behavioral therapy (CBT) is an evidence-based form of therapy that has successfully been used for several decades to treat mental disorders and is regarded as the treatment with the highest evidence for anxiety disorders [4]. The effectiveness of CBT in computerized and app-based form has already been proven to be beneficial for anxiety and studies with CBT delivered through chatbots showed promising results [13,19]. In a recent study the usability of voice assistant-based (VA-based) CBT was further rated higher as a comparable chatbot-based system due to the higher accessibility and faster interaction [34]. Additionally, a high acceptance of VA-based CBT could be shown for the target group of students [15]. This paper strives to investigate the usability and acceptance of a VA-based system capable of supporting students with test anxiety using selected CBT methods.

In Sect. 2 test anxiety as a mental disorder and the fundamentals of conversational agent-based (CA-based) CBT will be introduced, while incorporating the current state of research. Section 3 introduces system design and prototypical implementation of a VA capable of delivering selected methods for CBT-based interventions for test anxiety in students. Section 4 describes the methodology and results of a conducted study, followed by a thorough discussion. Section 5 draws a conclusion and indicates future work.

2 Preliminaries and Related Work

Test anxiety is a psychological condition expressed by a set of phenomenological, physiological, and behavioral responses that accompany concerns about possible adverse outcomes in examinations or other evaluative situations [37]. The symptoms vary from case to case and can occur on a physical, emotional, cognitive, and behavioral level. Consequences for the individual include e.g. increased heart rate and blood pressure [38], low self-esteem, fear of failure, decreased performance in exam situations [31], poor sleep quality [20], procrastination and avoidance of exam situations [35].

One treatment option for anxiety disorders, such as text anxiety, is the use of CBT. Originally introduced as a treatment method for depression by Aaron T. Beck [6], CBT has been proven to be effective for anxiety disorders as well and has successfully been used for the treatment of anxiety for decades. One main goal of CBT is the identification of cognitive distortions, such as negative beliefs and dysfunctional thought patterns, in patients [5]. With those cognitive distortions identified, the patient is made aware of their subjective nature, encouraged to critically challenge the justification of identified thought patterns, and led to cognitively reconstruct them into more functional thoughts and beliefs [5,6]. CBT furthermore offers different exercises for coping with acute stress and anxiety, such as relaxation and breathing exercises as well as meditation [10].

To cope with the shortage of face-to-face therapy options and the rising prevalence of mental disorders, research on computerized CBT approaches has been going on for several decades. In the form of online psychotherapy, cybertherapy as well as email, app, and chat-based therapy different solutions exist that differ in their approach. While some provide automated therapeutic methods for self-guided interventions, others function as a communication medium between therapist and patient and are intended to be used adjunct to therapy [7,23]. As they are easy to access and discrete in usage, those solutions provide one possible strategy to encounter the increasing prevalence of mental health disorders such as anxiety [3]. Furthermore, in recent years research on CA-based CBT delivery has gained in significance. Consequently, studies on the use of CA-based CBT for people with anxiety are presented in detail further below.

Fitzpatrick et al. [13] conducted a study with a chatbot called *Woebot* that is capable of delivering chosen CBT-based content to users. The authors evaluated the feasibility, acceptability, and preliminary efficacy of Woebot on a sample of college students with symptoms of anxiety and depression. The results indicated, Woebot could potentially be a suitable possibility to deliver CBT to students with anxiety and depression.

The chatbot-based system *Wysa* was used by Leo et al. [24] in a single-arm, prospective cohort study with adult participants who self-reported symptoms of anxiety and depression. The system was provided to participants for 2 months as a digital mental health intervention. The study measured the recruitment and retention rates, the engagement with the app's therapeutic tools, and the differences in mental and physical health scores at the 2-month follow-up between high and low users of the app as determined by a median split. Patient engagement exceeded industry standards and the group of high users showed improvements in anxiety scores when compared to the low usage group.

Oh et al. [29] developed a chatbot called *Todaki* capable of providing psychoeducational content on panic disorders, exercises on coping skills, and content based on chosen treatment methods that are deliverable in an app format. The system was used over 4 weeks in a prospective randomized controlled trial using a parallel-group design by adult patients with mild-to-severe panic symptoms. Whilst the experimental group used the application, the control group had access to a paperback book containing similar content. Results indicated that the use of the chatbot was more effective in reducing the severity of panic symptoms than the paperback book control condition.

Fulmer et al. [14] used a chatbot system called *Tess* in a study to investigate the efficacy of artificial intelligence-based conversational systems to reduce symptoms of depression and anxiety in college students. Tess was designed to deliver adaptive conversations based on expressed emotions and mental health concerns of participants and was used in a single-blind randomized user study with an information control group (receiving an educational ebook on the topic). Among other diagnostic tools, the Generalized Anxiety Disorder 7-item scale (GAD-7) [33] was used by the authors to measure the effects on anxiety in both groups over the course of 2 to 4 weeks. Results showed a significant reduction in symptoms of anxiety in the experimental group. Participants from the experimental group furthermore showed higher levels of engagement and user satisfaction than those from the control.

While mentioned studies showed promising results, more scientific evidence is needed in order to draw a stronger conclusion regarding the feasibility and efficacy of CA-based therapy approaches for anxiety disorders. Moreover, while some evidence exists that VAs may be preferable to chatbots for some user groups in the context of CA-based CBT [34] and while past studies indicated good usability and acceptance of VA-based CBT for the target group of students [15], research on VA-based systems is still sparse in comparison to chatbot-based CAs and the use of VA-based CBT for students with test anxiety has thus far not been investigated.

3   System Design and Implementation

To address this scientific gap, suitable CBT methods for VA-based interventions for anxiety disorders were identified based on the latest findings in behavioral and cognitive research. Consequently, a system for VA-based CBT for test anxiety was conceptualized using a user-centered design approach, while focusing on robust and natural dialog management for method delivery, and implemented as a high-fidelity prototype.

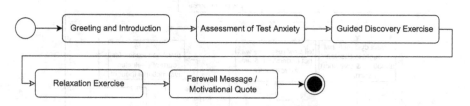

Fig. 1. Conceptualized structure of a VA-based CBT session for users with test anxiety.

While the goal is not to replace human-to-human therapy (as discussed later), the system nevertheless predominantly follows the structure of a classical CBT session (see Fig. 1). Hence, after a short introduction to the system, the mental state of users is assessed. To achieve this, the test anxiety questionnaire by Nist and Diehl [28] is utilized as a diagnostic tool, presented to the user in a dialog format and a resulting score is calculated by the system in order to approximate the level of test anxiety. Afterward, the user is led through a guided discovery exercise to identify dysfunctional thoughts [5] by presenting psychoeducational content regarding dysfunctional thought patterns and by asking specific questions about the feelings and thought processes of the user. Finally, the user is led through a breathing technique (4-7-8 breathing[1]) as a relaxation exercise that aims to address several of the symptoms of test anxiety. The chosen technique can be used to improve concentration, make it easier to fall asleep, and can be used as a coping strategy to dissolve tension and inner discomfort in exam situations [2, 26, 30]. An exemplary excerpt of dialog management can be seen in Fig. 2. The session is finished with an optional motivational quote and a farewell message.

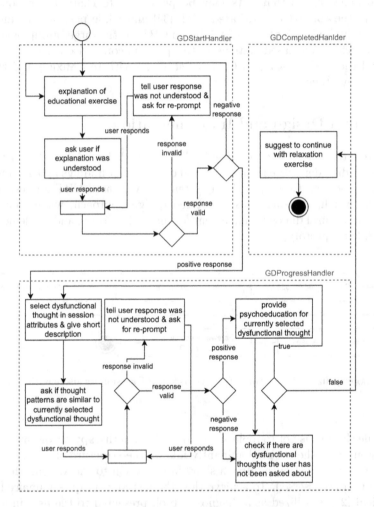

Fig. 2. Activity diagram showing the designed dialog management for the guided discovery exercise. The different handlers for the guided discovery (GD) intents are marked with dotted lines.

The objective pursued with regard to the developed concept is to conduct an initial study on the general acceptance and usability of voice assistants for this type of intervention against test anxiety for the defined target group. Accordingly, the concept is not claimed to be complete for a real-world application.

The conceptualized system was implemented using the Alexa Skills Kit[2]. Since the user study was conducted with German students, the systems utterances and natural language processing (NLP) models were created and trained in German.

4   Evaluation: Investigating Usability and Acceptance of the Designed System

To investigate the usability and acceptance of the developed system, a user study was conducted as a single-arm trial with participants from the target group.

4.1   Methods

20 subjects with an average age of 22.55 years participated in the study (12 males, 8 females). All participants had to sign a privacy policy and consent form to comply with data protection provisions.

Subjects were introduced to the topic and then tested the system in a laboratory setting without interference from the facilitator. The level of test anxiety was measured in subjects using the test anxiety questionnaire (TAQ) [28]. The partner model questionnaire (PMQ) [12] was used to measure usability as well as perceived competence, dependability, and human-likeness of the developed VA. As the PMQ was specifically developed for the evaluation of speech interfaces, it is particularly suitable for the evaluation of the created VA. To measure the acceptance of the developed system among the target group, the client satisfaction questionnaire adapted to internet-based health interventions (CSQi) [8] was used. As the technology affinity of a test subject could influence acceptance and perceived usability, the general technology acceptance (TA) and technology competence beliefs (TCB) were measured using sub-scales of the technology commitment model [27]. Furthermore, control questions on the intuitiveness, user-friendliness, and functionality of the system were administered in a 5-point Likert-Scale questionnaire. Finally, participants were asked open questions on the system's functionalities and possible improvements as a formative evaluation.

4.2   Results

All participants scored above average for the TA (mean (M) 15.55; standard deviation (SD) 2.92) and TCB (M 17.05; SD 2.67). Only one participant showed

---

[2] Amazon Alexa, https://developer.amazon.com/en-US/alexa/alexa-skills-kit, access date: 06.01.2023.

low levels of test anxiety in the TAQ results. 16 participants ranked in an average range of test anxiety and 3 participants showed severe levels of test anxiety. Participants assessed the system to be very competent and dependable (M 18.15; SD 4.33). The human-likeliness was rated above average (M 1.45; SD 6.41). The communicative flexibility factor of the PMQ showed room for improvement (M -2.00; SD 2.25). Participants found the system to be easy and intuitive to use (M 4.85, SD 0.48) and reported being able to start CBT-based exercises on the VA-based system without any problems (M 4.65; SD 0.73) in the 5-point Likert-Scale questionnaire. CSQi results indicate a high level of acceptance of the system (M 27.15; SD 3.00).

Table 1. Results of applied questionnaires. The possible range of result values for each questionnaire is presented in brackets.

Questionnaire	Mean	SD
Technology Acceptance [4;20] Technology Competence Beliefs [4;20]	15.55 17.05	2.92 2.67
Test Anxiety Questionnaire [10;50]	28.20	5.37
Client Satisfaction Questionnaire [8;32]	27.15	3.00
Partner Model Questionnaire 1. Communicative Competence/Dependability [-27;27] 2. Human-likeness in Communication [-18;18] 3. Communicative Flexibility [-9;9]	18.15 1.45 -2.00	4.33 6.41 2.26

4.3 Discussion

Overall, the PMQ results indicate good usability, as 14 of 18 questionnaire items were scored positively (compare [12]). Especially the communicative competence and dependability of the system stood out favorably. The communicative flexibility factor showed room for improvement and should be revised in future versions of the system. The acceptance of the system was high and slightly above comparable systems (cf. [15]). The control questions on the intuitiveness, user-friendliness, and functionality of the system are in line with the PMQ and CSQi results and indicate good usability. The open questions showed that all implemented exercises were well received by participants, with the breathing exercise being most positively mentioned (by 6 out of 20 participants).

The most mentioned point of criticism was that some utterances were not understood correctly by the system and that the number of accepted answers should be increased. This can be addressed in future iterations of the system by expanding the sample utterances the language model is trained on. In line with the results of related work [18], some participants found the system's responses to be too long. Accordingly, the VA's responses should be shortened and/or split into smaller chunks to be adaptable in length depending on the conversational flow.

Limitations

It should be pointed out that this study investigated the usability and acceptance of a VA-based CBT system for test anxiety after one-time use in a single-arm study design. Therefore, future studies should investigate the efficacy of the system in reducing symptoms of test anxiety. Moreover, the acceptance, usability, and adherence to this novel treatment approach should be investigated over a longer period while following the clinical guidelines for the monitoring of patients with anxiety disorders [21]. For digitized therapy approaches, especially in the case of semi or fully-automated approaches using CAs, ethical standards regarding privacy, confidentiality, and safety should be taken into account before systems, such as the here presented, are rolled out and applied in healthcare (cf. [22]). While all except one participant showed at least average levels of test anxiety, only 3 subjects indicated severe symptoms of test anxiety in the TAQ results. A follow-up study should include more participants with severe symptoms of test anxiety to make a statistical analysis of differences in acceptance, usability, efficacy, and adherence possible. Furthermore, future studies should use an evolved system, in terms of the mediated therapeutic content, to better convey the concept of VA-based CBT for test anxiety to participants.

Proposed Additional Features

Several additional features were suggested by participants. Namely, as the content of the guided discovery and psychoeducational exercise was particularly liked by participants (see Fig. 2), participants suggested an expansion of the delivered content regarding dysfunctional thought patterns. One subject was suffering from asthma and had found it difficult to follow the breathing exercise, therefore alternative relaxation exercises that are effective in reducing symptoms of test anxiety (such as progressive muscle relaxation [36]) should be made available as an alternative. Other suggested features by participants included a scheduling assistant to support the creation of a learning schedule, the possibility for open conversations with the system, reminder functionalities to encourage the daily practice of exercises, cognitive restructuring techniques such as the guided formulation of positive beliefs and the tracking of user data to see trends in the increase/decrease of anxiety symptoms. Especially for the last suggestion the aforementioned concerns for confidentiality and privacy should be taken into account.

5   Conclusion

In this paper, we presented a VA-based CBT and evaluated the usability and acceptance of the system. The results of the conducted user study indicate a high level of usability and acceptance among the target group of students. The system's flexibility can be enhanced in future iterations of the user-centered design cycle. Additionally, some improvements and additional features to the concept and the developed prototype were suggested by participants. Nevertheless, the results in this novel field of research on VA-based CBT seem promising. The results of the presented study confirm that VA-based CBT has good usability and acceptance for the target group of students (cf. [15] and indicate that VA-based CBT is also suitable to address test anxiety.

Acknowledgment. Preliminary work and execution of the presented study have been done by Jonas Richartz.

References

1. Adam-Gutsch, D., Paschel, F., Ophardt, D., Huck, J.: Studieren im Corona-Online-Semester: Bericht zur Befragung der Lehramtsstudierenden der Technischen Universität Berlin im Sommersemester 2020. Technische Universität Berlin (2021)
2. Aktaş, G.K., İlgin, V.E.: The effect of deep breathing exercise and 4-7-8 breathing techniques applied to patients after bariatric surgery on anxiety and quality of life. Obesity Surgery, pp. 1–10 (2022)
3. Auerbach, R.P., et al.: WHO world mental health surveys international college student project: prevalence and distribution of mental disorders. J. Abnormal Psychol. **127**(7), 623–638 (oct 2018)
4. Bandelow, B., Michaelis, S., Wedekind, D.: Treatment of anxiety disorders. Dialogues in Clinical Neuroscience (2022)
5. Beck, A.T.: Thinking and depression: I. idiosyncratic content and cognitive distortions. Archives of General Psychiatry **9**(4), 324–333 (1963)
6. Beck, A.T.: Cognitive models of depression. Clin. Adv. Psychother.: Theory Appl. **14**(1), 29–61 (2002)
7. Berger, T.: Internetbasierte Interventionen bei psychischen Störungen. Hogrefe Verlag, Fortschritte der Psychotherapie (2015)
8. Boß, L., et al.: Reliability and validity of assessing user satisfaction with web-based health interventions. J. Med. Internet Res. **18**(8), e5952 (2016)
9. Bundespsychotherapeutenkammer, B.: Bptk-auswertung: Monatelange wartezeiten bei psychotherapeut*innen - corona-pandemie verschärft das defizit an behandlungsplätzen (2021)
10. Craske, M.G.: Cognitive-behavioral therapy. Am. Psychol. Assoc. (2010)
11. Denecke, K., Vaaheesan, S., Arulnathan, A.: A mental health chatbot for regulating emotions (sermo) - concept and usability test. IEEE Trans. Emerg. Top. Comput. **9**(3), 1170–1182 (2021)
12. Doyle, P.R., Clark, L., Cowan, B.R.: What do we see in them? Identifying dimensions of partner models for speech interfaces using a psycholexical approach. In: Proceedings of the 2021 CHI Conference on Human Factors in Computing Systems, pp. 1–14 (2021)
13. Fitzpatrick, K.K., Darcy, A., Vierhile, M.: Delivering cognitive behavior therapy to young adults with symptoms of depression and anxiety using a fully automated conversational agent (woebot): a randomized controlled trial. JMIR Mental Health **4**(2), e7785 (2017)

14. Fulmer, R., Joerin, A., Gentile, B., Lakerink, L., Rauws, M., et al.: Using psychological artificial intelligence (tess) to relieve symptoms of depression and anxiety: randomized controlled trial. JMIR Mental Health **5**(4), e9782 (2018)
15. Gotthardt, M., Striegl, J., Loitsch, C., Weber, G.: Voice assistant-based CBT for depression in students: effects of empathy-driven dialog management. In: International Conference on Computers Helping People with Special Needs, pp. 451–461. Springer (2022). https://doi.org/10.1007/978-3-031-08648-9_52
16. Grobe, T.G., Steinmann, S., Szecsenyi, J.: Arztreport 2018 schriftenreihe zur gesundheitsanalyse. 'www' barmer. de, access July 17th (2018)
17. Gulliver, A., Griffiths, K.M., Christensen, H.: Perceived barriers and facilitators to mental health help-seeking in young people: a systematic review. BMC Psychiatry **10**(1), 1–9 (2010)
18. Haas, G., Rietzler, M., Jones, M., Rukzio, E.: Keep it short: a comparison of voice assistants' response behavior. In: CHI Conference on Human Factors in Computing Systems, pp. 1–12 (2022)
19. Inkster, B., Sarda, S., Subramanian, V., et al.: An empathy-driven, conversational artificial intelligence agent (wysa) for digital mental well-being: real-world data evaluation mixed-methods study. JMIR Mhealth Uhealth **6**(11), e12106 (2018)
20. Köse, S., Yılmaz, Ş.K., Göktaş, S.: The relationship between exam anxiety levels and sleep quality of senior high school students. J. Psychiatric Nursing (2018)
21. Kosteniuk, J., Morgan, D., D'Arcy, C.: Treatment and follow-up of anxiety and depression in clinical-scenario patients: survey of saskatchewan family physicians. Can. Fam. Physician **58**(3), e152–e158 (2012)
22. Kretzschmar, K., Tyroll, H., Pavarini, G., Manzini, A., Singh, I., Group, N.Y.P.A.: Can your phone be your therapist? young people's ethical perspectives on the use of fully automated conversational agents (chatbots) in mental health support. Biomedical Informatics Insights **11**, 1178222619829083 (2019)
23. Lattie, E.G., Adkins, E.C., Winquist, N., Stiles-Shields, C., Wafford, Q.E., Graham, A.K.: Digital mental health interventions for depression, anxiety, and enhancement of psychological well-being among college students: Systematic review. J. Med. Internet Res. **21**(7), e12869 (2019)
24. Leo, A.J., et al.: A digital mental health intervention in an orthopedic setting for patients with symptoms of depression and/or anxiety: feasibility prospective cohort study. JMIR Formative Res. **6**(2), e34889 (2022)
25. Liyanage, S., et al.: Prevalence of anxiety in university students during the Covid-19 pandemic: a systematic review. Int. J. Environ. Res. Public Health **19**(1), 62 (2021)
26. McFall, A., Jolivette, K.: Mindful breathing: a low-intensity behavior strategy for students with behavioral challenges. Preventing School Failure: Alternative Education for Children and Youth, pp. 1–7 (2022)
27. Neyer, F.J., Felber, J., Gebhardt, C.: Entwicklung und validierung einer kurzskala zur erfassung von technikbereitschaft. Diagnostica **58**(2), 87 (2012)
28. Nist, P., Diehl, M.: PHCC test anxiety questionnaire. Retrieved Aug 20, 2010 (1990)
29. Oh, J., Jang, S., Kim, H., Kim, J.J.: Efficacy of mobile app-based interactive cognitive behavioral therapy using a chatbot for panic disorder. Int. J. Med. Informat. **140**, 104171 (2020)
30. Pandekar, P.P., Thangavelu, P.D.: Effect of 4-7-8 breathing technique on anxiety and depression in moderate chronic obstructive pulmonary disease patients. Int. J. Health Sci. Res. **9**, 209 (2019). https://www.ijhsr.org

31. Rana, R., Mahmood, N.: The relationship between test anxiety and academic achievement. Bull. Educ. Res. **32**(2), 63–74 (2010)
32. Santomauro, D.F., et al.: Global prevalence and burden of depressive and anxiety disorders in 204 countries and territories in 2020 due to the covid-19 pandemic. The Lancet **398**(10312), 1700–1712 (2021)
33. Spitzer, R.L., Kroenke, K., Williams, J.B., Löwe, B.: A brief measure for assessing generalized anxiety disorder: the gad-7. Arch. Internal Med. **166**(10), 1092–1097 (2006)
34. Striegl, J., Gotthardt, M., Loitsch, C., Weber, G.: Investigating the usability of voice assistant-based CBT for age-related depression. In: International Conference on Computers Helping People with Special Needs, pp. 432–441. Springer, Cham (2022). https://doi.org/10.1007/978-3-031-08648-9_50
35. Wang, Y.: Academic procrastination and test anxiety: a cross-lagged panel analysis. J. Psychol. Counsellors Schools **31**(1), 122–129 (2021)
36. Zargarzadeh, M., Shirazi, M.: The effect of progressive muscle relaxation method on test anxiety in nursing students. Iranian J. Nurs. Midwifery Res. **19**(6), 607 (2014)
37. Zeidner, M.: Test anxiety: the state of the art. Springer Science & Business Media (1998)
38. Zhang, Z., Su, H., Peng, Q., Yang, Q., Cheng, X.: Exam anxiety induces significant blood pressure and heart rate increase in college students. Clin. Experimental Hypertens. **33**(5), 281–286 (2011)

The Relationship Between Pauses and Emphasis: Implications for Charismatic Speech Synthesis

Ning Wang[1]([✉]), Abhilash Karpurapu[2], Aditya Jajodia[3], and Chirag Merchant[1]

[1] University of Southern California, Los Angeles, USA
nwang@ict.usc.edu
[2] Amazon, Bellevue, USA
[3] Samsung Research, America, Mountain View, USA

Abstract. Animated voice is engaging, memorable, and entertaining. It is also an important aspect of charismatic behavior. For animated voices, the variations in speed, intensity, and intonation play a role in the perception of charisma. Changes in speed give rise to pauses. And speakers, especially charismatic ones, often use the silence created by pauses to contrast with the emphasis to follow, such as the words spoken with high intensity. How can we realize such behaviors in a virtual character? In this paper, we discuss our work toward the synthesis of charismatic speeches. We collected voice recordings of a tutorial on the human circulatory system in both charismatic and non-charismatic voices using actors from a crowd-sourcing platform. Those recordings were then annotated for occurrence of emphasis. In this paper, we present the analysis of the pauses and emphasis of charismatic and non-charismatic voice recordings, and discuss how they relate to each other and how such findings can inform the synthesis of charismatic speeches for virtual characters.

Keywords: charisma · prosody analysis · speech synthesis

1 Introduction

Charisma is one of the oldest and most effective forms of leadership. Early research considered charisma as a gift of the body and spirit not accessible to everybody [39,49]. It is believe to be personal characteristics and the behaviors employed by leaders to build emotional interactions with their followers [26]. Modern notions of charisma have departed from this conceptualization, and do not view charisma as a rare and unusual quality [7]. Instead, leaders are attributed charisma because they can communicate in vivid and emotional ways that federate collective action around a vision [16,20,42]. The influencing tactics used by charismatic leaders depend not only on the content (i.e., verbal) of what they say, but also on the delivery mode (i.e., nonverbal; [5]). Leaders often use verbal and nonverbal charismatic strategies [5,21,41,45,48] to make their messages memorable and inspiring [17,28]. The charismatic leadership tactics are very potent devices that affect followers' emotions and information processing.

© The Author(s), under exclusive license to Springer Nature Switzerland AG 2023
M. Kurosu and A. Hashizume (Eds.): HCII 2023, LNCS 14013, pp. 407–418, 2023.
https://doi.org/10.1007/978-3-031-35602-5_29

An important aspect of charismatic behavior is the use of animated voices. Research on perceived charisma in speech indicates that variations in pitch range and standard deviations are correlated with charisma [44]. Additionally, speech rate (speed and variation), intensity (loudness and variation), intonation (e.g., phrasal ending patterns, shape, variations), and vocal clarity also play a role in perception of charisma [15,38]. While different speech features might have different affective effects in different languages [37], researchers in expressive speech generally consider that pitch [50], loudness [22], spectral structure [31], voice quality [10,23], etc. as features relevant to perceived expressiveness (e.g., emotional states) in speech. Examples of variation in voice quality include breathy, whispery, creaky, tense, or harsh voice qualities [24].

Charismatic strategies are not always employed for the sake of perceived charisma, but as tools for effective communication. For example, varied speed, such as the insertion of pauses, and intensity, such as sudden increased in volume, can draw listeners' attention to the part of messages the speaker intended to. How can we realize charismatic speech in virtual characters and make them better communicators? Given the broad range of applications of virtual characters in, for example, health care [8], energy conservation [1], and education [33], being able to employ effective communication strategies such as charismatic speech can improve the virtual character's influence in learning and decision-making of their human interactants.

In this paper, we zoom in on two features in speech that can potentially have an impact on a speaker's perceived charisma and the listeners' emotions and information processing – pauses and emphasis. Changes in speech rate give rise to pauses. And speakers, especially charismatic ones, often use the silence created by pauses to contrast with the emphasis to follow, such as the words spoken with high intensity (e.g., loudness). How can we realize such behaviors in a virtual character? In this paper, we discuss our work toward the synthesis of charismatic speech. We developed a series of verbal charismatic strategies and implemented them in a tutorial on the human circulatory system. We then collected recordings of the tutorial in both charismatic and non-charismatic voice using actors from a crowd-sourcing platform (Study 1). Subsequently, we presented the charismatic recordings to human annotators and gathered data on emphasis in speech recording (Study 2). We conducted analyses on the pauses and emphasis in charismatic speech and their co-occurrences. We discuss how such findings can inform the synthesis of charismatic speeches for virtual characters.

2   Related Work

2.1   Charisma

Neocharismatic scholars have argued that there are nine verbal and three nonverbal strategies used by charismatic leaders [5,16,40]. Verbally, charisma is often expressed through the use of metaphors, which are very effective persuasion devices that affect information processing and framing by simplifying the message, stirring emotions, invoking symbolic meanings, and aiding recall [12,20,35].

Stories and anecdotes are also often employed as devices of charisma [21,45], by making the message understandable and easy to remember [9]. Rhetorical devices, such as contrasts (to frame and focus the message), lists (to give the impression of completeness), rhetorical questions (to create anticipation and puzzles that require an answer or a solution), are often used in charismatic communications as well [4,16,51].

In addition, charismatic speakers are skilled at expressing empathy [40], setting high expectations, demonstrating moral conviction [14,26], and sharing the sentiments of the collective [40,42]. Such an orientation aids in identification to the extent that the morals and sentiments overlap with those of followers, and the leader is seen as a representative of the group. Furthermore, these leaders set high expectations for themselves and their followers and communicate confidence that these goals can be met [26]. Theoretically, these strategies are catalysts of motivation [18,19,32] and increase self-efficacy belief [6,42]. Charismatic leaders are masters at conveying their emotional states, whether positive or negative, to demonstrate passion and obtain support for what is being said [21,48]. They use body gestures, as well as facial expressions [21,45,48] and an varied voice tone [21,45]. Interestingly, research suggests that many of these tactics can be manipulated and taught, allowing the learners to have profound impact on their listeners [3].

On a nonverbal level, of most relevance to this paper, charismatic speakers speak with varied pitch, amplitude, rate, fluency, emphasis, and an overall animated voice [21,45]—all aspects of speech commonly associated with a more engaged and lively style of speech and all predicting higher ratings of charisma [38]. Both the verbal and nonverbal behaviors make the message more memorable [9,12,20,34,35,48] and increase self-efficacy [3,21,45].

2.2 Pauses and Emphasis in Speech

Pauses in speech are often categorized into silent pauses, filler pauses, and breath pauses. Breath pauses are regular natural pauses caused by respiration activity. Filler pauses are pseudo-words, such as "Mmmm" and "Hmmmm", that do not affect the meaning of the sentence [27]. Filler pauses primarily occur in spontaneous speeches. While silent pauses can be indications of disfluencies, uncertainty, and hesitation, which occur more often in spontaneous speeches, they are primarily intentional stylistic pauses used purposely by professional speakers and the like [27]. There has been great debate since the 1970s s about the duration of silence that defines a silent pause [29]. Previous work has often adopted the convention of .2 to .25 s of silence (or longer) as indication of silent pauses, while those that fall below this threshold are often considered breath pauses [11,25,36]. In automated puncture detection in speech, it has been shown that over 95% of the pauses of .35 s or longer are the sentence boundaries [30]. Previous work on the relationship between pauses and emphasis in Swedish shows that most of the pauses (i.e. 67%) occur between the first noun and the verb, at the NP-VP (noun phases - verb phrase) boundary [43]. In the study, the experimenter attempted to induce increased levels of emphasis by telling the participants "I didn't get it. Could you repeat that again." followed by "I am sorry, but still I can't get it. Could you repeat that again." As a result, the study gathered data on emphasis on target words and phrases from low to medium and high levels. Results show that pauses are very few at the lower levels of emphasis; they appear at the higher levels of emphasis. Pause duration seems not to be affected by the level of emphasis. There is no trend of increased pause duration as a function of emphasis .

3   Previous Study on Perceived Charisma with Pre-recorded Voice

In order to isolate the effect of nonverbal strategies, such as those used in speech, on perceived charisma, we first conducted a study using a virtual human, which allows us to control and manipulate a number of verbal and nonverbal charismatic strategies. The virtual human gives a lecture on the human circulatory system inside a virtual classroom called ALIVE! (Fig. 1). Study participants interacted with the virtual human, giving a tutorial with or without verbal charismatic strategies, in a charismatic or non-charismatic voice recorded by human actors. Details of the study and the virtual human design are discussed here [47].

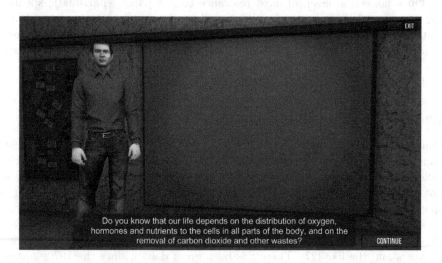

Fig. 1. The ALIVE! virtual classroom testbed with a virtual human tutor.

The results from the study suggest that the verbal strategies used by the virtual human made a significant impact on the perceived charisma. The use of such strategies also had a positive impact on the perceived effectiveness of the virtual human. This is aligned with previous work on the impact of a leader's charisma on the followers. Many charismatic strategies are used by leaders to make their messages "stick" to the followers, and to motivate them. Such strategies could indeed have an impact on the virtual human's effectiveness. However, the study also showed that there was no significant difference between the charismatic and non-charismatic voice used by the virtual human on the perceived charisma or the perceived competency of the virtual human. Interestingly, a follow-up analysis that compares the virtual human with and without a voice shows that the added voice, charismatic or not, did not make any significant difference on perceived charisma. However, when the virtual human spoke in a charismatic voice, there was a significant difference in perceived charisma between when the verbal charismatic strategies were present and absent in the lecture text. Such a difference was not observed when a non-charismatic voice was used. Given that the charismatic strategies used in the tutorial text alone had a significant impact on perceived charisma, this could mean that a non-charismatic voice, such as one that's flat and monotone, can potentially "wash out" any significant impact of verbal strategies used in the text of the lecture speech. This highlighted the negative impact when there is an absence of charismatic or animated voice for a virtual character; and the need to understand speech features contribute to perceived charisma that can be used for synthesis of charismatic speech. Given the number of speech features and values they can take on that can have potential impact on charisma, we started with the two that are among the most noticeable features by listeners – pauses and emphasis. In our in-lab testing of early synthesized charismatic speech by manipulating baseline synthesized speeches through statistical approaches, the insertion of pauses and the manipulation of speech intensity to emphasize part of speech made the most perceived improvement from baseline synthesized speech. Our previous analysis has focused on where pauses occur in charismatic speech [46]. Here, we extend the analysis to include emphasis and the relationship between these two features in charismatic speeches.

4   Emphasis and Pauses in Charismatic Speech

4.1   Study 1

Based on the research on charismatic speech, we developed a series of verbal strategies to express charisma, for example, the use of metaphor and analogies (e.g., "The major function of the blood is to be both the body's mailmen, delivering nutrients and oxygen to the cells, and its garbagemen, carrying away carbon dioxide and nitrogenous wastes from the cells") [21], stories (e.g., "My mother is still recovering from a heart attack she had when an artery got blocked, interrupting her coronary circulation.") [21,45], rhetorical questions (e.g., "As with all diffusion, molecules spread from an area of higher concentration on one side of the membrane to one of lower concentration on the other. After all, who wouldn't want to leave the crowded side?") [4], etc. Using these strategies, we re-wrote an existing tutorial on the human circulatory system [13,47]. Using the *charismatic* version of the tutorial (106 sentences, 1824 words), we gathered voice recordings from 13 participants, who read the tutorial out loud in both charismatic (e.g., animated) and non-charismatic (e.g., monotone) voice [46].

To gather the data, we first recruited 95 participants through a crowd-sourcing platform to record a snippet of the tutorial in charismatic and non-charismatic voices. Participants were given instructions that explain what is considered a charismatic vs. non-charismatic voice. For example,

- *"A voice conveys charisma is often considered to be varying in speed (e.g., sometimes fast, sometimes with pause), varying in energy (e.g., stress certain word or phrase), and varying in pitch (e.g., a more animated voice), compared to a mono-tone and mono-speed voice that often puts one to sleep. A charismatic speech inspires and motivates. "*
- *"A voice in contrast with a voice that conveys charisma is, for example, mono-tone, lack of emphasis, without changes in speed or pauses. And generally a voice that's boring and puts one to sleep. "*

Two members of the research team then selected the 13 participants whose recordings more closely followed the instructions, out of the 95 participants. The 13 participants then went on to create voice recordings of the tutorial in full length, in both charismatic and non-charismatic voices.

4.2   Study 1 Results

Pauses in speech are often categorized into silent pauses, filler pauses, and breath pauses [27]. Because our dataset consists of only prepared speeches, we did not include analysis of filler pauses, which primarily occur in spontaneous speeches. Previous work has often adopted the convention of .2 to .25 s of silence (or longer) as indication of silent pauses, while those that fall below this threshold are often considered breath pauses [11,25,36]. In our analysis, we define pauses as on silent pauses of .2 s or longer. We extracted the pauses (e.g., a silence of at least .2 s long) from the charismatic and non-charismatic speech recordings. A paired sample t-test that compares the number of silent pauses in charismatic and non-charismatic speech shows that there is no significant differences in the number of pauses between charismatic and non-charismatic speech ($M_C = 228.6, M_{NC} = 277.2, p = .214$). We also conducted a paired sample t-test to compare the number of breath pauses (a silence greater than .15 s but less than .2 s) in charismatic and non-charismatic speeches. Results show that there are significantly more breath pauses in non-charismatic speeches ($M_C = 122.1, M_{NC} = 193.2, p = .03$). Overall, there is a significant correlation of the number of silence pauses in charismatic and non-charismatic speeches ($r = .678, p = .011$). The correlation of the number of breath pauses in charismatic and non-charismatic speeches is also statistically significant ($r = .709, p = .007$). While it's not surprising that the same speaker may have a fixed habit on pause insertions, regardless of speaking styles (e.g., animated or monotone), the strength of the correlations here between those in charismatic and non-charismatic voices is only bordering medium to strong.

We also compared the mean pause durations, including both breath and silence pauses. While there is a statistically significant difference between charismatic and non-charismatic speeches, the difference is extremely small ($M_C =$

.203, $M_{NC} = .209, p = .023$). The correlation between the two is statistically significant as well ($r = .776, p = .002$). Interestingly, there is no statistically significant correlation between pause duration and speech rate ($r = -.03, p = .922$, speech rate calculated as word per minute, charismatic speech data only). In subsequent discussions of pause analysis, pauses are exclusively defined as silent pauses, with a duration of .2 s or longer.

4.3   Study 2

To understand where the emphasis occurs in the speech, we conducted a second study with participants from a crowd-sourcing platform to annotate where the emphasis occurred during the recorded *charismatic* speech gathered from study 1. We developed an online tool that allows users to play an audio recording and annotate on the transcript the words users believe to be emphasized. In the study, participants were asked to first listen to an audio recording of an utterance. After the audio recording has been played at least once, the participants were then asked to indicate which words they think that are emphasized. Each annotator listened to audio recordings of different sentences from different participants from Study 1, instead of annotating recordings of one participant reading the tutorial on human circulatory system from beginning to finish. This is to prevent the annotator from carrying the judgment of speaker charisma from one recording to the next. A total of 161 annotators were recruited to ensure each audio recording receives at least 3 annotations. After reviewing the annotations, data from 86 annotators were excluded. Excluded annotators either annotated all the words as emphasized words or none of the words as emphasized words. As a result, data from 75 annotators were included in the analysis.

4.4   Study 2 Results

Emphasis. Out of 13 charismatic audio recordings (each contains 1824 words from the charismatic text), a total of 660 recorded words were annotated as being emphasized. Note that the same word can appear in multiple recordings, e.g., the word "the" may appear in the text multiple times and recorded by 13 participants. Overall, there is very little inter-rater agreement on the emphasized words. Out of the 660 recorded words annotated as being emphasized, only 345 recorded words have the agreement from two annotators. In the subsequent analysis and unless specified otherwise, we will only consider a recorded word as being emphasized if it has the agreement of two annotators. The most commonly emphasized words are singular nouns (NN, 1643), plural nouns (NNS, 803), determiners, (DT, 671), prepositions (IN, 656), and adjectives, (JJ, 580). Compared to the non-emphasized words, the emphasized ones are spoken at higher energy ($p < .001$, Welch's t-test, given unequal emphasized and non-emphasized samples).

Emphasis and Pauses. We analyzed the relative location of pauses (annotation obtained from Study 1) and emphasized words (annotation obtained from Study 2) in charismatic speech recordings. Results show that there are a small percentage of pauses (48 out of 342) proceeding any given emphasized word. However, in our sample, there were no pauses immediately after an emphasized word. Even after relaxing the criteria for emphasized words (i.e., dropping the requirement for two-coder agreement), results still show that only a small percentage of pauses (102 out of 660) proceed any given emphasized word. Again, there was no pause immediately after an emphasized word.

5   Discussion

In this paper, we discussed two studies where we collected charismatic and non-charismatic speech samples, and subsequently gathered independent annotations of emphasis in the speech samples. Analysis of the data revealed that charismatic and non-charismatic speeches did not differ on the number of silent pauses but differed significantly on breath pauses. Not surprisingly, the number and duration of silent and breath pauses are correlated. However, pause duration is not correlated with overall speech rate.

The focus of the study, however, is on emphasis in speech and their relationship with pauses. Our data suggested that, first there is very low inter-rater agreement on the independent annotation of emphasis in speech. This could be influenced by the method used in Study 2 to present charismatic speech samples to the annotators. Instead of presenting the speech in its entirety from a given speaker, randomized selection and ordering of speech samples from different speakers were presented. This may give each annotator less time to adjust to the rhythm and flow a specific speaker uses to stress part of speech, and create difficulty in judging where the speaker intends to emphasize.

The result presented here also shows how often we emphasize without pauses proceeding or after. Interestingly, our result shows that when pauses are used together with emphasis, the pauses occur only *before* the emphasis occurs. This is in slight contradiction of previous studies on emphasis and pauses in Swedish, where pauses occur both before and after emphasis in speech [43]. Nevertheless, both studies highlighted the importance of inserting pauses immediately prior to intended emphasis. The contrast between silence (created by pause) and speech thereafter can help draw attention from the listeners, particularly on where the speaker intends to emphasize.

Pause and Emphasis Synthesis. Based on the analysis of pauses in our dataset, we have experimented with a number of ways to synthesize pauses and emphasis to express charisma. We first used a commercial speech synthesizer (Amazon Polly, [2]) to generate a baseline or neutral recording of the tutorial. Given that we used .2 s of silence as the threshold to extract pauses in our data, we then inserted silent pauses of .2 s into the baseline speech where pauses occurred in our dataset. We also applied a similar method to modify the baseline recording to emphasize part of the speech. At the word level, we experimented using build-in functions offered by commercial speech synthesizer, e.g., designating which word to emphasis, and allowing the synthesizer to adjust pitch, energy, and speed of the emphasized word. We have also experimented with manipulating these three features for emphasized words without the commercial platform and based on findings from our previous studies [46]. Anecdotal evidence suggests that both methods somewhat decreased the perceived naturalness of the synthesized speech, thus can potentially negatively impact the perceived charisma. We are currently conducting analysis of variations of pitch, energy and speed at the syllables level for the emphasized words, based on the observation that when a word is emphasized, the emphasis is often placed on the stressed syllables, and not necessarily the whole word. We are also experimenting with different functions to "smooth" the transition between emphasized and non-emphasized parts of speech, in order to improve the naturalness of the modified speech.

Limitations. One of the limitations of the study is that the charismatic speech samples are collected from non-actors. Professional actors are trained to speak and act with the audience in mind. In other words, actors act not just as expressions of their own, but how they should gesture and speak so that the audience can most accurately interpret what the actors want to express. Thus actors often act in a way more exaggerated from what we often experience in everyday life. They are also more skilled at delivering what they intend to deliver. It's possible that the charismatic recordings gathered through Study 1 are overall not as expressive in terms of charisma, from the perspective of listeners. Thus, it created difficulty for the annotators to determine occurrences of emphasis. As one of the next steps, we plan to extend the analysis to large publicly available speech datasets of charismatic speakers (e.g., speeches from past presidents, motivational speakers, etc.). This can also address one of the other limitations of the work presented here, that the pauses and emphasis analysis are specific to the tutorial text of interest to this project. Using datasets that include a larger vocabulary and greater varieties of sentence structures can allow us to better generalize where emphasis and pauses occur, and the interplay between these two features on perceived charisma.

Acknowledgement. This research was supported by the National Science Foundation under Grant #1816966. Any opinions, findings, and conclusions expressed in this material are those of the authors and do not necessarily reflect the views of the National Science Foundation.

References

1. Al Mahmud, A., Dadlani, P., Mubin, O., Shahid, S., Midden, C., Moran, O.: iParrot: towards designing a persuasive agent for energy conservation. In: de Kort, Y., IJsselsteijn, W., Midden, C., Eggen, B., Fogg, B.J. (eds.) PERSUASIVE 2007. LNCS, vol. 4744, pp. 64–67. Springer, Heidelberg (2007). https://doi.org/10.1007/978-3-540-77006-0_8

2. Amazon: Amazon Polly (2022). https://aws.amazon.com/polly/
3. Antonakis, J., Fenley, M., Liechti, S.: Can charisma be taught? tests of two interventions. Acad. Manage. Learn. Educ. **10**(3), 374–396 (2011)
4. Atkinson, J.M.: Lend me your ears: All you need to know about making speeches and presentations. Oxford University Press on Demand (2005)
5. Awamleh, R., Gardner, W.L.: Perceptions of leader charisma and effectiveness: the effects of vision content, delivery, and organizational performance. Leadersh. Q. **10**(3), 345–373 (1999)
6. Bandura, A., Walters, R.H.: Social Learning Theory, vol. 1. Prentice-hall Englewood Cliffs, NJ (1977)
7. Beyer, J.M.: Taming and promoting charisma to change organizations. Leadersh. Q. **10**(2), 307–330 (1999)
8. Bickmore, T.W., Pfeifer, L.M., Jack, B.W.: Taking the time to care: empowering low health literacy hospital patients with virtual nurse agents. In: Proceedings of the SIGCHI Conference on Human Factors in Computing Systems, pp. 1265–1274 (2009)
9. Bower, G.H.: Experiments on story understanding and recall. Q. J. Exp. Psychol. **28**(4), 511–534 (1976)
10. Burkhardt, F., Sendlmeier, W.F.: Verification of acoustical correlates of emotional speech using formant-synthesis. In: ISCA Tutorial and Research Workshop (ITRW) on Speech and Emotion (2000)
11. Campione, E., Véronis, J.: A large-scale multilingual study of silent pause duration. In: Speech prosody 2002, International Conference (2002)
12. Charteris-Black, J.: Politicians and rhetoric: The persuasive power of metaphor. Springer (2011)
13. Chi, M.T., Siler, S.A., Jeong, H., Yamauchi, T., Hausmann, R.G.: Learning from human tutoring. Cogn. Sci. **25**(4), 471–533 (2001)
14. Conger, J., Kanungo, R.: Behavioral dimensions of charismatic leadership'. in (eds, conger, ja and kanango, rn) charismatic leadership: The elusive factor in organizational effectiveness (1988)
15. DeGroot, T., Aime, F., Johnson, S.G., Kluemper, D.: Does talking the talk help walking the walk? an examination of the effect of vocal attractiveness in leader effectiveness. Leadersh. Q. **22**(4), 680–689 (2011)
16. Den Hartog, D.N., Verburg, R.M.: Charisma and rhetoric: communicative techniques of international business leaders. Leadersh. Q. **8**(4), 355–391 (1997)
17. Dumdum, U.R., Lowe, K.B., Avolio, B.J.: A meta-analysis of transformational and transactional leadership correlates of effectiveness and satisfaction: an update and extension. In: Transformational and Charismatic Leadership: The Road Ahead 10th Anniversary Edition, pp. 39–70. Emerald Group Publishing Limited (2013)
18. Eden, D.: Pygmalion, goal setting, and expectancy: compatible ways to boost productivity. Acad. Manag. Rev. **13**(4), 639–652 (1988)
19. Eden, D., et al.: Implanting pygmalion leadership style through workshop training: seven field experiments. Leadersh. Q. **11**(2), 171–210 (2000)
20. Emrich, C.G., Brower, H.H., Feldman, J.M., Garland, H.: Images in words: presidential rhetoric, charisma, and greatness. Adm. Sci. Q. **46**(3), 527–557 (2001)
21. Frese, M., Beimel, S., Schoenborn, S.: Action training for charismatic leadership: two evaluations of studies of a commercial training module on inspirational communication of a vision. Pers. Psychol. **56**(3), 671–698 (2003)
22. Frick, R.W.: Communicating emotion: the role of prosodic features. Psychol. Bull. **97**(3), 412 (1985)

23. Gobl, C., Bennett, E., Chasaide, A.N.: Expressive synthesis: how crucial is voice quality? In: Proceedings of 2002 IEEE Workshop on Speech Synthesis, 2002, pp. 91–94. IEEE (2002)
24. Gobl, C., Chasaide, A.N.: The role of voice quality in communicating emotion, mood and attitude. Speech Commun. **40**(1–2), 189–212 (2003)
25. Goldman-Eisler, F.: The distribution of pause durations in speech. Lang. Speech **4**(4), 232–237 (1961)
26. House, R.J.: A 1976 theory of charismatic leadership. working paper series, 76–06 (1976)
27. Igras-Cybulska, M., Ziółko, B., Żelasko, P., Witkowski, M.: Structure of pauses in speech in the context of speaker verification and classification of speech type. EURASIP J. Audio Speech Music Process. **2016**(1), 1–16 (2016). https://doi.org/10.1186/s13636-016-0096-7
28. Judge, T.A., Piccolo, R.F.: Transformational and transactional leadership: a meta-analytic test of their relative validity. J. Appl. Psychol. **89**(5), 755 (2004)
29. Kirsner, K., Dunn, J., Hird, K.: Language production: a complex dynamic system with a chronometric footprint (2005)
30. Lea, W.A.: Trends in speech recognition. Prentice Hall PTR (1980)
31. Lee, C.M., et al.: Emotion recognition based on phoneme classes. In: Eighth International Conference on Spoken Language Processing (2004)
32. Locke, E.A., Latham, G.P.: Building a practically useful theory of goal setting and task motivation: a 35-year odyssey. Am. Psychol. **57**(9), 705 (2002)
33. Martha, A.S.D., Santoso, H.B.: The design and impact of the pedagogical agent: a systematic literature review. J. Educators Online **16**(1), n1 (2019)
34. Mio, J.S.: Metaphor and politics. Metaphor and symbol **12**(2), 113–133 (1997)
35. Mio, J.S., Riggio, R.E., Levin, S., Reese, R.: Presidential leadership and charisma: the effects of metaphor. Leadersh. Q. **16**(2), 287–294 (2005)
36. Rochester, S.R.: The significance of pauses in spontaneous speech. J. Psycholinguist. Res. **2**(1), 51–81 (1973)
37. Roehling, S., MacDonald, B., Watson, C.: Towards expressive speech synthesis in english on a robotic platform. In: Proceedings of the Australasian International Conference on Speech Science and Technology, pp. 130–135 (2006)
38. Rosenberg, A., Hirschberg, J.: Charisma perception from text and speech. Speech Commun. **51**(7), 640–655 (2009)
39. Scott, M.G.: Max weber: On charisma and institution building (1970)
40. Shamir, B., Arthur, M.B., House, R.J.: The rhetoric of charismatic leadership: a theoretical extension, a case study, and implications for research. Leadersh. Q. **5**(1), 25–42 (1994)
41. Shamir, B., Arthur, M.B., House, R.J.: The rhetoric of charismatic leadership: a theoretical extension, a case study, and implications for research. In: Leadership Now: Reflections on the Legacy of Boas Shamir, pp. 31–49. Emerald Publishing Limited (2018)
42. Shamir, B., House, R.J., Arthur, M.B.: The motivational effects of charismatic leadership: a self-concept based theory. Organ. Sci. **4**(4), 577–594 (1993)
43. Strangert, E.: Emphasis by pausing. In: Proc. 15th ICPhS, Barcelona, pp. 2477–2480 (2003)
44. Touati, P.: Prosodic aspects of political rhetoric. In: ESCA Workshop on Prosody (1993)
45. Towler, A.J.: Effects of charismatic influence training on attitudes, behavior, and performance. Pers. Psychol. **56**(2), 363–381 (2003)

46. Wang, N., Karpurapu, A., Jajodia, A., Merchant, C.: Toward charismatic virtual agents: How to animate your speech and be charismatic. In: Human-Computer Interaction. User Experience and Behavior: Thematic Area, HCI 2022, Held as Part of the 24th HCI International Conference, HCII 2022, Virtual Event, June 26-July 1, 2022, Proceedings, Part III. pp. 580–590. Springer (2022)
47. Wang, N., Pacheco, L., Merchant, C., Skistad, K., Jethwani, A.: The design of charismatic behaviors for virtual humans. In: Proceedings of the 20th ACM International Conference on Intelligent Virtual Agents, pp. 1–8 (2020)
48. Wasielewski, P.L.: The emotional basis of charisma. Symb. Interact. 8(2), 207–222 (1985)
49. Weber, M.: The theory of social and economic organization. Simon and Schuster (2009)
50. Williams, C.E., Stevens, K.N.: Emotions and speech: some acoustical correlates. J. Acoustical Soc. Am. 52(4B), 1238–1250 (1972)
51. Willner, A.R.: The spellbinders: Charismatic political leadership. Yale University Press (1985)

Interacting in the Metaverse

Development of a VR Simulator for the Elder's Impaired Visual Function and the Investigation of the VR Objects Recognition with Visual Function Impairment

Masanao Koeda[1]([✉]), Kouhei Fukuroda[1], Sakae Mikane[1], Katsuhiko Onishi[2], Hiroshi Noborio[2], and Morihiro Tsujishita[3]

[1] Okayama Prefectural University, Okayama, Japan
koeda@ss.oka-pu.ac.jp
[2] Osaka Electro-Communication University, Osaka, Japan
[3] Nara Gakuen University, Nara, Japan

Abstract. Currently, we are developing a VR exposure system for improving post-fall syndrome for elderly fallers. However, it is difficult to recognize for young people whether an elderly person is more easily to fall in a fall-prone situation. In this study, we simulated blurred vision in VR in according with the visual impairment certification criteria. We conducted experiments that subjects walked through a space with steps in a VR space with blurred vision and estimated the height of the steps. The experimental results showed that the subjects considered the steps higher than actual height when the blurriness was stronger.

Keywords: Elder · Post-Fall Syndrome · Visual Function · Impairment · Blur · VR

1 Introduction

The elders are prone to falls because of the weakness in their legs and backs. Without injury, they may suffer post-fall syndrome, in which they lose confidence in walking due to fear and anxiety of falling. To treat post-fall syndrome, it is necessary to reduce the fear and improve confidence in walking. One treatment approach is exposure therapy. This method gradually exposes the patient to the fearful situation that caused the fearful stimulus. This allows the patient to recognize the irrationality of the fear and overcome the fear [2]. There are several methods of exposure therapy, including image exposure, in vivo exposure, and VR exposure.

Image exposure is a method to reduce patient's fear by imagining a fearful scene and repeating the feelings and sensations of the scene. However, some patients cannot imagine fearful scenes well, and there is some uncertainty in this method.

In vivo exposure is a method which uses real stimuli to reduce fearful memories by gradually approaching the feared situation. However, it is difficult to create a realistic fearful situation and make the patient experience it in the real situation.

M. Kurosu and A. Hashizume (Eds.): HCII 2023, LNCS 14013, pp. 421–430, 2023.
https://doi.org/10.1007/978-3-031-35602-5_30

VR Exposure is a method to create fearful scenes using computer graphics (CG) and treat patients by experiencing them in a VR space. This method is easy to create fearful scenes and can present fearful scenes to the patient with certainty.

Currently, we have been developing a VR exposures system for improving post-fall syndrome in elderly patients [1, 2]. However, we have not investigated the relationship between visual impairments and falls in the elderly. In this study, we simulate blurred vision, which is one of the visual impairments in elderly people, using VR, and conduct experiments by walking in a VR space with steps. We investigate how the visibility of steps changes depending on the intensity of blurred vision.

2   Blurred Vision Simulation in According with the Visual Impairment Certification Criteria

2.1   VR Simulation of the Elder's Impaired Visual Function

To simulate blurred vision in VR space, we developed a blur shader using a Gaussian operator based on [3]. This shader has the parameters Dispersion, Sampling Texel Amount, and Texel Interval, and by adjusting these parameters, the intensity of the blur can be controlled (Fig. 1).

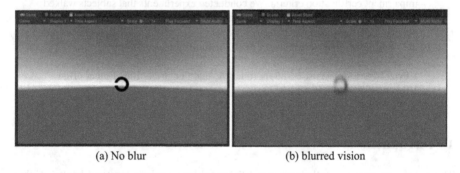

(a) No blur   (b) blurred vision

Fig. 1.   Generating a blurred vision in VR space

2.2   Adjustment of Eyesight in VR Space Based on the Visual Impairment Certification Criteria

Visual impairment certification criteria define the strength of visual impairment by the Japanese Ministry of Health, Labour and Welfare. This criteria has grades from 1 to 6, with the smaller the number indicating weaker vision (Table 1). To simulate blurred vision in accordance with this criterion in a VR space, we developed an eyesight adjustment system in a VR space.

Table 1. Visual impairment certification criteria

Level	Eyesight
1	The better eyesight is less than 0.01
2	1. The better eyesight is more than 0.02 and less than 0.03 2. The better eyesight is 0.04 and the other is less than hand motion
3	1. The better eyesight is more than 0.04 and less than 0.07 2. The better eyesight is 0.08 and the other is less than hand motion
4	The better eyesight is more than 0.08 and less than 0.1
5	The better eyesight is 0.2 and the other is less than 0.02
6	The better eyesight is more than 0.3 and less than 0.6, and the other is less than 0.02

2.3 Eyesight Adjustment System in a VR Space

A Landolt ring model (diameter: 10 mm, line width: 2 mm, slit width: 2 mm) shown in Fig. 2 is presented in the VR space with the size and orientation corresponding to each eyesight. The subject wears an HMD and sees the Landolt ring with blur. The aperture of the Landolt ring was changed randomly to the left and right, up and down, for about 5 s, and the subjects answered the direction of the aperture. More than 3/4 of the answers were correct, the subject was judged to have the same eyesight, and the blur intensity was logged.

The parameters of the blur shader are fixed at Dispersion = 8, Sampling Texel Amount = 4, and only the Texel Interval is changed.

Fig. 2. Landolt ring model

2.4   Experiment of Eyesight Adjustment in VR Space

We conducted a visual acuity adjustment experiment in a VR space. The subjects were five males (21, 19, 21, and 18 years old) with visual acuity of 2.0, 1.5, 1.0, 1.5, and 0.7 in real space, respectively. The experiment was conducted in VR space with Landolt rings of sizes corresponding to visual acuities of 0.01, 0.02, 0.05, and 0.1, using the same procedure as described above. Table 2 shows the results of Texel Interval for each subject. Although there are individual differences, the average value increases with each grade. We confirmed that eyesight in the VR space decreased in accordance with the intensity of the blurring.

Table 2. Texel Interval value for blur control

		Subject (Eyesight in real space)					
		Eyesight in VR	A (2.0)	B (1.5)	C (1.0)	D (1.5)	E (0.7)	Average
Level	1	0.01	8.0	9.0	9.0	9.0	8.0	8.60
	2	0.02	3.4	3.8	4.0	3.8	3.2	3.64
	3	0.05	2.4	2.4	2.4	2.6	1.8	2.32
	4	0.1	1.8	1.8	1.8	1.8	1.2	1.68

3   Investigation of the VR Objects Recognition with Visual Function Impairment

3.1   Experimental Environment and System Configuration

We installed three steps of different sizes in the corridor of the VR room (Fig. 3) developed in [1]. The width and length of the steps were 12 cm and 60 cm, respectively, and steps with heights of 1.5 cm, 4 cm, and 18.6 cm were created. Steps of 1.5 cm, 4.0 cm, and 18.3 cm were placed at intervals of 1.0 m in this order (Fig. 4). The height of the steps was referred to [4].

Meta Quest2 was used as the HMD, and the Meta Quest2 controller (hereinafter called "controller") was used to measure the position and posture of both feet of the subject. The attachment shown in [5] was mounted on a sandal, and the controller was attached to the sandal (Fig. 5). The subject wore the sandals during the experiment, and the lower leg model (Fig. 6), which moved in accordance with the subject's foot movements, was displayed in the VR space. The system was developed with Unity2021.2.14f1 using the PC shown in Table 3.

Fig. 3. VR room [1]

(a) Top view (18.3cm, 4.0cm, 1.5cm from the back)

(b) Side view (18.3cm, 4.0cm, 1.5cm from the left to right)

Fig. 4. Three steps of different sizes in the corridor of the VR room

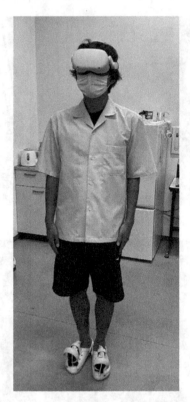

Fig. 5. A subject wearing the HMD and sandals with the controller

3.2 Experiment of Stepping Over Steps with Blurred Vision in VR Space

The subjects were tested to step over the steps in the VR space with blurred vision. The subjects' eyesight in the VR space was adjusted by the parameters described in the previous section, so that the subjects' eyesight in the VR space was adjusted to the same level.

Fig. 6. Lower leg model

Table 3. Specifications of the PC

Model	Mouse Computer H5-TGLBBW11
OS	Windows 11 Pro 64bit
CPU	Intel Core i7-11800 @ 2.30 GHz
Memory	64 GB

Subjects walked over steps in the following order: 1.5 cm, 4.0 cm, and 18.3 cm. The starting point was 1.0 m before the first step. The goal point was 1.0 m before the last step. Before crossing each step, the subjects were asked to answer how high each step seemed to be. The experiment was conducted in the following order:

1. Visual impairment level 1 (eyesight 0.01)
2. Visual impairment level 2 (eyesight 0.02)
3. Visual impairment level 3 (eyesight 0.05)
4. Visual impairment level 4 (eyesight 0.1)

Figure 7 shows an example of the visibility of the VR space at each visual impairment level. The subjects in this experiment are A, B, C, and D in Table 2.

3.3 Experimental Results

Figure 8 shows the results for each subject, and Fig. 9 shows the averages height evaluation of the steps. In both cases, the subjects tended to perceive steps as higher as their eyesight decreased.

(a) Level 1 (eyesight 0.01) (b) Level 2 (eyesight 0.02)

(c) Level 3 (eyesight 0.05) (d) Level 4 (eyesight 0.1)

Fig. 7. Visibility of the VR space at each visual impairment level

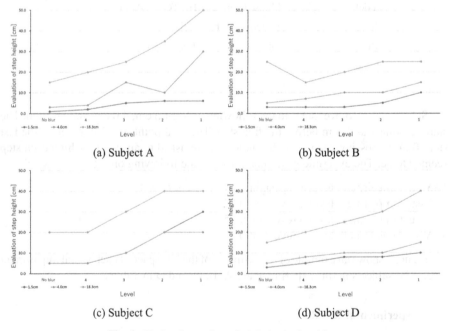

(a) Subject A (b) Subject B

(c) Subject C (d) Subject D

Fig. 8. Evaluations of step height by each subject

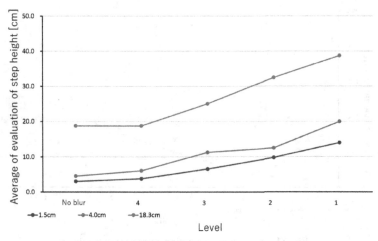

Fig. 9. Average of evaluation of step height

Figure 10 shows the evaluation errors for each subject, and Fig. 11 shows the averages of evaluation error. In both cases, as eyesight decreased, the error in the height of the steps tended to increase.

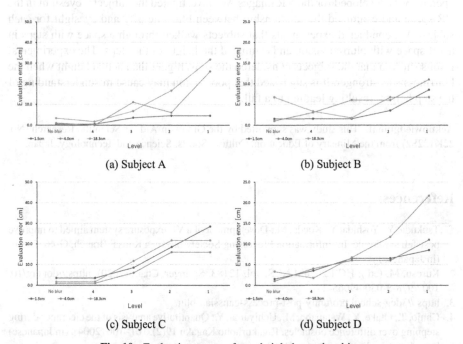

(a) Subject A

(b) Subject B

(c) Subject C

(d) Subject D

Fig. 10. Evaluations error of step height by each subject

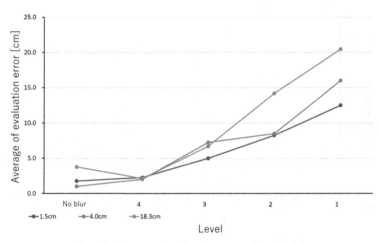

Fig. 11. Average of evaluation error of step height

4 Conclusion

In this study, we simulated blurred vision in VR in according with the visual impairment certification criteria. To simulate the blurred vision, a blur shader using a Gaussian operator was developed for the VR images. We investigated the subjects' eyesight in the VR space and examined the relationship between blur intensity and eyesight for each subject. We conducted experiments that subjects walked through a space with steps in a VR space with blurred vision and estimated the height of the steps. The experimental results showed that the subjects considered the steps higher than actual height when the blurriness was stronger. It is suggested that poor vision may cause misunderstanding of the step height, resulting leading to a fall.

Acknowledgment. This study was supported by the Grants-in-Aid for Scientific Research (No. 22K12282) from the Ministry of Education, Culture, Sports, Science and Technology, Japan.

References

1. Tsukuda, Y., Yoshida, Y., Koeda, M.: Development of a VR exposure system aimed to improve post-fall syndrome. In: Information Processing Society of Japan Kansai Branch, G-46 (2019). (in Japanese)
2. Kurosu, M. (ed.): HCII 2020. LNCS, vol. 12183. Springer, Cham (2020). https://doi.org/10.1007/978-3-030-49065-2
3. https://3dcg-school.pro/unity-post-process-gaussian-blur/
4. Chujo, T., Otake, Y., Watanabe, M., Uchiyama, Y.: Quantitative analysis of toe clearance during stepping over difference obstacles. Rigakurhoho Kagaku **19**(2), 101–106 (2004). (in Japanese)
5. https://protopedia.net/prototype/2660

System to Check Organs, Malignant Tumors, Blood Vessel Groups, and Scalpel Paths in DICOM with a 3D Stereo Immersive Sensory HMD

Takahiro Kunii[1]([✉]), Kaoru Watanabe[2], Michiru Mizoguchi[3], and Hiroshi Noborio[2]

[1] Kashina System Co., Hikone, Japan
kunii@tetera.jp

[2] Department of Computer Science, Osaka Electro-Communication University, Shijo-Nawate, Japan
nobori@osakac.ac.jp

[3] Faculty of Health Sciences, Department of Nursing, Naragakuen University, Tomigaoka, Nara, Japan
michiru-m@nara-su.ac.jp

Abstract. This study proposes a surgical simulator that generates a fused display of different DICOM [1] volumes, such as MRI and CT, and allows the user to experience and virtually operate a hole in the cranium, without the need for segmentation and with only a threshold level of adjustment, and take a peek inside it. We previously proposed an algorithm that uses DICOM as a 3D volume to find a cutting path from the malignancy to the organ surface, thereby avoiding vessel groups. Hence, in this study, we developed a surgical simulator that directly uses DICOM for this algorithm. This simulator uses the gesture function of the Meta Quest 2 HMD [11], an immersive head-mounted display, to freely manipulate the 3D volume of the DICOM and change the viewpoint and gaze. This system allows the user to view DICOM in the real world, completely different from surgical planning that is viewed with a keyboard, mouse, and 2D monitor. The current study is also linked to another study on DX Medicine, wherein the technique of attaching a pouch to a stoma was performed using the hand gestures described above. In that study, they attempted to use a VR model of their own stoma to enable remote practice as many times as needed. As a preliminary step, we made the system available to multiple participants on a local network. We build this model ensuring that it will allow multiple doctors and nurses to eventually collaborate in preoperative conferences and care training to plan highly accurate surgeries and fittings.

Keywords: Surgical path · Navigation · immersive HMD · User Experience

1 Introduction

We previously proposed an algorithm that uses a set of DICOM tomograms as a 3D volume to determine the cutting path from a malignant tumor to the organ surface, thereby avoiding a group of blood vessels [2]. In addition, for incorporating this algorithm, we developed a surgical simulator that directly utilizes DICOM tomograms without using a 3D mesh [3]. A surgical simulator that directly utilizes DICOM tomograms without 3D meshing was also developed to incorporate this algorithm [4]. This simulator uses an immersive head-mounted display (HMD) system [5] that allows the user to freely manipulate the DICOM 3D volume and change the viewpoint and gaze through the hand-gesture recognition function of the HMD. This system enables users to check the DICOM in the real world, unlike surgical planning that is performed using a keyboard, mouse, and 2D monitor. In addition, because this system was constructed as part of DX medicine, it will enable multiple physicians to collaborate remotely and realistically to plan and confirm surgical procedures.

On the other hand, this study is also linked to another DX (Digital transformation) [24] medicine study that performed the technique of attaching a pouch to a stoma using Oculus Quest 2 hand gestures and other techniques. A VR model of a stoma [6] can be used to perform the procedure remotely and as many times as required. As a preliminary step, we made the system available to multiple participants in a local network. The system is being developed with the expectation that multiple physicians will eventually collaborate at preoperative conferences to create highly accurate surgical plans.

Stereoscopic viewing with immersive HMDs is highly suitable for understanding 3D spaces, and studies are being conducted in various fields to effectively deal with stereoscopic images [7, 8]. In the medical field, a Medtronic Stealth Station Surgical Navigation System [9] is used to generate stereoscopic images from DICOM and display them on an immersive HMD. Moreover, studies are being conducted on remote collaboration using immersive HMDs [10]. In this context, we attempted to investigate the possibility of using an immersive HMD to display DICOM volumes for remote collaboration. Although we mentioned earlier that similar products are already available, the process of creating 3D images using DICOM is challenging to implement. We therefore develop a product that is slightly more easier to use as compared to the existing products; for example, the stereoscopic images can be displayed by simply specifying the DICOM and adjusting the threshold value for remote education. In this study, it is assumed in the development process that a single DICOM volume is displayed as a stereoscopic image and a skilled physician remotely instructs a student in neurosurgery. Meta Quest 2 [11] was used as the immersive HMD system for stereoscopic image displays. The hand-gesture recognition function of this system was also used, and a freehand operation was assumed. Currently, the system is limited to sharing a virtual space between two people and is being developed over an intranet using UDP (User Datagram Protocol) [25]. However, it will eventually be used over the Internet by several people using WebRTC [14].

We will hereafter refer to this surgical simulator as DICOM Surgical Instructions Communicator (Discom) because it is expected to serve as a surgical instruction communicator.

The remainder of this paper is structured as follows. First, the required goals, development environment, and equipment specifications of the Discom are discussed. Next, the measures taken to achieve these goals are explained. Subsequently, the communication between the two Discoms and the use of hand gestures for teacher-student are described. This is followed by a description of the support provided for immersive HMDs introduced for stereoscopic video displays and hand gestures. Next, an automatic segmentation method that extends the ray marching method and [18, 19] used in DICOM volume displays to simultaneously reference and display different DICOM volumes such as MRI [15] and CT is described [16]. Finally, the accuracy of the hand gesture and dedicated HMD controller is evaluated.

2 Discom Requirements Goals

A neurosurgeon who collaborated with us in this study expressed the following request for a simulator for educational use: "A simulator that can create a hole on the surface of the skin and look into the bone and the brain inside the bone". Discom has set the following requirements to make it a one-to-one communication tool in a virtual space that meets these requirements:

- Communicate between two Discoms
- Share the same virtual space
- Stereoscopic viewing of DICOM volume of human head is possible
- Freehand operation when using an immersive HMD
- Operation using a controller is possible
- Can be substituted with 2D monitor, mouse, and keyboard
- Two Discom, each of which can view the human head from different angles
- A hole drilled in one head can be displayed on the other head.
- The position indicated by one is also displayed on the other.
- Voice conversation is possible.

3 Development Environment and Equipment Specifications

Discom was developed by Unity [12]. The immersive HMD system utilizes Meta Quest 2 as a Windows PC peripheral and Meta's Oculus Integration Assets [13] provided by Meta for hand-gesture recognition capabilities using Meta Quest 2 in Unity. When the DICOM volume of a human head is displayed within the arm's reach (Fig. 1) with the following specifications, the drawing update rate is between 30 to 40 Hz, and therefore does not reach 75 Hz – this is considered ideal for HMDs. This issue should be addressed in future studies. The DICOM volume used 200 DICOM files of 512×512 pixels.

Development Environment
Windows 10 Pro 19045.2486.
Unity Version 2021.3.10f.
Oculus Integration Version 47.0
PC and HMD Specs
CPU 12th Gen Intel(R) Core(TM) i9-12900K 3.19 GHz.
Memory 64.0 GB.
GPU RTX2080S.
Meta Quest 2 (Use as a PC HMD using Oculus Link).

4 Sharing Virtual Space through Network Communication

Teachers and students use Discom individually. If the state of the virtual space needs to be shared, it is necessary to determine the state of each virtual space via network communication. In addition, Discom allows each person to view the human head displayed in the virtual space from any position and orientation. Therefore, instead of sending the image of one person to another, as in the case of videoconferencing, the position and posture of each person's head are sent to each other in the virtual space. The Discom sends the following information to the other party at a period of 15 Hz.

- Left hand, right hand, respective center position, and posture
- Cutting tool condition and cutting radius

In addition, the DICOM volume must be transmitted first; however, this requirement was omitted in this study. Although UDP is used as the communication standard, it is necessary to consider exchanging information on IP addresses and the ports used at the beginning if the system has to be used over the Internet. When supporting WebRTC, it is necessary to support these. However, this study uses fixed values for IP addresses and port numbers.

The position and posture were sent as affine matrices. This information was used to display the hand of the second party, as shown in Fig. 1. The cutting tool state and cutting radius are described as follows.

Second party's right hand   Second party' s left hand

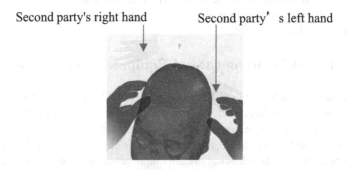

Fig. 1. State of dialogue with the other party in Discom.

The affine matrix to be transmitted was obtained based on the coordinate space of the human head. It was not based on the global space coordinates and allowed each human head to be rotated individually. For example, as shown in Fig. 2(a), if user A rotates the face toward himself/herself, the pointing position of user B's right hand will change if global spatial coordinates are used. To avoid this, the affine matrices of the left and right hands and cutting tools were based on the coordinate space of the head of the human body. This causes the hand of user A, as seen by user B, to move, as shown in Fig. 3(a), and the hand of user B, as seen by user A, to move by hooking onto the rotated head, as shown in Fig. 3(b).

Discom is being developed over an intranet using UDP; however, it will eventually be used over the Internet via WebRTC. To accommodate subsequent use by multiple

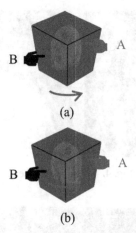

(a)

(b)

Fig. 2. (a) Head rotation by user A. (b) User B's viewpoint, where the head suddenly rotates and the pointing position changes.

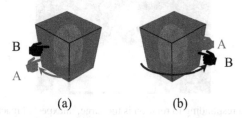

(a)   (b)

Fig. 3. From user B's perspective, user A's hand moves. (b) From user A's perspective, the head rotates and user B's hand moves.

people, it may be necessary to change the current peer-to-peer model into a server-client model in order to review the information to be exchanged. In this case, the UI of the virtual space may need to change.

5   Operation by Hand Gesture

Discom uses the hand-gesture recognition function of the HMD to enable the manipulation of the human head direction in the virtual space when wearing the HMD. Although other candidate methods exist for manipulating the human head, such as using both hands to zoom in and out (Fig. 4), we did not adopt it; this is because, according to the surgeons, it was not very important, and they also mentioned that they would rather not have the head direction change due to a malfunction in hand-gesture recognition.

Human head operation was therefore limited in that a plate placed under the head had to be turned to change direction. It would be more intuitive to allow the entire head to rotate, but doing so would result in several malfunctions, as shown in Fig. 5.

When drilling a hole in the head, the right hand has two modes, one for positioning and the other for cutting, and the user can switch between the two. The mode can usually

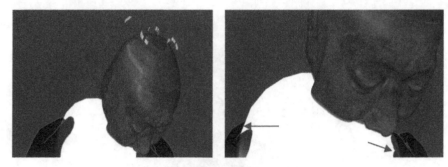

Fig. 4. Scaling of the head.

Fig. 5. If the area responding to rotation is too large, unexpected reactions may occur.

switched by pressing a button on the palette, but Discom displays the tool for cutting, and the user is in the cutting mode if he/she is holding onto the tool.

The cutting tool is picked up and moved by the fingers to cut around the cutting tool from the outer skin of the human head to the skull. When the cutting tool is released from the finger, it maintains its position (Fig. 6). The user who has released the cutting tool can point with his/her right hand to any location on the perforated cranium to communicate with the other person. They can then pick up the cutting tool again and move the drilling position. The drawing method for this cutout is described as follows.

Initially, we planned to adjust the cutting radius of the cutting tool by picking and moving the ring that appears on the right wrist when the cutting tool is held. However, we abandoned this idea because the hand-gesture recognition function often misrecognized both hands when they were placed too close to each other. Therefore, we decided to change the cutting radius according to the distance when the left-hand was brought closer than a certain distance to the head when using the cutting tool (Fig. 7). This required some initial explanation, but once understood, it was easy to adjust.

Although physicians have requested that cutting tools should be available in square, triangular, and round shapes, only those in round shapes are currently available. Our subsequent development will allow selection of another cutting tool; however, in that case, a plate for tool selection (Fig. 8) will be needed. When using a controller, a plate may be displayed on the right wrist to emphasize its relationship with the tool. However,

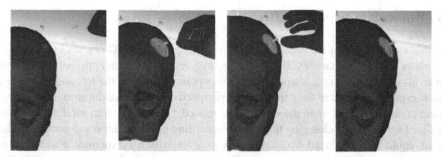

Fig. 6. Moving the cutting tool to specify the drilling position. The cutting tool remains at the point where it is released.

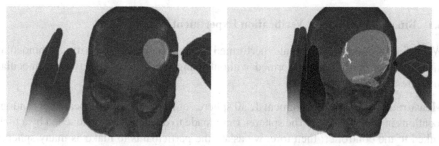

Fig. 7. Adjusting the cutting radius using the distance between the head and the left hand.

in the case of hand gestures, doing so would result in misrecognition or an unrecognizable state if the distance between the right and left hands is too small, as described above.

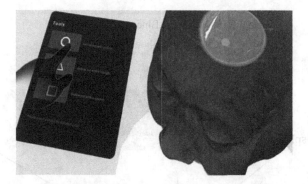

Fig. 8. Control plate placed away from the hand.

6   Binocular Disparity Effects

In this study, the term stereopsis refers to the recognition of 3D objects by binocular disparity and motion parallax. Binocular disparity refers to the perception of perspective in terms of changes in the shape of the gazing point as seen by the left and right eyes. Motion parallax refers to the perception of perspective in terms of the amount of movement of the gaze point when the viewpoint is moved. Of these, motion parallax, which is realized by the HMD changing the display according to the position and posture of the head, could be reproduced with some devices, even with a 2D monitor. Hand-gesture recognition is also possible without an HMD and only using LEAP Motion [23]. The following experiments confirm that it is useful for the remaining binocular parallax to accommodate the involvement of HMDs.

6.1   Binocular Disparity Verification Experiment

We refer to the measurements performed using binocular disparity as binocular measurements and those performed without using binocular disparity as monocular measurements.

Measurement 1. In Measurement 1, 30 spheres of random radius appeared at random locations in space (Fig. 9). The spheres were made to disappear when touched by a pick linked to the controller; therefore, we asked the participants to make as many spheres disappear as possible within 5 s and measured the number of spheres. The measurements were performed using a combination of four basic patterns: binocular, monocular, and with and without shadows (Table 1).

Table 1. Basic pattern of measurement 1.

Parallaxial format	Binocular/Monocular
Shadow	Show/Hide

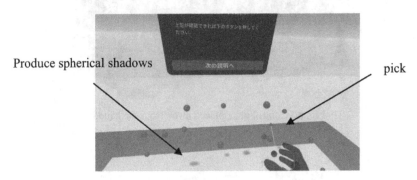

Produce spherical shadows   pick

Fig. 9. Erasing spheres.

To eliminate the differences in the 3D input devices for manipulating the picks, immersive HMDs were worn for both binocular and monocular measurements. In binocular measurements, the sphere was displayed in the same manner as it was in the immersed virtual space. In monocular measurement, the content of the 2D screen displayed changes in accordance with the movement of the subject's head, as if the subject was looking through a window; therefore, the same conditions apply to stereoscopic recognition by motion parallax (Fig. 10).

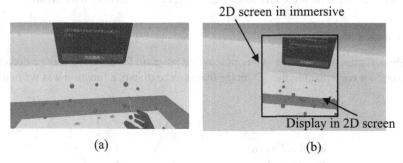

2D screen in immersive

Display in 2D screen

(a)   (b)

Fig. 10. (a) Binocular measurement. (b) Monocular measurement.

6.2 Evaluation of Measurement 1

Figure 11 shows the average measurements of the four subjects. The vertical axis of the measurement results indicates the number of spheres erased. The horizontal axis is the left monocular, and the right is binocular. Monocular and monocular data were analyzed using Wilcoxon's signed-rank sum test [20], with the significance level set at 5%. The results showed a significant difference between the two groups.

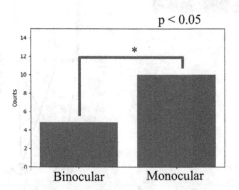

Fig. 11. Average of measured values.

7 Binocular Parallax Support for Immersive HMDs

Immersive HMDs enable stereoscopic viewing by rendering from the left eye, the right eye, and from each viewpoint. If the 3D mesh display rendering module, called a shader [17], is provided by Unity, it is already compatible with immersive HMDs, and if one uses the module provided by Unity, the display destination setting can be switched from a normal 2D monitor to immersive HMDs. Hence, binocular stereoscopic support can be achieved without any extra efforts. However, shaders for Discom's DICOM volume display do not exist on the Unity side. Therefore, custom shaders were created.

7.1 Custom Shader

The shaders are created as a drawing processing program for the GPU using a dedicated language: for each pixel in the 2D image that is to be drawn, a function was written that

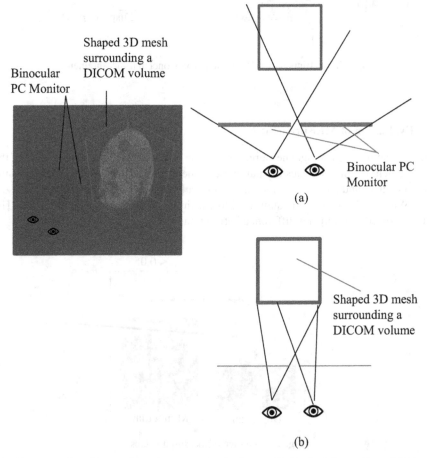

(a)

(b)

Fig. 12. (a) Designation to PC monitor screen for both eyes. (b) Designation to Shaped 3D mesh surrounding a DICOM volume.

receives information about which part of the 3D mesh surface the pixel is looking at, and from which angle, and returns the color to be drawn there. For the DICOM volume display in this study, colors are determined using the ray marching method, and there are two options for assigning this shader. The first option is to assign it to the binocular PC monitor screen and the second is to the 3D mesh shaped around the DICOM volume (Fig. 12).

In the case of designation on a PC monitor screen, for example, if multiple DICOM volumes are to be displayed in the future, each display must be handled simultaneously. In addition, it is necessary to determine whether the DICOM volume is in the current field of view. To avoid this, in this study, a cube, which is the basic shape of the Unity built-in mesh, was specified as the 3D mesh surrounding the DICOM volume, and shaders were assigned to it.

This allows Unity to determine whether the DICOM volume is in the current field of view. However, in this case, we needed a solution when the viewpoint was inside the cube.

If the viewpoint was inside the cube, Unity does not render the cube. This causes a loss of the DICOM volume (Fig. 13).

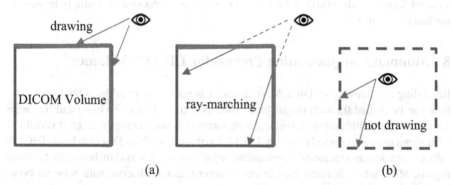

Fig. 13. (a) If the viewpoint is outside the cube, the cube is drawn. Therefore, ray marching is performed in the custom shader. (b) If the viewer is inside the cube, the cube is not drawn. Therefore, no custom shaders are executed.

This is a common process called culling, which eliminates implicit surfaces. However, in this study, we wanted to draw a view from this viewpoint, even if the viewpoint is inside a DICOM volume. In this respect, if the viewpoint is specified on the monitor screen, it is called unconditionally, and hence, there is no need to think about it; however, for the cube, it is necessary to think about how to deal with it.

7.2 Solution by Backside Drawing

We solved this problem by creating the backside of the drawing target. In this case, because it is the drawing of the backside that is called from Unity, the coordinates provided are the contact positions between the backside and the line of sight. Because nothing can be drawn by ray marching along the line of sight from this position, we return to the viewpoint along the line-of-sight direction and perform ray marching from there (Fig. 14).

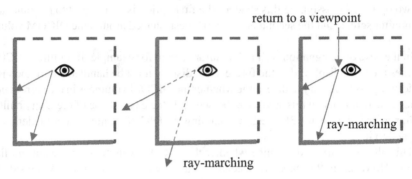

Fig. 14. Ray-marching after returning the starting position to the viewpoint.

This allows the user to stick their head inside the DICOM volume and investigate it, a useful feature of the HMD, a device that can be easily repositioned simply by moving the head close to it.

8   Automatic Segmentation Process for DICOM Volumes

Regarding the drawing of DICOM volumes, it is necessary to address the point that a hole can be drilled through the surface of the skin to look into the bone and the brain. This is not very difficult with surgical simulators that use 3D meshes, but it is difficult with simulators that directly display DICOM volumes, such as Discom. First, DICOM information does not include discriminative information, such as skin, bones, and internal organs. MRI, which is often used in neurosurgery, cannot discriminate between bones and other tissues based on numbers alone (Fig. 15).

Fig. 15. MRI shows the inside of the cranium at the threshold of bone identification.

Therefore, it is necessary for a human to specify and separate areas while viewing the screen display based on the measured values. This process is called segmentation, and a 3D mesh is the display that has undergone this process. To automate the segmentation process, research [21], such as classification using machine learning, is being conducted. Using such automated segmentation to color-code MRI images of the skin, bone, and visceral organs is desirable, but this is not feasible at this time.

Here, we propose a method of displaying MRIs while referring to CTs by incorporating a technique called fusion, which uses multiple DICOMs to create a single display [22], into the ray marching method used in this study.

8.1 Use of Two DICOM Volumes

First, bone segmentation can be clearly performed with CT using only a threshold (Fig. 16).

Hollow inside

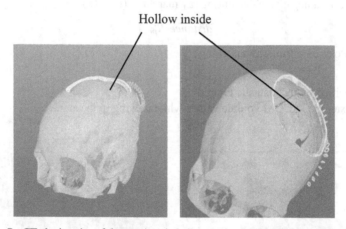

Fig. 16. On CT, the interior of the cranium is hollow at the threshold of bone identification.

Therefore, during ray marching on the MRI volume side, the CT volume side was referenced simultaneously, and if there was a value within the threshold range on the CT side, the value on the CT side was given priority and was displayed in the color of the bone (Fig. 17). After passing through the bone, the color assigned by MRI was changed to correspond to the epidermis and to the color change inside the brain.

Thus, by changing the display color of the MRI while referring to the CT region, rather than simply superimposing the two, the division into regions that conventionally had to be specified manually can now be performed with only a threshold adjustment (Fig. 18 b).

8.2 Application to Cutting Display

The drawing of the hole drilled into the head was achieved by not referring to the DICOM volume value while passing through the region where the distance function

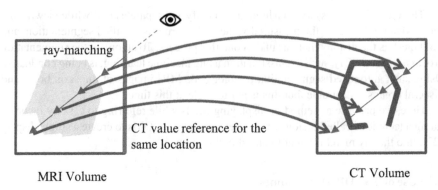

MRI Volume   CT Volume

Fig. 17. Simultaneous reference to the CT volume side during ray marching on the MRI volume side.

(Eq. 1) returns a negative value during ray marching (Fig. 18).

$$distance(R_{pos}) \tag{1}$$

R_{pos}: Position during ray marching

Area specified by the distance function:
Do not examine DICOM volume values while moving in the area.

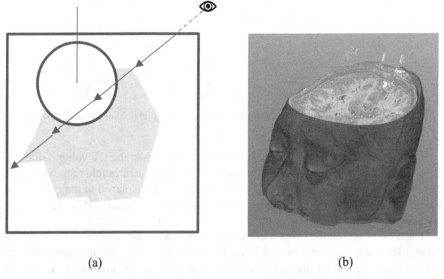

(a)   (b)

Fig. 18. (a) Ray marching does not refer to the DICOM volume value when the line of sight is within the region defined by the distance function. (b) The result. Here, the CT volume is also referenced to the same order.

In addition, the CT side volume was used to determine if the location of the ray marching was inside the skull. If it was inside the skull, the MRI side volume was also examined in the region where the distance function (Eq. 1) returns a negative value. In this manner, as shown in Fig. 19, only the brain inside the bone is displayed and the outside is not displayed.

If the information from the CT volume indicates that the patient is intracranial, DICOM volume values should be examined.

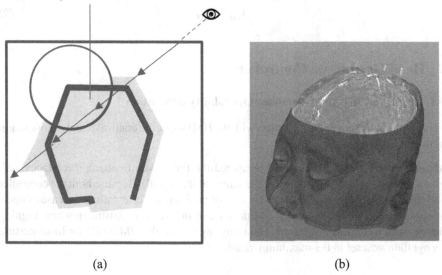

(a)   (b)

Fig. 19. (a) Decision including information on CT side volume. (b) Result.

8.3   Alignment of Two DICOM Volumes

Because they are not taken at the same time, the initial positions of the DICOMs taken by CT and MRI are not aligned. In fact, when the CT DICOM and MRI DICOM of the same patient used in this study were read as they were, the position, orientation, and size of the DICOM were also slightly different. This point was manually adjusted so that the DICOM on the CT side was aligned with that on the MRI side as a reference. There have been several studies on positioning, and we believe that automatic positioning will be possible in the future by incorporating such studies or by using the shape of the skin surface and a depth buffer; however, this is a future issue for this study.

8.4   Conversion from MRI Volume to CT Volume Coordinates

To produce the display that is the goal of this study with ray marching, it is necessary to enable the DICOM on the CT side to calculate and reference the corresponding internal position from the internal position of the DICOM of the MRI during ray marching. This is achieved by ensuring that the respective DICOM volumes taken by MRI and CT have tilt, position, and scale information in the virtual space. For this purpose, each

DICOM volume has an affine matrix, where the world coordinates are the virtual space coordinates to which the two DICOM volumes belong, and how much each is tilted, displaced from its origin, and scaled. For example, if the affine matrix for MRI is Amri and that for CT is Act, the affine matrix synthesized in Eq. 2 can be transformed from the position on the MRI side to the corresponding position on the CT side by applying it to the position coordinate vector of the ray marching.

$$A_{mri}^{-1}A_{ct} \qquad (2)$$

9   Hand Gesture vs. Controller

9.1   Hand Gesture and Controller Operability Evaluation

Finally, an evaluation of the operation with the HMD-specific controller and the operation with hand gestures is presented.

Measurement 2. Measurement 2 measured the time taken to attach three faces, red, green, and blue, to adjacent cubes of the same color (Fig. 20). Because both the controller and hand gestures could control the six axes of position and orientation, the ease of operation when grasping the surfaces and the ease of orientation adjustment when aligning the surfaces were to be evaluated. The sampling rate on the HMD side for hand-gesture recognition was set to the maximum value.

Fig. 20. Mounting of faces, white when position is matched.

9.2   Evaluation of Measurement 2

In the measurement results (Fig. 21), the vertical axis represents the time required to attach the three surfaces. The horizontal axis is the left controller use and the right is the hand gesture. The controller and hand gesture data were analyzed using Wilcoxon's signed-rank sum test with a significance level of 5%. The results showed a significant difference between the two groups.

The large difference between hand-gesture recognition and controller use can be attributed to the fact that the built-in gyro and acceleration sensors work effectively in

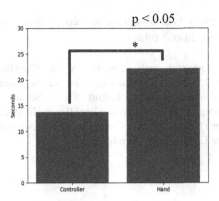

Fig. 21. Measurement results.

controllers. Because hand-gesture recognition uses image recognition by a camera built into the HMD to estimate posture, it is neither accurate nor fast.

Based on our observations, a significant amount of difference was not observed in the time taken to grab the board and bring it to the rectangular surface. The major difference lies in the operation used to adjust the orientation of the surface. Using the controller, the tilt could be changed responsively, but with hand gestures, the movement was significantly slower.

Considering these results, it was concluded that the controller is very effective in controlling posture owing to its internal sensors. In addition, since tactile feedback is possible, it is desirable to consider the use of controllers, while still being based on hand gesture operation.

10   Conclusions and Future Works

The fusion display of different DICOM volumes, such as MRI and CT, allows the user of this device to experience and virtually operate a hole in the cranium, without the need for segmentation and with only a threshold level of adjustment, and take a peek inside it. The stereoscopic effect of the binocular parallax of the newly introduced immersive HMD was confirmed to provide a user experience that was not possible with the 2D monitor. The hand-gesture operation, which does not require a controller, is easy to use, intuitive, and provides a UI that requires no learning curve. However, we also found that hand-gesture operations require special considerations. It is necessary to recognize that there are some limitations, such as the difficulty in recognizing overlapping hands before creating a UI. We are convinced that sharing such a virtual world between two people through network communication can contribute to the development of remote communication tools.

In the future, we plan to develop a faster display of this DICOM volume and investigate its further applications. In addition, we plan on extending the communication function to use WebRTC via the Internet to allow the product to be simultaneously used by multiple participants. Our goal is not to eliminate the use of controllers but to consider ways to use them to take advantage of their posture-recognition accuracy, and tactile feedback functions, among others.

Acknowledgment. This study was partly supported by the 2020 Grants-in-Aid for Scientific Research (C) (No. 20K12053) and the 2020 Grants-in-Aid for Scientific Research (C) (No. 20K04407) from the Ministry of Education, Culture, Sports, Science, and Technology, Japan. Further support was provided by the 2021 Specific Joint Research, Mechatronics Basic Research Laboratories, Osaka Electro Communication University. Finally, we would like to thank Editage (www.editage.com) for the English language editing.

References

1. DICOM https://en.wikipedia.org/wiki/DICOM
2. Kunii, T., Asano, M., Noborio, H.: Voxel-based route-search algorithm for tumour navigation and blood vessel avoidance. In: Kurosu, M. (ed.) HCII 2021. LNCS, vol. 12763, pp. 566–581. Springer, Cham (2021). https://doi.org/10.1007/978-3-030-78465-2_41
3. Polygon mesh. https://en.wikipedia.org/wiki/Polygon_mesh
4. Kunii, T., Asano, M., Noborio, H.: DICOM-based voxel-supported blood-vessel-avoiding scalpel navigation. In: Kurosu, M. (eds.) Human-Computer Interaction. Technological Innovation. HCII 2022. Lecture Notes in Computer Science, vol 13303. Springer, Cham (2022). https://doi.org/10.1007/978-3-031-05409-9_19
5. https://en.wikipedia.org/wiki/Head-mounted_display
6. Mizoguchi, M., Kayaki, M., Yoshikawa, T., Asano, M., Onishi, K., Noborio, H.: Selection and evaluation of color/depth camera for imaging surgical stoma. In: Kurosu, M. (ed.) HCII 2021. LNCS, vol. 12763, pp. 601–614. Springer, Cham (2021). https://doi.org/10.1007/978-3-030-78465-2_43
7. Hjellvik, S., Renganayagalu, S.K., Mallam, S., Nazir, S.: Immersive virtual reality in marine engineer education" Ergoship 2019 ISBN: 978-82-93677-04-8
8. Qi, W., Taylor II, R.M., Healey, C.G., Martens, J.-B.: A comparison of immersive HMD, fish tank VR and fish tank with haptics displays for volume visualization. APGV 2006: 51-58
9. https://www.medtronic.com/us-en/healthcare-professionals/products/neurological/surgical-navigation-systems/stealthstation.html
10. Celebi, K.C., Bailey, S.K.T., Burns, M.W., Bansal, K.: Is virtual reality streaming ready for remote medical education? measuring latency of stereoscopic VR for telementoring. In: Proceedings of the Human Factors and Ergonomics Society Annual Meeting 65(1), pp. 757–761, September 2021
11. https://www.meta.com/
12. Unity https://unity.com
13. https://assetstore.unity.com/packages/tools/integration/oculus-integration-82022
14. https://en.wikipedia.org/wiki/WebRTC
15. Magnetic resonance imaging https://en.wikipedia.org/wiki/Magnetic_resonance_imaging
16. CT scan https://en.wikipedia.org/wiki/CT_scan
17. https://docs.unity3d.com/2021.3/Documentation/Manual/SL-VertexFragmentShaderExamples.html
18. Bentoumi, H., Gautron, P., Bouatouch, K.: GPU-based volume rendering for medical imagery. Int. J. Electr. Comput. Syst. Eng. 4(1), 36–42 (2010)
19. Rasmussen, N., Nguyen, D.Q., Geiger, W., Fedkiw, R.: Smoke simulation for large-scale phenomena. In: Proceedings of SIGGRAPH 2003, pp. 703–707 (2003)

20. https://en.wikipedia.org/wiki/Wilcoxon_signed-rank_test
21. Khan, M.A., et al.: Multimodal brain tumor classification using deep learning and robust feature selection: a machine learning application for radiologists. Diagnostics **10**(8) (2020)
22. Saito, N., Kin, T., Oyama, H., et al.: Surgical simulation of cerebrovascular disease with multimodal fusion 3-dimensional computer graphics. Neurosurgery **60**(Suppl 1), 24–29 (2013)
23. https://www.ultraleap.com/
24. https://en.wikipedia.org/wiki/Digital_transformation
25. https://en.wikipedia.org/wiki/User_Datagram_Protocol

Mapping XR Platforms: Analyzing Immersion from the Designer's Perspective

Meng Li[1,2](✉) ⓘ, Daniel Houwing[2], Armagan Albayrak[2] ⓘ,
Mohammad Shidujaman[3] ⓘ, and Daan van Eijk[2] ⓘ

[1] Mechanical Engineering School, Xi'an Jiaotong University, Xianning Road 28, Xi'an 710049,
People's Republic of China
limeng.81@mail.xjtu.edu.cn
[2] Faculty of Industrial Design Engineering, Delft University of Technology, Landbergstraat 15,
2628 CE Delft, Netherlands
[3] Department of Computer Science and Engineering, Independent University,
16 Aftab Uddin Ahmed Rd, Dhaka 1229, Bangladesh
shantothusets@iub.edu.bd

Abstract. Understanding humans are the key to developing optimal design solutions for product-service systems. In this sense, the experiential approach is in line but might go beyond typical Human Centered Design (HCD) methods in that it focuses on generating positive experiences that contribute directly to human well-being. Extended Reality (XR) showed the potential to replicate or simulate experience as a whole and gained attention from design communities. XR platforms confused design practitioners due to their fast-advancing amounts and relevant experiences. Hence, this study introduced two surveys on XR platforms to clarify which experiences they could provide and when to implement them into HCD processes. Survey 1 categorized XR platforms according to their key attributes and mapped them into the Experience Matrix. Survey 2 invented two designer personas and a fictional project to analyze barriers and strategies to implement XR platforms into design processes. Eighty-eight XR platforms were categorized into nineteen clusters, where *creation* and *simulation* had the highest numbers. Regarding implementing XR in design practices, the cost is still the key concern and there's a trade-off between software cost and assets purchased for different types of designers.

Keywords: XR platforms · Immersion · Experience Design · Design Tools

1 Introduction

Understanding humans have been acknowledged as superior in creating better design solutions for product-service systems [1]. On one hand, designers use many methods and tools to understand human needs and requirements, particularly Human-Centered Design (HCD) methods [2]. On the other hand, HCD methods often focus on specific design elements instead of the entire episode of the human-system interaction. Most of the HCD models thus articulate more or less pragmatic and technology-focused design

© The Author(s), under exclusive license to Springer Nature Switzerland AG 2023
M. Kurosu and A. Hashizume (Eds.): HCII 2023, LNCS 14013, pp. 450–464, 2023.
https://doi.org/10.1007/978-3-031-35602-5_32

qualities, which can remove barriers to fulfilling human needs instead of targeting the positive experience itself. Experiential approaches are in line with but beyond typical HCD models (e.g., usability) as they generate positive experiences to contribute to human well-being. Extended Reality (XR) showed the potential to replicate or simulate the entire experience of product-service systems [3], thus gaining attention from design communities. However, the fast-growing XR platforms and their experiences confuse design practitioners and barrier their implementation. This study hence introduces two surveys to explore: (1) XR platforms and relevant experiences and (2) XR platforms and their suitable design phases.

Survey 1 aims at categorizing and mapping the authoring platforms of XR experiences. It will first investigate the state-of-the-art authoring platforms that can generate immersive experiences. These XR platforms then will be categorized according to their key characteristics. The categories of XR platforms are mapped with an experiential model to indicate the types of experiences these platforms might create.

The goal of Survey 2 is to link the XR platforms to an HCD process. To analyze the strategies in XR platforms' choices, the authors first invented two personas of designers with a fictional design project. A collection of XR platforms from the previous survey is made for these personas to complete the design project. Each XR platform is assigned to the process of an HCD model to support design methods or tools. In the end, the authors will discuss the strategies for implementing XR platforms.

2 Related Work

2.1 XR: A New Opportunity to Develop the User Experience in Product-Service Systems

Extended Reality (XR) as the key technological setting to generate immersive experiences, is more and more applied in the domains of interior design, architecture, product development, simulation, training, and education. The first-person immersion generated by XR platforms could enhance key components in creative and intuitive processes, like emotional engagement and multisensory solicitation [4]. Additionally, XR supports true-to-life simulations, which are as effective as corresponding experiences in the real world [5]. Studies have demonstrated the effectiveness of XR platforms for designing airport interiors [6], evaluating the ergonomics of machinery [7], as well as creative form-making in visual art [8]. Hence, a consensus in design communities is forming about the new opportunities XR platforms might bring, particularly for experience design [9]. Exploring XR in experience-driven design has been accelerated by the uncertainties of global crises like COVID-19 during the last two years [10].

2.2 The Problems of Designers to Introduce XR in Design Practices

Though technological advancement enables XR platforms to craft experiences with high fidelity, design professionals are unfamiliar with these platforms and thus do not clearly know what to expect. This induces a problem. Pilot studies revealed both enablers and barriers of XR platforms in product-service system design. Considering the different functionalities and pipelines of XR platforms, they may add value to several design stages and tasks but might be incompetent for the others in terms of time and cost. For example, Rieuf et al. investigated how XR augment the quality of design outcomes at the early design stages and found out that the XR experiences effectively enhance design qualities [11]. Kim et al. showed the advantages of XR simulation to enhance the aesthetics and originality of the final design [9]. When introducing XR during the development, it became however troublesome. For example, modelling is less intuitive and even more frustrating in VR than on the desktop [12]. The authors interviewed industry team leaders and showed that generative tasks (like modelling) seemed more difficult in XR than ideating tasks like brainstorming and sketching. Some design professionals who are keen to integrate XR into design practices felt frustrated, even if they used XR for sketching instead of modelling.

Without a clear overview, designers can hardly decide where and when it is necessary or beneficial to implement XR, resulting in skepticism and a low application rate [13]. It thus needs to be researched for which design stage XR brings opportunities and for which design challenges XR is not yet ready. By observing the curiosity and the struggles of design teams when applying XR, the authors hence find it necessary to analyze experiences from current XR platforms from the perspective of designers. The goal of this study is to realize an overview of XR platforms in terms of the categories of experiences and the HCD process, as well as recommendations for different designers. This overview surveys: (1) how XR platforms can be categorized according to their experiences in an experiential model, and (2) at which stages of HCD processes can different XR platforms be useful.

3 Surveys

3.1 Survey 1 – The Categories of XR Platforms Based on Their Experiences a Subsection Sample

Method
Selecting XR Platforms
The website, *XRcollaboration.com*[1], is a well-known, open dictionary to register the latest XR platforms, including development toolkits, digital galleries, or virtual campus/conferences both from big companies and start-ups. The XR platforms enrolled in this platform were the main source of this survey. These XR platforms are documented via a structured one-pager on the website. The authors collected the documents of seventy-one systems listed in the dictionary up to January 2022, whereas two systems are excluded because they are merely concepts, or their XR-relevant functions were too limited, such as a hidden VR plugin. Nineteen XR platforms from the interviews with team leaders were added when they were not listed but were well-known in the design community. Subsequently, eighty-eight systems are included in the analysis.

---
[1] https://xrcollaboration.com/directory/.

Defining Key Categories

To analyze the XR platforms concerning the categories of experiences, the first step is collecting their key attributes of them. At first, the one-pagers of each XR platform were reviewed and corresponding characteristics were collected in a spreadsheet following the six filters on the dictionary: *max. Collaborators and speculators, hardware support* (i.e., XR headsets), *collaboration types, OS platforms, features,* and *industry.* The one-sentence description of each platform from the one-pagers was recorded as well. The authors independently labelled each platform based on its description, collaboration types, and features. When the information of a platform from the dictionary is not sufficient to put a label, the authors searched for external sources (e.g., video demos) from its official website. Labelling XR platforms requires an iterative process. For example, there can be a lot of similarities between a platform tagged as 'Conference Room' and another one tagged as 'Roam & Discover'. After the first round of labelling, the authors put platforms with similar tags side-by-side and identified the differences: the platforms that have conference rooms but allow visitors to walk out and roam into a bigger world belong to the *Roam & Discover,* whereas the *Conference Room* is restricted to allowing a single meeting room. Thus, when the authors checked the key attributes to label the categories, they kept in mind that if the category seems to be ambiguous, look at similar categories. The final categories are labelled in such a way that they best describe the attributes of the category (shown in Fig. 1).

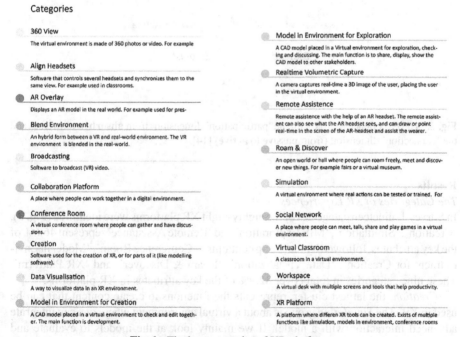

Categories

360 View

The virtual environment is made of 360 photos or video. For example

Align Headsets

Software that controls several headsets and synchronizes them to the same view. For example used in classrooms.

AR Overlay

Displays an AR model in the real world. For example used for pres-

Blend Environment

An hybrid form between a VR and real-world environment. The VR environment is blended in the real-world.

Broadcasting

Software to broadcast (VR) video.

Collaboration Platform

A place where people can work together in a digital environment.

Conference Room

A virtual conference room where people can gather and have discussions.

Creation

Software used for the creation of XR, or for parts of it (like modelling software).

Data Visualisation

A way to visualize data in an XR environment.

Model in Environment for Creation

A CAD model placed in a virtual environment to check and edit together. The main function is development.

Model in Environment for Exploration

A CAD model placed in a Virtual environment for exploration, checking and discussing. The main function is to share, display, show the CAD model to other stakeholders.

Realtime Volumetric Capture

A camera captures real-time a 3D image of the user, placing the user in the virtual environment.

Remote Assistence

Remote assistence with the help of an AR headset. The remote assistent can also see what the AR headset sees, and can draw or point real-time in the screen of the AR-headset and assist the wearer.

Roam & Discover

An open world or hall where people can roam freely, meet and discover new things. For example fairs or a virtual museum.

Simulation

A virtual environment where real actions can be tested or trained. For

Social Network

A place where people can meet, talk, share and play games in a virtual environment.

Virtual Classroom

A classroom in a virtual environment.

Workspace

A virtual desk with multiple screens and tools that help productivity.

XR Platform

A platform where differen XR tools can be created. Exists of multiple functions like simulation, models in environment, conference rooms

Fig. 1. The key categories of XR platforms

In the end, nineteen categories with specific names and synopses are identified and the numbers of XR platforms in each category were calculated. Each category is coded with different colors for the statistical analysis.

Mapping XR Platforms on the Experience Matrix
The authors applied the *Experience Matrix* by Pine and Gilmore to show the types of experiences that can be authorized via these XR platforms [14]. As a key step in the *Immersion Cycle* model, this well-known model (Fig. 2) explains the dimensions to engage the receiver of an experience [3]. The XR platforms are mapped into the four quadrants regarding the 'participation' and 'connection' dimensions. On the participation dimension (X-axis), the authors chose *supported hardware* (e.g., stereoscopic headsets) and *OS platforms* (e.g., smartphones or Web XR) to analyze whether an XR platform provides an absorptive or immersive experience; on the connection dimension (Y-axis), the authors selected *collaboration types* (e.g., co-working or lecture) and *features* (e.g., CAD images or 360 images) to analyze that an XR platform can support active or passive interactions.

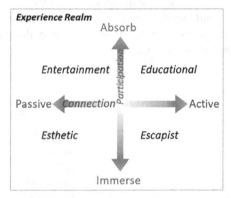

Fig. 2. The Experience Matrix with the 'participation' dimension (from **absorb** to **immerse**) and the 'connection' dimension (from **passive** to **active**) [14].

Results
The Categories of XR Experiences
In Survey 1, nineteen categories of the eighty-eight XR platforms were identified (Fig. 3). 'Creation', 'Simulation', 'MiE Exploration' and 'Remote Assistance' represent 46.6% of the key attributes, followed by the group containing 'Conference Room', 'Model in Environment for Creation', 'Data Visualization', 'Roam & Discover', and 'XR Platform'. These nine categories in total cover 82.9% of the key attributes in XR platforms.

Creation, the largest cluster, represents the functions to create content that can be used in XR. The *Simulation* group is about a virtual environment where one can integrate advanced interaction with a model. If we mainly look at the models to evaluate and explore in a virtual environment, then we get at the *Model in Environment for Exploration*. *Remote Assistance* seems like a popular way to use XR as well. The main goal is to help a remote expert in assisting a worker on location. For example, drawing in an AR application with motion tracking enables the drawing to remain on the object, and not move with the camera.

The *Conference Room* often provide a virtual space for co-working, meeting, and interpersonal interaction which can be accessed via multiple ends, such as XR goggles, tablets or smartphones. The *MiE Creation* is an extension of *MiE Exploration* where objects can also be edited. The *Data Visualization* category allows teams to visualize, manipulate and analyze data remotely and collectively. *Roam & Discover* is an open space where guests can roam freely, supporting collaboration, marketing, or showcases. The *XR Platform* are often a software development kit to create XR experiences focusing on specific fields, such as enterprise training, product visualization, or team collaboration.

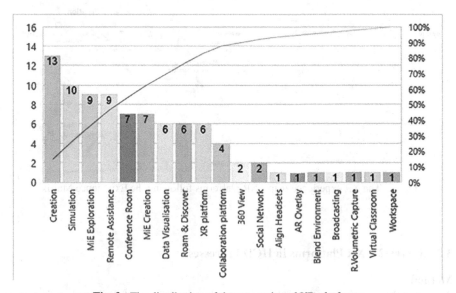

Fig. 3. The distribution of the categories of XR platforms

A Map of XR Experiences
When looking at the analysis in Fig. 4, what immediately stands out is the *escapist* quadrant is quite occupied. In this quadrant, the XR platform's experiences can immerse their receivers completely in virtual environments, where the receivers actively interact within these environments and memorize their visiting as 'places' instead of digital images.

In *simulating* scenarios that are complicated to build in the real-world, user tests might be done faster, easier, cheaper, and even remotely, especially for large-scale products, like aircraft interiors [15], ergonomic research [16], or urban planning [17]. Likewise, designing in XR can have benefits. Designer teams can work together globally and can test products with customers before major investments. *MiEE* is an interesting category for retail and design because the product can be seen in an intended environment, and it's even possible to turn, move or scale objects. Yet these are precisely where the interesting possibilities for the future lie. In addition, *Remote Assistance* can be advantageous by sharing the first-person view and involving stakeholders in contexts, where they can choose between immersive and non-immersive platforms. It would be beneficial for mutual understanding both assigning the designer's view to users and vice versa.

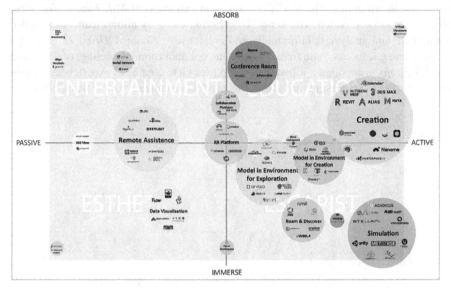

Fig. 4. The XR experience map - XR platforms following the Experience Matrix

3.2 Survey 2 – XR Platforms in HCD Processes

Method

As a thought experiment, the authors invented two personas of designers, a freelance designer and a corporate designer [18]. The freelance designer has a limited budget for software licenses and develops XR experiences by his/herself, while the corporate designer has more budget and can use commercial software and databases from the company. To clarify the differences between XR platform choices, a fictional design project is assigned to them, which requires creating an XR experience so that stakeholders can view a product in a particular context.

In Survey 2, the authors used a kitchen design as an example (see Fig. 5): CAD models simulated the requirements of a client, providing some parts in the kitchen, like a refrigerator and a stove. The cupboards need to be designed from scratch. It must be possible to interact with the drawers and kitchenware (like opening the fridge) in the VR demo. The authors discuss the general barriers of XR platforms and their implementation strategies according to the designer's personas.

The choice of XR platforms is then analyzed according to the two personas. XR platforms from the previous survey are analyzed to support HCD methods and tools in the fictional project. The XR platforms need to be assigned to the stages in the *Double-Diamond Model*: *Discover, Define, Develop* and *Deliver,* according to the methods and

Fig. 5. The fictional kitchen design project in virtual reality

tools listed in Table 1 [19]. If an XR platform is assigned to a certain stage, it means that it can support at least one or more design methods or tools at this stage. These XR platforms then are visualized on the DDM.

Table 1. The Double-Diamond Model and relevant design methods and tools [2]

Discover	Define	Develop	Deliver
- Observations	- Persona	- Brainstorming	- Storytelling
- Questionnaires	- Problem Definition	- Brain-drawing	- Comfort Evaluation
- Creating Focus Groups	- Function Analysis	- Morphological Chart	- 3D physical models
- SWOT analysis	- Product Life Cycle	- How-Tos	- Technical Documentation
- WWWWWH	- List of Requirements	- Design Drawing to Develop	- Design Drawing to Deliver
- Design Drawing to Discover	- Mind Mapping	- Harris Profile	- 3D Digital models
- Interviews	- Product Journey Mapping	- Usage analytics	
	- Future Visioning	- ViP	
	- Collage	- Cost-price estimation	
	- Storyboarding		
	- Scenario creation		
	- Design Drawing to Define		

As need fulfilment is key to generating positive experiences, the authors also analyzed the selected XR platforms to understand how they can support to understand users' needs and requirements [20]. A hierarchical model of goals from the *Action Theory* is used in this survey (see [21]). According to this theory, *be-goals* represent the universal needs and values of human beings, and they motivate actions and provide meaning to them; *do-goals* refer to the concrete outcomes that a user wants to attain in an action; *motor-goals* drive people to press a button or click an icon.

Results

The Barriers of XR Platforms and Their Implementation Strategies

A common problem faced by designers is the steep learning curve. In addition, the learning and developing hours can pile up when complex materials (e.g., mirrors) or interactions (e.g., interactive objects) are involved. Different types of designers developed diverse strategies to cope with it (Table 2).

Table 2. Strategies used by designer's personas when developing XR experiences

	Obtaining assets	Interacting assets	Texturing	Effects
Freelance designer	Purchasing models from *Sketchfab* or *Asset store*	Developing objectives using *Blender / Rhino*	Mapping textures with *Materialize* or *Substance*	Applying basic/designated templates in *Unity* or *Unreal Engine*
Corporate designer	Company's database of models and imagery	Autodesk toolkit including *Maya* (animation), *AutoCAD* (manufacturer), *Revit* (architecture), and *VREDD* (automotive)	Autodesk material library shared by *Maya*, Revit, and *AutoCAD* or creating materials with *Mudbox*	Outsourcing to XR developers

For freelance designers, it is advantageous to use open-source software so that they save on license costs, and can invest in assets or training to save time. Freelance designers need to allocate learning hours alongside production hours to explore alternative pipelines, especially finding formats that can transfer assets between different platforms errorless. Changing purchased assets might cause errors as well. The corporate designer has more resources at his/her disposal, and there is already a stock database for images and models. They can concentrate on sophisticated design solutions. The corporate designer probably already has a high budget for an XR project. For complicated XR experiences, outsourcing is a time-efficient option. However, corporate designers have limited capacity to reuse the XR experiences afterwards. Moreover, many 3D engines, like *Unreal Engine* or *Unity* are often not compatible with enterprise engineering software.

The situation is changing due to the increasing need for XR experiences. Many simulations are recently been included in open-source programs like *Rhinoceros*. Both freelance and corporate designers now can create enough relevant XR experiences to help clients clarify or promote their products when they can master alternative pipelines. For example, many XR platforms (e.g., *Unity, Unreal, Substances*, and *Autodesk*) offer asset stores where designers can purchase models or templates, which would save a lot of time on modelling and animating. This offers an option for freelancers, who would demand a budget from clients to purchase assets to save production hours. With the accumulated experience in developing XR experiences, the assets, i.e., models, materials, code, and environment, could be reused in different projects.

Different Ways for Choosing XR Platforms in an HCD Process
There are different ways of choosing XR platforms in the sense of time and budget. For example, freelance designers prefer open-source software such as *Blender*, which is free to use but very limited on technical support; whereas corporate designers are bound to enterprise software like *Autodesk* which a one-year subscription per package costs between two and three thousand Euros. These licenses usually are decided by the company and include different types of services from technical support to customized development. On the contrary, freelance designers have more flexibility in allocating learning and production hours, whereas for corporate designers, putting in extra hours to learn new tools requires an agreement at the organizational level. Moreover, XR developing skills serve as a new competence for freelancers as well.

The design tasks are different as well. The freelancers can easily do simple assignments, which are similar to the tutorial provided by each XR platform. As the complexity increases, such as multiple environments, interactive functionalities, or specific objects to be modelled, freelancers bear instant rises both in learning efforts and workloads. Precisely with these complex assignments, corporate designers benefit from licensed systems, like the Autodesk toolkit. It consists of a set of software that works in a smooth pipeline. For instance, exporting models to another program is effortless and simulations can be configured with 'one-click' functions. Hence, corporate designers can focus on more complex and detailed design tasks. Designers have different platforms at their disposal that can facilitate different design activities. The survey listed selected XR platforms following the *Double-Diamond Model* (Fig. 6).

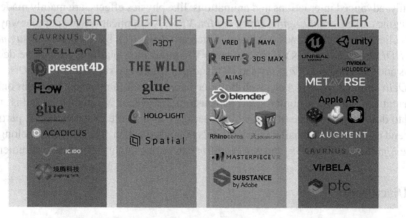

Fig. 6. The typical XR platforms in line with the DDM

The Discover Stage: IC.IDO, for example, supports replacing physical prototypes with interactive and digital mock-ups with real-time physics simulations in a team of six members. It enables remote observation with teams of up to twenty collaborators as well as a maximum of forty spectators. The platforms from the *Conference Room* category, like *glue,* focusing on casual co-working and review, which mostly share 2D video, presentation and desktop would be suitable for probe *be-goals* of users. The *Simulation* category with 360 videos and images, like the *IC.IDO* would help designers gain empathy under particular contexts. Other categories that help to understand be-goals are the *Data Visualization* and *XR platform.*

The Define Stage: Spatial.io is an online gallery supporting self-defined rooms for shared reviews with forty collaborators. *R3DT* and *the Wild* emphasize remote collaboration that allows a twenty-person team to use CAD data for visual prototypes. *Holo-light* can create co-work AR space to inspect, manipulate and share engineering designs. When a platform from the *Conference Room* or *Collaboration Platform* categories that share 3D assets or CAD images, like *the Wild,* it's suitable for defining a particular design problem and its relevant do-goals. The *MiE Creation* category (e.g., Holo-light) enabling visualizing, manipulating and sharing CAD data immersive could support the survey on do-goals alike.

The Develop Stage: The software, for modelling and prototyping, is *VRED, MAYA, ALIAS,* and *3DS Max,* or open-source software like *Blender* and *Rhinoceros. Substance* from Adobe focuses on 3D materials for photorealistic rendering. *SolidWorks* from Dassault Systems also puts efforts into direct modelling in VR. The XR interfaces of SolidWorks and Rhinoceros can help designers to check the ergonomic issues (like sizes, visibility, and reachability) with intuitions. When reviewing the early prototypes with stakeholders, designers can easily check the fulfilments of the *do-goals* and *motor-goals* with a specific design proposition.

The Deliver Stage: XR experiences need to be released across different hardware, where the most common ones are headsets, iOS/Android smartphones, or web browsers. Additionally, advanced interactions and animations, like physics effects, are mainly made via 3D engines, like *Unreal Engine, Unity,* or *MetaVRse.* AR applications are popular ways to reach clients on smartphones or tablets, which are developed by *Apple AR* or *Augment.* The *HOLODECK* from NVIDIA targets a VR innovation platform to involve design teams and stakeholders. *Cavrnus* and PTC *Vuforia Chalk* can support both the *Discover* and *Deliver* stage. *VirBELA* is a web-browser-based virtual campus that provides online presentations, meetings, conferences, and customized events. XR platforms at this stage need to deliver the essence of a specific experience as a whole to stakeholders, particularly end users, and thus shall review all levels of goals together. The platforms belonging to the *Simulation, Creation,* and *XR Platform* categories might fulfil this requirement.

4 Discussion

4.1 Survey 1

The categories of XR platforms still focus on *Creation* and *Simulation,* among which *Unity* or *Unreal Engine* are the most-used tools to create advanced interactions and narratives in XR experiences. As already explained, in the future the *Simulation* category will be helpful to train employees in different cases or test the experiences of product-service systems. It's worth noticing that the categories supporting remote collaboration in different levels of immersion, such as *MiE Exploration, Remote Assistance*, and *Conference Room*, become popular as well. A possible speculation is their attributes might link the design activities with marketing activities, which seems to accelerate iteration loops in design processes.

In the XR experience map, the *immerse-active* quadrant is more occupied compared to the other three quadrants. A possible explanation is that being immersed in a virtual environment is seen as active as you need to navigate and grab objects. Immersing and spatializing experience not only helps to transfer design problems to solutions but also enriches the emotional component of designers' work [11]. Compared to a real-life PowerPoint presentation, presenting in a virtual environment can be immersive to the receivers, but the presentation tools would be relatively absorptive compared to other XR platforms. Therefore, when it comes to immersion, the axis is relative to XR experiences as XR is generally seen as an immersive tool [22]. The absorptive experience is less represented by current platforms. Pine, B. J., & Gilmore, J. H. states: *"If the experience "goes into" guests, as when watching TV, then they are absorbing the experience (...)"* [14]. The absorption thus might as well invite high mental engagement which is very important in design communication. For instance, designers walk through an immersive environment while sharing their viewpoints with stakeholders on desktops or tablets to enhance mutual understanding.

4.2 Survey 2

To create a positive, valuable, and meaningful experience in a product-service system, it is important to satisfy universal needs and values, like emotional connection, affection and other experiential aspects [23]. Experience approaches thus show the possibility to solicit multisensory sensations, such as vision, audition, and touch. It might not only facilitate the assessment of pragmatic qualities, but also appraise the hedonic qualities, such as familiarity, pleasure, and communication [24]. Moreover, sometimes there are different conditions where the real-time involvement of stakeholders can be challenging [9], like limited time, accessibility of contexts, and ethical considerations [25]. There is thus a shift from the technology-focused perspective to experiential approaches, where the first-person perspective enables design professionals to collect subjective experiences as rich as possible for analysis [11, 26].

When it comes to implementing XR platforms in design, the first look is the costs. There's a trade-off between license expenses and asset purchases. For freelance designers, the expenses on licenses shall be as low as possible, while the budget for buying assets can be higher. To corporate designers, the situation is reversed because they already have enterprise dictionaries at their disposal. Design assignments leverage the license-asset balance as well. Thinking of a kitchen design as shown in Fig. 5, freelancers can produce XR experiences with standardized kitchen models and 'one-click' XR functions at a very low cost. As customized requirements increase, corporate designers have more resources that allow them to collaborate with colleagues and create detailed solutions that are impossible for freelancers.

In terms of time, designers so far probably need longer for learning than for producing at the beginning. When simulating sophisticated interactions, the learning curve can go even steeper. Another barrier, in terms of time, is the threshold to embed XR into design processes, in that design teams need a smooth workflow that links XR platforms with current pipelines. The errors occurring now frequently on incompatible file formats consume a lot of development hours. Regarding using XR in user testing, there's a learning gap as well because designers need to train users to understand the navigation and controls at first. Therefore, using XR platforms without thinking about them is the key to increasing the application rate.

5 Conclusion

Extended Reality, as a growing trend in digital transformation, is still evolving but has shown great potential for global economic and technological growth soon [27, 30]. Considering the rapid growth in computational power, especially in AI design [31] and graphic computing [28], it would be possible for everyone to create their own XR experiences soon. The next focus would be the improvements on interfaces of XR software and hardware, so it becomes intuitive both for ideating and developing tasks. More and more researchers put their efforts into the human factors of XR platforms, and many developments are expected in this area. It is therefore an interesting field to monitor in the coming years.

Several limitations in this work might pinpoint room for future studies: (1) Many simulation games or similar applications that serve as a good representative real-world experience are not included in this study. The analysis of how games can simulate corresponding experiences might be beneficial to designing relevant product-service experiences as well. (2) Experience by nature is memorable, as well as unique and irreducible [14, 29]. Hence, XR simulations should not merely focus on photorealistic appearances but also on generating relevant narratives. (3) The participation and connection axes of the experience model could be correlated. More specific analyses on immersive factors are needed. (4) Design agencies or small teams, who are both limited on time and budgets, are missing in this analysis. Further studies will involve different roles of designers to understand their needs and expectations of XR platforms.

The ability to observe from the first-person perspective, such as looking inwards, looking outwards, backwards into the past, and forward into the future, is as significant as the third-person view, like observing the user's eye movements, in understanding human needs and emotions [26]. XR platforms show the potential to integrate both of them in the future. Additionally, remote design is never as good as when people are together, but XR might offer a different solution. The authors can be cautiously optimistic that when the interfaces of XR hardware and software become intuitive, designers will be empowered to create what's impossible to experience now.

References

1. Stappers, P.J., Hekkert, P., Keyson, D.: Design for interaction: consolidating the user-centred focus in industrial design engineering. In: DS 43: Proceedings of E&PDE 2007, the 9th International Conference on Engineering and Product Design Education, University of Northumbria, Newcastle, UK, 13–14 September 2007

2. Van Boeijen, A., Daalhuizen, J., Zijlstra, J.: Delft Design Guide: Perspectives, Models, Approaches, Methods. BIS Publishers (2020)

3. Lingan, C.L., Li, M., Vermeeren, A.P.: The immersion cycle: understanding immersive experiences through a cyclical model. Proc. Des. Soc. **1**, 3011–3020 (2021)

4. Pietroni, E.: Experience design, virtual reality and media hybridization for the digital communication inside museums. Appl. Syst. Innov. **2**(4), 35 (2019)

5. Klahr, D., Triona, L.M., Williams, C.: Hands on what? the relative effectiveness of physical versus virtual materials in an engineering design project by middle school children. J. Res. Sci. Teach. **44**(1), 183–203 (2007)

6. Kefalidou, G., et al.: Designing airport interiors with 3D visualizations. In: Extended Abstracts of the 2019 CHI Conference on Human Factors in Computing Systems (2019)

7. Aromaa, S., Väänänen, K.: Suitability of virtual prototypes to support human factors/ergonomics evaluation during the design. Appl. Ergon. **56**, 11–18 (2016)

8. Keefe, D.F.: Creative 3d form-making in visual art and visual design for science. In: CHI 2009 Workshop on Computational Creativity Support: Using Algorithms and Machine Learning to Help People Be More Creative (2009)

9. Kim, K.G., et al.: Using immersive virtual reality to support designing skills in vocational education. Br. J. Edu. Technol. **51**(6), 2199–2213 (2020)

10. Corporation, I.D. Worldwide Spending on Augmented and Virtual Reality Forecast to Deliver Strong Growth Through 2024, 17 November 2020 [cited 17 January 2022]. https://www.idc.com/getdoc.jsp?containerId=prUS47012020

11. Rieuf, V., et al.: Emotional activity in early immersive design: Sketches and moodboards in virtual reality. Des. Stud. **48**, 43–75 (2017)

12. Toma, M.I., Girbacia, F., Antonya, C.: A comparative evaluation of human interaction for design and assembly of 3D CAD models in desktop and immersive environments. Int. J. Interact. Des. Manufact. - IJIDEM **6**(3), 179–193 (2012)

13. Armstrong, S.: Extended reality: what's stopping businesses from adoption? Raconteur Publishing 2018 November 29 [cited 17 January 2022]. https://www.raconteur.net/technology/vr-ar/extended-reality-barriers-adoption/

14. Pine, B.J., Gilmore, J.H.: The Experience Economy. Harvard Business Press (2011)

15. KLM. Kijk nu (zonder ticket) rond in alle KLM-vliegtuigen. 2019 [cited 18 January 2022]. https://blog.klm.com/nl/kijk-zonder-ticket-rond-alle-klm-vliegtuigen/

16. Whitman, L.E., et al.: Virtual reality: its usefulness for ergonomic analysis. In: 2004 Proceedings of the 2004 Winter Simulation Conference. IEEE (2004)

17. Schubert, T.: Virtual reality for smart cities and urban planning, 28 September 2017 [cited 14 January 2022]. https://esriaustralia.com.au/blog/virtual-reality-smart-cities-and-urban-planning

18. Miaskiewicz, T., Kozar, K.A.: Personas and user-centered design: how can personas benefit product design processes? Des. Stud. **32**(5), 417–430 (2011)

19. Council, D.: Eleven Lessons: Managing Design in Eleven Global Companies-Desk Research Report. Design Council (2007)

20. Hassenzahl, M.: Experience Design: Technology for All the Right Reasons. Synthesis Lectures on Human-Centered Informatics, vol. 3, pp. 1–95. Morgan & Claypool Publishers LLC. (2010)

21. Carver, C.S., Scheier, M.F.: Origins and functions of positive and negative affect: a control-process view. Psychol. Rev. **97**(1), 19–35 (1990)

22. Mbaabu, O.: Introduction to extended reality 2020, 5 November 2020 [cited 20 January 2022]. https://www.section.io/engineering-education/introduction-to-extended-reality/

23. Hassenzahl, M., Tractinsky, N.: User experience - a research agenda. Behav. Inf. Technol. **25**(2), 91–97 (2006)

24. Schifferstein, H.N., Desmet, P.M.: The effects of sensory impairments on product experience and personal well-being. Ergonomics **50**(12), 2026–2048 (2007)

25. Freina, L., Ott, M.: A literature review on immersive virtual reality in education: state of the art and perspectives. In: The International Scientific Conference eLearning and Software for Education (2015)

26. Xue, H., Desmet, P.M.: Researcher introspection for experience-driven design research. Des. Stud. **63**, 37–64 (2019)

27. Corporation, I.D. IDC Reveals 2021 Worldwide Digital Transformation Predictions; 65% of Global GDP Digitalized by 2022, Driving Over $6.8 Trillion of Direct DX Investments from 2020 to 2023. 2020 [cited 17 January 2022]. https://www.idc.com/getdoc.jsp?containerId= prUS46967420

28. Mims, C.: Huang's law is the new Moore's Law, and explains why Nvidia wants arm. Wall Street J. (2020)

29. McCarthy, J., Wright, P.: Technology as experience. Interactions **11**(5), 42–43 (2004)

30. Wang, K.J., Shidujaman, M., Zheng, C.Y., Thakur, P.: HRIpreneur thinking: strategies towards faster innovation and commercialization of academic HRI research. In: 2019 IEEE International Conference on Advanced Robotics and its Social Impacts (ARSO), pp. 219–226. IEEE, October 2019

31. Chen, W., Shidujaman, M., Tang, X.: AiArt: towards artificial intelligence art. In: ThinkMind // MMEDIA 2020, The Twelfth International Conference on Advances in Multimedia, February 2020

A Survey on When to Think About Talking to Users of the Work Immersion Time Presentation System in the Office

Soshi Nitta, Issei Yokota, Iori Okuno, and Takayoshi Kitamura$^{(\boxtimes)}$

Faculty of Engineering and Design, Kagawa University, Takamatsu, Japan
kitamura.takayoshi@kagawa-u.ac.jp

Abstract. While focusing on their own work (individual work), office workers contribute to the productivity of the entire organization by collaborating and cooperating with others in the same room, on the same floor, or on the same premises. However, it can be said that individual work with interruptions often requires more effort and time than uninterrupted individual work. For this reason, many studies have been conducted to estimate the decline in the state of concentration on individual work and to provide the timing of interruptions to the outside world. On the other hand, few studies have investigated how much such information is actually used as a reference. The purpose of this study is to investigate the relationship between "the timing when one is willing to talk to someone who declares immersion in work" and "the time when one thinks one can concentrate on work" in terms of the degree of intimacy and the time required for collaboration in an office. For this purpose, we first devised an application that allows workers to clearly indicate the time elapsed from the declaration of their own immersion in the work. Then, we conducted an experiment to examine the degree of elapsed time at which workers would be willing to talk to a person who is declaring work immersion, assuming both intimacy and the content of the intervening collaboration.

Keywords: Intellectual Productivity · Interruptions · Communication Enhancement

1 Introduction

While concentrating on their own work (individual work), people working in a business or research office contribute to the productivity of the entire organization by collaborating and cooperating with others in the same room, on the same floor, or on the same premises. For example, in offices (laboratories) set up for students in research and educational institutions such as universities, individual work at one's own seat, such as writing reports for assignments or developing programs for research, accounts for much of the time spent in the room. The content varies from those that require concentrated work, such as writing papers and making presentations, to those that can be accomplished in a relatively relaxed manner, such as making illustrations and conducting literature research. In addition, the office often involves conversation and collaboration with other

M. Kurosu and A. Hashizume (Eds.): HCII 2023, LNCS 14013, pp. 465–476, 2023.
https://doi.org/10.1007/978-3-031-35602-5_33

people in the same room. For example, they may ask each other questions, report on work-related issues, or ask for help with tasks that they cannot accomplish alone. In other words, the transition between individual work and conversational collaboration is repeated in the office [1].

There are two types of transitions from individual work to collaborative work: one in which a person interrupts his or her own individual work and transitions to collaborative work, and the other in which a person is asked to make a transition by another person. The factors that cause a person to interrupt his or her own individual work include the occurrence of unclear points during the work or the need for help in performing the work. On the other hand, when others request a transition, it may be because they need help or have something to do with the person who is working individually, or because they recognize the person who greeted them and remember what they have to do with that person. These examples of transitions between individual and collaborative work depend on the conditions of use, the relationship between the individual and the collaborators, and the context in which the individual works.

Interrupted individual work often requires more effort and time than uninterrupted individual work. This is due to the weakening or loss of temporary memory for the previously focused work by switching to another task. Temporary memory is a "memory for the moment" that is retained for a short period of time, and only about four items can be temporarily remembered [2], and the forgetting of temporary memory is influenced by the passage of time and the interference of memory by new input [3, 4]. Therefore, it is likely that individuals who are interrupted by other people's requests to switch from individual work to collaborative work will have to expend effort and time to recover lost temporary memories when they return to individual work.

Against this background, many studies have been conducted to provide the timing of interruptions by estimating the decline in the state of concentration on personal tasks [5–9]. On the other hand, whether the information about the decline in concentration state can support the decision whether to interrupt or not depends on various conditions, such as the human relationships in the office and the nature of the task to be interrupted. In addition, there are cases in which workers do not want to interrupt even when their concentration state is reduced. Therefore, it is necessary to accumulate knowledge about different cases in order to design an application that supports communication for interruptions.

The purpose of this study is to investigate the relationship between "when a worker is willing to talk to someone who declares immersion in the work" and "the time he/she thinks he/she can concentrate on the work" in terms of the degree of intimacy and the time required for collaboration in an office. For this purpose, we first developed an application that allows employees to clearly indicate the time elapsed since they declared their own immersion in the work. Then, we conducted an experiment to examine the degree of time elapsed before the worker wants to talk to the worker, assuming a situation in which the worker talks to the worker, and discussed the results.

2   Related Works

Research on improving cognitive productivity in offices includes approaches from various fields, such as management engineering and human interface studies, to increase the speed of work performance, i.e., to lead to profit. For example, management engineering approaches focus on increasing and maintaining employee motivation in the office [10–13], while human interface research approaches aim to improve cognitive productivity by controlling lighting and air conditioning [14–16]. Research on interrupting a person during personal work can be roughly divided into two categories: research that focuses on estimating the state of the person being interrupted, and research that focuses on supporting the decision of the person who wants to be interrupted.

In the research that focuses on estimating the state of the person being interrupted, Chen et al. [17] took the approach of estimating interruptibility based on physiological measures of heart rate variability and electromyography. Fogarty, J. et al. [18] are also working on a study that aims to infer the type of work and the context of a person at work by unevenly distributing different sensors in a room.

As research that focuses on supporting the decision of the person who wants to interrupt, Sakamoto, T. et al. [19] focus on the positional relationship between the two parties at the beginning of human communication and observe how they present considerations by assuming the internal state of the other party.

In addition, Tanaka, T. et al. [20] conducted research that considers the circumstances of both the person being interrupted and the person who wants to be interrupted, focusing on the degree of rejection of the person being interrupted. For example, they proposed an interaction initiation support method that estimates the degree of the user's refusal to be interrupted based on the work history of a PC and controls the presentation timing to reduce the loss of work efficiency due to interruption.

These studies on interrupting a person during personal work are expected to be applied to face-to-face communication in a near-future office with various sensing capabilities, and to office work in a metaverse with a head-mounted display that can collect biometric information. However, there are situations in individual work in which the worker may not welcome interruptions under any circumstances, because there are situations in which the worker must continue to work even if his or her state of concentration or refusal to be interrupted decreases. In addition, even if the timing of interruptions is known from the worker's concentration state and refusal level, there are few studies that focus on whether the interrupter really feels the need to talk to the worker, so it is necessary to accumulate more case studies.

3   Application for the Experiment

In this study, an application called MoguRun was developed to verify whether the user who wants to talk to the intruder really feels like talking to the intruder when the elapsed time since the intruder started concentrating on his work is presented to the intruder. MoguRun is an application that uses AR technology to create partitions around users who want to immerse themselves in their work, which can be checked with a smartphone or smart glasses. Figure 1 shows an image of MoguRun. By making a water tank appear around the user in the center, the room can be virtually divided into two parts: inside and outside. For example, a "person who wants to concentrate on his work" can use AR to set up a virtual water tank at his sitting position to present his state to the surrounding application users. The person who wants to talk to the other person can use AR to check the tank and decide when to talk to the other person. The person who wants to talk to the other person does not need to approach the other person and does not interfere with the visual and tactile information, which is thought to enable deliberation so as not to disturb the other person's concentration. The reason for adopting the water tank design is that there is a commonality in that there is a limit to how long one can concentrate on work and how long one can remain submerged in water. Note that the water tank in MoguRun does not disappear and remains displayed as long as the worker does not leave his seat, and the duration is not reset. In addition, although the original specifications call for the water in the tank to diminish as time passes, and for water to escape into the environment as the concentration decreases, we did not present such expressions in this experiment.

Fig. 1. Screen image of application 'MoguRun' using AR device.

4   Experiment

Using an aquarium-like partition that allows workers to show that they are concentrating on their work, and MoguRun, an application that can clearly display the elapsed time from the declaration of work immersion, we conducted an experiment assuming a situation in which workers talk to each other face-to-face to see how much elapsed time they are willing to talk to each other. We evaluated whether there was a difference in the intimacy and time required for joint work, and whether there was a correlation with the time that workers generally believed they could maintain concentration on their work.

4.1 Method

When the person to be talked to is a real person, there is a possibility that participants will make judgments based on other factors, such as whether or not the person is difficult to talk to. Figure 2 shows a schematic diagram of the positional relationship between the experimenter and the mannequin. Figure 3 shows a frontal view of the mannequin. Participants in the experiment were asked to control the mannequin sitting at a desk, assuming that they were using MoguRun from 5 m behind the mannequin, so that the mannequin would not interfere with their work. The scenario used in the experiment is "a situation in which the participant has something to do with the person he/she is working with, and after checking the person's status using MoguRun on a smartphone or tablet, the participant looks for the most appropriate moment to talk to the person". The experiment was conducted with the following procedure.

Step 1: The outline of MoguRun was explained to the participants.
Step 2: Participants were asked to stand at a predetermined point 5 m behind the mannequin and the scenario of the experiment was explained to them.
Step 3: The participants were instructed about the relationship with the other person and the content of what they are going to say to the mannequin.
Step 4: Participants are asked to answer when they are most likely to talk to the other person, assuming they will be using the application.
Step 5: After the answers are given, ask participants to indicate how often they have had similar experiences.
Step 6: Return to step 3 and repeat steps 4 and 5 until all situations are completed.
Step 7: Ask participants to indicate how long they think they can generally concentrate on the task (CT).
Step 8: Conduct a follow-up interview.

In Step 2, participants were told to assume that even if the person they were talking to showed the partition, they might not be able to concentrate on the task. The questionnaire format used in Step 4 is shown in Fig. 4. The situation assumed in this experiment is explained in Sect. 4.2. Since we did not know whether the time given in the answers in Step 4 was only a consideration of the partner's situation, we confirmed this in the post-interview in Step 8.

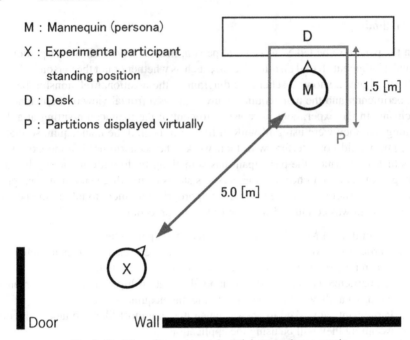

M : Mannequin (persona)

X : Experimental participant
   standing position

D : Desk

P : Partitions displayed virtually

D

M   1.5 [m]

P

5.0 [m]

X

Door   Wall

Fig. 2. Position of experimental participant and mannequin

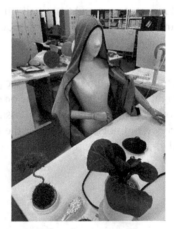

Fig. 3. Mannequin photographed from the front. The experimenter was supposed to call out to the mannequin from 5 m behind.

4.2 Assumed Situations

In this experiment we assumed a laboratory office for students studying media and product design at a university. Prior to the experiment, we discussed possible situations in which the transition from individual work to collaborative work might occur in a laboratory office for media and product design students. As a result, we derived three

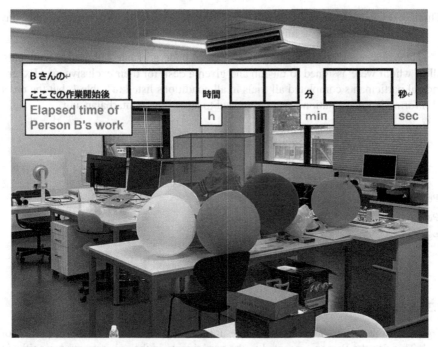

Fig. 4. Format in which participants in the experiment were asked to fill in their answers.

main types of intimacy that the participants of the experiment could easily imagine, and three types of errands for interruptions such as collaborative work that could be clearly imagined in terms of the amount of time involved. The following table shows the hypothetical persons with different levels of intimacy and the contents of errands that require different amounts of time. The following table shows the contents of errands for the hypothetical persons with different intimacy levels and different time requirements.

[Hypothetical people (with different intimacy levels)]

Person A: People of the same age and in the same class who go shopping together for personal use or for events, etc.
Person B: In the same group or next to each other in class, etc., they chat easily with each other.
Person C: People who have never met each other before, who just nod as they pass each other in the aisle.

[Tasks that require different amounts of time]

Thing 1: I need to know where to meet for tomorrow's event (he is the only person who might know).
Thing 2: I need 10 min of help with my survey.

Thing 3: I want to discuss the event we are going to do together in homeroom (this may take more than 30 min).

The experimental participants consisted of 24 undergraduate and graduate students, all of whom were assigned to the lab and given a desk for their exclusive use. Experimental participants completed all trials in all conditions listed in Table 1, but the order of information presentation was randomized to allow for counterbalancing.

Table 1. Suggested Information.

	Thing 1	Thing 2	Thing 3
Person A	A1	A2	A3
Person B	B1	B2	B3
Person C	C1	C2	C3

4.3 Results

Figure 5 shows a box-and-whisker plot summarizing the results of the responses of each Thing to the Person presented to the participants in the experiment. A significant difference was confirmed between the means of A1 and A3 and B1 and B3. A significant trend ($p < .10$) was found for the difference between the means of A1 and A2 and B1 and B2. On the other hand, there was no statistically significant difference between Person C's responses to the Thing.

Figure 6 shows a box-and-whisker plot of each person's responses to the Thing and the results of a multiple comparison test at the 5% level for the responses of Person 1, 2, and 3. A significant difference was confirmed between the means of A1 and C1, and A3 and C3. A significant trend ($p < .10$) was found for the difference between the means of B1 and C1, and A2 and C2.

Next, Spearman's rank correlation coefficients were calculated for CT (Concentrate Time) and other items, and as shown in Table 2, a relatively strong correlation was confirmed between CT and B3 and C3.

Table 2. The result of Spearman's rank correlation coefficient

	A1	B1	C1	A2	B2	C2	A3	B3	C3
CT	0.0901	0.0833	0.1825	−0.0218	0.1254	0.2101	0.3130	**0.4526**	**0.5298**
P-Value	0.6756	0.6988	0.3934	0.9196	0.5594	0.3243	0.1365	**0.0264**	**0.0077**

Table 3 shows some of the results from the interviews in which we asked the respondents why they gave the answers they did for the nine situations and the time responses for CT. In the interviews, 8 out of 24 participants answered that they made judgments

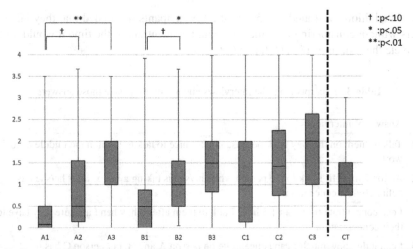

Fig. 5. Box-and-whisker diagram of the time answered for each **persona** (CT (Concentrate Time): The answer of "How long do you think you can maintain your concentration in general?". In this experiment, most of participants answered CT by imagining the amount of time they can concentrate on themselves. Note that multiple comparison tests between CT and the others (A1 to C3) were not conducted).

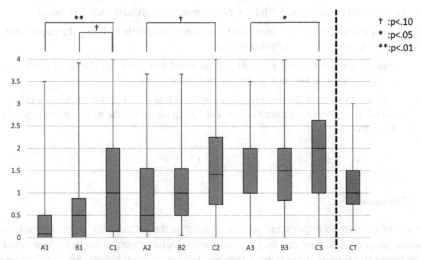

Fig. 6. Box-and-whisker diagram of the time answered for each **thing** (CT (Concentrate Time): The answer of "How long do you think you can maintain your concentra-tion in general?". In this experiment, most of participants answered CT by imagining the amount of time they can concentrate on themselves. Note that multiple comparison tests between CT and the others (A1 to C3) were not conducted).

based on the time they thought they would be able to concentrate on their work (e.g., 002, 003, 007, and 008). On the other hand, 11 participants answered that they expected a break in work (e.g., 005, 009, and 010) rather than concentration (e.g., 005, 009, and

010). In addition, we found that 5 out of 24 participants responded that they talked to others without considering the time they could concentrate or the time it would take to complete the task (e.g., 001, 004, and 006).

Table 3. Excerpts from the interviews about why they gave those answers.

ID	Answer of interview
001	Talk to them on the way back because it's not nice to talk to them in the middle of their work
002	As for Thing III, I talk to the person while he/she is taking a break, after he/she has definitely lost concentration
003	I can concentrate for about 1.5 h, so I talk to them after 2 h, when I am sure they have lost their concentration
004	I can judge how much I can concentrate on person A and B, but person C has no information at all, so I want to talk to her right away to finish my business
005	I am sorry if they have just started working, so I want to talk to them at a time when they have made some progress in their work
006	If I hesitate to talk to the person because of his condition, I have to keep thinking, "I'll have to ask again later," so I want to talk to him before I forget
007	Talk to them based on the 1.5 h I can concentrate, and talk to them if I exceed that
008	If it is a simple errand like Thing I and II, I want to talk to them during the elapsed time 0−20 min before they enter concentration
009	The class time at the university is 90 min, so if that much time has elapsed, I would judge that at least one task has been completed and talk to them
010	I don't want the other person to forget the original task because of my talking to him, so I avoid talking to him right after the start and talk to him when the work has progressed to some extent

4.4 Discussion

The aim of the current experiment was to investigate the relationship between the timing of when people think they can talk to those who declare themselves to be immersed in the task and the time that the person they are talking to thinks they can concentrate on the task.

In response to this objective, the results of the experiment did not confirm a significant difference in the mean value of the timing of the content of the conversation with Person C in Fig. 5. A possible reason for this could be the lack of a decision-making process for Person C, who is about to meet for the first time. This may be supported by the responses in the 004 interview. The high variance in the box-and-whisker plot for Person C suggests that differences in the way the experimental participants responded to the person close to their first meeting may have had an effect.

The results compared by intimacy in Fig. 6 show significant differences between the A1 and C1 and A3 and C3 conditions. Thus, it was confirmed that there was a difference in the timing of speaking to Person A and Person C in particular, depending on the level of intimacy. On the other hand, no differences could be observed between Person A and B and Person B and C. This raises the possibility that the difference was not observed because it was difficult to imagine the intimacy of Person B, who was set up to be able to chat comfortably but not to go shopping or to personal events together.

The results of Spearman's rank correlation coefficients for CT (Concentrate Time) and other items, which confirmed a relatively strong correlation between CT and B3 and C3, were divided into those that could be supported by the interview results (8 workers) and those that could not (16 workers). Therefore, it is considered that even if a worker is able to specify the time elapsed from the declaration of his own work immersion, it is not necessarily possible to realize an interruption that takes into account the concentration time of the other person. Therefore, it is considered that in order to support those who want to immerse themselves in work, a design that appeals to a stronger message to the environment is needed. In addition, responses 001, 004, and 006 differ in the reasoning behind their responses. This may be due to the personality of the participants in the experiment, such as their diplomacy and cooperativeness.

5 Conclusion

In this study, we conducted an experiment in a laboratory student office that focused on the relationship between "the time one is willing to talk to a person who declares to be immersed in work" and "the time one thinks one can concentrate on work" in terms of intimacy and the time required for collaboration. The results showed that although consideration was likely to be given to a person with high intimacy, interruptions were likely to occur when the time required to collaborate was at the level of light conversation. In addition, 8 out of 24 participants considered "the time when they think they can concentrate on the work" as a criterion, while 11 participants considered "when the work is finished" as a criterion, which resulted in a difference of opinion.

As a future prospect, we plan to conduct an additional survey to clarify the relationship with the personalities of the experiment participants. In addition, it will be necessary to compare the results with those of offices in different industries and to examine the effects of information other than the elapsed time from the declaration of work immersion.

Acknowledgement. This work was supported by JSPS KAKENHI Grant Number JP21K14392 and JP22K12701.

References

1. Sykes, E.R.: Interruptions in the workplace, a case study to reduce their effects. Int. J. Inf. Manage. **31**(4), 385–394 (2011)
2. Cowan, N.: The magical number 4 in short-term memory: a reconsideration of mental storage capacity. Behav. Brain Sci. **24**(1), 87–114 (2001)

3. Chen, D., Hart, J., Vertegaal, R.: Towards a physiological model of user interruptability. In: Baranauskas, C., Palanque, P., Abascal, J., Barbosa, S.D.J. (eds.) INTERACT 2007. LNCS, vol. 4663, pp. 439–451. Springer, Heidelberg (2007). https://doi.org/10.1007/978-3-540-74800-7_39

4. Reitman, J.S.: Mechanisms of forgetting in short-term memory. Cogn. Psychol. **2**, 185–195 (1971)

5. Reitman, J.S.: Without surreptitious rehearsal information in short-term memory decays. J. Verb. Learn. Verbal Behav. **13**, 365–377 (1974)

6. Fogarty, J., Lai, J., Christensen, J.: Presence versus availability: the design and evaluation of a context-aware communication client. Hum.-Comput. Stud. **61**, 299–317 (2004)

7. Erickson, T., Kellogg, W.A.: Social translucence: an approach to designing systems that support social processes. ACM Trans. Comput. Hum. Interact. **7**(1), 59–83 (2000)

8. Hincapie-Ramos, J.D., Voida, S., Mark, G.: A design space analysis of availability-sharing systems. In: UIST '11: Proceedings of the 24th Annual ACM Symposium on User Interface Software and Technology, pp. 85–96 (2011)

9. Kobayashi, Y., Tanaka, T., Aoki, T., Fujita, K.: Automatic delivery timing control of incoming email based on user interruptibility. In: CHI EA 2015: Proceedings of the 33rd Annual ACM Conference Extended Abstracts on Human Factors in Computing SystemsApril 2015, pp. 1779–1784 (2015)

10. Z¨uger, M., et al.: Reducing interruptions at work: a large-scale field study of FlowLight. In: CHI 2017: Proceedings of the 2017 CHI Conference on Human Factors in Computing Systems, pp. 61–72 (2017)

11. Knight, C., Haslam, S.A.: Your place or mine? organizational identification and comfort as mediators of relationships between the managerial control of workspace and employees' satisfaction and well-being. Br. J. Manag. **21**, 717–735 (2010)

12. Shanafelt, T.D, Trockel, M., Rodriguez, A., Logan, D.: Wellness-centered leadership: equipping health care leaders to cultivate physician well-being and professional fulfillment. Acad. Med. J. Assoc. Am. Med. Coll. **96**(5), 641 (2021)

13. Shanafelt, T.D., Noseworthy, J.H.: Executive leadership and physician well-being: nine organizational strategies to promote engagement and reduce Burnou. Mayo Clin. Proc. **92**, 129–146 (2017)

14. Roethlisberger, F.J., Dickson, W.J.: Management and the Worker? (2003)

15. Wargocki, P., Wyon, D.P., Fanger, P.O.: Productivity is affected by the air quality in offices. In: Proceedings of Healthy Buildings 2000, vol. 1, pp. 635–640 (2000)

16. Ishii, H., et al.: Intellectual productivity under task ambient lighting. Light. Res. Technol. **50**, 237–252 (2018)

17. Ueda, K., Yumura, K., Ishii, H., Shimoda, H., Obayashi, F.: An analysis of the effect of integrated thermal control on cognitive task performance using time-series changes in intellectual concentration. In: 13th AHFE International Conference, vol. 56, pp.205–210 (2022)

18. Fogarty, J., et al.: Predicting human interruptibility with sensors. ACM Trans. Comput.-Hum. Interact. **12**(1), 119–146 (2005)

19. Sakamoto, T., Sudo, A., Takeuchi, Y.: Investigation of model for initial phase of communication: analysis of humans interaction by robot. ACM Trans. Hum.-Robot Interact. **10**(2), 1–27 (2021)

20. Tanaka, T., Matsumura, K., Fujita, K.: Supporting acceptable dialogue start based on user uninterruptibility estimation for avatar-mediated multi-tasking online communication. In: Ozok, A.A., Zaphiris, P. (eds.) OCSC 2009. LNCS, vol. 5621, pp. 272–281. Springer, Heidelberg (2009). https://doi.org/10.1007/978-3-642-02774-1_30

Fashion Games, Fashion in Games and Gamification in Fashion. A First Map

Alice Noris[1]([✉]) [iD], Nadzeya Sabatini[1,2] [iD], and Lorenzo Cantoni[1] [iD]

[1] USI – Università della Svizzera italiana, Lugano, Switzerland
alice.noris@usi.ch
[2] Gdansk University of Technology, Gdansk, Poland

Abstract. Fashion companies have been using different forms of entertainment such as film and television, sport, music, museums, and photography as inspiration sources and as communication and marketing channels for decades. However, in recent years, they have also started to consider the gaming world. While gaming offers a potential revenue stream from sales of physical and digital clothing, change in it is also the gateway to access new opportunities of the so-called metaverse. Moreover, the development of mixed realities might, in a sense, "democratize" the industry by offering at a lower price the digital version of products that attract customers. Through an analysis of secondary data and the study of three cases, this research aims to understand how fashion companies adopt and adapt digital games to develop their communication and marketing strategies, and how gaming companies exploit fashion to develop their products. The main goal is to analyze from an academic perspective how the gaming industry represents a communication and marketing channel in which creative companies can produce immersive experiences different from those available through other means. Finally, this article provides a map of the relationships between fashion and gaming by proposing three categories: gamification in fashion, fashion games and fashion in games.

Keywords: Digital fashion · Fashion games · Gaming · Metaverse

1 Introduction

In recent years, the fashion world has been affected by a digital transformation that has been dramatically accelerated by the Covid19 pandemic. Fashion companies have become increasingly interested in the digital world through their appearance on social media, the creation of eCommerce platforms, and an increasing interest in the latest digital trends such as the Metaverse and gamification (Kalbaska et al. 2018; Kreutzer 2021; Noris et al. 2020; Noris & Cantoni 2021). The interest of fashion companies in gamification stems from the fact that they see gaming as a potential marketing channel where they can build their brand image and sell digital and/or physical collections (Kim et al. 2012). Gaming also presents a way for brands to extend themselves into virtual spaces where people spend a significant portion of their time (Bain 2021).

Some fashion houses, in fact, have chosen the use of gamification to attract and engage consumers and to be able to tell and express their values to young and tech-savvy

M. Kurosu and A. Hashizume (Eds.): HCII 2023, LNCS 14013, pp. 477–491, 2023.
https://doi.org/10.1007/978-3-031-35602-5_34

audience. Fashion brands on one hand are eager to communicate with that generation that will represent an important part of the customers in future years, Generation Z; on the other hand, players and fans of video games are proving to be fashion consumers, eager to buy products both in the game and in the real world.

Another aspect relates to the fact that there has been a surge of interest in the idea of the Metaverse: popular gaming platforms such as *Fortnite* and Roblox have emerged as sites where its foundations have been laid. More recently, Meta (formerly Facebook), has decided to invest billions in the attempt to make the Metaverse a reality (Bain 2021). Fashion companies, many of which have been slow to embrace eCommerce and have spent years building their digital presence, have decided to carve out their own place in this domain (Bain 2021).

The new partnerships between fashion brands and videogame designers are giving rise to great points of reflection and analysis. As it is a very recent phenomenon, there is a scarcity of academic research looking and studying the relationships and the interactions between these two domains, thus leaving a room for further investigation. Our research will start filling in this research gap, while proposing the first framework explaining the relationships between fashion and video gaming.

Subsequent paragraphs, however, are indented.

2   Literature Review

2.1   Framing Games

"Play" has been defined by Huizinga (1949) as an action, or a voluntary occupation, performed within certain defined limits of time and space, according to voluntarily assumed rules, and which nevertheless engages in an absolute way that is an end in itself; accompanied by a sense of tension and joy, and the consciousness of "being different" from "ordinary life". This definition encompasses all that is called play, whether by animals, children, or adults: games of skill, games of strength, games of intelligence, games of chance, representations, and performances.

More complex games, in order to exist, whether in a digital or analog formats, must be created by designers/teams of developers, and consumed by players (Hunicke et al. 2004). The MDA framework proposed by Hunicke et al. (2004) formalizes how games can be designed and described, outlining their Mechanics, Dynamics and Aesthetics.

According to Hunicke et al. (2004), mechanics describes the particular components of the game, at the level of data representation and algorithms. "Mechanics are the various actions, behaviors and control mechanisms afforded to the player within a game context. Together with the game's content (levels, assets and so on) the mechanics support overall gameplay dynamics" (Hunicke et al. 2004:3). Dynamics describes the real-time behavior of mechanics that act on player inputs and their respective outputs over time. According to Hunicke et al. (2004:3) "Dynamics work to create aesthetic experiences. For example, the challenge is created by the elements like time pressure and opponent play. Fellowship can be encouraged by sharing information across certain members of a session (a team) or supplying winning conditions that are more difficult to achieve alone (such as capturing an enemy base)". Finally, the "aesthetics describes the desirable emotional responses evoked by the player when interacting with the game system" (Hunicke et al. 2004:2).

2.2 Videogames: an Overview

Within the games' world, let's now focus our attention onto video games. According to Bergonse (2017:253) a videogame may be defined as: "... a mode of interaction between a player, a machine with an electronic visual display, and possibly other players, that is mediated by a meaningful fictional context, and sustained by an emotional attachment between the player and the outcomes of her actions within this fictional context".

As pointed out by Wolf and Perron (2003:2), "...the emerging field of video game theory is itself a convergence of a wide variety of approaches including film and television theory, semiotics, performance theory, game studies, literary theory, computer science, theories of hypertext, cybertext, interactivity, identity, postmodernism, ludology, media theory, narratology, aesthetics and art theory, psychology, theories of simulacra, and others".

Tekinbaş and Zimmerman (2003) add that digital games (computer, console and other electronic games) can be considered as a subset of games. The rise of academic interest in video games/digital games is relatively recent, especially when compared against the historical roots of video games, which can be traced back more than 70 years ago, to the first computer game "Noughts and Crosses" (or "OXO"), developed in 1952. Nevertheless, it was not until the late 1990s that social sciences and humanities began to approach digital games as an area of research (Mäyrä et al. 2013; Quandt et al. 2015).

In recent decades, digital gaming has transformed from a marginal leisure time activity of a small social group into a driving force in the entertainment industry and part of the mainstream culture of modern societies. Research also reveals that usage numbers are growing and that digital games are now played by large groups in society (Quandt et al. 2014). A 2021 report by Accenture (*Gaming the next Super Platform* 2021) showed that in 2021 the gaming market surpassed those of movies and music combined, while the estimated number of gamers in the world was 2.7 billion. It states that the number of subscribers on YouTube to the top 10 gaming influencers was 405 million, while the estimate of the direct and indirect value of the gaming industry was more than $300 billion.

For some time now, digital games have been found to be an attractive market, but what makes them unique as an object of study is that they are a leisure good purchased with disposable income. This aspect is of interest to both economists and socio-cultural researchers because it raises a number of interesting questions regarding value, consumer choices, networks, and so on (Bryce & Rutter 2006). Moreover, we are currently experiencing increasing virtualization and a rather unexpected *ludification* of the way we communicate, collaborate, learn, consume, or entertain. In this sense, for instance, developments in game technology have over time reinvigorated the discussion of the potential of digital games as vehicles for learning (Alexiou & Schippers 2018).

From the development of videogames/digital games comes gamification, which according to Huotari & Hamari (2017:25) can be defined as "a process of enhancing a service with affordances for gameful experiences in order to support users' overall value creation". This definition of gamification is agnostic to the nature of the core service being gamified, and it argues that gamification provides game-like experiences and sustains the customer's use value of the core service process (Huotari & Hamari 2017).

From a marketing and communication perspective, research on gaming is needed (Milanesi et al. 2022). In the field of fashion marketing and communication, studies on the use of gamification to facilitate sustainable fashion consumption (Waydel-Bendyk 2020), hybrid practices in fashion and game design, and the use of gamification as a tool to offer a digital luxury experience have been conducted, but more are needed to further frame the context and fill the research gap (Joy et al. 2022; Milanesi et al. 2022).

This article, through a careful analysis of the many relationships between fashion and gaming, aims to provide an initial map of their interactions.

3   Research Design and Methodology

This exploratory paper, through concept mapping, aims to determine the state of the art of fashion in relation to gamification and digital games, proposing a map of the interactions between gaming and fashion.

The goal is to answer the following research questions:

• Which are the possible relationships between fashion and gaming?
• How can they be mapped or framed?

To answer the questions, a map has been sketched trough a interpretative analysis of 24 qualitative cases. If still available the authors studied and firsthand experienced the digital games and gamification tools, if not, authors relied on secondary data. Three exemplary cases have been then selected, according to their meaningfulness for the research goal, to present the proposed map.

Authors opted for a qualitative multiple case studies approach, since it facilitates the exploration of a phenomenon within its context using a variety of data sources. Case studies ensure that the problem is not explored through a single lens, but rather through a variety of lenses that allow to reveal and understand several facets of the studied phenomenon (Baxter & Jack 2008). A multiple case study approach was chosen because it allows the researchers to explore differences within and across cases and to grasp similarities. This type of research design has advantages and disadvantages: evidence reached by it is considered robust and reliable (even if it cannot claim to be complete), but it can also be extremely time-consuming and expensive to conduct (Baxter & Jack 2008). This investigation was based on the case study methodology proposed by Yin (1994) which includes 6 steps: plan, design, preparation, data collection, analysis and reporting.

4   Examples of Fashion and Gaming Interactions

While the use of entertainment forms such as film, sports, and music as marketing channels in the fashion world began decades ago, digital games and gamification have only recently begun to attract attention (Bain 2021; Tepe & Koohnavard 2022). Fashion brands seem to be leveraging on existing video games to connect with new audiences and to make themselves known (Gibson 2021). More and more video games, including action or horror games such as *Grand Theft Auto, Dead by Daylight*, and *Fortnite*, have initiated collaborations and incorporated the concept of virtual clothing and cosmetics with which to customize characters (Allaire 2021). In the next paragraphs the 24 cases will be shortly presented.

Fortnite, for example, was one of the first gaming platforms to merge fashion with gaming. Among its collaborations is one with Balenciaga. Within the game, characters can buy and wear the brand's signature Triple-S sneakers and backpacks. The collaboration has introduced the Spanish fashion house to some 350 million gamers worldwide (Allaire 2021; Ryder 2022). Balenciaga, to mark the debut of the brand's fall 2021 collection, released a video game from its designer Demna Gvasalia's titled *Afterworld: The Age of Tomorrow*, in which characters from the game modeled his new garments (Allaire 2021).

In 2022, *Fortnite* has collaborated with Ralph Lauren to release a "phygital" fashion collection. The collaboration merged the gaming community with the real luxury audience, opting for a cross-border experience (Ryder 2022).

Recently also the Polish streetwear brand MISBHV has collaborated with the video game the *Grand Theft Auto V* to create virtual clothes. MISBHV designed graphic streetwear looks worn in the game by German DJ group Keinemusik (Allaire 2021).

Burberry is among the most active fashion brands in collaborating with video game platforms. After collaborations with other games, the fashion brand began working with *Minecraft* by launching *Burberry: Freedom To Go Beyond*, which includes a series of immersive in-game experiences with the launch of physical capsules available in seven stores worldwide (Ryder 2022). In 2021, Burberry introduced its first NFTs through a collaboration with *Blankos Block Party*, a game modeled after the vinyl toy industry, offering both characters and accessories in the form of NFTs (Mcdowell 2021).

In July 2022, Dior partnered with the *Gran Turismo* video game to launch *Gran Turismo 7 racing*. This game brought Dior's distinctive features to the virtual track, yellow uniforms, and a custom vintage car on which the brand iconic logo was affixed along with *Diorizon* shoes (Ryder 2022). In the same year, EA's *Need For Speed Unbound* in collaboration with the French brand Balmain has launched a series of limited in-game clothing on the channel, inspired by the couturier's most iconic designs (Ryder 2022).

Gucci and Vans have both recently strengthened a collaboration with Roblox, the first by launching the permanent residence *Gucci Town*, a development born in the wake of the Gucci Garden initiative and the second by presenting the Vans World, a virtual skatepark experience inspired by real-world exisiting destinations, such as the Vans Off the Wall Skatepark in California (Ryder 2022, *Vans World Roblox* n.d.).

Luxury accessories brand Bulgari has begun collaborating with Korean brand Zepeto, launching a virtual world on the Metaverse platform, complete with online and offline experiences. The goal is to strengthen its relationship with the Asian community by leveraging the video game's 150 million registered users (Ryder 2022).

In 2021, Louis Vuitton has started awarding its first NFTs to *Louis the Game* gamers. The game created to celebrate Louis Vuitton 200th anniversary sees the gamer accompany the avatar Vivienne to help her traverse a virtual world in which she has also to search for and find NFT postcards (Mcdowell 2021; Muhammad 2022).

The Nintendo Game *Animal Crossing* through the years partnered with many luxury labels including Sandy Liang, Marc Jacobs, and Valentino, which brought their designs to the game via virtual pop-ups and digital product drops (Pauly 2021).

There are also video game developers who make video games entirely dedicated to fashion. These include Magic Tavern, which has created the video game *Project Makeover*. The aim of the game is to complete a series of three-pair puzzles to win coins, mystery boxes, and gems to transform tasteless customers into stylish trendsetters by changing not only clothing and makeup, but also home and office decor (Magic Tavern n.d.; Project Makeover n.d.).

CrowdStar has developed *Covet Fashion*. The game allows gamers to dress different models by customizing their hair, makeup, and clothing. *Covet Fashion* uses clothes and accessories from real fashion brands and offers several themed challenges with special requirements to dress the chosen model, giving gamers a chance to win prizes in in-game currency and rare clothing items. Players vote on the challenges and determine the winners; they can also join fashion houses to socialize with other players and win more prizes (Covet Fashion n.d.).

Glu Mobile is the creator of the game *Kim Kardashian: Hollywood*. This is a role-playing game. The gamer starts as Kim Kardashian's assistant, creating various hairstyles and outfits, but dressing up and putting on makeup is not the only part of the game; in fact, the ultimate goal is to climb the ranks to become a celebrity like Kim Kardashian herself (Glu n.d.).

Fashion Empire – Boutique Sim is a game produced by Frenzoo, in which gamers enter the glamorous life by shopping, wearing fashionable clothes, attending beauty salons, hairdressers and numerous events. Within the game, however, work is also necessary: avatars choose their profession that will enable them a glamorous life. Their work activity is the starting point for selling high-fashion clothes. The gamer has to make strategic decisions, develop the store and make it grow by taking into consideration several factors. Gradually, the business has to be expanded, and the gamer can become the owner of many fashion venues and well-known personalities can visit them (GAMES.LOL n.d.).

Lady Popular, made by XS software, is a clothing game that offers the possibility of unlocking clothes, customizing one's character and performing a series of actions to unlock other items. The game offers new events every week or so, along with some competitive aspects (Hindy 2023).

There are also fashion brands that use game elements within their owned and earned media. Burberry and Ralph Lauren, for example, have joined forces with Snapchat; the former to create *Animal Kingdom*, an in-store game experience in which Snap codes invite consumers into the world of Burberry, the latter to create virtual clothing for personal Bitmojis (Sharbatian 2021). In 2011, Nike launched on its platforms a campaign to promote winter sportswear, creating an online game that allowed players to help athletes staying warm while training outdoors during wintertime. Players in addition to having the opportunity to assist an athlete of their choice among Greg Jennings, Alex Morgan, and Allyson Felix to "beat the cold" could purchase on the website Nike's winter apparel worn by the athletes themselves. The game required gamers to put their avatars' reflex speed to the test by completing various challenges to win a trip to meet one of the Nike athletes (Chou n.d.).

In 2011 as well, the luxury men's clothing company Bonobos chose to gamify some of its social media campaigns for Easter. In collaboration with the design network Not-Cot.org and using Twitter #secretcode, it launched an Easter egg-based campaign. On the NotCot and NotCouture sites, images of models dressed in Bonobos' signature pants were hidden, and visitors had to spot them. The first 50 people to find the images each day would receive a $25 Bonobos credit and free shipping (Chou n.d.).

In 2011, the Aldo Group (ALDO), known for its shoe and accessory stores, presented its *A is for Aldo* fragrance collection using elements of gamification. ALDO created the *A is for Aldo* website to present a number of fragrances: each fragrance was associated with a color that represented a type of personality. For women, three fragrances were created: red for the passionate woman, yellow for the chic, playful woman, and blue for the glamorous, seductive woman. For men, two proposals were offered: red for the modern classic man and yellow for the sporty yet casual man. The site invited customers to match their mood by playing a game on Facebook. After logging into Facebook, a series of images were presented to determine one's personality. After selecting 9 images, each user received his/her "mood board" which could be shared on his/her Facebook timeline or on other social media and matched with a specific fragrance and with a link to purchase from *A is for Aldo* (Chou n.d.).

In 2020, Karl Lagerfeld designed a gamified campaign by launching a *MAISON KARL LAGERFELD* game inspired by Pac-Man. The game was part of the campaign created for the launch of Lagerfeld's Pixel spring 2020 collection. People visiting the brand's eCommerce could impersonate Lagerfeld's cat, Choupette, and try to find their way around the iconic Karl Lagerfeld Maison in Paris. The goal was to avoid dogs and collect KARL Koins: those with the highest scores would be included in a weekly prize draw, which raffled off a shopping spree at a Karl Lagerfeld store in the UK and Europe (Eken 2021).

If Bonbos tried its hand at Easter eggs, jewelry retailer Taylor & Hart and Swaroski unveiled their digital advent calendars for 2022. The former counted down to Christmas by revealing on Instagram its new collection of engagement rings purchasable via an Instagram link in the stories (Butler 2022). The second launched an advent calendar on its website. For 24 days, users could open a window and play for a chance to win a selection of prizes that included: jewelry from Millenia, Constella, and Stella, the Annual Edition 2022 ornament, voucher codes to be used on Swarovski.com, and membership to the Swarovski Crystal Society (Swaroski n.d.). Also, the Swiss company Freitag in 2022 used gamification during Christmas season by creating the happy cycle. Taking advantage of the postscript in Freitag's manifesto quoting *Happiness is cyclical*, in the last days of December the company offered users the chance to receive some of its employees' unique private pieces. Starting on December 1, the company raffled off new bags every week until December 21 (*Happiness is cyclical* 2022).

Among the reasons fashion companies are expressing interest in the world of digital games and gamification is that games offer a potential revenue stream from sales of clothing and digital products and are a way for brands to extend themselves into the virtual spaces where people are spending an increasing proportion of their time (Bain

2021). In addition, they allow individuals to communicate who they are and who they would like to be (Noris & Cantoni 2020; Noris & Cantoni 2022): as with clothing in the real world, avatars can also be dressed in the digital world as a form of expression and immersion (Allaire 2021). Moreover, other reasons why fashion brands seem to be increasingly interested in the world of games lie in the fact that games can offer personalized, and engaging experiences increasing in-app purchase intentions, although some gamers might currently be too young to be able to buy certain products (Lau & Ki 2021; Ryder 2022), can enhance the online retail experience (Insley & Nunan 2014), can serve as platforms for brand co-creation experiences (Nobre & Ferreira 2017) and as a marketing tool to deliver an engaging digital experience in particular for luxury brands (Milanesi et al. 2022).

5   A Map and Three Cases Examples

The analysis of the 24 above-mentioned cases revealed three types of relationships between fashion companies and gaming:

- Gamification in Fashion
- Fashion in Games
- Fashion Games

The first layer is represented by *Gamification in Fashion*, which means the set of all those activities and strategies implemented by fashion brands using the main principles and features that are usually applied to video games in non-gaming contexts (eCommerce, newsletters, social media, etc.). Examples are short competitions, challenges, scoring systems whose purpose is to create engagement and consumer loyalty. Usually in this category the gamification strategy is developed by fashion companies within their digital channels.

The second layer named *Fashion in Games* refers to all those video games whose goal does not directly deal with the world of fashion but in which fashion is used as an enriching element and creates additional engagement. Examples are the possibility to use fashion products for one's avatar, fashion-related storytelling aspects, launch of fashion-related capsules and initiatives, NFT, etc. Typically, in this category, fashion companies collaborate with existing video games or even create their own games.

The third layer refers to *Fashion Games*: all those video games whose goal is closely related to the world of fashion: creation of characters to be dressed up, to be paraded, fashion-related work activities. The success of the game is closely related to the fashion world.

5.1   Gamification in Fashion

In the *Gamification in Fashion* category, all those gaming elements used by fashion brands outside video games are usually found. Within non-gaming contexts such as eCommerce, social media, newsletters and other communication channels, game elements, scores, rankings, competitions are inserted to attract visitors. The case chosen to

Fig. 1. Freitag newsletter.

present this category is that of Freitag, which in December 2022 launched its *Happiness is cyclical* campaign (*Happiness is cyclical* 2022).

Through the brand's website or through the newsletter (Fig. 1) users could access the game page (*Happiness is cyclical* 2022) .

In the last days of December, the brand offered the opportunity to play the game through its website (Fig. 2). The winner of the game could receive some of Freitag's employees private bag pieces. To get them, users had to write (in German or English) through a simple form to the chosen owner of the F-Crew bag how they would have used the bag to make someone else happy (Fig. 3). With a little luck the participant could have been selected in won the piece (*Happiness is cyclical* 2022).

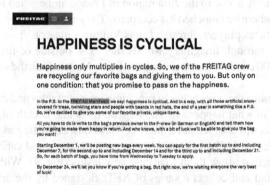

Fig. 2. Freitag's game rules.

As it can be noted, the strategy used by the Swiss brand is very simple and clear, it uses typical game elements such as fun, competition, time suitability, rewards and

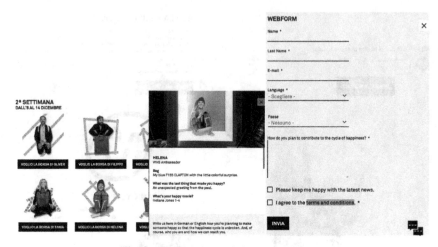

Fig. 3. Freitag's bags choice and webform.

storytelling to create engagement and attract more visitors to its website and eventually converge them into clients later.

5.2   Fashion in Games

Whether fashion brands collaborate with existing games such as *Blankos Block Party*, *Fortnite*, *Minecraft*, etc. or develop their own games, the present category represents all those games in which fashion is just an ancillary component. The case chosen to present the *Fashion in Games* category is *Louis the Game*. The adventure game, along with several initiatives, was launched in 2021 by Louis Vuitton to celebrate the brand's 200th anniversary and pays tribute to its founder by drawing inspiration from the journey Louis Vuitton took when he was 14 years old (De Klerk 2021; Northman 2021). Louis Vuitton left his family home in the Jura region of France alone when he was a teenager, arriving in Paris, where he launched his company. The smartphone app is inspired by this very journey and takes players, through Louis Vuitton's mascot Vivienne, on an action-packed adventure through imaginary worlds that exist outside of time, where gamers must collect the 200 candles to commemorate Louis Vuitton's birthday (De Klerk 2021; Northman 2021).

The game requires the own avatar to run, jump over obstacles and collect items along the way similarly to what happens in The Legend of Zelda: Breath of the Wild (Northman 2021). Players travel to reach birthday celebrations, collecting as many monogram candles as possible, while also obtaining a series of postcards and various items, as well as a series of keys that allow them to access new levels (Fig. 4). Within the game it is also possible to find and collect a series of NFTs designed by the artist Beeple. Each NFT is a collector's item that can only be found by playing the game and cannot be sold. The game is designed to be played with friends, who can be displayed in a global leaderboard. No premium version is offered.

Each character can be customized by choosing from a range of different Louis Vuitton-inspired monograms and colors and also choosing the type of backpacks (Fig. 5).

Fig. 4. Louise the Game user interfaces.

Fig. 5. Louise the Game personalization board

As it can be seen, the game is not about dressing up the character but about getting as many candles as possible to get through the levels and collecting various items for prizes. Louis Vuitton uses *Louis the Game* to create engagement with its audience and as a form of storytelling, since while collecting the various postcards little by little the story of the brand is revealed.

5.3 Fashion Games

The third category, *Fashion Games*, represents all those video games whose goal is strictly related to fashion. The purpose of the games in this category is the transformation of characters to be dressed up, beautified, paraded, and engaged in fashion-related work activities. Within this category are included games that use fashion as the main subject.

The case chosen to be present in this category is *Project Makeover*, a video game launched by Magic Tavern. The aim of the game is to complete a series of three-pair puzzles to win coins, mystery boxes and gems, and with the help of the stylist Gigi, the guru hairstylist Francis and the interior designer Derek it is possible to transform the assigned characters into fashion stars. Also featured within the game are Greta, the wicked and self-centered fashion icon who along with her secretary Michelle try to get in the players' way. The game alternates between three moments, the puzzle resolution phase to earn rewards and gems, the stylist and designer phase in which the assigned character through the gems and rewards earned by solving the puzzles can be dressed, beautified and the environment in which she lives improved, and the storytelling phase, in which the stories of Gigi, Francis, Derek, Greta and Michelle intertwine and alternate (Fig. 6).

Fig. 6. *Project Makeover* game design.

Each time a character's transformation is completed, the game moves on to the next level. The game does not have a premium version, but new lives or other game accelerators can be purchased in-game. Within the game real influencers can virtually come to life as avatars and brands can collaborate and integrate their products to make themselves known and to create a more customized experience.

The game focuses entirely on fashion, since the purpose of all elements and experiences is to earn as much money as possible to enable the character to achieve the goal of becoming a better person both in terms of clothing, beauty routine and the space in which he/she lives.

6   Conclusions, Limitations and Future Research

The paper through the analysis of three case studies purposefully selected from a sample of 24 presents how fashion companies and gaming platforms have, in recent years, intensified their relationships and collaborations. Fashion companies have understood the value of digital presence in the gaming sphere, beyond more traditional channels such as social media and eCommerce platforms. On the other hand, gaming platforms have evolved into digital social platforms where players can meet, communicate, make purchases, and also have discovered their audiences' interest in the world of fashion (*Gaming: The next super platform* 2021; Noris et al. 2020; Noris & Cantoni 2022).

All three identified categories Gamification in Fashion, Fashion in Games, and Fashion Games can be interpreted through the MDA framework: each player encounters the emotional/graphic side, then the dynamics and finally the set of mechanics that govern the system; the developer, on the other hand, defines the mechanics to bring to life dynamics that trigger aesthetics and emotions in the user/player.

Through the overview provided by this paper we might provide an interesting parallel dynamic. In photography and other communication media, for example, there has been a popularization of the sector over the years: initially only experienced people – professionals – could handle cameras or publish articles, while today anyone with a smart phone can take photos or videos or publish texts that could go viral. In the fashion world, on the other hand, in the past a large proportion of individuals knew how to mend and do fashion-related activities, even to the point of spinning and cutting clothes, with industrialization and the changing labor market there has been a shift to fewer and fewer skilled people. The digital world, however, seems to have allowed a return to the past and a re-popularization of garment making. It is not a dress that is manually cut and sewn to cover the physical body, but it is a digital dress to cover our avatars.

HCI brings back what was common in the past by popularizing it through digital affordances: allowing a pendulum that moved from a popularized practice to a specialized one (first industrial revolution), to change direction to a popularization of dress-making through the digital environment.

To conclude, it can be said that the relationship between fashion and gaming is becoming closer and closer, and at present there is a mutual curiosity to explore each other. While the relationship between these two worlds is intensifying, further studies are needed to fully understand the state of the art of this relationship. Despite the paper presents a rather innovative mapping of such relationship, the present research is not exempt from limitations. Based on this initial classification one could consider expanding the number of cases and conduct quantitative research mapping as many gaming experiences as possible. In addition, future studies could take into consideration the advent of the Metaverse, in particular Marck Zurckerberg's Worlds version, which is not yet available in the country where the authors are located, as well as other cases not considered by the authors. Finally, further studies could focus on user perceptions with respect to the three found categories.

References

Alexiou, A., Schippers, M.C.: Digital game elements, user experience and learning: a conceptual framework. Educ. Inf. Technol. **23**(6), 2545–2567 (2018). https://doi.org/10.1007/s10639-018-9730-6

Allaire, C.: Video Games Are Becoming a High-Fashion Playground (2021). https://www.vogue.com/article/video-game-fashion-designer-collaborations. Accessed Dec 2022

Bain, M.: How to How to Seize Fashion's Gaming Opportunity (2021). https://www.businessoffashion.com/case-studies/marketing-pr/fashion-technology-gaming-vans-balenciaga-benefit/. Accessed Dec 2022

Baxter, P., Jack, S.: Qualitative case study methodology: study design and implementation for novice researchers. Qual. Rep. **13**(4), 544–559 (2008)

Bergonse, R.: Fifty years on, what exactly is a videogame? an essentialistic definitional approach. Comput. Games J. **6**(4), 239–255 (2017). https://doi.org/10.1007/s40869-017-0045-4

Bryce, J., Rutter, J.: An introduction to understanding digital games. In: Rutter, J., Brice, J., (eds.), Understanding Digital Games. Sage Publications Ltd (2006). https://doi.org/10.4135/9781446211397

Butler, R.: Taylor & Hart unveils digital advent calendar. Professional Jeweller (2022). https://www.professionaljeweller.com/taylor-hart-unveils-digital-advent-calendar/. Accessed Jan 2023

Chou, Y.K.: Gamification & Behavioral Design. (n.d.). https://yukaichou.com/gamification-examples/top-10-ecommerce-gamification-examples-revolutionize-shopping/. Accessed Jan 2023

490   A. Noris et al.

Covet Fashion. (n.d.). https://www.covetfashion.com/about/. Accessed Jan 2023

de Klerk, A.: Louis Vuitton has launched a game as part of its founder's birthday celebrations. Harpers Bazar (2021). https://www.harpersbazaar.com/uk/fashion/fashion-news/a37218196/louis-vuitton-game/. Accessed Feb 2023

Eken, Y.: Gamification in eCommerce: Meaning, Examples and Uses. Segmentify (2021). https://www.segmentify.com/blog/best-uses-and-examples-of-gamification-in-ecommerce. Accessed Dec 2022

GAMES.LOL. (n.d.). https://games.lol/fashion-empire-boutique-sim/. Accessed Feb 2023

Gaming the next Super Platform (2021). Accenture. https://www.accenture.com/us-en/insights/software-platforms/gaming-the-next-super-platform. Accessed Jan 2023

Gibson, J.: When games are the only fashion in town: Covid-19, animal crossing, and the future of fashion. Queen Mary J. Intell. Property 11(2), 117–123 (2021)

GLU. (n.d.). https://www.glu.com/games/kim-kardashian-hollywood/. Accessed Feb 2023

Happiness is cyclical (2022). Freitag. https://www.freitag.ch/it/happycycle. Accessed Jan 2023

Hindy, J.: 10 best dress up games and fashion games for Android. Android Authority (2023). https://www.androidauthority.com/best-dress-up-games-android-1137263/. Accessed Feb 2023

Huizinga, J.: Homo Ludens. Routledge Kegan Paul Ltd (1949)

Hunicke, R., LeBlanc, M., Zubek, R.: MDA: a formal approach to game design and game research. In: Proceedings of the AAAI Workshop on Challenges in Game AI, vol. 4, no. 1, p. 1722 (2004)

Huotari, K., Hamari, J.: A definition for gamification: anchoring gamification in the service marketing literature. Electron. Mark. 27(1), 21–31 (2017). https://doi.org/10.1007/s12525-015-0212-z

Insley, V., Nunan, D.: Gamification and the online retail experience. Int. J. Retail Distrib. Manag. 42(5), 340–351 (2014). https://doi.org/10.1108/IJRDM-01-2013-0030

Joy, A., Zhu, Y., Peña, C., Brouard, M.: Digital future of luxury brands: metaverse, digital fashion, and non-fungible tokens. Strateg. Chang. 31(3), 337–343 (2022). https://doi.org/10.1002/jsc.2502

Kalbaska, N., Sádaba, T., Cantoni, L.: Editorial: Fashion communication: between tradition and digital transformation. Stud. Commun. Sci. 18(2), 269–285 (2018). https://doi.org/10.24434/j.scoms.2018.02.005

Kim, S.J., Kim, K.H., Mattila, P.: The role of fashion in the characters of online games. J. Glob. Fash. Market. 3(2), 81–88 (2012)

Kreutzer, R.T.: E-Commerce. In: Praxisorientiertes Online-Marketing, pp. 573–605. Springer, Wiesbaden (2021). https://doi.org/10.1007/978-3-658-31990-8_5

Lau, O., Ki, C.-W.: Can consumers' gamified, personalized, and engaging experiences with VR fashion apps increase in-app purchase intention by fulfilling needs? Fash. Text. 8(1), 1–22 (2021). https://doi.org/10.1186/s40691-021-00270-9

Magic Tavern (n.d.). https://www.magictavern.com. Accessed Feb 2023

Mäyrä, F., Van Looy, J., Quandt, T.: Disciplinary identity of game scholars: an outline. Digital Games Research Association, Proceedings. Presented at the Digital Games Research Association (DiGRA -: Atlanta. GA, USA (2013)

Mcdowell, M.: Why games became luxury fashion's NFT on-ramp. Vogue (2021). https://www.voguebusiness.com/technology/why-games-became-luxury-fashions-nft-on-ramp. Accessed Dec 2022

Milanesi, M., Guercini, S., Runfola, A.: Let's play! gamification as a marketing tool to deliver a digital luxury experience. Electron. Commer. Res. 1−18 (2022). https://doi.org/10.1007/s10660-021-09529-1

Muhammad, I.: Louis Vuitton's NFT Game Amasses More Than Two Million Downloads. Beyond Games.biz (2022). https://www.beyondgames.biz/22051/louis-vuittons-nft-game-amasses-more-than-2-million-downloads/. Accessed Feb 2023

Nobre, H., Ferreira, A.: Gamification as a platform for brand co-creation experiences. J. Brand. Manag. **24**, 349–361 (2017). https://doi.org/10.1057/s41262-017-0055-3

Noris, A., Cantoni, L.: COVID-19 outbreak and fashion communication strategies on instagram: a content analysis. In: Soares, M.M., Rosenzweig, E., Marcus, A. (eds.) HCII 2021. LNCS, vol. 12781, pp. 340–355. Springer, Cham (2021). https://doi.org/10.1007/978-3-030-78227-6_25

Noris, A., Cantoni, L.: Digital Fashion Communication. An Intercultural Perspective. Leiden, The Netherlands: Brill (2022). https://doi.org/10.1163/9789004523555

Noris, A., Nobile, T.H., Kalbaska, N., Cantoni, L.: Digital fashion: a systematic literature review. a perspective on marketing and communication. J. Glob. Fash. Mark. **12**(1), 32−46 (2020). https://doi.org/10.1080/20932685.2020.1835522

Noris, A., SanMiguel, P., Cantoni, L.: Localization and Cultural Adaptation on the Web: An Explorative Study in the Fashion Domain. In: Nah, FH., Siau, K. (eds) HCII 2020. LNCS, vol 12204, pp 474–492. Springer, Cham (2020). https://doi.org/10.1007/978-3-030-50341-3_36

Northman, T.: Louis Vuitton's New Game Is Better Than Fortnite. Highsnobiety (2021). https://www.highsnobiety.com/p/louis-vuitton-nft-game/. Accessed Feb 2023

Pauly, A.: Wait, Animal Crossing Fashion Collabs Are A Thing Again? Highsnobiety (2021). https://www.highsnobiety.com/p/animal-crossing-fashion/. Accessed Feb 2023

Project Makeover. (n.d.). https://www.projectmakeover.com. Accessed Jan 2023

Quandt, T., Chen, V., Mäyrä, F.,Van Looy, J.: (Multiplayer) gaming around the globe? a comparison of gamer surveys in four countries. In: Quandt, T., Kröger, S., (eds.), Multiplayer: The social Aspects of Digital Gaming, pp. 23–46. Routledge, London, England (2014)

Quandt, T., Van Looy, J., Vogelgesang, J., Elson, M., Ivory, J. D., Consalvo, M., Mäyrä, F.: Digital games research: a survey study on an emerging field and its prevalent debates. J. Commun. **65**(6), 975–996 (2015). https://doi.org/10.1111/jcom.12182

Ryder, B.: This Year, Fashion Gamified. But What Were The Best Luxury Fashion Gaming Collabs of 2022? Jing Daily (2022). https://jingdaily.com/best-luxury-fashion-gaming-collabs-2022/. Accessed Jan 2023

Sharbatian, A.-L.: The Future Of Fashion And Gaming: E-Commerce. Forbes (2021). Accessed Jan 2023

Swaroski. (n.d). https://www.swarovski.com/en_GB-GB/s-swarovski-advent-calendar/. Accessed Feb 2023

Tekinbaş, K.S., Zimmerman, E.: Rules of Play : Game Design Fundamentals. MIT Press (2003)

Tepe, J., Koohnavard, S.: Fashion and game design as hybrid practices: approaches in education to creating fashion-related experiences in digital worlds. Int. J. Fashion Des. Technol. Educ. 1–9 (2022)

Vans World Roblox. (n.d.). Vans. https://www.vans.co.uk/roblox-vans-world.html. Accessed Feb 2022

Waydel-Bendyk, M.: Evaluating potential of gamification to facilitate sustainable fashion consumption. In: Nah, F.-H., Siau, K. (eds.) HCII 2020. LNCS, vol. 12204, pp. 205–215. Springer, Cham (2020). https://doi.org/10.1007/978-3-030-50341-3_16

Wolf, M.J.P., Perron, B.: The Video Game Theory Reader. Routledge, London (2003)

Yin, R.K.: Case Study Research: Design and Methods (2nd ed.). Sage Publications (1994)

A Study on Measurement Method of User's Physiological Index in Rehabilitation Support System Using VR Environment

Katsuhiko Onishi[1]([✉]), Hiroki Arasuna[1], Masanao Koeda[2], Hiroshi Noborio[1], and Morihiro Tsujishita[3]

[1] Osaka Electro-Communication University, Osaka, Japan
onishi@osakac.ac.jp
[2] Okayama Prefectural University, Okayama, Japan
[3] Nara Gakuen University, Nara, Japan

Abstract. In recent years, the spread of VR technology has led to using VR environments composed of 3D CG models in various fields. For example, in medical and nursing care, VR is used in surgical simulations and navigation systems that utilize 3D data from CT/MRI images, etc. Because VR environments can reproduce matters that would not usually occur, simulation-based work support and training support have been widely used. However, these systems cannot produce the same situation as in the past. However, in many cases, these systems use images taken in advance, and certain limitations exist in reproducing an accurate site's realism. Furthermore, simulations that proceed according to predetermined scenarios are required in education and training, as training in the workplace.

Therefore, this study aims to construct a VR environment using 3D models and to build a training and education support system using this environment. The issues to be addressed include the study of methods for accurately measuring user behavior and the presentation of the VR environment. In addition, to reproduce a sense of realism, it is necessary to produce a VR environment and interaction system that allows the user to experience fear and other sensations in the same way as in the actual situation. This paper introduces examples of VR environments and describes the results of essential evaluations.

Keywords: VR exposure system · ECG evaluation · Training support system

1 Introduction

In recent years, the spread of VR technology has led to using VR environments composed of 3D CG models in various fields. For example, in the medical and nursing care fields, multiple applications such as surgical simulation, navigation systems, and training systems have been proposed and studied [1]. Since VR environments can reproduce matters that cannot usually occur, simulation-based work and training support has been actively used. However, these systems have certain limitations in creating a sense of presence that gives the viewer the feeling of being there. For this purpose, there is a need for more natural systems using input/output devices such as HMDs.

© The Author(s), under exclusive license to Springer Nature Switzerland AG 2023
M. Kurosu and A. Hashizume (Eds.): HCII 2023, LNCS 14013, pp. 492–501, 2023.
https://doi.org/10.1007/978-3-031-35602-5_35

Therefore, this study aims to build a VR environment using various 3D models and a system to support training and rehabilitation using this environment. The issues to be addressed include the study of accurate measurement methods for user behavior and the presentation method of the VR environment. In addition, to reproduce a sense of realism, it is necessary to produce a VR environment and interaction system that allows the user to experience fear and other sensations in the same way as in the actual situation. We focus on VR exposure therapy support systems as rehabilitation support systems. This paper introduces a case study of creating a VR environment and describes the results of a study of changes in physiological indices of users walking in an environment with stairs as an essential evaluation.

2   Rehabilitation Support System

2.1   Exposure Therapy

Exposure therapy [2, 3] is a method of erasing maladaptive reactions by exposing patients to situations that cause fear, anxiety, and avoidance behavior until they reduce their stress, etc. Exposure therapy includes the following various methods of exposure.

In Vivo Exposure
In vivo exposure is the most prevalent exposure therapy and refers to exposures performed with real-world stimuli.

Imaginal Exposure
Imaginal exposure is exposures in which the patient is asked to imagine a situation in which they feel fear or anxiety and is then exposed to the imagined stimulus. The imagination of each patient is independent of the efficacy of exposure therapy, and short-term treatment is more effective than in vivo exposure [4].

VR Exposure
VR exposure refers to exposures in which scary scenes are produced as virtual fear stimuli in 3DCG and are performed using incentives through input/output devices such as HMDs. The in vivo and VR exposures were similarly effective, with no significant differences between the two treatment conditions [5].
  In this study, we are investigating developing a system to support VR exposure therapy, the safest and most influential of these therapies.

2.2   Our Proposed VR Exposure Support Systems

This section describes specific VR environment examples of VR exposure support systems that have been produced.
  At first, we constructed a VR environment of a situation in the living room (Japanese-style room) of an elderly person who walks alone, which is the most common cause of falls among the elderly indoors. The elements that could induce accidents included a 4-cm-high threshold step between the Japanese-style room and the hallway, a power

cord, a zabuton (Japanese cushion), and some furniture. The size of the VR room was set to 3.64 m × 3.64 m, corresponding to an Edo-ma (8-mat room). The constructed virtual living room space is shown in Fig. 1, and the installed obstacles are shown in Fig. 2.

Fig. 1. Example scene of the living room.

(a) Steps between living room and hallway.   (b) A power codes.

Fig. 2. Examples of obstacles.

The second example of a VR environment is a staircase hall constructed, as shown in Fig. 3. The size of the staircase hall was set to 3 m × 4 m. This is because it was created concerning the size of stairs used in a typical Japanese house.

The final example is the damp and slippery bathroom and dressing room constructed, as shown in Fig. 4. The bathroom and changing room size is set at 4 m × 3 m, built in a slightly larger setting than a standard changing room or bathroom.

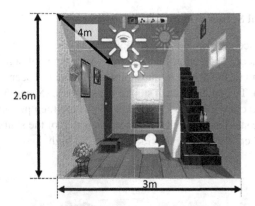

Fig. 3. Example scene of staircase hall.

Fig. 4. Example scene of bathroom and dressing room.

3 Experiments

3.1 Overview

To support VR exposure therapy using the environment created above, it is necessary to have a method to objectively evaluate the fear and other stresses that users are undergoing. Therefore, this paper made a new scene for experimentation to measure and objectively assess stress levels. We thought it might be possible to objectively evaluate fear by having the subjects walk in the created scenes and simultaneously measure and analyze their stress level. In this case, we will use a staircase scene that can express differences in elevation. We prepared two scenes with two stairs types and asked the subjects to walk and measure their ECGs. The experimental scene and procedures are described in the next section.

3.2   Experimental Scenes and Procedures

The experimental scene is set up as a walkable area 2 m × 4 m in length and width, and a staircase object is placed at that location. Two types of stairs with landings are provided: stairs with walls (Scene A) and stairs without walls (Scene B). They are shown in Fig. 5 and Fig. 6. The width of each step of the staircase (Scene A) with a wall should be 30 cm long, 100 cm wide, and 15 cm high. Walls are then provided on all sides and at the border of the staircase. And the width of each step of the stairs (Scene B) without walls should be 30 cm long, 105 cm wide, and 15 cm high.

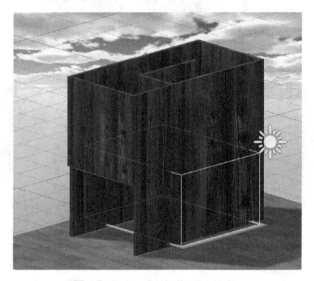

Fig. 5.   Stairs with walls (Scene A).

Fig. 6.   Stairs without walls (Scene B).

First, the subject is asked to wear an HMD and a tracker on their ankle to measure the position of their feet. Electrodes were then attached to the body to measure the ECG. The HMD and tracker utilized HTC VIVE and VIVE Tracker. In addition, BITalino [6, 7] was used for ECG measurements. The subjects during the experiment are shown in Fig. 7.

Fig. 7. The subjects during the experiment.

3.3 Experimental Results

This evaluation experiment used four healthy men in their 20s as subjects. From a position tracking device attached to both legs, the height at which the foot is raised during going up the stairs was measured to verify the difference in kinetic sensation from the motion of going up the stairs. Figure 8 shows the results representing the difference between the height at which the feet are raised at each step of the staircase and the actual step height. To measure the stress felt by the subjects during the experiment, a Poincare plot of the ECG measurement results is shown in Fig. 9.

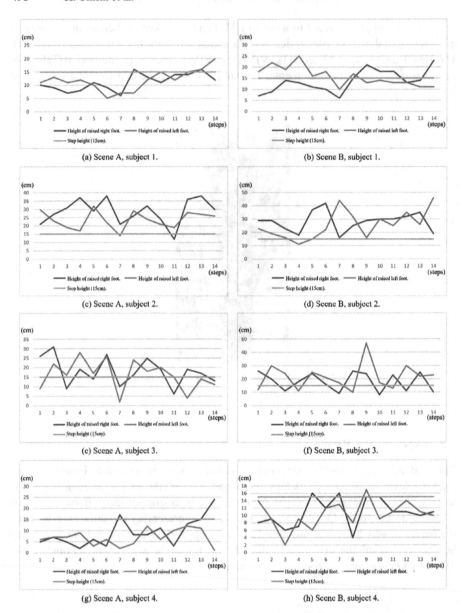

(a) Scene A, subject 1.

(b) Scene B, subject 1.

(c) Scene A, subject 2.

(d) Scene B, subject 2.

(e) Scene A, subject 3.

(f) Scene B, subject 3.

(g) Scene A, subject 4.

(h) Scene B, subject 4.

Fig. 8. The difference between the height at which the feet are raised at each step.

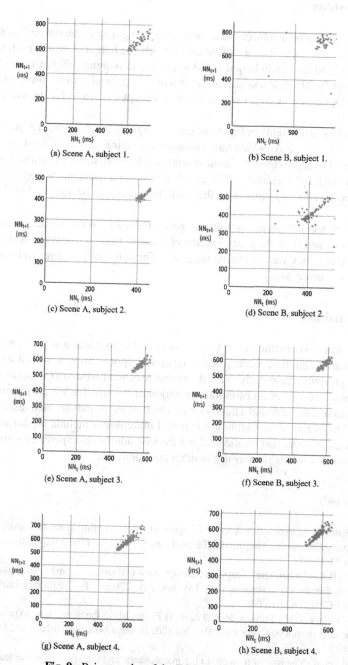

Fig. 9. Poincare plot of the ECG measurement results.

4 Discussions

From the height at which subjects raise their feet when going up the stairs (Fig. 8), it was found that there is a significant difference between the height at which each subject's feet are raised and the actual height of the steps. The maximum difference was found to be approximately 30 cm. It was also found that the height tended to be lower for the later foot, depending on the order in which the feet were placed, even for the same step-up motion.

The ECG measurements in Fig. 9 indicate no significant differences between Scene A and Scene B. Scene A, which has a smaller dispersion of points, tends to be more stress-loaded. For some subjects, Scene A tended to be more stress-loaded with a smaller distribution of data plot locations. This could be because some subjects may feel stressed by the oppressive feeling caused by the wall. This needs to be analyzed in detail as a future issue.

Also, in this experiment, the subjects go up the stairs in the scenes but walk on a flat floor. However, from the post-experiment questionnaire, some subjects commented that they felt like they were going up the stairs. The cause of this comment needs to be discussed as a future issue.

5 Conclusions

This study aims to construct a VR environment that reproduces a sense of realism and an interaction system for a training and education support system using VR technology. This paper presents a case study of a VR environment as a first step to achieving the goal. It describes the results of an essential evaluation of the stress a VR environment gives the user. As a result, we found a trend of stress load on users and obtained results that can be referred to as one of the future guidelines. Future issues include further analysis of the ECG measurement results and analysis through additional experiments considering experimental conditions such as use in other environments.

References

1. Antón-Sancho, Á., Fernández-Arias, P., Vergara, D.: Virtual reality in health science education: professors' perceptions. Multimodal Technol. Interact. **6**(12), 110 (2022). https://doi.org/10.3390/mti6120110
2. McNally, R.J.: Mechanisms of exposure therapy: how neuroscience can improve psychological treatments for anxiety disorders. Clin. Psychol. Rev. **27**(6), 750–759 (2007). https://doi.org/10.1016/J.CPR.2007.01.003
3. Becker-Haimes, E.M., Stewart, R.E., Frank, H.E.: It's all in the name: why exposure therapy could benefit from a new one. Curr Psychol (2022). https://doi.org/10.1007/s12144-022-03286-6
4. Hunt, M., et al.: The role of imagery in the maintenance and treatment of snake fear. J. Behav. Ther. Exp. Psychiatry **37**(4), 283–298 (2006). https://doi.org/10.1016/j.jbtep.2005.12.002
5. Emmelkamp, P.M., Krijn, M., Hulsbosch, A.M., de Vries, S., Schuemie, M.J., van der Mast, C.A.: Virtual reality treatment versus exposure in vivo: a comparative evaluation in acrophobia. Behav. Res. Ther. **40**(5), 509–516 (2002). https://doi.org/10.1016/s0005-7967(01)00023-7

6. Batista, D., Plácido da Silva, H., Fred, A.: Experimental characterization and analysis of the BITalino platforms against a reference device. In: 2017 39th Annual International Conference of the IEEE Engineering in Medicine and Biology Society (EMBC), pp. 2418–2421 (2017). https://doi.org/10.1109/EMBC.2017.8037344

7. Batista, D., Plácido da Silva, H., Fred, A., Moreira, C., Reis, M., Ferreira, H.A.: Benchmarking of the BITalino biomedical toolkit against an established gold standard. Healthcare Technol. Lett. 6(2), 32–36 (2019). https://doi.org/10.1049/htl.2018.5037

Being Elsewhere: An Information Architecture Approach to the Design of a Sense of Presence in XR Environments

Andrea Resmini[1]([⊠])(iD), Bertil Lindenfalk[2](iD), and Jussi Jauhiainen[3](iD)

[1] School of Information Technology, Halmstad University, Halmstad, Sweden
andrea.resmini@hh.se

[2] Jönköping Academy for the Improvement of Health and Welfare, School of Health and Welfare, Jönköping University, Jönköping, Sweden
bertil.lindenfalk@ju.se

[3] Department of Geography and Geology, University of Turku and Institute of Ecology and the Earth Sciences, University of Tartu, Turku, Finland
jusaja@utu.fi

Abstract. This paper frames extended reality (XR) as an information-based designed environment and argues that its design requires principles, tools and methods of digital design and experience design to be revisited and revised. Approaching the design of XR environments from the perspective of information architecture, the paper stipulates that the naturality commonly associated with a sense of presence in XR space cannot be achieved simply through the design or redesign of the visual interface layer, but rather requires a structural approach that leverages human embodiment and spatial thought. The paper tracks this conversation from interface to architecture by anchoring it to Bates' seminal work on information seeking strategies as exaptation and on her seminal intuition of the role that the environment plays in supporting human information needs; to Horan's definition of physical and digital space as elements in a continuum in which the ongoing expansion of digital is transforming the physical environment; to Benyon's conceptualization of blended space as the novel space emerging from the intimate commingling of digital with physical; and to Resmini and Rosati's heuristic information architecture principles for the design of digital/physical experiences. The paper then describes important structural challenges in the design of XR environments, illustrates the relevance of the framing introduced here by means of a brief case study, and concludes by offering a discussion and preliminary conclusions.

Keywords: Extended reality · Placemaking · Sense of presence · Information architecture · Experience design

1 Introduction

What has been dubbed the "fourth revolution" (Floridi 2014), the information revolution built on "everyware" (Greenfield 2006), the networked, pervasive, ambient and mobile computing we rely upon today has completely reshaped how we experience

© The Author(s), under exclusive license to Springer Nature Switzerland AG 2023
M. Kurosu and A. Hashizume (Eds.): HCII 2023, LNCS 14013, pp. 502–521, 2023.
https://doi.org/10.1007/978-3-031-35602-5_36

the world. Smartphones, tablets, sensors, ambient appliances, smart environments and wearables have become run-of-the-mill "objects", common occurrences, and "a dominant part of the cultural and social zeitgeist" (Resmini & Lindenfalk 2021). Information travels instantaneously from public spaces to someone's home, from offices to mountain tops, constantly crossing the the digital/physical divide and fueling conversations in that peculiar experiential place made of multiple platforms, locations, devices, apps, and information flows people have learned to know very well and to frequent often.

More recently, virtual reality (VR), augmented reality (AR), and mixed reality (MR), cumulatively referred to as extended reality (XR), have made their way first into gaming and entertainment (Gaudiosi 2015; Statista 2023) and then into work life and everyday activities (Johnson 2017), not always to everyone's satisfaction (Pahwa 2023). In 2022, Meta, the company behind Facebook, pivoted and refocused its strategy towards what they call the Metaverse (Carter & Egliston 2021; Brambilla Hall & Li 2021), a sprawling series of connected XR environments "that you can move seamlessly between" and the "successor to the mobile internet" where people will "connect, work, play, learn, shop" in the future (Meta 2023).

Design and design-adjacent disciplines such as experience design, interaction design, information architecture, human-computer interaction and service design have formalized several sets of principles, methods, and heuristics meant to address the human and experiential components of digital and digital/physical products and services. However, the applicability and fittingness of these principles, methods, and heuristics to XR environments is still an open question (Hillman 2021).

This paper intends to contribute to closing this gap by proposing a cohesive approach to the design of XR environments based on information architecture (Rosenfeld & Morville 2002; Resmini & Rosati 2011; Resmini 2021) and experience design theory and practice that considers embodiment, the spatial nature of XR environments, and the resulting sense of presence expressed in the experience as the core novel element of XR, and one for which most screen-based digital design disciplines are utterly unprepared. Not only does information conveyed in a 2D space obey different rules than information conveyed in a 3D space, but the structural role played by information in XR—from situating and visualizing dynamic information in the environment in AR to creating affordances for agency in MR to fully realizing the entirety of the space of action in VR—suggests that traditional digital design approaches, methods, and tools have to be revisited and revised.

Adapting Rosenfeld and Morville's initial definition of information architecture as the "structural design of an information space" (2002, p. 19) to include Resmini and Rosati's reframing of digital and physical environments as parts of that information space (2011), the paper argues that the type of consistency and "naturality" of the experience that a sense of presence in XR space suggests and requires cannot be achieved simply through the design or redesign of the interface layer: they require a structural approach. While a number of specific models have been proposed that approach XR space as information space, and thus structurally, including Parveau and Adda's recent information-interaction-immersion model (2019), the paper tracks the conversation from interface to architecture by anchoring it to Bates' work on information seeking strategies and her seminal intuition of their role in our "offloading of information into the environment"; to Horan's definition of physical and digital space as elements in a continuum in which digital is actively transforming physical; to Benyon's conceptualization of blended space as the novel space emerging from the intimate commingling of digital with physical; and to Resmini and Rosati's heuristic information architecture principles for the design of digital/physical experiences (2011).

2 Designing in the Digital/Physical Continuum

Discussing and describing information seeking strategies, Bates (2002) introduces a model that integrates social and cultural aspects of an experience with its underlying biological and physical layers. Bates considers such an approach necessary, since human behavior is "neither totally biological nor totally social, but a complex mixture of both". Bates' model describes information seeking strategies as four integrated but specific activities (Fig. 1) that are either directed or undirected, and active or passive: "searching" and "monitoring" are directed and respectively active and passive, and represent the way "we find information that we know we need to know"; "browsing", which is active, and "being aware", which is instead passive, are undirected and represent the "ways we find information that we do not know we need to know". The two passive modalities, awareness and monitoring, "provide the vast majority of information for most people during their lives" (Bates 2002).

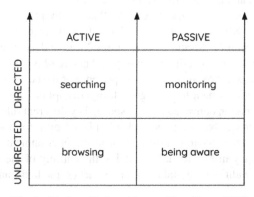

Fig. 1. Modes of information seeking (Bates 2002)

Searching, which is active and directed, is a resource-intensive activity in which the principle of least effort (Zipf 1949) plays an important role. According to Bates, this is why "we often arrange our physical and social environment so as to provide the information we need when we need it. From grocery lists to the arrangement of dials in airplane cockpits, to the physical placement and organization of tools and offices, we make it possible to be reminded, when we need reminding, of next steps or appropriate behaviors". Offloading information into the environment allows us to "(cut) down on the need for active information seeking" (Bates 2002).

In turn, environmental information produces "serendipitous encounters" that are the product of proximity and that rely on embodied activities such as "orientation, place-marking, comparison, resolution of anomalies" whose root can be identified in information foraging behaviors and their subsequent exaptation to what Bates calls "sample and select".

Horan (2000) introduces the concept of a "continuum of digital places" to examine and discuss the "interweaving of virtual and physical" and the way this interweaving is bound to influence and change the idea of what constitutes a human place in the physical world. Horan considers digital places "dynamic settings that evolve over time", a definition that today applies equally to a real-time public transport system, a social network, or a virtual reality environment. Digital places emerge along a continuum of technological integration: at one hand of the digital place continuum there are "unplugged" designs that "manifest little or no digital technology in their appearance and construction". The middle of the continuum is occupied by "adaptive" designs that "represent modest attempts to visibly incorporate electronic features into physical space". At the other end we find "transformative" designs, "rooms, buildings, or communities composed of truly interfaced physical and electronic spaces". While Horan is primarily looking at the integration of digital and physical from the perspective of the built environment, his effort to track the ongoing transformation of physical space clearly carries weight in the discourse on XR spaces, which are, in Horan's conceptualization, examples of transformative design.

Table 1. Stages in Horan's interweaving of digital and physical space

Principle or heuristic	Description	Example
Unplugged	Little or no digital technology is present in the environment	A forest trail
Adaptive	Some digital technology is integrated with physical space	A subway station
Transformative	Digital technology and physical space are fully integrated	The Void
Apply to	Primarily physical space	

Benyon defines a blended space as a space "where a physical space is deliberately integrated in a close-knit way with a digital space" (Benyon 2014, p. 79). This blended space is then a purposefully created space where a digital space commingles with a physical space, thus creating a new type of space with its own emergent structure and novel affordances that provide an entirely different experience. This experience is the result of the new properties that emerge from the combination of physical and digital and that create a new sense of presence and new possibilities for interaction. The higher the degree of integration, the richer the experience.

A blended space is characterized by four primary properties: (a) ontology, comprising the different elements that exist in the space and their semantic relationships; (b) topology, comprising the spatial relationships between the elements and between the elements and the space; (c) volatility, expressing the frequency of change in the elements, in their ontology, and in their topology; and (d) agency, the possibility for action that exists between elements within the space, including users.

In a blended space, one's embodiment and cognitive models contribute to create and sustain a sense of place and presence that erases the boundary between the digital and physical environments. The agency a person has inside the blended space, and the feedback mechanisms between space and agents, is what according to Benyon separates the conceptualization of blended space from initial conceptualizations of mixed reality or augmented reality. If we adopt Horan's framing, blended spaces can be considered to be an example of fully realized transformative spaces.

Table 2. Benyon's characteristics of blended space

Principle or heuristic	Description	Example
Ontology	i) the different elements that exist in the space, and ii) their semantic relationships	i) the pieces of furniture in a house, ii) the fact that the coffee table is by the armchair iii) and that coffee table and armchair are in the living room
Topology	i) the spatial relationships between the elements and ii) between the elements and the space	i) the distance between the TV and the sofa ii) and in which room and where in the room the TV and sofa are
Volatility	i) the frequency of change in the elements, in their ontology, and in their topology	i) how often the furniture changes place e.g. books or dishes are moved more frequently than a sofa
Agency	i) the possibility for action that exists between elements within the space, including users	i) if it's possible to ask Alexa, Siri or the Google voice assistant to turn on the lights in the kitchen
Apply to	Blended space constructs (AR, MR, HR)	

Resmini and Lindenfalk (2021) offer an example of how the properties of blended space concretely bear on the design of an AR/MR environment in their analysis of "Johann Sebastian Joust", a digital/physical video game of musical chairs for the Sony PS4 game console (Fig. 2).

"Johann Sebastian Joust"'s ontology contains the PlayStation game console, the game itself, the players, the Move controllers, and "what functions and facilities they have" (Benyon 2014, p. 80). Players and controllers, existing in physical space, are mirrored as "information artifacts" in the digital space of the game: their spatial relationships constitute the topology, which "remains relatively dense as the players cannot move too far away from each other".

Volatility, constrained in space by the topology, "varies greatly through time as the players react to the music and the controllers react to the action" producing the game's agency, which integrates the game's own rules and logic with the players' decision and opportunities for action in physical space.

Fig. 2. A game of Johann Sebastian Joust (Source: Die Gute Fabrik. Photo: B. Knepper)

In the experience design space, Resmini and Rosati (2011) propose a generative heuristic approach for digital/physical environments solidly anchored to contemporary information architecture principles (Resmini 2021). They argue that since "information architecture relies on principles that are largely independent from any specific medium", being concerned with the structuring of information space as much as architecture is concerned with structuring physical space, it "provides a flexible but solid conceptual model for helping design experiences which span different media and environments".

Addressing structural issues before considering interfaces allows the designers to create experiences that provide users with a constant, coherent cognitive framework regardless of how, where and when they engage in an experience or access a product or service: in support of this, Resmini and Rosati introduce five base heuristics that affect the foundational design of an experience. These heuristics are medium-nonspecific— that is, they apply equally to any possible individual instantiation of the final design, to a smartphone app as well as to a kiosk system or to an analog signage system—and are specifically aimed at the creation of a sense of permanence and presence across the entire duration of an experience.

Placemaking is the first heuristic introduced. It concerns the capability of an information architecture to create and sustain a sense of place and belonging to reduce disorientation, increase legibility, and facilitate navigation and way-finding across digital and physical environments. An example is how VR experiences allow users to navigate an immersive landscape by adopting well-known spatial schemas (Williams Goldhagen 2019; Tversky 2020), and return to it with some sense of temporary permanence by saving status and preserving changes. It is important to highlight how placemaking does not require a literal space: a sense of place can be established in writing, like in a novel, or by means of auditory or olfactory clues. In filmmaking, well understood semantic conventions such as cuts, fades, or specific types of shots, such as a shaky-cam shot, are used to establish the specific sense of presence and spatio-temporal cohesion of a given movie. Clubhouse (clubhouse.com), a drop-in audio chat platform for free-form conversations among peers, can be used to further illustrate how a digital-only environment can create its own sense of place without necessarily having to implement any type of literal physical space. As of February 2022, Clubhouse is home to approximately 10 million people (Dixon 2022) who meet on the platform to engage in non-structured conversations in "rooms" managed by moderators: attendees who want to speak up use a "raise hand" function and await the moderator's decision. Similar in functionality to the party lines of early telephony or to ham radio, Clubhouse is not really a clubhouse: its "rooms" are entirely built through soundscaping and a minimal information architecture that manages the basic function of joining, leaving, moderating, and peer contribution.

Consistency is the second heuristic. Consistency refers to the capability of an information architecture to provide and sustain experience-level coherence between its elements across the different media, devices, and environments in which the experience itself unfolds. It is important to note that consistency does not mean interface-level consistency, something already considered by design systems, UI guidelines, and style guides, but rather cognitive consistency. The interfaces for a game of chess might differ wildly depending on how the game is played: bodily interactions for a physical marble board, the feeling of size, weight and texture a primary concern; touch or gestures on a mobile app; voice for a live chess performance where moving real people by picking them up would be awkward and unwieldy; pen and paper, writing, pictures, or code ("bishop to E4") for a play-by-mail. On the other hand, the rules, the architecture of the game, remain constant, and thus not only they allow chess to be played at all, but they also allow people who know how to play to just play. As such, consistency has conceptual bearing also on the simple translation of the physical space of a house into its digital representation that we have in VR: a literal replica does not guarantee, in and of itself, a consistent experience.

Resilience is the capability of an information architecture to adapt to specific uses, needs, and seeking strategies, offer multiple pathways to perform a task or reach a goal, and improve its overall fitness-to-goals over time and use. An example of resilience in an XR environment is the way Google Maps' Live Street View uses AR technology to provide an augmented navigational experience while walking, offering one more option for orienting oneself and the possibility to gain new "abilities" and opportunities, for the serendipitous discovery of a food joint or an interesting but less traveled point of interest, by bringing in existing contextual information that can be accessed without much effort.

Reduction refers to the capability of an information architecture to minimize the stress and frustration associated with having to understand, handle, and navigate large information sets, favoring quality (the right information in the right place at the right time to the right user) over quantity. Reduction is an especially important heuristic for AR/MR environments, where additive overlaying or embedding is the norm. Well-proven design principles such as progressive disclosure should always be considered, as much as the possibility of spatially-based contextualization. An example of such an approach is provided by Spatial chat (spatialchat.com), an in-browser voice chat application, which uses the metaphor of personal proximity in space as a way to regulate voice input. Users can huddle together in groups by moving their avatars on the page representing the "chat room", and people not part of one's "chat table" will be heard at lower volumes while remaining close but disappear if they "step away" enough.

Correlation refers to the capability of an information architecture to make relevant connections among pieces of information explicit, visible, and actionable to help people achieve their stated goals and support any latent needs. Consider a traditional supermarket: having part of a shelf—or a visible, well-defined spot—dedicated to the week's specials or to a sale is to promote a system of suggestions and relationships. The digital analog of such a set up are the personalized lists pointing out that "if you like this item you may also like" or that "who bought this also bought…" made mainstream by Amazon. Taken one step further, such techniques could turn the information concerning sales, products, schedules, locations within the supermarket—the information architecture of specials—into a digital layer integral to the in-store information architecture, make it available to customers, and make it capable of preserving one's purchase history.

Table 3. Resmini and Rosati's information architecture heuristics

Principle/heuristic	Description	Example
Placemaking	How the environment creates a sense of presence, persistence, and belonging	Netflix remembers not only what one watches, but where they stopped watching and keeps tracks of progress across devices and through time
Consistency	How the environment provides a consistent mental model across locations, media, platforms, devices	Chess can be played on many different "platforms" while remaining chess
Resilience	How the environment adapts to non-standard behavior, allows for multiple ways-of-doing, and increases its robustness over time	Desire paths[a]; Real-time traffic flow and control systems[b]
Reduction	How the environment provides the right tools and the right information when, where, and to whom is necessary	Wayfinding signage in airports
Correlation	How the environment supports exploration and the widening of the user's possibilities of action	Amazon-like "if you like this you might also like that"
Apply to	Physical space, digital space (including VR), blended space (including AR/MR)	

[a] A desire path or desire line is "is a path created as a consequence of erosion caused by human or animal foot traffic. The path usually represents the shortest or most easily navigated route between an origin and destination" (Myhill 2004).
[b] See for example Stockholm Flows or Real Time Copenhagen, a collaboration between the MIT Senseable Lab and the cities of Stockholm and Copenhagen (http://senseable.mit.edu).

3   A Design Perspective of XR, VR, AR, and MR

Virtual Reality (VR) identifies a set of the technologies and the simulated 3D environments they originate that people can experience and inhabit by means of specialized head-mounted displays (Peddie 2017) or via CAVE-like room-scale setups (Cruz-Neira et al. 1992), and with which they can interact by means of movement, physical controllers, voice, or gestures. VR immerses users in a digital elsewhere, a realistic or imaginary world in which sight, sound, and haptic feedback are used to situate the experience and provide a sense of presence. It is important to remember that in mainstream VR applications, people immersed in the VR environment can still feel the ground under their feet and the temperature of the physical world around them, often hear non-VR sounds, be touched by others and, if in a room, bump into furniture or walls if they move around too much.

Augmented Reality (AR) is a set of techniques, and by extension the environment they create, to supplement an existing physical space and the objects it contains with digital, contextual information (visual, auditory, olfactory, haptic). This layer of overlaid or embedded information is usually additive and constructive, but could theoretically be ablative or destructive, and hide information objects belonging to the physical world (Hillman 2021). People experiencing an AR environment still proprioceptively perceive themselves present in the physical world.

Mixed Reality (MR), also called hybrid reality, refers to a form of AR where people in the environment can interact in real time with AR objects or an actionable AR overlay (Marr 2021).

From a design perspective, the goal of both VR and AR/MR is "to improve the user experience" (Parveau & Adda 2020), and they relate to human agency and perception rather similarly: they all offer six-degrees of freedom (6DOF) and, because of technical or practical constraints, a fixed focal length. They fundamentally differ only in the way they interact with the physical environment the person finds themselves in—substitution and augmentation or ablation, respectively—and in the degree they support digitally-focused agency—no support in AR, partial support in MR, full support in VR.

Extended reality (XR) is an umbrella term used to group together VR, AR and MR (Parveau & Adda 2020). It will be used throughout the paper when addressing concepts and design problems that apply or pertain, even if in different fashion or to a different degree, to all of these. The individual terms will be used when specifically discussing concepts and problems that only pertain to either VR, AR, or MR.

4   Embodiment and Spatiality in XR

Regardless of whether one is experiencing a physical space, for example a Romanesque church; a digital space, for example Facebook or a VR simulation; or a combination of these, either the AR/MR augmentation of a supermarket or the real-time sharing of one's experience at a holiday resort via a video call, one cannot escape the fact that all these are instantiations of human spaces. All designed space is human space, because it is the product of a human understanding and representation of spatial relationships based on our embodiment (Mallgrave 2013; Williams Goldhagen 2017). In this sense, digital space is no different from the built environment of a city: just like physical space and its structures—stairs, walls, slopes—digital space acts as a primary constraint that allows "certain patterns of events and make others less likely to occur" (Nitsche 2008, p. 160) and as an enabler whose "specific structures can help particular patterns evolve" (ibidem, p. 159). If spatial thinking guides our understanding of any given environment (Tversky 2019), including that of entirely digital spaces, then embodiment and embodied ways of doing become fundamental to the design of any experience that alters, augments or substitutes the spaces we inhabit, including XR environments. The fact that XR is characterized by a strong attention to the construction, deconstruction, modification, or substitution of the space in which people act makes architecting the fundamental structures of such space a primary element of their design.

At its simplest, embodiment can be said to be a conceptualization of how "our cognition is influenced, perhaps determined by, our experiences in the physical world" (McNerney 2011). Mind and body are parts of one single system and it is therefore impossible to separate cognition, how we think, from action, who we are and what we do.

Tversky (2019) considers moving in space the foundation of thought, and spatial thinking the root of abstract thought (p. 165): we experience and get to understand the world by moving and acting in it. Embodiment is then tightly coupled with our sense of spatiality and with the base spatial schemas that are developed during early childhood, such as "right-of", "away-from", or "inside-of". These are considered to be the building blocks for spatial primitives such as "proximity", "separation", "enclosure", "nesting", or "sequence" (Norberg-Schulz 1971) that structure not only the physical space of the built environment, but also all digital environments. For example, folders on a file system employ enclosure and nesting to provide structured access to individual files. Embodiment is also at the root of many of the metaphors we find in language, such as "affection is warmth", "up is control and down is being controlled", that emerge early in life and are based on a child's perception of the world: a parent's hug is warm, a child is small and not in control (Lakoff & Johnson 1980).

Current research in neurophysiology strongly hints at a fundamental equivalence between experiences happening in physical and digital space: they affect the same areas of the brain and are both fundamentally comprehended spatially (Benn et al. 2015; Aronov & Tank 2014). These base spatial elements are then used to form the basis of abstract cognition for three additional basic purposes: "to structure memory, to structure communication, and to structure reasoning" (Gattis 2001). Benn et al. maintain that findings support a neural explanation for the preference, documented multiple times, for navigation over search. They also provide an explanation, connected to the concept of cognitive load (Miller 1956; Sweller 1988), of the importance of this preference, and conclude that humans have developed mechanisms to retrieve any item from a specific location, either physical, digital, or mental, that rely on "navigating the same path followed in storing the information". These are "deep-rooted neurocognitive biases" that carry low cognitive loads as they trigger the automatic activation of retrieval routines that make minimal use of linguistic processes, "leaving the language system available for other tasks" (Benn et al. 2015).

We can synthetically express the relationship between embodiment, spatiality, and the design of XR environments as a system of nested spaces going from "being" to "understanding" to "making": embodiment—recognizing that apprehending oneself as a being "in a space" is the most fundamental human experience (Ryan et al. 2016); spatiality—being aware of the reason why spatial structures and spatial behaviors are the foundations of our "natural" understanding of the world (Tversky 2019); the design of XR environments—purposefully employing these interiorized spatial knowledge and spatial schemas (Gattis 2001; Williams Goldhagen 2017) to create meaningful environments with clear affordances.

Fig. 3. Moving an object on an horizontal plane in VR is a challenging task (Image: screen capture from Rick and Morty: Virtual Rick-ality, Adult Swim Games)

The use of objects as material anchors (Hutchins 2005) or physical avatars, mediators between a new digital experience and a well-known or relatable physical experience, is another way in which embodiment and spatiality are used to either facilitate the creation of a correct mental model in unfamiliar settings or to offer a recognizable affordance that successfully couples digital and physical space. Nonetheless, the role of sensory expectations and proprioception based on embodiment and spatiality should not be underestimated. An example is provided by the request to operate a virtual computer mouse in Adult Swim Games' VR game "Rick and Morty: Virtual Rick-ality" (Fig. 3), where the lack of an actual surface that constrains, supports and guides movement transforms what is a common interaction for a vast majority of people into a rather awkward task.

One of the primary challenges for XR experiences is to present users with a cognitively accessible experience, something that does not conflict with or contradict their existing mental model of how the world is. In this sense, operating a virtual mouse does not present particular conceptual problems, but, since cognition is a product of human embodiment and spatial knowledge (Tversky 2019), the missing embodied component, empty space where our muscle memory predicts resistance from a desk surface, is what creates friction. While constraints can be imposed on the virtual representation of the mouse, so that its movement is limited to a 2D plane, people interacting with it can still move in 3D space with 6DOF. They might then experience a mismatch between their possibility for action in physical space and what happens in VR that could be possibly solved by restructuring the space of the experience entirely so that it offers—in whatever way might be feasible—either an actual surface for the virtual mouse to rest on or a plausible, understandable reason for the mismatch.

Similarly, if one were to hand-write a note in VR, one would preferably write it as they would in the physical world, where it is a commonplace task. Being required to write something using a controller – which is nothing like a pen or a brush – on thin air, again with no surface feedback, causes discrepancies in the interpretation and performance of the task that are rooted in our embodiment and in our understanding of the world around us. The simple lack of the tactile and haptic feedback provided by a pen in the hand and by a surface that resists pressure, turns writing into a difficult activity that might take time to relearn. While this can be considered acceptable for activities performed routinely, such as those connected to a profession or a job, this is hardly anything a casual or occasional user would want to endure. This is an important aspect for education, entertainment, and those tasks, such as paying one's taxes for example, that are performed repeatedly but not frequently.

5   Experiential Challenges in XR

Designing XR environment then presents a number of experiential challenges related to immersing people in a dynamic information-rich or information-created 3D space in which they have 6DOF and the need to establish a sense of presence to be able to operate successfully. The simple naturalistic transliteration of physical into digital brings along problems related to underlying spatial schemas that relate to our sense of embodiment. An example can be made of how several VR environments present people with onboarding or loading spaces that recreate a house or other familiar space, with movement and interactions directly mapped to spatial metaphors such as those of rooms, activity areas, features and furniture. While this approach can be successfully applied to a limited set of tasks, mostly related to meta-activities such as modifying the parameters of the VR space, starting and stopping applications, and the like, the irreflective adoption of naturalistic 3D spaces in VR becomes problematic as soon as the size or scale of the environment change, introducing problems of cognitive load in relation to seeking behaviors and navigation, or the number and types of tasks, and thus complexity, increase. Walmart's recently resurfaced concept of the "VR supermarket" is an example of the former (Vincent 2022), and the reported dissatisfaction of Meta employees with Meta's own Horizon XR platform (Heath 2022) is an example of the latter.

Three XR experiential challenges—point of view, orientation, and locomotion—are especially worth of consideration as they primarily impact a person's sense of presence and embodiment and have strong structural design implications.

Point of view relates to the agency of the person in a volatile, changing XR environment. The semantic and visual grammar of filmmaking represent "a rich vocabulary available to use to create compelling stories" (Mateer 2017; Van Sijll 2005; Persson 1998). They were rapidly adopted and adapted by the video game industry (Wolf 1997;

Fassone et al. 2015) and then transported to the mise en scène of XR environments. The popularity of immersive shooting games (FPS) entirely presented from a first-person point of view, a type of shot that while "a part of conventional film grammar" has been "sparingly used", resulted in something new that still "reproduc(ed) the visual effects of a camera lens" while giving players an experience "very different from the camera-eye, and the associated editing, of mainstream cinema" (Brooker 2009). In traditional filmmaking, camera control and movement is the primary way the space of action is instantiated: in FPS games, and even more in XR space, "the free-ranging camera (…) breaks the rules of conventional cinema" (Brooker 2009). The person experiences space from an egocentric perspective (Landau 2002) which makes traditional camera control, techniques, movements, and composition problematic at the least. While differences exist between VR and AR/MR—the former still subject to some degree of control since the ontology and topology of the environment, if not the agency and volatility, are entirely designed; the latter a fundamentally open world whose ontology and topology are not under the designer's control—point of view control in XR is often limited to setting an entry view of the XR space, which has a bearing on orientation challenges, to generic consideration of embodiment related to scale and size, and to sustaining the egocentric perspective as a person exercises agency.

Orientation relates to a person's proprioception in XR space. Point of view, or better the preservation of the person's point of view across spaces and transitional moments—for example when moving between non-adjacent locations or when non-diegetic information is provided that occupies the person's field of view—plays an important role in avoiding spatial disorientation. The topology of the XR environment, which is a 6DOF space, also carries weight, and might produce interesting frictions between the digital and physical spaces part of the experience. A long-held assumption was that rotating one's body or point of view to orient or reorient oneself should happen naturally by physically turning around, since that is the modality that is less prone to break immersion. Again, while agency in XR space should not contradict embodiment, the context of physical engagement should be considered: for example, long VR sessions are often conducted while sitting, something which makes turning a more cumbersome movement and which contributed to the adoption of controller-driven ways to readjust one's orientation and point of view, called "snap rotation" or "viewpoint snapping". When snap rotating, the person's viewpoint is "snapped" a fixed amount of degrees in 3D space during fast movement to reduce the possibility of inconsistent displacement between optic flow and proprioception. Studies of viewpoint snapping indicate a reduction of cybersickness symptoms as well, especially in prolonged sessions (Farmani & Teather 2018). Cybersickness is the specific type of sickness one experiences as a result of exposure to immersive XR environments (Davis et al. 2014; Bender 2022; Garrido et al. 2022)—a problem affecting a sizable part of people and that still has not been entirely understood or resolved (Kim et al. 2018; Ohyama et al. 2007).

Locomotion relates to the topology and ontology of XR space. AR/MR environments do not present specific issues, but locomotion in VR remains at present a looming challenge introducing several limitations, due in part to technology, in part to our sensory-motor apparatus, and in part to the constraints of the physical space in which the person is located. Even without considering cybersickness, moving around in VR is currently a more complicated and less natural activity than moving around in physical space. The problem is somewhat exacerbated in educational or entertainment XR, where expectations are set for an engaging experience: it is not possible, convenient, or safe, for the person to actually climb a ladder or to jump across buildings in physical space, even though the person's avatar might just do that in VR space. This makes the relationship between environment and action across the two spaces a mediated one, rather than a simple transliteration of naturalistic behavior from one to the other. The use of VR omnidirectional treadmills (Darken et al. 1997), which have been entering the market in the past few years, presents practical challenges related to their cost and the space they require, but also in respect to their general adaptability to a variety of VR scenarios (Nabiyouni & Bowman 2016). Other technologies, such as circular floors or robotic tiles (Iwata et al. 2005), remain, for the time being at least, the purview of research.

Locomotion is also a "necessary" activity in physical space, one that aligns with the human idea of agency: one moves closer to the sofa to sit while the sofa stands still. Unsurprisingly though, unrealistic but effective locomotion techniques such as "teleportation"—which sees people simply disappear from one area and reappear in another, sometimes using predetermined mandatory "hotspots"—or "linear zipping", are preferred to the clumsiness of running-in-place techniques (Hillman 2021). The reason is that it is relatively easy, cognitively inexpensive, to adapt one's sense of presence to the novel affordances presented by the space—in terms of proprioception, movement, action—when they do not contradict, even though they might alter greatly, one's embodied sense of self. In this sense, teleportation provides a better fit for locomotion than flailing one's arms to run in place.

Immersion then results from the careful crafting of the designed space so that it supports the creation of a sense of presence (placemaking), works consistently and resiliently, and offers non-overwhelming opportunities for action (reduction, correlation): none of these hinge on absolute realism—as the success of locomotion via "linear zipping" or the adoption of "snap rotation" demonstrates—but they rather rely on a thoughtful (information) architecture that structures a sound ontology and topology, addresses volatility, and provides people with an opportunity for agency that does not contradict their embodiment.

With this framing in place, the paper briefly analyzes a commercial-scale augmented virtual reality experience to illustrate the way the structural and embodied approach described so far can contribute to foreground spatial structures and behaviors conducive to purposefully design around the current limitations, constraints, and shortcomings of XR environments.

6   An Information Architecture Analysis of "Star Wars: Secrets of the Empire"

The immersive "Star Wars: Secrets of the Empire" experience was one of a number of VR movie tie-ins in The Void's catalog (Bishop 2017). An on-site, location-based VR ride-like experience, "Secrets of the Empire" combined a generic physical environment consisting of a series of connected rooms and passages with a custom, a multi-user VR setup consisting of portable vest-mounted computing units and headsets whose task was to "paint over" walls, ceilings and floors, positional tracking and sensory feedback to immerse visitors in a Star Wars-themed narrative (Fig. 4).

Fig. 4. Players boarding a ship in The Void's Star Wars VR experience (Image: The Void)

Up to 4 people could team up and enter "Secrets of the Empire" as rebels disguised as stormtroopers, take a trip to the planet Mustafar to steal a secret weapon, shoot their way through the imperial base, and finally meet Darth Vader himself before being rescued at the very last minute. A large array of practical effects borrowed from the movie and theme park industry—from blowers to simulate the wind to heaters to simulate the hot vapors of flowing lava—was used to enhance and reinforce the affordances offered by walls, props, and machinery in the physical environment. This complex setup created an heightened immersive VR experience in which the carefully designed interplay of the digital and physical environment allowed patrons to augment their sense of presence by:

- feeling walls, going up stairs, waiting for a door to open, huddling up in the cargo bay of a ship, running for cover and crouching behind a make-shift shelter while seeing each other in complete stormtrooper garb and remaining able to talk to each other, touch each other, and feel each other's presence in the same physical space, contributing to placemaking;
- interacting with each other and with the environment without contradicting their embodiment: seats could be used for sitting, levers could be physically pulled, blasters could be fired and passed from hand to hand as they also were physical props overlaid with VR imagery. The reliability and predictability of these interactions increased consistency;
- exploring the space of the narrative by acting naturally and socially, increasing resilience and contributing to correlation;
- receiving narrative nudges to move forward at the right time and in the right place from the XR environment itself and via the careful employment of reduction;
- have actual agency in a physical and perceptible environment, thus solving the challenges relating to their individual point of view, locomotion, and orientation.

The synesthetic nature of the experience, "the entire body sensing and moving" (Casey 1996), made it possible to accomplish realistic immersion using comparatively lower-grade technology than what was already available at the time for home entertainment or business use for parts of the system. For example, the headsets could offer a relatively low resolution without fear of degrading the experience because of the additional proprioceptive, auditory and haptic enrichment provided by the XR environment.

7 Discussion

The concept of a "navigable space" rests on the foundations provided by embodiment and spatiality (Bates 2002; Nitsche 2008; Tversky 2019). Manovich argues that navigable space represents a larger cultural form that transcends digital culture and can be used to represent both physical spaces and abstract information spaces or, we could say, habitable spaces irregardless of whether or not they appear realistic, as in VR, or abstract, as in Facebook. For this reason, navigable and habitable space should not be intended to mean "life-like", "photorealistic", or even just plain "realistic". Immersion and presence have roots that go deeper than the interface layer. Even in experiences such as The Void's "Star Wars: Secrets of the Empire" what appears to be a "realistic" experience is really a mediated and designed construct that creates and sustains a sense of presence through careful crafting of its immersive narrative space. Mimicry, more than a technological or design problem, is a conceptual Borgesian map of the empire (Borges 1975, p. 131).

As outlined in this paper, focus should be directed instead to frame and design XR environments as transformative blended spaces (Horan 2000; Benyon 2014), carefully considering their nature of human spaces and addressing them from a structural perspective—such as the one introduced here and relying on information architecture heuristics rooted in embodiment and spatiality—that supports emergent, novel behavior.

Attention to the emergent nature of XR introduces an additional point for discussion that relates to the development of concepts such as the Metaverse, in which people access an online distributed array of XR spaces for more than just entertainment. In all likelihood, these spaces will be—at least initially—rather simple VR and AR experiences directed toward what is already known, well-established, and comprehensible, and only slowly will they transition towards what is not-yet-experienced. Here it is possible to imagine the possibility to move beyond XR and into some Expanded Reality (ER) in which people move, individually and collectively, toward whatever this not-yet-experienced will be, figuring out new heuristics, possibly leaving some of the spatial and embodiment constraints described in this paper behind and acquiring a different sense of presence and of self that defies gravity or subverts communication as we know it today. It is certainly possible to imagine that this ER will change, or get rid of, current hierarchies, conventions, and limitations, introducing the new ones which will characterize the end of the 21st century and the beginning of the 22nd.

8 Conclusions

In information-heavy XR environments, sense of presence is the result of the mediated interplay of a person's embodiment and spatial knowledge and their agency as it is constrained by the designed nature of the XR space itself.

As digital or digitally-enhanced designed spaces in the experience design domain, XR environments have primarily received attention as information-based artifacts, with important consequences due to the lack of specific expertise in digital design disciplines—game design being the exception—in dealing with spatiality and embodiment. Traditionally tasked with designing information environments deployed on the bidimensional flat space of a screen, the methods, tools, and mindsets of these disciplines are, as they stand, for the large part inadequate to solve the challenges of creating meaningful humane experiences in the 6DOF space of VR, AR and MR.

Referring to theories of information seeking as exaptation behavior and to theories of blended space as a transformative emergent space that establishes new affordances and a novel sense of presence, this paper introduced a cohesive set of information architecture heuristics for the design of XR spaces that are meant to structurally work across the digital / physical continuum and that place embodiment and spatiality at the forefront of the experience.

The adoption of Resmini and Rosati's heuristics as a reflective guide for the designer shifts the attention away from the visual layer of the interface to the deeper sitting architectures that shape the ontology and the topology of XR space (placemaking, consistency, resilience) and support people's agency (reduction, correlation), thus addressing the emergent volatility of the experience (resilience, consistency) and helping create more meaningful and humane extended realities.

References

Aronov, D., Tank, D.W.: Engagement of neural circuits underlying 2D spatial navigation in a rodent virtual reality system. Neuron **84**(2), 442–456 (2014). https://doi.org/10.1016/j.neuron.2014.08.042

Bates, M.J.: Toward an integrated model of information seeking and searching. New Rev. Inf. Behav. Res. **3**, 1–15 (2002). https://pages.gseis.ucla.edu/faculty/bates/articles/info_SeekSearch-i-030329.html

Bender, M.: Cybersickness Could Spell an Early Death for the Metaverse. The Daily Beast (2022). https://www.thedailybeast.com/cybersickness-could-spell-an-early-death-for-the-metaverse-and-virtual-reality

Benn, Y., et al.: Navigating through digital folders uses the same brain structures as real world navigation. Sci. Rep. **5**(1) (2015). https://doi.org/10.1038/srep14719

Benyon, D.: Spaces of interaction, places for experience. Syn. Lect. Hum. Centered Inf. **7**(2), 1–129. Morgan & Claypool (2014)

Bishop, B.: With Star Wars: Secrets of the Empire, virtual reality is finally ready for prime-time. The Verge (2017). https://www.theverge.com/2017/11/20/16678438/star-wars-secrets-of-the-empire-virtual-reality-disney-the-void-ilmxlab

Borges, J.L.: A Universal History of Infamy. Penguin Books (1975)

Brambilla, P., Hall, S., Li, C.: What is the metaverse? And why should we care? World Economic Forum (2021). https://www.weforum.org/agenda/2021/10/what-is-the-metaverse-why-care/

Karpouzis, K., Yannakakis, G.N. (eds.): Emotion in Games. SC, vol. 4. Springer, Cham (2016). https://doi.org/10.1007/978-3-319-41316-7

Carter, M., Egliston, B.: Facebook relaunches itself as 'Meta' in a clear bid to dominate the metaverse. The Conversation (2021). https://theconversation.com/facebook-relaunches-itself-as-meta-in-a-clear-bid-to-dominate-the-metaverse-170543

Casey, E.S.: How to get from space to place in a fairly short stretch of time. In: Feld, S., Basso, K.H. (eds.) Senses of Place. University of Washington Press (1996)

Cruz-Neira, C., Sandin, D.J., DeFanti, T.A., Kenyon, R.V., Hart, J.C.: The CAVE: audio visual experience automatic virtual environment. Commun. ACM **35**(6), 64–72 (1992). https://doi. org/10.1145/129888.129892

Darken, R.P., Cockayne, W.R., Carmein, D.: The omnidirectional treadmill: a locomotion device for virtual worlds. In: Proceedings of the 10th annual ACM Symposium on User Interface Software and Technology, pp. 213–221. ACM (1997)

Davis, S., Nesbitt, K., Nalivaiko, E.: A systematic review of cybersickness. In: Proceedings of the 2014 Conference on Interactive Entertainment, pp. 1–9 (2014). https://doi.org/10.1145/267 7758.2677780

Dixon, S.: Clubhouse. Statista (2022). https://www.statista.com/topics/7609/clubhouse/

Farmani, Y., Teather, R.J.: Viewpoint Snapping to reduce cybersickness in virtual reality. In: GI 2018: Proceedings of the 44th Graphics Interface Conference, pp. 168–175 (2018). https://doi. org/10.20380/GI2018.23

Fassone, R., Giordano, F., Girina, I.: Re-framing video games in the light of cinema. G|A|M|E Ital. J. Game Stud. **4** (2015). https://www.gamejournal.it/4_giordano_girina_fassone/

Floridi, L.: The Fourth Revolution. Oxford University Press (2014)

Garrido, L.E., et al.: Focusing on cybersickness: pervasiveness, latent trajectories, susceptibility, and effects on the virtual reality experience. Virtual Reality, 1–25 (2022). https://doi.org/10. 1007/s10055-022-00636-4

Gattis, M.: Spatial Schemas and Abstract Thought. The MIT Press (2001)

Gaudiosi, Why gamers are excited about virtual reality and augmented reality. Fortune (2015). https://fortune.com/2015/09/11/gamers-are-excited-about-vr-ar/

GreenField, A.: Everyware. New Riders (2006)

Heath, A.: Meta's flagship metaverse app is too buggy and employees are barely using it, says exec in charge. The Verge (2022). https://www.theverge.com/2022/10/6/23391895/meta-facebook-horizon-worlds-vr-social-network-too-buggy-leaked-memo

Hillmann, C.: The history and future of XR. In: UX for XR. DT, pp. 17–72. Apress, Berkeley, CA (2021). https://doi.org/10.1007/978-1-4842-7020-2_2

Horan, T.A.: Digital Places. Urban Land Institute (2000)

Hutchins, E.: Material anchors for conceptual blends. J. Pragmat. **37**(10), 1555–1577 (2005)

Iwata, H. et al.: Circulafloor: a locomotion interface using circulation of movable tiles. In: Proceedings of the 2005 IEEE Conference 2005 on Virtual Reality. IEEE Society (2005)

Johnson, C.: Virtual Reality is Here and It's a Huge Opportunity. Forbes (2017). https://www. forbes.com/sites/forbescommunicationscouncil/2017/11/15/virtual-reality-is-here-and-its-a-huge-opportunity/

Kim, H.K., Park, J., Choi, Y., Choe, M.: Virtual reality sickness questionnaire (VRSQ): motion sickness measurement index in a virtual reality environment. Appl. Ergon. **69**, 66–73 (2018). https://doi.org/10.1016/j.apergo.2017.12.016

Lakoff, G., Johnson, M.: Metaphors We Live by. University of Chicago Press (1980)

Bartolomeo, P., Mandonnet, E.: Spatial cognition. In: Mandonnet, E., Herbet, G. (eds.) Intraoperative Mapping of Cognitive Networks, pp. 59–76. Springer, Cham (2021). https://doi.org/10. 1007/978-3-030-75071-8_4

Mallgrave, H.F.: Architecture and Embodiment. Routledge (2013)

Manovich, L.: The Language of New Media. The MIT Press (2000)

Marr, B.: Extended Reality in Practice. Wiley (2021)

Mateer, J.: Directing for cinematic virtual reality: how the traditional film director's craft applies to immersive environments and notions of presence. J. Media Pract. **18**(1), 14–25 (2017). https:// doi.org/10.1080/14682753.2017.1305838

McNerney, S.: A Brief Guide to Embodied Cognition: Why You Are Not Your Brain. Scientific American (2011). https://blogs.scientificamerican.com/guest-blog/a-brief-guide-to-emb odied-cognition-why-you-are-not-your-brain/

Meta. What is the Metaverse (2023). https://about.meta.com/what-is-the-metaverse/

Mitchell, W.J.: Me++. The MIT Press (2004)

Miller, G.A.: The magical number seven, plus or minus two: some limits on our capacity for processing information. Psychol. Rev. **63**(2), 81–97 (1956). https://doi.org/10.1037/h0043158

Myhill, C.: Commercial success by looking for desire lines. In: Masoodian, M., Jones, S., Rogers, B. (eds.) APCHI 2004. LNCS, vol. 3101, pp. 293–304. Springer, Heidelberg (2004). https://doi.org/10.1007/978-3-540-27795-8_30

Nabiyouni, M., Bowman, D.A.: A Taxonomy for designing walking-based locomotion techniques for virtual reality. In: Proceedings of the 2016 ACM Companion on Interactive Surfaces and Spaces - ISS Companion 2016, pp. 115–121 (2016). https://doi.org/10.1145/3009939.3010076

Nitsche, M.: Video Game Spaces. The MIT Press (2008)

Norberg-Schulz, C.: Existence, Space, and Architecture. Littlehampton Book Services (1971)

Ohyama, S., et al.: Autonomic responses during motion sickness induced by virtual reality. Auris Nasus Larynx **34**(3), 303–306 (2007). https://doi.org/10.1016/j.anl.2007.01.002

Parveau, M., Adda, M.: Toward a user-centric classification scheme for extended reality paradigms. J. Ambient. Intell. Humaniz. Comput. **11**(6), 2237–2249 (2019). https://doi.org/10.1007/s12 652-019-01352-9

Pahwa, N.: The Often Maddening, Always Surreal Experience of Work Meetings in VR. Slate (2023). https://slate.com/technology/2023/01/vr-work-meetings-oculus-new-horizons-metave rse.html

Peddie, J.: Augmented Reality. Springer (2017)

Persson, P.: A Comparative study of digital and cinematic space with special focus on navigational issues. In: Dahlbäck, N. (ed.) Exploring Navigation: Towards a Framework for Design and Evaluation of Navigation in Electronic Spaces. Swedish Institute of Computer Science (1998)

Ramachandran, V.: Stanford researchers identify four causes for 'Zoom fatigue' and their simple fixes. Stanford News (2021). https://news.stanford.edu/2021/02/23/four-causes-zoom-fatigue-solutions/

Resmini, A.: Classical to contemporary: an M3-based model for framing change in information architecture. In: Resmini, A., Rice, S.A., Irizarry, B. (eds.) Advances in Information Architecture. HIS, pp. 9–17. Springer, Cham (2021). https://doi.org/10.1007/978-3-030-632 05-2_2

Resmini, A., Lindenfalk, B.: Mapping experience ecosystems as emergent actor-created spaces. In: Hameurlain, A., Tjoa, A.M., Chbeir, R. (eds.) Transactions on Large-Scale Data-and Knowledge-Centered Systems XLVII. LNCS, vol. 12630, pp. 1–28. Springer, Heidelberg (2021). https://doi.org/10.1007/978-3-662-62919-2_1

Resmini, A., Rosati, L.: Pervasive Information Architecture: Designing Cross-channel User Experiences. Morgan Kauffman (2011)

Rosenfeld, L., Morville, P.: Information Architecture for the World Wide Web (2nd ed). O'Reilly (2002)

Ryan, M-L., Foote, K., Azaryhau, M.: Narrating Architecture/Spatializing Narrative. Ohio State Press (2016)

Statista AR & VR – Worldwide (2023). https://www.statista.com/outlook/amo/ar-vr/worldwide# global-comparison

Sweller, J.: Cognitive load during problem solving: effects on learning. Cogn. Sci. **12**(2), 257–285 (1988). https://doi.org/10.1207/s15516709cog1202_4

Tversky, B.: Mind in Motion. Basic Books (2019)

Vincent, J.: That Walmart VR shopping video is old news — but so is the metaverse. The Verge (2022). https://www.theverge.com/tldr/2022/1/5/22868323/walmart-metaverse-shopping-video-viral-old

Zipf, G.K.: Human Behavior and the Principle of Least Effort: An Introduction to Human Ecology. Addison-Wesley (1949)

Van Sijll, J.: Cinematic Storytelling. Michael Wiese Productions (2005)

Williams Goldhagen, S.: Welcome to Your World. HarperCollins (2017)

Wolf, M.J.P.: Inventing space: toward a taxonomy of on- and off- screen space in video games. Film Q. 51(1), 11–23 (1997). https://doi.org/10.2307/1213527

High-Quality Synthetic Character Image Extraction via Distortion Recognition

Tomoya Sawada$^{(\boxtimes)}$, Marie Katsurai , and Masashi Okubo

Doshisha University, 1-3 Tatara Miyakodani, Kyotanabe 610-0394, Kyoto, Japan
{sawada,katsurai}@mm.doshisha.ac.jp, mokubo@mail.doshisha.ac.jp

Abstract. Digital avatars have become indispensable in the digital age. In Japan, virtual characters using illustration-style avatars have gained popularity and is generating large economic impact. However, the creation of such avatars is a time-consuming and costly process that requires a great deal of expertise. To support avatar creation, research of automatic generation of character design and textures for 3D models have emerged. However, deep learning-based generative models sometimes synthesize corrupted outputs. Methods to detect collapsed outputs from a generative model has not been explored, and users of the generator needs to manually exclude such outputs. In this paper, we propose a method to extract high-quality images from a set of synthetic illustrations, generated by a deep learning model, based on the degree of distortion of the images. As it is difficult to prepare real-world distorted images to train a distortion recognition model, we propose a simple procedure to create pseudo-distorted images. Experimental results showed superior results of the proposed method in distinguishing between human-drawn images and generated images, compared to baseline methods. Furthermore, we sorted the generated images using the confidence level of the trained distortion detection model, and qualitatively confirmed that the proposed method produces results closer to human perception.

Keywords: High-quality character image extraction · distortion recognition · deep learning

1 Introduction

Digital avatars play an essential role in games, films, and in recent years, Metaverse. In Japan, virtual YouTubers (VTubers) are one of the contents that is generated a large economic effect through the use of avatars. In addition to their activities on the video-sharing website YouTube, VTubers have recently appeared on television and been used in corporate advertisements. The appeal of using avatars for such activities is that, avatars can be not only abstractions of real-world figures, but can also be different from oneself or even illustrated characters that do not exist in the real world, which can contribute to the acquisition of new identities in the electronic world. In addition, avatars are being incorporated into many interfaces used for computer-mediated communication, and are

M. Kurosu and A. Hashizume (Eds.): HCII 2023, LNCS 14013, pp. 522–535, 2023.
https://doi.org/10.1007/978-3-031-35602-5_37

gaining ground as a communication tool in virtual space. However, the creation of avatars is not an easy task, as each step of the process requires specialized knowledge such as in sculpturing the shape of the character, drawing textures, and capturing the motion to move the avatar. Therefore, a method to easily synthesize digital avatars by using a deep learning-based generative models has been studied in recent years [13,36].

Generative models may synthesize data that are corrupted which makes the contents unrecognizable. Methods to detect these collapsed generated data are not well researched, and users need to manually exclude the collapsed data from the produced results. There is a research field called image quality assessment (IQA), which evaluates the quality of images, but most of these studies are conducted on natural images, and the behavior of IQA methods on synthetic data has not been examined in detail. In addition, it is pointed out that the results of IQA methods for illustration images differ from those of human perception, and IQA for illustration images is still a developing research field [39]. Therefore, it is difficult to use IQA to detect collapsed synthetic images, especially on unnatural images such as illustrations. A method to extract only high-quality images from a synthetic image set generated by a deep learning model would be very beneficial.

Corruption of synthesized data include creation of unnecessary objects, loss of necessary objects, unnatural textures, and distortions. Among them, we focused on distortion because it is a content-independent collapse. There are studies that focus on local distortion of synthetic images in the field of fake face detection. For example, Guo et al. discovered that human face images synthesized by deep generative models have irregular pupil shapes and proposed a method to automatically detect synthesized images by segmenting the pupil [10]. Detecting the distortions caused by the image generation model will contribute to evaluate the quality of the images according to the degree of the distortions.

We propose a novel approach for extracting high-quality character images from a synthetic image set to support deep learning-based creation of digital avatars. Specifically, we train a deep learning model to detect distorted images. Since it is difficult to collect distorted images in the real world, pseudo-distorted images are synthesized by applying transformations to undistorted images and used as training data. To extract high-quality images from synthetic images provided by and external generative model, we rank images based on probability value, which is the confidence when the distortion recognition model predicted inputs as distorted images. The proposed method was evaluated quantitatively and qualitatively. In the quantitative evaluation, we placed synthetic images in a set of human-drawn images and evaluated whether the synthetic image could be extracted from this set of images. In the qualitative evaluation, we sorted the generated images according to the confidence level of the model and observed the results. The proposed method showed superior results compared to baseline methods.

The main contributions of this paper are as follows:

- We propose a simple but effective method for extracting high-quality images from a set of synthetic images using a deep learning based distortion detection model.
- We apply simple transformation to real images to produce pseudo-distorted images to train a distortion recognition model. The proposed method is considered to be robust to the content of the synthetic data.

2 Related Works

2.1 Generative Models

Generative adversarial networks (GAN) was first proposed by Goodfellow et al. [8] as a generative model trained with adversarial supervision. GANs are trained using two deep learning models, a generator that synthesizes images and a discriminator that discriminates whether the input data is real or fake images. The generator receives a latent vector sampled from a probability distribution as the input and attempts to generate realistic images to fool the discriminator. By having the generators and discriminators compete with each other, the generator will eventually produce data of such high quality that they can be mistaken as real. Various studies have been conducted on GAN since its appearance, such as alternative or addition loss functions [1,9,22,23], methods to stabilize training [14,38,40], and also model architectures [2,17]. Karras et al. proposed a generator architecture based on neural style transfer literature, StyleGAN [15], which can automatically learn to separate high-level attributes and stochastic variations from an intermediate latent space. By analyzing generated images of StyleGAN, Karras et al. [16] proposed StyleGAN2, which improved the quality of the generated images by updating the generator and discriminator architectural terms. In most cases, systems designed to support the creation of illustrated characters use methods that have been proven effective on natural images with illustration datasets. In this study, StyleGAN2 is trained on whole body images of illustrated characters and used as an image generator in the experiments.

Diffusion models are rapidly developing in various research fields of deep learning, and generative diffusion models are the most actively studied [12,28]. In our experiments, we have evaluated the proposed method used synthesized images from a GAN model, but we believe our method can be used on images generated by other generative models such as diffusion models.

2.2 Assessing Quality of Synthetic Images

Metrics such as Inception score [30] and Fréchet Inception distance [11] are most commonly used to evaluate image generative models. Both metrics are based on a model called Inception v3 [32], which is trained on a large dataset of natural images called ImageNet [4]. These metrics evaluate the diversity of images produced by the generator and the degree of similarity between the synthetic images and the real images. However, these evaluation metrics cannot evaluate the visual quality of individual images. Blind IQA (BIQA) is a research field that aims to evaluate the quality of images on a piece-by-piece basis. BIQA is a fundamental metric in image processing operations such as image compression and transfer. Some methods are effective for natural images [37] or unnatural images such as computer graphics [25]. However, for illustrations, it has been reported that recent BIQA methods output results that differ from human perception [3]. In addition, since the validation of IQA methods when applied to synthetic data is still insufficient, the application of conventional IQA methods to our task will result in unintended behavior, such as judging low quality images as high quality and vice versa.

3   Distorted Image Recognition

This section describes how we detected high-quality illustrations from synthetic images, which were automatically produced by a GAN model. Our method is based on the assumption that the confidence of a deep learning model trained to detect distortions on images reflects the quality of the input images. First, we trained a distortion recognition model, which receives images and predict whether these input images were distorted or not. Though, it was difficult to collect real-world distorted illustrations as positive examples to train the distortion recognition model. Therefore, we applied a random transformation to human-drawn illustrations and created pseudo-distorted images to simulate corruptions on synthetic images produced by a generative model. Then, we input synthesized images to the trained model and sorted these images by the confidence of the predictions. We will explain the details in the following sections.

3.1   Pseudo Distorted Image Synthesis

This subsection describes the procedure to create pseudo-distorted images. The precedure to preprocess the input images is presented in Fig. 1. First, we sampled an image from the training set and randomly selected whether to apply transformation to this image. When the transformation was applied, the image was given a label representing the distorted class. The image that was not transformed was labeled as the non-distorted class. After the labeling, a transformation was uniformally selected from four spatial transformations. Sample images of the four transformations used in our experiments are presented on Fig. 2. The details of the transformations are described bellow:

Grid distortion divides an image into multiple grids and stretches or shrinks each grid vertically or horizontally. There are two parameters: the number of vertical and horizontal divisions, and the "limit" parameter that controls the maximum degree of expansion and contraction.

Elastic distortion [31] is a transform that moves image pixels within a local area using a displacement field. The distance that a pixel can move and the smoothness of the displacement field can be controlled by the parameters "alpha" and "sigma", respectively.

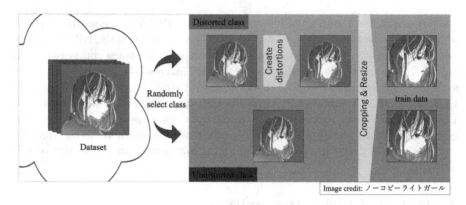

Image credit: ノーコピーライトガール

Fig. 1. Procedure of preprocessing images from the dataset as inputs to distortion detection model. Images labeled as distorted class is transformed using a spatial transformation method.

Table 1. Parameters used when applying the transform. When the "value" column is a range, a single value is uniformly sampled between the range.

transform	parameter	value
Grid distortion	number of grid divisions	15
	limit	0.6
Elastic distortion	alpha	200
	sigma	10
Piece-wise affine	number of rows and columns	$[3, 6]$
	scale	$[0.03, 0.05]$
Thin-plate-spline	initial point position	$[0.3, 0.7]$
	distance from initial point to the destination	$[-0.25, 0.25]$

Piece-wise affine transformation can create local distortions by randomly moving the neighbourhood of regularly placed grid of points via affine transformations. It is possible to control the number of rows and columns and also how much each point can be moved via "scale" parameter.

Thin-plate spline transformation is a method to warp an image by moving points on an image to another point and linearly interpolate the pixels between the points. Although the points and destinations to be moved are originally set manually, in this study they are uniformly sampled from a certain range.

The parameters used in the selected transformation were randomly sampled from a certain range for each training image. Table 1 are the parameters of each transform and the values we used in our experiments. Then, the images were randomly flipped horizontally. Finally, all images were resized and cropped to 224×224 pixels and the pixel values were normalized to $[-1, 1]$.

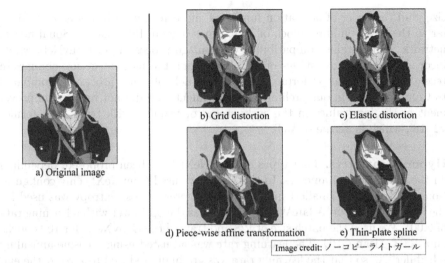

a) Original image

b) Grid distortion

c) Elastic distortion

d) Piece-wise affine transformation

e) Thin-plate spline

Image credit: ノーコピーライトガール

Fig. 2. Sample images of the four spatial transforms used to train our distortion recognition model.

We applied this distorted image creation pipeline while a batch of images was sampled as the input to the model. This made our method select the transformation and the parameters every time an image was sampled, which allowed us to prepare a pseudo-infinite number of distorted images. Creating distorted images on-the-fly, prevents the distortion recognition model from over-fitting to the training samples, and it also enables our method to be trained with limited amount of training data.

3.2 Training a Distortion Recognition Model

Model Architecture. The architectures of deep learning models have been remarkably developed since the advent of deep learning, and their performance has also been improved. Especially, the convolutional neural networks (ConvNets) which are composed of multiple convolutional layers has been useful in the field of image processing because of its superior compatibility with images. In this study, we adopt a type of ConvNet architecture called ConvNeXt presented by Liu et al. [19]. ConvNeXt is inspired by a deep learning model that employs an architecture which differs from that of ConvNet, called vision transformers (ViT) [5], while retaining ConvNet's compatibility with image processing. ViT has attracted attention in recent years and, like ConvNets, is used in various fields of image processing. ViT employs a mechanism called self-attention, which is capable of extracting global features of an image, in contrast to ConvNet, which uses convolution layers that are good at extracting local features. However, self-attention is computationally expensive and requires a longer time for training and testing. ConvNeXt, on the other hand, is a model in which self-attention is replaced by a depth-wise convolution layer with a large kernel size, and the order of activation functions and convolution layers is made similar to the basic building block of ViT. Since it is an fully convolutional neural network, it maintains compatibility with image processing of ConvNets, while incorporating the advantages of ViT by making the basic structure similar. In recent years, ViT has performed better in the field of image processing compared to ConvNets, but in our preliminary experiments, we did not find any improvement in the loss values in the early stages of training with Swin Transformer v2 [18], which is a type of ViT.

Hyper-parameters. Four types of ConvNeXt have been proposed, depending on the number of parameters. In this study, we used ConvNeXt-Tiny configuration, which has the smallest number of parameters. Cross entropy was used for the loss function, and AdamW [21] was used as the optimizer with a learning rate of 0.001. We used the batch size of 128 and trained the ConvNeXt for 100 epochs on a RTX Titan GPU. The learning rate was adjusted using a cosine annealing scheduler [20] so that the learning rate was gradually reduced to zero by the end of training. For the four spatial transforms, we selected one of the transforms to be applied with equal probability. The parameters for each transform were sampled uniformly from the ranges shown in Table 1 for each image.

Dataset. Our dataset consists of 260,000 images randomly selected from the Danbooru dataset[1], and divided into 250,000, 5,000, and 5,000 images for training, validation, and testing, respectively. We have limited the random selection of images from Danbooru dataset to those that have a source URL attached in their metadata. From the validation and testing set, 2,500 images each were randomly extracted before training the model and one of the four transforms was applied to each image. These transformed images were saved so that distorted and non-distorted classes were kept unchanged during training. For the training set, images were selected with a probability of 50% whether spatial transform was applied or not, so that the ratio of distorted images to undistorted images was 1 : 1.

Implementation Details. Among the four image transforms, grid distortion, elastic distortion and piece-wise affine transformation were performed using the implementation in albumentations[2], a library for image augmentation. For the thin-plate spline transformation, we modified an open-source implementation[3] to enable random selection of parameters. We used PyTorch [26], an deep learning library, for training the distortion recognition model. We used the implementation of ConvNeXt model in PyTorch's framework for modeling and training deep learning models, called transformers of huggingface [35]. To speed up the training, we used automatic mixed-precision [24], which is a method to stably train deep learning models using half-precision floating point numbers.

---

[1] https://www.gwern.net/Danbooru2021.

[2] https://albumentations.ai/.

[3] https://github.com/cheind/py-thin-plate-spline.

4   Evaluation

We evaluated the proposed method both quantitatively and qualitatively. For the quantitative evaluation, we put illustrations synthesized by the image generator into a set of real images drawn by illustrators and compared the performance of extracting the generated images. For the qualitative evaluation, we present and discuss the results of reordering of the synthesized images by the predicted visual quality using actual generated images. More detailed explanations are given in the following subsections.

For the image generator, we trained a well-known GAN model, Style-GAN2 [16] using illustrations of characters. The generator was capable of synthesize images of illustrated full-body characters with a resolution of 512×256 pixels.

4.1   Quantitative Evaluation

To quantitatively evaluate the proposed method, we conducted an experiment to predict the authenticity of illustration images. Specifically, we mixed synthetic images into a set of real illustrations collected from Shutterstock[4] with permission to use in publications. Then neural networks were used to predict whether the images were automatically generated or drawn by illustrators.

As comparison methods, we used Illustration2Vec (I2V) [29] and the discriminator used to train the image generator. I2V is a model for vectorizing illustrations proposed by Saito and Matsui. Since I2V uses image tagging as a learning task to train the vectorization network, it can not only vectorize illustrations but also assign appropriate tags according to their contents. In our experiments, among the 1,539 tags that I2V can assign, we used the tag "no human" which means that there is no human drawn in the image. If the model is convinced that this tag should be assigned, we could judge that the character in the image is collapsed. We used the pretrained model, distributed by the authors[5]. The discriminator was trained to discriminate whether the input images are from the dataset or generated images. Since the discriminator has knowledge about the generator, one criterion is to exceed the performance of the discriminator.

The output of each model for an input image was a probability value. Predictions for each model were defined as the result of thresholding this probability values. We used precision, recall, F1-score, and accuracy metric to evaluate the performance of the models. Precision measures the proportion of positive predictions that are actually correct. Recall, measures the proportion of actual positive examples that a classifier was able to identify correctly. The F1-score is an evaluation index that takes both precision and recall into account. The accuracy measures the percentage of correct predictions out of all predictions made by a classifier. Since the results change as the generated images change, the test was conducted on 5 different sets of randomly generated illustrations.

---

[4] https://www.shutterstock.com/.
[5] https://github.com/rezoo/illustration2vec.

Table 2. Results of the authenticity inference performance of the proposed and comparison methods. The number after @ indicates the threshold value and **bold** values indicate the best performing values.

model@threshold	Precision	Recall	F1-score	Accuracy
I2V@0.0001	0.671 ± 0.015	0.658 ± 0.017	0.652 ± 0.019	0.658 ± 0.017
Discriminator@0.5	0.692 ± 0.011	0.595 ± 0.012	0.536 ± 0.019	0.595 ± 0.012
Discriminator@0.3	0.705 ± 0.011	0.660 ± 0.014	0.640 ± 0.017	0.660 ± 0.014
ConvNeXt@0.5 (Ours)	0.765 ± 0.009	0.646 ± 0.017	0.601 ± 0.024	0.646 ± 0.017
ConvNeXt@0.3 (Ours)	$\mathbf{0.782 \pm 0.008}$	$\mathbf{0.688 \pm 0.015}$	$\mathbf{0.659 \pm 0.020}$	$\mathbf{0.688 \pm 0.015}$

Results. Table 2 presents the calculated metrics when thresholding with different values for each model. The values reported are the average and standard deviation of the results of five runs. It is shown that the proposed method with a threshold value of 0.3 has the best performance compared to the comparison method in all evaluation metrics.

Among the methods compared in this experiment, the discriminator had the lowest performance. This is due to the objective when training GANs, where the loss becomes low if the discriminator misidentifies synthesized images as real, even if these images are corrupted. The generator has the knowledge to fool the discriminator, which is independent of visual quality, and thus the results of the discriminator were less accurate than other methods. We further analyse this behavior in Sect. 4.2.

Using the thresholds of 0.3 and 0.5 for "no human" tag of I2V resulted to infer that all images contained human characters. Therefore, for I2V only, we selected an appropriate threshold value by inputting several images to the model and observing the output values. What should be noted in the results of I2V compared to the proposed method is that the evaluation was based on the contents in the images. We believe that better results can be obtained by considering both the quality of the image and its contents. This is an issue to be addressed in our future works.

4.2   Qualitative Evaluation

For qualitative evaluation, we generated several images and sorted them in the order of the probability that the proposed method classified them as the undistorted class. In the remainder of this subsection, we describe the images used in the evaluation, the results of the sorting, and the discussion on the results.

Non-duplicate Confirmation. In the research area of generative models, it has been pointed out that generators may synthesize copies of data that exist in the training set [6,33], which may lead to copyright issues. We confirmed that the generated images shown in the figures of this paper are not copies of the training data by using method for detecting data copies proposed by Pizzi

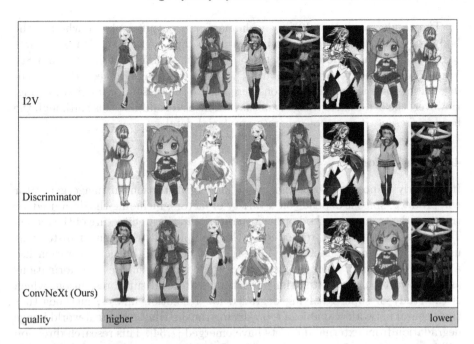

Fig. 3. Results of sorting synthetic images via the confidence of deep learning model's predictions. Images presented on this figure were confirmed that they are not replications of images in the training set. Zoom in for best view.

et al. [27]. Specifically, a deep learning model trained to detect copied images was used to embed arbitrary images to feature vectors, and these vectors can be used to calculate the similarity between other images. The feature vectors extracted from the synthesized images and the training data were used to calculate the cosine similarity. We observed the top 10 similar images sorted by the calculated cosine similarity and confirmed that the synthesized images were not copies of the training data.

Results. The sorted synthetic images for the three models used in our evaluation are presented in Fig. 3. The proposed method was able to reorder the images in an order close to that of human senses. The image in the 5th position is collapsed, but not distorted, so it may have been difficult to determine with the proposed method, which did not learn degradations of images other than distortion.

As we pointed out in Sect. 4.1, it can be seen that the generator was able to produce images that can fool the discriminator even though the images were collapsed. The character image sorted to be the highest quality of the discriminator has a silhouette that looks like a character, but the face and arms are not generated. Furthermore, the ranking of the 7th image is low despite the fact that it is a relatively clean synthesized image, since it has no missing body parts and the details of the face are clear.

The results show that I2V's "no human" tag output looks at whether the body parts are aligned. This can be seen from the fact that the 5th image was ranked higher than the other methods. The images ranked 6th, 7th, and 8th have simplified body parts or no arms, whereas the image ranked 5th has well-defined legs and arms, which is considered to be the reason for its high ranking. However, the 5th-ranked image is not favorable as a result, because although the head is present, it does not generate any facial details.

4.3   Limitation

It is nearly impossible to predict what kind of distortion an image generator will produce, since it depends on a variety of factors, including the data used for training, the training method of the generator, and the architecture of the model. There are limitations to reproducing this complex distribution of distortions using only parametric methods. The study of degraded image restoration has a similar limitation, since images are degraded using simple transformations and used to train the restoration model. In real-world super resolution, which is the study of super-resolving degraded low-resolution images, methods that train neural networks capable of reproducing the distribution of real-world image degradation from external datasets have emerged [7,34]. This research direction will improve the performance of our task. In addition, as mentioned in Sect. 4.1, the proposed method evaluates high quality images by considering only spatial distortion, therefore the aggregation with the content-aware method is our future issue.

5   Conclusion and Future Works

In this study, we presented a distortion recognition-based method for extracting high-quality images from a synthetic image set. We transformed images from the training data to automatically synthesize distorted image samples to train the classification model. We demonstrated that simple spatial transformation methods can adequately simulate distortions on synthetic data produced by deep learning-based generative models. Moreover, our method can be trained without any knowledge of the synthetic data, therefore has some robustness in the contents of the synthesized images. We believe that this study will help to create high-quality avatars, which have become an important communication tool in virtual spaces.

We used distortion as the corruption on synthesized images, but other corruptions can be compared to find more effective transformations to improve our method. Also, our method uses the visual quality as the basis for the ranking, but we believe that methods focusing on the contents can also be explored. In our future work, we will study methods that take both content of the image and visual quality into account.

References

1. Arjovsky, M., Chintala, S., Bottou, L.: Wasserstein generative adversarial networks. In: Proceedings of the 34th International Conference on Machine Learning (ICML), pp. 214–223 (2017)
2. Brock, A., Donahue, J., Simonyan, K.: Large scale GAN training for high fidelity natural image synthesis. In: International Conference on Learning Representations (ICLR) (2019). https://openreview.net/forum?id=B1xsqj09Fm
3. Chen, Y., Zhao, Y., Li, S., Zuo, W., Jia, W., Liu, X.: Blind quality assessment for cartoon images. IEEE Trans. Circuits Syst. Video Technol. **30**, 3282–3288 (2020). https://doi.org/10.1109/TCSVT.2019.2931589
4. Deng, J., Dong, W., Socher, R., Li, L.J., Li, K., Fei-Fei, L.: Imagenet: a large-scale hierarchical image database. In: IEEE Conference on Computer Vision and Pattern Recognition (CVPR), pp. 248–255 (2009)
5. Dosovitskiy, A., et al.: An Image is Worth 16 × 16 Words: transformers for image recognition at scale. In: International Conference on Learning Representations (ICLR) (2020). https://openreview.net/forum?id=YicbFdNTTy
6. Feng, Q., Guo, C., Benitez-Quiroz, F., Martinez, A.M.: When Do GANs replicate? on the choice of dataset size. In: Proceedings of the IEEE/CVF International Conference on Computer Vision (ICCV), pp. 6701–6710 (2021)
7. Fritsche, M., Gu, S., Timofte, R.: Frequency separation for real-world super-resolution. In: IEEE/CVF International Conference on Computer Vision Workshop (ICCVW), pp. 3599–3608 (2019). https://doi.org/10.1109/ICCVW.2019.00445
8. Goodfellow, I., et al.: Generative adversarial nets. In: Advances in Neural Information Processing Systems (NeurIPS), vol. 27, pp. 2672–2680 (2014)
9. Gulrajani, I., Ahmed, F., Arjovsky, M., Dumoulin, V., Courville, A.C.: Improved Training of Wasserstein GANs. In: Guyon, I., Luxburg, U.V., Bengio, S., Wallach, H., Fergus, R., Vishwanathan, S., Garnett, R. (eds.) Advances in Neural Information Processing Systems, pp. 5767–5777 (2017)
10. Guo, H., Hu, S., Wang, X., Chang, M.C., Lyu, S.: Eyes tell all: irregular pupil shapes reveal GAN-generated faces. In: IEEE International Conference on Acoustics, Speech and Signal Processing (ICASSP), pp. 2904–2908 (2022). https://doi.org/10.1109/ICASSP43922.2022.9746597
11. Heusel, M., Ramsauer, H., Unterthiner, T., Nessler, B., Hochreiter, S.: GANs trained by a two time-scale update rule converge to a local nash equilibrium. In: Advances in Neural Information Processing Systems, vol. 30, pp. 6626–6637 (2017)
12. Ho, J., Jain, A., Abbeel, P.: Denoising Diffusion Probabilistic Models. In: Advances in Neural Information Processing Systems (NeurIPS), vol. 33, pp. 6840–6851 (2020)
13. Hong, F., Zhang, M., Pan, L., Cai, Z., Yang, L., Liu, Z.: AvatarCLIP: zero-shot text-driven generation and animation of 3D avatars. ACM Trans. Graph. **41** (2022). https://doi.org/10.1145/3528223.3530094
14. Karras, T., Aittala, M., Hellsten, J., Laine, S., Lehtinen, J., Aila, T.: Training generative adversarial networks with limited data. In: Advances in Neural Information Processing Systems, pp. 12104–12114 (2020)
15. Karras, T., Laine, S., Aila, T.: A style-based generator architecture for generative adversarial networks. In: Proceedings of the IEEE/CVF Conference on Computer Vision and Pattern Recognition (CVPR), pp. 4401–4410, June 2019
16. Karras, T., Laine, S., Aittala, M., Hellsten, J., Lehtinen, J., Aila, T.: Analyzing and improving the image quality of StyleGAN. In: Proceedings of the IEEE/CVF Conference on Computer Vision and Pattern Recognition (CVPR), pp. 8110–8119, June 2020

17. Liu, B., Zhu, Y., Song, K., Elgammal, A.: Towards Faster and Stabilized GAN Training for High-fidelity Few-shot Image Synthesis. In: International Conference on Learning Representations (ICLR) (2021). https://openreview.net/forum?id=1Fqg133qRaI
18. Liu, Z., et al.: Swin transformer V2: scaling up capacity and resolution. In: Proceedings of the IEEE/CVF Conference on Computer Vision and Pattern Recognition (CVPR), pp. 12009–12019 (2022)
19. Liu, Z., Mao, H., Wu, C.Y., Feichtenhofer, C., Darrell, T., Xie, S.: A ConvNet for the 2020s. In: Proceedings of the IEEE/CVF Conference on Computer Vision and Pattern Recognition (CVPR), pp. 11976–11986 (2022)
20. Loshchilov, I., Hutter, F.: SGDR: stochastic gradient descent with warm restarts. In: International Conference on Learning Representations (ICLR) (2017). https://openreview.net/forum?id=Skq89Scxx
21. Loshchilov, I., Hutter, F.: Decoupled weight decay regularization. In: International Conference on Learning Representations (ICLR) (2018). https://openreview.net/forum?id=Bkg6RiCqY7
22. Mao, X., Li, Q., Xie, H., Lau, R.Y., Wang, Z., Paul Smolley, S.: Least squares generative adversarial networks. In: Proceedings of the IEEE International Conference on Computer Vision (ICCV), pp. 2794–2802 (2017)
23. Mescheder, L., Geiger, A., Nowozin, S.: Which Training Methods for GANs do actually Converge? In: Proceedings of the 35th International Conference on Machine Learning (ICML), vol. 80, pp. 3481–3490 (2018)
24. Micikevicius, P., et al.: Mixed Precision Training. In: International Conference on Learning Representations (ICLR) (2018). https://openreview.net/forum?id=r1gs9JgRZ
25. Ni, Z., Zeng, H., Ma, L., Hou, J., Chen, J., Ma, K.K.: A gabor feature-based quality assessment model for the screen content images. IEEE Trans. Image Process. **27**, 4516–4528 (2018). https://doi.org/10.1109/TIP.2018.2839890
26. Paszke, A., et al.: PyTorch: an imperative style, high-performance deep learning library. In: Advances in Neural Information Processing Systems (NeurIPS). 32, pp. 8026–8037 (2019). https://proceedings.neurips.cc/paper/2019/file/bdbca288fee7f92f2bfa9f7012727740-Paper.pdf
27. Pizzi, E., Roy, S.D., Ravindra, S.N., Goyal, P., Douze, M.: A self-supervised descriptor for image copy detection. In: Proceedings of the IEEE/CVF Conference on Computer Vision and Pattern Recognition (CVPR), pp. 14532–14542, June 2022
28. Rombach, R., Blattmann, A., Lorenz, D., Esser, P., Ommer, B.: High-resolution image synthesis with latent diffusion models. In: Proceedings of the IEEE/CVF Conference on Computer Vision and Pattern Recognition (CVPR), pp. 10684–10695 (2022)
29. Saito, M., Matsui, Y.: Illustration2Vec: a semantic vector representation of illustrations. In: SIGGRAPH Asia 2015 Technical Briefs, pp. 1–4 (2015). https://doi.org/10.1145/2820903.2820907
30. Salimans, T., et al.: Improved techniques for training GANs. In: Advances in Neural Information Processing Systems (NeurIPS), vol. 29, pp. 2234–2242 (2016)
31. Simard, P.Y., Steinkraus, D., Platt, J.C., et al.: Best practices for convolutional neural networks applied to visual document analysis. In: International Conference on Document Analysis and Recognition (ICDAR), vol. 3, pp. 958–963 (2003)
32. Szegedy, C., Vanhoucke, V., Ioffe, S., Shlens, J., Wojna, Z.: Rethinking the inception architecture for computer vision. In: Proceedings of the IEEE Conference on Computer Vision and Pattern Recognition (CVPR), pp. 2818–2826, June 2016

33. Tinsley, P., Czajka, A., Flynn, P.: This Face Does Not Exist... But It Might Be Yours! Identity Leakage in Generative Models. In: Proceedings of the IEEE/CVF Winter Conference on Applications of Computer Vision (WACV), pp. 1320–1328 (2021)
34. Wei, Y., Gu, S., Li, Y., Timofte, R., Jin, L., Song, H.: Unsupervised real-world image super resolution via domain-distance aware training. In: Proceedings of the IEEE/CVF Conference on Computer Vision and Pattern Recognition (CVPR), pp. 13385–13394 (2021)
35. Wolf, T., et al.: Transformers: state-of-the-art natural language processing. In: Proceedings of the 2020 Conference on Empirical Methods in Natural Language Processing: System Demonstrations, pp. 38–45 (2020), https://www.aclweb.org/anthology/2020.emnlp-demos.6
36. Wu, Y., Deng, Y., Yang, J., Wei, F., Chen, Q., Tong, X.: AniFaceGAN: animatable 3D-aware face image generation for video avatars. In: Oh, A.H., Agarwal, A., Belgrave, D., Cho, K. (eds.) Advances in Neural Information Processing Systems (2022). https://openreview.net/forum?id=LfHwpvDPGpx
37. Yang, X., Li, F., Liu, H.: A survey of DNN methods for blind image quality assessment. IEEE Access 7, 123788–123806 (2019). https://doi.org/10.1109/ACCESS.2019.2938900
38. Zhao, S., Liu, Z., Lin, J., Zhu, J.Y., Han, S.: Differentiable augmentation for data-efficient GAN training. In: Advances in Neural Information Processing Systems (NeurIPS), vol. 33, pp. 7559–7570 (2020)
39. Zhao, Y., Ren, D., Chen, Y., Jia, W., Wang, R., Liu, X.: Cartoon image processing: a survey. Int. J. Comput. Vision 130, 2733–2769 (2022). https://doi.org/10.1007/s11263-022-01645-1
40. Zhao, Z., Singh, S., Lee, H., Zhang, Z., Odena, A., Zhang, H.: Improved consistency regularization for gans. In: Proceedings of the AAAI Conference on Artificial Intelligence, vol. 35, pp. 11033–11041 (2021)

Barriers of Design Management in AR/VR Startups: Interview and Discussion

Jiahao Wang[1], Chuntie Chen[2], and Yuan Liu[3]($\boxtimes$)

[1] Polytechnic University of Milan, 20133 Milan, Italy
jiahao.wang@mail.polimi.it
[2] Metaself Technology Pte. Ltd, Singapore 757022, Singapore
keem@metaself.tech
[3] Beijing Institute of Fashion Technology, Beijing 100029, China
yuan.liu@polimi.it

Abstract. DM plays an important role in improving innovation and seeking business opportunities, but in new startups, they face the problem of timing limitation and product design. This phenomenon is even more pronounced in tech companies since the new technology is premature, and the market adoption barrier is presented. In this paper, we interviewed four CEOs from hi-tech startups, in which three of them from AR/VR startups, explored their application of design management and design thinking at all enterprise levels. They had difficulties in expanding the client base and must constantly change their products to meet market trends. According to the findings, a new DMC framework for hi-tech startups has been formed. As a tool and mindset, DT is introduced to empower enterprise management and innovation models and launch products that meet market demand as soon as possible, to extend their lifespan and shorten their business incubation process.

Keywords: Virtual Reality · Design Management · Design Thinking

1 Introduction

Design management (DM) is essential for innovation and obtaining business opportunities (Acklin & Fust 2014). However, new startups face the dual problems of correctly timing product release and creating an effective product design (Öndas & Akipinar 2021). These issues are more pronounced in tech companies due to the premature state of the technology and the adoption barriers in the market (Kuester et al. 2012). In this study, we specifically focus on AR/VR startups due to their high future values (Savin 2022). We interviewed 3 CEOs from AR/VR startups and one CEO from 3D printing startups for additional information. The current barriers in AR/VR startups and their opinion of DT are questioned. We found their difficulties in expanding their user base, integrating technology products with design, managing the communication among designers, and other company functions. Then the barriers are organized into three categories: market, product, and managerial. In addition, the interviewees all agreed that design thinking (DT) should be applied across the various departments of an enterprise. Specifically, it can be integrated into the organizational culture to keep the team creative and open-minded.

© The Author(s), under exclusive license to Springer Nature Switzerland AG 2023
M. Kurosu and A. Hashizume (Eds.): HCII 2023, LNCS 14013, pp. 536–549, 2023.
https://doi.org/10.1007/978-3-031-35602-5_38

As for the findings, a new DMC framework for high-tech startups will be formed and the relationships between DM, DT, and high-tech startups will be discussed. As a tool and mindset, DT is introduced to support enterprise management and innovation models, also to expedite the launch of products that attend to market demand, to extend their lifespan and shorten the business incubation process.

More specifically, this study aims to achieve two outcomes:

First, high-tech startups' current barriers using four dimensions (product, market, financial, managerial) are defined by carrying out a secondary study and pilot study with relevant CEOs. Therefore, the understanding of new DMCs is enriched by studying interaction relationships with DM and DT. Moreover, identifying barriers to DM will allow them to be addressed, thus deepening its impact on companies.

Second, new DT tools/methods will be developed to strengthen the ability of DT in design management in high-tech startups. Specifically, we envision that the developed tools will assist and manage the involvement of different company functions to fully exploit DT without incurring cost and time implications. We also explore new technologies related to DT tool innovation and investigate their impact on company culture.

2 Literature Review

2.1 The Opportunity and Challenge of AR/VR Startup

Understanding the entrepreneurial process and entrepreneurial performance are integral aspects of broader entrepreneurial studies (Venkataraman 1997). We consider Eisenmann's (2013) formulation, which is the most concise, widely used definition. Entrepreneurship is defined as the pursuit of opportunity beyond what resources are controlled. Tech (2018) defined two critical aspects of high-tech startups: First, their key offering includes physical hardware that must be manufactured. Second, they fall within one of the OECD's 13 high-tech industry categories (OECD 2011, 2014). As they promise future growth and employment possibilities, such companies play an essential role in economic development (Suleyman et al. 2014).

A recent estimate by The Insight Partners (Alsop, 2022) forecasts that AR and VR are expected to grow into a $252 billion market by 2028. At present, industries in the creative economy—specifically, gaming, live events, video entertainment, and retail— currently generate the most substantial demand for the technologies, though a broader range of applications will develop over time, in industries as diverse as healthcare, education, real estate, and the military (Bellini, Chen, Sugiyama, Shin, Alam & Takayama 2016). Besides, AR/VR startups are a growing trend in the broader field of tech startups (Savin 2022). Nearly $1.9 billion of venture capital was channeled into startups in the virtual and augmented reality software and hardware space—the highest for any quarter to date (Metinko 2022).

However, tech startups are well known for their high failure rate. Statistics show that about three-quarters of high-tech startups fail during their first year of operation, whilst 90% cease operations after five years (Aminova & Marchi 2021; US Bureau of Labor Statistics 2020). Öndas and Akipinar's analysis (2021) outlines four potential causes of failure for high-tech startups, namely: product problems, market problems, financial problems, and managerial problems. To be precise, in terms of product issues, they will initially face high production costs and long production cycles due to the immaturity of their technology. In terms of marketing issues, they will start with a small customer base and a lack of understanding of new technologies, which will compound difficulties in expanding to new user groups. Liu (2021) posited that the main barriers hindering tech startups from employing design function are establishing design collaboration, positioning design function in an organization, the lack of ability to manage designers, and insufficient professional knowledge.

Additionally, for a company that launches its products and attempts to reach its target market, there are potential barriers to product diffusion (Kuester et al. 2012), which must be overcome to avoid failure. These barriers are the lack of knowledge adoption barrier (Vowles, Thirkell & Sinha 2011), the competitiveness barrier (Debruyne et al. 2002), and the pricing barrier (Smith 2011). To prevent failure of this kind, Öndas and Akipinar (2021) suggest that the high-tech startup should work to ensure they have a team that possesses the skills needed to design the product and manage the design process. According to the interviews, companies with design-led initiatives address technical shortcomings through design innovation.

The XR Industry Insider 2021 AR/VR/XR Survey (Ho, Soderquist & Schneiderman 2021) found that user experience is the more significant barrier to the greater adoption of XR. Astari (2020) outlined several challenges faced when creating augmented and virtual reality applications, including barriers to understanding the overall landscape of virtual reality technology and so on. As is reflected in the literature, the technical difficulties of ARVR are mainly related to those technologies that provide immersive experiences and the content that supports their adaptability to a diverse range of disciplines (Ho, Soderquist & Schneiderman 2021; Laurell et al. 2019). The opportunities are reflected in becoming the next computing platform (Bellini, Chen, Sugiyama, Shin, Alam & Takayama 2016), and to feature a design that provides high-value service experiences (Sherman & Craig 2003).

2.2 New DMCs Transformation in New Tech Startup

Design management is a tool that can be strategically deployed to prevent startup failure, improve innovation, and seek out business opportunities (Acklin & Fust 2014). Specifically, it pertains to the ongoing management and leadership of design organizations, processes, and outcomes (Cooper, Junginger & Lockwood 2009). Raymond Turner (2013) argues that design management success in business is more covered with attitudes and behavior than practices, it can create added value during the incubation phase of high-tech startups (Acklin & Wanner 2017).

Design management capability (DMC) refers to the capability of managers to dynamically deploy design resources (Fernández-Mesa et al. 2013; Teece, Pisano & Shuen 1997). It is distributed in different stages of a company. There are several ways to define the stages tech startups move through as they develop, Tech (2018) define startups as having four stages of development: the seed stage, startup stage, growth stage, and later stage. During the seed stage, the startup team aims to create a successful business. In the startup stage, entrepreneurs mainly focus on prototyping. In the growth stage, the startup seeks and reaches out to angel investors, early venture capital firms, and possibly even corporate venture capital firms for investment. This stage is characterized by scaling production and refinement. The startup transitions to its later stage when it reaches maturity and turns its attention to diversification and internationalization. Focusing on design management capabilities in entrepreneurial design management, Liu & Rieple (2019) arranged such capabilities in three stages: formation, validation, and growth. The DMCs include involving customers, setting up a working pattern, and reconfiguring resources, amongst others.

2.3 The Value of Design Thinking in DMCs and AR/VR Startup

Design Thinking and Tech Startup. Design thinking refers to design practices and competence that include uses beyond design context and also includes individuals with non-professional design backgrounds. Kimball (2020) describes design thinking in three ways: design thinking as a cognitive style (Schön 1983; Rowe 1991; Lawson 2005; Cross 2006; Dorst 2006), design thinking as a general theory of design (Buchanan 1992) and design thinking as an organizational resource (Dunne & Martin 2006; Brown 2009; Martin 2009; Bauer and Eagan 2008).

Design thinking is attractive for both scholars and practitioners due to the applicability of design methods for promoting innovation (de Mozota 2006; Martin 2009) and its applicability across many areas, such as in business (Seidel & Fixson 2013). Design thinking has been readily deployed in technology companies to achieve IT development (Linberg, Meinel & Wagner 2011), engineering design (Skogstad & Leifer 2011), create virtual collaboration environments (Hirschfeld, Steinert & Lincke 2011), and produce complex software system models (Gabrysiak Giese & Seibel 2011). It should be noted that the design thinking literature tends to focus on larger organizations (Acklin 2013), this is problematic as there are notable differences between large organizations and startups. Tech startups might have to navigate barriers relating to the market, and staff competence (Matejun 2016). There has also been discussion of design thinking in startups set in an entrepreneurial context. Nielsen and Christensen (2014) suggest that, given the similarities between reasoning and design and entrepreneurship, design associated with "wicked problems" is closely related to entrepreneurship. Additionally, both have a fuzzy front-end process (Stevenson & Jarillo 2007) and a common objective: creating value (Liedtka 2014). Considering the above discussion, it can be concluded that design thinking can create value in tech startups.

Design Thinking and Design Management. Design thinking has been described as the best way to create, innovate (Johansson-Sköldberg, Woodilla & Çetinkaya 2013), and pursue a human-centered approach to innovation (Brown 2009). As part of the management discourse, Hassi (2011) propose a framework in which the identified elements of design thinking are categorized into three dimensions: practices, thinking styles, and mindsets. Chasanidou et al. (2015) provide practical guidelines for utilizing design thinking methods and tools in innovation projects. The tools selected are personas, stakeholder maps, customer journey maps, service blueprints, business model innovation, and rapid prototyping.

The connection between design management and design thinking is strong. Design management can be divided into four main phases: simple, integrated, dynamic, and entrepreneurial. In the integrated stage, design managers infuse design thinking into the companies' planning, approaches, and activities (Acklin 2011). In the dynamic phase, design thinking is mainly used to achieve product innovation (Acklin 2013). In the entrepreneurial design management phase, design thinking is widely deployed at the executive level in various non-design disciplines to uncover and define problems and seek solutions (Liu & Rieple 2019).

A field study found that design thinking positively affects managers' sensing, seizing, and transformation of opportunities, which in turn stimulate innovation amongst their teams and strengthen team operational capabilities (Kurtmollaiev et al. 2018). It is undergoing a transition from managing tangible products to service design and organizational management. At the same time, design thinking is providing ideas and approaches to solve wicked problems at the organizational level during this transition.

The benefits of applying a design thinking approach in design management in AR/VR startups, from our point of view, include:

- improve capabilities in seeking market opportunities
- improve capabilities in innovation
- improve capabilities in organization management

It should also be noted that some researchers argue that design thinking can negatively impact team execution. For example, making changes to the teams' routines may not be conducive to strengthening their dynamic capacities (Kurtmollaiev et al. 2018). Elsewhere, other researchers are concerned about the immediate suitability of design thinking for improving an organization's operational capabilities (Kolko 2015). These arguments will also be covered during the discussion.

3   Method

We aim to understand the current barriers faced by high-tech startups. There is a lack of research on the difficulties faced by virtual technology startups, and our interest is on how startups with a virtual reality technology background deal with development barriers compared to other high-tech startups. We hoped to identify opportunities for new design research that could help virtual reality startups to work more effectively, so that their innovation capacity can be enhanced, and the company incubation process can be shortened.

Table 1. Basic information of interviewees.

Partecipants	Professional Role	Name of the Company	Company Size	Example company project	Education
Chuntie Chen	CEO	Zanvr	10-100 employees	Virtual reality training classrooms at universities	Mechanical Engineering
Wubo Zhou	CEO	Micia	10-100 employees	International NFT marketplace	Management Engineering
Wentong Huang	Co-Founder & Art Director	Morpha Design	Under 10 employees	Web 3D & AR solution	Product Design
Xiaobu Jia	Co-Founder	Scrat 3D	10-100 employees	3D printed children's shoes	Product Design

Data collection was based on longitudinal semi-structured interviews conducted in 2022 with senior company managers of high-tech startups. According to a purposive protocol, interview candidates were chosen and contacted based on their capacity to provide pertinent information. Morpha Design received numerous awards, including the TCL AWARD 2021, the Reddot Award (best of the best), and the DIA Design Intelligence Award. In order to have more knowledge about high-tech startups, we also interviewed the CEO of a 3d printing startup Scrat 3D, who has more than ten years of working experience.

We chose semi-structured interviews because, with open-ended questions, individuals' thoughts with details and richness can be provided (Newcomer et al. 2015). The semi-structured interviews also gave the interviewees the possibility to provide extensive information. We have 4 participants, which all are managing high-tech startups as CEOs or co-founders. Three virtual reality startups offer different kinds of products/service compared to each other. Zanvr is a Beijing Zhongguancun high-tech enterprises association member and a VR training provider certified by the Chinese Ministry of Education. MICIA is an international NFT marketplace linked to China, created by HuanCheng Digital Technology and in collaboration with Tencent Cloud, whose CEO, Mr. Zhou, has 5 years of international management experience (China, EU, Africa). Table 1 give specific information about the participants' backgrounds and their companies' projects.

The questions for the interviews were divided into two main sections. In the first section we asked about the challenges for virtual reality technology startups. Based on their descriptions and our preliminary investigation, the entrepreneurship phase of the company was determined. We then interviewed them about the key challenges they had encountered in their companies' development concerning management, particularly the unique challenges to virtual reality technology startups. Afterward, to learn more about the difficulties related to design management, we asked questions based on the previous literature on DMCs (Liu & Rieple 2019), the new DMCs, and the company's entrepreneurship phase. We probed them to get details on their challenges and current solutions. In the second section, we asked participants about the possibilities and challenges of applying DT in the company's management.

All interviews were recorded and transcribed. Then, using affinity diagrams to synthesize across the interviews and extract critical insights, we went over the transcripts to find thematic patterns. Models are set to describe how the various problems developed and how the managers worked with various company departments. Grounded theory was rejected in favor of affinity diagrams and models for several reasons.

Our goal wasn't to develop a thorough theory of the modern design techniques used by a very small percentage of managers. Instead, we opted for a more practice-based strategy since concepts that could benefit practitioners are essential.

4   Findings: Barriers Within High-Tech Startups

We organized our findings around three themes: market problem, product problem, managerial problem. There are overlaps between two or all three of these themes, so they are not mutually exclusive.

Besides, we observed two distinct academic backgrounds that significantly affected how participants worked. In the detailed findings below, we note where this difference impacted their understanding of DM.

4.1 Barrier 1: Market Problem

The preliminary conclusion of the interview: The market problem is divided into the problem of user demand research and the problem of expanding the user base. Participants almost all stated the customers' needs are *"fundamental"* for high-tech startups. When asked about the reasons for the company's success, P1 said, *"We are a company that relies entirely on the user to support our development, so we must think about the user, so the fundamental words of all this is entirely to solve the user's problems"*. The current method of researching user needs for high-tech startups are divided into push, pull and interactive. P2 said, *"The company is based on Web 3.0 and decentralization, so we will have a community. Inside the community we will have a product manager, who our users directly face. There are always community discussions with users, in which they will take the initiative to propose a feature out"*. P1 mentioned that *"normally we first simulate a demand, then we will solve the demand pain points of such a group of users. With the research we will tell them that we have such a program can solve your problem"*. P4 mentioned that they will extract the reviews of the goods being sold from Taobao to form a professional report. P3 said he would not do questionnaires due to the lack of large data volume, and usually put the product into the market first and then see the market reaction.

However, the current methods are problematic. P2 pointed out that *"push and pull are ineffective, such as questionnaires, because the company does not understand the actual context of the user. Interactive is the best, but it takes a long time."* Most participants agreed that another problem is that users cannot clearly express their needs, a problem that is even more pronounced in high-tech startups. Since most high-tech startups are based on brand-new technology, the public does not have a deep understanding of this technology. The lack of sufficient understanding of new technology leads to the fact that when users express their needs to the company, they do not professionally express themself, and the company's solutions may not meet their needs. Educating the market is one of the fundamental ways to get the market to express its needs correctly as P2 described *"In fact, we try to educate this group of our users to make them more professional, so that they can communicate with us more smoothly."* Hosting a speech or event is a common method of educating for these companies.

All companies have expressed their desire to expand their user base. Currently, the companies are limited to a small user base and finds it difficult to increase the number of users due to *"a few classic cases about related industries"* (P1), *"the placid state of the market"* (P4), *"imperfect policies"* (P2), and *"technical limitations"* (P3 & P4). The approach to business expansion includes word-of-mouth and networking events such as the metaverse art gallery.

4.2 Barrier 2: Product Problem

The preliminary conclusion of the interview: The limitation of the new technology is one of the fundamental reasons why the quality of the finished product is not as good as expected. Since the new technology is not yet mature, the cost, production cycle, and output cannot be guaranteed, resulting in a gap with the initial product concept. P1 expressed that the current products lack the combination of technology and art and hope to expand from product design to interaction design and service design. P3 said the main challenge they encounter unlike other startups was that the infrastructure was not as good as expected. They were currently finding that 5G penetration and speeds were still too low. Because of the real-time nature of augmented reality, it relied on proven network speeds. Too low internet speeds lead to a lack of product experience. Currently P3 said their solution was to take advantage of the design to optimize the model, but "we can indeed make our model 10 times smaller than our peers, but we can do it on the premise that we also have to do it manually, which is the biggest problem".

In the interviews, the problem of immaturity of technology is more evident in the entity industry. It leads to low accuracy and high cost (P4). In addition, P4 proposed 3D printing on behalf of the customization model was still not established. Difficulties are mainly reflected in the accuracy of data collection and the lack of big data processing method. The hindrance in the development of customization leads to the current solution was first not to advertise customization and sell shoes according to the average size, and second to let parents take photos of the soles of their babies' feet to do a small amount of simple customization.

4.3 Barrier 3: Managerial Problem

The preliminary conclusion of the interview: The managerial problem is mainly reflected in two aspects. First, the lack of understanding of design by management function may lead to a lack of clarity in recruiting suitable designers and experience whether the product is in line with the trend. The second is the communication conflict between the design department and other departments, such as marketing or engineering. In the first aspect, we found that respondents with engineering backgrounds find it more challenging to perceive design aesthetics than respondents with design backgrounds due to their educational experiences being different from design.

"We wouldn't be able to assess too well at the selection stage whether the candidate was suitable for such a position. Then this is the first one. The second is process management, such as whether the aesthetic sense aligns with a trend." (P1)

P1 also mentioned that it is complicated to monitor senior managers or master artists. Even respondents with design education have difficulty managing the process, mainly due to design uncertainty. On design projects, if a new idea comes up while the project is going in the original direction, P2 said he's "torn" between following the original plan or following the new path (P2).

In the second aspect, people with different responsibilities in different industries naturally have different backgrounds and knowledge systems, so there are naturally communication problems. In high-tech startups, all interviewees reported that they have flat personnel structures due to the characteristics of small companies. In virtual reality startups, designers have conflicts mainly with the technical department. One of the biggest reasons is the workload assessment (P2). The design department may have difficulties with the solutions proposed by the marketing department due to design difficulties and other considerations. The design department may have difficulties with the solutions proposed by the marketing. The sales department may believe that the designer cannot complete the sales strategy.

Currently, on the employee selection program, P1 said that they sorted into a kind of model and then standardized his position through the model as much as possible. All interviewees indicated that their management approach was developed gradually in process management. P1 uses agile thinking management, creating a simple feature first, and if the opportunity is good, it can continue to evolve. P2 said cost and duration are the focus of his consideration. *"If the cost is too high, the development process will be pushed back. The relevant part of the process must be cut. I can compromise that (the aesthetic is) good or bad, but the cost and the duration can never be touched, so this is one of our processes"* (P2). In the face of design uncertainty, P3 believes that they will consider other options only after they have come up with one that feels *"safe"*. He also emphasized the importance of extra ideas because a lot of worthwhile projects are created from those ideas rather than follow the process step by step out of the road.

We asked what their current solution was to resolve interdepartmental conflicts. Most respondents said designers, technology, and sales departments should improve their knowledge and change their work strategies appropriately. Designers should understand the technology and its possibilities and limitations (P4). A little sense of beauty and design is required in the technical department (P2). Sales should change the traditional sales mindset and recognize the natural characteristics of the technology. For example, 3d printing can claim the concept of new technology instead of a bargain because it is expensive (P4).

4.4   Findings: The Role of DM, DT to Gap the Barriers

During the interview, the companies all expressed the hope that design thinking would become part of the company culture, stimulate creativity in all departments while keeping costs low and encourage diverse and exploratory ways of thinking, identify and understand design thinking from the heart. P2 and P4 indicate that design thinking is present in every department in the company. Design thinking is used more in the daily management and communication of the team, and it will make colleagues work easier and more smoothly (P2). Including managers will use design thinking methods, such as brainstorming. Brainstorming is used at the start of a project, usually two to three times, mainly for sorting user requirements in the requirements pool, and then after a guided meeting, conclusions are drawn using management tools.

Depending on the company's size or the management approach, the interviewees are indirectly or directly involved in design management. Still, they generally have an open attitude toward design work. P1 indicated that since the company's work is mainly virtual scene building, the designers do script planning according to client requirements, which is managed by the planning manager and discussed in the weekly meetings. Since P2's company is in the digital collection field with more designers or artists, they will be more respectful of the designers in many cases. *"We had 3 designers come up with 4 sets of proposals during the UI design, then our major shareholder agreed with one version, but no one didn't like it. In the end, everyone voted, including our technical developers"*. P3 will not be directly involved in the design work but will observe and suggest solutions when the project is in distress.

When we asked respondents about the future role of design in the company, P2, P3, and P4 all mentioned that they wanted the company to be design-driven because *"the user experience that comes out of design is completely different from what comes out of technology and management."* P4 said the future of Morpha is a design-driven technology company. P2 revealed that many startups and large companies want to be design-driven, but the biggest bottleneck is the lack of leaders who have design and management skills and think in terms of design and cost. Universities should tell students the rules of how a business works. He suggested that students should train themselves in practice.

With web 3.0 and decentralization trends, design thinking will become essential to the corporate culture. DT can stimulate greater creativity (P1). To achieve this, all departments in the company should truly understand DT rather than simply using design thinking methods. For DT-led design management, the future of DM should be the trend of decentralization. The manager's job is to provide a relatively orderly framework for team members to play a certain role in the project chain. What managers manage is their output, packaged into a logical, commercialized idea to export to clients." (P3).

5 Discussion

This paper discusses DT-related content and tool innovation, also redefines the characteristics and practical tools of an enterprise in three stages. We aim to bridge the current gap between DT and new tech startups by analyzing the DMC innovative application framework of AR and VR-related startups. Moreover, attention will be paid to probing the new problems they face at this stage (market, product, and management), which are discovered by literature review and semi-structured interviews. The problems include understanding user's needs, expanding the client base, combining technology and design in a systematic way to receive innovative outcome and communication among design and other departments. The DMCs in the VR/AR startup change in response to specific challenges.

These DMCs include:

- Involving customers in VR/AR experience creation and testing (Astari 2020; Sherman & Craig 2003).
- Establishing working patterns with other functions to efficiently develop virtual reality products (Astari 2020; Liedtka & Ogilvie 2011).
- Reconfiguring resources to provide an overall landscape of virtual reality technology (Hassi 2011)
- Designing immersive experiences (Ho, Soderquist & Schneiderman 2021; Sherman & Craig 2003)
- Devising and implementing design standards for both hardware and software products (Astari 2020; Bellini, Chen, Sugiyama, Shin, Alam & Takayama 2016)
- Building knowledge and cultivating a responsible brand image (Astari 2020; Dick, 2021)
- Designing hardware/software to sustain competitiveness (Astari 2020; Bellini, Chen, Sugiyama, Shin, Alam & Takayama 2016)

For the purposes of the present study, design thinking refers to design activities that have a human-centered approach that are used beyond a design context and exhibit characteristics and features related to the practices, mindsets, and conceptions of design thinking. By combining the framework for design thinking by Hassi (2011), guidelines for design thinking by Chasanidou et al. (2015), and entrepreneurial design management capabilities by Liu & Rieple (2019), a framework for applying design thinking to entrepreneurial design management capabilities is accordingly proposed.

The entry point for this study is also divided into three parts:

- **Formation stage**

    The startup focuses on seeking business opportunities and innovating. Divergent thinking is encouraged at this stage. Since survival is the main goal for startups during this time (Tech 2018), a practical side of design thinking is suitable. Startups benefit from using concrete design thinking tools in design management, such as personas, rapid prototyping, and business model innovation (Chasanidou et al. 2015).

- **Validation stage**

    The product/service provided by the startup is accepted by an initial group of customers, though the quality of the product needs to be improved, necessitating that a working pattern for design should be established (Liu & Rieple (2019). The practice and thinking style dimension of design thinking are helpful in this stage. At this point, novice multidisciplinary teams might participate in the design process. Applying more sections of traditionally creative processes like brainstorming corresponds to lower performance (Seidel & Fixson 2013). Efficiency of communication among teams is essemtial for formulating a working pattern. Such individuals are more likely to be successful in applying design thinking when they can be guided to combine methods and more- to less-reflexive practices (Seidel & Fixson 2013). Some tools inspiring convergent and divergent thinking are put forward, such as customer journey maps and stakeholder maps (Chasanidou et al. 2015). These items provide an overall visual representation of the various connections between the company, stakeholders, and customers. For example, using a stakeholder map when reconfiguring DMC resources can help individuals to better understand the current relationship with stakeholders and maximize the current value.

- **Growth stage**

    At this point, the company has received funding from various sources. People from different functions and nations participate in the design process. It would be noted that the mindset dimension of design thinking is considerable at this point. Using design thinking tools facilitates the development of organizational cultures defined by openness to become ambiguous and engage in risk-taking (Elsbach & Stigliani 2018). This open culture helps develop DMCs, such as knowledge building and brand upgrading (Table 2).

Two distinguishing traits of the new DMCs are found by contrasting the newly reported DMCs in this research with the DMCs in the two earlier models. First off, the new DMCs streamline the descriptions of the DMCs from the earlier studies. The new DMCs are more specific and concentrated on AR/VR startups than the previous DMCs. For instance, the new DMC of "creating immersive experience" attempts to enhance the user experience of virtual reality during the validation stage.

Furthermore, the new DMC incorporates the remedy or course of action inside DT dimensions. To sum up, in conclusion, the new DMCs cover the three stages of AR/VR

Table 2. The framework for design thinking applied in design management innovation.

	New DMC	DT dimension	DT method
Formation	• Involving customers in VR/AR experience, creating	Practice	Personas, rapid prototyping, and business model innovation
Validation	• Involving customers in VR/AR experience testing • Setting up the working pattern with other functions for efficient virtual reality product development • Reconfiguring resources to provide an overall landscape of virtual reality technology designing immersive experiences	Practice and thinking style	Customer journey map and stakeholder map
Growth	• Design standards for both hardware and software products • Knowledge building, building responsible brand image design hardware/software to sustain competitiveness	Mindset	Design thinking culture

startups better than the DMCs in the earlier studies. Additionally, it offers DT techniques that are simple to use in practice.

The efficiency of DT in design management should be investigated and evaluated in the following studies. Researchers can also examine how businesses quickly grasp the DT approach to increase its efficacy. In order to increase the longevity of AR/VR firms, our findings provide points of reference for entrepreneurship design management research and tool development. We want to spark a thoughtful debate about how DT research may more effectively assist actual design management practice through this effort.

References

Acklin, C.: The absorption of design management capabilities in SMEs with little or no prior design experience. Nordes, (4) (2011)

Acklin, C.: Design management absorption model: a framework to describe and measure the absorption process of design knowledge by SMEs with little or no prior design experience. Creativity Innov. Manag. **22**(2), 147–160 (2013)

Acklin, C., Fust, A.: Towards a dynamic mode of design management and beyond (2014)

Acklin, C., Wanner, A.: Design and design management in the incubation phase of high-tech start-ups. Des. J. **20**(sup1), S469–S478 (2017)

Alsop, T.: Augmented Reality and Virtual Reality Market Size & Share Report 2028. The Insight Partners (2022)

Aminova, M., Marchi, E.: The role of innovation on startup failure vs. its success. Int. J. Bus. Ethics Gov. **4**(1), 41–72 (2021)

Ashtari, N., Bunt, A., McGrenere, J., Nebeling, M., Chilana, P.K.: Creating augmented and virtual reality applications: current practices, challenges, and opportunities. In: Proceedings of the 2020 CHI Conference on Human Factors in Computing Systems, pp. 1–13 (April 2020)

Bauer, R., Eagen, W.: Design thinking: epistemic plurality in management and organization. Aesthesis Int. J. Art Aesthetics Manag. Organ. Life **2**(3), 568–596 (2008)

Bellini H., Chen W., Sugiyama M., Shin S., Alam, S., Takayama D.: Goldman Sachs (2016)

Borja de Mozota, B.: The four powers of design: a value model in design management (2006)

Brown, T.: Change by design: how design thinking transforms organizations and inspires innovation. New York Bus. Rev. **61**(3), 30–50 (2009)

Buchanan, R.: Wicked problems in design thinking. Des. Issues **8**(2), 5–21 (1992)

Chasanidou, D., Gasparini, A.A., Lee, E.: Design thinking methods and tools for innovation. In: Marcus, A. (ed.) DUXU 2015. LNCS, vol. 9186, pp. 12–23. Springer, Cham (2015). https://doi.org/10.1007/978-3-319-20886-2_2

Cooper, R., Junginger, S., Lockwood, T.: Design thinking and design management: a research and practice perspective. Des. Manag. Rev. **20**(2), 46–55 (2009)

Cross, N.: Understanding design cognition. Designerly Ways Knowing, 77–93 (2006)

Daniel, A.D.: Fostering an entrepreneurial mindset by using a design thinking approach in entrepreneurship education. Ind. High. Educ. **30**(3), 215–223 (2016)

De Mozota, B.B.: The four powers of design: a value model in design management. Des. Manag. Rev. **17**(2), 44–53 (2006)

Debruyne, M., Moenaertb, R., Griffinc, A., Hartd, S., Hultinke, E.J., Robben, H.: The impact of new product launch strategies on competitive reaction in industrial markets. J. Prod. Innov. Manag. **19**, 159–170 (2002)

Dick, E.: Balancing user privacy and innovation in augmented and virtual reality. Inf. Technol. Innov. Fondation (2021)

Dorst, K.: Design problems and design paradoxes. Des. Issues **22**(3), 4–17 (2006)

Dunne, D., Martin, R.: Design thinking and how it will change management education: an interview and discussion. Acad. Manag. Learn. Educ. **5**(4), 512–523 (2006)

Eisenmann, T.R.: Entrepreneurship: a working definition. Harv. Bus. Rev. **10**, 2013 (2013)

Elsbach, K.D., Stigliani, I.: Design thinking and organizational culture: a review and framework for future research. J. Manag. **44**(6), 2274–2306 (2018)

Fernández-Mesa, A., Alegre-Vidal, J., Chiva-Gómez, R., Gutiérrez-Gracia, A.: Design management capability and product innovation in SMEs. Manag. Decis. (2013)

Gabrysiak, G., Giese, H., Seibel, A.: Towards next generation design thinking: scenario-based prototyping for designing complex software systems with multiple users. In: Meinel, C., Leifer, L., Plattner, H. (eds.) Design Thinking. Understanding Innovation, pp. 219–236. Springer, Berlin, Heidelberg (2011). https://doi.org/10.1007/978-3-642-13757-0_13

Hassi, L., Laakso, M.: Conceptions of design thinking in the design and management discourse. In: Proceedings of IASDR2011, pp. 1–10 (2011)

Hirschfeld, R., Steinert, B., Lincke, J.: Agile software development in virtual collaboration environments. In: Design Thinking, pp. 197–218. Springer, Berlin, Heidelberg (2011)

Ho, C., Soderquist K.A., Schneiderman, J.: XR Industry Insider 2021 AR/VR/XR Survey (2021). https://www.perkinscoie.com/en/ar-vr-survey-results/2021-augmented-and-virtual-reality-survey-results.html

Hyytinen, A.: Shared problem solving and design thinking in entrepreneurship research. J. Bus. Ventur. Insights **16**, e00254 (2021)

Johansson-Sköldberg, U., Woodilla, J., Çetinkaya, M.: Design thinking: past, present and possible futures. Creativity Innov. Manag. **22**(2), 121–146 (2013)

Kimball, L.: Rethinking design thinking. Ann. Rev. Policy Des. **8**(1), 1–20 (2020)

Kolko, J.: Design thinking comes of age. Harv. Bus. Rev. **93**(9), 66–71 (2015)

Kuester, S., Homburg, C., Hess, S.C.: Externally directed and internally directed market launch management: the role of organization factors in influencing new product success. J. Prod. Innov. Manag. **29**, 38–52 (2012)

Kurtmollaiev, S., Pedersen, P.E., Fjuk, A., Kvale, K.: Developing managerial dynamic capabilities: a quasi-experimental field study of the effects of design thinking training. Acad. Manag. Learn. Educ. **17**(2), 184–202 (2018)

Laurell, C., Sandström, C., Berthold, A., Larsson, D.: Exploring barriers to adoption of virtual reality through social media analytics and machine learning–an assessment of technology, network, price and trialability. J. Bus. Res. **100**, 469–474 (2019)

Lawson, B.: How Designers Think. Routledge (2006)

Liedtka, J., Ogilvie, T.: Designing for Growth: A Design Thinking Tool Kit for Managers. Columbia Business School Publishing, New York (2011)

Liedtka, J.: Perspective: linking design thinking with innovation outcomes through cognitive bias reduction. J. Prod. Innov. Manag. n/a–n/a **32**(6), 925–938 (2014)

Liu, S.X.: Barriers to bringing design function into technology start-ups: a survey on the incubation programme of Hong Kong science park. Des. J. **24**(5), 807–828 (2021)

Liu, S., Rieple, A.: Design management capability in entrepreneurship: a case study of Xiaomi. Int. J. Des. **13**(3), 125–138 (2019)

Mansoori, Y., Lackéus, M.: Comparing effectuation to discovery-driven planning, prescriptive entrepreneurship, business planning, lean startup, and design thinking. Small Bus. Econ. **54**(3), 791–818 (2019). https://doi.org/10.1007/s11187-019-00153-w

Martin, R.: The Design of Business: Why Design Thinking Is the Next Competitive Advantage. Harvard Business School Press, Boston (2009)

Matejun, M.: Barriers to development of technology entrepreneurship in small and medium enterprises. Res. Logist. Product. **6**(3), 269–282 (2016)

Newcomer, K.E., Hatry, H.P., Wholey, J.S. (eds.): Handbook of Practical Program Evaluation, p. 492. John Wiley & Sons, USA (2015)

Nielsen, S.L., Christensen, P.R.: The wicked problem of design management: perspectives from the field of entrepreneurship. Des. J. **17**(4), 560–582 (2014)

OECD: Technology Intensity Definition—Classification of Manufacturing Industries into Categories based on R&D Intensities. OECD, Paris (2011)

OECD: OECD Science, Technology and Industry Outlook 2014. OECD, Paris (2014)

Öndas, V., Akpinar, M.: Understanding high-tech startup failures and their prevention. In: Proceedings of Research in Entrepreneurship and Small Business Conference, RENT XXXV: Inclusive Entrepreneurship, 18–19 November 2021, Turku, Finland (2021)

Rowe, P.G.: Design Thinking. MIT Press (1991)

Savin, I., Chukavina, K., Pushkarev, A.: Topic-based classification and identification of global trends for startup companies. Small Bus. Econ. 1–31 (2022). https://doi.org/10.1007/s11187-022-00609-6

Schon, D.A.: The reflective practitioner. Ashgate Publishing (1991)

Seidel, V.P., Fixson, S.K.: Adopting design thinking in novice multidisciplinary teams: the application and limits of design methods and reflexive practices. J. Prod. Innov. Manag. **30**, 19–33 (2013)

Sherman, W.R., Craig, A.B.: Understanding Virtual Reality: Interface, Application, and Design. Morgan Kaufmann (2018)

Skogstad, P., Leifer, L.: A unified innovation process model for engineering designers and managers. In: Meinel, C., Leifer, L., Plattner, H. (eds.) Design Thinking. Understanding Innovation, pp. 19–43. Springer, Berlin, Heidelberg (2011). https://doi.org/10.1007/978-3-642-13757-0_2

Smith, T.J.: Price Strategy – Setting Price Levels, Managing Price Discounts, & Establishing Price Structures, International South-Western, Cengage Learning, USA (2011)

Stevenson, H.H., Jarillo, J.C.: A paradigm of entrepreneurship research: entrepreneurial management. Strateg. Manag. J. **11**, 17–27 (2007)

Sulayman, M., Mendes, E., Urquhart, C., Riaz, M., Tempero, E.: Towards a theoretical framework of SPI success factors for small and medium web companies. Inf. Softw. Technol. **56**(7), 807–820 (2014)

Tech, R.: Financing High-Tech Startups. Springer, Berlin, Heidelberg (2018)

Teece, D.J., Pisano, G., Shuen, A.: Dynamic capabilities and strategic management. Strateg. Manag. J. **18**(7), 509–533 (1997)

Turner, R.: Design Leadership: Securing the Strategic Value of Design (1st ed.). Routledge (2013)

US Bureau of Labor Statistics. Table 7. Survival of private sector establishments by opening year (2020). https://www.bls.gov/bdm/us_age_naics_00_table7.txt. Accessed 12 Sept 2022

Venkataraman, S.: The distinctive domain of entrepreneurship research. Emerald Publishing Limited, In Seminal ideas for the next twenty-five years of advances (2019)

Vowles, N., Thirkell, P., Sinha, A.: Different determinants at different times: B2B adoption of a radical innovation. J. Bus. Res. **64**(11), 1162–1168 (2011)

Zhang, S.X., Van Burg, E.: Advancing entrepreneurship as a design science: developing additional design principles for effectuation. Small Bus. Econ. **55**(3), 607–626 (2019). https://doi.org/10.1007/s11187-019-00217-x

Author Index

Printed in the United States
by Baker & Taylor Publisher Services